S0-BDP-013

america
at odds

fourth edition

edward sidlow
Eastern Michigan University

beth henschen

WADSWORTH

Australia • Canada • Mexico • Singapore • Spain • United Kingdom • United States

For Sarah

Publisher: Clark Baxter
Acquiring Editor: David Tatom
Development Editor: Stacey Sims
Editorial Assistant: Reena Thomas
Assistant Editor: Heather Hogan
Technology Project Manager: Melinda Newfarmer
Marketing Manager: Janise Fry
Marketing Assistant: Mary Ho
Executive Project Manager: Nathaniel Bergson-Michelson
Project Editor: Ann Borman
Print Buyer: Karen Hunt

Permissions Editor: Sarah Harkrader
Senior Project Manager: Bill Stryker
Text and Cover Design: Bill Stryker
Illustrator: Bill Stryker
Photo Researcher: Anne Sheroff
Copy Editor: Pat Lewis
Cover Image: © 2003 Chad McNeeley. All Rights Reserved.
Text and Cover Printer: Von Hoffmann
Compositor: Parkwood Composition Service
Indexer: Bob Marsh

OPYRIGHT © 2004 Wadsworth, a division of Thomson Learning, Inc. Thomson Learning™ is a trademark used herein under license.

ALL RIGHTS RESERVED. No part of this work covered by the copyright hereon may be reproduced or used in any form or by any means—graphic, electronic, or mechanical, including photocopying, recording, taping, Web distribution, or information storage and retrieval systems—without the written permission of the publisher.

Printed in the United States
1 2 3 4 5 6 7 07 06 05 04 03

For more information about our products, contact us at:
Thomson Learning Academic Resource Center
1-800-423-0563
For permission to use material from this text, contact us by:
Phone: 1-800-730-2214
Fax: 1-800-730-2215
Web: http://www.thomsonrights.com

ExamView® and ExamView Pro® are registered trademarks of FSCreations, Inc. Windows is a registered trademark of the Microsoft Corporation used herein under license. Macintosh and Power Macintosh are registered trademarks of Apple Computer, Inc. Used herein under license.

COPYRIGHT 2004 Thomson Learning, Inc. All Rights Reserved. Thomson Learning Web Tutor™ is a trademark of Thomson Learning, Inc.

Library of Congress Control Number: 2003107137
ISBN: 0–534–57521–8

Wadsworth/Thomson Learning
10 Davis Drive
Belmont, CA 94002-3098
USA

International Headquarters
Thomson Learning
International Division
290 Harbor Drive, 2nd Floor
Stamford, CT 06902-7477
USA

UK/Europe/Middle East/South Africa
Thomson Learning
Berkshire House
168-173 High Holborn
London WC1V 7AA
United Kingdom

Asia
Thomson Learning
60 Albert Street, #15-01
Albert Complex
Singapore 189969

Canada
Nelson Thomson Learning
1120 Birchmount Road
Toronto, Ontario M1K 5G4
Canada

Credits for chapter-opening photos appear on the page following the index.

contents in brief

contents

PART ONE
THE FOUNDATIONS OF OUR AMERICAN SYSTEM

v

CHAPTER 2 FEATURES

PERCEPTION VERSUS REALITY
Was the Constitution Favored by a Majority? 37

THE POLITICS OF HOMELAND SECURITY
Tampering with the System of Checks and Balances 39

WHY DOES IT MATTER?
The Constitution and Your Everyday Life 45

CHAPTER TWO
The Constitution 19

PART TWO
OUR LIBERTIES AND RIGHTS

CHAPTER 4
Civil Liberties 73

CHAPTER 5
Civil Rights 99

CHAPTER 5 FEATURES

PERCEPTION VERSUS REALITY
Are America's Schools Integrated? 106

THE POLITICS OF HOMELAND SECURITY
Racial Profiling in the War on Terrorism 115

WHY DOES IT MATTER?
Civil Rights and Your Everyday Life 124

PART THREE
THE POLITICS OF DEMOCRACY

CHAPTER 6
Interest Groups   129

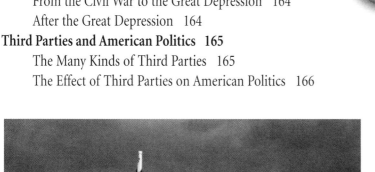

CHAPTER 8
Public Opinion and Voting 175

CHAPTER 9
Campaigns and Elections 201

CHAPTER 10 FEATURES

THE POLITICS OF HOMELAND SECURITY
Saturation News Coverage 227

PERCEPTION VERSUS RELAITY
Does Online Information Mean the Death of Traditional News? 238

COMPARATIVE POLITICS
Cyber Activism in South Korea 241

WHY DOES IT MATTER?
Politics, the Media, and Your Everyday Life 242

CHAPTER 10
Politics and the Media 223

PART FOUR
INSTITUTIONS

CHAPTER 12
The Presidency 271

CHAPTER 13
The Bureaucracy 299

CHAPTER 14
The Judiciary 323

PART FIVE
PUBLIC POLICY

CHAPTER 16 FEATURES

THE POLITICS OF HOMELAND SECURITY
Does the Threat of Terrorism Justify Preemptive War? 390

WHY DOES IT MATTER?
Foreign Policy and Your Everyday Life 394

CHAPTER 16
Foreign Policy 371

It does not take long for a student of American government to get the message: Americans are at odds over numerous political issues. Political conflict is certainly not new to this country. During the confusing aftermath of the 2000 elections, for example, many people thought that the United States might be facing a constitutional crisis. The war on terrorism that began on September 11, 2001, also created new challenges for American democracy, as you will read throughout this text. Yet our democracy continues to endure, and the U.S. Constitution has been the model for most of the world's new democracies in the 1990s and early 2000s.

Political conflict and divergence of opinion have always helped to forge our political traditions and way of governing. For example, in 2003, Americans were deeply divided over taking action against Saddam Hussein without the backing of the United Nations. Protests against the second Gulf War continued even when American troops were in harm's way, fighting in Iraq.

America at Odds: An Introduction to American Government, Fourth Edition, looks at government and politics in this country as a series of conflicts that have led to compromises. Along the way, your students will sometimes encounter a bit of irreverence—none of us should take ourselves so seriously all of the time!

This text was written with today's generation of students in mind. As such, it does the following:

- Forthrightly presents different perspectives on key issues being debated today, including some of the issues raised during the war on terrorism, such as how to ensure our security while protecting our civil liberties.
- Helps your students test their beliefs and assumptions.
- Assists your students in forming enlightened political values and opinions.
- Uses a thematic as well as an analytical approach, with emphasis on the various challenges that face our enduring democracy.
- Fully explains the major problems facing the American political system today.
- Integrates the global connections that exist between American politics and those of the rest of the world.
- Captures the excitement of cyberspace with respect to its effect on American politics and makes available numerous Web resources, ranging from a book-specific site to the online library of InfoTrac® College Edition.
- Offers links to an issues-driven, fully interactive CD-ROM.

Politics in a Cyber Age

Cyberspace affects not only our home lives and the way we do business but also American politics. *America at Odds,* Fourth Edition, fully integrates the world of cyberspace into the study of American politics.

Throughout this text, your students are exposed to the numerous political issues that have arisen because of the rapid changes in communications technology. For example, Chapter 1 explores the question of how data-mining technology is being used in the war on terrorism. Chapter 4 examines the issues of online obscenity and the erosion of privacy rights in an era of e-commerce.

Politics on the Web

The amount of information available to students of American government on the Web is almost without limits. Where do they start? And where do they go? We solve this thorny problem by providing, at the end of each chapter, an entire section entitled *Politics on the Web.* There your students can discover the best Web sites for each chapter's subject matter. Many of those Web sites offer additional hot links.

Web Exercises on Your CD-ROM

This edition of *America at Odds* also offers Web exercises on the topics covered in each chapter. In these exercises, the student is asked to access certain Web sites, read or analyze the materials presented on the sites, and answer specific, critical-thinking questions about those materials. Links to these online exercises are included in the CD-ROM that accompanies *America at Odds,* Fourth Edition, which is seamlessly integrated with the Internet. (The CD-ROM and its contents will be discussed shortly.)

The *America at Odds,* Fourth Edition, Web Site

In addition to the *Politics on the Web* section and the Web exercises on the CD-ROM, there is an *America at Odds* companion Web site at:

http://politicalscience.wadsworth.com/sidlow04

Here you and your students will find a wealth of information developed specifically for *America at Odds.* The Web site offers numerous helpful resources, including the following:

- Chapter-by-chapter tutorial quizzes that allow students to test their knowledge.
- Hyperlinks to relevant Web sites for each chapter—including URLs that update materials in the text and the CD-ROM.
- Internet and InfoTrac® activities that relate to each chapter's material.

InfoTrac® for Real Research on the Internet

Many professors require their students to undertake research projects. Users of this text are fortunate to have at their disposal the finest existing search system on the Internet for questions relating to American government and politics. Wadsworth Publishing Company has an exclusive agreement with InfoTrac®, the premier research service on the Web, developed by Information Access Corporation. InfoTrac® lets your students ask specific questions. Through exclusive search agreements with many important political science journals and other related sources, the system takes the student to exactly where he or she needs to go to find the relevant information, including full-text articles. When full text is available, the student prints it directly. Otherwise, the full text can be sent to the student's e-mail address.

In this Fourth Edition of *America at Odds,* we have included at the end of each chapter a special InfoTrac® section. This section lists the titles of articles relevant to the chapter topic that can be accessed using InfoTrac. We also give the key words to be searched when accessing each article.

Professors who use this book can order a one-month free subscription to this service. If the professor requests that the service be bundled with each student copy of the text (for a nominal fee), then he or she will receive a four-month free subscription. Ask your sales representative for your free password to log on at **http://infotrac.thomsonlearning.com** on the Web.

InfoTrac® Resource Guide

This online guide to InfoTrac®, your twenty-four-hour-a-day reference resource, contains approximately fifteen articles tied to each of the twenty major topics in the text. Activities that include exercises in obtaining research materials are also included. The guide is updated quarterly to keep you up to date with the latest news.

Internet Activities

To make sure that your students not only master the Web but at the same time improve their understanding of American politics, we have a specially designed booklet that you can order for them. It is called *American Government Internet Activities,* Third Edition. Each exercise relates to topics that are covered in the text. The exercise takes your students on a navigation path and then asks them to complete various exercises related to the data that they discover.

A Fully Interactive CD-ROM

Free with *America at Odds,* Fourth Edition, is a fully interactive CD-ROM. Students will find values inventories, dialogues and debates, participation activities, video clips, and other activities for each chapter in the text. Seamlessly integrated with the Internet, the CD-ROM provides students with access to links related to chapter material, Internet and InfoTrac® activities on the text's companion Web site, and all of the resources at Wadsworth's American Government Resource Center (at **http://politicalscience.wadsworth.com/amgov**), including simulations, MicroCase activities, and more.

The Modern Text—Features That Teach

Any American government text must present the basics of the American political process and its institutions. Any *modern* American government text, however, must go further; it must excite and draw the student into the subject materials. That is exactly what we do in *America at Odds,* Fourth Edition. Among other things, the Fourth Edition of *America at Odds* deals with current issues and events that are familiar to students. For example, in virtually every chapter there is a reference to, or discussion of, some aspect of the 2000 and 2002 campaigns, elections, or election results.

Additionally, we present many of today's controversial political issues in special features. Each of these features is referred to within the text itself so that the student understands the connection between the feature and the topic being discussed. We describe below the various types of features that we have included in *America at Odds,* Fourth Edition.

■ *America at Odds*—This chapter-opening feature examines a major controversy over which the public is divided and has strong views. Each of these features concludes with a section entitled *Where Do You Stand?* These sections, which consist of two questions, invite the student to form or express his or her own opinions on the arguments presented in the feature.

Students can explore the issue further by accessing additional resources on the *America at Odds* CD-ROM. Students can take the CD's "Values Inventory" quizzes at the beginning and end of each chapter's work to evaluate whether their exploration of the chapter's material has changed their personal stance on the topics presented in the *America at Odds* features. "Dialogues" present students with debates on the feature's topic. Each debate involves three hypothetical students and challenges students to generate arguments of their own and decide where they stand on the issue.

Some of the titles of these chapter-opening *America at Odds* features are:

- Are We Becoming Too Patriotic? (Chapter 1).
- Should Hate Speech on Campus Be Banned? (Chapter 4).
- Should Affirmative Action Be Abolished? (Chapter 5).
- What Is the Media's Role in Wartime? (Chapter 10).
- Should Presidents Be Able to Go to War on Their Own? (Chapter 12).

- **In-Chapter** *America at Odds*—The theme of controversy continues in shorter features, new to the Fourth Edition, that are integrated within the text of every chapter. Each in-chapter *America at Odds* briefly introduces students in a concise yet thought-provoking manner to an issue that divides Americans. These features will keep your students thinking and questioning their own political attitudes and values. Some titles of these features include:

- Should the Government Pay Reparations for Slavery? (Chapter 2).
- Is America One Nation "under God"? (Chapter 4).
- Should Bilingual Education Be Abolished? (Chapter 5).
- Should Third-Party Candidates Debate? (Chapter 7).
- Do the Federal Courts Wield Too Much Power? (Chapter 14).

- *The Politics of Homeland Security*—These features, which are also new to the Fourth Edition, are designed to focus on the political implications of the effort to secure the homeland from terrorist attacks. At the end of each of these features is a thought-provoking question that challenges students to consider whether we are safer as a result of a particular homeland security measure. Some of the titles of these features are as follows:

- How Much Federal Control over the "First Responders"? (Chapter 3).
- Should We Carry National Identification Cards? (Chapter 4).
- Racial Profiling and the War on Terrorism (Chapter 5).
- "Selling" Terrorism Insurance (Chapter 6).
- Presidential Power in a Time of Crisis (Chapter 12).

- *Why Does It Matter?*—This feature gives a number of specific examples showing how the topic under study affects the student's everyday life. Each feature carries a subtitle including the chapter topic. For example, in Chapter 11 the feature's title is *Why Does It Matter? Congress and Your Everyday Life*. At the end of each feature is a section entitled *Taking Action*. These sections illustrate how ordinary Americans have made their voices heard on issues of importance to them.

- *Perception versus Reality*—Perhaps nowhere in our media-generated view of the world are there more misconceptions than in the area of American government and politics. This feature tries to help your students understand the difference between the public's general perception of a particular political event or issue and the reality of the situation. The perception is often gleaned from responses to public opinion surveys. The reality usually is presented in the form of objective data that show that the world is not quite what the public often thinks it is. At the end of each of these features is a section entitled *What's Your Opinion?*, which encourages the student to think about why there is such a disparity between the perception and the reality. Some of the titles of these features are as follows:

- Who Rules in Our "Representative" Democracy? (Chapter 1).
- Who's Paying for All Those Issue Ads? (Chapter 6).
- What Do Americans Really Know about the U.S. Constitution? (Chapter 8).
- Who Makes the Law? (Chapter 13).
- Crime in the Schools (Chapter 15).

- *Comparative Politics*—One of the best ways to understand the American political system is by comparing it with other political systems. Students need to know that in much of the world, the political process is different. By understanding this, they can better understand and appreciate what goes on in this country, both in Washington, D.C., and in state capitals. Nearly every chapter has at least one of these features. At the end of each of these features, the student is asked to further examine some part of the argument in a question "For Critical Analysis." Some examples of the *Comparative Politics* features are as follows:

- Life in a Unitary System (Chapter 3).
- Church and State in Other Countries (Chapter 4).
- Gun Control in Britain and the United States (Chapter 6).
- The German Greens (Chapter 7).
- Cyber Activism in South Korea (Chapter 10).

- *Chapter Objectives*—Every chapter-opening page includes a list of five learning objectives that let students know what concepts will be covered in the chapter.

Chapter-Ending Issues and Pedagogy

Every chapter ends with the following sections:

- **Key Terms.** This is a list of the terms that were boldfaced and defined within the chapter. Each term in the list is followed by the page number on which it first appeared and was defined.
- **Chapter Summary.** This point-by-point feature summarizes every important topic covered in the chapter.
- **Selected Readings.** Several books of recent scholarship, as well as some classic texts, are listed at the end of each chapter, along with annotations describing each book.
- **InfoTrac® Citations.** As already mentioned, this section lists the titles of relevant articles that students can access through InfoTrac®.
- **Politics on the Web.** As explained earlier, this section gives selected Web sites that students can access for more information.
- **Web Resources on Your CD-ROM.** This section lists the various chapter-related Web resources that students can access using the CD-ROM.

The Supplements

Both instructors and students today expect, and indeed require, a variety of accompanying supplements to teach and learn about American government. *America at Odds,* Fourth Edition, takes the lead in providing the most comprehensive and user-friendly supplements package on the market today. These supplements include those listed below.

Printed Materials for Instructors

- *Instructor's Manual with Test Bank and Multimedia Guide,* written by Beth Henschen.

Multimedia Supplements for Instructors

- An online Resource Center for political science at

    http://politicalscience.wadsworth.com

- A special, book-specific Web site for *America at Odds,* Fourth Edition, which can be accessed through the Resource Center or at

    http://politicalscience.wadsworth.com/sidlow04

- 2004 American Government Multimedia Manager—A one-stop digital library and presentation tool that makes it easy to assemble, edit, publish, and present custom lectures—bringing together art from this CD-ROM, the Web, and your own material.
- WebTutor™, available on WebCT and Blackboard—A Web-based teaching and learning tool that allows you to provide virtual office hours, post your syllabi, set up threaded discussions, track student progress with the quizzing material, and more.
- *CNN Today: American Government videos,* Volumes 1, 2, and 3.

- A video library, including new selections.
- Online Instructor's Manual, Test Bank, and Multimedia Guide.
- ExamView® for Macintosh/Windows.
- American Government Transparency Acetate Package.
- InfoTrac® College Edition.
- InfoTrac® Resource Guide.

Lecture Launchers—Video Case Studies in American Government

This set of twelve video case studies, produced by Baker/Losco Multimedia in 2002, won the Bronze Telly Award for outstanding video production. Now available to qualified adopters in both video and DVD formats, topics include affirmative action and money and the 2000 presidential campaigns, among others. A free *Instructor's Manual* provides brief summaries of each video, a set of key terms, three to five activities for each video, and suggestions on how best to use this exciting new collection.

Printed Materials for Students

- *Study Guide,* written by Beth Henschen.
- *Readings in American Government,* Fourth Edition, edited by Mack C. Shelley, Jamie Swift, and Steffen W. Schmidt, all of Iowa State University.
- *An Introduction to Critical Thinking and Writing in American Politics.*
- *American Government Internet Activities,* Third Edition.
- *Handbook of Selected Legislation and Other Documents.*
- *Handbook of Selected Court Cases.*
- *College Survival Guide.*
- *Thinking Globally, Acting Locally.*

Multimedia Supplements for Students

- *America at Odds* Interactive CD-ROM, included free.
- A special online Resource Center for American government at

  http://politicalscience.wadsworth.com/amgov

- A special, book-specific Web site for *America at Odds,* Fourth Edition, which can be accessed through the Resource Center or at

  http://political science.wadsworth.com/sidlow04

- InfoTrac® College Edition, offering a fully searchable online library of readings.
- InfoTrac® Resource Guide.
- *American Government: Using MicroCase® ExplorIt,* Eighth Edition—The Eighth Edition of this popular ancillary for American government courses includes computer-based assignments, a student version of MicroCase's ExplorIt software, and current real data sets. Each assignment is packed with dozens of issues that are guaranteed to grab student interest.
- WebTutor™ on WebCT and Blackboard, a Web-based teaching and learning tool.

What's New in the Fourth Edition?

We thought that those of you who have used the Third Edition of *America at Odds* would like to know what changes have been made for the Fourth Edition. Generally, all of the text, tables, figures, and features in this book have been rewritten or updated as necessary to reflect the most recent developments in American government and politics. The Fourth Edition incorporates the results of the most recent presidential and congressional elections throughout the text as they relate to chapter topics. This edition also presents the most up-to-the-minute discussion of the war on terrorism and the second Gulf War. Other key changes and additions for the Fourth Edition include those described below.

Special New Features and Pedagogy

The Fourth Edition of *America at Odds* includes a large number of newly written features. In addition, the following special new features and pedagogy have been added:

- In-Chapter *America at Odds*—A new feature that fully integrates the theme of controversy and debate throughout the main text of each chapter.
- *The Politics of Homeland Security*—This feature, designed to illustrate the political implications of defending the homeland against terrorism, replaces the *American Political Perspectives* of the Third Edition.
- *Taking Action* sections of the chapter-ending *Why Does It Matter?* features—These sections tell the story of real Americans who have made their voices heard on important political issues.

Significant Changes to the Chapters

As already indicated, each chapter in *America at Odds,* Fourth Edition, has been updated and revised in order to reflect the most current developments in American politics and government. When appropriate, new features have been added, and references to new laws and court decisions have been included. Throughout the text, we have incorporated references to the 2000 and 2002 elections as appropriate. Here we list some other significant changes made to selected chapters.

- Chapter 1 (America in the Twenty-First Century)—This chapter includes new sections on American political values, multiculturalism, and patriotism. The chapter also incorporates sections that were part of the Third Edition's chapter on political culture and ideology, which has been deleted from the Fourth Edition.
- Chapter 3 (Federalism)—This chapter includes a new feature on unitary systems, as well as discussions of federalism and the welfare state, picket-fence federalism, and competitive federalism. The chapter also explores the Bush administration's approach to federalism.
- Chapter 4 (Civil Liberties)—This chapter contains discussions of the most recent court cases involving civil liberties, including the "virtual" child pornography case, cases related to privacy rights at abortion clinics, and the case concerning the words "under God" in the Pledge of Allegiance. This chapter also specifically addresses the threats to civil liberties presented by the war on terrorism.
- Chapter 5 (Civil Rights)—This chapter was reorganized to present a clearer and more detailed history of the struggle by African Americans for civil rights. There is also a new section on immigrants' rights, particularly since the war on terrorism began.
- Chapter 6 (Interest Groups)—This chapter contains a new section on how interest groups form. It also contains the latest information on efforts to regulate lobbying.
- Chapter 7 (Political Parties)—The section on the two-party system has been revised to clarify how the American electoral system tends to support the two major parties' hold on power. A new section on the positions of the two major parties on impotant issues facing the nation has also been added.
- Chapter 8 (Public Opinion and Voting)—The section on public opinion polling has been thoroughly revised, and a new table has been added on how to evaluate the quality of public opinion polls. A new section on ideology has also been added, drawn from the Third Edition's chapter on political culture and ideology.
- Chapter 10 (Politics and the Media)—This chapter contains a new section on the role of the media in a democracy and on the media's agenda-setting function. The section on media bias has been thoroughly revised and updated.
- Chapter 11 (Congress)—This chapter contains expanded sections on the power of incumbency and the debates over term limits. It also includes a new section on Congress's power of investigation and oversight and Congress's relationship to the executive branch.

- Chapter 12 (The Presidency)—The sections on presidential roles and presidential powers have been thoroughly revised, with new discussions of the president's war powers, the pardon power, and executive privilege. A new section on congressional and presidential relations explores this pivotal relationship in American government.
- Chapter 13 (The Bureaucracy)—This chapter includes discussions of the new Department of Homeland Security, recent trends in privatization of the bureaucracy, and new material on the 2002 farm bill.
- Chapter 14 (The Judiciary)—A new section on judicial activism and judicial restraint has been added, as well as a discussion of the power and ideology of the federal courts.
- Chapter 16 (Foreign Policy)—Major new sections have been added to this chapter that focus on the war on terrorism, the proliferation of weapons of mass destruction, and the second Gulf War. The chapter also addresses the issues of unilateralism and preemption in the foreign policy of the Bush administration.

Acknowledgments

A number of political scientists reviewed the previous editions of *America at Odds*. We remain indebted to the following scholars for their thoughtful suggestions on how to create a text that best suits the needs of today's students and faculty:

Weston H. Agor
University of Texas, El Paso

Ross Baker
Highland Park, New Jersey

Glenn Beamer
University of Virginia

Lynn Brink
Northlake College, Texas

John Francis Burke
University of Houston

Rebecca Cartwright
Montgomery College

Brian Cherry
Northern Michigan University

Richard G. Chesteen
University of Tennessee at Martin

Richard Christofferson
University of Wisconsin, Stevens Point

Lane Crothers
Illinois State University

Larry Elowitz
Georgia College and State University

Craig Emmert
Texas Tech University

Terri Fine
University of Central Florida

Scott R. Furlong
University of Wisconsin, Green Bay

John Geer
Vanderbilt University

Christian Goergen
College of DuPage, Illinois

Paul Goren
Southern Illinois University

Jim Graves
Kentucky State University

Joanne Green
Texas Christian University

Marianne Ide
Monterey Peninsula College, California

William E. Kelly
Auburn University, Alabama

Matt Kerbel
Villanova University, Pennsylvania

James D. King
University of Wyoming

Steven A. Light
University of North Dakota

James J. Lopach
University of Montana

Sam W. Mckinstry
East Tennessee State University

William McLauchlan
Purdue University, Indiana

Paz Pena
Austin Community College

Paul Savoie
Long Beach City College, California

Wendy E. Scattergood
University of Wisconsin, Green Bay

Linda J. Simmons
Northern Virginia Community College

Ruth Ann Strickland
Appalachian State University,
North Carolina

Gabriel Ume
Palo Alto College, Texas

Sharon G. Whitney
Tennessee Technological University

Bruce M. Wilson
University of Central Florida

J. David Woodard
Clemson University, South Carolina

Michele Zebich-Knos
Kennesaw State University, Georgia

In preparing the Fourth Edition of *America at Odds*, we benefited from the criticism and comments of a number of users and reviewers of the Third Edition. We thank the following reviewers for their conscientious work:

David Gray Adler
Idaho State University

Terri Fine
University of Central Florida

Paul D. Foote
Abraham Baldwin Agricultural College, Georgia

Gail E. Garbrandt
University of Akron, Ohio

J. Tobin Grant
Southern Illinois University

Richard Himelfarb
Hofstra University, New York

Brian Kessel
Columbia College, Maryland

Mel Laracey
University of Texas at San Antonio

Steven A. Light
University of North Dakota

Larry Taylor
Georgia Southern University

Our styles of teaching and mentoring students were shaped in important ways by our graduate faculty at Ohio State University. We thank Lawrence Baum, Herbert Asher, Elliot Slotnick, and Randall Ripley for lessons well taught. The students we have had the privilege of working with at many fine universities during our careers have also taught us a great deal. We trust that some of what appears on these pages reflects their insights, and we hope that what we have written will capture the interest of current and future students. Of course, we owe an immeasurable debt to our families, whose divergent views on political issues reflect an America at odds.

We thank Susan Badger, president of Wadsworth Publishing Company, for all of her encouragement and support throughout our work on this project. We were also fortunate to have the editorial advice of Clark Baxter, publisher, and David Tatom, executive editor, and the assistance of Stacey Sims, senior developmental editor, who supervised all aspects of the supplements and the text. We thank Heather Hogan, assistant editor, for her handling of the supplements and related items. We also thank Lavina Leed Miller and Erin Wait for their tremendous help in coordinating the project and for their research, copyediting, and proof-reading assistance. We received additional copyediting and proofreading assistance from Pat Lewis and Suzie DeFazio. We are also grateful to Sue Jasin of K&M Consulting and Roxie Lee. With their help, we were able to meet our ambitious publishing schedule. We appreciate the enthusiasm of Janise Fry, our hard-working marketing manager, and the cheerful support of Ann Borman, our project editor, at Wadsworth Publishing Company. We would also like to acknowledge Bill Stryker, our designer and production manager for producing the most attractive and user-friendly American government text on the market today.

Finally, we are indebted to others who worked on various supplements for *America at Odds*. For their tireless and expert work on the CD-ROM that accompanies this text, we would like to give special thanks to Melinda Newfarmer (technology project manager) and Imagix Studios. Melinda Newfarmer also handled the development of the *America at Odds* Web site. We also thank the contributors to the CD-ROM: Larry Elowitz of Georgia College and State University; John Soares; Brigid Harrison of Montclair State University; and Anthony Simones.

If you or your students have ideas or suggestions, you can write us directly or send us information through Wadsworth Publishing Company.

E.I.S.
B.M.H.

chapter 1

america in the twenty-first century

CHAPTER OBJECTIVES

After reading this chapter, you should be able to . . .

Explain what is meant by the terms *politics* and *government*.

Describe the four basic functions of government.

Identify the various types of government systems.

Distinguish between a direct democracy and a representative democracy.

Summarize some of the basic principles of American democracy.

Identify the basic American political values.

Are We Becoming Too Patriotic?

According to a study of patriotism by the National Opinion Research Center at the University of Chicago, Americans are prouder of their country than are people in any other country in the world.[1] The survey, which compared patriotism in twenty-three nations, revealed that nearly 90 percent of Americans would rather be citizens of the United States than of any other country. According to the director of the survey project, Tom Smith, "[A]n important element of idealism . . . spurs pride in the U.S." Smith notes that unlike most nations, which were "built up around a primordial tribe," the United States was from the outset a nation "based on a set of shared ideals." In this chapter, you will read more about the origins and types of political ideals that Americans share.

Patriotism Symbolizes National Unity

At its core, patriotism means "love of country." Some people would add to this the passion that drives one to serve one's country and perhaps die for it. A vast majority of Americans are patriotic, although the precise qualities that they love about this country and the ways in which they feel compelled to serve it may differ. After the terrorist attacks of September 11, 2001, 82 percent of Americans said that they had displayed the flag.[2] Such outpourings of patriotism sustained Americans through their mourning after September 11 and have inspired feelings of belonging and national unity.

Patriotic Symbols Inflame Americans' Differences of Opinion

Critics of patriotic displays such as flag waving argue that they are sometimes used aggressively, not patriotically. For example, a student might put up a flag in his or her dorm room to express solidarity with the nation and sadness for the victims of September 11. Another student might put up a flag because she has argued with international students down the hall about American foreign policy. At that point, the flag waving may cross the line from patriotism to harassment.

"[T]his country has been neatly divided between aggressive flag wavers and those suspicious of aggressive flag wavers," says Wallace Baine, a writer for the *Santa Cruz Sentinel.* American patriots, argues Baine, express their love of country in a variety of ways, from playing the blues, to hiking the John Muir trail, to serving in the American military. "Those genuinely moved by

. . . traditional expressions of patriotism need to understand something about those of us who aren't. We aren't hostile or even indifferent to your values; we are dismayed that our own aren't being recognized."[3]

This cultural divide in the way Americans express their patriotism has been seen most dramatically on college campuses. At Florida Gulf Coast University, library employees were asked to remove "Proud to Be an American" stickers from their work areas to avoid offending international students.[4] At Central Michigan University, a residential adviser said that pro-American items in dorm rooms were offensive.[5]

American Patriotism Viewed from Abroad

Around the world, there was an initial outpouring of public sympathy for America following the September 11, 2001, terrorist attacks. Since then, however, global public opinion of the United States has fallen. And this has occurred not only in developing nations or nations in the Middle East, but also among the citizens of our traditional allies, such as Canada, Germany, and France.

Americans seem oblivious to other nations' views of the United States. Whereas citizens of most other countries say that the United States fails to consider the interests of other countries in its foreign policy, a solid majority of Americans think that the government does consider other countries' interests. Eighty percent of Americans believe that it is a good thing that U.S. ideas and customs are spreading around the world, but most of those polled in other countries resent the influence of American culture in their societies.[6]

Where Do You Stand?

1. Do you believe symbols of American patriotism unite the nation or accentuate Americans' cultural and political differences?

2. Do you think it matters that American expressions of patriotism following the September 11 attacks may have offended people from other countries?

Interacting with Your CD-ROM Resources

Use your CD-ROM to access resources on the Web, simulations, participation exercises, and video clips. Important resources related to this feature include:
- **Values Inventory**—Political Ideology: Are We Becoming Too Patriotic?
- **Where Do You Stand?**—Dialogue: Are We Becoming Too Patriotic?
- **Web Resources**—Internet Activities: The USA Patriot Act of 2001; What Is Patriotism?; The New American Patriotism.

INTRODUCTION

Regardless of how Americans feel about government, one thing is certain: they can't live without it. James Madison (1751–1836) once said, "If men were angels, no government would be necessary." Today, his statement still holds true. People are not perfect. People need an organized form of government and a set of rules by which to live.

Note, though, that even if people were perfect, they would still need to establish rules to guide their behavior. They would somehow have to agree on how to divide up a society's resources, such as its land, among themselves and how to balance individual needs and wants against those of society generally. These perfect people would also have to decide *how* to make these decisions. They would need to create a process for making rules and a form of government to enforce those rules. It is thus not difficult to understand why government is one of humanity's oldest and most universal institutions. No society has existed without some form of government. The need for authority and organization will never disappear.

As you will read in this chapter, a number of different systems of government exist in the world today. In the United States, we have a democracy, in which decisions about pressing issues ultimately are made by the people, through their representatives in government. Because people rarely have identical thoughts and feelings about issues, it is not surprising that in any democracy citizens are often at odds with one another. Certainly, Americans are at odds over many political and social issues, including the issue discussed in the chapter-opening feature. Americans were also seriously at odds in 2002 and 2003 over whether the United States should unilaterally—that is, without the support of the global community, as represented by the United Nations—invade Iraq with U.S. ground troops to remove Saddam Hussein from power. Many Americans favored giving diplomatic efforts more time to be effective. Others favored immediate invasion, while still others believed the United States should never invade Iraq without a broad international coalition.[7] Throughout the pages of this text, you will read about other issues that divide Americans.

Realize, though, that the aim of this book is not to depict a nation that is falling apart at the seams. Rather, it is to place the conflicting views currently being expressed by Americans in a historical perspective. Having citizens at odds with one another is nothing new in this country. Indeed, throughout this nation's history, Americans have had strikingly different ideas about what decisions should be made and by whom. Differences in opinion are part and parcel of a democratic government. Ultimately, these differences are resolved, one way or another, through the American political process and our government institutions.

John Locke (1632–1704), an English philosopher. Locke argued that human beings were equal and endowed by nature with certain rights, such as the right to life, liberty, and property. The purpose of government, according to Locke, was to protect those rights. Locke's theory of natural rights and his contention that government stemmed from a social contract among society's members were an important part of the political heritage brought to this country by the English colonists. (The Granger Collection)

What Are Politics and Government?

Politics means many things to many people. To some, politics is an expensive and extravagant game played in Washington, D.C., in state capitols, and in city halls, particularly during election time. To others, politics involves all of the tactics and maneuvers carried out by the president and Congress.

Most formal definitions of politics, however, begin with the assumption that **social conflict**—disagreements among people in a society over what the society's priorities should be—is inevitable. Conflicts will naturally arise over how the society should use its scarce resources and who should receive various benefits, such as wealth, status, health care, and higher education. Resolving such conflicts is the essence of **politics**. Political scientist Harold Lasswell perhaps said it best when he defined politics as the process of determining "who gets what, when, and how" in a society.[8]

There are also many different notions about the meaning of government. From the perspective of political science, though, **government** can best be defined as the individuals and institutions that make society's rules and that also possess the *power* and *authority* to enforce those rules.

Although this definition of government sounds remote and abstract, what the government does is very real indeed. As one scholar put it, "Make no mistake. What Congress does directly and powerfully affects our daily lives."[9] The same can be said for decisions made by state

SOCIAL CONFLICT Disagreements among people in a society over what the society's priorities should be with respect to the use of scarce resources.

POLITICS The process of resolving conflicts over how society should use its scarce resources and who should receive various benefits, such as public health care and public higher education. According to Harold Lasswell, politics is the process of determining "who gets what, when, and how" in a society.

GOVERNMENT The individuals and institutions that make society's rules and that also possess the power and authority to enforce those rules.

legislators and local government officials, as well as for decisions rendered by the courts—the judicial branch of government. There remains, of course, a key question: How do specific individuals obtain the power and authority to govern? As you will read shortly, the answer to this question varies from one type of political system to another.

What Does Government Do?

The first step in understanding how government works is to understand what it actually does for people and society. Generally, in any country government serves four major purposes: (1) it resolves conflicts; (2) it provides public services; (3) it sets goals for public policies; and (4) it preserves culture.

POWER The ability to influence the behavior of others, usually through the use of force, persuasion, or rewards.

AUTHORITY The ability to exercise power, such as the power to make and enforce laws, legitimately.

Resolving Conflicts   Even though people have lived together in groups since the beginning of time, none of these groups has been free of social conflict. As mentioned, disputes over how to distribute a society's valued resources inevitably arise because valued resources, such as property, are limited, while people's wants are unlimited. To resolve such disputes, people need ways to determine who wins and who loses, and how to get the losers to accept those decisions. Who has the legitimate power and authority to make such decisions? This is where government steps in.

Governments decide how conflicts will be resolved so that public order can be maintained. Governments have **power**—the ability to influence the behavior of others. Power is getting someone to do something he or she would not do otherwise. Power may involve the use of force (often called coercion), persuasion, or rewards. Governments also have **authority,** which they can exercise only if their power is legitimate. As used here, the term *legitimate power* means power that is collectively recognized and accepted by society as legally and morally correct. Power and authority are central to a government's ability to resolve conflicts by making and enforcing laws, placing limits on what people can do, and developing court systems to make final decisions.

For example, the judicial branch of government—specifically, the United States Supreme Court—resolved the conflict over whether the votes in certain Florida counties could be recounted after the 2000 presidential elections. Because of the Court's stature and authority as a government body, there was virtually no resistance to the Court's decision not to allow the recounting—although the decision was strongly criticized by many.

PUBLIC SERVICES Essential services that individuals cannot provide for themselves, such as building and maintaining roads, providing welfare programs, operating public schools, and preserving national parks.

Providing Public Services   Another important purpose of government is to provide **public services**—essential services that many individuals cannot provide for themselves. Governments undertake projects that individuals usually would not or could not do on their own, such as building and maintaining roads, providing welfare programs, operating public schools, and preserving national parks. Governments also provide such services as law enforcement, fire protection, and public health and safety programs. As Abraham Lincoln once stated:

> The legitimate object of government is to do for a community of people whatever they need to have done but cannot do at all, or cannot so well do for themselves in their separate and individual capacities. But in all that people can individually do for themselves, government ought not to interfere.

Some public services are provided equally to all citizens of the United States. For example, government services such as national defense and domestic law enforcement allow all citizens, at least in theory, to feel that their lives and property are safe. Laws governing clean air and safe drinking water benefit all Americans. Other services are provided only to citizens who are in need at a particular time, even though they are paid for by all citizens through taxes. Examples of such services include Medicare, welfare benefits, and public housing. Laws such as the Americans with Disabilities Act explicitly protect the rights of people with disabilities, although all Americans pay for such protections whether they are disabled or not.

Historically, matters of national security and defense have been given high priority by governments and have demanded considerable time, effort, and expense. The U.S. government provides for the common defense and national security with its Army, Navy, Air Force, Marines, and Coast Guard. The State Department, Defense Department, Homeland Security

Department, Central Intelligence Agency, National Security Agency, and other agencies also contribute to this defense network. As part of an ongoing policy of national security, many departments and agencies in the federal government are constantly dealing with other nations. The Constitution gives our national government exclusive power over relations with foreign nations. No individual state can negotiate a treaty with a foreign nation.

Setting Goals for Public Policies Governments set goals designed to improve the lives of their citizens. These goals may affect the people on a local, state, or national scale. On setting these goals, governments design plans of action, known as **public policies,** to support or achieve the goals. Public-policy goals may be short term, such as improving a city's educational system by adding new classes, or long term, such as discovering new energy sources.

Public policymaking is a difficult and complex undertaking. In part, this is because policy decisions ultimately involve difficult choices. Because resources are limited, establishing one policy goal, such as tax cuts, may mean sacrificing another, such as using tax revenues to improve education.

Preserving Culture A nation's culture includes the customs, language, beliefs, and values of its people. Governments have worked to preserve their nations' cultures in ways that citizens cannot. For example, the observance of Independence Day on July 4 in the United States helps carry on a tradition that celebrates our history. In France, Bastille Day is celebrated every year on July 14. In the People's Republic of China, National Day is celebrated on October 10.

Of course, a government also helps to preserve a nation's culture, as well as its integrity as an independent unit, by defending the nation against attacks by other nations. Failure to defend successfully against foreign attacks may have significant results for a nation's culture. For example, consider what happened in Tibet. When the former government of that country was unable to defend itself against the People's Republic of China in the 1950s, the conquering Chinese set out on a systematic program to destroy Tibet's culture.

One of the primary purposes of government is, of course, to resolve conflicts in society. Governments also serve other purposes, however, one of which is to provide public services that individuals cannot provide for themselves. Providing for national defense is an activity that only the federal government can undertake. (AP Photo/Evan Vucci)

PUBLIC POLICIES Plans of action to support or achieve government goals that are designed to improve the lives of citizens.

Different Systems of Government

Through the centuries, the functions of government just discussed have been performed by many different types of government structures. A government's structure is influenced by a number of factors, such as history, customs, values, geography, climate, resources, and human experiences and needs. No two nations have exactly the same form of government. Over time, however, political analysts have developed various ways of classifying different systems of government. One of the most meaningful ways of classifying governments is according to *who* governs. Who has the power to make the rules and laws that all must obey?

Rule by One: Autocracy

In an **autocracy,** the power and authority of the government are in the hands of a single person. At one time, autocracy was a common form of government, and it still exists in some parts of the world. Autocrats usually obtain their power either by inheriting it (as the heir to a divine right monarchy, for example) or by force.

AUTOCRACY A form of government in which the power and authority of the government are in the hands of a single person.

Monarchy One form of autocracy, known as a **monarchy,** is government by a king, queen, emperor, empress, tsar, or tsarina. In a monarchy, the monarch, who usually acquires power through inheritance, is the highest authority in the government.

Historically, many monarchies were *absolute monarchies,* in which the ruler held complete and unlimited power as a matter of divine right. Prior to the eighteenth century, the theory of

MONARCHY A form of autocracy in which a king, queen, emperor, empress, tsar, or tsarina is the highest authority in the government; monarchs usually obtain their power through inheritance.

One of the ways that we preserve our unique American political culture is through celebrating important historical events, such as the date we declared independence from Britain. Fourth of July parades, such as the one shown here, remind Americans of their history and contribute to feelings of patriotism. (AP Photo/ *Newport News-Daily Press*, Heather Charles)

DIVINE RIGHT THEORY A theory that the right to rule by a king or queen was derived directly from God rather than from the consent of the people.

divine right was widely accepted in Europe. The **divine right theory,** variations of which had existed since ancient times, held that God gave those of royal birth the unlimited right to govern other men and women. In other words, those of royal birth had a "divine right" to rule. According to this theory, only God could judge those of royal birth. Thus, all citizens were bound to obey their monarchs, no matter how unfair or unjust they seemed to be. Challenging this power was regarded not only as treason against the government but also as a sin against God.

Most modern monarchies, however, are *constitutional monarchies,* in which the monarch shares governmental power with elected lawmakers. The monarch's power is limited, or checked, by other government leaders and perhaps by a constitution or a bill of rights. These constitutional monarchs serve mainly as *ceremonial* leaders of their governments, as in Great Britain, Denmark, and Sweden.

DICTATORSHIP A form of government in which absolute power is exercised by a single person who has usually obtained his or her power by the use of force.

Dictatorship
Another form of autocracy is a **dictatorship,** in which a single leader rules, although not through inheritance. Dictators often gain supreme power by using force, either through a military victory or by overthrowing another dictator or leader. Dictators hold absolute power and are not accountable to anyone else.

A dictatorship can also be *totalitarian,* which means that the leader (or group of leaders) seeks to control almost all aspects of social and economic life. The needs of the nation come before the needs of individuals, and all citizens must work for the common goals established by the government. Examples of this form of government include Adolf Hitler's government in Nazi Germany from 1933 to 1945, Benito Mussolini's rule in Italy from 1923 to 1943, and Josef Stalin's rule in the Soviet Union from 1929 to 1953. More contemporary examples of totalitarian dictators include Fidel Castro in Cuba, Kim Jong Il in North Korea, and, until his government was dismantled in 2003, Saddam Hussein in Iraq.

Rule by Many: Democracy

The most familiar form of government to Americans is **democracy,** in which the supreme political authority rests with the people. The word *democracy* comes from the Greek *demos,* meaning "the people," and *kratia,* meaning "rule." The main idea of democracy is that government exists only by the consent of the people and reflects the will of the majority.

DEMOCRACY A system of government in which the people have ultimate political authority. The word is derived from the Greek *demos* (people) and *kratia* (rule).

DIRECT DEMOCRACY A system of government in which political decisions are made by the people themselves rather than by elected representatives. This form of government was practiced in some areas of ancient Greece.

The Athenian Model of Direct Democracy
Democracy as a form of government began long ago. **Direct democracy** exists when the people participate directly in government decision making. In its purest form, direct democracy was practiced in Athens and

other ancient Greek city-states about 2,500 years ago. Every Athenian citizen participated in the governing assembly and voted on all major issues. Although some consider the Athenian form of direct democracy ideal because it demanded a high degree of citizen participation, others point out that most residents in the Athenian city-state (women, foreigners, and slaves) were not deemed to be citizens and thus were not allowed to participate in government.

Clearly, direct democracy is possible only in small communities in which citizens can meet in a chosen place and decide key issues and policies. Nowhere in the world does pure direct democracy exist today. Some New England town meetings, though, and a few of the smaller political subunits, or cantons, of Switzerland still use a modified form of direct democracy. (See this chapter's *Comparative Politics* feature.)

Representative Democracy   Although the founders of the United States were aware of the Athenian model and agreed that government should be based on the consent of the governed, many feared that a pure, direct democracy would deteriorate into mob rule. They believed that large groups of people meeting together would ignore the rights and opinions of people in the minority and would make decisions without careful thought. They concluded that a representative democracy would be the better choice because it would enable public decisions to be made in a calmer and more deliberate manner.

In a **representative democracy,** the will of the majority is expressed through a smaller group of individuals elected by the people to act as their representatives. These representatives are responsible to the people for their conduct and can be voted out of office. Our founders preferred to use the term **republic,** which means essentially a representative democracy. As our population grew, this republic became increasingly removed from the Athenian model. (Some contend that our republic has also become increasingly removed from the people. See this chapter's *Perception versus Reality* feature on the following page for a discussion of this issue.)

In the modern world, there are two forms of representative democracy: presidential and parliamentary. In a *presidential democracy,* the lawmaking and law-enforcing branches of government are separate but equal. For example, in the United States, Congress is charged with the power to make laws, and the president is charged with the power to carry them out. In a *parliamentary democracy,* the lawmaking and law-enforcing branches of government overlap. In Great Britain, for example, the prime minister and the cabinet are members of the legislature, called Parliament. Parliament thus both enacts the laws and carries them out.

This New Hampshire town meeting is an example of direct democracy. (Farrell Grehan, Photo Researchers)

REPRESENTATIVE DEMOCRACY A form of democracy in which the will of the majority is expressed through smaller groups of individuals elected by the people to act as their representatives.

REPUBLIC Essentially, a term referring to a representative democracy—in which the will of the majority is expressed through smaller groups of individuals elected by the people to act as their representatives.

comparative politics

Direct Democracy in Switzerland

There is a belief that in a modern democracy every qualified adult is entitled to an equal say in the conduct of public affairs. Nowhere in the modern world has this idea been taken further than in Switzerland, a country in which direct democracy reigns. In that country, only 50,000 signatures—about 1 percent of the qualified voters—are needed on a petition to bring a new countrywide law passed by the parliament before the vote of the whole people for a possible recall. If 150,000 signatures can be gathered, a proposal that the parliament has not even considered can be brought before the whole people. By their votes, the people can either reject the proposal or adopt it as law.

Since the current system was instituted in Switzerland 130 years ago, over 450 questions have been the subjects of nationwide referenda. Three or four times a year, all Swiss citizens are invited to read detailed documents sent to them in the mail, presented on TV, or available on the Internet that set forth arguments for and against as many as a dozen different issues.

One recent issue involved an attempt to toughen Switzerland's political asylum laws. As a neutral country, Switzerland has long attracted refugees seeking political asylum. This referendum was rejected in 2002 by a margin of merely 3,422 votes out of 2.2 million votes cast. Another issue concerned the legalization of abortion. Although the nation's ban on abortion had been widely ignored for years, many groups favored officially lifting the ban. The referendum passed with 72 percent of the popular vote.

Swiss voters have accepted about half of the laws passed by the parliament that were put before the people for a vote. But the voters have turned down nine-tenths of the proposed new legislation.

For Critical Analysis

Is direct democracy compatible with a strong legislature? Would direct democracy be practical in the United States?

perception versus REALITY

Who Rules in Our "Representative" Democracy?

As you read elsewhere in this chapter, the founders of this nation chose not to create a direct democracy, in which citizens directly participate in government decisions. Rather, they established a representative democracy, in which citizens elect representatives to make decisions on their behalf. The question is, do these representatives really represent the people's interests?

THE PERCEPTION

For many Americans, the government in Washington, D.C., is a faceless, anonymous entity. Polls in recent years have shown that about two-thirds of Americans do not even know the names of their representatives in Congress. This lack of interest stems, in part, from a fairly widespread notion that the individual is powerless to control what goes on in the nation's capital. Decisions made there do not reflect the voters' wishes, but rather the influence of elite, monied interest groups. In other words, America is not truly a "representative" democracy, in which those elected by the voters represent the people's views. The real rulers of this country are the rich and powerful.

THE REALITY

To be sure, campaign contributions carry a lot of clout, as you will read in Chapters 6 and 9, and money does talk—in the halls of Congress as elsewhere. Yet there is also much evidence that rich special interests do not really rule America.

Consider an example. If wealthy Americans are so powerful, why is their tax burden increasing, rather than decreasing? According to the Congressional Budget Office, the wealthiest groups of Americans have paid a growing share of federal taxes since the mid-1980s. About 1.2 million families with average incomes of $768,000 now pay about 21 percent of all federal taxes, up from 15 percent in the mid-1980s. In contrast, taxes for the poorest group of Americans dropped from 22 to 17 percent of total taxes during the same period. Clearly, the wealthiest Americans do not have the political power to protect themselves against higher taxes, so do they really dominate Washington?

Consider also that Congress spends a good deal of federal tax revenues on programs, such as Medicare, Social Security, and Medicaid, that benefit the middle and poorer classes in American society.[10]

It is true that wealthy interests clearly buy "access" to members of Congress through campaign contributions and that they do influence lawmaking to a significant extent. Yet, at least to date, they have not been able to "buy" Congress and really rule the country.[11]

What's Your Opinion?

Does the fact that someone does not know the name of his or her congressional representatives necessarily mean that that person is not interested in what goes on in Congress? Explain.

American Democracy

> This country, with all its institutions, belongs to the people who inhabit it. Whenever they shall grow weary of the existing government, they can exercise their constitutional right to amend it, or their revolutionary right to dismember or overthrow it.

With these words, Abraham Lincoln underscored the most fundamental concept of American government: that the people, not the government, are ultimately in control.

Principles of American Democracy

American democracy is based on five fundamental principles:

- *Equality in voting.* Citizens need equal opportunities to express their preferences about policies or leaders.
- *Individual freedom.* All individuals must have the greatest amount of freedom possible without interfering with the rights of others.
- *Equal protection of the law.* The law must entitle all persons to equal protection of the law.
- *Majority rule and minority rights.* The majority should rule, while guaranteeing the rights of minorities so that the latter may sometimes become majorities through fair and lawful means.
- *Voluntary consent to be governed.* The people who make up a democracy must agree voluntarily to be governed by the rules laid down by their representatives.

These principles frame many of the political issues that you will read about in this book. They also frequently lie at the heart of America's political conflicts. Should the principle of

The American flag symbolizes not only our independence but also such ideals as equality, liberty, and limited government. The original Stars and Stripes came about as a result of a resolution offered by the Marine Committee of the Second Continental Congress in Philadelphia on June 14, 1777. The current fifty-star flag of the United States was raised for the first time officially at 12:01 A.M. on July 4, 1960, at Fort McHenry National Monument in Baltimore, Maryland. (AP Photo/*The News-Times,* Douglas Healey)

minority rights mean that minorities should receive preferential treatment in hiring and fir-ing decisions? Should the principle of individual freedom mean that individuals can say what-ever they want on the Internet, including hateful, racist comments? Such conflicts over individual rights and freedoms and over society's priorities are natural and inevitable. Resolving these conflicts is what politics is all about. What is important is that Americans are able to reach acceptable compromises—because of their common political heritage.

American Political Values

One of the forces that unites Americans is a common **political culture,** which can be defined as a patterned set of ideas, values, and ways of thinking about government and politics. Despite the flaws and weaknesses of the American political system, most Americans are proud of their country and support it with their obedience to its laws, their patriotism, and their votes.

The shared political beliefs at the core of our political culture were summarized in the **American Creed,** written by William Tyler Page (1868–1942) in 1917.

> I believe in the United States of America as a government of the people, by the people, and for the people; whose just powers are derived from the consent of the governed; a democracy in a Republic; a sovereign Nation of many sovereign States; a perfect Union, one and inseparable; established upon those principles of freedom, equality, justice, and humanity for which American patriots sacrificed their lives and fortunes.
>
> I therefore believe it is my duty to my country to love it; to support its Constitution; to obey its laws; to respect its flag; and to defend it against all enemies.

These ideals and standards are also embodied in the Declaration of Independence, one of the founding documents of this nation, which is discussed further in Chapter 2 and presented in its entirety in Appendix B. The political values outlined in the Declaration of Independence include natural rights (to life, liberty, and the pursuit of happiness), equality under the law, government by the consent of the governed, and limited government powers. In some ways, the Declaration of Independence defines Americans' sense of right and wrong. It presents a challenge to anyone who might wish to overthrow our democratic processes or deny our cit-izens their natural rights.

POLITICAL CULTURE The set of ideas, values, and attitudes about government and the political process held by a community or nation.

AMERICAN CREED The principles set forth in a document written by William Tyler Page in 1917 and based on the Declaration of Independence.

AMERICA at odds

The Flag as a National Symbol

Because of the importance of our basic political values, Americans attach great meaning to national symbols, as you read in the chapter-opening *America at Odds* feature. The American flag, for example, represents not only independence, but also everything that Americans fought for during the Revolutionary War, including liberty, equality, and limited government. For this reason, flag burning as a gesture of protest does not sit well with many Americans. Indeed, in 1989 Congress even passed a law prohibiting such actions.[12] The Supreme Court, however, held that the law was unconstitutional because it violated the freedom of expression protected by the First Amendment (which is discussed in Chapter 4).[13]

Another controversial issue involving a flag as a symbol relates to the Confederate flag, the symbol of the southern states that broke away from the Union in 1860, triggering the Civil War. Those who display the Confederate flag today elicit hostility from many Americans who view that flag as a symbol of slavery—part of the political culture of the Old South. Others believe that states in the South should have the right to display the Confederate flag because it is a symbol of old southern traditions. In 2000, the state of South Carolina refused to lower the Confederate flag from the top of its state capitol building. Hundreds of thousands of people marched in protest on Martin Luther King Day in 2000. Later that year, the South Carolina legislature decided to remove the flag from its statehouse, although the flag continues to fly on statehouse grounds. Other southern states have faced similar controversies.[14]

This Atlanta couple is proud of their heritage and the Confederate "Stars and Bars" that symbolizes it. Others believe that the Confederate flag should not be displayed because it is too closely linked to the institution of slavery. (J. Van Hasselt/CORBIS Sygma)

Liberty, Equality, and Property

Fundamental political values shared by most Americans include liberty, equality, and property. These values provide a basic framework for American political discourse and debate because they are shared by most Americans, yet individual Americans often interpret their meaning quite differently.

LIBERTY The freedom of individuals to believe, act, and express themselves freely so long as doing so does not infringe on the rights of other individuals in the society.

Liberty   The term **liberty** refers to a state of being free from external controls or restrictions. In the United States, the Constitution sets forth our civil liberties. These liberties include the freedom to practice whatever religion we choose and to be free from any state-imposed religion. They also include the freedom to speak freely on any topics and issues, including government actions. Because people cannot govern themselves unless they are free to voice their opinions, freedom of speech is a basic requirement in a true democracy.

Clearly, though, if we are to live together with others, there have to be some restrictions on individual liberties. If people were allowed to do whatever they wished, without regard for the rights or liberties of others, pandemonium would result. Hence, a more accurate definition of liberty would be as follows: *liberty is the freedom of individuals to believe, act, and express them-*

The POLITICS of HOMELAND SECURITY

Total Information Awareness

In the aftermath of the terrorist attacks on September 11, 2001, government officials and citizens alike asked why government agencies designed to protect us had failed to stop the terrorists before they acted. As information about the terrorists' actions before September 11 was revealed, the government's answer was that it "failed to connect the dots." Since then, the government has been working on systems that could "connect the dots"— that could monitor the actions of potential terrorists and thwart a terrorist attack before it occurs.

To tie together the actions of hundreds, if not thousands, of potential terrorists would require a sophisticated computer database that could track everything from applications for passports, visas, and driver's licenses to credit-card transactions, car rentals, airline ticket purchases, gun purchases, arrest records, e-mail, and more. And to monitor the activity of every potential terrorist, the government would need to monitor the activity of, well, just about everyone. The government is creating such a "data-mining" system. It is called the Total Information Awareness system, or TIA.

LIBERTY VERSUS NATIONAL SECURITY

In this chapter, you have read that a fundamental political value of all Americans is liberty—the freedom of individuals to believe, act, and express themselves freely. As you will read in Chapter 4, this political value is protected by the Constitution and its first ten amendments, known as the Bill of Rights. If the government creates a system that could monitor the transactions, purchases, and records of all Americans, this fundamental tenet of our democracy could be violated. Yet part of the definition of liberty is that one person's freedom should not infringe on the rights of others, such as the right to be secure in our persons. How can the government balance the need to protect our liberties with its duty to provide national security?

TECHNOLOGY IS VITAL IN THE WAR ON TERRORISM

In countries with fewer constitutionally protected rights than we enjoy, the war against terrorism has been proceeding more quickly. According to Philip Zelikow of the University of

Virginia's Miller Center, "The paradox is that once someone enters the United States, they become invisible, shielded by all our laws and restraints. The National Security Agency and the CIA can keep tabs on people around the world—but not here. We just caught a terrorist in Pakistan. Had he been in America, he'd have been safe."[15] Zelikow and other observers argue that homeland security must necessarily involve combining the most modern technology with intelligence gathering. "[T]echnology is our strength, our asymmetric capability to defeat terrorism," says retired Colonel Edward Badolato, former deputy secretary of energy focusing on counterterrorism.[16]

EXACTLY WHO IS "BIG BROTHER"?

Some of the most vocal criticism of the TIA project has targeted not its intent but the person managing it, retired admiral John Poindexter. Poindexter is most famous for his role in what was known as the Iran-Contra scandal. While serving as national security adviser to President Ronald Reagan, Poindexter became involved in secretly selling weapons to Iran as ransom for hostages and using the proceeds to support rebels in Nicaragua. He was convicted in 1990 on five felony counts of misleading Congress and making false statements, but the conviction was overturned because Congress had given him immunity in exchange for his testimony.

Poindexter's critics say that someone with such contempt for government openness and congressional oversight should not be in charge of a computerized dossier on every American's private life. The political backlash against Poindexter was so great that in late 2002, Senator Charles Schumer (D., N.Y.) demanded that Defense Secretary Donald Rumsfeld replace him as director of the Information Awareness office that oversees TIA. "If we need a Big Brother, John Poindexter is the last guy on the list that I would choose," said Schumer.[17]

Are We Safer?

Do you believe that a government database system that looks for patterns of behavior among thousands, if not millions, of people will be able to anticipate and stop terrorist acts before they happen?

selves freely so long as doing so does not infringe on the rights of other individuals in the society. (Another reason liberty is sometimes curtailed is to ensure the security of all Americans. See this chapter's *The Politics of Homeland Security* feature for a discussion of this issue.)

Equality   The goal of **equality** has always been a central part of American political culture. Many of the first settlers came to this country to be free of unequal treatment and persecution. They sought the freedom to live and worship as they wanted. They believed that anyone who worked hard could succeed, and America became known as the "land of opportunity." The Declaration of Independence confirmed the importance of equality to early Americans by stating, "We hold these Truths to be self-evident, that all Men are created equal." Because of the goal of equality, the Constitution prohibited the government from granting titles of nobility. Article I, Section 9, of the Constitution states, "No Title of Nobility shall be granted by the United States." (The Constitution did not prohibit slavery, however—see Chapter 2.)

EQUALITY A concept that holds, at a minimum, that all people are entitled to equal protection under the law.

But what, exactly, does equality mean? Does it mean simply political equality—the right to vote and run for political office? Does it mean that individuals should have equal opportunities to develop their talents and skills? What about those who are poor, suffer from disabilities, or are otherwise at a competitive disadvantage? Should it be the government's responsibility to ensure that these groups also have equal opportunities? Although most Americans believe that all persons should have the opportunity to fulfill their potential, few contend that it is the government's responsibility to totally eliminate the economic and social differences that lead to unequal opportunities. Indeed, some contend that efforts to achieve equality, in the sense of equal justice for all, are misguided attempts to create an ideal society that can never exist.[18]

Property   The English philosopher John Locke (1632–1704) asserted that people are born with "natural" rights and that among these rights are life, liberty, and *property*. The Declaration of Independence makes a similar assertion: people are born with certain "unalienable" rights, including the right to life, liberty, and the *pursuit of happiness*. For Americans, property and the pursuit of happiness are closely related. Americans place a great value on land ownership, on material possessions, and on the monetary value of their jobs. Property gives its owners political power and the liberty to do whatever they want—within limits.

"The American Story"—What Values and Ideals Should Be Included?

You can tell a lot about a nation's political values by reading its history books. As you will learn in Chapter 8, our schools play an important part in the process of political socialization—the passing on of political values from one generation to the next. You can also tell a lot about a person's political ideals and values by asking her or him which themes should be stressed in the teaching of American history.

What themes should be stressed in teaching "the American story" to schoolchildren? To learn the answer to that question, the Roper Center conducted a survey, the results of which are shown in Table 1–1. The answers show that the respondents clearly placed a high value on

TABLE 1–1
The Teaching of American History

Question: In teaching the American story to children, how important is the following theme . . . ?

	ESSENTIAL/VERY IMPORTANT	SOMEWHAT IMPORTANT	SOMEWHAT UNIMPORTANT/ VERY UNIMPORTANT/LEAVE IT OUT OF THE STORY
With hard work and perseverance, anyone can succeed in America.	83%	14%	4%
American democracy is only as strong as the virtue of its citizens.	83	14	4
Our founders limited the power of government, so government would not intrude too much into the lives of its citizens.	74	19	8
America is the world's greatest melting pot in which people from different countries are united into one nation.	73	21	5
America's contribution is one of expanding freedom for more and more people.	71	22	6
From its start, America had a destiny to set an example for other nations.	65	22	13
Our nation betrayed its founding principles by cruel mistreatment of blacks and American Indians.	59	24	17
Our nation was founded upon biblical principles.	58	26	15
Ours has been a history of war and aggression—our expansion occurred at the cost of much suffering.	58	26	16
America has a special place in God's plan for history.	50	22	29
Our founders were part of a male-dominated culture that gave important roles to men while keeping women in the background.	38	28	35

SOURCE: *The Public Perspective*, April/May 1999.

such ideals as democracy, limited government, liberty, and equality. The results also indicate that a majority of Americans want their children to know that this nation "was founded upon biblical principles" and that "America has a special place in God's plan for history." The inclusion of religious values in the American story should not come as a surprise, for Americans continue to express a high degree of association with religion and religious groups.

Political Values in a Multicultural Society

From the earliest British and European settlers to the numerous cultural groups who today call America their home, American society has always been a multicultural society. Until recently, most Americans viewed the United States as the world's melting pot. They accepted that American society included numerous ethnic and cultural groups, but they expected that the members of these groups would abandon their cultural distinctions and assimilate the language and customs of Americans. One of the outgrowths of the civil rights movement of the 1960s, however, was an emphasis on *multiculturalism,* the belief that the many cultures that make up American society should remain distinct and be protected—and even encouraged—by our laws.

The ethnic make-up of the United States has changed dramatically in the last two decades, however, and will continue to change (see Figure 1–1). During the 1990s, more immigrants entered the United States than at any time since the 1910s, and the majority were not Europeans but rather Asians and Latin Americans. Already, whites are a minority in California. For the nation as a whole, non-Hispanic whites will be in the minority by the year 2060 or shortly thereafter. As immigration rates increased during the 1990s, some Americans feared that rising numbers of immigrants would threaten traditional American political values and culture. Among other things, this fear led to growing criticism of multiculturalist goals and policies.

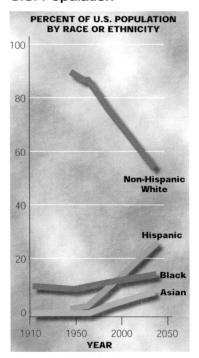

FIGURE 1–1
Racial and Ethnic Composition of the U.S. Population

SOURCE: U.S. Bureau of the Census.

AMERICA at odds

A Nation Divided?

Supporters of multiculturalist policies believe that Americans must be tolerant of other cultures and ways of life. They argue that in the past, too much of what was taught in our educational institutions about history, art, and literature dealt with the achievements of "dead white men." Consequently, they have supported the elimination of standard Western civilization requirements at colleges and universities in favor of more emphasis on American minority groups and non-Western cultures. Multiculturalists have also been among the strongest supporters of bilingual education (see Chapter 5).

Opponents of multiculturalism argue that such policies promote moral relativism by implying that no one group's values are superior to those of another. They argue that all groups should accept certain fundamental American values, including individual liberty, equality between men and women, freedom to voice unpopular opinions, freedom of religion, and so on. Furthermore, the emphasis on diversity is creating a nation divided at a time when the nation needs to be united against its common enemies.

Despite the fears that cultural diversity and increased tolerance for different cultural groups will destroy American values, there is no real evidence that these fears are being realized. In fact, the ties that bind the nation may be stronger than is often thought. According to a poll by Public Agenda, a nonpartisan research group in New York, over 80 percent of all groups in this country (whites, blacks, Hispanics, and so on) felt that it is "absolutely essential" for schools to teach students that "whatever their ethnic or racial background, they are all part of one nation." Similarly, a large majority of respondents, regardless of their ethnic backgrounds or whether they were recent immigrants, believed that "to graduate from high school, students should be required to show they understand the common history and ideas that tie all Americans together."[19]

Reciting the Pledge of Allegiance in school is one way that American children learn about their political heritage and values. (Bob Daemmrich/Stock Boston)

American Democracy at Work

By now, you may have decided that Americans are at odds over every possible issue. But even the most divisive issues can be and are resolved through the political process. How does this process work? Who are the key players? These questions will be answered in the remaining chapters of this book. In the meantime, though, it is helpful to have some kind of a "road map" to guide you through these chapters so that you can see how each topic covered in the text relates to the big picture.

The Big Picture

The U.S. Constitution is the supreme law of the land. It sets forth basic governing rules by which Americans, when they ratified the Constitution, agreed to abide. It is appropriate, then, that we begin this text, following this introductory chapter, with a discussion of how and why the Constitution was created, the type of governing structure it established, and the rights and liberties it guarantees for all Americans. These topics, covered in Chapters 2 through 5, are necessarily the point of departure for any discussion of our system of government. As you will see, some of the most significant political controversies today have to do with how various provisions in this founding document should be applied, over two hundred years later, to modern-day events and issues.

Who Governs?

Who acquires the power and authority to govern, and how do they obtain that power and authority? Generally, of course, the "winners" in our political system are the successful candidates in elections. But the electoral process is influenced by more than just the issue positions taken by the candidates. As you read Chapters 6 through 10, keep the following questions in mind: How do interest groups influence elections? How essential are political parties to the electoral process? To what extent do public opinion and voting behavior play a role in determining who the winners and losers will be? Why are political campaigns so expensive, and what are the implications of high campaign costs for our democracy? Finally, what role do the media play in fashioning the outcomes of campaigns?

Once a winning candidate assumes a political office, that candidate becomes a part of one of the institutions of government. In Chapter 11 and the remaining chapters of this text, we examine these institutions and the process of government decision making. You will learn how those who govern the nation make laws and policies to decide "who gets what, when, and how" in our society. Of course, the topics treated in these chapters are not isolated from the materials covered earlier in the text. For example, when formulating and implementing federal policies, as well as state and local policies, the wishes of interest groups cannot be ignored, particularly those of wealthy groups that can help to fund policymakers' reelections. And public opinion and the media not only affect election outcomes but also influence which issues will be included on the policymaking agenda.

The political system established by the founders of this nation has endured for over two hundred years. The question facing Americans now is whether it will continue to endure.

why does it MATTER?

American Politics and Your Everyday Life

From the time you are born until you reach your final resting place, government affects your everyday life. This was not always the case. In the early years of this nation, government at both the state and federal levels was a relatively small undertaking. The extensive presence of government in the average American's everyday life truly began only in the twentieth century, when, as the nation grew and faced new problems, the government began to regulate economic and social life. Today, government affects virtually all of your activities.

The American government provides the essential framework for nearly everything you do, and in turn American political culture provides the essential framework for American government. Virtually all Americans believe in private property. Most believe in freedom of speech and religion. Few Americans today would advocate the violent overthrow of the government. Almost no Americans believe that taxes are theft. Universal education is accepted by all. The peaceful transition from one administration to the next is taken as a given. For the most part, decisions made by the Supreme Court are accepted, even if reluctantly, by those they concern.

Thus, in spite of Americans' diverse backgrounds, we share certain beliefs about the role of government and citizens in the United States. This common political culture creates an environment that maximizes the possibility that Americans will live peaceful and fulfilling lives.

Taking Action

Although the government of the United States is a *representative* democracy, our political culture encourages *direct* participation in government by citizens. Much is said in the media about low voter turnout in elections and other examples of Americans' lack of political participation. In fact, though, Americans have, and take advantage of, a vast array of methods for influencing their government. In the remaining chapters of this book, *Why Does It Matter?* features will discuss how government and politics affect your daily life. These features will also give examples of how, when citizens are at odds with their government on an issue, they can take action to make a difference.

Key Terms

American Creed 9	direct democracy 6	monarchy 5	public services 4
authority 4	divine right theory 6	political culture 9	representative democracy 7
autocracy 5	equality 11	politics 3	republic 7
democracy 6	government 3	power 4	social conflict 3
dictatorship 6	liberty 10	public policies 5	

Chapter Summary

1 Politics can be formally defined as the process of resolving social conflict—disagreements over how the society should use its scarce resources and who should receive various benefits, such as wealth, status, health care, and higher education.

2 Government can be defined as the individuals and institutions that make society's rules and that also possess the power and authority to enforce those rules. Government serves four major purposes: (1) it resolves conflicts; (2) it provides public services; (3) it sets goals for public policies; and (4) it preserves culture.

3 In an autocracy, the power and authority of the government are in the hands of a single person. Monarchies and dictatorships, including totalitarian dictatorships, are all forms of autocracy. In a constitutional monarchy, however, the monarch shares power with elected lawmakers.

4 Democracy is a form of government in which the government exists only by the consent of the people and reflects the will of the majority. In a direct democracy, the people participate directly in government decision making. In a representative democracy, or

republic, people elect representatives to government office to make decisions for them. Forms of representative democracy include presidential democracy and parliamentary democracy.

5 The five principles of American democracy are (1) equality in voting, (2) individual freedom, (3) equal protection of the law, (4) majority rule and minority rights, and (5) voluntary consent to be governed.

6 A political culture can be defined as a patterned set of ideas, values, and ways of thinking about government and politics. Three deeply rooted values in American political culture are liberty, equality, and property.

7 Americans seem to be in agreement as to what the basic political values of this country are. Polls show that Americans continue to place a high value on such ideals as democracy, limited government, individual liberty, and equality. Although many Americans have expressed fears that multiculturalist policies and programs tend to erode American political values, there is no evidence that this has happened.

RESOURCES FOR FURTHER STUDY

Selected Readings

Cullen, Jim. *The American Dream: A Short History of an Idea That Shaped a Nation.* New York: Oxford University Press, 2003. The author explores the history of "the American dream," how the dream has evolved, and how it remains an expression of Americans' shared ideals.

D'Souza, Dinesh. *What's So Great about America?* Washington, D.C.: Regnery Publishing, 2002. The author presents his arguments, from the perspective of an immigrant and now a citizen, for why America is "the greatest, freest, and most decent society in existence."

Skocpol, Theda, and Morris Fiorina, eds. *Civic Engagement in American Democracy.* Washington, D.C.: Brookings Institution Press, 1999. This collection of essays examines citizen participation in America in the search for why Americans are withdrawing from involvement with community affairs and politics.

InfoTrac Citations

Using your InfoTrac password, access the InfoTrac database at **http://infotrac.thomsonlearning.com**. Once at the site, you can do "key word" searches to locate the following articles, each of which deals with a topic covered in this chapter. The key words to use in your search are indicated in parentheses.

- "Saudi Arabia: The Rules May Be Severe, but This Monarchy's Oil Profits Support a Cushy Lifestyle" (Absolute Monarchy)

- "Voters Take the Initiative: Voters in 42 States Had the Opportunity to Bypass Representative Democracy and Vote Directly on 202 Different Statewide Measures (Representative Democracy)

- "The American Paradox: The Country with the Most Patents, Nobel Laureates, and Millionaires Is Also the Country with the Highest Levels of Poverty, Homicide, and Infant Mortality among Modern Democracies: A Case for Revising Our Social Contract" (Social Contract)

- "Historical Hopes, Media Fears, and the Electronic Town Meeting Concept: Where Technology Meets Democracy or Demagogy? (Teledemocracy)

Politics on the Web

Each chapter of *America at Odds,* Fourth Edition, concludes with a list of Internet resources and addresses. Once you are on the Internet, you can use the addresses, or uniform resource locators (URLs), listed in the *Politics on the Web* sections in this book to access the ever-growing number of resources available on the Internet relating to American politics and government.

Internet sites tend to come and go, and there is no guarantee that a site included in some of the *Politics on the Web* features will be there by the time this book is in print. We have tried, though, to include sites that have so far proved to be fairly stable. If you do have difficulty reaching a site, do not immediately assume that the site does not exist. First, recheck the URL shown in your browser. Remember, you have to type the URL exactly as written: upper case and lower case are important. If the URL appears to be keyed in correctly, then try the following technique: delete all of the information to the right of the forward slash mark that is farthest to the right in the address, and press enter. Sometimes, this will allow you to reach a home page from which you can link to the topic at issue.

A seemingly infinite number of sites on the Web offer information on American government and politics. A list of even the best sites would fill pages. For reasons of space, in this chapter and in those that follow, the *Politics on the Web* sections will include references to only a few selected sites. Following the links provided by these sites will take you to a host of others. The Web sites listed below all provide excellent points of departure for those who wish to learn about American government and politics today.

- The U.S. government's "official" Web site provides extensive information on the national government and the services it provides for citizens. To access this site, go to
  http://www.firstgov.gov

- National Issues, a nonpartisan Web site, provides articles discussing the pros and cons of several controversial issues currently facing Americans. The URL for this site's home page is
  http://www.nationalissues.com

- Another nonpartisan site dealing with current political questions is This Nation. To access this site, go to
  http://www.thisnation.com

- To find news on the Web, you can go to the site of any major news organization or even your local newspaper. Links to online newspapers, both within the United States and in other countries, are available at
  http://www.newspapers.com

- Additionally, CNN's AllPolitics offers a wealth of news, news analysis, polling data, and news articles dating back to 1996. Go to
  http://www.cnn.com/ALLPOLITICS

- To learn how new computer and communications technologies are affecting the constitutional rights and liberties of Americans, go to the Web site of the Center for Democracy and Technology at
  http://www.cdt.org

- The Pew Research Center for the People and the Press offers survey data online on a number of topics relating to American politics and government. The URL for the center's site is
  http://people-press.org

- Yale University Library, one of the great research institutions, has an excellent collection of sources relating to American politics and government. Go to
  http://www.library.yale.edu/socsci

Web Resources on Your CD-ROM

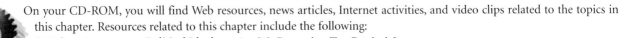

On your CD-ROM, you will find Web resources, news articles, Internet activities, and video clips related to the topics in this chapter. Resources related to this chapter include the following:
- **Values Inventory**—Political Ideology: Are We Becoming Too Patriotic?
- **Why Does It Matter?**—Discuss Patriotism on a Newsgroup.
- **Updates**—Keep up with the issues in this chapter!
- **Web Resources**—Internet Activities: The USA Patriot Act of 2001; What Is Patriotism?; The New American Patriotism.
- **Where Do You Stand?**—Dialogue: Are We Becoming Too Patriotic?
- **Comparative Politics**—Democracy: Global Trends.
- **Video**—Desires of the Founders.
- **NewsEdge**—Visit this global resource for current events related to this chapter.

chapter 2
the constitution

CHAPTER OBJECTIVES

After reading this chapter, you should be able to . . .

- Describe some of the influences on the American political tradition in the colonial years.

- Indicate why and how Americans achieved independence from Great Britain.

- Summarize the strengths and weaknesses of the Articles of Confederation.

- List some of the major compromises made by the delegates at the Constitutional Convention.

- Discuss the Federalist and Anti-Federalist positions with respect to ratifying the Constitution.

19

Would a Direct Democracy Be Better?

How could it happen? A candidate for the presidency wins the most votes and yet ends up losing the election. It has happened in America several times, most recently in the 2000 presidential elections.

How can it be? In 1998, a majority of Americans did not want to see President Bill Clinton impeached by the House of Representatives. Nonetheless, the members of that chamber impeached him.

What is wrong with this picture? Should the wishes of a majority of Americans have more influence in government?

Over two hundred years ago, at the Constitutional Convention, the founders of this nation created a republic in which representatives elected by the people make government decisions. Today, we refer to the government created by the founders as a *representative democracy*. The founders did not want a *direct democracy*, in which the people directly control government decision making. True, direct democracy might not be possible in a large country such as the United States. Yet some people maintain that we could and should allow Americans to have a more direct voice in their government.

We Should Have More "Government by the People," Say Some

Many Americans believe that we should get rid of the electoral college. After all, until the 2000 presidential elections, most Americans had not realized that when they vote in November for a presidential candidate, they are voting for a slate of electors who will cast their votes in the electoral college on a date several weeks after the elections—in 2000, the date was December 18. Just taking the one step of abolishing the electoral college could quickly give the people a sense that they have a more direct voice in government.

The people would also have more say in government if members of Congress were forced to follow the wishes of their constituents (those who elect them into office) instead of voting with their consciences, as they did when they impeached President Bill Clinton in 1998. At a minimum, members of Congress should not be influenced by groups whose interests are contrary to those of the members' constituents. If members of Congress voted the will of the people, we would have stronger gun control laws, more social services available, and better schools.

Finally, whenever significant policy issues are before Congress, Congress should put those issues before the people. The states do this already via referenda and voter initiatives. This may sound implausible, but it really is not in today's online world. Most Americans now have access to the Internet, either at home or where they work. Members of Congress could obtain instant feedback from the population via the Internet about any significant legislative proposal.

Representative Democracy Is Better, Say Others

Those Americans who are in favor of keeping the status quo argue that the founders never intended us to have a direct democracy. They feared that a pure direct democracy would deteriorate into mob rule—the tyranny of the majority. Under any type of majoritarian system with no constraints, the rights and opinions of people in the minority would not be protected.

Imagine what would happen if the opinion of a majority of Americans, perhaps expressed through the Internet, determined everything. What would stop the majority from passing new laws directed against those in the minority camp? What would stop the majority from restricting the free speech rights of those in the minority, for example? Also, how could we maintain stability in government? After all, majorities come and go over time, and laws passed by one majority group could be quickly overturned by a new majority.

Representative democracy shields us from these possible dangers of a direct democracy. To be sure, congressional representatives do not always follow the wishes of their constituents, but this is good. A Congress driven only by the will of the members' constituents would not be able to exercise reasoned judgment. In contrast, representative democracy allows for more deliberation in the legislative process.

Where Do You Stand?

1. Political participation is at an all-time low. Do you think that if we had more of a direct democracy, more Americans would participate in governmental decision making?

2. Is it necessarily true that if members of Congress listened more to their constituents and less to their consciences, we would see the tyranny of the majority become a reality?

Interacting with Your CD-ROM Resources

Use your CD-ROM to access resources on the Web, simulations, participation exercises, and video clips. Important resources related to this feature include:
- **Values Inventory**—Political Ideology: Direct Democracy.
- **Where Do You Stand?**—Dialogue: Would a Direct Democracy Be Better?
- **Web Resources**—Internet Activities: The National Initiative for Democracy; Frequently Asked Questions about the NID.

INTRODUCTION

Whether Americans should have more say in government is just one of the many debates concerning the type of government established by the U.S. Constitution. The Constitution, which was written over two hundred years ago, continues to be the supreme law of the land. Time and again, its provisions have been adapted to the changing needs and conditions of society. The challenge before today's citizens and political leaders is to find a way to apply those provisions to an information age that could not possibly have been anticipated by the founders. Will the Constitution survive this challenge? Most Americans assume that it will—and with good reason: no other written constitution in the world today is as old as the U.S. Constitution. To understand why, you have to go back to the beginnings of our nation's history.

The Beginnings of American Government

When the framers of the Constitution met in Philadelphia in 1787, they brought with them some valuable political assets. One asset was their English political heritage. Another was the hands-on political experience they had acquired during the colonial era. Their political knowledge and experience enabled them to establish a constitution that could meet not only the needs of their own time but also the needs of generations to come.

The British Legacy

In writing the Constitution, the framers incorporated two basic principles of government that had evolved in England: *limited government* and *representative government.* In a sense, then, the beginnings of our constitutional form of government are linked to events that occurred centuries earlier in England. They are also linked to the writings of European philosophers, particularly the English political philosopher John Locke. From these writings, the founders of our nation derived ideas to justify their rebellion against Britain and the establishment of a "government by the people."

Limited Government   At one time, the English monarch had virtually unrestricted powers. This changed in 1215, when King John was forced by his nobles to sign the Magna Carta, or Great Charter. This monumental document provided for a trial by a jury of one's peers (equals). It prohibited the taking of a person's life, liberty, or property except by the lawful judgment of that person's peers. The Magna Carta also forced the king to obtain the nobles' approval of any taxes he imposed on his subjects. Government thus became a contract between the king and his subjects.

The importance of the Magna Carta to England cannot be overemphasized, because it clearly established the principle of **limited government**—a government on which strict limits are placed, usually by a constitution. Hence, the Magna Carta signaled the end of the monarch's absolute power. Although the rights provided under the Magna Carta originally applied only to the nobility, it formed the basis of the future constitutional government for all individuals in England and eventually in the United States.

The Magna Carta
(The National Archives)

LIMITED GOVERNMENT A form of government based on the principle that the powers of government should be clearly limited either through a written document or through wide public understanding; characterized by institutional checks to ensure that government serves public rather than private interests.

The principle of limited government was expanded four hundred years later, in 1628, when Charles I signed the Petition of Rights. Among other things, this petition prohibited the monarch from imprisoning political critics without a jury trial. Perhaps more important, the petition declared that even the king or queen had to obey the law of the land.

In 1689, the English Parliament (described shortly) passed the English Bill of Rights, which further extended the concept of limited government. This document included several important ideas:

- The king or queen could not interfere with parliamentary elections.
- The king or queen had to have Parliament's approval to levy (collect) taxes or to maintain an army.
- The king or queen had to rule with the consent of the people's representatives in Parliament.
- The people could not be subjected to cruel or unusual punishment or to excessive fines.

The English colonists in North America were also English citizens, and thus the English Bill of Rights of 1689 applied to them as well. As a result, virtually all of the major concepts in the English Bill of Rights became part of the American system of government.

Representative Government

REPRESENTATIVE GOVERNMENT A form of government in which representatives elected by the people make and enforce laws and policies.

In a **representative government,** the people, by whatever means, elect individuals to make governmental decisions for all of the citizens. Usually, these representatives of the people are elected to their offices for specific periods of time. In England, this group of representatives is referred to as **Parliament,** which is a **bicameral** (two-house) **legislature** consisting of an upper chamber (the House of Lords) and a lower chamber (the House of Commons). The English form of representative government provided a model for Americans to follow. Many of the American colonies had bicameral legislatures—as did, eventually, the U.S. Congress that was established by the Constitution.

PARLIAMENT The name of the national legislative body in countries governed by a parliamentary system, as in Britain and Canada.

BICAMERAL LEGISLATURE A legislature made up of two chambers, or parts. The United States has a bicameral legislature, composed of the House of Representatives and the Senate.

Political Philosophy—Social Contract and Natural Rights

SOCIAL CONTRACT A voluntary agreement among individuals to create a government and to give that government adequate power to secure the mutual protection and welfare of all individuals.

Our democracy resulted from what can be viewed as a type of **social contract** among early Americans to create and abide by a set of governing rules. Social contract theory was developed in the seventeenth and eighteenth centuries by philosophers such as John Locke (1632–1704) and Thomas Hobbes (1588–1679) in England and Jean-Jacques Rousseau (1712–1778) in France. According to this theory, individuals voluntarily agree with one another, in a "social contract," to give up some of their freedoms to obtain the benefits of orderly government; the government is given adequate power to secure the mutual protection and welfare of all individuals. Generally, social-contract theory, in one form or another, provides the theoretical underpinnings of most modern democracies, including that of the United States.

NATURAL RIGHTS Rights that are not bestowed by governments but are inherent within every single man, woman, and child by virtue of the fact that he or she is a human being.

Although Hobbes and Rousseau also posited social contracts as the bases of governments, neither theorist was as influential in America as John Locke was. John Locke argued that people are born with **natural rights** to life, liberty, and property. He theorized that the purpose of government was to protect those rights; if it did not, it would lose its legitimacy and need not be obeyed. Locke's assumption that people, by nature, are rational and are endowed with certain rights is an essential component of his theory that people can govern themselves. As you will see, when the American colonists rebelled against British rule, such concepts as "natural rights" and a government based on a "social contract" became important theoretical tools in justifying the rebellion.

Politics and Practices in the American Colonies

The American colonies were settled by individuals from many nations, including England, France, Spain, Holland, Sweden, and Norway. The majority of the colonists, though, came from England. The British colonies in North America were established by private individuals and private trading companies and were under the rule of the British Crown. The British colonies, which were located primarily along the Atlantic seaboard of today's United States, eventually numbered thirteen.

Although American politics owes much to the English political tradition, the colonists actually derived most of their understanding of social compacts, the rights of the people, limited government, and representative government from their own experiences. Years before Parliament adopted the English Bill of Rights or John Locke wrote his *Two Treatises on Government* (1690), the American colonists were putting the ideas expressed in those documents into practice.

The First British Settlements

In the 1580s, Sir Walter Raleigh convinced England's queen, Elizabeth I, to allow him to establish the first English outpost in North America on Roanoke Island, off the coast of what was to become North Carolina. The attempted settlement was unsuccessful, however. The first permanent English settlement in North America was Jamestown, in what is now Virginia.[1] Jamestown was established in 1607 as a trading post of the Virginia Company of London.[2]

The Plymouth Company founded the first New England colony in 1620 at the site of what is now Plymouth, Massachusetts. The settlers at Plymouth, who called themselves Pilgrims, were a group of English Protestants who came to the New World on the ship *Mayflower*. Even before the Pilgrims went ashore, they drew up the **Mayflower Compact,** in which they set up a government and promised to obey its laws. The reason for the compact was that the group was outside the jurisdiction of the Virginia Company, which had arranged for them to settle in Virginia, not Massachusetts. Fearing that some of the passengers might decide that they were no longer subject to any rules of civil order, the leaders on board the *Mayflower* agreed that some form of governmental authority was necessary. The Mayflower Compact, which was essentially a social contract, has historical significance because it was the first of a series of similar contracts among the colonists to establish fundamental rules of government.[3]

The Massachusetts Bay Company established another trading outpost in New England in 1630. In 1639, some of the Pilgrims at Plymouth, who felt that they were being persecuted by the Massachusetts Bay Colony, left Plymouth and settled in what is now Connecticut. They developed America's first written constitution, which was called the Fundamental Orders of Connecticut. This document called for the laws to be made by an assembly of elected representatives from each town. The document also provided for the popular election of a governor and judges. Other colonies, in turn, established fundamental governing rules. The Massachusetts Body of Liberties protected individual rights. The Pennsylvania Frame of Government, passed in 1682, and the Pennsylvania Charter of Privileges of 1701 established principles that were later expressed in the U.S. Constitution and **Bill of Rights** (the first ten amendments to the Constitution).

By 1732, all thirteen colonies had been established, each with its own political documents and a constitution (see Figure 2–1).

Colonial Legislatures

As mentioned, the British colonies in America were all under the rule of the British monarchy. Britain, however, was thousands of miles away (it took two months to sail across the Atlantic). Thus, to a significant extent, colonial legislatures carried on the "nuts and bolts" of colonial government. These legislatures, or *representative assemblies,* consisted of representatives elected by the colonists. The earliest colonial legislature was the Virginia House of Burgesses, established in 1619. By the time of the American Revolution, all of the colonies had representative assemblies, many of which had been in existence for more than a hundred years.

Through their participation in colonial governments, the colonists gained crucial political experience. Colonial leaders became familiar with the practical problems of governing. They learned how to build coalitions among groups with diverse interests and how to make compromises. Indeed, according to Yale University professor Jon Butler, by the time of the American Revolution in 1776 Americans had formed a complex, sophisticated political system. They had also created a wholly new type of society characterized, among other things, by ethnic and religious diversity.[4] Because of their political experiences, the colonists were quickly able to set up their own constitutions and state systems of government—and eventually a new national government—after they declared their independence from Great Britain in 1776.

MAYFLOWER COMPACT A document drawn up by Pilgrim leaders in 1620 on the ship *Mayflower.* The document stated that laws were to be made for the general good of the people.

BILL OF RIGHTS The first ten amendments to the U.S. Constitution. They list the freedoms—such as the freedoms of speech, press, and religion—that a citizen enjoys and that cannot be infringed on by the government.

FIGURE 2–1
The Thirteen Colonies

Georgia, the last of the thirteen colonies, was established in 1732. By this time, each of the thirteen colonies had developed its own political system, complete with necessary political documents and a constitution.

* Maine was under the governance of Massachusetts until 1832.

The Rebellion of the Colonists

Scholars of the American Revolution point out that, by and large, the American colonists did not want to become independent of Great Britain. For the majority of the colonists, Britain was the homeland, and ties of loyalty to the British monarch were strong. Why, then, did the colonists revolt against Britain and declare their independence? What happened to sever the political, economic, and emotional bonds that tied the colonists to Britain? The answers to these questions lie in a series of events in the mid-1700s that culminated in a change in British policy with respect to the colonies. Table 2–1 shows the chronology of the major political events in early U.S. political history.

One of these events was the Seven Years' War (1756–1763) between Britain and France, which Americans often refer to as the French and Indian War. The Seven Years' War and its aftermath permanently changed the relationship between Britain and the American colonists. To pay its war debts and to finance the defense of its expanded empire, Britain needed revenues. The British government decided to obtain some of these revenues by imposing taxes on the American colonists and exercising more direct control over colonial trade. At the same time, Americans were beginning to distrust the British. Having fought alongside British forces, Americans thought they deserved some credit for the victory. The British, however, attributed the victory solely to the British war effort.

Additionally, Americans began to develop a sense of identity separate from the British. Americans were shocked at the behavior of some of the British soldiers and the cruel punishments meted out to enforce discipline among the British troops. The British, in turn, had little good to say about the colonists with whom they had fought, considering them brutish, uncivilized, and undisciplined. It was during this time that the colonists began to use the word *American* to describe themselves.

"Taxation without Representation"

In 1764, in an effort to obtain needed revenues, the British Parliament passed the Sugar Act, which imposed a tax on all sugar imported into the American colonies. Some colonists, particularly in Massachusetts, vigorously opposed this tax and proposed a boycott of certain British imports. This boycott launched a "nonimportation" movement that soon spread to other colonies.

The Stamp Act of 1765   The following year, Parliament passed the Stamp Act, which imposed the first direct tax on the colonists. Under the act, all legal documents, newspapers, and other items, including playing cards and dice, had to use specially embossed (stamped) paper that was purchased from the government.

The Stamp Act generated even stronger resentment among the colonists than the Sugar Act had aroused. James Otis, Jr., a Massachusetts attorney, declared that there could be "no taxation without representation." The American colonists could not vote in British elections and therefore were not represented in the British Parliament. They viewed Parliament's attempts to tax them as contrary to the principle of representative government. The British saw the matter differently. From the British perspective, it was only fair that the colonists pay taxes to help support the costs incurred by the British government in defending its American territories and maintaining the troops that were permanently stationed in the colonies following the Seven Years' War.

In October 1765, nine of the thirteen colonies sent delegates to the Stamp Act Congress in New York City. The delegates prepared a declaration of rights and grievances, which they sent to King George III. This action marked the first time that a majority of the colonies had joined together to oppose British rule. The British Parliament repealed the Stamp Act.

Further Taxes and the Coercive Acts   Soon, however, Parliament passed new laws designed to bind the colonies more tightly to the central government in London. Laws that imposed taxes on glass, paint, lead, and many other items were passed in 1767. The colonists protested by boycotting all British goods. In 1773, anger over taxation reached a powerful climax at the Boston Tea Party, in which colonists dressed as Mohawk Indians dumped almost 350 chests of British tea into Boston Harbor as a gesture of tax protest.

TABLE 2–1

Significant Events in Early U.S. Political History

1585	British outpost set up in Roanoke.
1607	Jamestown established; Virginia Company lands settlers.
1620	Mayflower Compact signed.
1630	Massachusetts Bay Colony set up.
1639	Fundamental Orders of Connecticut adopted.
1641	Massachusetts Body of Liberties adopted.
1682	Pennsylvania Frame of Government passed.
1701	Pennsylvania Charter of Privileges written.
1732	Last of thirteen colonies established.
1756	French and Indian War declared.
1765	Stamp Act; Stamp Act Congress meets.
1770	Boston Massacre.
1773	Boston Tea Party.
1774	First Continental Congress.
1775	Second Continental Congress; Revolutionary War begins.
1776	Declaration of Independence signed.
1777	Articles of Confederation drafted.
1781	Last state signs Articles of Confederation.
1783	"Critical period" in U.S. history begins; weak national government until 1789.
1786	Shays' Rebellion.
1787	Constitutional Convention.
1788	Ratification of Constitution.
1791	Ratification of Bill of Rights.

The British Parliament was quick to respond to the Tea Party. In 1774, it passed the Coercive Acts (sometimes called the "Intolerable Acts"), which closed the harbor and placed the government of Massachusetts under direct British control.

The Continental Congresses

In response to the "Intolerable Acts," Rhode Island, Pennsylvania, and New York proposed a colonial congress. The Massachusetts House of Representatives requested that all colonies select delegates to send to Philadelphia for such a congress.

Patrick Henry addressing the First Continental Congress. (Bettmann/CORBIS)

The First Continental Congress
On September 5, 1774, the **First Continental Congress** met at Carpenter's Hall in Philadelphia. Of the thirteen colonies, Georgia was the only one that did not participate. The First Continental Congress decided that the colonies should send a petition to King George III to explain their grievances, which they did. The congress also passed other resolutions continuing the boycott of British goods and requiring each colony to establish an army.

To enforce the boycott and other trading sanctions against Britain, the delegates to the First Continental Congress urged that "a committee be chosen in every county, city and town, by those who are qualified to vote for representatives in the legislature, whose business it shall be attentively to observe the conduct of all persons." Over the next several months, all colonial legislators supported this action. The committees of "safety" or "observation," as they were called, organized militias, held special courts, and suppressed the opinion of those who remained loyal to the British Crown. Committee members spied on neighbors' activities and reported to the press the names of those who violated the trading sanctions against Britain. The names were then printed in the local papers, and the transgressors were harassed and ridiculed in their communities.

FIRST CONTINENTAL CONGRESS The first gathering of delegates from twelve of the thirteen colonies, held in 1774.

The Second Continental Congress
Almost immediately after receiving the petition, the British government condemned the actions of the First Continental Congress as open acts of rebellion. Britain responded with even stricter and more repressive measures. On April 19, 1775, British soldiers (Redcoats) fought with colonial citizen soldiers (Minutemen) in the towns of Lexington and Concord in Massachusetts, the first battles of the American Revolution. The battle at Concord was memorialized by the poet Ralph Waldo Emerson as the "shot heard round the world." Less than a month later, delegates from all thirteen colonies gathered in Pennsylvania for the **Second Continental Congress,** which immediately assumed the powers of a central government. The Second Continental Congress declared that the militiamen who had gathered around Boston were now a full army. It also named George Washington, a delegate to the Second Continental Congress who had some military experience, as its commander in chief.

The delegates to the Second Continental Congress still intended to reach a peaceful settlement with the British Parliament. One declaration stated specifically that "we [the congress] have not raised armies with ambitious designs of separating from Great Britain, and establishing independent States." The continued attempts to effect a reconciliation with Britain, even after the outbreak of fighting, underscore the colonists' reluctance to sever their relationship with the home country. As one scholar put it, "Of all the world's colonial peoples, none became rebels more reluctantly than did Anglo-Americans in 1776."[5]

SECOND CONTINENTAL CONGRESS The congress of the colonies that met in 1775 to assume the powers of a central government and establish an army.

Breaking the Ties: Independence

Public debate about the problems with Great Britain continued to rage, but the stage had been set for declaring independence. One of the most rousing arguments in favor of independence was presented by Thomas Paine, a former English schoolmaster and corset maker,[6] who wrote a pamphlet called *Common Sense.* In that pamphlet, which was published in Philadelphia in

Thomas Paine (1737–1809). In addition to his successful pamphlet *Common Sense,* Paine also wrote a series of sixteen pamphlets, under the title *The Crisis,* during the American Revolution. He returned to England and, in 1791 and 1792, wrote *The Rights of Man,* in which he defended the French Revolution. Paine returned to the United States in 1802. (Library of Congress)

January 1776, Paine addressed the crisis using "simple fact, plain argument, and common sense." He mocked King George III and attacked every argument that favored loyalty to the king. He called the king a "royal brute" and a "hardened, sullen-tempered Pharaoh [Egyptian king in ancient times]."[7]

Paine's writing went beyond a personal attack on the king. He contended that America could survive economically on its own and no longer needed its British connection. He wanted the developing colonies to become a model nation for democracy in a world in which other nations were oppressed by strong central governments.

None of Paine's arguments was new; in fact, most of them were commonly heard in tavern debates throughout the land. Instead, it was the pungency and eloquence of Paine's words that made *Common Sense* so effective:

> A government of our own is our natural right: and when a man seriously reflects on the precariousness of human affairs, he will become convinced, that it is infinitely wiser and safer, to form a constitution of our own in a cool and deliberate manner, while we have it in our power, than to trust such an interesting event to time and chance.[8]

Many historians regard Paine's *Common Sense* as the single most important publication of the American Revolution. The pamphlet became a best seller; more than 100,000 copies were sold within a few months after its publication.[9] It put independence squarely on the agenda. Above all, *Common Sense* severed the remaining ties of loyalty to the British monarch, thus removing the final psychological barrier to independence. Indeed, later John Adams would ask,

> What do we mean by the Revolution? The War? That was no part of the Revolution. It was only an effect and consequence of it. The Revolution was in the minds of the people, and this was effected, from 1760 to 1775, in the course of fifteen years before a drop of blood was drawn at Lexington.[10]

The Resolution of Independence

In June 1776, Richard Henry Lee of Virginia introduced the Resolution of Independence into the Second Continental Congress. By this time, the congress had already voted for free trade at all American ports for all countries except Britain. The congress had also suggested that all colonies establish state governments separate from Britain. On July 2, 1776, the congress adopted the Resolution of Independence:

> RESOLVED, That these United Colonies are, and of right ought to be free and independent States, that they are absolved from allegiance to the British Crown, and that all political connection between them and the state of Great Britain is, and ought to be, totally dissolved.

Although it was not legally binding, the Resolution of Independence was one of the first necessary steps to establish the legitimacy of the new nation in the eyes of foreign governments. The new nation required supplies for its armies and commitments of foreign military aid. Unless officials of foreign nations believed that this new land was truly independent from Britain, they would not support its new leaders.

The committee chosen to draft a declaration of independence is shown at work in this nineteenth-century engraving. They are, from the left, Benjamin Franklin, Thomas Jefferson, John Adams, Philip Livingston, and Roger Sherman. (AP Photo)

The Declaration of Independence

Immediately after adopting the Resolution of Independence, the congress was ready to pass a full declaration. On July 4, 1776, the Declaration of Independence finally became law in the new nation. On that day, King George III, unaware of the events taking place three thousand miles away, wrote in his diary, "Nothing of importance happened today."

Minor changes to the Declaration of Independence were made during the next two weeks. On July 19, the modified draft became the "Unanimous Declaration of the Thirteen United States of America."[11] On August 2, the members of the Second Continental Congress signed the document. The first official printed version carried only the signatures of the congress's president, John Hancock, and of its secretary, Charles Thompson.

The Significance of the Declaration of Independence

The Declaration of Independence is one of the world's most famous documents. Like Paine, Thomas Jefferson, who wrote most of the document, elevated the dispute between Britain and the American colonies to a universal level. Jefferson opened the second paragraph of the declaration with the following words, which have since been memorized by countless American schoolchildren and admired the world over:

> We hold these Truths to be self-evident, that all Men are created equal, that they are endowed by their Creator with certain unalienable Rights, that among these are Life, Liberty, and the Pursuit of Happiness— That to secure these Rights, Governments are instituted among Men, deriving their just Powers from the Consent of the Governed, that whenever any Form of Government becomes destructive of these Ends, it is the Right of the People to alter or to abolish it, and to institute new Government . . . .

The concepts expressed in the Declaration of Independence clearly reflect Jefferson's familiarity with European political philosophy, particularly the works of John Locke.[12] Locke's philosophy, though it did not cause the American Revolution, provided the philosophical underpinnings by which it could be justified.

AMERICA at odds

What Happened to the Promise of Equality?

For some Americans, the political concepts that are set forth in the Declaration of Independence—particularly the concept of equality—have become standards by which American institutions should be measured. For example, as you will see, the Constitution did not allow for equal treatment for many Americans, including African Americans (who were not considered citizens) and women. The disparity between the declaration's promise of equality and the Constitution's unequal treatment of Americans set the stage for future conflicts over the issue of equality.

Neither Thomas Jefferson nor the framers of the Constitution interpreted the word *equality* to mean equal income. Rather, they envisioned a nation in which all citizens had what we would now call equal opportunity. Equal opportunity promotes other American ideals, such as individualism and self-reliance. It also often leads to a meritocracy based on individual talent and effort. Those who have the advantage of more education, more money to invest in an enterprise, greater talent, and higher levels of energy will have a competitive edge and come out the winners.

In recent times, some people have been unwilling to accept the results of simple equality of opportunity if it creates a gross maldistribution of wealth. Some have argued that the founders, who lived in a largely agrarian economy, could not have envisioned the huge disparities in income in an industrial age and certainly would not have thought them consistent with democratic government.[13] Some reformers have thus backed the creation of a welfare safety net by which the government protects and promotes the economic security of its citizens. Other reformers have tried to level the playing field through programs known as "affirmative action." These programs give preferences to minorities and other groups to make up for past discrimination. Those who favor affirmative action view its opponents as heartless individualists, who would let other Americans remain in poverty because they lack the talent, luck, or education to rise above it. Opponents of affirmative action argue that such programs perpetuate unequal treatment and emphasize racial divisions in society. We discuss this debate further in Chapter 5.

From Colonies to States

Even prior to the Declaration of Independence, some of the colonies had transformed themselves into sovereign states with their own permanent governments. In May 1776, the Second Continental Congress had directed each of the colonies to form "such government as shall . . . best be conducive to the happiness and safety of their constituents [those represented by the government]." Before long, all thirteen colonies had created constitutions. Eleven of the colonies had completely new constitutions; the other two colonies, Rhode Island and Connecticut, made minor modifications to old royal charters. Seven of the new constitutions contained bills of rights that defined the personal liberties of all state citizens. All constitutions called for limited governments.

Many citizens were fearful of a strong central government because of their recent experiences under the British Crown. They opposed any form of government that resembled monarchy in any way. Consequently, wherever such antiroyalist sentiment was strong, the legislature—composed of elected representatives—itself became all-powerful. In Pennsylvania and Georgia, for example, **unicameral** (one-house) **legislatures** were unchecked by any executive authority. Indeed, antiroyalist sentiment was so strong that the executive branch was extremely weak in all thirteen states. This situation would continue until the ratification of the U.S. Constitution.

UNICAMERAL LEGISLATURE A legislature with only one chamber.

The Confederation of States

Antiroyalist sentiments also influenced the thinking of the delegates to the Second Continental Congress, who formed a committee to draft a plan of confederation. A **confederation** is a voluntary association of *independent* states (see Chapter 3). The member states agree to let the central government undertake a limited number of activities, such as forming an army, but the states do not allow the central government to place many restrictions on the states' own actions. The member states typically can still govern most state affairs as they see fit.

CONFEDERATION A league of independent states that are united only for the purpose of achieving common goals.

On November 15, 1777, the Second Continental Congress agreed on a draft of the plan, which was finally signed by all thirteen colonies on March 1, 1781. The **Articles of Confederation,** the result of this plan, served as this nation's first national constitution and represented an important step in the creation of our governmental system.[14]

ARTICLES OF CONFEDERATION The nation's first national constitution, which established a national form of government following the American Revolution. The articles provided for a confederal form of government in which the central government had few powers.

The Government of the Confederation

The Articles of Confederation established the Congress of the Confederation as the central governing body. This congress was a unicameral assembly of representatives, or ambassadors, as they were called, from the various states. Although each state could send anywhere from two to seven ambassadors, or representatives, to the congress, each state, no matter what its size, had only one vote. The issue of sovereignty was an important part of the Articles of Confederation:

> Each State retains its sovereignty, freedom and independence, and every power, jurisdiction, and right, which is not by this Confederation expressly delegated to the United States in Congress assembled.

The structure of government under the Articles of Confederation is shown in Figure 2–2.

FIGURE 2-2
American Government under the Articles of Confederation

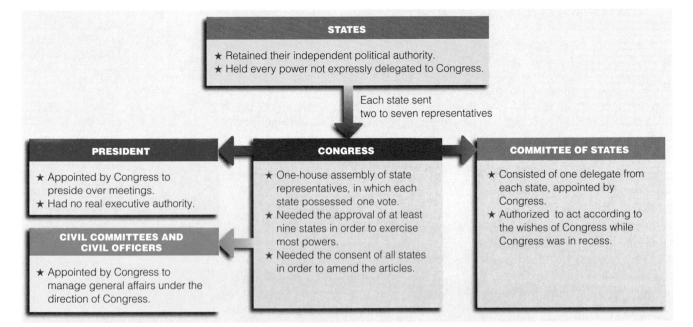

STATES
★ Retained their independent political authority.
★ Held every power not expressly delegated to Congress.

Each state sent two to seven representatives

PRESIDENT	CONGRESS	COMMITTEE OF STATES
★ Appointed by Congress to preside over meetings. ★ Had no real executive authority.	★ One-house assembly of state representatives, in which each state possessed one vote. ★ Needed the approval of at least nine states in order to exercise most powers. ★ Needed the consent of all states in order to amend the articles.	★ Consisted of one delegate from each state, appointed by Congress. ★ Authorized to act according to the wishes of Congress while Congress was in recess.

CIVIL COMMITTEES AND CIVIL OFFICERS
★ Appointed by Congress to manage general affairs under the direction of Congress.

Strengths of the Government of the Confederation

Congress had several powers under the Articles of Confederation, and these enabled the new nation to achieve a number of accomplishments, as shown in Figure 2–3. Not only did the Northwest Ordinance settle states' claims to western land, but it also established a basic pattern for the government of new territories. Furthermore, the 1783 peace treaty negotiated with Great Britain granted to the United States all of the territory from the Atlantic Ocean to the Mississippi River and from the Great Lakes and Canada to what is now northern Florida.

The Articles of Confederation proved to be a good "first draft" for the Constitution, and at least half of the text of the articles would later appear in the Constitution. The articles were an unplanned experiment that tested some of the principles of government that had been set forth earlier in the Declaration of Independence. Some argue that without the experience of government under the Articles of Confederation, it would have been difficult, if not impossible, to arrive at the compromises that were necessary to create the Constitution several years later. The articles, though, had some important weaknesses.

Weaknesses of the Government of the Confederation

In spite of its accomplishments, the central government created by the Articles of Confederation was, in fact, quite weak. The articles also had other major weaknesses, which are listed in Figure 2–4 on the following page. These weaknesses stemmed from the fact that the Confederation was made up of independent states that had no intention of giving up their sovereignty.

As you can see from Figure 2–4, much of the functioning of the government under the Articles of Confederation depended on the goodwill of the states. Article 3, for example, simply established a "league of friendship" among the states, with no central government intended.

A Time of Crisis—The 1780s

The Revolutionary War ended on October 18, 1781. The Treaty of Paris, which confirmed the colonies' independence from Britain, was signed in 1783. Peace with the British may have been won, but peace within the new nation was hard to find. The states bickered among themselves and refused to support the new central government in almost every way. As George Washington stated, "We are one nation today and thirteen tomorrow. Who will treat us on such terms?"

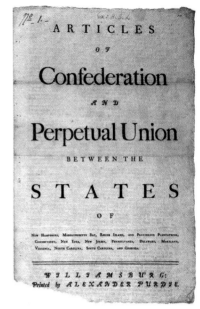

Articles of Confederation and Perpetual Union between the states of New Hampshire, Massachusetts Bay, Rhode Island and Providence Plantations, Connecticut, New York, New Jersey, Pennsylvania, Delaware, Maryland, Virginia, North Carolina, South Carolina, and Georgia. (Williamsburg: Printed by Alexander Purdie [1777].) (Library of Congress)

STRENGTH	ACCOMPLISHMENT
Congress could establish and control the armed forces, declare war, and make peace.	The United States won the Revolutionary War.
Congress could enter into treaties and alliances.	Congress negotiated a peace treaty with Great Britain.
Congress could settle disputes among the states under certain circumstances.	Congress passed the Northwest Ordinance, which settled certain states' land claims.
Congress could regulate coinage (but not paper money) and set standards for weights and measures.	Congress carried out these functions, but the inability to regulate paper money proved a major weakness.
Congress could borrow money from the people.	Congress did borrow money, but without the power to tax, it had trouble repaying the loans or obtaining new ones.
Congress could create a postal system, courts to address issues related to ships at sea, and government departments.	Congress created a postal system and departments of foreign affairs, finance, and war.

FIGURE 2-3

Strengths of the Articles of Confederation

Although the Articles of Confederation were later scrapped, they did allow the early government of the United States to achieve several important goals, including winning the Revolutionary War.

FIGURE 2-4
Weaknesses of the Articles of Confederation

The weaknesses of the Articles of Confederation taught the framers of the Constitution several important lessons, which helped them create a more effective government under that new document.

WEAKNESS	RESULT
Congress could not force the states to meet military quotas.	The central government could not draft soldiers to form a standing army.
Congress could not regulate commerce between the states or with other nations.	Each state was free to set up its own system of taxes on goods imported from other states. Economic quarrels among the states broke out. There was difficulty in trading with other nations.
Congress could enter into treaties, but could not enforce its power or control foreign relations.	The states were not forced to respect treaties. Many states entered into treaties independent of Congress.
Congress could not directly tax the people.	The central government had to rely on the states to collect and forward taxes, which the states were reluctant to do. The central government was always short of money.
Congress had no power to enforce its laws.	The central government depended on the states to enforce its laws, which they rarely did.
Nine states had to approve any law before it was enacted.	Most laws were difficult, if not impossible, to enact.
Any amendment to the articles required all thirteen states to consent.	The powers of the central government could not be changed in practice.
There was no national judicial system.	Most disputes among the states could not be settled by the central government.
There was no executive branch.	Coordinating the work of the central government was almost impossible.

The states also increasingly taxed each other's imports and at times even prevented trade altogether. By 1784, the new nation was suffering from a serious economic depression. States started printing their own money at dizzying rates, which led to inflation. Banks were calling in old loans and refusing to issue new ones. Individuals who could not pay their debts were often thrown into prison.

Shays' Rebellion   The tempers of angry farmers in western Massachusetts reached the boiling point in August 1786. Former Revolutionary War captain Daniel Shays, along with approximately two thousand armed farmers, seized county courthouses and disrupted the debtors' trials. Shays and his men then launched an attack on the national government arsenal in Springfield. **Shays' Rebellion** continued to grow in intensity and lasted into the winter, when it was finally stopped by the Massachusetts volunteer army, paid by private funds.

SHAYS' REBELLION A rebellion of angry farmers in western Massachusetts in 1786, led by former Revolutionary War captain Daniel Shays. This rebellion and other similar uprisings in the New England states emphasized the need for a true national government.

Similar disorders occurred throughout most of the New England states and in some other areas as well. The upheavals, and particularly Shays' Rebellion, were an important catalyst for change. The revolts scared American political and business leaders and caused more and more Americans to realize that a *true* national government had to be created.

The Annapolis Meeting   The Virginia legislature called for a meeting of representatives from all of the states at Annapolis, Maryland, on September 11, 1786, to address the problems facing the nation. Five of the thirteen states sent delegates, two of whom were Alexander Hamilton of New York and James Madison of Virginia. Both of these men favored a strong central government.[15] They persuaded the other delegates to issue a report calling on the states to hold a convention in Philadelphia in May of the following year.

The Congress of the Confederation at first was reluctant to give its approval to the Philadelphia convention. By mid-February 1787, however, seven of the states had named delegates to the Philadelphia meeting. Finally, on February 21, the congress called on the states to send delegates to Philadelphia "for the sole and express purpose of revising the Articles of Confederation." That Philadelphia meeting became the **Constitutional Convention.**

Drafting the Constitution

Although the convention was supposed to start on May 14, 1787, few of the delegates had actually arrived in Philadelphia on that date. The convention formally opened in the East Room of the Pennsylvania State House on May 25, after fifty-five of the seventy-four delegates had arrived.[16] Only Rhode Island, where feelings were strong against creating a more powerful central government, did not send any delegates.

Who Were the Delegates?

Among the delegates to the Constitutional Convention were some of the nation's best-known leaders. George Washington was present, as were Alexander Hamilton, James Madison, George Mason, Robert Morris, and Benjamin Franklin (then eighty-one years old), who had to be carried to the convention on a portable chair. Some notable leaders were absent, including Thomas Jefferson and John Adams, who were serving as ambassadors in Europe, and Patrick Henry, who did not attend because he "smelt a rat." (Henry favored local government and was wary that the convention might favor a stronger central government.)

For the most part, the delegates were from the best-educated and wealthiest classes. Thirty-three delegates were lawyers, nearly half of the delegates were college graduates, three were physicians, seven were former chief executives of their respective states, six owned large plantations, at least nineteen owned slaves, eight were important business owners, and twenty-one had fought in the Revolutionary War. In other words, the delegates to the convention constituted an elite assembly. No ordinary farmers, workers, women, African Americans, or Native Americans were present.

Indeed, in his classic work on the Constitution, Charles Beard maintained that the Constitution was produced primarily by wealthy property owners who wanted a stronger government that could protect their property rights.[17] (Whether the Constitution was favored by a majority of Americans is the topic of the *Perception versus Reality* feature later in this chapter on page 37.)

The Virginia Plan

James Madison had spent months reviewing European political theory before he went to the Philadelphia convention. When his Virginia delegation arrived before anybody else, he immediately put its members to work. On the first day of the convention, Governor Edmund Randolph of Virginia was able to present fifteen resolutions outlining what was to become known as the Virginia Plan. This was a masterful political stroke on the part of the Virginia delegation. Its proposals immediately set the agenda for the remainder of the convention.

The fifteen resolutions contained in the Virginia Plan proposed an entirely new national government under a constitution. The plan, which favored large states such as Virginia, called for the following:

- A bicameral legislature. The lower house was to be chosen by the people. The smaller upper house was to be chosen by the elected members of the lower house. The number of representatives would be in proportion to each state's population (the larger states would have more representatives). The legislature could void any state laws.
- A national executive branch, elected by the legislature.
- A national court system, created by the legislature.

CONSTITUTIONAL CONVENTION The convention (meeting) of delegates from the states that was held in Philadelphia in 1787 for the purpose of amending the Articles of Confederation. In fact, the delegates wrote a new constitution (the U.S. Constitution) that established a federal form of government to replace the governmental system that had been created by the Articles of Confederation.

James Madison (1751–1836). Madison's contributions at the Constitutional Convention in 1787 earned him the title "Master Builder of the Constitution." As a member of Congress from Virginia, he advocated the Bill of Rights. He was secretary of state under Thomas Jefferson (1801–1809) and became our fourth president in 1809. (Library of Congress)

The smaller states immediately complained because they would have fewer representatives in the legislature. After two weeks of debate, they offered their own plan—the New Jersey Plan.

The New Jersey Plan

William Paterson of New Jersey presented an alternative plan favorable to the smaller states. He argued that because each state had an equal vote under the Articles of Confederation, the convention had no power to change this arrangement. The New Jersey Plan proposed the following:

- Congress would be able to regulate trade and impose taxes.
- Each state would have only one vote.
- Acts of Congress would be the supreme law of the land.
- An executive office of more than one person would be elected by Congress.
- The executive office would appoint a national supreme court.

The Compromises

Most delegates were unwilling to consider the New Jersey Plan. When the Virginia Plan was brought up again, delegates from the smaller states threatened to leave, and the convention was in danger of dissolving. On July 16, Roger Sherman of Connecticut broke the deadlock by proposing a compromise plan. Compromises on other disputed issues followed.

The Connecticut Plan: The Great Compromise

Sherman's plan, which has become known as the **Great Compromise** (or the Connecticut Compromise), called for a legislature with two houses:

- A lower house (the House of Representatives), in which the number of representatives from each state would be determined by the number of people in that state.
- An upper house (the Senate), which would have two members from each state; the members would be elected by the state legislatures.

The Great Compromise gave something to both sides: the large states would have more representatives in the House of Representatives than the small states, yet each state would be granted equality in the Senate—because each state, regardless of size, would have two senators. The Great Compromise thus resolved the small-state/large-state controversy.

The Three-Fifths Compromise

A second compromise settled a disagreement over how to count slaves for the purposes of determining how many representatives each state would have in the House and how to count slaves for tax purposes. Although slavery was legal in parts of the North, most slaves and slave owners lived in the South. The southern states wanted slaves to be counted equally in determining representation in Congress but not for tax purposes.

Because they did not have many slaves, the northern states took the opposite position. They wanted slaves to be counted for tax purposes but not for representation. The **three-fifths compromise** settled this deadlock. Three-fifths of the slaves were to be counted for both tax purposes and representation. (The three-fifths compromise was eventually overturned in 1868 by the Fourteenth Amendment, Section 2.)

The Slavery Question

The three-fifths compromise did not satisfy everyone at the Constitutional Convention. Many delegates wanted slavery to be banned completely in the United States. The delegates compromised on this question by agreeing that Congress could limit the number of slaves imported into the country after 1808. The issue of slavery itself, however, was never really addressed by the dele-

GREAT COMPROMISE A plan for a bicameral legislature in which one chamber would be based on population and the other chamber would represent each state equally. The plan, also known as the Connecticut Compromise, resolved the small-state/large-state controversy.

THREE-FIFTHS COMPROMISE A compromise reached during the Constitutional Convention by which it was agreed that three-fifths of all slaves were to be counted both for tax purposes and for representation in the House of Representatives.

This woodcut of slaves prior to the Civil War shows the slave overseer with a whip in his hand. During the fifteenth and sixteenth centuries, the British, French, Dutch, Spanish, and Portuguese engaged in a brutal slave trade along the African coast. Slaves were first brought to Virginia in 1619. Britain outlawed the slave trade in 1807 and abolished slavery in the entire British Empire in 1833. (Granger Collection)

gates to the Constitutional Convention. As a result, the South won twenty years of unrestricted slave trade and a requirement that escaped slaves who had fled to the northern states be returned to their owners. Domestic slave trading was untouched.

Banning Export Taxes The South's economic health depended in large part on its exports of agricultural products. The South feared that the northern majority in Congress might pass taxes on these exports. This fear led to yet another compromise: the South agreed to let Congress have the power to regulate **interstate commerce** as well as commerce with other nations; in exchange, the Constitution guaranteed that no export taxes would ever be imposed on products exported by the states. Today, the United States is one of the few countries that does not tax its exports.

INTERSTATE COMMERCE Trade that involves more than one state.

The Final Draft Is Approved

The Great Compromise was reached by mid-July. Still to be determined was the make-up of the executive branch and the judiciary. A five-man Committee of Detail undertook the remainder of this work and on August 6 presented a rough draft to the convention. On September 8, a committee was named to "revise the stile [style] of, and arrange the Articles which had been agreed to" by the convention. The Committee of Stile was headed by Gouverneur Morris of Pennsylvania.[18] On September 17, 1787, the final draft of the Constitution was approved by thirty-nine of the remaining forty-two delegates.

Looking back on the drafting of the Constitution, an obvious question emerges: Why didn't the founders ban slavery outright? Certainly, as already mentioned, many of the delegates thought that slavery was morally wrong and that the Constitution should ban it entirely. This group, as well as many other Americans, regarded the framers' failure to deal with the slavery issue as a betrayal of the Declaration of Independence, which proclaimed that "all Men are created equal." Others pointed out how contradictory it was that the framers of the Constitution complained about being "enslaved" by the British yet ignored the problem of slavery in this country.

Perhaps the most compelling argument supporting the framers' action (or lack of it) with respect to slavery is that they had no alternative but to ignore the issue. If they had taken a stand on slavery, the Constitution certainly would not have been ratified. Indeed, if the antislavery delegates had insisted on banning slavery, the delegates from the southern states might have walked out of the convention—and there would have been no Constitution to ratify. Many delegates, including Benjamin Franklin, thought that any government would be a blessing for the people, so long as it was not despotic. Perhaps delegate Gunning Bedford said it best when he stated, "The condition of the United States requires that something should be immediately done. It will be better that a defective plan should be adopted, than that none should be recommended."[19]

AMERICA at odds

Should the Government Pay Reparations for Slavery?

By failing to address slavery in the Constitution, the framers turned slavery into a government-sanctioned institution. For this, many have argued over the years that the government ought to repay African Americans. "When government participates in a crime against humanity, and benefits from it, then that government is under the law obliged to make the victims whole," argues Randall Robinson, author of *The Debt: What America Owes to Blacks*.20 When slavery was finally abolished and four million slaves freed after the Civil War (1861–1865), General William Tecumseh Sherman was the first to propose reparations for former slaves. He promised forty acres and a mule for each former slave and confiscated southern land to pay for it. But President Andrew Johnson (1865–1869) put an end to the proposal and took back land that had already been distributed.

A Methodist pastor from Los Angeles calls for reparations for slavery at a demonstration in Washington, D.C., in August 2002. Hundreds of African Americans attended the rally, contending that it is long past time to compensate them for the ills of slavery. (AP Photo/Pablo Martinez Monsivais)

In recent years, the notion of reparations has become a familiar concept to many Americans. The U.S. government paid reparations to Japanese Americans interned in camps during World War II (1941–1945). European countries and corporations have paid reparations to Holocaust survivors. Although no formal reparations have been paid to descendants of slaves in this country, formal apologies have been issued in some instances. Aetna, an insurance company, apologized in March 2000 for having sold policies to slave owners insuring the lives of their slaves. The *Hartford Courant* newspaper apologized for having run advertisements of slaves for sale more than 150 years ago.[21] Today, prominent African American lawyers are part of an effort to sue the federal government and American corporations for damages, alleging that they profited from slavery. "The history of slavery in America has never been fully addressed in a public forum. Litigation will show what slavery meant, how it was profitable, and how the issue of white privilege is still with us," says Charles Ogletree, a professor at Harvard Law School and co-chair of the Reparations Coordinating Committee.[22]

Of course, opponents of slavery reparations are equally vocal. Even among African Americans, the issue is controversial. "If the government got the money from the tooth fairy or Santa Claus, that'd be great. But the government has to take the money from citizens, and there are no citizens alive today who were responsible for slavery," says Walter E. Williams, an African American economics professor at George Mason University. He further argues that the reparations movement is a waste of effort. "The resources that are going into the fight for reparations would be far more valuably spent making sure that black kids have a credible education."[23] As you will read further in Chapter 5, the legacy of slavery in America continues to divide the nation nearly 150 years after it was abolished.

FEDERALISTS A political group, led by Alexander Hamilton and John Adams, that supported the adoption of the Constitution and the creation of a federal form of government.

ANTI-FEDERALISTS A political group that opposed the adoption of the Constitution because of the document's centralist tendencies and because it did not include a bill of rights.

The Debate over Ratification

The ratification of the Constitution set off a national debate of unprecedented proportions. The battle was fought chiefly by two opposing groups—the **Federalists** (those who favored a strong central government and the new Constitution) and the **Anti-Federalists** (those who opposed a strong central government and the new Constitution).

The Federalists Argue for Ratification

In the debate over ratification, the Federalists had several advantages. They assumed a positive name, leaving their opposition with a negative label. The Federalists also had attended the Constitutional Convention and thus were familiar with the arguments both in favor of and against various constitutional provisions. The Anti-Federalists, in contrast, had no actual knowledge of those discussions because they had not attended the convention. The Federalists also had time, money, and prestige on their side. Their impressive list of political thinkers and writers included Alexander Hamilton, John Jay, and James Madison. The Federalists could communicate with each other more readily because they were mostly bankers, lawyers, and merchants who lived in urban areas, where communication was easier. The Federalists organized a quick and effective ratification campaign to elect themselves as delegates to each state's ratifying convention.

The *Federalist Papers*

Alexander Hamilton, a leading Federalist, started answering the Constitution's critics in New York by writing newspaper columns under the pseudonym "Caesar." The Caesar letters appeared to have little effect, so Hamilton switched his pseudonym to "Publius" and enlisted John Jay and James Madison to help him write the papers. In a period of less than a year, these three men wrote a series of eighty-five essays in defense of the Constitution. These essays, which were printed not only in New York newspapers but also in other papers throughout the states, are collectively known as the *Federalist Papers*.

FACTION A group of persons forming a cohesive minority.

TYRANNY The arbitrary or unrestrained exercise of power by an oppressive individual or government.

Allaying the Fears of the Constitution's Critics

Generally, the papers attempted to allay the fears expressed by the Constitution's critics. One fear was that the rights of minority groups would not be protected. Another was that a minority might block the passage of measures that the majority felt were in the national interest. Many critics also feared that a republican form of government would not work in a nation the size of the United States. Various groups, or **factions,** would struggle for power, and chaos would result. Madison responded to the latter argument in *Federalist Paper* No. 10 (see Appendix F or your CD-ROM), which is considered a classic in political theory. Among other things, Madison argued that the nation's size was actually an advantage in controlling factions: in a large nation, there would be so many diverse interests and factions that no one faction would be able to gain control of the government.[24]

The Anti-Federalists' Response

Perhaps the greatest advantage of the Anti-Federalists was that they stood for the status quo. Usually, it is more difficult to institute changes than it is to stay with what is already known, experienced, and understood. Among the Anti-Federalists were such patriots as Patrick Henry and Samuel Adams. Patrick Henry said of the proposed Constitution: "I look upon that paper as the most fatal plan that could possibly be conceived to enslave a free people."

This satirical eighteenth-century engraving touches on some of the issues in Connecticut politics on the eve of the Constitution's ratification. The two factions shown are the "Federals," who represented the trading interests and were for tariffs on imports, and the "Antifederals," who favored agrarian interests and were more receptive to paper money. The artist clearly sides with the Federalist cause. (National Archives)

In response to the *Federalist Papers,* the Anti-Federalists published their own essays, using such pseudonyms as "Montezuma" and "Philadelphiensis." They also wrote brilliantly, attacking nearly every clause of the new document. Many Anti-Federalists contended that the Constitution had been written by aristocrats and would lead the nation to aristocratic **tyranny** (the exercise of absolute, unlimited power). Other Anti-Federalists feared that the Constitution would lead to an overly powerful central government that would limit personal freedom.[25]

The Anti-Federalists strongly argued that the Constitution needed a bill of rights. They warned that without a bill of rights, a strong national government might take away the political rights won during the American Revolution. They demanded that the new Constitution clearly guarantee personal freedoms. The Federalists generally did not

In 1789, during a celebration of the Constitution's ratification, the ship *Hamilton* passes by a fort in New York City. Members of Congress gathered at the fort to greet the procession. (Bettmann/CORBIS)

think that a bill of rights was all that important. Nevertheless, to gain the necessary support, the Federalists finally promised to add a bill of rights to the Constitution as the first order of business under the new government. This promise turned the tide in favor of the Constitution.

Ratification

The contest for ratification was close in several states, but the Federalists finally won in all of the state conventions. After unanimous ratifications in Delaware, New Jersey, and Georgia, Pennsylvania voted in favor of the Constitution by a margin of two to one, and Connecticut by a margin of three to one. Even though the Anti-Federalists were perhaps the majority in Massachusetts, a successful political campaign by the Federalists led to ratification by that state on February 6, 1788.

New Hampshire became the ninth state to ratify the Constitution on June 21, 1788, by a fifty-seven to forty-six margin, thus formally putting the Constitution into effect. New York and Virginia had not yet ratified, however, and without them the Constitution would have no true power. Those worries were dispelled in the summer of 1788, when both Virginia and New York ratified the new Constitution. North Carolina waited until November 21 of the following year to ratify the Constitution, and Rhode Island did not ratify until May 29, 1790. (For ideas on how democratic ratification really was, see this chapter's *Perception versus Reality* feature.)

The Constitution's Major Principles of Government

The framers of the Constitution were fearful of the powerful British monarchy, against which they had so recently rebelled. At the same time, they wanted a central government strong enough to prevent the kinds of crises that had occurred under the weak central authority of the Articles of Confederation. The principles of government expressed in the Constitution reflect both of these concerns.

Limited Government and Popular Sovereignty

The Constitution incorporated the principle of limited government, which means that government can do only what the people allow it to do through exercise of a duly developed system of laws. This principle can be found in many parts of the Constitution. For example, while Articles I, II, and III indicate exactly what the national government *can* do, the first nine amendments to the Constitution list the ways in which the government *cannot* limit certain individual freedoms.

Implicitly, the principle of limited government rests on the concept of popular sovereignty. Remember the phrases that frame the Preamble to the Constitution: "We the People of the

perception versus REALITY

Was the Constitution Favored by a Majority?

We think of our government as being formed by the will of the people. But who were the "people" who ratified the U.S. Constitution? Was the Constitution really favored by a majority of Americans?

THE PERCEPTION

Many Americans never question the idea that the Constitution resulted from a democratic process and was favored by a majority of Americans. After all, the state conventions that ratified the Constitution consisted of representatives of the people. Thus, the process of adopting the Constitution was essentially democratic. If the majority had not favored the Constitution, the state conventions would not have adopted it.

THE REALITY

In reality, the evidence points to the contrary. There was never any popular vote on whether to hold a constitutional convention in the first place. Furthermore, only male property owners were eligible to vote. This means that most people in the country (white males without property, women, African Americans, and Native Americans) had no say in the matter. Additionally, of the white males who were eligible to vote, only about one-sixth of them actually voted for ratification. In all, the delegates at the various state ratifying conventions had been selected by only about 150,000 of the approximately four million citizens of that time. Even Federalist John Marshall, who became chief justice of the Supreme Court after serving as John Adams's secretary of state, believed that in some of the adopting states a majority of the people opposed the Constitution.[26] If a public opinion poll could have been taken at that time, those supporting the Anti-Federalists' position would probably have outnumbered those supporting the Federalists' arguments.[27]

What's Your Opinion?

Does it really matter whether a majority of Americans supported the Constitution when it was adopted?

United States . . . do ordain and establish this Constitution for the United States of America." In other words, it is the people who form the government and decide on the powers that the government can exercise. If the government exercises powers beyond those granted to it by the Constitution, it is acting illegally. The idea that no one is above the law, including government officers, is often called the **rule of law.**

The Principle of Federalism

The Constitution also incorporated the principle of federalism. In a **federal system** of government, the central (national) government shares sovereign powers with the various state governments. Federalism was the solution to the debate over whether the national government or the states should have ultimate sovereignty.

The Constitution gave to the national government significant powers—powers that it had not had under the Articles of Confederation. For example, the Constitution expressly states that the president is the nation's chief executive as well as the commander in chief of the armed forces. The Constitution also declares that the Constitution and the laws created by the national government are supreme—that is, they take precedence over conflicting state laws. Other powers given to the national government include the power to coin money, to levy and collect taxes, and to regulate interstate commerce, granted by the **commerce clause.** Finally, the national government was authorized to undertake all laws that are "necessary and proper" to carrying out its expressly delegated powers.

Because the states feared too much centralized control, the Constitution also allowed for numerous states' rights. These rights include the power to regulate commerce within state borders and generally the authority to exercise any powers that are not delegated by the Constitution to the central government. (See Chapter 3 for a detailed discussion of federalism.)

Checks and Balances

As James Madison (1751–1836) once said, after you have given the government the ability to control its citizens, you have to "oblige it to control itself." To force the government to "control itself" and to prevent the rise of tyranny, Madison devised a scheme, the **Madisonian Model,** in which the powers of the national government were separated into different

RULE OF LAW A basic principle of government that requires both those who govern and those who are governed to act in accordance with established law.

FEDERAL SYSTEM A form of government that provides for a division of powers between a central government and several regional governments. In the United States, the division of powers between the national government and the fifty states is established by the Constitution.

COMMERCE CLAUSE The clause in Article I, Section 8, of the Constitution that gives Congress the power to regulate interstate commerce (commerce involving more than one state).

MADISONIAN MODEL The model of government devised by James Madison in which the powers of the government are separated into three branches: executive, legislative, and judicial.

branches: the legislative, executive, and judicial.[28] The legislative branch (Congress) passes laws; the executive branch (the president) administers and enforces the laws; and the judicial branch (the courts) interprets the laws. By separating the powers of government, no one branch would have enough power to dominate the others. This principle of **separation of powers** is laid out in Articles I, II, and III.

The separation of powers is part of a system of **checks and balances** that was devised to ensure that no one group or branch of government can exercise exclusive control. Even though each branch of government is independent of the others, it can also check the actions of the others. (See the feature *The Politics of Homeland Security* for a discussion of the system of checks and balances in the war on terrorism.) Look at Figure 2–5, and you can see how this is done. As the figure shows, the president checks Congress by holding a **veto power,** which is the ability to return bills to Congress for reconsideration. Congress, in turn, controls taxes and spending, and the Senate must approve presidential appointments. The judicial branch of government can also act as a check on the other branches of government through its power of *judicial review*—the power to rule congressional or presidential actions unconstitutional.[29] In turn, the president (and the Senate) exercise some control over the judiciary through the president's power to appoint federal judges and the Senate's role in confirming presidential appointments.

Among the other checks and balances built into the American system of government are staggered terms of office. Members of the House of Representatives serve for two years, members of the Senate for six, and the president for four. Federal court judges are appointed for life but may be impeached and removed from office by Congress for misconduct. Staggered terms and changing government personnel make it difficult for individuals within the government to form controlling factions. The American system of government also includes numerous other checks and balances, many of which you will read about in later chapters of this book. We look next at another obvious check on the powers of government: the Bill of Rights.

SEPARATION OF POWERS The principle of dividing governmental powers among the executive, the legislative, and the judicial branches of government.

CHECKS AND BALANCES A major principle of American government in which each of the three branches is given the means to check (to restrain or balance) the actions of the others.

VETO POWER A constitutional power that enables the chief executive (president or governor) to reject legislation and return it to the legislature with reasons for the rejection. This prevents or delays the bill from becoming law.

FIGURE 2-5
Checks and Balances among the Branches of Government

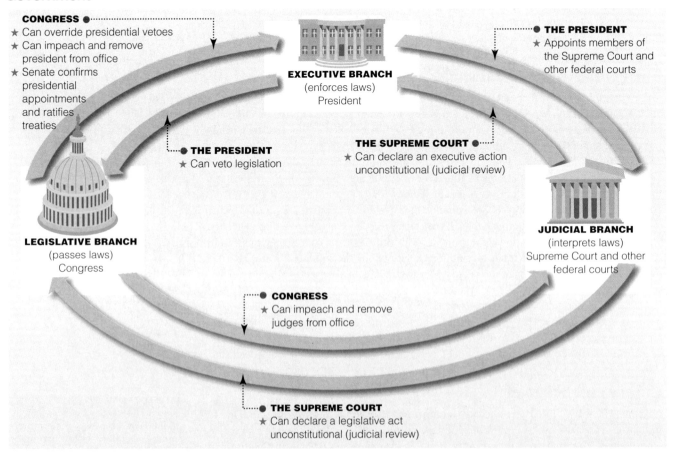

CONGRESS
★ Can override presidential vetoes
★ Can impeach and remove president from office
★ Senate confirms presidential appointments and ratifies treaties

EXECUTIVE BRANCH
(enforces laws)
President

THE PRESIDENT
★ Appoints members of the Supreme Court and other federal courts

THE PRESIDENT
★ Can veto legislation

THE SUPREME COURT
★ Can declare an executive action unconstitutional (judicial review)

LEGISLATIVE BRANCH
(passes laws)
Congress

JUDICIAL BRANCH
(interprets laws)
Supreme Court and other federal courts

CONGRESS
★ Can impeach and remove judges from office

THE SUPREME COURT
★ Can declare a legislative act unconstitutional (judicial review)

The POLITICS of HOMELAND SECURITY

Tampering with the System of Checks and Balances

As you will read in Chapters 12 and 13, the executive branch of the government has grown considerably since 1789. The Constitution did not specify the number or size of departments in the executive branch. Each president has had to turn to Congress to authorize and fund the creation of executive departments. In November 2002, the largest reorganization of the executive branch since 1947 took place with the creation of the Department of Homeland Security. Many observers questioned whether a reorganization of the bureaucracy would provide Americans with more security. Supporters countered that the new department would streamline the efforts of the many agencies that protect the homeland. Republicans, traditionally the foes of "big government," defended the department; Democrats argued that its size and scope would upset the system of checks and balances established by the Constitution.

THE SIZE AND POWER OF THE NEW DEPARTMENT

In 2002, President George W. Bush proposed a new department that would incorporate some of the largest agencies in government, including the Immigration and Naturalization Service, the Coast Guard, the Secret Service, and the Federal Emergency Management Agency. Some of the earliest protests from Congress concerned the size and power of the new department. In the end, Congress acquiesced to most of the president's requests, creating a department with 170,000 employees from twenty-two federal agencies, commanding a budget of nearly $38 billion. It instantly became the third largest of the fifteen cabinet departments.

President Bush also proposed that the secretary of the new department be granted more flexibility in managing employees than the heads of other departments have. The shifting threats to homeland security require this flexibility, the president argued. One of the most contentious debates concerned whether the department's employees would be covered by civil service protections, such as protection from arbitrary discharge. Shouldn't the president have complete control over federal employees working on tasks essential to the nation's security? Democrats initially resisted this argument, calling it "union busting." When they lost control of the Senate in the 2002 elections, however, they compromised with the Republicans: although the final form of the act allows for some civil service protections, they do not apply to intelligence and law enforcement personnel.

CONGRESSIONAL OVERSIGHT MAINTAINS BALANCE

Another early proposal for the department gave the new secretary the power to sell or exchange property and equipment owned by the department without congressional oversight. With the absorption of so many large agencies, the department acquired control of valuable assets. The law requires that money from the sale or lease of such assets be deposited in the U.S.

President George W. Bush, center, speaks at a ceremony marking the first day of the Homeland Security Department as the head of this new cabinet department, Tom Ridge, second from left, looks on. Twenty-two agencies and 170,000 workers who patrol America's borders, secure computer networks, check for contamination of crops, and otherwise help guard against terrorism were officially folded into the new department on March 1, 2003, in the largest government reorganization since the Defense Department was created in 1947. (AP Photo/Charles Dharapak)

Treasury and spent only with congressional approval, through what is called *appropriation* of funds. Congress's ability to appropriate funds, or control the purse strings of government, is one of its most powerful checks on the other two branches of government. Commenting on the flexibility in funding the new department, David R. Obey (D., Wisc.), a member of the House Appropriations Committee, declared: "Any executive branch would love the opportunity to be unchained from the troubles of democracy. But the need for this department does not give the administration the freedom to reign as kings."[30]

On this point, even Republicans on the Appropriations Committee agreed. An amendment was added to the bill banning "overly broad" funding authority. In the words of the House Select Committee on Homeland Security, "Congress serves as a check on the powers of the executive branch. These protections ensure the balance of power is not upset."[31] With this added protection, the Homeland Security Act of 2002 passed by a large margin, 299 to 121 in the House, 90 to 9 in the Senate.

Are We Safer?

Do you think that the creation of this new department will better ensure Americans' safety from terrorist attacks? Do you think that it gives too much power to the president?

The Bill of Rights

To secure the ratification of the Constitution in several important states, the Federalists had to provide assurances that amendments would be passed to protect individual liberties against violations by the national government. At the state ratifying conventions, delegates set forth specific rights that should be protected. James Madison considered these recommendations as he labored to draft what became the Bill of Rights.

After sorting through more than two hundred state recommendations, Madison came up with sixteen amendments. Congress tightened the language somewhat and eliminated four of the amendments. Of the remaining twelve, two—one dealing with the apportionment of representatives and the other with the compensation of the members of Congress—were not ratified by the states during the ratification process.[32] By 1791, all of the states had ratified the ten amendments that now constitute our Bill of Rights. Table 2–2 presents the text of the first ten amendments to the Constitution, along with explanatory comments. (Note that neither a constitution nor a bill of rights, in itself, is any guarantee that rights will be enforced. See this chapter's *Comparative Politics* feature for a discussion of this topic.)

comparative politics

Democracy and Civil Rights

Today, Americans tend to take their democracy for granted. They are not surprised to see a peaceful transfer of power from one group of leaders to another after elections. Even in the confusion caused by the 2000 presidential election outcomes, most Americans were not seriously worried. They assumed that government bodies—courts and legislatures—would find an acceptable solution. As mentioned elsewhere, James Madison had hoped that the Constitution would be a "document for the ages"—although he and others had their doubts. If Madison could see the world today, he would indeed be amazed at how successful the founders' experiment in democracy turned out to be. He would probably be even more astonished at how democracy has swept across the world in the past two centuries.

THE GLOBAL REACH OF DEMOCRACY

Since the Constitution was drafted, the world has been transformed politically—from a world in which the majority of people lived under divine right monarchs or dictators to one in which democracy prevails. Today, the majority of the world's people are governed by democratic regimes. The effect on other countries of the success of democracy in the United States cannot be overstated. Indeed, because the U.S. Constitution has withstood the test of time, it has become the most imitated constitution in the world. It has served as a model for constitutions in at least 174 countries.

Realize, though, that having a constitution establishing a democratic or republican form of government and setting forth basic rights and liberties of citizens is no guarantee that the people's rights and liberties will be respected by a nation's government. Consider such countries as the "republics" of Iraq, when Iraq was still ruled by Saddam Hussein, and China. Iraq's constitution provided for a number of basic freedoms—including the freedoms of speech, religion, and assembly—similar to those found in the U.S. Bill of Rights.[33] Yet Iraq was ruled not by the people, but by a dictator. Similarly, China calls itself a "People's Republic" and has a constitution setting forth various rights (and duties) of citizens, including the rights of free speech, religion, and assembly. Yet, in fact, the Chinese government prohibits speech that is critical of the socialist system or that might harm the nation's interests in some way—a determination that is made by government officials.[34]

POLITICAL TRADITION IS IMPORTANT

The United States, in contrast, is known the world over for the extensive rights and liberties enjoyed by its citizens. Clearly, the Constitution and the Bill of Rights are important elements in the American political system. Yet it is also evident that it takes more than a written constitution and a bill of rights to create and maintain a government that protects the basic rights of its citizens. The truth is, political traditions play an important role in determining whether citizens of a given nation will enjoy civil rights and liberties. In the United States, the courts traditionally have zealously guarded the rights and protections for Americans that are set forth in the Bill of Rights. Ultimately, it may be that, as American federal court judge Learned Hand once said, "Liberty lies in the hearts of men and women; when it dies there, no constitution, no law, no court can ever do much to help it."

For Critical Analysis

Which do you think is more important for Americans' civil rights and liberties, the written Bill of Rights or the American political tradition?

TABLE 2-2

The Bill of Rights

Amendment I.
Religion, Speech, Press, Assembly, and Petition

Congress shall make no law respecting an establishment of religion, or prohibiting the free exercise thereof; or abridging the freedom of speech, or of the press; or the right of the people peaceably to assemble, and to petition the Government for a redress of grievances.

Congress may not create an official church or enact laws limiting the freedom of religion, speech, the press, assembly, and petition. These guarantees, like the others in the Bill of Rights (the first ten amendments), are not absolute—each may be exercised only with regard to the rights of other persons.

Amendment II.
Militia and the Right to Bear Arms

A well regulated Militia, being necessary to the security of a free State, the right of the people to keep and bear Arms, shall not be infringed.

To protect itself, each state has the right to maintain a volunteer armed force. States and the federal government regulate the possession and use of firearms by individuals.

Amendment III.
The Quartering of Soldiers

No Soldier shall, in time of peace be quartered in any house, without the consent of the Owner, nor in time of war, but in a manner to be prescribed by law.

Before the Revolutionary War, it had been common British practice to quarter soldiers in colonists' homes. Military troops do not have the power to take over private houses during peacetime.

Amendment IV.
Searches and Seizures

The right of the people to be secure in their persons, houses, papers, and effects, against unreasonable searches and seizures, shall not be violated, and no Warrants shall issue, but upon probable cause, supported by Oath or affirmation, and particularly describing the place to be searched, and the persons or things to be seized.

Here the word warrant *means "justification" and refers to a document issued by a magistrate or judge indicating the name, address, and possible offense committed. Anyone asking for the warrant, such as a police officer, must be able to convince the magistrate or judge that an offense probably has been committed.*

Amendment V.
Grand Juries, Self-Incrimination, Double Jeopardy, Due Process, and Eminent Domain

No person shall be held to answer for a capital, or otherwise infamous crime, unless on a presentment or indictment of a Grand Jury, except in cases arising in the land or naval forces, or in the Militia, when in actual service in time of War or public danger; nor shall any person be subject for the same offense to be twice put in jeopardy of life or limb; nor shall be compelled in any criminal case to be a witness against himself, nor be deprived of life, liberty, or property, without due process of law; nor shall private property be taken for public use, without just compensation.

There are two types of juries. A grand jury considers physical evidence and the testimony of witnesses, and decides whether there is sufficient reason to bring a case to trial. A petit jury hears the case at trial and decides it. "For the same offense to be twice put in jeopardy of life or limb" means to be

tried twice for the same crime. A person may not be tried for the same crime twice or forced to give evidence against herself or himself. No person's right to life, liberty, or property may be taken away except by lawful means, called the due process of law. Private property taken for public purposes must be paid for by the government.

Amendment VI.
Criminal Court Procedures

In all criminal prosecutions, the accused shall enjoy the right to a speedy and public trial, by an impartial jury of the State and district wherein the crime shall have been committed, which district shall have been previously ascertained by law, and to be informed of the nature and cause of the accusation; to be confronted with the witnesses against him; to have compulsory process for obtaining witnesses in his favor, and to have the Assistance of Counsel for his defence.

Any person accused of a crime has the right to a fair and public trial by a jury in the state in which the crime took place. The charges against that person must be so indicated. Any accused person has the right to a lawyer to defend him or her and to question those who testify against him or her, as well as the right to call people to speak in his or her favor at trial.

Amendment VII.
Trial by Jury in Civil Cases

In Suits at common law, where the value in controversy shall exceed twenty dollars, the right of trial by jury shall be preserved, and no fact tried by a jury, shall be otherwise re-examined in any Court of the United States, than according to the rules of the common law.

A jury trial may be requested by either party in a dispute in any case involving more than $20. If both parties agree to a trial by a judge without a jury, the right to a jury trial may be put aside.

Amendment VIII.
Bail, Cruel and Unusual Punishment

Excessive bail shall not be required, nor excessive fines imposed, nor cruel and unusual punishments inflicted.

Bail is that amount of money that a person accused of a crime may be required to deposit with the court as a guarantee that she or he will appear in court when requested. The amount of bail required or the fine imposed as punishment for a crime must be reasonable compared with the seriousness of the crime involved. Any punishment judged to be too harsh or too severe for a crime shall be prohibited.

Amendment IX.
The Rights Retained by the People

The enumeration in the Constitution, of certain rights, shall not be construed to deny or disparage others retained by the people.

Many civil rights that are not explicitly enumerated in the Constitution are still held by the people.

Amendment X.
Reserved Powers of the States

The powers not delegated to the United States by the Constitution, nor prohibited by it to the States, are reserved to the States respectively, or to the people.

Those powers not delegated by the Constitution to the federal government or expressly denied to the states belong to the states and to the people. This clause in essence allows the states to pass laws under their "police powers."

The Constitution Compared to the Articles of Confederation

As mentioned earlier, the experiences under the government of the Confederation, particularly the weakness of the central government, strongly influenced the writing of the U.S. Constitution. The Constitution shifted many powers from the states to the central government—the Constitution's division of powers between the states and the national government is discussed at length in Chapter 3.

One of the weaknesses of the Confederation had been the lack of an independent executive authority. The Constitution remedied this problem by creating an independent executive—the president—and by making the president commander in chief of the army and navy and of the state militias when called into national service. The president was also given extensive appointment powers, although Senate approval was required for certain appointments.

Another problem under the Confederation was the lack of a judiciary that was independent of the state courts. The Constitution established the United States Supreme Court and authorized Congress to establish other "inferior" federal courts.

To protect against possible wrongdoing, the Constitution also provided for a way to remove federal officials from office—through the impeachment process. The Constitution provides that a federal official who commits "Treason, Bribery, or other high Crimes and Misdemeanors" may be impeached (accused, or charged with wrongdoing) by the House of Representatives and tried by the Senate. If found guilty of the charges by a two-thirds vote in the Senate, the official can be removed from office and prevented from ever assuming another federal government post. The official may also face judicial proceedings for the alleged wrongdoing after removal from office.

The Constitution— A Document for the Ages

The Constitution that was drafted by the framers and ratified by the states has proved to be a lasting foundation for American government. At the time the Constitution was created, however, there was a great deal of doubt about whether the arrangement would actually work. James Madison, among others, hoped that the framers had created a government "for the ages." Indeed, Madison's vision has been realized, in large part because of the checks and balances that were incorporated in the Constitution and that have safeguarded the nation from tyranny—one of the greatest fears of the founders.

Another reason for the Constitution's long life is the brevity of its wording. Rather than set forth the details of government, the founders established broad principles that could—and have been—applied to changing conditions over time. Moreover, for all the stress on private property in the founding era, the framers did not require any property qualification for holding political office. The Constitution also provides that compensation be given for elective posts, meaning that, at least in theory, anyone—no matter how poor—could hold a federal office.

The Constitution also provided for an easier amendment process than that provided under the Articles of Confederation. Under the Articles of Confederation, amendments to the articles required the unanimous consent of the states. As a result, it was virtually impossible to amend the articles. The framers of the Constitution provided for an amendment process that required the approval of only three-fourths of the states. While the process is still extraordinarily cumbersome, it does make changes to the Constitution easier than they were under the Articles of Confederation.

Amending the Constitution

Since the Constitution was written, more than 11,000 amendments have been introduced in Congress. Sometimes, amendments have been proposed to counter perceived antimajoritarian provisions of the Constitution. Immediately after the 2000 elections, for example, an amendment was introduced in Congress to abolish the electoral college, which many Americans

The electoral college came under strong criticism after the 2000 presidential elections, in which Al Gore won the popular vote but the electoral vote went to George W. Bush. Some people, including the protesters shown here, contended that the Supreme Court, by refusing to allow vote recounts in certain Florida counties, effectively handed the presidency to Bush. (AFP Photo/Tim Sloan/CORBIS)

believe is an archaic institution that thwarts the popular will. After all, Democratic candidate Al Gore received a half-million more popular votes than George W. Bush, yet the electoral college vote, not the popular vote, determined the outcome of the race. Other suggested amendments have called for term limits for members of Congress, prayer in the public schools, English as the nation's official language, the prohibition of flag-burning, the banning of abortion, equal rights for women, and rights for crime victims during criminal proceedings.

It is often contended that members of Congress use the amendment process simply as a political ploy. By proposing an amendment, a member of Congress can show her or his position on an issue, knowing that the odds *against* the amendment's being adopted are high. After all, in the years since the ratification of the Bill of Rights, the first ten amendments to the Constitution, only seventeen proposed amendments have actually survived the amendment process and become a part of our Constitution.

One of the reasons there are so few amendments is that the framers, in Article V, made the formal amendment process extremely difficult—although it was much easier than it was under the Articles of Confederation, as just discussed. There are two ways to propose an amendment and two ways to ratify one. As a result, there are only four possible ways for an amendment to be added to the Constitution.

Methods of Proposing an Amendment

The two methods of proposing an amendment are as follows:

1. A two-thirds vote in the Senate and in the House of Representatives is required. All of the twenty-seven existing amendments have been proposed in this way.
2. If two-thirds of the state legislatures request that Congress call a national amendment convention, then Congress could call one. The convention could propose amendments to the states for ratification. There has yet to be a successful amendment proposal using this method.

The notion of a national amendment convention is exciting to many people. Many national political and judicial leaders, however, are uneasy about the prospect of convening a body that conceivably could do what the Constitutional Convention did—create a new form of government.

In two separate instances, the call for a national amendment convention almost became reality. Between 1963 and 1969, thirty-three state legislatures (out of the necessary thirty-four) attempted to call a convention to amend the Constitution to eliminate the Supreme

FIGURE 2–6
**The Process of
Amending the
Constitution**

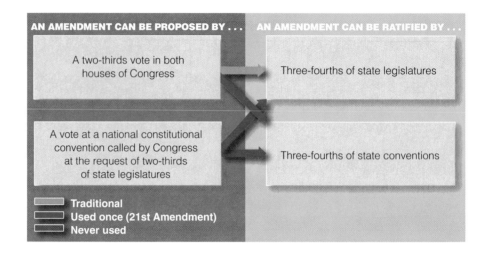

FIGURE 2–6
The Process of Amending the Constitution

Court's "one person, one vote" decisions (see Chapter 11). Since 1975, thirty-two states have asked for a national convention to propose an amendment requiring that the federal government balance its budget. Generally, the major national convention campaigns have reflected dissatisfaction, on the part of certain conservative and rural groups, with the national government's social and economic policies.

Methods of Ratifying an Amendment

There are two methods of ratifying a proposed amendment:

1. Three-fourths of the state legislatures can vote in favor of the proposed amendment. This method is considered the "traditional" ratification method and has been used twenty-six times.
2. The states can call special conventions to ratify the proposed amendment. If three-fourths of the states approve, the amendment is ratified. This method has been used only once—to ratify the Twenty-first Amendment.

You can see the four methods for proposing and ratifying amendments in Figure 2–6. As you can imagine, to meet the requirements for proposal *and* ratification, any amendment must have wide popular support in all regions of the country. This is why many scholars have concluded that the proposed amendment to abolish the electoral college has little chance of succeeding—see the chapter-opening *America at Odds* feature in Chapter 9 for a further discussion of this issue.

why does it MATTER?

The Constitution and Your Everyday Life

The U.S. Constitution is the supreme law of the land. Perhaps this is not enough to convince you that the Constitution is important to you and does affect your everyday life. To show that the Constitution does matter and that it directly affects your daily life, we look here at just two constitutional provisions—it would take a book to discuss them all.

Congress Regulates Interstate Commerce

Article 1, Section 8, Clause 3, of the Constitution expressly delegates to the national government the power:

> [T]o regulate Commerce with foreign Nations, and among the several States, and with the Indian Tribes.

The framers included this clause, known as the commerce clause, to prevent states from establishing laws or regulations that would interfere with trade among the states, as had happened under the Articles of Confederation. But the commerce clause has had much broader implications. Today, it applies to nearly every aspect of your life.

- If you had breakfast this morning, chances are the food you ate was inspected by a federal government agency.
- As for the clothes you wear, the federal government regulates the way the fabric is manufactured and the way clothes are shipped to the store where you buy them.
- If you have a job, your workplace is governed by myriad federal laws and regulations, such as laws protecting employees against unsafe working conditions and against discriminatory treatment in the workplace.

Such a list could fill all the pages in this book. Suffice it to say that the power granted to the national government by the commerce clause and broadly interpreted by the Supreme Court affects every American throughout his or her life.

You Can Move from State to State and Not Lose Any of Your Rights

Consider Article IV, Section 1, Clause 1, which states as follows:

> Full Faith and Credit shall be given in each State to the Public Acts, Records, and judicial Proceedings of every other State.

Now consider the words of Article IV, Section 2, Clause 1:

> The Citizens of each State shall be entitled to all Privileges and Immunities of Citizens in the several States.

These clauses concern relationships among the states in our system of government. Among other things, the "full faith and credit" clause means that if you are married in one state, you are considered legally married in all other states. If you are divorced in one state, you are considered divorced in all states. If you have signed a contract in one state, such as to purchase a car, that contract is valid no matter where you move within the United States.

The "privileges and immunities" clause means that if you need police protection while visiting another state, that state cannot deny you such protection simply because you are a nonresident. If you apply for a job in another state, that state cannot discriminate against you simply because it would prefer to hire only state citizens in order to reduce the state's unemployment rate. In short, states normally must consider actions legally undertaken in other states to be valid and cannot discriminate against out-of-state residents.

Taking Action

As you have read, the founders envisioned that the Constitution, to remain relevant, would need to be changed over time. It has been amended twenty-seven times, but many more amendments have been proposed. You can take action to change the Constitution by supporting an amendment, such as the proposed amendment granting rights to crime victims. In the photo below, President George W. Bush and Attorney General John Ashcroft acknowledge applause after Bush made a speech on victims' rights in April 2002. Bush endorsed a constitutional amendment that would guarantee rights to crime victims, including possible payments by criminals, stating that this was "one of those rare instances where amending the Constitution is the right thing to do." (AP Photo/ Ron Edmonds)

Key Terms

Anti-Federalists 34	faction 35	Mayflower Compact 23	Shays' Rebellion 30
Articles of Confederation 28	federal system 37	natural rights 22	social contract 22
bicameral legislature 22	Federalists 34	Parliament 22	three-fifths compromise 32
Bill of Rights 23	First Continental Congress 25	representative government 22	tyranny 35
checks and balances 38	Great Compromise 32	rule of law 37	unicameral legislature 28
commerce clause 37	interstate commerce 33	Second Continental Congress 25	veto power 38
confederation 28	limited government 21	separation of powers 38	
Constitutional Convention 31	Madisonian Model 37		

Chapter Summary

1 The British legacy to the American form of government consisted of two principles of government: (1) limited government, or a government whose powers are strictly limited, usually by a constitution; and (2) representative government, or a system of government in which the people elect individuals to make governmental decisions for all citizens.

2 The first successful English colonies were established at Jamestown (Virginia) in 1607 and at Plymouth (Massachusetts) in 1620. The Mayflower Compact created the first formal government in the colonies. By 1732, all thirteen colonies had been established.

3 For all their distance from Britain, the colonists had strong ties of loyalty to the home country and to the British monarch. A series of events during and following the Seven Years' War (1756–1763) served to loosen, and finally sever, these ties.

4 The colonies eventually transformed themselves into sovereign states, each having its own permanent government. The first national government was created by the Articles of Confederation.

5 General dissatisfaction with the Articles of Confederation prompted the states to send delegates to a meeting in Philadelphia in 1787, which is now referred to as the Constitutional Convention. The Constitution created by the convention delegates provided for limited government and popular sovereignty; a federal system of government; and a system of checks and balances, including the

separation of government powers among the three branches of government.

6 The Federalists, who favored a strong central government, and the Anti-Federalists, who opposed ratification, intensely debated the ratification issue. By 1790, however, all of the states had ratified the Constitution. The Anti-Federalists' fears of a strong central government prompted the addition of the Bill of Rights (the first ten amendments) to the Constitution.

7 The Constitution addressed several problems that the Articles of Confederation had not resolved and shifted many powers from the states to the central government.

8 A constitutional amendment may be proposed either by a two-thirds vote in each house of Congress or by a national convention called by Congress at the request of two-thirds of the state legislatures. Ratification of an amendment can occur either by a positive vote in three-fourths of the legislatures of the various states or by a positive vote in three-fourths of special conventions called in the states for the specific purpose of ratifying the proposed amendment.

9 The broad language of the Constitution means that it can be interpreted in different ways. As a result, Americans have been—and continue to be—at odds over the meaning of certain constitutional provisions. Whether the Constitution is a stumbling block to democracy is another issue over which Americans are at odds.

RESOURCES FOR FURTHER STUDY

Selected Readings

Dahl, Robert A. *How Democratic Is the American Constitution?* New Haven, Conn.: Yale University Press, 2002. The author compares the American Constitution—the world's first great democratic experiment—to other democratic systems. He focuses on the more unusual, and potentially undemocratic, aspects of the American system, such as federalism and the electoral college.

Hamilton, Alexander, James Madison, and John Jay. *The Federalist Papers.* Cambridge, Mass.: Harvard University Press, 1961. The book contains the complete set of columns from the *New York Packet* defending the new Constitution.

Storing, Herbert J. *The Complete Anti-Federalist.* 7 vols. Chicago: University of Chicago Press, 1981. An analysis of the views of those who argued against the adoption of the Constitution.

Whittington, Keith E. *Constitutional Construction: Divided Powers and Constitutional Meaning.* Cambridge, Mass.: Harvard University Press, 2001. This book argues that the Constitution is not only the basis for judicial review of laws but also permeates politics itself by guiding and constraining political actors in the very process of making public policy.

InfoTrac Citations

Using your InfoTrac password, access the InfoTrac database at **http://infotrac.thomsonlearning.com**. Once at the site, you can do "key word" searches to locate the following articles, each of which deals with a topic covered in this chapter. The key words to use in your search are indicated in parentheses.

- "To Secure the Blessings of Liberty: The Making of the Constitution—The Infant American Nation Weathered Tremendous Obstacles in Order to Form a Constitutional Union" (First Continental Congress)

- "Congress: The First 200 Years" (Articles of Confederation)

- "The Power of the Powerless: The Fierce and Forgotten Battle for the Bill of Rights" (Anti-Federalists)

- "The Second Amendment in Historical Context" (Second Amendment Historical)

Politics on the Web

The World Wide Web version of the Constitution provides hypertext links to amendments and other changes. Go to **http://www.law.cornell.edu/ constitution/constitution. overview.html**

- The home page of Emory University School of Law offers access to a number of early American documents, including scanned originals of the Constitution, the Bill of Rights, the Declaration of Independence, and Jefferson's draft of that document. This page is located at **http://www.law.emory.edu/FEDERAL**

- The National Constitution Center in Philadelphia has a Web page at **http://www.constitutioncenter.org**

  The site offers an online version of the *Federalist Papers,* a Constitution quiz, basic facts about the Constitution, and other information.

- James Madison's notes are one of our most important sources for the debates and exchanges that took place during the Constitutional Convention. These notes are now online at **http://www.thisnation.com/library/madison/index.html**

- An online version of the Anti-Federalist Papers is now available at the Web site of the West El Paso Information Network (WEPIN). Go to **http://wepin.com/articles/afp/index.htm**

- For information on the effect of new computer and communications technologies on the constitutional rights and liberties of Americans, go to the Center for Democracy and Technology at **http://www.cdt.org**

- The Cyberspace Law Institute (CLI) also focuses on law and communications technology. Go to **http://www.cli.org/papers.html**

- The constitutions of almost all of the states are now online. You can find them at **http://www.findlaw.com/11stategov**

- To find historical documents from the founding period, including the charter to Sir Walter Raleigh in 1584, the Royal Proclamation of 1763, and writings by Thomas Paine, go to **http://www.yale.edu/lawweb/avalon/alfalist.htm**

- You can find constitutions for other countries at **http://oefre.unibe.ch/law/icl/home.html**

Web Resources on Your CD-ROM

On your CD-ROM, you will find Web resources, news articles, Internet activities, and video clips related to the topics in this chapter. Resources related to this chapter include the following:
- **Values Inventory**—Political Ideology: Direct Democracy.
- **Why Does It Matter?**—Write a Letter about Your Views on Direct Democracy.

- **Updates**—Keep up with the issues in this chapter!
- **Web Resources**—Internet Activities: The National Initiative for Democracy; Frequently Asked Questions about the NID.
- **Where Do You Stand?**—Dialogue: Would a Direct Democracy Be Better?
- **Comparative Politics**—The Declaration of the Rights of Man, 1789; and the Declaration of the Rights of Women, 1791.
- **Videos**—Federalist Compromise; Constitution and Impeachment.
- **NewsEdge**—Visit this global resource for current events related to this chapter.

chapter **3**
federalism

CHAPTER OBJECTIVES

After reading this chapter, you should be able to . . .

▶ Explain what federalism means and why it exists in the United States.

▶ Indicate how the Constitution divides governing powers in our federal system.

▶ Summarize the evolution of federal-state relationships in the United States over time.

▶ Distinguish between the "new federalism" of today and earlier forms of federalism.

▶ Explain what is meant by the term *fiscal federalism*.

Should the States Take Orders from the National Government?

In recent years, voters in several states approved laws permitting the use of marijuana for medicinal purposes. Such laws would allow physicians to prescribe marijuana for patients suffering from AIDS (acquired immune deficiency syndrome) or other terminal or chronic illnesses.

Shortly after its passage in 1996, the medicinal marijuana law in California was challenged in court. Although a federal appellate court upheld the constitutionality of the law, the Clinton administration asked the United States Supreme Court to intervene, arguing, among other things, that the distribution of marijuana would promote disregard for federal laws combating illegal drug trafficking. Ultimately, the Supreme Court held, in May 2001, that the courts could not make a "medical necessity" exception to the federal law prohibiting the manufacture and sale of marijuana.[1] How can this be? Don't the voters in California (and elsewhere) have the right to regulate drug policy within their borders?

The answer to this question is yes—but only to the extent that state laws do not conflict with national drug policy. In all states, the possession of marijuana continues to be subject to a national law governing drugs: the Comprehensive Drug Abuse Prevention and Control Act of 1970, as amended. The national government's authority to control drugs is laid out very specifically in that law. The fact is, drug strategy in the United States is fundamentally a policy of the national government, although each state has its own drug laws that operate concurrently with national law.

Let the States Control

Those in favor of permitting the medicinal use of marijuana are only one part of a larger group who think that the national government should get out of the drug control business altogether. This group argues that drug policy should be formed by the states, cities, and neighborhoods where we live, rather than by the national government. State and local governments could then tailor drug policies to reflect local views and interests.

At least one federal court agrees with aspects of this argument. After California passed its medicinal marijuana law in 1996, the federal government tried to circumvent it by threatening to revoke physicians' licenses if they recommended marijuana use to chronically or terminally ill patients. Physicians and patients sued the federal government, arguing that these threats violated physicians' First Amendment right to free speech. In a 2002 decision, a federal appeals court agreed. "Being a member of a regulated profession does not, as the government suggests, result in the surrender of First Amendment rights. . . . Our decision is consistent with principles of federalism that have left states as the primary regulators of professional conduct."[2] The decision supports the notion that regulating physicians is the province of state governments, not the federal government.

Those who support state and local control over drug policy would also like states to have more flexibility in imposing penalties for drug possession. Indeed, in 2000 voters in California passed a ballot initiative that replaces current mandatory jail sentences for nonviolent drug possession offenses with a required drug treatment program and probation. The law authorizes the dismissal of charges against those who successfully complete the program. It is possible that this law may be challenged in court as contrary to federal policy.

Let the National Government Control

Many Americans believe that it is in the best interests of the country, not just of each state, to have a national drug policy. That way, American citizens, regardless of which state they live in, will be protected uniformly from the consequences of drug possession and the crimes that result from drug use and distribution. The argument is that illegal drug use and drug trafficking are nationwide problems. In any given year, more than forty million Americans violate some drug law at least once, and the number of crimes associated with illegal drugs continues to increase.

Many state legislators and governors are reluctant to tackle the drug problem by themselves. Consequently, the resources of the national government must be used in the fight against illegal drug manufacturing, importation, shipment, and use.

Where Do You Stand?

1. What would result if the states were allowed to control drug policy?

2. If the states exercised ultimate control over drug policy, how could they arrange to handle the problem of interstate drug trafficking?

Interacting with Your CD-ROM Resources

Use your CD-ROM to access resources on the Web, simulations, participation exercises, and video clips. Important resources related to this feature include:

- **Values Inventory**—Political Ideology: Medical Marijuana?
- **Where Do You Stand?**—Dialogue: Should States Take Orders from the National Government?
- **Web Resources**—Internet Activities: The International Medical Marijuana Association; The Science of Medical Marijuana.

INTRODUCTION

Whether drug policy should be controlled by the national government or by state governments is just one example of how different levels of government in our federal system can be at odds with one another. Let's face it. Those who work for the national government based in Washington, D.C., probably would not like to see power taken away from Washington and given to the states. At the same time, those who work in state governments don't like to be told what to do by the national government. Finally, those who work in local governments would like to run their affairs with the least amount of interference from both their state governments and the national government.

Such conflicts arise because our government is based on the principle of **federalism,** which means that government powers are shared by the national government and the states. When the founders of this nation opted for federalism, they created a practical and flexible form of government capable of enduring for centuries. At the same time, however, they planted the seeds for future conflict between the states and the national government over how government powers should be shared. As you will read in this chapter—and throughout this book—many of today's most pressing issues have to do with which level of government should exercise certain powers, such as the power to control drug policy.

The relationship between the national government and the governments at the state and local levels has never been free of conflict. Indeed, even before the Constitution was adopted, the Federalists and Anti-Federalists engaged in a heated debate over the issue of national versus state powers. As you learned in Chapter 2, the Federalists won the day, in terms of convincing Americans to adopt the Constitution. The Anti-Federalists' concern for states' rights, however, has surfaced again and again in the course of American history. Today, for example, we see the concern for states' rights reflected in arguments supporting **devolution**—the transfer to the states of some of the responsibilities assumed by the national government since the 1930s.

FEDERALISM A way of organizing separate states into a single political system in such a way that each can maintain its fundamental political identity. Federalism emphasizes negotiated policymaking among the member states. The United States has a truly federal system because the Constitution specifically describes how power to make and implement policy should be shared by the national government and the state governments.

DEVOLUTION In the context of American politics, the transfer to the states of some of the responsibilities assumed by the national government since the 1930s.

Federalism and Its Alternatives

There are various ways of ordering relations between central governments and local units. Federalism is one of these ways. Learning about federalism and how it differs from other forms of government is important to understanding the American political system.

Who should control public policy—the national government or the states? This question is at the heart of the *devolution* movement in the United States. One example of an attempt by the states to "control their own destinies" involves the legalization of the medicinal use of marijuana, as discussed in the *America at Odds* feature opening this chapter. (PhotoEdit)

| TABLE 3-1 |
| **Countries That Have a Federal System Today** |

COUNTRY	POPULATION (IN MILLIONS)
Argentina	36.9
Australia	19.2
Austria	8.1
Brazil	172.9
Canada	31.3
Germany	82.8
India	1,014.0
Malaysia	21.8
Mexico	100.3
Switzerland	7.3
United States	285.0

SOURCE: Central Intelligence Agency, *The World Fact Book, 2001* (Washington, D.C.: U.S. Government Printing Office, 2000); plus authors' update.

What Is Federalism?

Nowhere in the Constitution does the word *federalism* appear. This is understandable, given that the concept of federalism was an invention of the founders. Since the Federalists and the Anti-Federalists argued more than two hundred years ago about what form of government we should have, hundreds of definitions of federalism have been offered. Basically, though, as mentioned in Chapter 2, in a *federal system,* government powers are divided between a central government and regional, or subdivisional, governments.

Although this definition seems straightforward, its application certainly is not. After all, virtually all nations—even the most repressive totalitarian regimes—have some kind of subnational governmental units. Thus, the existence of national and subnational governmental units by itself does not make a system federal. *For a system to be truly federal, the powers of both the national units and the subnational units must be specified in a constitution.* Under true federalism, individuals are governed by two separate governmental authorities (national and state authorities) whose expressly designated constitutional powers cannot be altered without rewriting or altering (by amendment, for example) the constitution. The Central Intelligence Agency estimates that only eleven countries, constituting 32 percent of the world's population, have a truly federal system (see Table 3–1).

Federalism in theory is one thing; federalism in practice is another. As you will read shortly, the Constitution sets forth specific powers that can be exercised by the national government and provides that the national government has the implied power to undertake actions necessary to carry out its expressly designated powers. All other powers are "reserved" to the states. The broad language of the Constitution, though, has left much room for debate over the specific nature and scope of certain powers, such as the national government's implied powers and the powers reserved to the states. Thus, the actual workings of our federal form of government have depended, to a great extent, on the historical application of the broad principles outlined in the Constitution.

To further complicate matters, the term *federal government,* as it is currently used, refers to the national, or central, government. When individuals talk of the federal government, they mean the national government; they are not referring to the federal *system* of government, which is made up of both the national government and the state governments.

Alternatives to Federalism

UNITARY SYSTEM A centralized governmental system in which local or subdivisional governments exercise only those powers given to them by the central government.

Most of the nations in the world today have a **unitary system** of government. In such a system, the constitution vests all powers in the national government. If the national government so chooses, it can delegate certain activities to subnational units. The reverse is also true: the national government can take away, at will, powers delegated to subnational governmental units. In a unitary system, any subnational government is a "creature of the national govern-

Great Britain has a unitary system of government, in which governmental power is centralized at the national level. The key government institution in that country is Parliament, the origins of which go back to the medieval Great Council—a body of noble and church advisers to the monarch that eventually became the House of Lords (the upper chamber of Parliament). Today, only the House of Commons (the lower chamber of Parliament) exercises significant power. (David Levenson/Stock Photo)

ment." The governments of Britain, France, Israel, Japan, and the Philippines are examples of unitary systems. In the United States, because the Constitution does not mention local governments (cities and counties), we say that city and county governmental units are "creatures of state government." That means that state governments can—and do—both give powers to and take powers from local governments. (For further discussion of how unitary systems differ from federal systems, see this chapter's *Comparative Politics* feature.)

The Articles of Confederation created a confederal system (see Chapter 2). In a **confederal system,** the national government exists and operates only at the direction of the subnational governments. Few true confederal systems are in existence today.

CONFEDERAL SYSTEM A league of independent sovereign states, joined together by a central government that has only limited powers over them.

Federalism—An Optimal Choice for the United States?

The Articles of Confederation failed because they did not allow for a sufficiently strong central government. The framers of the Constitution, however, were fearful of tyranny and a too-powerful central government. The natural outcome had to be a compromise—a federal system.

The appeal of federalism was that it retained state powers and local traditions while establishing a strong national government capable of handling common problems, such as national defense. A federal form of government also furthered the goal of creating a division of powers (to be discussed shortly). There are other reasons why the founders opted for a federal system, and a federal structure of government continues to offer many advantages (as well as some disadvantages) for U.S. citizens.

comparative politics

Life in a Unitary System

Even in a country with a unitary system, the central government must delegate some power to regional or local administrative units. No matter how small the country, it usually doesn't make sense for the central government to decide such things as the speed limit on every city street. Note, though, that under a unitary system, once the decision about speed limits is made on the local level, the central government can override that decision if it chooses. Local governments in a unitary system have only as much or as little power as the central government decides they should have, and the central government can give or take away that power at its discretion.

AN EXAMPLE—JAPAN'S POSTWAR CONSTITUTION

Japan contains forty-seven prefectures—subdivisional units that manage local affairs—but the central government maintains a large amount of control over them. Japan's present constitution was written in 1946 when the country was under U.S. occupation following World War II. The United States, therefore, greatly influenced Japan's postwar constitution. Despite the U.S. preference for a federal system, however, the tradition of strong central power in Japan prevailed. The Japanese islands were unified 1,500 years ago and were ruled by an emperor, considered divine by the Japanese people. After World War II, the emperor renounced his divinity and today serves only as a political figurehead, but centuries of centralized government left their mark on Japan.

The 1946 constitution created a representative democracy in which the National Diet, elected by the people, wields legislative power. A prime minister and cabinet are chosen by the Diet from its own members. As is typical in a unitary system, the central government in Japan controls local taxation, collecting nearly two-thirds of the nation's taxes and sending half back to local governments. These transferred revenues are targeted for specific programs that reflect national policies, not local initiatives.

EVEN UNITARY SYSTEMS ARE DECENTRALIZING

In spite of Japan's unitary system, its prefectures collect one-third of the taxes for local use, and the constitution does prescribe certain autonomous functions for local government. Such decentralization is also occurring in other countries with unitary systems such as France and Great Britain. France has recently decreased the degree of its government centralization, and Britain has allowed a degree of regional autonomy in Northern Ireland, Wales, and Scotland.

The key difference between a federal and a unitary system, then, is that the central government in a unitary system has the power to grant, and to take away, local autonomy.

For Critical Analysis

Why might the central government in a unitary system relinquish some of its power over regional governments? Conversely, why might the central government take power away from regional governments?

Advantages of Federalism   One of the reasons a federal form of government is well suited to the United States is its size relative to that of many other countries. Even in the days when the United States consisted of only thirteen colonies, its geographic area was larger than that of France or England. In those days, travel was slow, and communication was difficult, so people in outlying areas were isolated. The news of any particular political decision could take several weeks to reach everyone. Therefore, even if the framers of the Constitution had wanted a more centralized system (which most of them did not), such a system would have been unworkable.

Look at Figure 3–1. As you can see, to a great extent the practical business of governing this country takes place not in Washington, D.C., but in state and local government units. Federalism, by providing a multitude of arenas for decision making, keeps government closer to the people and helps make democracy possible.

The existence of numerous government subunits in the United States also makes it possible to experiment with innovative policies and programs at the state or local level. Many observers, including Supreme Court Justice Louis Brandeis, have emphasized that in a federal system, state governments can act as "laboratories" for public-policy experimentation. When a state adopts a program that fails, any negative effects are relatively limited. A program that succeeds can be copied by other states. For example, several states today are experimenting with new educational programs, including voucher systems. Depending on the outcome of a specific experiment, other states may (or may not) implement similar programs. State innovations can also serve as models for federal programs. For example, California was a pioneer in air-pollution control. Many of that state's regulations were later adapted by the federal government to federal regulatory programs.

We have always been a nation of different political subcultures. The Pilgrims who founded New England were different from the settlers who established the agricultural society of the South. Both of these groups were different from those who populated the Middle Atlantic states. The groups who founded New England were religiously oriented, while those who populated the Middle Atlantic states were more business oriented. Those who settled in the South were more individualistic than the other groups; that is, they were less inclined to act as a unit and more inclined to act independently of each other. A federal system of government allows the political and cultural interests of regional groups to be reflected in the laws governing those groups.

Some Drawbacks to Federalism   Federalism offers many advantages, but it also has some drawbacks. For example, although federalism in many ways promotes greater self-rule, or democracy, some scholars point out that local self-rule may not always be in society's

---

FIGURE 3-1

Governmental Units in the United States Today

The most common type of governmental unit in the United States is the special district, which is generally concerned with issues such as solid waste disposal, mass transportation, fire protection, or similar matters. Often, the jurisdiction of special districts crosses the boundaries of other governmental units, such as cities or counties. They also tend to have fewer restrictions than other local governments as to how much debt they can incur and so are created to finance large building projects.

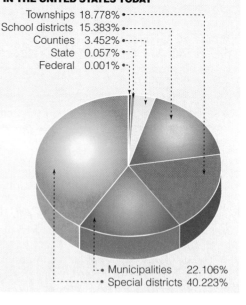

THE NUMBER OF GOVERNMENTS IN THE UNITED STATES TODAY

Government	Number
Federal government	1
State governments	50
Local governments	
Counties	3,034
Municipalities (mainly cities or towns)	19,431
Townships (less extensive powers)	16,506
Special districts (water, sewer, and so on)	35,356
School districts	13,522
Subtotal local governments	87,849
Total	**87,900**

SOURCE: U.S. Census Bureau, *Preliminary Report, 2002 Census of Governments.*

PERCENTAGE OF ALL GOVERNMENTS IN THE UNITED STATES TODAY

Townships 18.778%
School districts 15.383%
Counties 3.452%
State 0.057%
Federal 0.001%

Municipalities 22.106%
Special districts 40.223%

best interests. These observers argue that the smaller the political unit, the higher the probability that it will be dominated by a single political group, which may or may not be concerned with the welfare of the majority of the local unit's citizens. For example, entrenched segregationist politicians in southern states denied African Americans their civil rights and voting rights for decades, as you will read further in Chapter 5.

Federalism also poses the danger that national powers will be expanded at the expense of the states. President Ronald Reagan (1981–1989) once said, "The Founding Fathers saw the federalist system as constructed something like a masonry wall. The States are the bricks, the national government is the mortar. . . . Unfortunately, over the years, many people have increasingly come to believe that Washington is the whole wall."[3]

At the same time, powerful state and local interests can block progress and impede national plans. State and local interests often diverge from those of the national government. For example, as you will read later in this chapter, the state of Oregon and the federal government are at odds over Oregon's physician-assisted suicide law. Finding acceptable solutions to such a conflict has not always been easy. Indeed, as you will read shortly, in the 1860s, war—not politics—decided the outcome of a struggle over states' rights.

Federalism has other drawbacks as well. One of them is the lack of uniformity of state laws, which can complicate business transactions that cross state borders. Another problem is the difficulty of coordinating government policies at the national, state, and local levels. Regulation of business by all levels of government creates considerable red tape that imposes substantial costs on the business community.

The Constitutional Division of Powers

The founders created a federal form of government by dividing sovereign powers into powers that could be exercised by the national government and powers that were to be reserved to the states. Although there is no systematic explanation of this **division of powers** between the national and state governments, the original Constitution, along with its amendments, sets forth what the national and state governments can (and cannot) do.

DIVISION OF POWERS A basic principle of federalism established by the U.S. Constitution. In a federal system, powers are divided between units of government (such as the federal and state governments).

The Powers of the National Government

The Constitution delegates certain powers to the national government. It also prohibits the national government from exercising certain powers.

Powers Delegated to the National Government The Constitution delegates three types of powers to the national government: expressed powers, implied powers, and inherent powers. Article I, Section 8, of the Constitution expressly enumerates twenty-seven powers that Congress may exercise. Two of these **expressed powers** are the power to coin money and the power to regulate interstate commerce. Constitutional amendments have provided for other expressed powers. For example, the Sixteenth Amendment, added in 1913, gives Congress the power to impose a federal income tax. Article II, Section 2, of the Constitution expressly delegates certain powers to the president. These powers include making treaties and appointing certain federal officeholders.

The constitutional basis for the **implied powers** of the national government is found in Article I, Section 8, Clause 18, often called the **necessary and proper clause.** This clause states that Congress has the power to make "all Laws which shall be necessary and proper for carrying into Execution the foregoing [expressed] Powers, and all other Powers vested by this Constitution in the Government of the United States, or in any Department or Officer thereof." The necessary and proper clause is often referred to as the *elastic clause,* because it gives elasticity to our constitutional system.

The national government also enjoys certain **inherent powers**—powers that governments have simply to ensure the nation's integrity and survival as a political unit. For example, any national government must have the inherent ability to make treaties, regulate immigration, acquire territory, wage war, and make peace. Although the national government's inherent powers are few, they are important.

EXPRESSED POWERS Constitutional or statutory powers that are expressly provided for by the Constitution or by congressional laws.

IMPLIED POWERS The powers of the federal government that are implied by the expressed powers in the Constitution, particularly in Article I, Section 8.

NECESSARY AND PROPER CLAUSE Article I, Section 8, Clause 18, of the Constitution, which gives Congress the power to make all laws "necessary and proper" for the federal government to carry out its responsibilities; also called the elastic clause.

INHERENT POWERS The powers of the national government that, although not expressly granted by the Constitution, are necessary to ensure the nation's integrity and survival as a political unit. Inherent powers include the power to make treaties and the power to wage war or make peace.

One of the expressed powers of Congress is the power to coin money. On April 2, 1792, Congress established the Mint of the United States in Philadelphia. Today, the U.S. Bureau of the Mint also maintains mints in Denver and San Francisco. The earliest mints were started in ancient Greece. The name *mint* comes from the Roman temple of Juno Moneta (*moneta* is Latin for *mint*), where silver coins were made as early as 269 B.C.E. (AP Photo/Dan Loh)

Powers Prohibited to the National Government   The Constitution expressly prohibits the national government from undertaking certain actions, such as imposing taxes on exports, and from passing laws restraining certain liberties, such as the freedom of speech or religion. Most of these prohibited powers are listed in Article I, Section 9, and in the first eight amendments to the Constitution. Additionally, the national government is prohibited from exercising powers, such as the power to create a national public school system, that are not included among its expressed and implied powers.

The Powers of the States

The Tenth Amendment to the Constitution states that powers that are not delegated to the national government by the Constitution, nor prohibited to the states, "are reserved to the States respectively, or to the people."

Police Powers   The Tenth Amendment thus gives numerous powers to the states, including the power to regulate commerce within their borders and the power to maintain a state militia. In principle, each state has the ability to regulate its internal affairs and to enact whatever laws are necessary to protect the health, morals, safety, and welfare of its people. These powers of the states are called **police powers.** The establishment of public schools and the regulation of marriage and divorce are uniquely within the purview of state and local governments.

POLICE POWERS The powers of a government body that enable it to create laws for the protection of the health, morals, safety, and welfare of the people. In the United States, most police powers are reserved to the states.

States have the power to protect the health, safety, morals, and welfare of their citizens. (Myrleen Ferguson Cate/PhotoEdit)

Because the Tenth Amendment does not specify what powers are reserved to the states, these powers have been defined differently at different times in our history. In periods of widespread support for increased regulation by the national government, the Tenth Amendment tends to recede into the background of political discourse. When the tide turns the other way, as it has in recent years (see the discussion of the new federalism later in this chapter), the Tenth Amendment is resurrected to justify arguments supporting increased states' rights. Because the Supreme Court is the ultimate arbiter of the Constitution, the outcome of disputes over the extent of state powers often rests with the Court.

Powers Prohibited to the States   Article I, Section 10, denies certain powers to state governments, such as the power to tax goods that are transported across state lines. States also are prohibited from entering into treaties with other countries. In addition, the Thirteenth, Fourteenth, Fifteenth, Nineteenth, Twenty-fourth, and Twenty-sixth Amendments also prohibit certain state actions. (The complete text of these amendments is included in Appendix A.)

Concurrent Powers

Concurrent powers can be exercised by both state governments and the federal government. Generally, a state's concurrent powers apply only within the geographic area of the state and do not include functions that the Constitution delegates exclusively to the national government, such as the coinage of money and the negotiation of treaties. An example of a concurrent power is the power to tax. Both the states and the national government have the power to impose income taxes—and a variety of other types of taxes. States, however, are prohibited from imposing tariffs (taxes on imported goods), and the federal government may not tax articles exported by any state. Figure 3–2, which summarizes the powers granted and denied by the Constitution, lists other concurrent powers.

The Supremacy Clause

The Constitution makes it clear that the federal government holds ultimate power. The **supremacy clause** in Article VI, Clause 2, states that the U.S. Constitution and the laws of the

CONCURRENT POWERS Powers held by both the federal and state governments in a federal system.

SUPREMACY CLAUSE Article VI, Clause 2, of the Constitution, which makes the Constitution and federal laws superior to all conflicting state and local laws.

FIGURE 3-2
The Constitutional Division of Powers

As illustrated here, the Constitution grants certain powers to the national government and to the state governments, while denying them other powers. Some powers, called *concurrent powers,* can be exercised at either the national or the state level, but generally the states can exercise these powers only within their own borders.

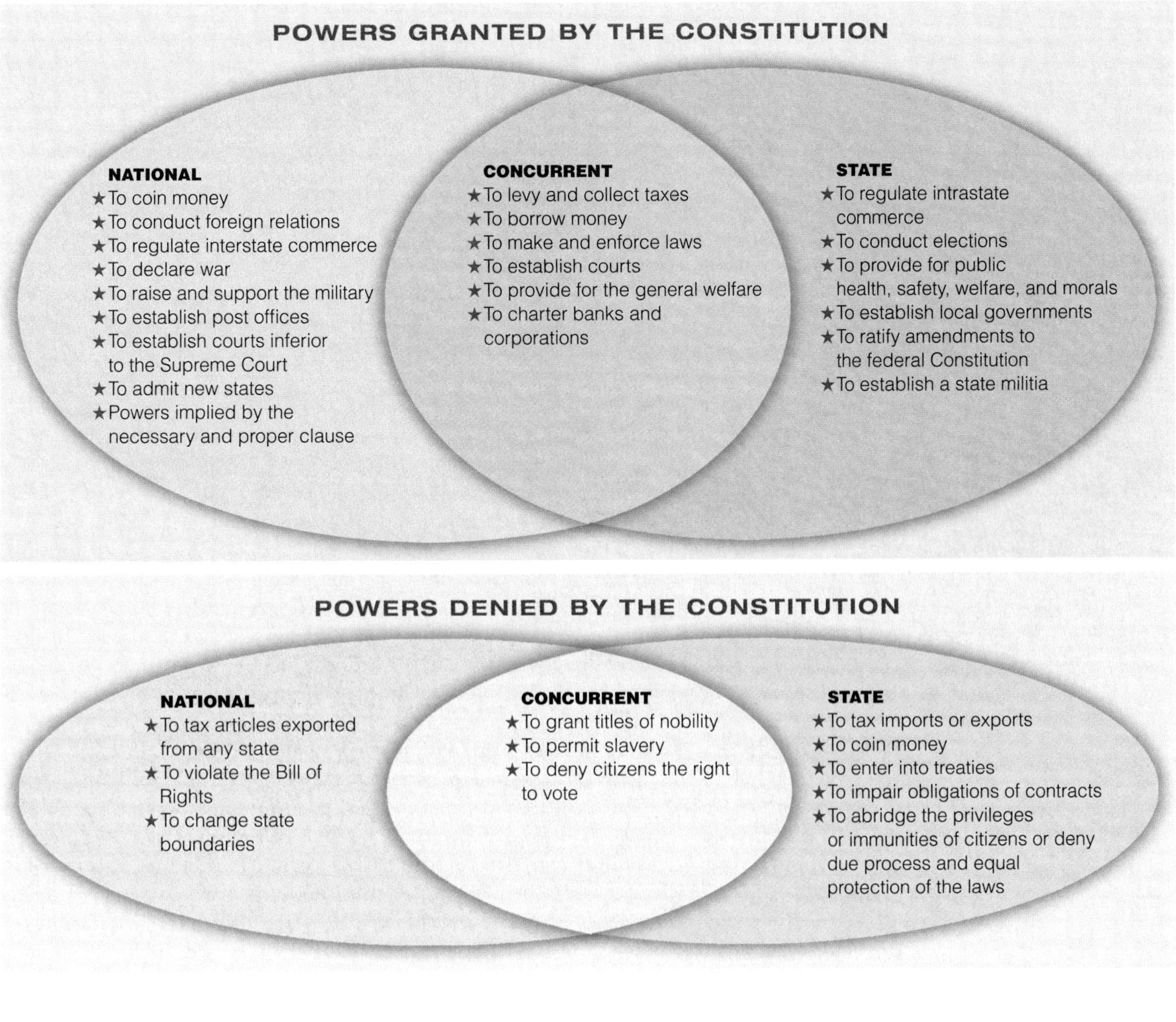

POWERS GRANTED BY THE CONSTITUTION

NATIONAL
- ★To coin money
- ★To conduct foreign relations
- ★To regulate interstate commerce
- ★To declare war
- ★To raise and support the military
- ★To establish post offices
- ★To establish courts inferior to the Supreme Court
- ★To admit new states
- ★Powers implied by the necessary and proper clause

CONCURRENT
- ★To levy and collect taxes
- ★To borrow money
- ★To make and enforce laws
- ★To establish courts
- ★To provide for the general welfare
- ★To charter banks and corporations

STATE
- ★To regulate intrastate commerce
- ★To conduct elections
- ★To provide for public health, safety, welfare, and morals
- ★To establish local governments
- ★To ratify amendments to the federal Constitution
- ★To establish a state militia

POWERS DENIED BY THE CONSTITUTION

NATIONAL
- ★To tax articles exported from any state
- ★To violate the Bill of Rights
- ★To change state boundaries

CONCURRENT
- ★To grant titles of nobility
- ★To permit slavery
- ★To deny citizens the right to vote

STATE
- ★To tax imports or exports
- ★To coin money
- ★To enter into treaties
- ★To impair obligations of contracts
- ★To abridge the privileges or immunities of citizens or deny due process and equal protection of the laws

federal government "shall be the supreme Law of the Land." In other words, states cannot use their reserved or concurrent powers to counter national policies. Whenever state or local officers, such as judges or sheriffs, take office, they become bound by an oath to support the U.S. Constitution. National government power always takes precedence over any conflicting state action.[4]

The Struggle for Supremacy

Much of the political and legal history of the United States has involved conflicts between the supremacy of the national government and the desires of the states to remain independent. The most extreme example of this conflict was the Civil War in the 1860s. Through the years, because of the Civil War and several key Supreme Court decisions, the national government has increased its power.

Early Supreme Court Decisions

Two Supreme Court cases, both of which were decided in the early 1800s, played a key role in establishing the constitutional foundations for the supremacy of the national government. Both decisions were issued while John Marshall was chief justice of the Supreme Court. In his thirty-four years as chief justice (1801–1835), Marshall did much to establish the prestige and the independence of the Court. In *Marbury v. Madison*,[5] he clearly enunciated the principle of judicial review, which has since become an important part of the checks and balances in the American system of government. Under his leadership, the Supreme Court also established, through the following cases, the superiority of federal authority under the Constitution.

McCulloch v. Maryland (1819)
The issue in *McCulloch v. Maryland*,[6] a case decided in 1819, involved both the necessary and proper clause and the supremacy clause. When the state of Maryland imposed a tax on the Baltimore branch of the Second Bank of the United States, the branch's chief cashier, James McCulloch, decided not to pay the tax. The state court ruled that McCulloch had to pay it, and the national government appealed to the United States Supreme Court. The case involved much more than a question of taxes. At issue was whether Congress had the authority under the Constitution's necessary and proper clause to charter and contribute capital to the Second Bank of the United States. A second constitutional issue was also involved: If the bank was constitutional, could a state tax it? In other words, was a state action that conflicted with a national government action invalid under the supremacy clause?

Chief Justice Marshall pointed out that no provision in the Constitution grants the national government the expressed power to form a national bank. Nevertheless, if establishing such a bank helps the national government exercise its expressed powers, then the authority to do so could be implied. Marshall also said that the necessary and proper clause included "all means that are appropriate" to carry out "the legitimate ends" of the Constitution.

Having established this doctrine of implied powers, Marshall then answered the other important constitutional question before the Court and established the doctrine of national supremacy. Marshall declared that no state could use its taxing power to tax an arm of the national government. If it could, the Constitution's declaration that the Constitution "shall be the supreme Law of the Land" would be empty rhetoric without meaning. From that day on, Marshall's decision became the basis for strengthening the national government's power.

Gibbons v. Ogden (1824)
As you learned in Chapter 2, Article I, Section 8, gives Congress the power to regulate commerce "among the several States." But the framers of the Constitution did not define the word *commerce*. At issue in *Gibbons v. Ogden*[7] was how the *commerce clause* should be defined and whether the national government had the exclusive power to regulate commerce involving more than one state. The New York legislature had given Robert Livingston and Robert Fulton the exclusive right to operate steamboats in New York waters, and they licensed Aaron Ogden to operate a ferry between New York and New Jersey. Thomas Gibbons, who had a license from the U.S. government to operate boats in

interstate waters, decided to compete with Ogden, but he did so without New York's permission. Ogden sued Gibbons in the New York state courts and won. Gibbons appealed.

Chief Justice Marshall defined *commerce* as including all business dealings, including steamboat travel. Marshall also stated that the power to regulate interstate commerce was an *exclusive* national power and had no limitations other than those specifically found in the Constitution. Since this 1824 decision, the national government has used the commerce clause numerous times to justify its regulation of virtually all areas of economic activity.

The Ultimate Supremacy Battle—The Civil War

In part, the Civil War (1861–1865) was a fight to free the slaves. Although freedom for the slaves was an important aspect of the war, it was not the only one—or even necessarily the most important one, according to many scholars. At the heart of the controversy that led to the Civil War was the issue of states' rights versus national supremacy. The war brought to a bloody climax the ideological debate that had been outlined by the Federalist and Anti-Federalist factions even before the Constitution was ratified.

As just discussed, the Supreme Court headed by John Marshall interpreted the commerce clause in such a way as to increase the power of the national government at the expense of state powers. By the late 1820s, however, a shift back to states' rights began, and the question of the regulation of commerce became one of the major issues in federal-state relations. When the national government, in 1823 and again in 1830, passed laws imposing tariffs (taxes) on goods imported into the United States, the southern states objected, believing that such taxes were against their best interests.

One southern state, South Carolina, attempted to *nullify* the tariffs, or to make them void. South Carolina claimed that in conflicts between state governments and the national government, the states should have the ultimate authority to determine the welfare of their citizens. Additionally, some southerners believed that democratic decisions could be made only when all the segments of society affected by those decisions were in agreement. Without such agreement, a decision should not be binding on those whose interests it violates. This view was used to justify the **secession**—withdrawal—of the southern states from the Union.

When the South was defeated in the war, the idea that a state has a right to secede from the Union was defeated also. Although the Civil War occurred because of the South's desire for

SECESSION The act of formally withdrawing from membership in an alliance; the withdrawal of a state from the federal Union.

The Civil War is known in the South as the War between the States, but the official Union designation was the War of the Rebellion. Certainly, the question of slavery and its extension into new territories was an important cause of this conflict. Equally important, though, was the fundamental disagreement about the relative powers of the federal government and the state governments—or the issue of states' rights. Efforts toward a peaceful solution to the conflict failed, and ultimately the issue was decided by war. The first shot of the Civil War was fired on April 12, 1861, at Fort Sumter, South Carolina. (Library of Congress)

increased states' rights, the result was just the opposite—an increase in the political power of the national government.

Federalism from the Civil War to the 1930s

DUAL FEDERALISM A system of government in which both the federal and state governments maintain diverse but sovereign powers.

Scholars have devised various models to describe the relationship between the states and the national government at different times in our history. These models are useful in describing the evolution of federalism after the Civil War. The model of **dual federalism** assumes that the states and the national government are more or less equals, with each level of government having separate and distinct functions and responsibilities. The states exercise sovereign powers over certain matters, and the national government exercises sovereign powers over others.

For much of our nation's history, this model of federalism prevailed. Certainly, after the Civil War the courts tended to support the states' rights to exercise their police powers and concurrent powers to regulate intrastate activities. In 1918, for example, the Supreme Court ruled unconstitutional a 1916 federal law excluding from interstate commerce the products created through the use of child labor. The law was held unconstitutional because it attempted to regulate a local problem.[8] The era of dual federalism came to an end in the 1930s, when the United States was in the depths of the greatest economic depression it had ever experienced.

Cooperative Federalism and the Growth of the National Government

COOPERATIVE FEDERALISM The theory that the states and the federal government should cooperate in solving problems.

The model of **cooperative federalism,** as the term implies, involves cooperation by all branches of government. This model views the national and state governments as complementary parts of a single governmental mechanism, the purpose of which is to solve the problems facing the entire United States. For example, federal law enforcement agencies, such as the Federal Bureau of Investigation (FBI), lend technical expertise to solve local crimes, and local officials cooperate with federal agencies.

Cooperative federalism grew out of the need to solve the pressing national problems caused by the Great Depression, which began in 1929. In 1933, to help bring the United States out of the depression, President Franklin D. Roosevelt (1933–1945) launched his **New Deal,** which involved many government spending and public-assistance programs. Roosevelt's New Deal legislation not only ushered in an era of cooperative federalism, which has more or less continued until the present day, but also marked the real beginning of an era of national supremacy.

NEW DEAL A program ushered in by the Roosevelt administration in 1933 to bring the United States out of the Great Depression. The New Deal included many government spending and public-assistance programs, in addition to thousands of regulations governing economic activity.

Was the Expansion of National Powers Inevitable? Some scholars argue that even if the Great Depression had not occurred, we probably would still have witnessed a growth in the powers of the national government. As the country became increasingly populated, industrialized, and interdependent with other nations, problems and situations that once were treated locally began to have a profound impact on Americans hundreds or even thousands of miles away. Environmental pollution does not respect state borders, nor do poverty, crime, and violence. National defense, space exploration, and an increasingly global economy also call for national—not state—action. Thus, the ascendancy of national supremacy in the twentieth century had a logical set of causes.

Cooperative Federalism and the Welfare State Certainly, the 1960s and 1970s saw an even greater expansion of the national government's role in domestic policy. The Great Society legislation of President Lyndon Johnson's administration (1963–1969) created Medicaid, Medicare, the Job Corps, Operation Head Start, and other programs. The Civil Rights Act of 1964 prohibited discrimination in public accommodations, employment, and other areas on the basis of race, color, national origin, religion, or gender. In the 1970s, national laws protecting consumers, employees, and the environment imposed further regulations on the economy. Today, few activities are beyond the reach of the regulatory arm of the national government.

Nonetheless, the massive social programs undertaken in the 1960s and 1970s also precipitated greater involvement by state and local governments. The national government simply could not implement those programs alone. For example, Head Start, a program that provides preschool services to children of low-income families, is administered by local nonprofit organizations and school systems, although it is funded by federal grants. When every level of government is involved in implementing a policy, this is sometimes referred to as **picket-fence federalism.** In this model, the policy area is the vertical picket on the fence, while the levels of government are the horizontal support boards. America's welfare system has relied on this model of federalism, although, as you will read, recent reforms have attempted to give more power to the state and local levels.

Supreme Court Decisions and Cooperative Federalism

The two Supreme Court decisions discussed earlier became the constitutional cornerstone of the regulatory powers the national government enjoys today. From the 1930s to the mid-1990s, the Supreme Court consistently upheld Congress's power to regulate domestic policy under the commerce clause. Even activities that occur entirely within a state were rarely considered outside the regulatory power of the national government. For example, in 1942 the Supreme Court held that wheat production by an individual farmer intended wholly for consumption on his own farm was subject to federal regulation, because the home consumption of wheat reduced the demand for wheat and thus could have a substantial effect on interstate commerce.[9]

By 1980, the Supreme Court acknowledged that the commerce clause had "long been interpreted to extend beyond activities actually in interstate commerce to reach other activities, while wholly local in nature, which nevertheless substantially affect interstate commerce."[10] Today, Congress can regulate almost any kind of economic activity, no matter where it occurs. Increasingly, though, as you will read shortly, the Supreme Court is curbing Congress's regulatory powers under the commerce clause.

John Marshall's validation of the supremacy clause of the Constitution has also had significant consequences for federalism. One important effect of the supremacy clause today is that the clause allows for federal **preemption** of certain areas in which the national government and the states have concurrent powers. When Congress chooses to act exclusively in an area in which the states and the national government have concurrent powers, Congress is said to have *preempted* the area. When Congress preempts an area, such as aviation, the courts have held that a valid federal law or regulation takes precedence over a conflicting state or local law or regulation covering the same general activity. Since the 1960s, the use of federal preemption has been popular, as you can see in Figure 3–3.

President Johnson displays his signature on the War on Poverty bill after he signed it into law in a ceremony in the Rose Garden at the White House on August 20, 1964. (Getty News Images)

PICKET-FENCE FEDERALISM A model of federalism in which specific policies and programs are administered by all levels of government—national, state, and local.

PREEMPTION A doctrine rooted in the supremacy clause of the Constitution that provides that national laws or regulations governing a certain area take precedence over conflicting state laws or regulations governing that same area.

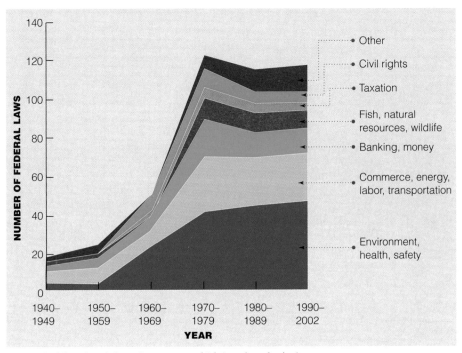

FIGURE 3-3

Federal Preemption from 1940 to the Present

This graph shows the number of federal laws that preempt state authority. As you can see, the greatest growth in federal preemption is in laws regulating the environmental, health, or safety areas. Laws affecting commerce, energy, labor, and transportation run a close second.

Federalism Today

By the 1970s, some Americans began to question whether the national government had acquired too many powers. Had the national government gotten too big? Was it too deeply in debt as a result of annual budget deficits that resulted in a national debt running into the trillions? Should steps be taken to reduce the regulatory power and scope of the national government edifice? Today's model of federalism reflects these concerns.

The New Federalism—More Power to the States

NEW FEDERALISM A plan to limit the federal government's role in regulating state governments and to give the states increased power to decide how they should spend government revenues.

During the 1970s and 1980s, several administrations attempted to revitalize the doctrine of dual federalism, which they renamed the "new federalism." The **new federalism** involves a shift from *nation-centered* federalism to *state-centered* federalism. One of the major goals of the new federalism is to return to the states certain powers that have been exercised by the national government since the 1930s. The term *devolution*—the transfer of powers to political subunits—is often used to describe this process. Although a product of conservative thought and initiated by Republicans, the devolutionary goals of the new federalism were also espoused by the Clinton administration (1993–2001).

An example of the new federalism is the welfare reform legislation passed by Congress in 1996, which gave the states more authority over welfare programs. In the late 1990s, Congress also managed to balance its budget for the first time in decades, but deficits returned in the 2000s. As you will read in Chapter 13, reducing the size of the national government has proved difficult, as have attempts to reduce government spending—a topic discussed in this chapter's *Perception versus Reality* feature.

perception versus REALITY

Devolution?

When the Republicans took control of Congress in 1995, both the Clinton administration and the Republican-dominated Congress promised a historic transfer of power from Washington, D.C., to the states. Spending by the national government would thus be reduced, numerous federal programs would no longer be necessary, and so on. Has this promise been realized?

THE PERCEPTION

Many Americans believe that there has been a historic transfer of power to the states. Since 1995, the states have gained control in a number of areas, most notably in the area of welfare. The federal welfare reform legislation of 1996 transferred significant powers to the states, which now have much more discretion over how welfare programs are administered. The states can determine who is eligible for welfare benefits and on what conditions. Although the national legislation put a lifetime limit on how long people could stay on welfare, the states can extend this period—as long as state funds are used to pay for the benefits.

Since 1995, the states have also gained control over other programs. For example, they now have the ability to expand children's health insurance and the option of enrolling Medicaid clients in managed-care programs.

THE REALITY

A close look at what has actually happened since 1995 reveals a different picture. After taking control of Congress in 1995, the Republican leadership promised, among other things, to eliminate ninety-five major programs. Yet far from being eliminated, these programs' combined budgets have increased by 13 percent since 1995. When President Bill Clinton proposed that the government spend $592 billion from its discretionary accounts in fiscal year 2000, Congress went even further—it upped the amount to $617 billion. In all, in the last three years of the Clinton administration, the Republican-dominated Congress approved discretionary spending that exceeded President Clinton's requests by more than $30 billion!

What happened here? Why is it apparently so difficult to give the states more control over their affairs? Some scholars contend that a large part of the problem has been the failure of the Republican leadership in Congress to defend the principle of devolution.[11] Others suggest that it is only natural for policymakers in the nation's capital to push for federal legislation rather than turn over funds to the states to accomplish the same ends. Federal legislators who want to be reelected like to claim credit for passing laws or instituting programs in areas of public concern, such as educational reform and crime, so that they look good in the eyes of their constituents.[12]

What's Your Opinion?

Should the states be more willing to let the federal government regulate areas, such as education and crime, that have traditionally been regulated by state governments? Why or why not?

The Supreme Court and the New Federalism

During and since the 1990s, the Supreme Court has played a significant role in furthering the cause of states' rights. In a landmark 1995 decision, *United States v. Lopez*,[13] the Supreme Court held, for the first time in sixty years, that Congress had exceeded its constitutional authority under the commerce clause. The Court concluded that the Gun-Free School Zones Act of 1990, which banned the possession of guns within one thousand feet of any school, was unconstitutional because it attempted to regulate an area that had "nothing to do with commerce." In a significant 1997 decision, the Court struck down portions of the Brady Handgun Violence Prevention Act of 1993, which obligated state and local law enforcement officers to do background checks on prospective handgun buyers until a national instant check system could be implemented. The Court stated that Congress lacked the power to "dragoon" state employees into federal service through an unfunded mandate of this kind.[14]

In its 2000–2001 term, the Court continued to limit the national government's regulatory powers. In 2000, for example, the Court invalidated a key provision of the federal Violence Against Women Act of 1994, which allowed women to sue in federal court when they were victims of gender-motivated violence, such as rape. According to the Court, the commerce clause did not justify national regulation of noneconomic, criminal conduct.[15]

AMERICA at odds

Should State Employees Have Fewer Rights than Other Americans?

Continuing the trend of Supreme Court decisions favoring states' rights, the Court has issued a number of rulings in recent years defending states' sovereign immunity—the notion that sovereign governments can shield themselves from lawsuits. The concept that states are shielded from being sued in federal courts is embodied in the Eleventh Amendment to the Constitution. But the Supreme Court has further enunciated the view that the Constitution also makes the states immune from private lawsuits brought in state courts to enforce a federal right.

For example, many years ago Congress passed a law guaranteeing Americans the right to overtime pay. In 1999, however, the Supreme Court ruled that you cannot take your employer to court for violating this right if your employer is the sovereign state of Maine or, by extension, any other state. The Court held, in *Alden v. Maine*,[16] that state immunity from such lawsuits "is a fundamental aspect of the sovereignty which [the states] enjoyed before the ratification of the Constitution, and which they retain today." The Court voiced this view again in 2000, when it held that state university employees in Florida could not sue the state to enforce federal age discrimination laws.[17] In early 2001, the Court further held that the state of Alabama was immune from lawsuits involving rights granted to persons with disabilities under federal law.[18]

These rulings do not prohibit the federal government from making these laws; nor do they liberate the states from having to follow them. The rulings simply say that Americans cannot sue the states for failing to follow federal laws. Are Americans in danger of losing their civil rights? Curt Levey, of the Center for Individual Rights in Washington, D.C., points out that state constitutions also protect civil rights, often providing greater protection than federal laws do. No one is prevented from suing in state court to enforce a state-conferred right.[19] Others disagree. They argue that with these rulings the Supreme Court has sanctioned a serious erosion of Americans' civil rights.

The Shifting Boundary between Federal and State Authority

Clearly, the boundary between federal and state authority is shifting. Notably, issues relating to the federal structure of our government, which in the past several decades have not been at

Promoting his "No Child Left Behind" education agenda, President Bush tours Clarke Street Elementary School in Milwaukee, Wisconsin, on May 8, 2002. The second graders demonstrated their reading proficiency for the president. This was Bush's fifth visit as president to Wisconsin, a crucial electoral state that he narrowly lost to Al Gore in 2000. (AP Photo/J. Scott Applewhite)

the forefront of the political arena, are now the subject of heated debate among Americans and their leaders. The federal government and the states seem to be in a constant tug of war over federal regulation, federal programs, and federal demands on the states.

Federalism under the Bush Administration   For example, at the beginning of George W. Bush's administration, the new president announced the creation of a task force on federalism that would consult with governors on federal rulemaking and draft an executive order on federalism requiring federal departments and agencies to "respect the rights of our states and territories."[20] The executive order was never issued, however.

Since the September 11, 2001, terrorist attacks, the Bush administration has increased demands on state and local governments to participate in homeland security, yet by 2003 Congress had failed to provide a promised $3.5 billion to the states to pay for homeland security. (For more on how homeland security efforts have influenced the balance of power between the federal government and the states, see this chapter's *The Politics of Homeland Security* feature.) Furthermore, in 2002, President Bush signed a sweeping new education bill, called the No Child Left Behind Act (NCLB), which significantly expands the federal government's role in education, an area long regarded as the purview of the states. The NCLB Act requires schools to provide public school choice for students in failing schools, to issue annual report cards on schools, and to implement annual, standards-based assessment tests. It also sets strict time lines for the states to show improvement in poorly performing schools. The federal government will spend $26.5 billion to help the states implement the act.

Federalism and Public Opinion   Although many U.S. political leaders, as well as many average Americans, believe that the national government does too much and has too much power, the issues become more complex when it comes to specific government programs. According to one study, most Americans support government spending on such programs as job training, medical research, subsidies for teachers, aid for college students, clean air standards, Head Start, job-safety regulations, Medicaid, and housing assistance. In all, fewer than 10 percent of those interviewed wanted the government to do or spend less on these programs, and about half of those interviewed thought the government should do more.[21]

The Fiscal Side of Federalism

As everybody knows, big government is costly. But how can government spending be reduced without sacrificing government programs that many feel are essential? This question, which to a significant extent frames the debate over federalism today, requires an understanding of the fiscal side of federalism.

Since the advent of cooperative federalism in the 1930s, the national government and the states have worked hand in hand to implement programs mandated by the national government. Whenever Congress passes a law that preempts a certain area, the states are, of course, obligated to comply with the requirements of that law. A requirement that a state provide a service or undertake some activity in order to meet the national standards specified by the

The POLITICS of HOMELAND SECURITY

How Much Federal Control over the "First Responders"?

As you have read, the United States is composed not of one government, but of more than 87,000. Each of these governments plays a role in preventing terrorist attacks and will be involved in responding to an attack if one occurs. Experts agree that in a terrorist attack, no matter how large the scale, the first responders will be local. The question that is often raised, however, is as follows: How much control can and should the federal government have over these first responders?

A federal system of government inherently creates competition among the national, state, and local governments. Local governments don't like being told what to do by state governments, and neither state nor local governments like orders coming down from the federal level. Nonetheless, in the war on terrorism, the federal government may obtain information about a terrorist threat and need to share it with states and cities, to put police and hospitals on high alert, and to assure that these first responders are properly equipped and trained. At other times, information about potential terrorists may be gained at the local level and will have to be communicated in an efficient manner through a chain of command to the federal level. If even one scrap of evidence or information falls through bureaucratic cracks, the results could be catastrophic.

MORE FEDERAL BUREAUCRACY WILL NOT SOLVE THE PROBLEM

When state and local governments compete for "turf," the federal government may need to take the lead in ensuring that cooperation, and not competition, prevails. One of the aims in creating the Department of Homeland Security was to provide a single department to which all state, local, and national governments and agencies involved in the war on terrorism can turn. But the new department may not solve the problem of bureaucratic turf battles. Donald F. Kettl, director of the Century Foundation's Working Group on Federalism Challenges in Homeland Security, notes that it may do the opposite. "The [Bush] administration's plan will provoke fierce bureaucratic battles, and these battles will end up defining the plan. Instead, we should figure out how to solve the basic problems and organize the government accordingly. Restructuring should be the last step—not the first."[22]

Kettl gives as examples the gaps in local preparedness revealed by the September 11 attacks, and by the anthrax attacks of October and November 2001. On September 11, New York Mayor Rudolph Giuliani struggled to reach the White House by cell phone. In addition, the New York fire department acknowledged after the attacks that communication breakdowns on the morning of September 11 caused serious problems at the World Trade Center. Two months later, when Wisconsin state and local officials faced hundreds of anthrax hoaxes, firefighters and police officers failed to call the appropriate public health specialists to crime scenes. When public health officials did arrive, they were not allowed to cross the crime scene tape because they lacked proper identification. Kettl argues that the govern-

Director of Homeland Security Tom Ridge presents the Homeland Security Advisory System to the media at Constitution Hall in Washington, D.C., on March 12, 2002. "The advisory system is based on five threat conditions or five different alerts: low, guarded, elevated, high, and severe," said Ridge. "It empowers government and citizens to take actions to address the threat." (White House photo/Paul Morse.)

ment should address these areas of homeland security rather than creating a huge, albeit reorganized, bureaucracy at the federal level.

TAKE CONTROL NOW . . . OR LATER

Others disagree with Kettl's assessment. Daniel Henninger, a writer for the *Wall Street Journal,* recognizes the threat that the creation of a huge new federal department represents to the balance of power between Washington, D.C., and the states. But, he argues, it is a necessary measure in the war on terrorism. "The Department of Homeland Security . . . is the sophisticated solution. The crude one would be to wait for the hit, then impose martial law, for as long as necessary. Amid a biological attack, no one would question such measures. We'd muddle through. The resulting political system would be a secondary disaster."[23]

The federal government, Henninger and others argue, must take a leading role in preventing an attack. Because the federal government will pay the largest part of the cost, it will insist on shaping the new system of homeland security. We simply cannot afford turf battles and local rivalries when homeland security is at stake.

Are We Safer?

Do you think that your city government is prepared to respond to a terrorist attack in the event that one hits your city? Do you think information about potential terrorist threats can be effectively shared at all levels of government?

FEDERAL MANDATE A requirement in federal legislation that forces states and municipalities to comply with certain rules.

federal law is referred to as a **federal mandate.** Many federal mandates concern civil rights or environmental protection. Recent federal mandates require the states to provide persons with disabilities with access to public buildings, sidewalks, and other areas; to establish minimum water-purity and air-purity standards for specific localities; and to extend Medicaid coverage to all poor children.

To help the states pay for some of the costs associated with implementing national policies, the national government gives back some of the tax dollars it collects to the states—in the form of grants. As you will see, the states have come to depend on grants as an important source of revenue.

Federal Grants

Even before the Constitution was adopted, the national government granted lands to the states for the purpose of financing education. Using the proceeds from the sale of these lands, the states were able to establish elementary schools and later, *land-grant colleges.* Cash grants started in 1808, when Congress gave money to the states to pay for the state militias. Federal grants were also made available for other purposes, such as building roads and railroads.

Only in the twentieth century, though, did federal grants become an important source of funds to the states. The major growth began in the 1960s, when the dollar amount of grants quadrupled to help pay for the Great Society programs of the Johnson administration. Grants became available for education, pollution control, conservation, recreation, highway construction and maintenance, and other purposes.

CATEGORICAL GRANT A federal grant targeted for a specific purpose as defined by federal law.

There are two basic types of federal grants: categorical grants and block grants. A **categorical grant** is targeted for a specific purpose as defined by federal law—the federal government defines hundreds of categories of state and local spending. Categorical grants give the national government control over how states use the money by imposing certain conditions. For example, a categorical grant may require that the funds not be used for purposes that discriminate against any group or for construction projects that pay below the local union wage. Depending on the project, the government might require that an environmental impact statement be prepared.

BLOCK GRANT A federal grant given to a state for a broad area, such as criminal justice or mental health programs.

In contrast, a **block grant** is given for a broad area, such as criminal justice or mental-health programs. First started in 1966, block grants now constitute a growing percentage of all federal aid programs. The block grant is one of the tools of the new federalism because it gives

Many public services and projects carried out by the states are actually funded, at least in part, by federal grants. Our interstate highway system is a case in point. (Mark C. Burnett/ Stock Boston)

the states more discretion over how the funds will be spent. Nonetheless, the federal government can exercise control over state decision making through these grants by using *cross-cutting requirements*. Title VI of the 1964 Civil Rights Act, for example, bars discrimination in the use of all federal funds, regardless of their sources.

Bridging the Tenth Amendment—Fiscal Federalism

Grants of funds to the states from the national government are one way that the Tenth Amendment to the U.S. Constitution can be bridged. Remember that the Tenth Amendment reserves all powers not delegated to the national government to the states and to the people. You might well wonder, then, how the federal government has been able to exercise control over matters that traditionally have been under the control of state governments, such as the minimum drinking age. The answer involves the giving or withholding of federal grant dollars. The power of the national government to influence state policies through grants is often referred to as **fiscal federalism.**

For example, during President Ronald Reagan's administration (1981–1989), the national government wanted the states to raise the minimum drinking age to twenty-one years. States that refused to do so were threatened with the loss of federal highway construction funds. The threat worked—it was not long before all states had changed their minimum-drinking-age laws accordingly.[24] In the 1990s, Congress used this same threat to encourage the states to lower their blood-alcohol limits for drunk driving to .08 percent by 2004. Those states that failed to comply with the .08 percent limit would face reductions in federal highway funds. The education reforms embodied in the NCLB Act rely on fiscal federalism for their implementation. The states will receive block grants for educational purposes and, in return, must meet federally imposed standards relating to testing and accountability.

FISCAL FEDERALISM The power of the national government to influence state policies through grants.

The Cost of Federal Mandates

As mentioned, when the national government passes a law preempting an area in which the states and the national government have concurrent powers, the states must comply with that law in accordance with the supremacy clause of the Constitution. Thus, when such laws require the states to implement certain programs, the states must comply—but compliance with federal mandates can be costly.

For example, the estimated total cost of complying with federal mandates concerning water purity, over just a four-year period, is in the vicinity of $29 billion. In all, the estimated cost of federal mandates to the states in the early 2000s was over $70 billion annually. Although Congress passed legislation in 1995 to curb the use of "unfunded" federal mandates (that is, mandates that are not funded by the federal government), the legislation was more rhetoric than reality.

AMERICA at odds

Controversy over Federal Mandates

Many states are at odds with the federal government over the issue of federal preemption—and particularly the use of federal mandates. Not only are mandates costly for the states, but they also prevent state and local governments from setting their own priorities. Those who oppose federal preemption argue that policy should be established by the level of government that implements the policy. Additionally, if the national government wants a particular policy result, it should pay for that result, rather than pass the costs on to other levels of government (or even the private sector, for that matter).

The controversy over the cost of unfunded federal mandates sometimes masks the importance of these mandates in creating a level playing field among the states. Consider an example. One of the most costly unfunded federal mandates for the states of Tennessee and Mississippi in the early 1990s was the requirement that states could no longer impose sales taxes on foods purchased with federally funded food stamps. These states had been imposing a 7 percent and 8 percent tax, respectively, on such foods. As a result, food stamps in those states did not purchase as much food as in other states, and poor families consequently found it more difficult to obtain as much food as they could if they lived elsewhere. Thus, in some instances, unfunded federal mandates force the states to pay their share of the costs involved in improving the welfare of the nation's citizens.

Consider another example—the problem of environmental pollution. What if the national government left environmental regulation entirely to the states? States with less stringent environmental regulations would attract more businesses because businesses in those states could avoid some of the costs imposed by environmental regulations (such as the cost of installing pollution-control equipment). Yet pollution by those firms could affect the environmental health of other states, and those states would call on the federal government to impose regulations.

Competitive Federalism

The debate over federalism is sometimes reduced to a debate over taxes. Which level of government will raise taxes to pay for government programs, and which will cut services to avoid raising taxes?

How states answer that question gives citizens an option: they can move to a state with fewer services and lower taxes, or to a state with more services but higher taxes. Political scientist Thomas R. Dye calls this model of federalism **competitive federalism.** State and local governments compete for business and citizens. If the state of Ohio offers tax advantages for locating a factory there, for example, a business may be more likely to do so, providing more jobs for Ohio residents. If Ohio has very strict environmental regulations, however, that same business may choose not to build its factory there, no matter how beneficial the tax advantages, because complying with the regulations will be costly. Although Ohio citizens lose the opportunity for more jobs, they may enjoy better air and water quality than citizens of the state where the new factory is ultimately built.

Some observers consider the competitive nature of federalism an advantage: Americans have several variables to consider when they choose the state where they live. Others consider it a disadvantage: a state that offers more social services or lower taxes may suddenly experience an increase in population as people "vote with their feet" to take advantage of that state's laws. This population increase can overwhelm the state's resources and force it to cut social services or raise taxes.

It appears likely, then, that the debate over how our federal system functions, as well as the battle for control between the states and the federal government, will continue. The Supreme Court, which has played "umpire" in this battle, will also likely continue to issue rulings that influence the balance of power.

COMPETITIVE FEDERALISM A model of federalism devised by Thomas R. Dye in which state and local governments compete for businesses and citizens, who in effect "vote with their feet" by moving to jurisdictions that offer a competitive advantage.

why does it MATTER?

Federalism and Your Everyday Life

Most students of American government believe that the rather abstract concept of federalism has nothing to do with the realities they encounter in their everyday lives. Nothing could be further from the truth. On a broad scale, the fact that we have a federal form of government allows the fifty states to have significant influence over such matters as the level of taxation, the regulation of business, the creation and enforcement of criminal laws, and so on. What does that mean for you, as an individual? Most important, it means that you can pack up and move from one state to another in search of a business or working environment, a social and moral environment, or a legal environment that is more appealing to you than the one offered by your state.

Consider some examples of how state laws differ. In Nevada, you can purchase alcoholic beverages 24 hours a day, 365 days a year. In the neighboring state of Utah, the purchase of alcoholic beverages is severely restricted. With respect to so-called soft drugs, such as marijuana, there are also differences in state laws. Many states now do not prosecute an individual who is found with a small amount of marijuana. (Federal law still has not decriminalized marijuana.) Certainly, your ability to carry a gun or to be protected from those who do carry guns is a function of the state where you live. This is because in our federal system, the

states can currently regulate the sale and use of concealed firearms. In some states, concealed firearms are allowed; in others, they are strictly forbidden. You have the ability under our federal system to move to a jurisdiction that suits your tastes.

In nations that have a unitary form of government, such as France, this is not the case. Basically, you pay the same taxes no matter where you live in France. You go to exactly the same school system, and you face exactly the same criminal laws no matter where you live in that country.

Taking Action

As you have read, our federal system frequently creates tension between state or local concerns and national priorities. Often, individuals and groups take the initiative to assure that state or local governments respond to their particular wishes, regardless of how the nation as a whole might feel about it. The issue of physician-assisted suicide is a case in point. Oregonians have repeatedly voted for the right for terminally ill patients to seek help from a physician in ending their lives. In 2001, however, U.S. Attorney General John Ashcroft issued a directive prohibiting physicians from prescribing lethal doses of federally controlled drugs. In response to this attempt, James Romney, shown in the photo on the left, took action. He brought a suit in federal court, claiming that the federal government did not have the authority to nullify Oregon's law. The court agreed with Romney and issued a restraining order against the federal government. (AP Photo/ Don Ryan)

Key Terms

block grant 66	division of powers 55	inherent powers 55	preemption 61
categorical grant 66	dual federalism 60	necessary and proper clause 55	secession 59
competitive federalism 68	expressed powers 55	New Deal 60	supremacy clause 57
concurrent powers 57	federal mandate 66	new federalism 62	unitary system 52
confederal system 53	federalism 51	picket-fence federalism 61	
cooperative federalism 60	fiscal federalism 67	police powers 56	
devolution 51	implied powers 55		

Chapter Summary

1 The United States has a federal form of government, in which governmental powers are shared by the national government and the states. Alternatives to federalism include a unitary system and a confederal system. Federalism has been viewed as well suited to the United States for several reasons, but it also has some drawbacks.

2 The powers delegated by the Constitution to the national government include expressed powers, such as the power to coin money and to regulate interstate commerce; implied powers, or powers that are "necessary and proper" to the carrying out of the expressed powers; and inherent powers, which are necessary for any nation to survive and be a member of the community of nations.

3 All powers not delegated to the national government are "reserved" to the states, or to the people. State powers include police powers, which enable the states to enact whatever laws are necessary to protect the health, safety, morals, and welfare of their citizens. The Constitution prohibits both the national government and the states from exercising certain powers and provides for concurrent powers—powers that can be exercised by both state governments and the national government. The supremacy clause provides that national laws are supreme—they take priority over any conflicting state laws.

4 Two early Supreme Court cases that increased the powers of the national government are *McCulloch v. Maryland* (1819) and *Gibbons v. Ogden* (1824). The power struggle between the states and the national government ultimately resulted in the Civil War.

5 Federalism has evolved through several stages since the Civil War, including dual federalism, which prevailed until the 1930s, and cooperative federalism, which involves cooperation by all branches of government and launched an era of national government growth. The new federalism, which involves returning to the states some of the powers assumed by the national government, dates to the 1970s and has continued, in varying degrees, to the present.

6 For much of the twentieth century, the Supreme Court by and large held that the national government had not overreached the powers given to it by the commerce clause and the supremacy clause of the Constitution. In the 1990s and early 2000s, however, a more conservative Supreme Court has shown a willingness to support the new federalism by holding certain national government actions unconstitutional and emphasizing state sovereignty.

7 To help the states pay for the costs associated with implementing policies mandated by the national government, the national government awards grants to the states. Through the awarding of grants, the federal government can also influence activities that constitutionally are regulated by the states under their reserved powers.

8 Today, the federal government and the states seem to be in a constant tug of war over power, with the Supreme Court sometimes acting as umpire. Although the Supreme Court has ruled in favor of state sovereignty in many cases, the federal government continues to wield enormous power. Controversial issues today concern federal preemption of state laws and the use of unfunded federal mandates. Homeland security concerns have also led the federal government to impose greater demands on the states.

RESOURCES FOR FURTHER STUDY

Selected Readings

Liebmann, George W. *Solving Problems without Large Government: Devolution, Fairness, and Equality.* Westport, Conn.: Praeger, 2000. The author examines the merits of devolution from a practical point of view.

Light, Paul Charles. *Government's Greatest Achievements: From Civil Rights to Homeland Defense.* Washington, D.C.: Brookings Institution Press, 2002. The author acknowledges that the federal government is rarely credited with policy successes, particularly in the debate over how much power it should share with the states. Nonetheless, the federal government has made achievements, and they are chronicled in this book.

Nagel, Robert F. *The Implosion of American Federalism.* New York: Oxford University Press, 2002. The author argues that even recent Supreme Court decisions returning some power to the states will not save the nation from the dangers of increasingly centralized power. Indeed, he argues, the Court cannot, and is not, leading a revival of federalism.

Simon, James F. *What Kind of Nation: Thomas Jefferson, John Marshall, and the Epic Struggle to Create a United States.* New York: Simon & Schuster, 2002. The author compares the states' rights views of Jefferson and the Federalist beliefs of Marshall in the early decades of the nation and describes how Marshall's views eventually prevailed.

InfoTrac Citations

Using your InfoTrac password, access the InfoTrac database at **http://infotrac.thomsonlearning.com**. Once at the site, you can do "key word" searches to locate the following articles, each of which deals with a topic covered in this chapter. The key words to use in your search are indicated in parentheses.

- "State Internet Regulation and the Dormant Commerce Clause" (Commerce Clause)

- "National-State Relations: Cooperative Federalism in the Twentieth Century" (Cooperative Federalism)

- "President Bush Touts Era of 'New Federalism'" (New Federalism)

- "Schools Unclear on Federal Mandate's Definition of Qualified Teachers" (Federal Mandate)

Politics on the Web

To learn more about the founders' reasons for creating a federal form of government, you can access the *Federalist Papers* online at
http://www.law.emory.edu/FEDERAL

- You can also access the *Federalist Papers,* as well as state constitutions, information on the role of the courts in determining issues relating to federalism, and information on international federations, at the following site:
http://www.constitution.org/cs_feder.htm

- You can find information on state governments, state laws and pending legislation, and state issues and initiatives at
http://www.statescape.com

- Supreme Court opinions, including those discussed in this chapter, can be found at the Court's official Web site. Go to
http://www.supremecourtus.gov

- A good source for information on state governments and issues concerning federalism is the Web site of the Council of State Governments. Go to
http://www.statenews.org

- The Electronic Policy Network offers "timely information and leading ideas about federal policy and politics." It also has links to dozens of sites providing materials on federalism and public policy. Go to
http://www.movingideas.org

- The Brookings Institution, the nation's oldest think tank, is a good source for information on emerging policy challenges, including those relating to federal-state issues, and for practical recommendations for dealing with those challenges. To access the institution's home page, go to
http://www.brook.edu

- If you are interested in a libertarian perspective on issues such as federalism, the Cato Institute has a Web page at
http://www.cato.org

Web Resources on Your CD-ROM

On your CD-ROM, you will find Web resources, news articles, Internet activities, and video clips related to the topics in this chapter. Resources related to this chapter include the following:
- **Values Inventory**—Political Ideology: Medical Marijuana?
- **Why Does It Matter?**—Write a Letter to Your Congressperson about Your Views on State Drug Laws.
- **Updates**—Keep up with the issues in this chapter!
- **Web Resources**—Internet Activities: The International Medical Marijuana Association; The Science of Medical Marijuana.
- **Where Do You Stand?**—Dialogue: Should States Take Orders from the National Government?
- **Comparative Politics**—The German Constitution.
- **Videos**—*McCulloch v. Maryland;* States' Rights.
- **NewsEdge**—Visit this global resource for current events related to this chapter.

chapter 4
civil liberties

CHAPTER OBJECTIVES

After reading this chapter, you should be able to . . .

▷ Define the term *civil liberties* and explain how civil liberties differ from civil rights.

▷ Describe how the courts have interpreted and applied the freedom of religion guaranteed by the First Amendment.

▷ Indicate what forms of free speech will not be constitutionally protected, and why.

▷ Discuss why Americans are increasingly concerned about privacy rights.

▷ Summarize how the Constitution and the Bill of Rights protect the rights of accused persons.

Should Hate Speech on Campus Be Banned?

Most Americans consider the right to free speech one of the most treasured rights in the Constitution. But does freedom of speech mean that anybody can say anything, anywhere? Certainly not. No one is allowed to yell "fire" in a crowded theater as a joke. A more difficult question, faced by many universities today, is whether the right to free speech includes the right to make hateful remarks about others based on their race, gender, or sexual orientation.

Some claim that allowing people with extremist views to voice their opinions can lead to violence. For example, after antiabortion activists distributed "wanted" posters of two abortion physicians, both physicians were shot and killed. A judge for the Ninth Circuit Court of Appeals ruled that other similar posters were not mere expressions of speech. "While advocating violence is protected, threatening a person with violence is not."[1] How can society decide when speech has crossed the line from political hyperbole or abusive language to threats of violence? Should all hate speech be banned?

Hate Speech on College Campuses Should Be Banned

In response to this question, some universities have gone so far as to institute racial- and sexual-harassment rules to minimize the disturbances that hate speech can cause. We need more civility in campus discourse, argue those who favor campus speech codes. Some speech in the classroom does rise to the level of veiled or overt threats, and some speech constitutes sexual harassment, which most universities are required by law to prevent.[2] Considering that universities function best when students can engage in a free exchange of ideas, students need to learn to express their opinions without offending, threatening, or harassing others. "A certain level of civility, . . . being considerate of other folks in the room, is something that's good to work at," says Martha A. Field, a constitutional law specialist at Harvard University.[3] The student assembly at Wesleyan University agreed, passing a resolution in 2002 stating that the "right to speech comes with implicit responsibilities to respect community standards."[4]

The issue has also been raised on high school campuses, particularly in the wake of several school shootings. School officials take even the most veiled threats seriously. For example, when a student arrived at school on Halloween dressed in overalls and a straw hat, with black face and a noose around his neck, he was sent home and suspended. School officials later banned students from wearing clothing that "creates ill will or hatred," such as T-shirts with the Confederate flag or with jokes or statements on them that might be offensive to some groups.[5]

Speech Must Remain Free

Other Americans believe that there should be as few restrictions as possible on speech. They point out that free speech, even speech to which some may vehemently object, is essential to a democratic government. Campus rules governing speech and expression foster the idea that "good" speech should be protected, but "bad" speech should not. Who is to decide what is good and bad speech? Leaving this decision to a majority of university administrators, a majority of students, or a majority on the Supreme Court would lead to the "tyranny of the majority" so feared by the founders. What about the rights of minority groups to have their say?

"The remedy for silly, extreme, or offensive ideas is not less free speech, but more," reads Georgetown University's student handbook on speech and expression.[6] Harvard professor Alan Dershowitz agrees. Although he demanded that the Harvard English Department reinstate an invitation to a controversial poet accused of anti-Semitic views, he planned to picket outside the speech, arguing that the proper reaction to that kind of speech is answering it.

Where Do You Stand?

1. Would banning hate speech on university campuses help to create a student body more tolerant of diversity?

2. If you felt threatened by a fellow student's statement in class, would you want your college or university to institute a speech code in an effort to ensure that students feel safer on campus?

Interacting with Your CD-ROM Resources

Use your CD-ROM to access resources on the Web, simulations, participation exercises, and video clips. Important resources related to this feature include:
- **Values Inventory**—Political Ideology: Banning Hate Speech on Campus.
- **Where Do You Stand?**—Dialogue: Should Hate Speech on Campus Be Banned?
- **Web Resources**—Internet Activities: AAUP Statement on "Freedom of Expression and Campus Speech Codes"; The Price of Free Speech: Campus Hate Speech Codes—A Pro/Con Debate.

INTRODUCTION

The debate over hate speech on college campuses is but one of many controversies concerning our civil liberties. **Civil liberties** are legal and constitutional rights that protect citizens from government actions. For example, the First Amendment to the U.S. Constitution prohibits Congress from making any law that abridges the right to free speech. The First Amendment also guarantees freedom of religion, freedom of the press, and freedom to assemble (to gather together for a common purpose, such as to launch a protest against a government policy or action). These and other freedoms and guarantees set forth in the Constitution and the Bill of Rights are essentially *limits* on government action.

Perhaps the best way to understand what civil liberties are and why they are important to Americans is to look at what might happen if we did not have them. If you were a student in China, for example, you would have to exercise some care in what you say and do. That country prohibits speech that is contrary to the socialist ideology or the cultural aims of the nation. If you criticized the government in e-mail messages to your friends or on your Web site, you could end up in court on charges that you had violated the law—and perhaps even go to prison.

Note that some Americans confuse civil liberties (discussed in this chapter) with civil rights (discussed in the next chapter), and use the terms interchangeably. Nonetheless, scholars make a distinction between the two. They point out that whereas civil liberties are limitations on government action, setting forth what the government *cannot* do, civil rights specify what the government *must* do—to ensure equal protection under the law for all Americans, for example.

> **CIVIL LIBERTIES** Individual rights protected by the Constitution against the powers of the government.

The Constitutional Basis for Our Civil Liberties

The founders believed that the constitutions of the individual states contained ample provisions to protect citizens from government actions. Therefore, the founders did not include many references to individual civil liberties in the original version of the Constitution. These references were added by the Bill of Rights, ratified in 1791. Nonetheless, the original Constitution did include some safeguards to protect citizens against an overly powerful government.

Safeguards in the Original Constitution

Article I, Section 9, of the Constitution provides that the writ of *habeas corpus* (a Latin phrase that roughly means "produce the body") will be available to all citizens except in times of rebellion or national invasion. A **writ of *habeas corpus*** is an order requiring that an official bring a specified prisoner into court and show the judge why the prisoner is being kept in jail. If the court finds that the imprisonment is unlawful, it orders the prisoner to be released. If our country did not have such a constitutional provision, political leaders could jail their opponents without giving them the opportunity to plead their cases before a judge. Without this opportunity, many opponents might conveniently disappear or be left to rot away in prison.

> **WRIT OF *HABEAS CORPUS*** An order that requires an official to bring a specified prisoner into court and explain to the judge why the person is being held in prison.

The Constitution also prohibits Congress and the state legislatures from passing *bills of attainder*. A **bill of attainder** is a legislative act that directly punishes a specifically named individual (or a group or class of individuals) without a trial. For example, your state's legislature cannot pass a law that automatically sentences high school students who drive over the speed limit to one night in jail.

> **BILL OF ATTAINDER** A legislative act that inflicts punishment on particular persons or groups without granting them the right to a trial.

The Constitution also prohibits Congress from passing *ex post facto* laws. The Latin term *ex post facto* roughly means "after the fact." An ***ex post facto* law** punishes individuals for committing an act that was legal when it was committed but that has since become a crime.

> ***EX POST FACTO* LAW** A criminal law that punishes individuals for committing an act that was legal when the act was committed but that has since become a crime.

The Bill of Rights

As you read in Chapter 2, one of the contentious issues in the debate over ratification of the Constitution was the lack of protections for citizens from government actions. Although many state constitutions provided such protections, the Anti-Federalists wanted more. The promise of the addition of a Bill of Rights to the Constitution assured its ratification.

The Bill of Rights was ratified by the states and became part of the Constitution on December 15, 1791. Look at the text of the Bill of Rights in Chapter 2 on page 41. As you can see, the first eight amendments grant the people specific rights and liberties. The remaining two amendments reserve certain rights and powers to the people and to the states.

Basically, in a democracy, government policy tends to reflect the view of the majority. A key function of the Bill of Rights, therefore, is to protect the rights of minority groups against the will of the majority. When there is disagreement over how to interpret the Bill of Rights, the courts step in—particularly the Supreme Court, which has become known as the guardian of individual liberties. Ultimately, though, the responsibility for protecting minority rights lies with the American people. Each generation has to learn anew how it can uphold its rights by voting, expressing opinions to elected representatives, and bringing cases to the attention of the courts when constitutional rights are threatened.

The Incorporation Issue

For many years the protections against government actions in the Bill of Rights were applied only to actions of the federal government, not those of state or local governments. The founders believed that the states, being closer to the people, would be less likely to violate their own citizens' liberties. Moreover, state constitutions, most of which contain bills of rights, protect citizens against state government actions.

DUE PROCESS CLAUSE The constitutional guarantee, set out in the Fifth and Fourteenth Amendments, that the government will not illegally or arbitrarily deprive a person of life, liberty, or property.

DUE PROCESS OF LAW The requirement that the government use fair, reasonable, and standard procedures whenever it takes any legal action against an individual; required by the Fifth and Fourteenth Amendments.

The Right to Due Process
In 1868, three years after the end of the Civil War, the Fourteenth Amendment was added. The **due process clause** of this amendment ensures that state governments will protect their citizens' rights. The due process clause reads, in part, as follows:

> No State shall . . . deprive any person of life, liberty, or property, without due process of law.

The right to **due process of law** is simply the right to be treated fairly under the legal system. That system and its officers must follow "rules of fair play" in making decisions, in determining guilt or innocence, and in punishing those who have been found guilty. Generally, due process means that whenever the government takes a person's life, liberty, or property, the government must follow the correct procedures and give the person an equal opportunity to be heard.

Other Liberties Incorporated
The Fourteenth Amendment also states that no state "shall make or enforce any law which shall abridge the privileges or immunities of citizens of the United States." For some time, the Supreme Court considered the "privileges and immunities" referred to in the amendment to be those conferred by state laws or constitutions, not the federal Bill of Rights.

Starting in 1925, however, the Supreme Court gradually began using the due process clause to say that states could not abridge a civil liberty that the national government could not abridge. In other words, the Court *incorporated* the protections guaranteed by the national Bill of Rights into the liberties protected under the Fourteenth Amendment. As you can see in Table 4–1, the Supreme Court was particularly active during the 1960s in broadening its interpretation of the due process clause to assure that states and localities cannot infringe on civil liberties protected by the Bill of Rights. Today, the liberties not incorporated relate to the right to bear arms, the right to refuse to quarter soldiers, and the right to a grand jury hearing.

ESTABLISHMENT CLAUSE The section of the First Amendment that prohibits Congress from passing laws "respecting an establishment of religion." Issues concerning the establishment clause often center on prayer in public schools, the teaching of fundamentalist theories of creation, and government aid to parochial schools.

FREE EXERCISE CLAUSE The provision of the First Amendment stating that the government cannot pass laws "prohibiting the free exercise" of religion. Free exercise issues often concern religious practices that conflict with established laws.

Freedom of Religion

The First Amendment prohibits Congress from passing laws "respecting an establishment of religion, or prohibiting the free exercise thereof." The first part of this amendment is known as the **establishment clause.** The second part is called the **free exercise clause.**

TABLE 4–1

Incorporating the Bill of Rights into the Fourteenth Amendment

YEAR	ISSUE	AMENDMENT INVOLVED	COURT CASE
1925	Freedom of speech	I	*Gitlow v. New York,* 268 U.S. 652.
1931	Freedom of the press	I	*Near v. Minnesota,* 283 U.S. 697.
1932	Right to a lawyer in capital punishment cases	VI	*Powell v. Alabama,* 287 U.S. 45.
1937	Freedom of assembly and right to petition	I	*De Jonge v. Oregon,* 299 U.S. 353.
1940	Freedom of religion	I	*Cantwell v. Connecticut,* 310 U.S. 296.
1947	Separation of church and state	I	*Everson v. Board of Education,* 330 U.S. 1.
1948	Right to a public trial	VI	*In re Oliver,* 333 U.S. 257.
1949	No unreasonable searches and seizures	IV	*Wolf v. Colorado,* 338 U.S. 25.
1961	Exclusionary rule	IV	*Mapp v. Ohio,* 367 U.S. 643.
1962	No cruel and unusual punishments	VIII	*Robinson v. California,* 370 U.S. 660.
1963	Right to a lawyer in all criminal felony cases	VI	*Gideon v. Wainwright,* 372 U.S. 335.
1964	No compulsory self-incrimination	V	*Malloy v. Hogan,* 378 U.S. 1.
1965	Right to privacy	Various	*Griswold v. Connecticut,* 381 U.S. 479.
1966	Right to an impartial jury	VI	*Parker v. Gladden,* 385 U.S. 363.
1967	Right to a speedy trial	VI	*Klopfer v. North Carolina,* 386 U.S. 213.
1969	No double jeopardy	V	*Benton v. Maryland,* 395 U.S. 784.

That the freedom of religion was the first freedom mentioned in the Bill of Rights is not surprising. After all, many colonists came to America to escape religious persecution. Nonetheless, these same colonists showed little tolerance for religious freedom within the communities they established. For example, in 1610 the Jamestown colony enacted a law requiring attendance at religious services on Sunday "both in the morning and the afternoon." Repeat offenders were subjected to particularly harsh punishments. For those who twice violated the law, for example, the punishment was a public whipping. For third-time offenders, the punishment was death. The Maryland Toleration Act of 1649 declared that anyone who cursed God or denied that Jesus Christ was the son of God was to be punished by death. In all, nine of the thirteen colonies had established official religions by the time of the American Revolution.

This context is helpful in understanding why, in 1802, President Thomas Jefferson, a great proponent of religious freedom and tolerance, wanted the establishment clause to be "a wall of separation between church and state." The context also helps to explain why even state leaders who supported state religions might have favored the establishment clause—to keep the national government from interfering in such state matters. After all, the First Amendment states only that *Congress* can make no law respecting an establishment of religion; it says nothing about whether the *states* could make such laws. And, as noted earlier, the protections in the Bill of Rights initially applied only to actions taken by the national government, not the state governments.

The Establishment Clause

The establishment clause forbids the government to establish an official religion. This makes the United States different from countries that are ruled by religious governments, such as the Islamic government of Iran (see this chapter's *Comparative Politics* feature on the following page). It also makes us different from nations that have in the past strongly discouraged the practice of any religion at all, such as the People's Republic of China.

What does this separation of church and state mean in practice? For one thing, religion and government, though constitutionally separated in the United States, have never been

Church and State in Other Countries

Americans are often surprised to learn that many countries do not provide for the separation of church and state. In fact, the separation of church and state is more the exception than the rule. For example, in many Latin American countries, the Catholic Church is the state church. Many European countries also had state churches for much of their history. Consider Sweden. For more than four centuries, to be Swedish was to be Lutheran. Newborn babies were automatically registered as members of the Church of Sweden, the nation's official Lutheran denomination. Government officials appointed the bishops of the church, and any changes in the prayer books required an act of Parliament. The government collected mandatory "church taxes" from the citizens. Only, in 2000, did the government "disestablish" itself from the church.

The union between church and state is particularly strong in Muslim (Islamic) countries. In most of these countries, government and religion are intertwined to a degree that is quite startling to both Europeans and Americans. This lack of any separation between church and state in the legal systems of these countries is a feature that can be difficult for Americans to understand.

For Critical Analysis

Is the union of religion and law incompatible with a democratic form of government?

According to the Constitution as well as numerous Supreme Court decisions, there must be a separation of church and state in this country. Nonetheless, references to God are common in public life. Here you see a reference to God on a coin. It is also common for most public gatherings to open with prayer and references to God. Certainly, every recent presidential candidate has felt compelled to refer to God in public speeches.

enemies or strangers. The establishment clause does not prohibit government from supporting religion *in general;* it remains a part of public life. Most government officials take an oath of office in the name of God, and our coins and paper currency carry the motto "In God We Trust." Clergy of different religions serve with each branch of the armed forces. Public meetings and even sessions of Congress open with prayers. Indeed, the establishment clause often masks the fact that Americans are, by and large, religious and would like their political leaders to be people of faith.

The "wall of separation" that Thomas Jefferson referred to, however, does exist and has been upheld by the Supreme Court on many occasions. An important ruling by the Supreme Court on the establishment clause came in 1947 in *Everson v. Board of Education.*[7] The case involved a New Jersey law that allowed the state to pay for bus transportation of students who attended parochial schools (schools run by churches or other religious groups). The Court stated as follows: "No tax in any amount, large or small, can be levied to support any religious activities or institutions." The Court upheld the New Jersey law, however, because it did not aid the church *directly* but provided for the safety and benefit of the students. The ruling both affirmed the importance of separating church and state and set the precedent that not *all* forms of state and federal aid to church-related schools are forbidden under the Constitution.

A full discussion of the various church-state issues that have arisen in American politics would fill volumes. Here we examine three of these issues: prayer in the schools, evolution versus creationism, and government aid to parochial schools.

Prayer in the Schools

On occasion, some schools have promoted a general sense of religion without proclaiming allegiance to any particular church or sect. Whether the states have a right to allow this was the main question presented in 1962 in *Engel v. Vitale,*[8] also known as the "Regents' Prayer case." The State Board of Regents in New York had composed a nondenominational prayer (a prayer not associated with any particular religion) and urged school districts to use it in classrooms at the start of each day. The prayer read as follows:

> Almighty God, we acknowledge our dependence upon Thee, and we beg Thy blessings upon us, our parents, our teachers, and our Country.

Some parents objected to the prayer, contending that it violated the establishment clause. The Supreme Court agreed and ruled that the Regents' Prayer was unconstitutional. Speaking for the

Is prayer permissible in school? This thorny issue continues to come to the fore in public debate and court cases. Public schools, according to the majority of Supreme Court decisions, cannot sponsor religious activities. Nonetheless, individuals can pray when and as they choose in any place. (Karim Shambi-Basha/CORBIS Sygma)

majority, Justice Hugo Black wrote that the First Amendment must at least mean "that in this country it is no part of the business of government to compose official prayers for any group of the American people to recite as a part of a religious program carried on by government."

Prayer in the Schools—The Debate Continues   Since the *Engel v. Vitale* ruling, the Supreme Court has continued to shore up the wall of separation between church and state in a number of decisions. Generally, the Court has had to walk a fine line between the wishes of those who believe that religion should have a more prominent place in our public institutions and those who do not. For example, in a 1980 case, *Stone v. Graham,*[9] the Supreme Court ruled that a Kentucky law requiring that the Ten Commandments be posted in all public schools violated the establishment clause. Many groups around the country opposed this ruling. Currently, a number of states have passed or proposed laws permitting (but not *requiring,* as the Kentucky law did) the display of the Ten Commandments on public property, including public schools. Supporters of such displays contend that they will help reinforce the fundamental religious values that are a part of the American heritage. Opponents claim that the displays blatantly violate the establishment clause.

Another controversial issue is whether "moments of silence" in the schools are constitutional. In 1985, the Supreme Court ruled that an Alabama law authorizing a daily one-minute period of silence for meditation and voluntary prayer was unconstitutional. Because the law specifically endorsed prayer, it appeared to support religion.[10] Since then, the lower courts have generally held that a school may require a moment of silence but only if it serves a clearly secular purpose (such as to meditate on the day's activities).[11] Yet another issue concerns prayers said before public school sporting events, such as football games. In 2000, the Supreme Court held that student-led pre-game prayer using the school's public-address system was unconstitutional.[12]

In sum, the Supreme Court has ruled that the public schools, which are agencies of government, cannot sponsor religious activities. It has *not,* however, held that individuals cannot pray, when and as they choose, in schools or in any other place. Nor has it held that the Bible cannot be studied as a form of literature in the schools. (Furthermore, as indicated in this chapter's *Perception versus Reality* feature on the next page, even when the Court does rule that a certain state law is unconstitutional, there is no guarantee that the ruling will actually be followed by all Americans.)

The Supreme Court and Prayer in the Schools

Since the beginning of this nation, the Supreme Court has been the ultimate interpreter of our constitutional liberties, including the freedom of religion. Once the Supreme Court speaks on a constitutional issue, that ruling becomes the law on the matter.

THE PERCEPTION

The general public widely perceives the Supreme Court to be the final arbiter of national laws. Through its power of judicial review (the power to decide whether a law is or is not constitutional—see Chapter 14), the Court can wield enormous powers. It can determine the nation's policy in regard to such matters as religion in the schools, abortion, the right to die, the rights of criminal defendants, and hundreds of other issues that affect our daily lives. Understandably, many Americans also assume that if the Court decides that a particular law or practice, such as school prayer, is in violation of the Constitution, the dispute over the matter is laid to rest.

THE REALITY

In reality, the Supreme Court has no tangible enforcement mechanisms. If a Supreme Court decision is noticeably at odds with public opinion, persons affected by the decision may simply ignore it. Suppose, for example, that a teacher continues to lead her or his students in prayer every day despite the Supreme Court ruling that such a practice violates the establishment clause. What can the courts do in this situation? Unless some-

one complains about the teacher's actions and initiates a lawsuit, the courts can do nothing.

Similarly, what if a state passes a law that directly challenges a Supreme Court decision on the practice regulated by the law? What can the courts do? Again, the answer is nothing—unless the law is challenged in court.

Additionally, Supreme Court rulings are made in actual cases involving specific circumstances. For example, as mentioned on the previous page, in 2000 the Court ruled that students in a Texas public high school could not use the school's public-address system to lead fans in prayer before the first football game of the season. But what if a pre-game prayer is transmitted using a local radio broadcaster's microphone and the fans listen to the prayer via radios brought to the game for that purpose—as happened recently in a North Carolina school? This is a completely different scenario, and the Court's ruling on pre-game prayer using a publicly owned public-address system does not apply. A number of other communities in the South have similarly shown considerable ingenuity in devising ways to skirt the Court's ruling on pre-game prayers.

What's Your Opinion?

Should the framers of the Constitution have given the Supreme Court enforcement powers?

Evolution versus Creationism   Certain religious groups, particularly in the southern states, have long opposed the teaching of evolution in the schools. These groups contend that evolutionary theory, a scientific theory with overwhelming support, directly counters their religious belief that human beings did not evolve but were created fully formed, as described in the biblical story of the creation. The Supreme Court, however, has held unconstitutional state laws that forbid the teaching of evolution in the schools.

For example, in *Epperson v. Arkansas*,[13] a case decided in 1968, the Supreme Court held that an Arkansas law prohibiting the teaching of evolution violated the establishment clause because it imposed religious beliefs on students. In 1987, the Supreme Court also held unconstitutional a Louisiana law requiring that the biblical story of the creation be taught along with evolution. The Court deemed the law unconstitutional, in part because it had as its primary purpose the promotion of a particular religious belief.[14] In another case from Louisiana, a school board required all teachers in the district to recite a disclaimer, before teaching evolution, that instruction in evolutionary theory was "not intended to influence or dissuade the Biblical version of Creation or any other concept." In 2000, a federal appellate court held that this disclaimer violated the establishment clause because its effect was to give protection to a particular religious viewpoint.[15]

State and local groups in the so-called Bible Belt, however, continue their efforts against the teaching of evolution. Recently, for example, Alabama approved a disclaimer to be inserted in biology textbooks, stating that evolution is "a controversial theory some scientists present as a scientific explanation for the origin of living things." A school district in Georgia adopted a policy that creationism could be taught along with evolution. No doubt, these laws and policies will eventually be challenged on constitutional grounds.

Aid to Parochial Schools

Americans have long been at odds over whether public tax dollars should be used to fund activities in parochial schools—private schools that have religious affiliations. Over the years, the courts have often had to decide whether specific types of aid do or do not violate the establishment clause. Aid to church-related schools in the form of transportation, equipment, or special educational services for disadvantaged students has been held permissible. Other forms of aid, such as funding teachers' salaries and paying for field trips, have been held unconstitutional.

Since 1971, the Supreme Court has held that, to be constitutional, a state's school aid must meet three requirements: (1) the purpose of the financial aid must be clearly secular (not religious); (2) its primary effect must neither advance nor inhibit religion; and (3) it must avoid an "excessive government entanglement with religion." The Court first used the test in *Lemon v. Kurtzman*,[16] and hence it is often referred to as the **Lemon test.** In the *Lemon* case, the Court denied public aid to private and parochial schools for the salaries of teachers of secular courses and for textbooks and instructional materials in certain secular subjects. The Court held that the establishment clause is designed to prevent three main evils: "sponsorship, financial support, and active involvement of the sovereign [the government] in religious activity."

Recent Applications of the *Lemon* Test

In 2000, the Supreme Court applied the *Lemon* test to a federal law that gives public school districts federal funds for special services and instructional equipment. The law requires that the funds be shared with all private schools in the district. A central issue in the case was whether using the funds to supply computers to parochial schools had a clearly secular purpose. Some groups claimed that it did not, because students in parochial schools could use the computers to access religious materials online. Others, including the Clinton administration, argued that giving high-tech assistance to parochial schools did have a secular purpose and was a religiously neutral policy. The Supreme Court sided with the latter argument and held that the law did not violate the establishment clause.[17]

School Voucher Programs

Another contentious issue has to do with school vouchers—educational certificates provided by state governments that students can use at any school, public or private. In an effort to improve their educational systems, several school districts have been experimenting with voucher systems. President George W. Bush also proposed vouchers as part of his plan to reform education. The courts, however, have been

LEMON TEST A three-part test enunciated by the Supreme Court in the 1971 case of *Lemon v. Kurtzman* to determine whether government aid to parochial schools is constitutional. To be constitutional, the aid must (1) be for a clearly secular purpose; (2) in its primary effect, neither advance nor inhibit religion; and (3) avoid an "excessive government entanglement with religion." The *Lemon* test has also been used in other types of cases involving the establishment clause.

School voucher proponent Jackie Meeks of Cleveland takes part in a rally outside the U.S. Supreme Court in February 2002, when the Court heard arguments on Cleveland's six-year-old school voucher program. The Supreme Court subsequently ruled that the program was constitutional. (AP Photo/Rick Bowmer)

divided on the issue of whether school vouchers violate the establishment clause when they enable public funds to be used to pay for education at parochial schools.

For example, in one case a federal appellate court held that a voucher program in Cleveland, Ohio, was unconstitutional. Under the program, the state provided up to $2,250 to low-income families, who could use the funds to send their children to either public or private schools. The court held that the program did not meet the three prongs of the *Lemon* test and thus violated the establishment clause.[18] The case was appealed to the United States Supreme Court, and in 2002 the Court ruled that the Ohio voucher program was constitutional. The Court concluded that the taxpayer-paid voucher program does not unconstitutionally entangle church and state because the funds go to parents, not to schools. The parents theoretically can use the vouchers to send their children to secular private academies or charter schools, even though 95 percent use the vouchers at religious schools.[19]

Despite the Supreme Court ruling, several constitutional questions surrounding school vouchers remain unresolved. For example, some state constitutions are more explicit in denying the use of public funds for religious education than is the federal Constitution. Even after the Supreme Court ruling in the Ohio case, a Florida court ruled in 2002 that a voucher program in that state violated Florida's constitution.[20]

AMERICA at odds

Is America One Nation "under God"?

Although by law no person can be required to say the Pledge of Allegiance, children routinely recite it in classrooms across the nation every day. When the pledge was first published in a youth magazine in 1892, it did not contain the words "under God." Those were added by congressional legislation in 1954, at the urging of President Dwight D. Eisenhower (1952–1961). In 2002, however, the Ninth Circuit Court of Appeals, using the *Lemon* test, ruled that the words "under God" in the pledge violated the establishment clause of the First Amendment.

Michael Newdow, the plaintiff in the case, argued that his daughter's constitutional rights were violated when she was forced to "watch and listen" as her teacher led her classmates "in a ritual proclaiming that there is a God."[21] The federal appellate court agreed, stating that "a profession [declaration] that we are a nation 'under God' is identical, for Establishment Clause purposes, to a profession that we are a nation 'under

Michael Newdow filed suit against the Elk Grove Unified School District in Sacramento, California, because his second-grade daughter was required to say the Pledge of Allegiance. Here, Newdow in shown talking to reporters outside his home in June 2002, after a federal appellate court ruled that requiring public school children to recite the Pledge was unconstitutional. (AP Photo/Rich Pedroncelli)

Jesus,' a nation 'under Vishnu,' a nation 'under Zeus,' or a nation 'under no god,' because none of these professions can be neutral with respect to religion." The court further argued that to recite the pledge "is to swear allegiance to the values for which the flag stands: unity, indivisibility, liberty, justice, and—since 1954—monotheism."

In contrast, proponents of the pledge as it now reads argue that the words "under God" merely acknowledge the religious heritage of the nation. Other proponents say the pledge is purely ceremonial—it recognizes a higher power that supports the nation but does not endorse any particular religious belief.[22] In a *Newsweek* poll following the appellate court's decision, 87 percent of respondents said they support including "under God" in the pledge, and 84 percent said they think references to God are acceptable in schools, government buildings, and other public settings, so long as no specific religion is mentioned.[23] Nonetheless, 29 million Americans identify themselves as nonreligious, atheist, or agnostic, and another one million are affiliated with religions generally not considered monotheistic, such as Buddhism or Hinduism. If the Supreme Court agrees to review the Ninth Circuit's decision, the justices are likely to overturn it. The question thus remains whether such a public ritual proclaiming the existence of a God can be religiously neutral to the 30 million Americans who disagree.

The Free Exercise Clause

As mentioned, the second part of the First Amendment's statement on religion consists of the free exercise clause, which forbids the passage of laws "prohibiting the free exercise of religion." This clause protects individuals' right to worship or believe as they wish without government interference. No law or act of government may violate this constitutional right.

Belief and Practice Are Distinct

The free exercise clause does not necessarily mean that individuals can act in any way they want on the basis of their religious beliefs. There is an important distinction between belief and practice. The Supreme Court has ruled consistently that the right to hold any *belief* is absolute. The government has no authority to compel you to accept or reject any particular religious belief. The right to *practice* one's beliefs, however, may have some limitations. As the Court itself once asked, "Suppose one believed that human sacrifice were a necessary part of religious worship?"

The Supreme Court first dealt with the issue of belief versus practice in 1878 in *Reynolds v. United States*.[24] Reynolds was a Mormon who had two wives. Polygamy, or the practice of having more than one spouse at a time, was encouraged by the customs and teachings of this religion. Polygamy was also prohibited by federal law. Reynolds was convicted and appealed the case, arguing that the law violated his constitutional right to freely exercise his religious beliefs. The Court did not agree. It said that to allow Reynolds to practice polygamy would be to make the doctrines of religious beliefs superior to the law.

Religious Practices and the Workplace

The free exercise of religion in the workplace was bolstered by Title VII of the Civil Rights Act of 1964, which requires employers to accommodate their employees' religious practices unless such accommodation causes an employer to suffer an "undue hardship." Thus, if an employee claims that his or her religious beliefs prevent him or her from working on a particular day of the week, such as Saturday or Sunday, the employer must attempt to accommodate the employee's needs.

Several cases have come before lower federal courts concerning employer dress codes that contradict the religious customs of employees. For example, in 1999 the Third Circuit Court of Appeals ruled in favor of two Muslim police officers in Newark, New Jersey, who claimed that they were required by their faith to wear beards and would not shave them to comply with the police department's grooming policy. A similar case was brought in 2001 by Washington, D.C., firefighters who were suspended for violating their department's safety regulations regarding long hair and beards. Muslims, Rastafarians, and others refused to change the grooming habits required by their religion and were successful in court.[25]

Ku Klux Klan members burning a cross.
(Bettmann/CORBIS)

Freedom of Expression

No one in this country seems to have a problem protecting the free speech of those with whom they agree. The real challenge is protecting unpopular ideas. The protection needed is, in Justice Oliver Wendell Holmes's words, "not free thought for those who agree with us but freedom for the thought that we hate." The First Amendment is designed to protect the freedom to express *all* ideas, including those that may be unpopular or different.

The First Amendment has been interpreted to protect more than merely spoken words; it also protects **symbolic speech**—speech involving actions and other nonverbal expressions. Some common examples include picketing in a labor dispute or wearing a black armband in protest of a government policy. Even burning the American flag as a gesture of protest has been held to be protected by the First Amendment.

The Right to Free Speech Is Not Absolute

Although Americans have the right to free speech, not *all* speech is protected under the First Amendment. Our constitutional rights and liberties are not absolute. Rather, they are what the Supreme Court—the ultimate interpreter of the Constitution—says they are. Although the Court has zealously safeguarded the right to free speech, at times it has imposed limits on speech in the interests of protecting other rights of Americans. These rights include security against harm to one's person or reputation, the need for public order, and the need to preserve the government.

Generally, throughout our history, the Supreme Court has attempted to balance our rights to free speech against these other needs of society. As Justice Holmes once said, even "the most stringent protection of free speech would not protect a man in falsely shouting fire in a theatre and causing a panic."[26] We look next at some of the ways that the Court has limited the right to free speech.

SYMBOLIC SPEECH The expression of beliefs, opinions, or ideas through forms other than speech or print; speech involving actions and other nonverbal expressions.

ESPIONAGE The practice of spying, on behalf of a foreign power, to obtain information about government plans and activities.

SABOTAGE A destructive act intended to hinder a nation's defense efforts.

TREASON As enunciated in Article III, Section 3, of the Constitution, the act of levying war against the United States or adhering (remaining loyal) to its enemies.

SEDITIOUS SPEECH Speech that urges resistance to lawful authority or that advocates the overthrowing of a government.

Early Restrictions on Expression

At times in our nation's history, various individuals have not supported our form of democratic government. Our government, however, has drawn a fine line between legitimate criticism and the expression of ideas that may seriously harm society. Clearly, the government may pass laws against violence, espionage, sabotage, and treason. **Espionage** is the practice of spying for a foreign power. **Sabotage** involves actions normally intended to hinder or damage the nation's defense or war effort. **Treason** is specifically defined in the Constitution as levying war against the United States or adhering (remaining loyal) to its enemies (Article III, Section 3). But what about **seditious speech,** which urges resistance to lawful authority or advocates overthrowing the government?

As early as 1798, Congress took steps to curb seditious speech when it passed the Alien and Sedition Acts, which made it a crime to utter "any false, scandalous, and malicious" criticism against the government. The acts were considered unconstitutional by many but were never tested in the courts. Several dozen individuals were prosecuted under the acts, and some were actually convicted. In 1801, President Thomas Jefferson pardoned those sentenced under the acts, and Congress soon repealed them. During World War I, Congress passed the Espionage Act of 1917 and the Sedition Act of 1918. The 1917 act prohibited attempts to interfere with the operation of the military forces, the war effort, or the process of recruitment. The 1918 act made it a crime to "willfully utter, print, write, or publish any disloyal, profane, scurrilous [insulting], or abusive language" about the government. More than two thousand persons were tried and convicted under this act, which was repealed at the end of World War I.

In 1940, Congress passed the Smith Act, which forbade people from advocating the violent overthrow of the U.S. government. The Supreme Court first upheld the constitutionality of the Smith Act in *Dennis v. United States,*[27] which involved eleven top leaders of the Communist

Party who had been convicted of violating the act. The Court found that their activities went beyond the permissible peaceful advocacy of change. According to the Smith Act, these activities threatened society's right to national security. Subsequently, however, the Court modified its position. Since the 1960s, the Court has defined seditious speech to mean only the advocacy of imminent and concrete acts of violence against the government.[28]

Limited Protection for Commercial Speech

Advertising, or **commercial speech,** is also protected by the First Amendment, but not as fully as regular speech. Generally, the Supreme Court has considered a restriction on commercial speech to be valid as long as the restriction "(1) seeks to implement a substantial government interest, (2) directly advances that interest, and (3) goes no further than necessary to accomplish its objective." Problems arise, though, when restrictions on commercial advertising achieve one substantial government interest yet are contrary to the interest in protecting free speech and the right of consumers to be informed. In such cases, the courts have to decide which interest takes priority.

Liquor advertising is a good example of this kind of conflict. For example, in one case, Rhode Island argued that its law banning the advertising of liquor prices served the state's goal of discouraging liquor consumption (because the ban discouraged bargain hunting and thus kept liquor prices high). The Supreme Court, however, held that the ban was an unconstitutional restraint on commercial speech. The Court stated that the First Amendment "directs us to be especially skeptical of regulations that seek to keep people in the dark for what the government perceives to be their own good."[29] In contrast, restrictions on tobacco advertising are the result of a policy choice that free speech can be restrained in the interests of protecting the health of society, particularly the health of young Americans.

COMMERCIAL SPEECH Advertising statements that describe products. Commercial speech receives less protection under the First Amendment than ordinary speech.

Unprotected Speech

Certain types of speech receive no protection under the First Amendment. These types of speech include libel and slander, "fighting words," and obscenity.

Libel and Slander   No person has the right to libel or slander another. **Libel** is a published report of a falsehood that tends to injure a person's reputation or character. **Slander** is the public utterance (speaking) of a statement that holds a person up for contempt, ridicule, or hatred. To prove libel and slander, however, certain criteria must be met. The statements made must be untrue, must stem from an intent to do harm, and must result in actual harm.

The Supreme Court has ruled that public figures (public officials and others in the public limelight) cannot collect damages for remarks made against them unless they can prove the remarks were made with "reckless" disregard for accuracy. Generally, it is believed that because public figures have greater access to the media than ordinary persons do, they are in a better position to defend themselves against libelous or slanderous statements.

LIBEL A published report of a falsehood that tends to injure a person's reputation or character.
SLANDER The public utterance (speaking) of a statement that holds a person up for contempt, ridicule, or hatred.

"Fighting Words"   Another form of speech that is not protected by the First Amendment is what the Supreme Court has called **"fighting words."** This is speech that is so inflammatory that it will provoke the average listener to violence. The Court has ruled that fighting words must go beyond merely insulting or controversial language. The words must be a clear invitation to immediate violence or breach of the peace. As mentioned in the opening *America at Odds* feature, however, determining when hateful speech becomes an actual threat against a person or an invitation to start a riot can be difficult. For example, an individual was arrested for allegedly praising the World Trade Center terrorist attacks to a crowd in Times Square just a few days after September 11, 2001. His arrest was upheld in court by a judge who noted that his words "were plainly intended to incite the crowd to violence, and not simply to express a point of view." Nonetheless, some legal experts argue that upholding this arrest on the "fighting words" doctrine is untenable because the defendant was expressing political speech.[30]

"FIGHTING WORDS" Words that, when uttered by a public speaker, are so inflammatory that they could provoke the average listener to violence.

OBSCENITY Indecency or offensiveness in speech or expression, behavior, or appearance; whether specific expressions or acts constitute obscenity normally is determined by community standards.

Obscenity

Obscene speech is another form of speech that is not protected under the First Amendment. Although the dictionary defines **obscenity** as that which is offensive and indecent, the courts have had difficulty defining the term with any precision. Supreme Court Justice Potter Stewart's famous statement, "I know it when I see it," certainly gave little guidance on the issue.

One problem in defining obscenity is that what is obscene to one person is not necessarily obscene to another; what one reader considers indecent, another reader might see as "colorful." Another problem is that society's views on obscenity change over time. Major literary works of such great writers as D. H. Lawrence (1885–1930), Mark Twain (1835–1910), and James Joyce (1882–1941) were once considered obscene in most of the United States.

After many unsuccessful attempts to define obscenity, in 1973 the Supreme Court came up with a three-part test in *Miller v. California*.[31] The Court decided that a book, film, or other piece of material is legally obscene if it meets the following criteria:

1. The average person applying contemporary [present-day] standards finds that the work taken as a whole appeals to the prurient interest—that is, tends to excite unwholesome sexual desire.
2. The work depicts or describes, in a patently [obviously] offensive way, a form of sexual conduct specifically prohibited by an antiobscenity law.
3. The work taken as a whole lacks serious literary, artistic, political, or scientific value.

The very fact that the Supreme Court has had to set up such a complicated test shows how difficult defining obscenity is. The Court went on to state that, in effect, local communities should be allowed to set their own standards for what is obscene. What is obscene to many people in one area of the country might be perfectly acceptable to those in another area.

Obscenity in Cyberspace

One of the most controversial issues in regard to free speech in cyberspace concerns obscene and pornographic materials. Such materials can be easily accessed by anyone of any age anywhere in the world via numerous World Wide Web sites. Many strongly believe that the government should step in to prevent obscenity on the Internet. Others believe, just as strongly, that speech on the Internet should not be regulated.

The issue came to a head in 1996, when Congress passed the Communications Decency Act (CDA). The law made it a crime to transmit "indecent" or "patently offensive" speech or images to minors (those under the age of eighteen) or to make such speech or images available online to minors. Violators of the act could be fined up to $250,000 or imprisoned for up to two years. In 1997, the Supreme Court held that the law's sections on indecent speech were unconstitutional. According to the Court, those sections of the CDA were too broad in their

Reprinted with special permission of King Features Syndicate.

scope and significantly restrained the constitutionally protected free speech of adults.[32] Congress made a further attempt to regulate Internet speech in 1998 with the Child Online Protection Act. The act imposed criminal penalties on those who distribute material that is "harmful to minors" without using some kind of age-verification system to separate adult and minor Web users. The law has been under a court injunction barring its enforcement until the First Amendment issues are resolved in the courts.[33]

Having failed twice in its attempt to regulate online obscenity, Congress decided to try a different approach. In late 2000, it passed the Children's Internet Protection Act. This act requires schools and libraries to use Internet **filtering software** to protect children from pornography or risk losing federal funds for technology upgrades. In 2002, a federal three-judge panel sitting in the Eastern District of Pennsylvania found that the law was unconstitutional when applied to libraries but not when applied to schools.[34] The case is currently pending before the United States Supreme Court.

In 1996, with the Child Pornography Prevention Act, Congress also attempted to prevent the distribution and possession of "virtual" child pornography—computer-generated images of children engaged in lewd and lascivious behavior. These images, when digitally rendered, are amazingly real, even though they are created entirely on a computer, with no child actors involved. In 2002, the Supreme Court reviewed the 1996 act and found it unconstitutional. The Court ruled that the act did not establish the necessary link between "its prohibitions and the affront to community standards prohibited by the obscenity definition."[35]

FILTERING SOFTWARE Computer programs designed to block access to certain Web sites.

Freedom of the Press

The framers of the Constitution believed that the press should be free to publish a wide range of opinions and information, and generally the free speech rights just discussed also apply to the press. The courts have placed certain restrictions on the freedom of the press, however. Over the years, the Supreme Court has developed various guidelines and doctrines to use in deciding whether freedom of speech and the press can be restrained.

Clear and Present Danger

One guideline the Court has used resulted from a case in 1919, *Schenck v. United States*.[36] Charles T. Schenck was convicted of printing and distributing leaflets urging men to resist the draft during World War I. The government claimed that his actions violated the Espionage Act of 1917, which made it a crime to encourage disloyalty to the government or resistance to the draft. The Supreme Court upheld both the law and the convictions. Justice Holmes, speaking for the Court, stated as follows:

> The question in every case is whether the words used are used in such circumstances and are of such a nature as to create a *clear and present danger* that they will bring about the substantive evils that Congress has a right to prevent. It is a question of proximity [closeness] and degree. [Emphasis added.]

Thus, according to the *clear and present danger test*, government should be allowed to restrain speech only when that speech clearly presents an immediate threat to public order. It is often hard to say when speech crosses the line between being merely controversial and being a "clear and present danger," but the principle has been used in many cases since *Schenck*.

The clear and present danger principle seemed too permissive to some Supreme Court justices. Several years after the *Schenck* ruling, in the case of *Gitlow v. New York*,[37] the Court held that speech could be permissibly curtailed even if it had only a *tendency* to lead to illegal action. Since the 1920s, however, this guideline, known as the *bad-tendency test*, has generally not been supported by the Supreme Court.

The Preferred-Position Doctrine

Another guideline, called the *preferred-position doctrine*, states that certain freedoms are so essential to a democracy that they hold a preferred position. According to this doctrine, any law that limits these freedoms should be presumed unconstitutional unless the government can show that the law is absolutely necessary. Thus, freedom of speech and the press should rarely, if ever, be diminished, because spoken and printed words are the prime tools of the democratic process.

Prior Restraint

Stopping an activity before it actually happens is known as *prior restraint*. With respect to freedom of the press, prior restraint involves *censorship*, which occurs when an official removes objectionable materials from an item before it is published or broadcast. An example of censorship and prior restraint would be a court's ruling that two paragraphs in an upcoming article in the local newspaper had to be removed before the article could be published. The Supreme Court has generally ruled against prior restraint, arguing that the government cannot curb ideas *before* they are expressed.

On some occasions, however, the Court has allowed prior restraints. For example, in a 1988 case, *Hazelwood School District v. Kuhlmeier*,[38] a high school principal deleted two pages from the school newspaper just before it was printed. The pages contained stories on students' experiences with pregnancy and discussed the impact of divorce on students at the school. The Supreme Court, noting that students in school do not have exactly the same rights as adults in other settings, ruled that high school administrators *can* censor school publications. The Court said that school newspapers are part of the school curriculum, not a public forum. Therefore, administrators have the right to censor speech that promotes conduct inconsistent with the "shared values of a civilized social order."

Freedom of Assembly

The First Amendment also protects the right of the people "peaceably to assemble" and communicate their ideas on public issues to government officials, as well as to other individuals. Parades, marches, protests, and other demonstrations are daily events in this country and allow groups to express and publicize their ideas. The Supreme Court often has put this freedom of assembly, or association, on a par with freedom of speech and freedom of the press. In the interests of public order, however, the Court has allowed municipalities to require permits for parades, sound trucks, demonstrations, and the like.

Like unpopular speech, unpopular assemblies or protests often generate controversy. One controversial case arose in 1977, when the American Nazi Party decided to march through the largely Jewish suburb of Skokie, Illinois. The city of Skokie enacted three ordinances designed to prohibit the types of demonstrations that the Nazis planned to undertake. The American Civil Liberties Union (ACLU) sued the city on behalf of the Nazis, defending their right to march (in spite of the ACLU's opposition to the Nazi philosophy). A federal district court

The Constitution guarantees freedom of assembly. Does that mean that any group should be allowed to stage a protest or hold a parade? Many Americans would like to prevent the Ku Klux Klan (KKK) from marching in downtown areas, such as in Austin, Texas, as seen here. Nonetheless, the Supreme Court has upheld the First Amendment rights of such marchers. (AP Photo/Rogelio Solis)

agreed with the ACLU and held that the city of Skokie had violated the Nazis' First Amendment guarantees by denying them a permit to march. The appellate court affirmed that decision. The Supreme Court refused to review the case, thus letting the lower court's decision stand.[39]

What about laws that prevent gang members from assembling on city streets? Do such laws violate the gang members' First Amendment rights or other constitutional guarantees? Courts have answered this question differently, depending in part on the nature of the laws in question.

In some cases, for example, "antiloitering" laws have been upheld by the courts. In others, they have not. In 1999, the Supreme Court held that Chicago's antiloitering ordinance violated the right to due process because, among other things, it left too much "lawmaking" power in the hands of the police, who were left to decide what constitutes "loitering."[40] How a particular court balances gang members' right of assembly against the

Members of the Crips gang gather in San Fernando, California. (A. Ramey/PhotoEdit)

rights of society may also come into play. In 1997, for example, the California Supreme Court had to decide whether court injunctions barring gang members from appearing in public together in certain areas of San Jose, California, were constitutional. The court upheld the injunctions, declaring that society's rights to peace and quiet and to be free from harm outweighed the gang members' First Amendment associational rights.[41]

The Right to Privacy

Supreme Court Justice Louis Brandeis stated in 1928 that the right to privacy is "the most comprehensive of rights and the right most valued by civilized men."[42] The majority of the justices on the Supreme Court at that time did not agree. In the 1960s, though, the justices on the Supreme Court began to hold that a right to privacy is implied by other constitutional rights guaranteed in the First, Third, Fourth, Fifth, and Ninth Amendments. For example, consider the words of the Ninth Amendment: "The enumeration in the Constitution, of certain rights, shall not be construed to deny or disparage others retained by the people." In other words, just because the Constitution, including its amendments, does not specifically mention the right to privacy does not mean that this right is denied to the people.

Since then, the government has also passed laws ensuring the privacy rights of individuals. For example, in 1966 Congress passed the Freedom of Information Act, which, among other things, allows any person to request copies of any information about her or him contained in government files. In 1974, Congress passed the Privacy Act, which restricts government disclosure of data to third parties. In 1994, Congress passed the Driver's Privacy Protection Act, which prevents states from disclosing or selling a driver's personal information without the driver's consent.[43] In late 2000, the federal Department of Health and Human Services issued a regulation ensuring the privacy of a person's medical information. Health-care providers and insurance companies are restricted from sharing confidential information about their patients.

Although Congress and the courts have acknowledged a constitutional right to privacy, the nature and scope of this right are not always clear. For example, Americans continue to debate whether the right to privacy includes the right to have an abortion or the right of terminally ill persons to commit physician-assisted suicide. Americans are also at odds over how to deal with what is perhaps one of the most difficult challenges of our time—how to protect privacy rights in cyberspace. Since the terrorist attacks of September 11, 2001, another pressing privacy issue has been how to monitor potential terrorists to prevent another attack without violating the privacy rights of all Americans.

The Abortion Controversy

One of the most divisive and emotionally charged issues being debated today is whether the right to privacy means that women can choose to have abortions.

Abortion and Privacy   In 1973, in the landmark case of *Roe v. Wade*,[44] the Supreme Court held that it did. According to the Court, the "right of privacy . . . is broad enough to encompass a woman's decision whether or not to terminate her pregnancy." The right is not absolute throughout pregnancy, however. The Court also said that any state could impose certain regulations to safeguard the health of the mother after the first three months of pregnancy and, in the final stages of pregnancy, could act to protect potential life.

Since the *Roe* decision, the Supreme Court has adopted a more conservative approach and has upheld restrictive state laws requiring counseling, waiting periods, notification of parents, and other actions prior to abortions.[45] Yet the Court has never overturned the *Roe* decision. In fact, in 1997 and again in 2000, the Supreme Court upheld laws requiring "buffer zones" around abortion clinics to protect those entering the clinics from unwanted counseling or harassment by pro-life groups.[46] Additionally, in 2000, the Supreme Court invalidated a Nebraska statute banning "partial-birth" abortions, a procedure used during the second trimester of pregnancy.[47]

Even with the *Roe* decision intact and the Court's rulings upholding "buffer zones," a woman's right to privacy in seeking an abortion remains an issue before the courts. Since 2001, protesters opposed to abortions have positioned themselves outside abortion clinics with cameras, photographed clinic patients, and then posted the photos, along with license-plate numbers and other identifying information, on Web sites. At least one case alleging that this tactic violates patients' privacy rights is pending before an Illinois court. The question that the courts face is whether women entering a clinic lose their privacy protection because they are in a public place or, to the contrary, are afforded additional privacy protection because they are seeking medical attention.[48]

Abortion and Politics   American opinion on the abortion issue has become more nuanced than the labels "pro-life" and "pro-choice" would indicate. For example, about half of the respondents in a 2000 *Los Angeles Times* poll thought that abortion should be illegal in all circumstances, or legal only in cases of rape, incest, or when a woman's life is in danger. At the same time, more than two-thirds said that regardless of their own feelings on the subject, an abortion decision should be a private one, to be made by a woman and her physician. Even more notably, while 57 percent of the respondents said that they consider abortion to be mur-

The abortion controversy was certainly not put to rest by the *Roe v. Wade* decision in 1973. Americans continue to express their differing views on this subject passionately, as shown in this photo. Abortion was long practiced as a form of birth control until pressure from the Roman Catholic Church and changing public opinion led to the passage of strict antiabortion laws in the nineteenth century. By the 1970s, though, abortion had been legalized not only in the United States but also in most European countries and in Japan. In recent years, abortion opponents in the United States have resorted to militant tactics in attempts to disrupt abortion clinics; some have even resorted to bombings and murders. (Christopher Brown/Stock Boston)

der, more than half of that group thought that a woman should have the right to an abortion. Understandably, politicians find it difficult to respond to these conflicting perspectives.

Some scholars contend, though, that the election of George W. Bush in 2000 and the Republican victories in the Senate in 2002 presage a shift in the ideological bent of federal judges. More conservative judges, opposed to abortion rights, are more likely to be nominated to the Supreme Court and approved by the Senate. Some observers have even predicted that *Roe v. Wade* could be overturned.

Do We Have the "Right to Die"?

Whether it is called euthanasia (mercy killing), assisted suicide, or a dignified way to leave this world, it all comes down to one basic question: Do terminally ill persons have, as part of their civil liberties, a right to die and to be assisted in the process by physicians or others? Phrased another way, are state laws banning physician-assisted suicide in such circumstances unconstitutional?

In 1997, the issue came before the Supreme Court, which characterized the question as follows: Does the liberty protected by the Constitution include a right to commit suicide, which itself includes a right to assistance in doing so? The Court's clear and categorical answer to this question was no. To hold otherwise, said the Court, would be "to reverse centuries of legal doctrine and practice, and strike down the considered policy choice of almost every state."[49] (Suicide, including attempts to aid or promote suicide, is defined as a crime in most, if not all, states.) Although the Court upheld the states' rights to ban such a practice, the Court did not hold that state laws *permitting* assisted suicide were unconstitutional. In 1997, Oregon became the first state—and so far, the only one—to implement such a law.

The Supreme Court's enunciation of its opinion on this topic has not ended the debate, though, just as the debate over abortion did not stop after the 1973 *Roe v. Wade* decision legalizing abortion. And Americans continue to be at odds over this issue.

Privacy Rights in an Information Age

Perhaps one of the most pressing issues facing Americans and their political leaders today is how to protect privacy rights in cyberspace. Indeed, in today's online world, some people believe that privacy rights are quickly becoming a thing of the past. "Cookies" tell the hosts of a Web site what you did the last time you visited their site. Furthermore, any person who wants to purchase goods from online merchants or auctions inevitably must reveal some personal information, including (often) a credit-card number. One of the major concerns of consumers in recent years has been the increasing value of personal information for online marketers— who are willing to pay a high price to those who collect and sell them such information.

The problem for today's citizens is that they cannot even know what kind of information on their personal lives and preferences is being collected by Internet companies and other online users. Nor can they know how that information will be used. According to a report recently published by the University of California at Los Angeles (UCLA), Americans are quite aware of—and concerned about—their lack of privacy on the Internet. The study found that almost two-thirds (63.6 percent) of Internet users and more than three-quarters (76.1 percent) of nonusers either agreed or strongly agreed with the statement that "people who go online put their privacy at risk."[50]

The federal government has yet to take any decisive step toward regulating the acquisition and sale of personal information by online businesses. This is largely because most Web firms have implemented privacy policies on their Web sites that inform Internet users as to how their personal information will and will not be used and sometimes allow users to opt out of any disclosure of personal information. Additionally, new software has been developed that will crush or filter out "cookies," thus allowing Internet users to surf the Web anonymously. In view of these developments, the Federal Trade Commission has decided to allow the online industry to regulate itself, with only minimal oversight by the federal government.

Personal Privacy and National Security

Since the terrorist attacks of September 11, 2001, one of the most common debates in the news media and on Capitol Hill has been how the United States can address the urgent need to strengthen national security while still protecting civil liberties, particularly the right to privacy. As you will read throughout this book, various programs have been proposed or attempted, and some have already been dismantled after public outcry. For example, the Homeland Security Act passed in late 2002 included language explicitly prohibiting a controversial program called Operation TIPS (Terrorism Information and Prevention System). Operation TIPS was proposed to create a national reporting program for "citizen volunteers" who regularly work in neighborhoods and communities, such as postal carriers and meter readers, to report suspicious activity to the government. The public backlash against the program was quick and resolute—neighbors would not spy on neighbors.

Other programs that infringe on Americans' privacy rights were enacted in the months following the September 11 attacks, however. The Federal Bureau of Investigation (FBI) sought and received legislation permitting "roving" wiretaps, which allow the government to monitor a person under suspicion no matter what form of electronic communication he or she uses. When, how, and where such roving wiretaps are used is left entirely up to the FBI. Such taps may lead to the invasion of the privacy of hundreds of third parties who believe their telephone conversations or e-mails are private. Another type of monitoring system that has been much debated since September 11 is the use of national identification cards. We explore this issue in *The Politics of Homeland Security* feature.

Concerns over privacy rights have been so pronounced that in 2002 both the House and the Senate proposed bills that would require all federal agencies putting forward new rules or regulations to produce a "privacy impact analysis" explaining how the new rules will affect Americans' privacy. Some civil libertarians are so concerned about the erosion of privacy rights that they wonder why the public outcry has not been even more vehement.

AMERICA at odds

Should Americans Be More Concerned about the Erosion of Privacy Rights?

Even before September 11, some scholars detected a certain complacency in Americans' attitudes toward the erosion of privacy rights. Yale Law School professor Jeffrey Rosen noted that Americans seem to believe that a kind of "technological determinism" is at work today: as surveillance becomes more intrusive, people become more used to it.[51] Since September 11, 2001, Americans seem even more willing to give up some personal freedoms to feel safer. In his study of the use of closed-circuit television surveillance in Britain, Rosen questioned whether America might take a similar path. "Will America be able to resist the pressure to follow the British example and wire itself up with surveillance cameras? Before September 11, I was confident that we would. . . . After September 11, however, everything has changed."[52]

Some Americans believe that people who are most concerned about privacy rights are probably doing something they should not be doing. Someone holding this view would likely argue, "Why are they so concerned about privacy if they have nothing to hide?" The problem with this view, according to Rosen, is that uncertainty about whether our actions are observed or tracked by others causes us to lead more restricted lives. "The cameras are not consistent with the values of an open society. They are technologies of classification and exclusion. They are ways of putting people in their place, of deciding who gets in and who stays out, of limiting people's movement and restricting their opportunities."[53]

Clearly, Americans need to decide just how much privacy they should demand, and whether—and to what extent—privacy should be sacrificed to achieve other goals. As sociologist Amitai Etzioni of George Washington University acknowledges, "without privacy, no society can long remain free." Yet Etzioni and others believe that at times serv-

The POLITICS of HOMELAND SECURITY

Should We Carry National Identification Cards?

Most of you probably carry a driver's license, a Social Security card, a student identification card, credit cards, and possibly even a passport. Today, the majority of these cards contain a magnetic strip that can be scanned to access your data from the relevant database and add new information about you. With so much information about all of us readily available, why does the issue of a national identification card continue to resurface?

ID CARDS WILL CATCH MORE TERRORISTS

The most common argument in favor of a national identification system is that, using appropriate technology, it will help the government monitor the activities of potential terrorists and catch them before they act. "Smart cards" that use some type of biometric identification system, such as face scans, retinal scans, or thumbprints, will reduce the prevalence of forged ID cards. In addition, sophisticated "back-end" technology will ensure that when you board a plane, buy a gun, or cross a border, your ID card is linked to a central database that will prove you are not a threat.

Steven Brill, an author and columnist, suggests that even a voluntary system of ID cards might give us a measure of security. Those who know they have nothing to hide could obtain the card, while those who do not want a card could go without and face stricter scrutiny when boarding planes or entering or exiting the country. "Fifteen months after September 11, the idea that some people are less of a threat than others—and that they should be able to carry a credible card that verifies that— should not be kept under wraps for fear of offending those who oppose a government ID card," argues Brill.[54]

ID CARDS AND PRIVACY RIGHTS

If we had a national ID card system, your ID card could be requested at any time or any place and scanned into a master database that logs your movements, your purchases, your deposits at your bank—almost everything about you. Even if safeguards were put in place to prevent such intrusive uses of the system, those safeguards could be ignored or abandoned months or years from now, especially if the terrorist threat becomes more severe. The original Social Security Act prohibited using Social Security cards for unrelated purposes, but those strictures are routinely ignored today. Consider how often you use your Social Security number as your student ID or are asked for part or all of your number by your bank or credit-card company.

In many countries, citizens are required to carry national ID cards. Here, Pakistani voters, holding up their identity cards, stand in a line to cast their vote outside a polling station in Lahore on April 30, 2002. (AP Photo/Khalid Mehmood Chaudary)

DISCRIMINATION

In addition, a national ID card system would likely increase the harassment of minorities and foreigners. If identity checks were left to the discretion of police, banks, and merchants, then the likely targets would be people who look or sound "foreign." The American Civil Liberties Union, one of the most vocal opponents of national ID cards, argues, "The stigma and humiliation of constantly having to prove that they are Americans or legal immigrants would weigh heavily on such groups. . . . Rather than eliminating discrimination, as some have claimed, a national identity card would foster new forms of discrimination and harassment."[55]

The political wrangling over ID cards has become so bitter that the law creating the Department of Homeland Security provided that "nothing in this act shall be construed to authorize the development of a national identification system or card." Even before the passage of the bill, Tom Ridge, the head of the White House Office of Homeland Security (now the Department of Homeland Security), was told that the issue of national ID cards was so politically sensitive that he should not even use the term.[56]

Are We Safer?

Would a national ID card system be such a threat to our privacy rights that Americans are safer by avoiding a public debate over the issue? Do you think a national ID card system could prevent a terrorist attack?

ing the common good should take priority. Etzioni feels that we need a new conception of privacy, a new privacy doctrine that protects individuals from irresponsible government and snooping corporations but that also surrenders individual privacy when public health and safety are at stake.[57]

The Rights of the Accused

The United States has one of the highest violent crime rates in the industrialized world. It is therefore not surprising that many Americans have extremely strong opinions about the rights of persons accused of criminal offenses. Indeed, some Americans complain that criminal defendants have too many rights.

Why do criminal suspects have rights? The answer is that all persons are entitled to the protections afforded by the Bill of Rights. If criminal suspects were deprived of their basic constitutional liberties, all people would suffer the consequences. In fact, these liberties take on added significance in the context of criminal law. After all, in a criminal case, a state official (such as the district attorney, or D.A.) prosecutes the defendant, and the state has immense resources that it can bring to bear against the accused person. By protecting the rights of accused persons, the Constitution helps to prevent the arbitrary use of power on the part of the government.

The Rights of Criminal Defendants

The basic rights, or constitutional safeguards, provided for criminal defendants are set forth in the Bill of Rights. These safeguards include the following:

- The Fourth Amendment protection from unreasonable searches and seizures.

PROBABLE CAUSE Cause for believing that there is a substantial likelihood that a person has committed or is about to commit a crime.

- The Fourth Amendment requirement that no warrant for a search or an arrest be issued without **probable cause** (cause for believing that there is a substantial likelihood that a person has committed or is about to commit a crime).
- The Fifth Amendment requirement that no one be deprived of "life, liberty, or property, without due process of law." (As discussed earlier in this chapter, this requirement is also included in the Fourteenth Amendment, which protects persons against actions by state governments.)

DOUBLE JEOPARDY To prosecute a person twice for the same criminal offense; prohibited by the Fifth Amendment in all but a few circumstances.

- The Fifth Amendment prohibition against **double jeopardy** (being tried twice for the same criminal offense).

SELF-INCRIMINATION Providing damaging information or testimony against oneself in court.

- The Fifth Amendment provision that no person can be required to be a witness against (incriminate) himself or herself. (This is often referred to as the constitutional protection against **self-incrimination.** It is the basis for a criminal suspect's "right to remain silent" in criminal proceedings.)
- The Sixth Amendment guarantees of a speedy trial, a trial by jury, a public trial, the right to confront witnesses, and the right to counsel at various stages in some criminal proceedings. (The right to counsel was established in 1963 in *Gideon v. Wainwright.*[58] The Supreme Court held that if a person is accused of a felony and cannot afford an attorney, an attorney must be made available to the accused person at the government's expense.)
- The Eighth Amendment prohibitions against excessive bail and fines and against cruel and unusual punishments.

The Exclusionary Rule

Any evidence obtained in violation of the constitutional rights spelled out in the Fourth Amendment normally is not admissible at trial. This rule, which has been applied in the federal courts since at least 1914, is known as the **exclusionary rule.** The rule was extended to state court proceedings in 1961.[59] The reasoning behind the exclusionary rule is that it forces law enforcement personnel to gather evidence properly. If they do not, they will be unable to introduce the evidence at trial to convince the jury that the defendant is guilty.

EXCLUSIONARY RULE A criminal procedural rule requiring that any illegally obtained evidence not be admissible in court. The rule is based on Supreme Court interpretations of the Fourth and Fourteenth Amendments.

The *Miranda* Warnings

In the 1950s and 1960s, one of the questions facing the courts was not whether suspects had constitutional rights—that was not in doubt—but how and when those rights could be exercised. For example, could the right to remain silent (under the Fifth Amendment's prohibition against self-incrimination) be exercised during pretrial interrogation proceedings or only during the trial? Were confessions obtained from suspects admissible in court if the suspects

This police officer is reading the accused his *Miranda* warnings. Since the 1966 *Miranda* decision, the Supreme Court has relaxed its requirements in some situations, such as when a criminal suspect who is not under arrest enters a police station voluntarily. (Elena Rooraid/ PhotoEdit)

had not been advised of their right to remain silent and other constitutional rights? To clarify these issues, in 1966 the Supreme Court issued a landmark decision in *Miranda v. Arizona.*[60] In that case, the Court enunciated the ***Miranda*** **warnings** that are now familiar to virtually all Americans:

> Prior to any questioning, the person must be warned that he has a right to remain silent, that any statement he does make may be used against him, and that he has a right to the presence of an attorney, either retained or appointed.

MIRANDA WARNINGS A series of statements informing criminal suspects, on their arrest, of their constitutional rights, such as the right to remain silent and the right to counsel; required by the Supreme Court's 1966 decision in *Miranda v. Arizona.*

The Erosion of *Miranda*

As part of a continuing attempt to balance the rights of accused persons against the rights of society, the Supreme Court has made a number of exceptions to the *Miranda* ruling. In 1986, for example, the Court held that a confession need not be excluded even though the police failed to inform a suspect in custody that his attorney had tried to reach him by telephone.[61] In an important 1991 decision, the Court stated that a suspect's conviction will not be automatically overturned if the suspect was coerced into making a confession. If the other evidence admitted at trial was strong enough to justify the conviction without the confession, then the fact that the confession was obtained illegally can be, in effect, ignored.[62] In yet another case, in 1994, the Supreme Court ruled that a suspect must unequivocally and assertively state his right to counsel in order to stop police questioning. Saying, "Maybe I should talk to a lawyer" during an interrogation after being taken into custody is not enough. The Court held that police officers are not required to decipher the suspect's intentions in such situations.[63]

In 1999, the U.S. Court of Appeals for the Fourth Circuit stunned the nation's legal establishment by enforcing a long-forgotten provision, Section 3501, of the Omnibus Crime Control Act of 1968. Congress passed the act two years after the Supreme Court's *Miranda* decision in an attempt to reinstate a rule that had been in effect for 180 years before *Miranda*—namely, that statements by defendants can be used against them as long as they are voluntarily made. The Justice Department immediately disavowed Section 3501 as unconstitutional. The Fourth Circuit, however, could see no reason not to enforce the provision. After all, Congress has the "unquestioned power to establish the rules of procedure and evidence in federal courts," and there is no explicit constitutional requirement that defendants be told of their rights to counsel and to remain silent. In 2000, however, when the Supreme Court reviewed the case, the high court held that the *Miranda* rights were based on the Constitution. Thus, these rights could not be overruled by legislative act.[64]

why does it MATTER?

Civil Liberties and Your Everyday Life

The sad fact is that most Americans take their civil liberties so much for granted that they do not even consider how these liberties affect their everyday lives. But they do. The Bill of Rights—the first ten amendments to the Constitution—sets forth a number of basic liberties that are enjoyed by all Americans. Because our civil liberties are so important to our everyday lives, individuals and organizations are constantly fighting to make sure that federal, state, and local governments do not infringe on those liberties. Consider some obvious ones:

■ Freedom of speech—We all take for granted that we can read just about any point of view that we want to in newspapers, magazines, and even brochures. What you read every day of your life is clearly a function of our freedom of speech. Throughout history, many nations have severely curtailed this important civil liberty. Today, citizens of the United States still enjoy perhaps the freest press in the world.

■ Freedom of religion—We have enjoyed religious freedom for so long that we tend to take this liberty for granted. Although there are restrictions on how the state can or cannot be involved in religious activities, virtually any of you can practice just about any religion you wish. For many Americans, that is an important aspect of their everyday lives. In contrast, in some countries—for example, Iran and Saudi Arabia—an official state religion dominates all aspects of everyday life. In other countries—for example, Cuba and the People's Republic of China—religious activities are often curtailed by government.

Taking Action

Americans frequently get involved in protecting their civil liberties. Some have said it is part of the American character to fight the intrusion of government into our private lives. Groups such as the American Civil Liberties Union (ACLU), the Center for Democracy and Technology, and the Electronic Privacy Information Center (EPIC) monitor government regulation and pending legislation, organize letter-writing campaigns and protests, and bring law-

suits—all in defense of our civil liberties. But even individuals acting alone can make a difference. For example, Cliff Cookman, shown in the photo above, is a junior at Manhattan High School in Manhattan, Kansas, and a self-proclaimed priest of Satanism. He decided to wear his "priestly vestments" to school, believing that he had a right, under the First Amendment, to express his beliefs through his clothing. His high school principal disagreed, however, and told him that he would have to change his clothes. The ACLU is now assisting Cookman in asserting his right to wear his priestly symbols in school. (AP Photo/*The Manhattan Mercury*, Rod Mikinski)

Key Terms

bill of attainder 75	establishment clause 76	libel 85	slander 85
civil liberties 75	*ex post facto* law 75	*Miranda* warnings 95	symbolic speech 84
commercial speech 85	exclusionary rule 94	obscenity 86	treason 84
double jeopardy 94	"fighting words" 85	probable cause 94	writ of *habeas corpus* 75
due process clause 76	filtering software 87	sabotage 84	
due process of law 76	free exercise clause 76	seditious speech 84	
espionage 84	*Lemon* test 81	self-incrimination 94	

Chapter Summary

1 The Bill of Rights (the first ten amendments to the Constitution) sets forth our civil liberties. Other civil liberties are specified in the Constitution itself. Although originally the Bill of Rights limited only the power of the national government, not that of the states, today most of the liberties guaranteed by the national Constitution apply to state government actions as well.

2 The First Amendment prohibits government from passing laws "respecting an establishment of religion, or prohibiting the free exercise thereof." The first part of this statement is referred to as the establishment clause; the second part is known as the free exercise clause. Issues involving the establishment clause often focus on prayer in the schools, the teaching of evolutionary theory, and aid to parochial schools.

3 Although citizens have an absolute right to hold any religious beliefs they choose to hold, their right to engage in religious practices may be limited if those practices violate the laws or threaten the health, safety, or morals of the community. Employers must accommodate the religious needs of employees unless to do so would cause the employer to suffer an "undue hardship."

4 The First Amendment also protects freedom of speech, including symbolic (nonverbal) speech, although the Supreme Court has at times imposed limits on speech in the interests of protecting other rights of society. Some forms of speech—including libel and slander, "fighting words," and obscenity—are not protected by the First Amendment.

5 The First Amendment freedom of the press generally protects the right to publish a wide range of opinions and information. Guidelines have been developed by the courts to decide in what situations freedom of expression can be restrained.

6 The Supreme Court has held that a right to privacy is implied by other constitutional rights set forth in the Bill of Rights. The nature and scope of this right are not always clear, however. Whether this right encompasses a right to have an abortion or to commit assisted suicide, and how privacy rights can be protected while increasing national security, are issues on which Americans have still not reached consensus.

7 The Fourth, Fifth, Sixth, and Eighth Amendments protect the rights of persons accused of crimes. Any evidence obtained in violation of the constitutional rights of criminal defendants normally is not admissible in court.

RESOURCES FOR FURTHER STUDY

Selected Readings

Bollinger, Lee C., and Geoffrey R. Stone, eds. *Eternally Vigilant: Free Speech in the Modern Era.* Chicago: University of Chicago Press, 2002. This book examines the philosophical underpinnings of free speech. It also contains a history of some of the most contentious free speech disputes, drawing on the work of several legal scholars.

Etzioni, Amitai. *The Limits of Privacy.* New York: Basic Books, 1999. The author argues that although privacy is vital to ensuring freedom, some social concerns should outweigh privacy rights. For example, Etzioni argues that the government's role in protecting society from terrorists justifies such actions as issuing national ID cards to all Americans.

Gottlieb, Roger S. *Joining Hands: Politics and Religion Together for Social Change.* Bounder, Colo.: Westview Press, 2002. In this book, the author examines such movements for social change as the civil rights movement, feminism, and environmentalism to reveal how religion and progressive politics share a common vision.

Shiell, Timothy C. *Campus Hate Speech on Trial.* Lawrence, Kans.: University Press of Kansas, 1998. Shiell contends that American colleges and universities, which are ostensibly committed to free speech and the open exchange of ideas, betray this commitment when they implement hate speech codes. The author believes that the principle of free speech must be upheld, even if it means tolerating hate speech.

InfoTrac Citations

Using your InfoTrac password, access the InfoTrac database at **http://infotrac.thomsonlearning.com**. Once at the site, you can do "key word" searches to locate the following articles, each of which deals with a topic covered in this chapter. The key words to use in your search are indicated in parentheses.

- "Church, State, and the Faith-Based Initiative: A Historical Perspective" (Faith Based Initiative)

- "Is Hate Free Speech? Does the First Amendment Protect Something as Offensive as Burning a Cross? The Supreme Court Will Decide" (Hate Speech Free Speech)

- "The U.S. Supreme Court Addresses the Child Pornography Prevention Act and Child Online Protection Act in *Ashcroft v. Free Speech Coalition* and *Ashcroft v. American Civil Liberties Union*" (Child Online Pornography Act)

- "Are Police Free to Disregard *Miranda?*" (Exclusionary Rule)

Politics on the Web

Almost three dozen First Amendment groups have launched the Free Expression Clearinghouse, which is a Web site designed to feature legislation updates, legal briefings, and news on cases of censorship in local communities. Go to **http://www.FREEExpression.org**

- The leading civil liberties organization, the American Civil Liberties Union (ACLU), can be found at **http://www.aclu.org**

- A group named the Liberty Counsel calls itself "a nonprofit religious civil liberties education and legal defense organization established to preserve religious freedom." You can access this organization's home page at **http://www.lc.org**

- For information on the effect of new computer and communications technologies on the constitutional rights and liberties of Americans, go to the Center for Democracy and Technology at **http://www.cdt.org**

- For information on privacy issues relating to the Internet, go to the Electronic Privacy Information Center's Web site at **http://www.epic.org/privacy**

- To access Supreme Court decisions on civil liberties, go to the Supreme Court's official Web site at **http://supremecourtus.gov**

Web Resources on Your CD-ROM

On your CD-ROM, you will find Web resources, news articles, Internet activities, and video clips related to the topics in this chapter. Resources related to this chapter include the following:
- **Values Inventory**—Political Ideology: Banning Hate Speech on Campus.
- **Why Does It Matter?**—Discuss Civil Liberties on a Newsgroup.
- **Updates**—Keep up with the issues in this chapter!
- **Web Resources**—Internet Activities: AAUP Statement on "Freedom of Expression and Campus Speech Codes"; The Price of Free Speech: Campus Hate Speech Codes—A Pro/Con Debate.
- **Where Do You Stand?**—Dialogue: Should Hate Speech on Campus Be Banned?
- **Comparative Politics**—Civil Liberties and Civil Rights in Other Countries.
- **Videos**—Privacy Rights.
- **NewsEdge**—Visit this global resource for current events related to this chapter.

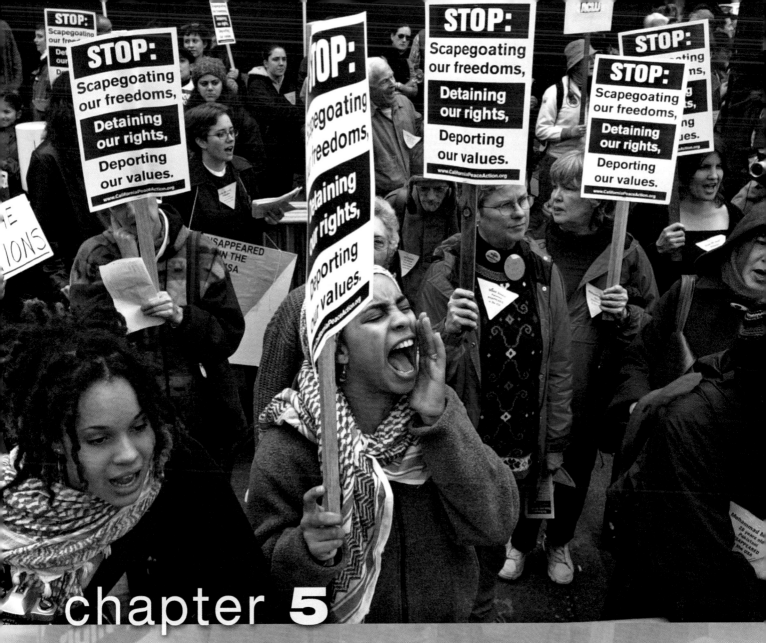

chapter 5
civil rights

CHAPTER OBJECTIVES

After reading this chapter, you should be able to . . .

▸ Define the term *civil rights* and explain the constitutional basis for laws prohibiting discrimination.

▸ Discuss the reasons for the civil rights movement and the changes it effected in American politics and government.

▸ Describe the political and economic achievements of women in this country over time and identify some obstacles to equality that they continue to face.

▸ Summarize the struggles faced by other minority groups in America.

▸ Explain what affirmative action is and why it has been so controversial in this country.

99

Should Affirmative Action Be Abolished?

The phrase "affirmative action" was first used by President Lyndon Johnson (1963–1969) in a 1965 executive order that required federal contractors to "take affirmative action" to ensure that neither applicants nor employees are treated differently because of race or national origin. Since then, the federal government—and many state and local governments as well—has embraced the notion that not only should racial discrimination be eliminated, but the effects of past discrimination should be reversed wherever possible. Today, the term *affirmative action* applies to various programs of preferences and quotas that benefit minorities and women in hiring, granting of government contracts, and awarding of college admissions. The problem is that any program that involves preferences necessarily means that some people will be aggrieved. Whites resent preferences being given to African Americans and Hispanics. Men resent being displaced by women.

After more than three decades of affirmative action programs, voters and the courts are beginning to eliminate racial preferences. California and Washington voters ended affirmative action programs by all state employers in those states. Several cases involving racial preferences in college admissions have also come before the courts. In 2003, the Supreme Court heard oral arguments in two cases involving preferences in college admissions.[1] By the time you read this book, the Court will have issued its ruling in those cases.

It's Time to Put an End to Affirmative Action

A growing number of Americans argue that we should end affirmative action because racial and gender preferences do not equate to the empowerment of minorities and women. In fact, preferences inject a dose of poison into the body politic, they argue. Minorities resent the stereotype that they were admitted to universities or offered jobs because of affirmative action, rather than because of their true abilities and qualifications. Many minority students admitted to predominantly white colleges report feeling isolated. African Americans are singled out by professors in class to represent "the black opinion," for example. Some minorities have found the atmosphere on campuses so hostile that they have left their universities. The racial divide that separates Americans is thereby increased.

Affirmative action has run its course, opponents argue. To see real improvement in our race relations, we must stop focusing on what divides us and instead focus on what unites us.

Affirmative Action Is Still Justified

Many other Americans have come to the defense of affirmative action, arguing that it is still necessary to combat the effects of past discrimination. They point out that minorities and women have made great strides in both education and the work force in the last thirty years, in large part because of the effectiveness of affirmative action programs in countering racial and gender bias. True, such bias still exists, but this is a reason to continue affirmative action—not a reason to abandon it.

Proponents argue that to abolish affirmative action would destroy everything that it has accomplished in the last several decades. As former Harvard University president Neil L. Rudenstine has written, "Diversity is the substance from which much human learning, understanding, and wisdom derive. It offers one of the most powerful ways of creating the intellectual energy and robustness that lead to greater knowledge, and to the tolerance and mutual respect so essential to the maintenance of our civic society."[2] A reversal of the policies that have helped to create more diversity in universities and workplaces could be devastating to America's race relations.

Where Do You Stand?

1. If it were up to you to decide whether to continue or abandon affirmative action, what would your decision be? Why?

2. If the government, by means of affirmative action, cannot end racial and gender bias in American institutions, who can?

Interacting with Your CD-ROM Resources

Use your CD-ROM to access resources on the Web, simulations, participation exercises, and video clips. Important resources related to this feature include:

- **Values Inventory**—Political Ideology: Affirmative Action.
- **Where Do You Stand?**—Dialogue: Should Affirmative Action Be Abolished?
- **Web Resources**—Internet Activities: Affirmative Action: Objections and an Alternative; Affirmative Action Tests: *Gratz v. Bollinger; Grutter v. Bollinger.*

INTRODUCTION

Affirmative action programs are one issue in an ongoing debate over the nature of our civil rights. As noted in Chapter 4, people sometimes confuse civil rights with civil liberties. Generally, though, the term **civil rights** refers to the rights of all Americans to equal treatment under the law, as provided for by the Fourteenth Amendment. One of the functions of our government is to ensure—through legislation or other actions—that this constitutional mandate is upheld.

Although the democratic ideal is for all people to have equal rights and equal treatment under the law, and although the Constitution guarantees those rights, this ideal has often remained just that—an ideal. It is people who put ideals into practice, and as James Madison (1751–1836) once pointed out (and as we all know), people are not angels. As you will read in this chapter, the struggle of various groups in American society to obtain equal treatment has been a long one, and it still continues today.

In a sense, the history of civil rights in the United States is a history of discrimination against various groups. Discrimination against women, African Americans, and Native Americans dates back to the early years of this nation, when the framers of the Constitution refused to grant these groups rights that were granted to others (that is, to white, property-owning males). During our subsequent history, as peoples from around the globe immigrated to this country at various times and for various reasons, each of these immigrant groups has faced discrimination in one form or another. More recently, other groups, including older Americans, persons suffering from disabilities, and gay men and lesbians, have had to struggle for equal treatment under the law.

Central to any discussion of civil rights is the interpretation of the equal protection clause of the Fourteenth Amendment to the Constitution. For that reason, we look first at that clause and how the courts, particularly the Supreme Court, have interpreted it and applied it to civil rights issues.

CIVIL RIGHTS The rights of all Americans to equal treatment under the law, as provided for by the Fourteenth Amendment to the Constitution.

The Equal Protection Clause

Equal in importance to the due process clause of the Fourteenth Amendment is the **equal protection clause** in Section 1 of that amendment, which reads as follows: "No State shall . . .

EQUAL PROTECTION CLAUSE Section 1 of the Fourteenth Amendment, which states that no state shall "deny to any person within its jurisdiction the equal protection of the laws."

Hundreds of pro–affirmative action demonstrators gather outside the U.S. Supreme Court in Washington, D.C., on April 1, 2003. The Court was hearing arguments about whether the University of Michigan's undergraduate college and law school should be allowed to use race as a factor in admissions. (AP Photo/Teru Iwasaki)

deny to any person within its jurisdiction the equal protection of the laws." Section 5 of the amendment provides a legal basis for federal civil rights legislation: "The Congress shall have power to enforce, by appropriate legislation, the provisions of this article."

The equal protection clause has been interpreted by the courts, and especially the Supreme Court, to mean that states must treat all persons in an equal manner and may not discriminate *unreasonably* against a particular group or class of individuals unless there is a sufficient reason to do so. The task of distinguishing between reasonable discrimination and unreasonable discrimination is difficult. Generally, in deciding this question, the Supreme Court balances the constitutional rights of individuals to equal protection against government interests in protecting the safety and welfare of citizens. Over time, the Court has developed various tests, or standards, for determining whether the equal protection clause has been violated.

Strict Scrutiny

FUNDAMENTAL RIGHT A basic right of all Americans, such as all First Amendment rights. Any law or action that prevents some group of persons from exercising a fundamental right will be subject to the "strict-scrutiny" standard, under which the law or action must be necessary to promote a compelling state interest and must be narrowly tailored to meet that interest.

SUSPECT CLASSIFICATION A classification based on race, for example, that provides the basis for a discriminatory law. Any law based on a suspect classification is subject to strict scrutiny by the courts—meaning that the law must be justified by a compelling state interest.

If the law or action prevents some group of persons from exercising a **fundamental right** (such as all First Amendment rights), the law or action will be subject to the "strict-scrutiny" standard. Under this standard, the law or action must be necessary to promote a *compelling state interest* and must be narrowly tailored to meet that interest. A law based on a **suspect classification,** such as race, is also subject to strict scrutiny by the courts, meaning that the law must be justified by a compelling state interest.

Intermediate Scrutiny

Because the Supreme Court had difficulty deciding how to judge cases in which men and women were treated differently, another test was developed—the "intermediate-scrutiny" standard. Under this standard, laws based on gender classifications are permissible if they are "substantially related to the achievement of an important governmental objective." For example, a law punishing males but not females for statutory rape is valid because of the important governmental interest in preventing teen-age pregnancy in those circumstances and because virtually all of the harmful and identifiable consequences of teen-age pregnancy fall on the young female.[3] A law prohibiting the sale of beer to males under twenty-one years of age and to females under eighteen years would not be valid, however.[4]

Generally, since the 1970s, the Supreme Court has scrutinized gender classifications closely, and many gender-based laws have been declared unconstitutional. In 1979, the Court held that a state law allowing wives to obtain alimony judgments against husbands but preventing husbands from receiving alimony from wives violated the equal protection clause.[5] In 1982, the Court declared that Mississippi's policy of excluding males from the School of Nursing at Mississippi University for Women was unconstitutional.[6] In a controversial 1996 case, *United States v. Virginia,*[7] the Court held that Virginia Military Institute, a state-financed institution, violated the equal protection clause by refusing to accept female applicants. The Court said that the state of Virginia had failed to provide a sufficient justification for its gender-based classification. Nonetheless, the goal of equal treatment for women, which dates back to the Constitution, has yet to be fully achieved.

The Rational Basis Test (Ordinary Scrutiny)

RATIONAL BASIS TEST A test (also known as the "ordinary-scrutiny" standard) used by the Supreme Court to decide whether a discriminatory law violates the equal protection clause of the Constitution. Few laws evaluated under this test are found invalid.

A third test used to decide whether a discriminatory law violates the equal protection clause is the **rational basis test.** When applying this test to a law that classifies or treats people or groups differently, the justices ask whether the discrimination is rational. In other words, is it a reasonable way to achieve a legitimate government objective? Few laws tested under the rational basis test—or the "ordinary-scrutiny" standard, as it is also called—are found invalid, because few laws are truly unreasonable. A municipal ordinance that prohibits certain vendors from selling their wares in a particular area of the city, for example, will be upheld if the city can meet this rational basis test. The rational basis for the ordinance might be the city's legitimate government interest in reducing traffic congestion in that particular area.

African Americans

The equal protection clause was originally intended to protect the newly freed slaves after the Civil War (1861–1865). In the early years after the war, the U.S. government made an effort to protect the rights of blacks living in the former states of the Confederacy. The Thirteenth Amendment (which granted freedom to the slaves), the Fourteenth Amendment (which guaranteed equal protection under the law), and the Fifteenth Amendment (which stated that voting rights could not be abridged on account of race) were part of that effort. By the late 1880s, however, southern legislatures began to pass a series of segregation laws—laws that separated the white community from the black community. Such laws were commonly called "Jim Crow" laws (from a song that was popular in black minstrel shows). Some of the most common Jim Crow laws involved the use of public facilities such as schools, railroads, and, later, buses. They also affected housing, restaurants, hotels, and many other facilities.

Separate but Equal

In 1892, a group of Louisiana citizens decided to challenge a state law that required railroads to provide separate railway cars for African Americans. A man named Homer Plessy, who was seven-eighths Caucasian and one-eighth African, boarded a train in New Orleans and sat in the railway car reserved for whites. When Plessy refused to move at the request of the conductor, he was arrested for breaking the law.

Four years later, in 1896, the Supreme Court provided a constitutional basis for these segregation laws. In *Plessy v. Ferguson*,[8] the Court held that the law did not violate the equal protection clause because *separate* facilities for blacks were *equal* to those for whites. The lone dissenter, Justice John Marshall Harlan, disagreed: "Our Constitution is colorblind, and neither knows nor tolerates classes among citizens." The majority opinion, however, established the **separate-but-equal doctrine,** which was used to justify segregation in many areas of American life for nearly sixty years.

In the late 1930s and 1940s, the Supreme Court gradually moved away from this doctrine. The major breakthrough, however, did not come until 1954, in a case involving an African American girl who lived in Topeka, Kansas.

The *Brown* Decisions and School Integration

In the 1950s, Topeka's schools, like those in many cities, were segregated. Mr. and Mrs. Oliver Brown wanted their daughter, Linda Carol Brown, to attend a white school a few blocks from their home instead of an all-black school that was twenty-one blocks away. With the help of lawyers from the National Association for the Advancement of Colored People (NAACP), Linda's parents sued the Board of Education to allow their daughter to attend the nearby school.

In *Brown v. Board of Education of Topeka*,[9] the Supreme Court reversed *Plessy v. Ferguson*. The Court unanimously held that segregation by race in public education was unconstitutional. Chief Justice Earl Warren wrote as follows:

> Does segregation of children in public schools solely on the basis of race, even though the physical facilities and other "tangible" factors may be equal, deprive the children of the minority group of equal educational opportunities? We believe that it does . . . . [Segregation generates in children] a feeling of inferiority as to their status in the community that may affect their hearts and minds in a way unlikely ever to be undone. . . . We conclude that in the field of public education the doctrine of "separate but equal" has no place. Separate educational facilities are inherently unequal.

The following year, in *Brown v. Board of Education*[10] (sometimes called *Brown II*), the Supreme Court ordered desegregation to begin "with all deliberate speed," an ambiguous phrase that could be (and was) interpreted in a variety of ways.

Reactions to School Integration
The Supreme Court ruling did not go unchallenged. Bureaucratic loopholes were used to delay desegregation. Another reaction was "white flight." As white parents sent their children to newly established private schools, some

Signs such as the ones shown here over the drinking fountains in the Dougherty County Courthouse, in Albany, Georgia, were commonplace in the South from the 1870s to the 1960s. The "separate-but-equal" doctrine, enunciated by the Supreme Court in 1896, justified "Jim Crow" laws that permitted racial segregation. (Library of Congress, photo by Danny Lyon, 1963)

SEPARATE-BUT-EQUAL DOCTRINE A Supreme Court doctrine holding that the equal protection clause of the Fourteenth Amendment did not forbid racial segregation as long as the facilities for blacks were equal to those provided for whites. The doctrine was overturned in the *Brown v. Board of Education of Topeka* decision of 1954.

President Bill Clinton, Arkansas governor Mike Huckabee, and Little Rock Mayor Jim Daley (top row, going from right to left) stand on the steps of Central High School in Little Rock, Arkansas, behind the "Little Rock Nine." The occasion was the fortieth anniversary of the integration of the high school. All nine of the black students who entered the all-white high school under armed escort in 1957 attended the 1997 anniversary ceremony. (AP Photo/Danny Johnston)

DE JURE SEGREGATION Racial segregation that is legally sanctioned—that is, segregation that occurs because of laws or decisions by government agencies.

DE FACTO SEGREGATION Racial segregation that occurs not as a result of deliberate intentions but because of past social and economic conditions and residential patterns.

BUSING The transportation of public school students by bus to schools physically outside their neighborhoods to eliminate school segregation based on residential patterns.

formerly white-only public schools became 100 percent black. Arkansas's Governor Orval Faubus used the state's National Guard to block the integration of Central High School in Little Rock in 1957, which led to increasing violence in the area. The federal court demanded that the troops be withdrawn. Only after President Dwight D. Eisenhower federalized the Arkansas National Guard and sent in troops to help quell the violence did Central High finally become integrated.

By 1970, school systems with **de jure segregation**—segregation that is legally sanctioned—had been abolished. That is not to say that **de facto segregation** (actual segregation, produced by circumstances even though no law requires it) was eliminated. It meant only that no public school could legally identify itself as being reserved for all whites or all blacks.

Busing   Attempts to eliminate *de facto* segregation have included redrawing school district lines and reassigning pupils. **Busing**—the transporting of students by bus to schools physically outside their neighborhoods—to achieve racially desegregated schools has also been tried. The Supreme Court first sanctioned busing in 1971 in a case involving the school system in Charlotte, North Carolina.[11] Following this decision, the Court upheld busing in several northern cities, as well as in Denver, Colorado.[12] Proponents believe that busing improves the educational and career opportunities of minority children and also enhances the ability of children from different ethnic groups to get along with each other.

Opposition to Busing   Nevertheless, busing was unpopular with many groups from its inception. Parents and children complained that they lost the convenience of neighborhood schools. Local governments and school boards resented having the courts tell them what to do. Some black parents argued that busing exposed their children to the hostility of white students in the schools to which they were bused. Some blacks also resented the implication that minority children can learn only if they sit next to white children. Opposition to busing was so pronounced in some areas that bused students had to be escorted by police to prevent potential violence.

By the mid-1970s, the courts had begun to retreat from their former support for busing. In 1974, the Supreme Court rejected the idea of busing children across school district lines.[13] In 1986, the Court refused to review a lower court decision to end a desegregation plan in Norfolk, Virginia.[14] By the 1990s, some large-scale busing programs were either being cut back or terminated. In *Missouri v. Jenkins*[15] in 1995, the Supreme Court ruled that the state of Missouri could stop spending money to attract a multiracial student body through major educational improvements, called magnet schools. Today, busing orders to end *de facto* segre-

In the left-hand photo, you see a police escort of buses carrying African American students to South Boston High in 1974. Busing was initiated in the late 1960s and early 1970s as a means to integrate public schools. A more common sight today is a public school bus transporting children of different racial and ethnic backgrounds, as in the photo on the right. (left: UPI/Corbis-Bettmann; right: Michael Newman/PhotoEdit)

gation are not upheld in court. As you will read in this chapter's *Perception versus Reality* feature on the next page, *de facto* segregation in America's schools is still widespread.

The Civil Rights Movement

In 1955, one year after the first *Brown* decision, an African American woman named Rosa Parks, a long-time activist in the NAACP, boarded a public bus in Montgomery, Alabama. When it became crowded, she refused to move to the "colored section" at the rear of the bus. She was arrested and fined for violating local segregation laws. Her refusal and arrest spurred the local African American community to organize a year-long boycott of the entire Montgomery bus system. The protest was led by a twenty-seven-year-old Baptist minister, Dr. Martin Luther

This is a photo of National Guard members blocking the entrance to Beale Street in Memphis, Tennessee, on March 29, 1968. Many of the civil rights advances made in the 1960s resulted from peaceful demonstrations such as the one shown here. (Bettmann/CORBIS)

perception
versus REALITY

Are America's Schools Integrated?

Tremendous progress has been made in integrating America's public school system since the two *Brown* decisions. African Americans have more educational opportunities today than ever before. But are America's schools fully integrated?

THE PERCEPTION

There is a perception, more prevalent among white Americans than among Americans of color, that the process of racial desegregation in America is complete. *De jure* segregation, the legal segregation of public facilities by race, no longer exists. A Brookings Institution study of the 2000 census data concludes that segregation in America's metropolitan areas is at its lowest level since 1920.[16] In addition, African Americans are experiencing high levels of academic achievement: 80 percent of African Americans hold a high school diploma, and in the past twenty years, the number of African American college graduates has doubled. With so much progress, the perception is that past efforts by Congress, the courts, and even the state legislatures have succeeded in creating an integrated society in the United States.

THE REALITY

The reality is that while the numbers sound promising, many public schools, colleges, and professions remain, for all intents and purposes, segregated. For example, the number of African American lawyers has more than tripled since 1960, but that means only that the percentage of black lawyers in America increased from 1.3 percent to 5.1 percent.[17]

De facto segregation in public schools is the norm in many parts of the country. In Cleveland, Ohio, 61 percent of public school students attend schools that are racially segregated—meaning that more than 90 percent of the students are of the same racial or ethnic background.[18]

A report by Harvard University's Civil Rights Project shows that public schools are not integrated. Rather, they are actually becoming more segregated, particularly in the South. Resegregation has been increasing since the mid-1980s. Central-city school districts also tend to be very segregated. The fifteen school districts with the lowest percentages of white students are located in an inner city, where African American and Hispanic students attend schools with only 5 percent white (non-Hispanic) students.[19]

One explanation of persistent segregation in public schools is that patterns of segregation by race are strongly linked to segregation by poverty. This turns out to be a weak explanation of the reality today. The authors of Harvard's study conclude that the desegregation efforts of the 1960s and 1970s achieved substantial results that have been reversed with the end of court-mandated, or even voluntary, desegregation plans.

What's Your Opinion?

Studies show that the advantages of attending a school with a racially diverse population are multifold. Do you think school districts should enact voluntary desegregation plans to assure integration? Do you think the government should intervene and mandate desegregation of public schools through such programs as busing?

CIVIL RIGHTS MOVEMENT The movement in the 1950s and 1960s, by minorities and concerned whites, to end racial segregation.

King, Jr. During the protest period, he was jailed and his house was bombed. Despite the hostility and the overwhelming odds, the protesters were triumphant.

In 1956, a federal court prohibited the segregation of buses in Montgomery, and the era of the **civil rights movement**—the movement by minorities and concerned whites to end racial segregation—had begun. The movement was led by a number of diverse groups and individuals, including Dr. Martin Luther King and his Southern Christian Leadership Conference (SCLC). Other groups, such as the Congress of Racial Equality (CORE), the NAACP, and the Student Nonviolent Coordinating Committee (SNCC), also sought to secure equal rights for African Americans.

CIVIL DISOBEDIENCE The deliberate and public act of refusing to obey laws thought to be unjust.

Nonviolence as a Tactic   Civil rights protesters in the 1960s began to apply the tactic of nonviolent **civil disobedience**—the deliberate and public refusal to obey laws considered unjust—in civil rights actions throughout the South. For example, in 1960, in Greensboro, North Carolina, four African American students sat at the "whites only" lunch counter at Woolworth's and ordered food. The waitress refused to serve them and the store closed early, but more students returned the next day to sit at the counter, with supporters picketing outside. **Sit-ins** spread to other lunch counters across the South. In some cases, students were heckled or even dragged from the store by angry whites. But the protesters never reacted with violence. They simply returned to their seats at the counter, day after day. Within months of the first sit-in, lunch counters began to reverse their policies of segregation.

SIT-IN A tactic of nonviolent civil disobedience. Demonstrators enter a business, college building, or other public place and remain seated until they are forcibly removed or until their demands are met. The tactic was used successfully in the civil rights movement and other protest movements in the United States.

Civil rights activists were trained in the tools of nonviolence—how to use nonthreatening body language, how to go limp when dragged or assaulted, and how to protect themselves from clubs or police dogs. As the civil rights movement gained momentum, the media images of nonviolent protesters being attacked by police, sprayed with fire hoses, and attacked by dogs shocked and angered Americans nationwide. This public backlash led to nationwide demands for reform. The March on Washington for Jobs and Freedom, led by Martin Luther King, Jr., in 1963, aimed in part to demonstrate the widespread public support for legislation to ban discrimination in all aspects of public life.

Civil Rights Legislation in the 1960s   As the civil rights movement demonstrated its strength, Congress began to pass civil rights laws. It became clear that while the Fourteenth Amendment prevented the *government* from discriminating against individuals or groups, the private sector—businesses, restaurants, and so on—could still freely refuse to employ and serve nonwhites.

A group of black students from North Carolina A&T College, who were refused service at a lunch counter reserved for white customers, staged a sit-down strike at the F. W. Woolworth store in Greensboro on February 2, 1960. (Library of Congress)

The Civil Rights Act of 1964 was the first and most comprehensive civil rights law. It forbade discrimination on the basis of race, color, religion, gender, and national origin. The major provisions of the act were as follows:

- It outlawed discrimination in public places of accommodation, such as hotels, restaurants, snack bars, movie theaters, and public transportation.
- It provided that federal funds could be withheld from any federal or state government project or facility that practiced any form of discrimination.
- It banned discrimination in employment.
- It outlawed arbitrary discrimination in voter registration.
- It authorized the federal government to sue to desegregate public schools and facilities.

Other significant laws passed by Congress during the 1960s included the Voting Rights Act of 1965, which made it illegal to interfere with anyone's right to vote in any election held in this

This photo shows Martin Luther King, Jr., shaking hands with President Lyndon B. Johnson at the White House on July 2, 1964. Johnson had just signed into law the Civil Rights Act, the most comprehensive civil rights law of our country's modern era. At the signing, Johnson asked all Americans to join in his effort "to bring justice and hope to all of our people and to bring peace to our land." (Bettmann/CORBIS)

Black Muslim leader Malcolm X speaks to an audience at a Harlem rally in 1963. His talk, in which he restated the Muslim theme of complete separation of whites and Negroes, outdrew a nearby rally sponsored by a civil rights group ten to one. (Bettmann/CORBIS)

country (see Chapter 8 for a discussion of the historical restrictions on voting that African Americans faced), and the Civil Rights Act of 1968, which prohibited discrimination in housing.

The Black Power Movement   Not all African Americans embraced nonviolence. Several outspoken leaders in the mid-1960s were outraged at the slow pace of change in the social and economic status of blacks. Malcolm X, a speaker and organizer for the Nation of Islam, rejected the goals of integration and racial equality espoused by the civil rights movement. He called instead for black separatism and black pride. Although he later moderated some of his views, his rhetorical style and powerful message influenced many African American young people. Among them was Stokely Carmichael. Carmichael had been a leader in the civil rights movement, a freedom rider, and later chairman of SNCC, but by 1966 he had become frustrated with the tactic of nonviolence. He began to exhort civil rights activists to defend themselves, to demand political and economic power, and to demonstrate racial pride.

By the late 1960s, with the assassinations of Malcolm X in 1965 and Martin Luther King, Jr., in 1968, the era of mass acts of civil disobedience in the name of civil rights came to an end. Some civil rights leaders ceased to believe that further change was possible. Some left the United States altogether. Stokely Carmichael emigrated to Guinea in West Africa. Others entered politics and worked to advance the cause of civil rights from within the system.

Political Participation

As you will read in Chapter 8, African Americans were restricted from voting for many years after the Civil War, despite the Fifteenth Amendment (1870). These discriminatory practices persisted in the twentieth century. In the early 1960s, only 22 percent of African Americans of voting age in the South were registered to vote, compared with 63 percent of voting-age whites. In Mississippi, the most extreme example, only 6 percent of voting-age African Americans were registered to vote. Such disparities led to the enactment of the Voting Rights Act of 1965, which ended discriminatory voter-registration tests and gave federal voter registrars the power to prevent racial discrimination in voting.

Today, the percentages of voting-age blacks and whites registered to vote is nearly equal, at about 65 percent.[20] As a result of this dramatic change, political participation by African Americans has increased, as has the number of African American elected officials. Today, more than 8,500 African Americans serve in elective office in the United States. At least one congressional seat in each southern state is held by an African American, as are more than 15 percent of the state legislative seats in the South.

Nonetheless, only one African American has been elected to a state governorship, and only two African Americans have been elected to the U.S. Senate since 1900. Although several African Americans have aspired to the presidency, none has come close to winning the nomination of one of the major political parties. Like school desegregation, discussed in this chapter's *Perception versus Reality* feature on page 106, the increase in political participation by African Americans is somewhat more illusory than the numbers suggest. Some argue that a great deal more progress needs to be made.

Equal Treatment for Women

In 1776, Abigail Adams, anticipating that new laws would probably be necessary after the Declaration of Independence was issued, asked her husband, John Adams, to "remember the ladies." Despite this request, women, although considered citizens in the early years of the nation, had no political rights. Of course, neither did women in other countries—but the United States was different. Americans were not bound as tightly to age-old traditions and laws that allowed only men to fully participate in the political arena. During the revolutionary era, for example, women had played a significant political role, particularly in organizing boycotts against British imports and making substitute goods.

In this context, Abigail Adams's request is not all that surprising. The failure of the framers of the Constitution to give women political rights was viewed by many early Americans as an act of betrayal. Not only did the Constitution betray the Declaration of Independence's promise of equality, but it also betrayed the women who had contributed to the making of that independence during the Revolutionary War. Nonetheless, not until the 1840s did women's rights groups begin to form.

The Struggle for Voting Rights

In 1848, Lucretia Mott and Elizabeth Cady Stanton organized the first woman's[21] rights convention in Seneca Falls, New York. The three hundred people who attended approved a Declaration of Sentiments: "We hold these truths to be self-evident: that all men *and women* are created equal." In the following years, other women's groups held conventions in various cities in the Midwest and the East. With the outbreak of the Civil War, though, women's rights advocates devoted their energies to the war effort.

Abigail Adams, left (The Granger Collection); Lucretia Mott, center (The Granger Collection); and Elizabeth Cady Stanton, right (Bettmann/CORBIS).

TABLE 5-1

Years, by Country, in Which Women Gained the Right to Vote

1893: New Zealand
1902: Australia
1913: Norway
1918: Britain
1918: Canada
1919: Germany
1920: United States
1930: South Africa
1932: Brazil
1944: France
1945: Italy
1945: Japan
1947: Argentina
1950: India
1952: Greece
1953: Mexico
1956: Egypt
1963: Kenya
1971: Switzerland
1984: Yemen

SUFFRAGE The right to vote; the franchise.

House Minority Leader Nancy Pelosi (D., Calif.) addresses the Democratic National Committee at the party's meeting in Washington, D.C., in 2003. Pelosi called on Democrats "to expose the rhetorical gap between George Bush's lofty rhetoric and the harsh reality of his policies."
(AP Photo/Charles Dharapak)

The movement for political rights again gained momentum in 1869, when Susan B. Anthony and Elizabeth Cady Stanton formed the National Woman Suffrage Association. **Suffrage**—the right to vote—became their goal. For members of the National Woman Suffrage Association, suffrage was only one step on the road toward greater social and political rights for women. Lucy Stone and other women, who had founded the American Woman Suffrage Association, thought that the right to vote should be the only goal. By 1890, the two organizations had joined forces, and the resulting National American Woman Suffrage Association had indeed only one goal—the enfranchisement of women. When little progress was made, small, radical splinter groups took to the streets. Parades, hunger strikes, arrests, and jailings soon followed.

World War I (1914–1918) marked a turning point in the battle for women's rights. The war offered many opportunities for women. Thousands of women served as volunteers, and about a million women joined the work force, holding jobs vacated by men who entered military service. After the war, President Woodrow Wilson wrote to Carrie Chapman Catt, one of the leaders of the women's movement, "It is high time that [that] part of our debt should be acknowledged." Two years later, in 1920, seventy-two years after the Seneca Falls convention, the Nineteenth Amendment to the Constitution was ratified: "The right of citizens of the United States to vote shall not be denied or abridged by the United States or by any State on account of sex." Although the United States may seem slow in having given women the vote, it was really not far behind the rest of the world (see Table 5–1).

Women in American Politics Today

More than ten thousand members have served in the U.S. House of Representatives. Only 1 percent of them have been women. Women continue to face a "men's club" atmosphere in Congress, although in 2002, for the first time in history, a woman, Nancy Pelosi (D., Calif.), was elected minority leader of the House of Representatives. In the 108th Congress, 14 percent of the 435 members of the House of Representatives and 13 percent of the 100 members of the Senate are women. Considering that eligible female voters outnumber eligible male voters, women are vastly underrepresented in the U.S. Congress.

The same can be said for the number of women receiving presidential appointments to federal offices. Franklin Roosevelt (1933–1945) appointed the first woman to a cabinet post—Frances Perkins, who was secretary of labor from 1933 to 1945. In recent administrations, several women have held cabinet posts. In addition, Ronald Reagan (1981–1989) appointed the first woman ever to sit on the Supreme Court, Sandra Day O'Connor. Bill Clinton (1993–2001) appointed Ruth Bader Ginsburg to the Supreme Court, and, in his second term, he appointed Madeleine Albright as secretary of state, the first woman to hold that position. President George W. Bush went even further: he appointed three women to cabinet positions and two women to other significant federal offices.

Women have made greater progress at the state level, and the percentage of women in state legislatures has been rising steadily. Women now constitute nearly one-fourth of state legislators. Notably, in recent elections gender seemed to be less of an issue than it had been in the past. In fact, in 1998, women won races for each of the top five offices in Arizona, the first such occurrence in U.S. history. Generally, women have been more successful politically in the western states than elsewhere. In Washington, over one-third of the state's legislative seats are now held by women. At the other end of the spectrum, though, are states such as Alabama. In that state, less than 10 percent of the lawmakers are women.

Today, various women's organizations are attempting to increase the number of women in government. These organizations include the National Coalition for Women's Appointments, the Women's Political Caucus, Black Women Organized for Action, and the Fund for a Feminist Majority. Additionally, women have formed political action committees (PACs—discussed in Chapter 6) to support female candidates for political office. One of the largest PACs is EMILY's List, which promotes and supports Democratic women candidates running for seats in Congress and state governorships. (EMILY is an acronym for the phrase "Early Money Is Like Yeast—It Makes the Dough Rise.")

Women in the Workplace

An ongoing challenge for American women is to obtain equal pay and equal opportunity in the workplace. In spite of federal legislation and programs to promote equal treatment of women in the workplace, women continue to face various forms of discrimination.

Wage Discrimination   In 1963, Congress passed the Equal Pay Act. The act requires employers to pay an equal wage for substantially equal work—males cannot be paid more than females who perform essentially the same job. The following year, Congress passed the Civil Rights Act of 1964, Title VII of which prohibits employment discrimination on the basis of race, color, national origin, gender, and religion. Women, however, continue to face wage discrimination.

It is estimated that for every dollar earned by men, women earn about 76 cents. Although the wage gap has narrowed significantly since 1963, when the Equal Pay Act was enacted (at that time women earned 58 cents for every dollar earned by men), it still remains. Moreover, since 1993 the gap has begun to widen slightly. Also, when a large number of women are in a particular occupation, the wages that are commanded in that occupation continue to be relatively low.

Additionally, even though an increasing number of women now hold business and professional jobs once held by men, relatively few of these women are able to rise to the top of the career ladder in their firms due to the lingering bias against women in the workplace. This bias has created the so-called **glass ceiling**—the often subtle obstacles to advancement that professional women encounter on the job. A recent study conducted by the U.S. Census Bureau, however, shows that the glass ceiling may be "cracking." The study found that over seven million women now hold managerial positions in the United States—nearly one-third more than did so in 1993.

GLASS CEILING The often subtle obstacles to advancement faced by professional women in the workplace.

Sexual Harassment   Title VII's prohibition of gender discrimination has also been extended to prohibit sexual harassment. **Sexual harassment** occurs when job opportunities, promotions, salary increases, or even the ability to retain one's job depends on whether an employee complies with demands for sexual favors. A special form of sexual harassment, called hostile-environment harassment, occurs when an employee is subjected to sexual conduct or comments in the workplace that interfere with the employee's job performance or that create an intimidating, hostile, or offensive environment.

SEXUAL HARASSMENT Unwanted physical contact, verbal conduct, or abuse of a sexual nature that interferes with a recipient's job performance, creates a hostile environment, or carries with it an implicit or explicit threat of adverse employment consequences.

The Supreme Court has upheld the right of persons to be free from sexual harassment on the job on a number of occasions. In 1986, the Court indicated that creating a hostile environment by sexual harassment violates Title VII, even when job status is not affected, and in 1993 the Court held that to win damages in a suit for sexual harassment a victim did not need to prove that the harassment caused psychological harm.[22] In 1998, the Court made it clear that sexual harassment includes harassment by members of the same sex.[23] In the same year, the Court held that employers are liable for the harassment of employees by supervisors in their workplaces *unless* the employers can show that (1) they exercised reasonable care in preventing such problems (by implementing antiharassment policies and procedures, for example) and (2) the employees failed to take advantage of any corrective opportunities provided by the employers.[24] Additionally, the Civil Rights Act of 1991 greatly expanded the remedies available for victims of sexual harassment. The act specifically states that victims can seek damages in addition to back pay, job reinstatement, and other remedies previously available.

On two occasions, sexual-harassment claims have had serious political repercussions. In 1991, Anita Hill claimed that Supreme Court nominee Clarence Thomas had sexually harassed her when she and Thomas were both employees of the Equal Employment Opportunity Commission. Thomas's nomination to the Supreme Court was confirmed, but the publicity given to the Senate's hearings on this harassment issue inspired a host of other sexual-harassment lawsuits around the country. In 1994, Paula Corbin Jones sued President Clinton, claiming that Clinton had sexually harassed her while he was governor of Arkansas and she was a state employee. This suit, before ultimately being dismissed for lack of evidence, led to a precedent-setting Supreme Court decision that a sitting president could be subject to a civil lawsuit—a ruling that could have serious implications at some point in the future. Additionally, testimony taken prior to the suit's dismissal pointed to the president's relationship with White House intern Monica Lewinsky. It was the testimony given in this lawsuit that ultimately led to Clinton's impeachment in 1998 (see Chapter 12).

Hispanics

Like African Americans and women, other groups in American society continue to fight for equal treatment. Hispanics, or Latinos, as they are often called, constitute the largest ethnic minority in the United States. Whereas African Americans represent about 12.1 percent of the U.S. population, Hispanics now constitute about 12.5 percent of the population (see Figure 5–1). Each year, the Hispanic population grows by nearly one million people, one-third of whom are newly arrived legal immigrants. By 2050, Hispanics are expected to constitute about one-fourth of the U.S. population.

To classify Hispanics as a single minority group is misleading. Spanish-speaking individuals do not refer to themselves as Hispanics but rather identify themselves by their country of origin. The largest Hispanic group consists of Mexican Americans, who constitute slightly over 60 percent of the Hispanic population living in the United States. About 15 percent of Hispanics are Puerto Ricans, and approximately 6 percent are Cuban Americans. Other, smaller groups include many individuals who have fled from Latin American countries for political reasons, hoping to find refuge in the United States.

Economically, Hispanic households seem to have become entrenched as this country's working poor. About 22 percent of Hispanic families now live below the poverty line, compared with 8 percent of white families. Researchers have found it difficult to pinpoint any reasons for such extensive poverty among Hispanics. Hispanic leaders, however, tend to attribute the low income levels to language problems, lack of job training, and continuing immigration. (Immigration disguises statistical progress because language problems and lack of job training are usually more notable among new immigrants than among those who have lived in the United States for several years.)

Party Identification and Electoral Significance

With respect to party identification, Hispanics tend to follow some fairly well-established patterns. Generally, Mexican Americans and Puerto Ricans tend to identify with the Democratic

FIGURE 5-1

The U.S. Population in 1990 and 2000

As this chart shows, between 1990 and 2000 the Hispanic population of the United States grew significantly. By 2000, Hispanics had surpassed African Americans as the nation's largest minority group.

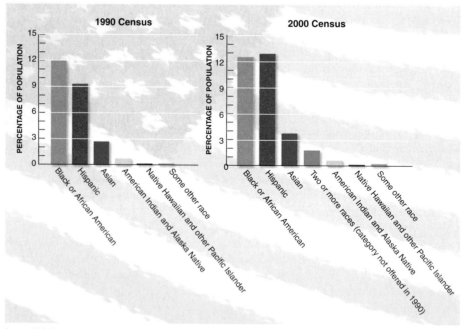

SOURCE: U.S. Census Bureau, 2001.

President Bush listens to Sara Martinez Tucker, president of the National Hispanic Scholarship Fund, prior to his speech to the group in 2001. The National Hispanic Scholarship Fund is the largest Hispanic scholarship-granting organization in the nation. (AP Photo/Ron Edmonds)

Party, which traditionally has favored more government assistance and support programs for disadvantaged groups. Cubans, in contrast, tend to identify with the Republican Party. This is largely because of a different history. Cuban émigrés fled from that country during and after the Communist revolution led by Fidel Castro. The strong anti-Communist sentiments of the Cubans propelled them toward the more conservative party—the Republicans. Today, relations with Castro-led Cuba continue to be the dominant political issue for Cuban Americans.

Given their increasing numbers, the electoral importance of Hispanics cannot be denied. Significantly, Latinos tend to be located in some of the most populous states, including California, Florida, New York, Illinois, and Texas. In the 2000 elections, these states accounted for 166 electoral college votes. Understandably, in the 2000 presidential campaigns both candidates tried to woo Hispanic voters. Among other things, both candidates spoke of liberalizing immigration laws; candidate Al Gore even supported an amnesty program for illegal immigrants. At the Republican National Convention, a speech was delivered entirely in Spanish.

Political Participation

Generally, Hispanics in the United States have a comparatively low level of political participation. Voter turnout among Hispanics is only about 27 percent, compared with about 50 percent for the population at large. Yet the Hispanic voting rate is rising as more immigrants become citizens and as more Hispanics reach voting age. Notably, when comparing citizens of equal incomes and educational backgrounds, Hispanic citizens' participation rate is higher than average. Even poor Hispanics are more likely to vote than poor whites.

Increasingly, Hispanics are holding political offices, particularly in those states with large Hispanic populations. Today, more than 5 percent of the state legislators in Arizona, California, Colorado, Florida, New Mexico, and Texas are of Hispanic ancestry. Cuban Americans have been notably successful in gaining local political power, particularly in Dade County, Florida. Hispanics have been less successful in winning congressional seats, however. Although their numbers in Congress are increasing, only about 5 percent of the members of the 108th Congress are Hispanic. President George W. Bush appointed Mel Martinez to head the Department of Housing and Urban Development, and another Hispanic, Alberto Gonzales, now serves as White House Counsel.

Asian Americans

Asian Americans have also suffered, at times severely, from discriminatory treatment. The Chinese Exclusion Act of 1882 prevented persons from China and Japan from coming to the United States to prospect for gold or to work on the railroads or in factories in the West. After 1900, immigration continued to be restricted—only limited numbers of persons from China and Japan were allowed to enter the United States. Those who were allowed into the country faced racial prejudice by Americans who had little respect for their customs and culture. In 1906, after the San Francisco earthquake, Japanese American students were segregated into special schools so that white children could use their buildings.

The Japanese bombing of Pearl Harbor in 1941, which launched the entry of the United States into World War II, intensified Americans' fear of the Japanese. Actions taken under an executive order issued by President Franklin Roosevelt in 1942 subjected many Japanese Americans to curfews, excluded them from certain "military areas," and evacuated them to internment camps (also called "relocation centers").[25] In 1988, Congress provided funds to compensate former camp inhabitants—$1.25 billion for approximately 60,000 people.

Today, Japanese Americans and Chinese Americans lead other ethnic groups in median income and median education. Indeed, Asians who have immigrated to the United States since 1965 represent the most highly skilled immigrant group in American history. Nearly 40 percent of Asian Americans over the age of twenty-five have college degrees.

More recently, immigrants from Asia, particularly from Southeast Asia, have faced discrimination. Over a million Indochinese war refugees, most of them from Vietnam, have immigrated to the United States since the 1970s. Like their predecessors, the newer immigrants quickly increased their median income. Most came with relatives and were sponsored by American families or organizations. Thus, they had good support systems to help them get started.

In what many consider to be one of America's low points, 120,000 Japanese Americans were moved to "internment camps" during World War II. Shown here is Manzanar Camp in California. The internees suffered property losses estimated at over $400 million (several billion in today's dollars). The last camp was closed in March 1946.
(Library of Congress)

Immigrants' Rights

Hispanic Americans and Asian Americans are joined every day by a steady stream of immigrants to the United States, some also from Latin America and Asia and others from the Middle East, Africa, and Europe. Approximately 1.5 million immigrants entered the United States in 2001. Thirty-three million people born outside the United States currently live here, the highest percentage of foreign-born residents since 1930. The percentage of immigrants who eventually become citizens has been on the rise in recent years. Today, naturalized citizens account for approximately 6 percent of eligible voters. This trend has focused more political attention on the rights of immigrants. Issues such as access to public services, health care, and education have dominated the debate. As you will read shortly, one issue over which Americans are at odds is whether bilingual education should be offered to the children of immigrants.

Immigrants' Rights and the War on Terrorism

The terrorist attacks of September 11, 2001, focused particular attention on U.S. immigration policy and the rights of immigrants. Several of the hijackers were here legally on student visas. In the weeks following the attacks, the federal government detained nearly 1,500 immigrants of Middle Eastern descent. Although many civil rights advocates decry the treatment of Arab Americans and immigrants, the response of the nation as a whole has been muted because the fear of future terrorist attacks is so great.

RACIAL PROFILING A form of discrimination in which law enforcement assumes that people of a certain race are more likely to commit crimes. Racial profiling has been linked to more frequent traffic stops of African Americans by police and increased security checks in airports of Arab Americans.

Racial profiling, a form of discrimination that occurs when, for example, a police officer pulls a driver over for no reason other than the driver's skin color, has received attention mainly in how it has been applied to African Americans. The practice has also been used in the prosecution of the war on terrorism. Civil rights groups claim that immigrants from the Middle East, North Africa, India, Pakistan, Indonesia, and the Philippines have been singled out by airport security workers, border guards, and immigration officials for searches and detention. Airlines have removed passengers from flights solely because they were of Middle Eastern or Asian appearance. Five civil rights lawsuits raising this issue were filed in 2002. We examine the issue of racial profiling and the war on terrorism further in this chapter's *The Politics of Homeland Security* feature.

The POLITICS of HOMELAND SECURITY

Racial Profiling in the War on Terrorism

Racial profiling by police has been a controversial practice for several years. Civil rights groups, the media, and politicians have decried it as an unconstitutional form of discrimination as it has been applied to African Americans and Hispanics. Since September 11, 2001, Arab Americans have also become victims of this practice, but with little public outcry. Airline passengers, airport security screeners, and officials of the Immigration and Naturalization Service (INS) have "profiled" people of Middle Eastern appearance as potential terrorists. At issue is whether this violates their constitutionally protected civil rights.

RACIAL PROFILING AT AIRPORTS

Not surprisingly, several cases of racial profiling of Arab Americans have taken place at airports. On September 20, 2001, four men "of Middle Eastern appearance" were removed from a Northwest Airlines flight when passengers complained that the men looked suspicious. As John Derbyshire, a columnist for the *National Review,* points out, being "of Middle Eastern appearance," or OMEA, as Derbyshire abbreviates it, "is perhaps a more dubious description even than 'black' or 'Hispanic.'"[26] Many physical characteristics can make a person OMEA. For example, on December 31, 2001, three men were removed from a Continental Airlines flight after a passenger told the captain that "those brown-skinned men are behaving suspiciously." In fact, none of the men was an Arab: one was Filipino, one Sri Lankan, and one Latino. Of the many passengers removed from airplanes since September 11, none have been charged with a crime or with terrorist connections.

RACIAL PROFILING BY THE INS

In December 2002, the INS began implementing the National Security Entry-Exit Registration System, which requires foreign visitors from Middle Eastern and certain other countries[27] to report to an INS office to register. Registrants are fingerprinted and photographed, and some are forced to answer questions under oath about their religious beliefs and political affiliation. In its first month of operation, the system led to the detention of hundreds of people, mostly on minor immigration violations. Many registrants reported mistreatment. A class-action lawsuit filed by immigrants' rights groups alleges that the INS is targeting people for arrest solely on the basis of race, religion, or national origin.

RACIAL PROFILING BY THE JUSTICE DEPARTMENT

A thornier legal issue has been making its way through the courts: how to treat U.S. citizens found to be associated with al Qaeda. Two American citizens fighting with the Taliban in Afghanistan were captured and detained, but they have been treated quite differently under the law. One, John Walker Lindh, is from a white, middle-class family from affluent Marin County, California. He converted to Islam as a teen-ager and later moved to Yemen. Lindh was charged with conspiring to kill Americans and received legal counsel. With the aid of legal

Samar Kaukab, right, and Harvey Grossman of the American Civil Liberties Union filed a suit against the Illinois National Guard and O'Hare International Airport security officers. The Muslim woman alleged that she was strip-searched at the Chicago airport before a flight simply because she was wearing a Muslim head scarf, or *hijab.* (AP Photo/Charles Bennett)

representation, he pled guilty to a lesser charge of supplying services to the Taliban and is now serving twenty years in prison. The other, Yassir Hamdi, was born in the United States to Saudi parents and moved to Saudi Arabia as a child. He has been held as an "enemy combatant" without being charged with a crime and thus has been denied access to an attorney. A third man, Jose Padilla, a U.S. citizen of Hispanic descent, was detained in Chicago for allegedly planning to build a "dirty" (radiological) bomb. He has also been held as an enemy combatant, without being charged with a crime, and is being denied access to an attorney.

Legal scholars have questioned the disparate treatment of these three men: charging Lindh, the only white suspect, and thus giving him the full protections of the American criminal justice system, but not charging Hamdi and Padilla, and thus denying them the basic constitutional rights to counsel and a hearing.

Are We Safer?

Do you think that targeting people of Middle Eastern appearance for greater scrutiny by airport officials and the INS will help prevent future terrorist attacks?

AMERICA at odds

Should Bilingual Education Be Abolished?

In the 1960s, many Americans became concerned over the language difficulties faced by immigrant children. In an effort to accommodate these children, bilingual schools were established. Because Hispanics form the largest non-English-speaking group in the United States, the majority of these schools were created to teach Spanish-speaking immigrant children. The long-term benefits of bilingual education have never been proved, however. Some argue that bilingual education has actually impeded children's progress in learning English—and thus made it difficult for them to compete in college and in the job market. Others disagree.

Proponents of bilingual education point out that the United States has a history of multilingual education. In the 1800s, children were taught in a variety of languages, including German, Dutch, and Polish. During World War I, anti-German sentiment led most states to prohibit schools from teaching in a language other than English. But in 1968, Congress passed the Bilingual Education Act, which was intended to help Hispanic children learn English. In *Lau v. Nichols*,[28] the Supreme Court ordered a California school district to provide special programs for Chinese students with limited English proficiency. English will always be the language of the nation, say bilingual education supporters. Teaching students to be proficient in more than one language will not change that fact, but it may help students in the long run.

Opponents of bilingual education argue that schools should be concerned only with their students' achievement levels and not with maintaining cultural ties or family relationships, which are among the benefits touted by bilingual education supporters. As a result of a 1998 ballot initiative banning bilingual education in California, in that state children who did not speak English were placed in "English-immersion" programs. Two years later, test results showed dramatic improvement in English-language proficiency. Even the co-founder of the California Association of Bilingual Educators, Ken Noonan, admitted that if the new law had not passed, "We would not have learned how quickly and how well kids can learn English."

Parents and students from across Colorado march and voice their opposition to Amendment 31 at a rally in Denver prior to the November 2002 elections. The amendment, which failed to pass, would have changed the state constitution to require schools to replace bilingual education with an intensive English-immersion program aimed at getting students into regular classrooms after one year. (AP Photo/*The Denver Post,* Andy Cross)

Native Americans

Today, more than two million people in the United States identify themselves as Native Americans. Most Native Americans live in Oklahoma, New Mexico, Arizona, and California; about half of them live on reservations. Of all of the groups that have suffered discriminatory treatment in the United States, Native Americans stand out because of the unique nature of their treatment.

In 1789, Congress designated the Native American tribes as foreign nations so that the government could sign land and boundary treaties with them. As members of foreign nations, Native Americans had no civil rights under U.S. laws. This situation continued until 1924, when citizenship rights were extended to all persons born in the United States.

Here, young men from a variety of tribes pose for a photograph in 1872 on their arrival at the Hampton Institute in Virginia, a boarding school for Native Americans. Later, they donned school uniforms, and another photo was taken (to be used for "before and after" comparisons). This was a typical practice at Native American boarding schools. (Library of Congress)

Early Policies toward Native Americans

The Northwest Ordinance, passed by the Congress of the Confederation in 1787, stated that "the utmost good faith shall always be observed towards the Indians; their lands and property shall never be taken from them without their consent; and in their property, rights, and liberty, they shall never be invaded or disturbed, unless in just and lawful wars authorized by Congress." Over the next hundred years, many agreements were made with the Indian tribes; many were also broken by Congress, as well as by individuals who wanted Indian lands for settlement or exploration.

In the early 1830s, the government followed a policy of separation. To prevent conflicts, boundaries were established between lands occupied by Native Americans and those occupied by white settlers. In 1830, Congress instructed the Bureau of Indian Affairs (BIA), which had been established in 1824 as part of the War Department, to remove all tribes to lands (reservations) west of the Mississippi River in order to free land east of the Mississippi for white settlement.

In the late 1880s, the U.S. government changed its policy. The goal became the "assimilation" of Native Americans into American society. Each family was given a parcel of land within the reservation to farm. The remaining acreage was sold to whites, thus reducing the number of acres in reservation status from 140 million to about 47 million acres. Tribes that would not cooperate with this plan lost their reservations altogether. To further the goal of cultural assimilation, agents from the BIA, which runs the Indian reservation system with the tribes, set up Native American boarding schools for the children to remove them from their parents' influence. In these schools, Native American children were taught to speak English, to practice Christianity, and to dress like white Americans.

Native Americans Today

Native Americans have always found it difficult to obtain political power. In part, this is because they have no official representation. Additionally, the tribes are small and scattered, making organized political movements difficult. Today, Native Americans remain a fragmented political group because large numbers of their population live off the reservations. Nonetheless, by the 1960s, some Native Americans succeeded in forming organizations to strike back at the U.S. government and to reclaim their heritage, including their lands.

The first militant organization was called the National Indian Youth Council. In the late 1960s, a small group of persons identifying themselves as Indians occupied Alcatraz Island, claiming that the island was part of their ancestral lands. Other militant actions followed. For example, in 1973, supporters of the American Indian Movement took over Wounded Knee, South Dakota, where about 150 Sioux Indians had been killed by the U.S. Army in 1890.[29] The occupation was undertaken to protest the government's policy toward Native Americans and to call attention to the injustices they had suffered.

A dealer named Michaela works behind a blackjack table at Casino Hollywood on New Mexico's Pueblo San Felipe. Today, many Native American tribes run lucrative gambling operations. Some critics of such institutions argue that these operations are wrongfully transforming the traditional Native American way of life. (Miguel Gandert/CORBIS)

Compensation for Past Injustices

As more Americans became aware of the concerns of Native Americans, Congress started to compensate them for past injustices. In 1990, Congress passed the Native American Languages Act, which declared that Native American languages are unique and serve an important role in maintaining Indian culture and continuity. Under the act, the government and the Indian community share responsibility for the survival of native languages and native cultures. Courts, too, have shown a greater willingness to recognize Native American treaty rights. For example, in 1985, the Supreme Court ruled that three tribes of Oneida Indians could claim damages for the use of tribal land that had been unlawfully transferred in 1795.[30]

The Indian Gaming Regulatory Act of 1988 allows Native Americans to have gambling operations on their reservations. Although the profits from casino gambling operations have helped to improve the economic and social status of many Native Americans, some Native Americans feel that the casino industry has irreparably hurt traditional culture. Poverty and unemployment remain widespread on the reservations.

Securing Rights for Other Groups

In addition to those groups already discussed, other groups in American society have faced discriminatory treatment. Older Americans have been victims of discrimination. So have persons with disabilities and gay men and lesbians.

Protecting Older Americans

Today, about 35 million Americans (13 percent of the population) are aged sixty-five or over. By the year 2040, it is estimated that this figure will more than double. Clearly, as the American population grows older, the problems of aging and retirement will become increasingly important national issues. Because many older people rely on income from Social Security, the funding of Social Security benefits continues to be a major issue on the national political agenda.

Many older people who would like to work find it difficult because of age discrimination. Some companies have unwritten policies against hiring, retaining, or promoting people they feel are "too old," making it impossible for some older workers to find work or to continue with their careers. At times, older workers have fallen victim to cost-cutting efforts by employers. To reduce operational expenses, companies may replace older, higher-salaried employees with younger workers who are willing to work for less pay. As part of an effort to protect the rights of older Americans, Congress passed the Age Discrimination in Employment Act (ADEA) in 1967. This act prohibits employers, employment agencies, and labor organizations from discriminating against individuals over the age of forty on the basis of age.

As noted in Chapter 3, in 2000 the Supreme Court limited the applicability of the ADEA somewhat when it held that lawsuits under this act could not be brought against a state government employer.[31] Essentially, this means that this act does not protect state employees against age-based discrimination by their state employers. (Note, though, that most states also have laws prohibiting age-based discrimination, and state employees can sue in state courts under those laws.)

Obtaining Rights for Persons with Disabilities

Like age discrimination, discrimination based on disability crosses the boundaries of race, ethnicity, gender, and religion. Persons with disabilities, especially physical deformities or severe mental impairments, have to face social bias against them simply because they are "different." Although attitudes toward persons with disabilities have changed considerably in the last several decades, persons with disabilities continue to suffer from discrimination in all its forms.

Persons with disabilities first became a political force in this country in the 1970s, and in 1973, Congress passed the first legislation protecting this group of persons—the Rehabilitation Act. This act prohibited discrimination against persons with disabilities in programs receiving federal aid. In 1975, Congress passed the Education for All Handicapped Children Act, which guarantees that all children with disabilities will receive an "appropriate" education. Further legislation in 1978 led to regulations for ramps, elevators, and the like in all federal buildings. The Americans with Disabilities Act (ADA) of 1990, however, is by far the most significant legislation protecting the rights of this group of Americans.

Americans with disabilities demonstrate in Washington, D.C., in support of the Americans with Disabilities Act (ADA), which was signed into law by President George H. W. Bush in 1990. The ADA requires that all public buildings and public services be accessible to persons with disabilities. The act also prohibits discrimination against a "qualified individual with a disability" with regard to job application and hiring procedures, training, compensation, fringe benefits, advancement, and other terms or conditions of employment. The ADA requires that employers "reasonably accommodate" the needs of employees or job applicants with disabilities. (Terry Ashe/Getty News Images)

The ADA requires that all public buildings and public services be accessible to persons with disabilities. The act also mandates that employers "reasonably accommodate" the needs of workers or job applicants with disabilities who are otherwise qualified for particular jobs unless to do so would cause the employer to suffer an "undue hardship." The ADA defines persons with disabilities as persons who have physical or mental impairments that "substantially limit" their everyday activities. Health conditions that have been considered disabilities under federal law include blindness, alcoholism, heart disease, cancer, muscular dystrophy, cerebral palsy, paraplegia, diabetes, and acquired immune deficiency syndrome (AIDS). The ADA, however, does not require employers to hire or retain workers who, because of their disabilities, pose a "direct threat to the health or safety" of their co-workers.

The Supreme Court recently reviewed a case raising the question of whether suits under the ADA could be brought against state employers. The Court concluded, as it did with respect to the ADEA, that states are immune from lawsuits brought to enforce rights under this federal law.[32]

Gay Men and Lesbians

Until the late 1960s and early 1970s, gay men and lesbians tended to keep quiet about their sexual preferences because to expose them usually meant facing harsh consequences. This attitude began to change after a 1969 incident in New York City, however. When the police raided the Stonewall Inn—a bar popular with gay men and lesbians—on June 27 of that year, the bar's patrons responded by throwing beer cans and bottles at the police. The riot continued for two days. The Stonewall Inn incident launched the gay power movement. By the end of the year, gay men and lesbians had formed fifty organizations, including the Gay Activist Alliance and the Gay Liberation Front.

A Changing Legal Landscape
The number of gay and lesbian organizations has grown from fifty in 1969 to several thousand today. These groups have exerted significant political pressure on legislatures, the media, schools, and churches. Since the 1970s, twenty-five states plus the District of Columbia have repealed their sodomy laws—laws that prohibited homosexual conduct. Such laws have been invalidated by the courts in seven other states. The Civil Service Commission eliminated its ban on the employment of gay men and lesbians, and in 1980, the Democratic Party platform included a gay rights plank.

Today, eleven states and over 160 cities and counties in the United States have laws prohibiting discrimination against homosexuals in housing, education, banking, employment, and public accommodations. In a landmark case in 1996, *Romer v. Evans*,[33] the Supreme Court held that a Colorado amendment that would have invalidated all state and local laws protecting homosexuals from discrimination violated the equal protection clause of the Constitution. The Court stated that the amendment would have denied to homosexuals in Colorado—but to no other Colorado residents—"the right to seek specific protection from the law."

Changing Attitudes
Laws and court decisions protecting the rights of gay men and lesbians reflect social attitudes that are much changed from the days of the Stonewall incident. Liberal political leaders have been supporting gay rights for at least two decades. In 1984, presidential candidate Walter Mondale openly sought the gay vote, as did Jesse Jackson in his 1988 presidential campaign. President Bill Clinton strongly supported gay rights.

Even conservative politicians have softened their stance on the issue. For example, in 2000 during his presidential campaign, George W. Bush met with representatives of gay groups to discuss issues important to them. Although Bush stated that he was opposed to the idea of gay marriage, he promised that he would not disqualify anyone from serving in his administration on the basis of sexual orientation. To the surprise of many, during his confirmation hearings before the Senate, attorney general designee John Ashcroft, long an opponent of gay rights, stated that he would "enforce the law equally without regard to sexual orientation. It will not be a consideration of hiring at the Department of Justice."

AMERICA at odds

Should Gay and Lesbian Couples Be Allowed to Marry?

Perhaps the most controversial issue with respect to gay rights is whether gay and lesbian couples should have the right to marry legally. The controversy over this issue was fueled in 1993 when the Hawaii Supreme Court ruled that Hawaii's law banning same-sex marriages violated the state constitution's equal protection clause. Although Hawaiians voted in 1998 to amend their constitution to allow such a ban, the 1993 ruling aroused considerable reaction across the country. Thirty-five states subsequently passed laws that prohibit same-sex marriages, and in 1996 Congress passed the Defense of Marriage Act, which allows states to refuse to recognize same-sex marriages. The controversy was reignited in 1999, however, by a Vermont Supreme Court ruling similar to Hawaii's. To the surprise of many, the Vermont legislature reacted by allowing same-sex couples to form "civil unions."

Gay and lesbian rights groups hailed the Vermont law as a major step toward a long-sought goal—the right of same-sex couples to enjoy the full legal rights of marriage. The next step should be to allow legal marriage and to rid the legal system of a "separate-but-equal" standard in regard to homosexual couples. Furthermore, supporters argue, laws permitting same-sex marriages foster family values and stable relationships among gay and lesbian couples.

Much of the opposition to gay marriage comes from conservative Christian groups that claim that the Bible regards homosexual conduct as sinful. Leaders of the Christian Right argue that to allow homosexuals to marry would pervert the purpose of marriage, which is procreation. It would also further erode traditional American family values. The issue continues to be a divisive one, particularly as gay couples form civil unions in Vermont but choose to live outside the state.

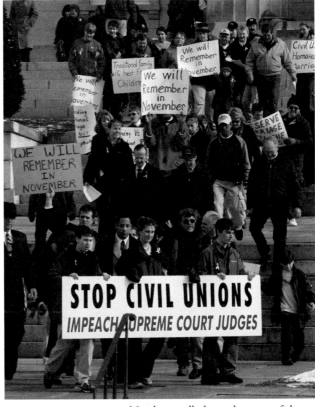

Marchers walk down the steps of the state house in Montpelier, Vermont, during a protest against same-sex marriage on April 6, 2000. (AP Photo/Toby Talbot)

Beyond Equal Protection— Affirmative Action

One provision of the Civil Rights Act of 1964 called for prohibiting discrimination in employment. As you read in the opening *America at Odds* feature, the federal government began to legislate programs of **equal employment opportunity** soon thereafter. Such programs require that employers' hiring and promotion practices guarantee the same opportunities to all individuals. Experience soon showed that minorities often had fewer opportunities to obtain education and relevant work experience than did whites. Because of this, they were still excluded from many jobs. Even though discriminatory practices were made illegal, the change in the law did not make up for the results of years of discrimination. Consequently, a new strategy was developed.

Initiated by President Lyndon B. Johnson, the new strategy came to be called **affirmative action,** a policy that requires employers to take positive steps to remedy *past* discrimination. Affirmative action programs involve giving preference, in jobs and college admissions, to members of groups that have been discriminated against in the past. All public and private employers who receive federal funds, until recently, have been required to adopt and implement these programs. Thus, the policy of affirmative action has been applied to all agencies of the federal, state, and local governments and to all private employers who sell goods to or

EQUAL EMPLOYMENT OPPORTUNITY A goal of the 1964 Civil Rights Act to end employment discrimination based on race, color, religion, gender, or national origin and to promote equal job opportunities for all individuals.

AFFIRMATIVE ACTION A policy calling for the establishment of programs that give preference, in jobs and college admissions, to members of groups that have been discriminated against in the past.

perform services for any agency of the federal government. In short, it has covered nearly all of the nation's major employers and many of its smaller ones.

Affirmative Action Tested

The Supreme Court first addressed the issue of affirmative action in 1978 in *Regents of the University of California v. Bakke.*[34] Allan Bakke, a white male, had been denied admission to the University of California's medical school at Davis. The school had set aside sixteen of the one hundred seats in each year's entering class for applicants who wished to be considered as members of designated minority groups. Many of the students admitted through this special program had lower test scores than Bakke. Bakke sued the university, claiming that he was a victim of **reverse discrimination**—discrimination against whites. Bakke argued that the use of a **quota system,** in which a specific number of seats was reserved for minority applicants only, violated the equal protection clause.

The Supreme Court was strongly divided on the issue. Some justices believed that Bakke had been denied equal protection and should be admitted. A majority on the Court, however, concluded that both the Constitution and the Civil Rights Act of 1964 allow race to be used as a factor in making admissions decisions, although race could not be the *sole* factor. Because the university's quota system was based solely on race, it was unconstitutional.

Affirmative Action under Attack

Although the *Bakke* case and later court decisions alleviated the harshness of the quota system, today's courts seem to be going even further in questioning the constitutional validity of affirmative action. Affirmative action has also been attacked at the ballot box.

REVERSE DISCRIMINATION The assertion that affirmative action programs that require preferential treatment for minorities discriminate against those who have no minority status.

QUOTA SYSTEM A policy under which a specific number of jobs, promotions, or other types of selections, such as university admissions, must be given to members of selected groups.

© The Cartoon Bank. Used with permission.

B. Smaller

"Larry is a white male, but he hasn't been able to do much with it."

The Courts Retrench   In 1995, the Supreme Court issued a landmark decision in *Adarand Constructors, Inc. v. Peña*.[35] The Court held that any federal, state, or local affirmative action program that uses racial classifications as the basis for making decisions is subject to "strict scrutiny" by the courts. As discussed earlier in this chapter, this means that, to be constitutional, a discriminatory law or action must be narrowly tailored to meet a *compelling* government interest. In effect, the *Adarand* decision narrowed the application of affirmative action programs. An affirmative action program can no longer make use of quotas or preferences for less qualified persons and cannot be maintained simply to remedy past discrimination by society in general. It must be narrowly tailored to remedy actual discrimination that has occurred, and once the program has succeeded, it must be changed or dropped.

Since the *Adarand* decision, a question before several lower courts has been whether affirmative action programs designed to achieve diversity on college campuses are constitutional. For example, in a 1996 case, *Hopwood v. State of Texas*,[36] two white law school applicants sued the University of Texas School of Law in Austin, claiming that they had been denied admission because of the school's affirmative action program. The program allowed admissions officials to take racial and other factors into consideration when determining which students would be admitted. A federal appellate court held that the program violated the equal protection clause because it discriminated in favor of minority applicants. In its decision, the court directly challenged the *Bakke* decision by stating that the use of race even as a means of achieving diversity on college campuses "undercuts the Fourteenth Amendment." In other words, race could never be a factor, even though it was not the sole factor, in such decisions.

More recent decisions by the federal courts show that the courts are divided on the issue, however.[37] As mentioned in this chapter's opening *America at Odds* feature, the issue is now before the Supreme Court, which will render its decision in 2003 concerning the admissions policy of the University of Michigan.

State Initiatives   On November 5, 1996, the citizens of California voted on a civil rights initiative to amend their state constitution. That initiative, which appeared on the ballot as Proposition 209, read in part as follows:

> The state shall not discriminate against, or grant preferential treatment to, any individual or group on the basis of race, sex, color, ethnicity, or national origin in the operation of public employment, public education, or public contracting.

Of the nearly 9 million Californians casting ballots, over 4.7 million (54 percent) voted in favor of the initiative.

The ink was barely dry on the new constitutional amendment when several groups and individuals filed a lawsuit in a federal court to prevent the amendment from being enforced. These groups claimed that the law was unconstitutional because, among other things, it denied to racial minorities and women the equal protection of the laws guaranteed by the Fourteenth Amendment. The federal judge granted the groups' request for a temporary restraining order, which meant that the law could not be enforced until further proceedings. On appeal, however, the federal appellate court reversed the lower court's decision.[38] The case was appealed to the United States Supreme Court, but the Court declined to review the case.

In 1997, the leader of the movement to pass Proposition 209, Ward Connerly, launched the American Civil Rights Institute. Its purpose is to lobby for federal legislation to ban affirmative action and to help garner support for measures similar to Proposition 209 that are on other states' ballots. Soon after the organization was started, a dozen states asked for help in putting anti–affirmative action propositions on their ballots. In 1998, voters in one of these states, Washington, approved a ballot measure ending all state-sponsored affirmative action in that state.

Civil Rights and Your Everyday Life

In the twenty-first century, we tend to take for granted the civil rights of virtually all Americans, including women, African Americans, Hispanics, and all other minorities. Yet these rights, relatively speaking, are of fairly recent vintage. We all know, of course, that compared to hundreds of years ago, when only white males had full civil rights, the rights that citizens enjoy today are extensive. But consider what America was like a little over fifty years ago, in 1950.

- In 1950, the prevailing view was that "a woman's place is in the home." Women in the workplace faced far more discrimination than they do today, and there was no such thing as a lawsuit for gender discrimination or sexual harassment.
- At that time, segregation in public schools and in colleges and universities was pervasive—and legal. Today, segregation in public schools cannot be required by law.
- There were no laws requiring that special accommodations be made for persons with disabilities. Today, several laws and policies protect this group of Americans.
- Older Americans who were fired from their jobs and replaced with younger workers had little recourse under the law. Today, both federal and state laws prohibit age discrimination in employment.
- Gay males and lesbians had no political voice; there were no special laws protecting their rights, and many laws outlawed certain forms of homosexual behavior. Today, these groups have much more protection against discrimination.
- There were no equal employment opportunity guarantees for minorities and women. Today, equal employment opportunity for all is required by law.
- At that time, few civil and political rights were guaranteed for minority groups. Today, equal rights for minority groups are mandated by federal laws and by many state laws.

Your Educational Everyday Life

Because of changing laws and changing court interpretations of the laws, you most likely are going to school in a much different environment than students experienced fifty years ago. Indeed, it is probably hard for you to imagine a college classroom in which all students are of the same race or ethnic background. Yet if our laws and their application had not changed, it is likely you would be surrounded on a daily basis by only those of your same race. You would not be exposed to the cultural backgrounds of mem-

bers of other minority groups. Now, this is not to say that all of you are attending institutions whose student bodies are fully diversified. But certainly, the majority of American college and university students find themselves surrounded by more ethnic diversity than their counterparts did fifty years ago.

Taking Action

Despite the progress that has been made toward attaining equal treatment for all groups of Americans, much remains to be done. Discriminatory practices have not vanished from the nation, to be sure. Countless activist groups continue to pursue the goal of equality for all Americans. Individuals also can take action in various ways to make their voices heard. For example, James Justin Wilson, shown in the photo below, made his views on affirmative action known to all who came near the steps of the Student Union on the University of Michigan campus. Wilson was reacting to a federal appellate court's decision, which had upheld the university's use of preferences in admissions. The issue is now before the United States Supreme Court. (AP Photo/Danny Moloshok)

Key Terms

affirmative action 121

busing 104

civil disobedience 106

civil rights 101

civil rights movement 106

de facto segregation 104

de jure segregation 104

equal employment
   opportunity 121

equal protection clause 101

fundamental right 102

glass ceiling 111

quota system 122

racial profiling 114

rational basis test 102

reverse discrimination 122

separate-but-equal
   doctrine 103

sexual harassment 111

sit-in 106

suffrage 110

suspect classification 102

Chapter Summary

1 Civil liberties limit the government by stating what the government cannot do. Civil rights, in contrast, are constitutional provisions and laws specifying what the government must do. Generally, civil rights refer to the right to equal treatment under the laws, as guaranteed by the Fourteenth Amendment to the Constitution.

2 The Fourteenth Amendment was added in 1868 to protect the newly freed slaves from discriminatory treatment. Soon, however, southern states began to pass laws that required racial segregation ("Jim Crow" laws). In 1896, the Supreme Court held that "separate-but-equal" treatment of the races did not violate the equal protection clause. The separate-but-equal doctrine justified segregation for the next sixty years.

3 In the landmark case of *Brown v. Board of Education of Topeka,* the Supreme Court held that segregation in the schools violated the equal protection clause. Forced integration of the schools was begun, and court-ordered busing of schoolchildren from white to black schools and vice versa was undertaken in an attempt to integrate the schools. By the 1980s and 1990s, the courts were allowing cities and states to discontinue busing efforts.

4 The civil rights movement was a movement by minorities and concerned whites to end racial segregation. In response, Congress passed a series of civil rights laws, including the Civil Rights Act of 1964, the Voting Rights Act of 1965, and the Civil Rights Act of 1968.

5 The struggle of women for equal treatment initially focused on gaining the franchise—voting rights. In 1920, the Nineteenth Amendment, which granted voting rights to women, was ratified. Today, women remain vastly underrepresented in Congress and political offices, even though eligible female voters outnumber male voters. In the workplace, women continue to face discrimination in the form of sexual harassment and wage discrimination.

6 Hispanics, or Latinos, constitute the second-largest minority group in the United States, and their numbers are climbing. The largest Hispanic groups are Mexican Americans, Puerto Ricans, and Cuban Americans. Relative to other groups, a disproportionate number of Hispanics live below the poverty line. Politically, Hispanics have been gaining power in some states, and their electoral significance is increasing.

7 Asian Americans have suffered from racial bias and discrimination since they first began to immigrate to this country in the late 1800s. The worst treatment of Japanese Americans occurred during World War II, when they were placed in "internment camps." Economically, Asian Americans have the highest median income and median education of any ethnic group in the United States.

8 The United States absorbs more than 1.5 million new immigrants every year. New immigrants lack citizenship and voting rights, but they are still guaranteed equal protection under the laws. Since September 11, 2001, the civil rights of immigrants have been particularly threatened, as they face arbitrary and sometimes discriminatory changes in immigration laws and the fear and hostility of some Americans worried about future terrorist attacks.

9 U.S. policy toward Native Americans was first one of separation—removing them to lands separate from those occupied by whites—and then one of "assimilation." By the late 1980s and 1990s, federal policy had changed, and legislation was passed that allowed gambling on reservation lands and encouraged the survival of Native American languages.

10 Other groups have also suffered discrimination and unequal treatment in America. The Age Discrimination in Employment Act of 1967 was passed in an attempt to protect Americans over the age of forty from age discrimination in employment. The Americans with Disabilities Act of 1990 provided significant protection for persons with disabilities. Since 1969, gay rights groups have become a significant political force, and social attitudes toward these groups are changing. Many states and cities now have laws specifically protecting the rights of gay men and lesbians. Whether same-sex couples should be allowed to marry is an issue that has divided society.

11 Affirmative action programs, because they involve unequal treatment of different groups of Americans, have always been controversial. Today, California and Washington have laws outlawing affirmative action programs in their states, and some lower courts have held that such programs are unconstitutional. In 2003, the Supreme Court once again addressed the issue of affirmative action in college admissions.

RESOURCES FOR FURTHER STUDY

Selected Readings

Brown, Dee. *Bury My Heart at Wounded Knee.* New York: Holt, Rinehart & Winston, 1971. This is an important examination of the treatment of Native Americans as the frontier pushed westward.

Freedman, Estelle B. *No Turning Back: The History of Feminism and the Future of Women.* New York: Ballantine Books, 2002. This book summarizes the history of the women's movement using an interdisciplinary approach—examining the historical, economic, and cultural implications of feminism. The author employs a narrative style that makes this book highly readable.

Guerrero, Andrea. *Silence at Boalt Hall: The Dismantling of Affirmative Action.* Berkeley: University of California Press, 2002. The author was a student admitted to the University of California at Berkeley's prestigious law school, Boalt Hall, under affirmative action. In this book, she gives an insider's view into the controversy surrounding the end of affirmative action policies there.

Irons, Peter H. *Jim Crow's Children: The Broken Promises of the Brown Decision.* New York: Viking Press, 2002. This book looks at the process of desegregation since the Supreme Court's *Brown* decision. The author presents numerous examples of how the Court, state governments, and other institutions have delayed or evaded the ruling and continue to allow segregated schools.

Woodward, C. Vann. *The Strange Career of Jim Crow.* New York: Oxford University Press, 1957. This is the classic study of segregation in the southern United States.

InfoTrac Citations

Using your InfoTrac password, access the InfoTrac database at **http://infotrac.thomsonlearning.com**. Once at the site, you can do "key word" searches to locate the following articles, each of which deals with a topic covered in this chapter. The key words to use in your search are indicated in parentheses.

- "Awaiting Judgment Day: *Lawrence v. Texas* Could Take Out Sodomy Laws for Good—Or It Could Set a Precedent for Increased Infringement of Gays Rights" (Lawrence v. Texas)

- "Peer Sexual Harassment Outlawed" (Davis v. Monroe)

- "English Lesson in California: In the Face of a Ballot Challenge, Support for Bilingual Education is Wavering" (Latinos Bilingual Education)

- "Are Asians Black? The Asian American Civil Rights Agenda and the Contemporary Significance of the Black/White Paradigm" (Asian American Rights)

Politics on the Web

Stanford University's Web site contains primary documents written by Martin Luther King, Jr., as well as secondary documents written about King. The URL for the "Martin Luther King Directory" is **http://www.stanford.edu/group/King**

- If you are interested in learning more about the Equal Employment Opportunity Commission (EEOC), the laws it enforces, how to file a charge with the EEOC, and general information about this agency, go to **http://www.eeoc.gov**

- The home page for the National Association for the Advancement of Colored People (NAACP), which contains extensive information about African American civil rights issues, is **http://www.naacp.org**

- For information on Hispanics in the United States, Latino Link is a good source. You can find it at **http://www.latinolink.org**

- The most visible and successful advocacy group for older Americans is the AARP (formerly known as the American Association of Retired Persons). Its home page contains helpful links and much information. Go to **http://www.aarp.org**

- The home page of the National Organization for Women (NOW) has links to numerous resources containing information on the rights and status of women both in the United States and around the world. You can find NOW's home page at **http://www.now.org**

- You can access the Web site of the Women's Web World, which focuses on equality for women, at **http://www.feminist.org**

- For information on the Americans with Disabilities Act (ADA) and its enforcement, go to the Justice Department's "ADA Home Page" at
http://www.usdoj.gov/crt/ada/adahom1.htm

- The Lesbian and Gay Alliance against Defamation has an online News Bureau. To find this organization's home page, go to
http://www.glaad.org

Web Resources on Your CD-ROM

On your CD-ROM, you will find Web resources, news articles, Internet activities, and video clips related to the topics in this chapter. Resources related to this chapter include the following:
- **Values Inventory**—Political Ideology: Affirmative Action.
- **Why Does It Matter?**—Read about Five Civil Rights Bills and Write to Your Representatives in Congress about Them.
- **Updates**—Keep up with the issues in this chapter!
- **Web Resources**—Internet Activities: Affirmative Action: Objections and an Alternative; Affirmative Action Tests: *Gratz v. Bollinger; Grutter v. Bollinger.*
- **Where Do You Stand?**—Dialogue: Should Affirmative Action Be Abolished?
- **Comparative Politics**—Women's Rights around the World.
- **Videos**—The *Hopwood* case: Affirmative Action on Campus.
- **NewsEdge**—Visit this global resource for current events related to this chapter.

chapter 6
interest groups

CHAPTER OBJECTIVES

After reading this chapter, you should be able to . . .

▷ Explain what an interest group is and how interest groups form.

▷ Indicate how interest groups function in American politics and how they differ from political parties.

▷ Identify various types of interest groups.

▷ Discuss how the activities of interest groups help to shape government policymaking.

▷ Describe how interest groups are regulated by government.

Gun Control: Do We Need an Armed Citizenry?

One of the most successful interest groups in American history has been the National Rifle Association (NRA). Partly because of the Second Amendment to the U.S. Constitution, which guarantees the right to bear arms, and partly because of the effectiveness of NRA lobbying, the United States has the laxest gun control laws in the developed world.

To some extent, the general public is at odds with the very effective lobbying results of the NRA. The cry for more gun control legislation intensified after the killings at Columbine High School in Littleton, Colorado, in 1999, which followed a number of other high school shootings around the country. A series of sniper shootings in the Washington, D.C., area in 2002 also renewed the demand for gun-control measures. Recent polls show that about 80 percent of Americans want gun control laws tightened.

Yes, We Need More Control on Guns

Let there be no doubt about it, contend those in favor of more gun control, the United States has the most heavily armed population in the world. The result, they say, is the highest murder rate in the developed world.

The Constitution's Second Amendment, which guarantees the right to bear arms, was never meant to allow private citizens to keep firearms in their homes but only to allow citizens to bear firearms in the event that they were called to be part of a state-sponsored militia.[1]

The massive amount of firepower in the hands of criminals in the United States is a direct result of our lax gun control laws. Under what circumstances, ask those in favor of more gun control, would any American need a semiautomatic weapon for protection? Under what circumstances would individuals use automatic or semiautomatic weapons in sports shooting? A gun in the home is many times more likely to kill a family member than to stop a criminal. Furthermore, armed citizens are not a deterrent to crime.

The gun control lobby has had some striking successes in its fight against the opponents of gun control, such as the NRA. For example, in 1993 the gun control lobby was an effective force in convincing Congress to pass the Brady Handgun Violence Prevention Act (although the Supreme Court declared key provisions of the act unconstitutional in 1997[2]). In 1994, Congress also passed a ban on nineteen types of semiautomatic weapons.

We Have a Constitutional Right to Bear Arms

The NRA is the most outspoken interest group in the United States with respect to fighting gun control laws. The NRA claims a membership of over four million target shooters, hunters, gun collectors, gunsmiths, police, and others interested in firearms. The NRA includes the following statement in its "Ten Myths about Gun Control": "The Second Amendment contains no qualifiers, no 'buts,' or 'excepts.' It affirms people's right to possess firearms."[3]

The Second Amendment is one of the most powerful arguments that opponents of gun control can muster. The right to bear arms is not only a constitutional right in the United States, but it was also a traditional right in England.[4]

Indeed, a U.S. court has held that the Second Amendment allows individuals, and not states, to have the right to possess weapons. In 1999, a U.S. district court judge in Texas stated that "[t]he right to bear arms is a protected individual right and not just a right belonging to a militia."[5]

Those who are against further gun control also argue that the registration and licensing of guns will have no effect on crime. After all, criminals, by definition, do not obey laws. Furthermore, convicted felons are prohibited by law from possessing firearms, so they would not register anyway.

In any event, more than 99 percent of all privately owned handguns in the United States are not used for criminal purposes. At least half of the handgun owners in the United States keep guns for protection and security. Indeed, events such as the September 11 terrorist attacks and the sniper shootings in the Washington, D.C., area have led to increased gun purchases and applications for concealed-weapons permits. During the sniper attacks in the Washington, D.C., area, officials reported a 500 percent increase in applications for concealed-weapons permits.[6]

Where Do You Stand?

1. Do you think that gun control laws should be stricter in the United States? Why or why not?

2. "If guns are outlawed, only criminals will have guns." Do you accept this reasoning? Explain.

Interacting with Your CD-ROM Resources

Use your CD-ROM to access a values inventory, participation exercises, resources on the Web, and video clips. Important resources related to this feature include:

- **Values Inventory**—Political Ideology: Gun Control.
- **Where Do You Stand?**—Dialogue: Do We Need an Armed Citizenry?
- **Web Resources**—Internet Activities: Original Intent and Purpose of the Second Amendment; Milestones in Federal Gun Control Legislation.

INTRODUCTION

The groups supporting and opposing gun control provide but one example of how Americans form groups to pursue or protect their interests. All of us have interests that we would like to have represented in government: farmers want higher prices for their products, young people want good educational opportunities, environmentalists want clean air and water, and the homeless want programs that provide food and shelter.

The old adage that there is strength in numbers is certainly true in American politics. The right to organize groups is even protected by the Constitution, which guarantees people the right "peaceably to assemble, and to petition the Government for redress of grievances." The Supreme Court has defended this important right over the years.

Special interests significantly influence American government and politics. Some Americans think that this influence is too great and jeopardizes representative democracy. Others maintain that interest groups are a natural consequence of democracy. After all, throughout our nation's history, people have organized into groups to protect special interests. Because of the important role played by interest groups in the American system of government, in this chapter we focus solely on such groups. We look at what they are, why they are formed, and how they influence policymaking.

Interest Groups and American Government

An **interest group** is an organization of people sharing common objectives who actively attempt to influence government policymakers through direct and indirect methods. Whatever their goals—more or fewer social services, higher or lower prices—interest groups pursue these goals on every level and in every branch of government.

On any given day in Washington, D.C., you can see national interest groups in action. If you eat breakfast in the Senate dining room, you might see congressional committee staffers reviewing testimony with representatives from women's groups. Later that morning, you might visit the Supreme Court and watch a civil rights lawyer arguing on behalf of a client in a discrimination suit. Lunch in a popular Washington restaurant might find you listening in on a conversation between an agricultural lobbyist and a congressional representative.

That afternoon you might visit an executive department, such as the Department of Labor, and watch bureaucrats working out rules and regulations with representatives from a labor interest group. Then you might stroll past the headquarters of the NRA, the AARP (formerly the American Association of Retired Persons), or the National Wildlife Federation.

INTEREST GROUP An organized group of individuals sharing common objectives who actively attempt to influence policymakers in all three branches of the government and at all levels.

Charlton Heston, then president of the National Rifle Association, addresses gun owners during a "get-out-the-vote" rally in New Hampshire a few weeks before the 2002 elections. (AP Photo/Jim Cole)

Alexis de Tocqueville (1805–1859) was a well-known French political historian. His best-known work is *Democracy in America,* which was published in 1835. In that book, he stated, "If men are to remain civilized or to become civilized, the art of association must develop and improve among them at the same speed as equality of conditions spreads." (Vol. 2, Part II, Chapter 5) (The Granger Collection)

PATRON An individual or organization that provides financial backing to an interest group.

FREE RIDER PROBLEM The difficulty faced by interest groups that lobby for a public good. Individuals can enjoy the outcome of the group's efforts without having to contribute, such as by becoming members of the group.

TABLE 6-1
Percentage of Americans Belonging to Various Groups

Health organizations	16%
Social clubs	17
Neighborhood groups	18
Hobby, garden, and computer clubs	19
PTA and school groups	21
Professional and trade associations	27
Health, sport, and country clubs	30
Religious groups	61

SOURCE: AARP.

How Interest Groups Form

Interest groups form in response to change: a political or economic change, a dramatic shift in population or technology that affects how people live or work, or a change in social values or cultural norms. Some groups form to support the change or even speed it along, while others form to fight change. For example, during the economic boom of the 1990s, interest groups formed to support easing immigration restrictions on highly skilled workers who were in great demand in technology industries. After the terrorist attacks of September 11, 2001, however, other groups formed to support more restrictions on immigration.

As you will read shortly, there are many different types of interest groups—some represent the interests of a particular industry, while others lobby on behalf of employees. Some interest groups promote policies to protect the environment, and others seek to protect consumers. These types of groups may be interested in a broad array of issues. A consumer group may want to protect consumers from dangerous products as well as high prices. Other groups form in response to a single issue, such as a proposed treaty or a potential highway project. These groups are sometimes more successful than multi-issue groups.

Financing   To have much success in gaining members and influencing policy, an interest group must have **patrons**—people or organizations willing to finance the group. Although groups usually collect fees or donations from their members, few can survive without large grants or donations. The level of financing required to form and expand an interest group successfully depends on the issues involved and the amount of lobbying the group needs to do. A group that pays professional lobbyists to meet with lawmakers in Washington, D.C., will require more funding than a group that operates with leaflets printed out from a Web site and distributed by volunteers.

As you can see in Figure 6–1 on page 135, the budgets of different interest groups can vary widely. The AARP's budget surpasses $500 million, while the League of Women Voters operates with only $3 million. Some interest groups can become very powerful very quickly if they have wealthy patrons. Other groups can raise money in a hurry if a particular event galvanizes public attention on an issue. For example, the impending war against Iraq brought thousands of dollars into peace groups in 2002 and 2003.

Incentives to Join a Group   The French political observer and traveler Alexis de Tocqueville wrote in 1835 that Americans have a tendency to form "associations" and have perfected "the art of pursuing in common the object of their common desires." "In no other country of the world," said Tocqueville, "has the principle of association been more successfully used or applied to a greater multitude of objectives than in America."[7] Of course, Tocqueville could not foresee the thousands of associations that now exist in this country. Surveys show that over 85 percent of Americans belong to at least one group. Table 6–1 shows the percentage of Americans who belong to various types of groups today.

This penchant for joining groups is just part of the story, however. Americans have other incentives for joining interest groups. Some people enjoy the camaraderie and sense of belonging that comes from associating with other people who share their interests and goals. Some groups offer their members material incentives for joining: discounts on products, subscriptions, or group insurance programs, for example. But sometimes these incentives are not enough to persuade people to join.

The Free Rider Problem   Many people recognize that a public good is not excludable—they cannot be excluded from enjoying the good just because they didn't pay for it. If an interest group is successful in lobbying for laws that will improve air quality, for example, everyone who breathes that air will benefit, whether they paid for the lobbying effort or not. This is called the **free rider problem.** In some instances, the free rider problem can be overcome. For example, social pressure may persuade some people to join or donate to a group for fear of being ostracized. The government can also step in to ensure that the burden of lobbying for the public good is shared by all. When the government classifies interest groups as nonprofit organizations, it confers on them tax-exempt status. The groups' operating costs are reduced because they do not have to pay taxes, and the impact of the government's lost revenue is absorbed by all taxpayers.

How Interest Groups Function in American Politics

Despite the bad press that interest groups tend to get in the United States, they do serve several purposes in American politics:

- ■ Interest groups help bridge the gap between citizens and government and enable citizens to explain their views on policies to public officials.
- ■ Interest groups help raise public awareness and inspire action on various issues.
- ■ Interest groups often provide public officials with specialized and detailed information that might be difficult to obtain otherwise. This information may be useful in making policy choices.
- ■ Interest groups serve as another check on public officials to make sure that they are carrying out their duties responsibly.

Access to Government   In a sense, the American system of government invites the participation of interest groups by offering many points of access for groups wishing to influence policy. Consider the possibilities at just the federal level. An interest group can lobby members of Congress to act in the interests of the group. If the Senate passes a bill opposed by the group, the group's lobbying efforts can shift to the House of Representatives. If the House passes the bill, the group can try to influence the new law's application by lobbying the executive agency that is responsible for implementing the law. The group might even challenge the law in court, directly (by filing a lawsuit) or indirectly (by filing a brief as an *amicus curiae*,[8] or "friend of the court").

Pluralist Theory   The **pluralist theory** of American democracy focuses on the participation of groups in a decentralized structure of government that offers many points of access to policymakers. According to the pluralist theory, politics is a contest among various interest groups. These groups vie with each other—at all levels of government—to gain benefits for their members. Pluralists maintain that the influence of interest groups on government is not undemocratic because individual interests are indirectly represented in the policymaking process through these groups. Although not every American belongs to an interest group, inevitably some group will represent each individual's interests. Each interest is satisfied to some extent through the compromises made in settling conflicts among competing interest groups.[9]

Pluralists also contend that because of the extensive number of interest groups vying for political benefits, no one group can dominate the political process. Additionally, because most people have more than one interest, conflicts among groups do not divide the nation into hostile camps. Not all scholars agree that this is how interest groups function, however.

PLURALIST THEORY A theory that views politics as a contest among various interest groups—at all levels of government—to gain benefits for their members.

AMERICA at odds

Can We Control the "Mischiefs of Factions"?

Interest groups were a cause of concern even before the Constitution was ratified. Recall from Chapter 2 that those opposed to the Constitution (the Anti-Federalists) claimed that a republican form of government could not work in a country this size because so many factions—interest groups—would be contending for power. The result would be anarchy and chaos.

James Madison attempted to allay these fears in *Federalist Paper* No. 10 (presented in Appendix F) by arguing that the "mischiefs of factions" could be controlled. Madison pointed out that factions would be inevitable in a democratic form of government. After all, different groups in society have different interests, and all citizens have the right to express their views and petition the government for redress. Yet precisely because of the large size of the United States, there would be so many diverse interests and factions that no one faction would be able to gain control of the government. Small factions could simply be outvoted, thus eliminating the possibility that they could impose the will of a minority on the majority. Large factions would be neutralized by other large factions, which would emerge in a large republic.

What Madison did not foresee is that small, intensely focused interest groups can indeed affect policymaking in the United States. The most powerful groups—those with the most resources and political influence—are primarily business, trade, or professional groups. Some of the most successful groups are those that focus on very specific issues—such as tobacco farming, funding of abortions, or handgun control. If very small groups of Americans can have such a profound influence on public policy, do we have a democracy at all?

How Do Interest Groups Differ from Political Parties?

Although interest groups and political parties are both groups of people joined together for political purposes, they differ in several important ways. As you will read in Chapter 7, a political party is a group of individuals outside government who organize to win elections, operate the government, and determine policy. Interest groups, in contrast, do not seek to win elections or operate the government. Clearly, though, they do seek to influence policy. Interest groups also differ from political parties in other ways including the following:

- Interest groups are often policy *specialists*, whereas political parties are policy *generalists*. Political parties are broad-based organizations that must attract the support of many opposing groups and consider a large number of issues. Interest groups, in contrast, have only a handful of key policies to push. An environmental group will not be as concerned about the economic status of Hispanics as it is about polluters. A manufacturing group is more involved with pushing for fewer regulations than it is with inner-city poverty.
- Interest groups are usually more tightly organized than political parties. They are often financed through contributions or dues-paying memberships. Organizers of interest groups communicate with members and potential members through conferences, mailings, newsletters, and electronic formats, such as e-mail.
- A political party's main sphere of influence is the electoral system; parties run candidates for political office. Interest groups try to influence the outcome of elections, but unlike parties, they do not compete for public office. Although a candidate for office may be sympathetic to—or even be a member of—a certain group, he or she does not run for election as a candidate of that group.

Different Types of Interest Groups

American democracy embraces almost every conceivable type of interest group, and the number is increasing rapidly. No one has ever compiled a *Who's Who* of interest groups, but you can get an idea of the number and variety by looking through the annually published *Encyclopedia of Associations*. Look at Figure 6–1 to see profiles of some selected important interest groups.

Some interest groups have large memberships. The AARP, for example, has about 35 million members. Others, such as the Tulip Growers Association, have as few as fourteen members. Some, such as the NRA, are household names and have been in existence for many years, while others crop up overnight. Some are highly structured and run by professional, full-time staffs, while others are loosely structured and informal.

The most common interest groups are private-interest groups, which seek public policies that benefit the economic interests of their members and work against policies that threaten those interests. Other groups, sometimes called **public-interest groups,** are formed with the broader goal of working for the "public good"; the American Civil Liberties Union and Common Cause are examples.

Business Interest Groups

Business has long been well organized for effective action. Hundreds of business groups are now operating in Washington, D.C., in the fifty state capitals, and at the local level across the country. Two umbrella organizations that include small and large corporations and businesses

PUBLIC-INTEREST GROUP An interest group formed for the purpose of working for the "public good"; examples of public-interest groups are the American Civil Liberties Union and Common Cause.

The Elizabeth Senior Dancers from North Nashville, Tennessee, perform at the War Memorial auditorium in Nashville on March 20, 2002, as part of the AARP's festivities. Hundreds of members of the AARP flooded Tennessee's capital on that date, urging lawmakers to support tax reform and improve nursing-home care. (AP Photo/*The Tennessean,* Eric Parsons)

are the U.S. Chamber of Commerce and the National Association of Manufacturers (NAM). In addition to representing about 200,000 individual businesses, the Chamber has nearly 3,000 local, state, and regional affiliates. It has become a major voice for the nation's thousands of small businesses. The NAM chiefly represents big business and has about 14,000 members.

The hundreds of **trade organizations** are far less visible than the Chamber of Commerce and the NAM, but they are also important in seeking policy goals for their members. Trade organizations usually support policies that benefit specific industries. For example, people in the oil industry work for policies that favor the development of oil as an energy resource.

TRADE ORGANIZATION An association formed by members of a particular industry, such as the oil industry or the trucking industry, to develop common standards and goals for the industry. Trade organizations, as interest groups, lobby government for legislation or regulations that specifically benefit their groups.

FIGURE 6-1
Profiles of Selected Interest Groups

AARP

Name: The AARP
Founded: 1958
Membership: 35,000,000 working or retired persons 50 years of age or older.
Description: The AARP strives to better the lives of older people, especially in the areas of health care, worker equity, and minority affairs. The AARP sponsors community crime prevention programs, research on the problems associated with aging, and a mail-order pharmacy.
Budget: $544,000,000
Address: 601 E St. N.W., Washington, DC 20049
Phone: (202) 434–3741
Web site: http://www.AARP.org

LWV

Name: League of Women Voters of the United States (LWVUS)
Founded: 1920
Membership: 130,000 members and supporters.
Description: The LWVUS promotes active and informed political participation. It distributes candidate information, encourages voter registration and voting, and takes action on issues of public policy. The group's national interests include international relations, natural resources, and social policy.
Budget: $3,000,000
Address: 1730 M St. N.W., Washington, DC 20036
Phone: (202) 429–1965
Web site: http://www.lwv.org

Name: National Education Association (NEA)
Founded: 1857
Membership: 2,600,000 elementary and secondary school teachers, college and university professors, academic administrators, and others concerned with education.
Description: The NEA's committees investigate and take action in the areas of benefits, civil rights, educational support, personnel, higher education, human relations, legislation, minority affairs, and women's concerns.
Budget: $267,000,000
Address: 1201 16th St. N.W., Washington, DC 20036
Phone: (202) 833–4000
Web site: http://www.nea.org

Name: National Rifle Association (NRA)
Founded: 1871
Membership: 4,300,000 persons interested in firearms.
Description: The NRA promotes rifle, pistol, and shotgun shooting, as well as hunting, gun collecting, and home firearm safety. It educates police firearm instructors and sponsors teams to participate in international competitions.
Budget: $156,500,000
Address: 11250 Waples Mill Road, Fairfax, VA 22030
Phone: 1–800–NRA–3888
Web site: http://www.nra.org

Name: The Sierra Club (SC)
Founded: 1892
Membership: 700,000 persons concerned with the interrelationship between nature and humankind.
Description: The Sierra Club endeavors to protect and conserve natural resources, save endangered areas, and resolve problems associated with wilderness, clean air, energy conservation, and land use. Its committees are concerned with agriculture, economics, environmental education, hazardous materials, the international environment, Native American sites, political education, and water resources.
Budget: $52,000,000
Address: 85 2d St., 2d Floor, San Francisco, CA 94105
Phone: (415) 977–5500 **Web site:** http://www.sierraclub.org

Membership in a labor union allows employees to bargain collectively with their employer to obtain higher salaries, improved working conditions, and so on. Here, airline pilots exercise a union's ultimate right—the right to strike when labor-management negotiations fail to result in a satisfactory outcome. (AP Photo/Al Behrman)

LABOR FORCE All of the people over the age of sixteen who are working or actively looking for jobs.

Other business groups have worked for policies that favor the development of coal, solar power, and nuclear power. Trucking companies would work for policies that would result in more highways being built. Railroad companies would, of course, not want more highways built because that would hurt their business.

Traditionally, business interest groups have been viewed as staunch supporters of the Republican Party. This is because Republicans are more likely to promote a "hands-off" government policy toward business. Over the last decade, however, donations from corporations to the Democratic National Committee more than doubled. Why would business groups make contributions to the Democratic National Committee? Fred McChesney, a professor of law and business at Emory University's School of Law, offers an interesting answer to this question. He argues that campaign contributions are often made not for political favors but rather to avoid political disfavor. Just as government officials can take away wealth from citizens (in the form of taxes, for example), politicians can extort from private parties payments *not* to expropriate private wealth.[10]

Labor Interest Groups

Interest groups representing labor have been some of the most influential groups in our country's history. They date back to at least 1886, when the American Federation of Labor (AFL) was formed. The largest and most powerful labor interest group today is the AFL–CIO (the American Federation of Labor–Congress of Industrial Organizations), an organization that includes nearly ninety unions representing more than 13 million workers. Several million additional workers are members of other unions (not affiliated with the AFL–CIO), such as the United Electrical Workers.

Like labor unions everywhere, American labor unions press for policies to ensure improved working conditions and better pay for their members. On some issues, however, unions may take opposing sides. For example, separate unions of bricklayers and carpenters may try to change building codes to benefit their own members even though the changes may hurt other unions. Unions may also compete for new members. In many states, the National Education Association and the AFL–CIO's American Federation of Teachers compete fiercely for members. Also, organized labor represents less than 13 percent of the **labor force**, or all of the people over the age of sixteen who are working or actively looking for a job.

Although unions were highly influential in the late 1800s and the early 1900s, their strength and political power have waned in the last several decades, as you can see in Figure 6–2. Nonetheless, they are still a powerful lobbying force and continue to work in support of their members' interests.

FIGURE 6–2

Union Membership, 1952 to Present

This figure shows the percentage of the work force represented by unions since 1952. As you can see, union membership has declined significantly over the past several decades.

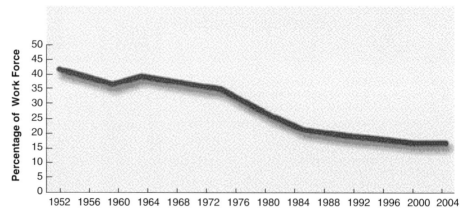

Agricultural Interest Groups

Many groups work for general agricultural interests at all levels of government. Three broad-based agricultural groups represent millions of American farmers, from peanut farmers to dairy producers to tobacco growers. They are the American Farm Bureau Federation, the National Grange, and the National Farmers' Union. The Farm Bureau, with over 4.9 million members, is the largest and generally the most effective of the three. Founded in 1919, the Farm Bureau achieved one of its greatest early successes when it helped to obtain government guarantees of "fair" prices during the Great Depression of the 1930s.[11] The Grange, founded in 1867, is the oldest group. It has a membership of about 300,000 rural families. The National Farmers' Union comprises approximately 12,250 smaller farmers.

A number of national interest groups protect the interests of farmers. Through their lobbying efforts and campaign contributions, these groups have wielded significant influence on congressional policymaking with respect to agricultural subsidies and other forms of assistance. (PhotoDisc)

Like special interest labor groups, producers of various specific farm commodities, such as dairy products, soybeans, grain, fruit, corn, cotton, beef, sugar beets, and so on, have formed their own organizations. These specialized groups, such as the Associated Milk Producers, Inc., also have a strong influence on farm legislation. Like business and labor groups, farm organizations sometimes find themselves in competition. In some western states, for example, barley farmers, cattle ranchers, and orchard owners may compete to influence laws governing water rights. Different groups also often disagree over the extent to which the government should regulate farmers.

Consumer Interest Groups

Groups organized for the protection of consumer rights were very active in the 1960s and 1970s. Some are still active today. The best known and perhaps the most effective are the public-interest consumer groups organized under the leadership of consumer activist Ralph Nader. Another well-known consumer group is Consumers Union, a nonprofit organization started in 1936. In addition to publishing *Consumer Reports,* Consumers Union has been influential in pushing for the removal of phosphates from detergents, lead from gasoline, and pesticides from food. Consumers Union strongly criticizes government agencies when they act against consumer interests.

In each city, consumer groups have been organized to deal with such problems as poor housing, discrimination against minorities and women, discrimination in the granting of credit, and business inaction on consumer complaints.

Senior Americans can access the AARP's Web site to learn how various policy proposals will affect them.

Senior Citizen Interest Groups

While the population of the nation as a whole has tripled since 1900, the number of elderly has increased eightfold. Persons over the age of sixty-five now account for 13 percent of the population, and many of these people have united to call attention to their special needs and concerns. Interest groups formed to promote the interests of the elderly have been very outspoken and persuasive. As pointed out before, the AARP has about 35 million members. It has become a potent political force.

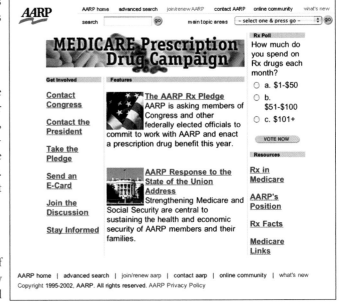

Environmental Interest Groups

With the current concern for the environment, the membership of established environmental groups has blossomed, and many new groups have formed. They are becoming some of the most powerful interest groups in Washington, D.C. The National Wildlife Federation has about 4.5 million members. Table 6–2 lists some of the major environmental groups and the number of members in each group.

Environmental groups have organized to support pollution controls, wilderness protection, and clean-air legislation. They have opposed strip-mining, nuclear power plants, logging activities, chemical waste dumps, and many other potential environmental hazards.

Professional Interest Groups

Most professions that require advanced education or specialized training have organizations to protect and promote their interests. These groups are concerned mainly with the standards of their professions, but they also work to influence government policy. Some also function as labor unions. Four major professional groups are the American Medical Association, representing physicians; the American Bar Association, representing lawyers; and the National Education Association and the American Federation of Teachers, both representing teachers. In addition, there are dozens of less well known and less politically active professional groups, such as the Screen Actors Guild, the National Association of Social Workers, and the American Political Science Association.

How Interest Groups Shape Policy

Interest groups operate at all levels of government and use a variety of strategies to steer policies in ways beneficial to their interests. They sometimes attempt to directly influence the policymakers themselves, while at other times they try to indirectly influence policymakers by shaping public opinion. The extent and nature of the groups' activities depend on their goals and their resources.

Direct Techniques

DIRECT TECHNIQUE Any method used by an interest group to interact with government officials directly to further the group's goals.

LOBBYING All of the attempts by organizations or by individuals to influence the passage, defeat, or contents of legislation or to influence the administrative decisions of government.

LOBBYIST An individual who handles a particular interest group's lobbying efforts.

Lobbying and providing election support are two important **direct techniques** used by interest groups to influence government policy.

Lobbying   Today, **lobbying** refers to all of the attempts by organizations or individuals to influence the passage, defeat, or contents of legislation or to influence the administrative decisions of government. (The term *lobbying* arose because, traditionally, individuals and groups interested in influencing government policy would gather in the foyer, or lobby, of the legislature to corner legislators and express their concerns.) A **lobbyist** is an individual who han-

TABLE 6–2
Selected Environmental Interest Groups

NAME OF GROUP	YEAR FOUNDED	NUMBER OF U.S. MEMBERS
Environmental Defense Fund	1967	300,000
Greenpeace USA	1971	250,000
Izaak Walton League of America	1922	50,000
League of Conservation Voters	1970	35,000
National Audubon Society	1905	600,000
National Wildlife Federation	1936	4,500,000
The Nature Conservancy	1951	1,000,000
The Sierra Club	1892	700,000
The Wilderness Society	1935	200,000
The World Wildlife Fund	1948	1,000,000

SOURCES: Foundation for Public Affairs, 1996; plus authors' update.

dles a particular interest group's lobbying efforts. Most of the larger interest groups have lobbyists in Washington, D.C. These lobbyists often include former members of Congress or former employees of executive bureaucracies who are experienced in the methods of political influence and who "know people." Many lobbyists also work at state and local levels. In fact, lobbying at the state level has increased in recent years as states have begun to play a more significant role in policymaking. Table 6–3 summarizes some of the basic methods by which lobbyists directly influence legislators and government officials.

The Effectiveness of Lobbying Lobbying is one of the most widely used and effective ways to influence legislative activity. For example, Mothers Against Drunk Driving has had many lobbying successes at both the state and federal levels. The NRA has successfully blocked most proposed gun control laws, even though a majority of Americans are in favor of such laws. An NRA brochure describes its lobbying operation as "the strongest, most formidable grassroots lobby in the nation." As mentioned in the chapter-opening feature, the NRA has occasionally been defeated in its lobbying efforts by interest groups that support gun control. (For a comparison of the U.S. and British approaches to gun control, see the *Comparative Politics* feature on the following page.)

Lobbyists often line up in the "lobbies," or halls, of Congress while awaiting their turns to consult with members of Congress. The term *lobby* comes from the medieval Latin *lobia,* which referred to a monastic cloister. The word began to be used in U.S. politics in the 1830s, when agents gathered in the lobbies of both Congress and state legislatures to press their causes. (Paul Conklin/ PhotoEdit)

TABLE 6–3
Direct Lobbying Techniques

TECHNIQUE	DESCRIPTION
Making Personal Contacts with Key Legislators	A lobbyist's personal contacts with key legislators or other government officials—in their offices, in the halls of Congress, or on social occasions, such as dinners, boating expeditions, and the like—are one of the most effective direct lobbying techniques. The lobbyist provides the legislators with information on a particular issue in an attempt to convince them to support the interest group's goals.
Providing Expertise and Research Results for Legislators	Lobbyists often have knowledge and expertise that are useful in drafting legislation, and this expertise can be a major strength for an interest group. Because many harried members of Congress cannot possibly be experts on everything they vote on and therefore eagerly seek information to help them make up their minds, some lobbying groups conduct research and present their findings to those legislators.
Offering "Expert" Testimony before Congressional Committees	Lobbyists often provide "expert" testimony before congressional committees for or against proposed legislation. A bill to regulate firearms, for example, might concern several interest groups. The NRA would probably oppose the bill, and representatives from the interest group might be asked to testify. Groups that would probably support the bill, such as law enforcement personnel or wildlife conservationists, might also be asked to testify. Each side would offer as much evidence as possible to support its position.
Providing Legal Advice or Assistance to Legislators and Bureaucrats	Many lobbyists assist legislators or bureaucrats in drafting legislation or prospective regulations. Lobbyists are a source of ideas and sometimes offer legal advice on specific details.
Following Up on Legislation	Because executive agencies responsible for carrying out legislation can often increase or decrease the power of the new law, lobbyists may also try to influence the bureaucrats who implement the policy. For example, beginning in the early 1960s, regulations outlawing gender discrimination were broadly outlined by Congress. Both women's rights groups favoring the regulations and interest groups opposing the regulations lobbied for years to influence how those regulations were carried out.

Gun Control in Britain and the United States—A Tale of Two Lobbies

In March 1995, a former Boy Scout leader named Thomas Hamilton acquired four high-powered rifles and took them to a primary school in a peaceful Scottish village named Dunblane. There he methodically slaughtered sixteen small children and their teacher. Gun violence was no longer something the British could dismiss as a uniquely American problem.

Less than a year and a half later, the government in London responded by banning virtually all handguns except .22 caliber and smaller guns, which later were also banned. Under these laws, which are said to be among the toughest gun control laws in the world, British residents face the prospect of up to ten years in prison if they fail to give up their weapons.

TWO DIFFERENT GUN CULTURES

The United States has experienced many "slaughters" similar to the one in Dunblane, Scotland, and yet our gun control laws do not come close to those of Britain. As Table 6–4 shows, the United States and Britain also differ considerably in both the number of guns owned and the number of murders committed with guns.

TABLE 6-4
Ownership of Firearms and Number of Murders in the United States versus Britain

	UNITED STATES	BRITAIN
Total firearms	222,000,000	409,000
Firearms per capita	0.853	0.006
Total firearm murders per year	14,000	80
Firearm murders per year per 100,000 people	5.25	0.116

SOURCES: Bureau of Justice Statistics (United States); Home Office (Britain).

A DIFFERENT MENTALITY OR JUST DIFFERENT LOBBYING?

The British have had a long history of stringent gun control laws. In the past, anyone seeking a gun in Britain had to obtain a certificate from the police and demonstrate a need for the weapon. Whereas 50 percent of private citizens in the United States have guns in their homes, fewer than 5 percent of British citizens do.

Prior to the ban on guns in Britain, an opinion poll showed that British citizens favored such a ban by 81 percent to 15 percent.[12] Similarly, in the United States a majority of citizens would like stricter gun control laws; yet such laws have not been passed in this country. Why not?

The answer to this question, at least in part, is the effective lobbying efforts of the NRA, which strongly opposes any gun control legislation. One of the NRA's most effective techniques continues to be grassroots lobbying: encouraging members to get involved in the legislative process through letter writing, e-mail, and phone calls to legislators.

In contrast, the most important gun lobby in Britain is primarily concerned with protecting the group's interest in sports shooting. Sports shooting in Britain is associated with landowning. Joining a good shooting club gives rural residents a step up the social ladder in the British countryside. Those who shoot typically use shotguns, which have escaped bans in Britain. Thus, the gun lobby in Britain has been effective in protecting this niche interest in sports shooting, but it has expended much less effort than the NRA in mounting massive grassroots campaigns to protect gun ownership overall.

For Critical Analysis

Opponents of the British handgun ban argued that in 1996, 41 percent of homicides were from knives; 29 percent were from blunt objects, hitting, and kicking; and 18 percent were from strangulation. That leaves only 12 percent from guns.[13] Do these statistics represent a valid argument against the British handgun ban? Explain.

As another example of how effective lobbying can help special interest groups, consider the minimum wage bill passed in 1996. Virtually everyone was certain that President Bill Clinton would sign the bill; therefore, any special interest legislation attached to the bill would be passed along with it. So lobbyists went to work in the Senate and succeeded in getting the following provisions tacked on to the minimum wage bill:

■ A provision that shielded insurance companies from new, costly lawsuits.

■ Larger tax write-offs for small businesses.

■ Tax deductions for Alaskan fisheries (for example, the ability to claim deductions on the cost of all meals the fishers eat while at sea).

■ Extension of tax credits for companies that hire disadvantaged people.

■ Deductions for companies that underwrite their employees' college education, plus a second credit to employees attending graduate school.

■ A provision to reduce the excise tax on hard-cider producers.

■ A provision backed by the securities industry that allowed all homemakers to deposit $2,000 annually, tax free, into an individual retirement account.

■ A renewal of the 20 percent tax credit for corporate research and development.

Lobbying can be directed not only at the legislative branch of government but also at administrative agencies and even at the courts. For example, individuals stricken with AIDS formed a strong lobby in the early 1990s to force the Food and Drug Administration to allow patients to use experimental drugs to treat AIDS before the drugs were fully tested. Lobbying can also be directed at changing international policies. For example, after political changes had opened up Eastern Europe to business in the late 1980s and early 1990s, intense lobbying by Western business groups helped persuade the United States and other industrial powers to reduce controls on the sale of high-technology products, such as personal computers, to Eastern European countries.

Providing Election Support   Interest groups often become directly involved in the election process. Many interest group members join and work with political parties in order to influence party platforms and the nomination of candidates. Interest groups provide campaign support for legislators who favor their policies and sometimes urge their own members to try to win posts in party organizations. Most important, interest groups urge their members to vote for candidates who support the views of the group. They can also threaten legislators with the withdrawal of votes. No candidate can expect to have support from *all* interest groups, but if the candidate is to win, she or he must have support (or little opposition) from the most powerful ones.

Since the 1970s, federal laws governing campaign financing have allowed corporations, labor unions, and special interest groups to raise funds and make campaign contributions through **political action committees (PACs).** Both the number of PACs and the amount of money they spend on elections have grown astronomically in recent years. There were about a thousand PACs in 1976; today, there are more than four thousand PACs. In 1973, total spending by PACs amounted to $19 million; in recent elections, total spending by PACs has reached nearly $600 million.[14] We discuss PACs in more detail in Chapter 9.

Although campaign contributions do not guarantee that officials will vote the way the groups wish, contributions usually do ensure that the groups will have the ear of the public officials they have helped to elect. PACs have also succeeded in bypassing campaign-contribution limits, thereby obtaining the same type of "vote-buying" privileges that wealthy individual contributors enjoyed in the past.

POLITICAL ACTION COMMITTEE (PAC) A committee that is established by a corporation, labor union, or special interest group to raise funds and make contributions on the establishing organization's behalf.

INDIRECT TECHNIQUE Any method used by interest groups to influence government officials through third parties, such as voters.

Indirect Techniques

Interest groups also try to influence public policy indirectly through third parties or the general public. Such **indirect techniques** may appear to be spontaneous, but they are generally as well planned as the direct lobbying techniques just discussed. Indirect techniques can be particularly effective because public officials are often more impressed by contacts from voters than from lobbyists.

Shaping Public Opinion   Public opinion weighs significantly in the policymaking process, so interest groups cultivate their public images carefully. If public opinion favors a certain group's interests, then public officials will be more ready to listen and more willing to pass legislation favoring that group. To cultivate public opinion, an interest group's efforts may include television publicity, newspaper and magazine advertisements, mass mailings, and the use of public-relations techniques to improve the group's public image.

For example, environmental groups run television ads to dramatize threats to the environment. Oil companies respond to criticism about increased gasoline prices with advertising showing their concern for the public welfare. The goal of all these activities is to influence public opinion and bring grassroots pressure to bear on officials. (For another example of how interest groups attempt to influence public opinion, see this chapter's *The Politics of Homeland Security* feature on the following page.)

Interest groups often use celebrities to help promote their causes to the public. This video still of actor Will Smith holding a booster seat helps Ford Motor Company convince the public to support state legislation requiring booster seats for children who are too large for child-safety seats but too small to use adult seat belts. (Ford Motor Company)

The POLITICS of HOMELAND SECURITY

"Selling" Terrorism Insurance

Individuals, businesses, and even governments purchase insurance to protect themselves against catastrophic losses. Certainly, one of the most dramatic instances of a catastrophic loss—$40 billion worth—occurred as a result of the terrorist attacks on September 11, 2001. Yet the American insurance industry has faced similar monumental losses on several occasions. In 1992, for example, Hurricane Andrew resulted in $30 billion in property damage in South Florida. After that event, certain homeowners in Florida had to pay higher premiums when they renewed their insurance policies. After September 11, building owners and others desiring insurance protection against another terrorist attack similarly expected higher premiums.

INSURANCE LOBBYING BEGAN IMMEDIATELY

The U.S. insurance industry also knew that the long-run consequences of the terrorist attacks would be higher rates. Higher rates would allow the affected insurance companies to recoup their major losses and enable all companies to build up their reserves for the possibility of another attack. Naturally, the insurance industry looked to Congress for additional help. The industry's lobbyists, together with lobbyists for banks and realtors, argued before Congress that if the federal government did not agree to be the "insurer of last resort" in the event of a future terrorist attack, a financial meltdown would occur. Why? According to the insurance companies, their reserves would be so depleted by the attacks on September 11 that there would be nothing left to pay claims if another attack occurred. Consequently, the federal government had to "do something."

By the summer of 2002, no such financial meltdown had occurred. Nevertheless, still wanting some help from the government, the insurance industry came up with the idea of linking the terrorism insurance bill to jobs in the construction industry.

Thus, the insurance companies argued that many large construction projects, particularly those for high-rise buildings, were being held up because of lack of terrorism insurance. The Bush administration and Congress were persuaded by this argument. The result was a $300 billion terrorism insurance bill signed by the president on November 26, 2002.

THE REAL FACTS

Arguing that the terrorism insurance bill was a job-creation bill (or at least a bill to prevent job losses in the construction industry) was a stroke of genius, even though the facts did not support this line of reasoning. By the summer of 2002, no major

Key legislators applaud President Bush after he signed the terrorism insurance bill into law on November 26, 2002. Terrorism insurance had been a top priority for the president since shortly after the September 11 terrorist attacks. (AP Photo/J. Scott Applewhite)

construction projects had been halted or slowed down because owners could not obtain terrorism insurance. Michael Dugan of the State Building and Construction Trades Council of California asked, "Do we know of a single job being delayed because of [lack of terrorism insurance]? The answer is, 'no.'"

Within the insurance industry itself, a strong market for terrorism insurance was already emerging. Nevertheless, the federal government—the taxpayers—has assumed that burden. As J. Robert Hunter of the Consumer Federation of America said, "While some problems exist in Manhattan . . . , taxpayers should not be forced to foot the bill for businesses and insurers that have already found terrorism insurance coverage." If another terrorist attack occurs, taxpayers will have to cover up to $300 billion of losses.

Are We Safer?

You probably have car insurance, renters' insurance, or other property insurance. Do you feel safer knowing that federal terrorism insurance will protect your insurance company in the event of catastrophic losses? Who should be responsible for verifying the facts used by lobbyists to support the passage of a bill?

RATING SYSTEM A system by which a particular interest group evaluates (rates) the performance of legislators based on how often the legislators have voted with the group's position on particular issues.

Some interest groups also try to influence legislators through **rating systems.** A group selects legislative issues that it feels are important to its goals and rates legislators according to the percentage of times they vote favorably on that legislation. For example, a score of 90 percent on the Americans for Democratic Action (ADA) rating scale means that the legislator supported that group's position to a high degree. Other groups tag members of Congress who support (or fail to support) their interests to a significant extent with telling labels. For instance, the Communications Workers of America refers to policymakers who take a position consistent with its members' own views as "Heroes" and those who take the opposite position as "Zeroes." Needless to say, such tactics can be an effective form of indirect lobbying, particularly with legislators who do not want to earn a low ADA score or be placed on the "Zeroes" list.

Mobilizing Constituents   Interest groups sometimes urge members and other constituents to contact government officials—by letter, e-mail, or telephone—to show their support for or opposition to a certain policy. Large interest groups can generate hundreds of thousands of letters, e-mail messages, and calls. Interest groups often provide form letters or postcards for constituents to fill out and mail. The NRA has successfully used this tactic to fight strict federal gun control legislation by delivering half a million letters to Congress within a few weeks. Policymakers recognize that the letters were initiated by an interest group, but they are still made aware of an issue that is important to that group.

Going to Court   The legal system offers another avenue for interest groups to influence the political process. Civil rights groups paved the way for interest group litigation in the 1950s and 1960s with major victories in cases concerning equal housing, school desegregation, and employment discrimination. Environmental groups, such as the Sierra Club, have also successfully used litigation to protect their interests. For example, an environmental group might challenge in court an activity that threatens to pollute the environment or that will destroy the natural habitat of an endangered species. The legal challenge forces those engaging in the activity to bear the costs of defending themselves and possibly delays their project. In fact, much of the success of environmental groups has been linked to their use of lawsuits.

Interest groups can also influence the outcome of litigation without being a party to a lawsuit. As you read earlier in this chapter, interest groups often file *amicus curiae* ("friend of the court") briefs in appellate courts. These briefs state the group's legal argument in support of their desired outcome in the case. For example, in the affirmative action cases before the Supreme Court in 2003, dozens of *amicus* briefs were filed by various groups, including the National Association of Scholars, the Center for New Black Leadership, the American Council on Education, the National Urban League, and the Clinical Legal Education Association, as well as General Motors Corporation. Often, interest groups have statistics and research that support their position on a certain issue, and this research can have considerable influence on the justices deciding the case. Also, filing a brief in a case gives the group publicity, which aids in promoting its causes.

Demonstration Techniques   Some interest groups stage protests to make a statement in a dramatic way. The Boston Tea Party of 1773, in which American colonists dressed as Native Americans and threw tea into Boston Harbor to protest British taxes, is testimony to how long this tactic has been around. Over the years, many groups have organized protest marches and rallies to support or oppose such issues as legalized abortion, busing, gay and lesbian rights, government assistance to farmers, the treatment of Native Americans, restrictions on the use of federally owned lands in the West, trade relations with China, and the activities of global organizations, such as the World Trade Organization.

AMERICA at odds

Should Issue Ads Be Regulated?

One of the most powerful indirect techniques used by interest groups is issue ads—television and radio ads supporting or opposing a particular issue. The Supreme Court has made it clear that the First Amendment's guarantee of free speech protects interest groups' rights to set forth their positions on issues. Nevertheless, issue advocacy is controversial because the funds spent to air issue ads have had a clear effect on the outcome of elections, yet until recently, such spending was not regulated by the laws governing campaign financing.

Both parties have been helped by such interest group spending. In many instances, the sponsors of the ads are clearly identified, as required by the Federal Communications Commission. Sometimes, however, the group behind the ads is not always clear, as discussed in this chapter's *Perception versus Reality* feature. A study by the Brennan Center Policy Committee on Political Advertising found that the true sponsorship of issue ads was impossible to discern in at least 25 percent of the ads studied.[15] The Brennan Center also found that ads are sometimes aired by "front groups" that have been set up to disguise the true identity of the sponsors. For example, prescription drug companies and pharmaceutical trade groups have created seemingly independent groups, such as the Alliance for Better Medicare and Citizens for the Right to Know, to promote their issues.[16]

The Bipartisan Campaign Reform Act of 2002 attempted to address the power of issue ads, as you will read in Chapter 9. One of its key provisions prohibits interest groups' issue ads that refer to a clearly identified candidate from being aired within sixty days of a general election or thirty days of a primary election. This provision faces a serious court challenge as an unconstitutional restriction of free speech. The Brennan Center favors more strict enforcement of existing disclosure requirements for issue ads. Clearly, this is a concern with which Americans will struggle in future elections.

Today's Lobbying Establishment

Without a doubt, interest groups and their lobbyists have become a permanent feature in the landscape of American government. The major interest groups all have headquarters in Washington, D.C., close to the center of government. Professional lobbyists and staff members of various interest groups move freely between their groups' headquarters and congressional offices and committee rooms. Interest group representatives are routinely consulted when Congress drafts new legislation. As already mentioned, interest group representatives are frequently asked to testify before congressional committees or subcommittees on the effect or potential effect of particular legislation or regulations. In a word, interest groups have become an integral part of the American government system.

As interest groups have become a permanent feature of American government, lobbying has developed into a profession. A professional lobbyist—one who has mastered the techniques of lobbying discussed earlier in this chapter—is a valuable ally to any interest group seeking to influence government. Professional lobbyists can and often do move from one interest group to another.

The "Revolving Door" between Interest Groups and Government

In recent years, it has become increasingly common for those who leave positions with the federal government to become lobbyists or consultants for the private-interest groups they helped to regulate. Former government officials, particularly those who held key positions in Congress or the executive branch, have little difficulty finding work as lobbyists. For one thing, they often have inside information that can help an interest group's efforts. More important, they normally have an established network of personal contacts, which is a great political asset.

In spite of legislation and regulations that have been created in an attempt to reduce this "revolving door" syndrome, it is still functioning quite well. When Representative Sam Gibbons (D., Fla.) retired, he went to work as a lobbyist on the same tax and trade issues he had handled as a member of the House Ways and Means Committee. Representative Bill Brewster (D., Okla.) stated that when he retired, he planned to work on the same health-care and energy issues he worked on in Congress. Even though current law requires former lawmakers and aides to wait a year before directly lobbying their former colleagues, the restrictions have had little discernible effect. On average, about one in four former lawmakers becomes a lobbyist.

A lobbyist talks with a member of Congress outside the congressperson's office. Interest groups often hire former members of Congress to serve as lobbyists, thus creating a "revolving door" between interest groups and government. (Spencer Grant/Photo Edit)

perception versus REALITY

Who's Paying for All Those Issue Ads?

Each election cycle, various interest groups sponsor "issue" ads—ads that support a particular candidate's position. As mentioned elsewhere, under the laws governing campaign financing, issue ads are perfectly legal so long as they do not *expressly* support a particular candidate. Who's sponsoring these ads?

THE PERCEPTION

Most Americans believe, understandably, that the organizations promoting and paying for such ads are what they say they are. For example, consider an ad that was televised in several key election states during the 2000 presidential campaigns. In the ad, a cancer survivor, Ardell DeCarlo, described how medicine saved her life but said that if Congress passed proposed legislation to regulate prescription drug prices, others might not be so lucky. "My fear is," she stated, "if the government takes control of this, it is going to hurt a lot of people." The ad concluded with a statement urging people to take action: "Tell Congress. The . . . prescription plan is no cure for America's seniors."

Most viewers probably assumed that the Citizens for Better Medicare, the ad's sponsor, was what it described itself to be—a grassroots organization fighting for better drug coverage. Certainly, the ad was effective—thousands of people called or sent letters to their congressional representatives urging them not to pass the bill.[17]

Similarly, most viewers probably concluded that the Alliance for Quality Nursing Home Care, which aired ads in several states opposing further government involvement in nursing-home operations, was a patients' advocacy group.

THE REALITY

In reality, American viewers were not told who was really behind these and numerous other issue ads that appeared to represent grassroots or consumer interests. For example, Citizens for Better Medicare is funded almost entirely by the pharmaceutical industry, which has long fought congressional efforts to regulate drug prices. The Alliance for Quality Nursing Home Care was not an organization advocating patients' rights but a group of nursing-home owners and administrators who did not want further government interference in their operations. The American Federation of State, County, and Municipal Employees ran ads supporting Democratic presidential candidate Al Gore's positions on certain issues through a front group called American Family Voices.[18]

What's Your Opinion?

"People have a right to speak and to advocate, but listeners have a right to know who the speaker is." Do you agree with this statement? Why or why not?

Why Do Interest Groups Get Bad Press?

Despite their importance to democratic government, interest groups, like political parties, are sometimes criticized by both the public and the press. Our image of interest groups and their special interests is not very favorable. You may have run across political cartoons depicting lobbyists standing in the hallways of Congress with briefcases stuffed with money, waiting to lure representatives into a waiting limousine.

These cartoons are not entirely factual, but they are not entirely fictitious either. President Richard Nixon (1969–1974) was revealed to have yielded to the campaign contributions of milk producers by later authorizing a windfall increase in milk subsidies. In 1977, "Koreagate," a scandal in which a South Korean businessman was accused of offering lavish "gifts" to several members of Congress, added to the view that politicians were too easily susceptible to the snares of special interests. In the early 1990s, it was revealed that a number of senators who received generous contributions from one particular savings and loan association turned around and supported a "hands-off" policy by savings and loan regulators. The savings and loan association in question later got into financial trouble, costing the taxpayers billions of dollars.

As you will read shortly, Congress has tried to impose stricter regulations on lobbyists. For example, in the wake of numerous scandals over the years, in 1996 both the House and the Senate passed a set of rules that prohibited members of Congress from accepting free trips, meals, and gifts from interest group lobbyists. The most important legislation regulating lobbyists was passed in 1946 and revised in 1995. The problem with stricter regulation is that it could abridge First Amendment rights.

The Regulation of Interest Groups

In an attempt to control lobbying, Congress passed the Federal Regulation of Lobbying Act in 1946. The major provisions of the act are as follows:

- Any person or organization that receives money to be used principally to influence legislation before Congress must register with the clerk of the House and the secretary of the Senate.
- Any group or persons registering must identify their employer, salary, amount and purpose of expenses, and duration of employment.
- Every registered lobbyist must give quarterly reports on his or her activities, which are to be published in the *Congressional Quarterly*.
- Anyone failing to satisfy the specific provisions of this act can be fined up to $10,000 and be imprisoned for up to five years.

The act was very limited and did not succeed in regulating lobbying to any great degree for several reasons. First, the Supreme Court restricted the application of the law only to those lobbyists who seek to influence federal legislation directly.[19] Any lobbyist seeking to influence legislation indirectly through public opinion did not fall within the scope of the law. Second, only persons or organizations whose principal purpose was to influence legislation were required to register. Many groups avoided registration by claiming that their principal function was something else. Third, the act did not cover lobbying directed at agencies in the executive branch or lobbyists who testified before congressional committees. Fourth, the public was almost totally unaware of the information in the quarterly reports, and Congress created no agency to oversee interest group activities. Not until 1995 did Congress finally address these loopholes by enacting new legislation.

The Lobbying Disclosure Act of 1995

In 1995, Congress passed new lobbying legislation that reformed the 1946 act in the following ways:

- Strict definitions now apply to determine who must register with the clerk of the House and the secretary of the Senate as a lobbyist. A lobbyist is anyone who either spends at least 20 percent of his or her time lobbying members of Congress, their staffs, or executive-

"A very special interest to see you, Senator."

Drawing by Joseph Farris © 1994 The New Yorker Magazine, Inc.

branch officials, or is paid more than $5,000 in a six-month period for such work. Any organization that spends more than $20,000 in a six-month period conducting such lobbying activity must also register.

- Lobbyists must report their clients, the issues on which they lobbied, and the agency or house they contacted, although they do not need to disclose the names of individuals they contacted.

Tax-exempt organizations, such as religious groups, were exempted from these provisions, as were organizations that engage in grassroots lobbying, such as a media campaign that asks people to write or call their congresspersons. Nonetheless, the number of registered lobbyists nearly doubled in the first few years of the new legislation.

why does it MATTER?

Interest Groups and Your Everyday Life

Interest groups exist in our political arena for only one reason: to influence political outcomes. The goal of interest groups is to inform the public and lobby the politicians about the good or bad aspects of some proposed policy. In addition, some interest groups may propose policies and then seek support from the public and politicians for those proposals. The success of interest groups is usually measured by the extent to which their members benefit from legislation. Realize, though, that any law passed by Congress affects not only the members of the interest group or groups that lobbied for the law's passage but all Americans. Therefore, interest group activities very much affect your everyday life. At times, you might be among the Americans who benefit from a particular interest group's activities, even though you are not a member of that interest group. At other times, you may be affected adversely by legislation resulting from interest groups lobbying Congress. Consider some examples:

- The lobbying efforts of labor unions over the years have led to improved conditions in the workplace for all American workers, not just for union members. At the same time, labor interest groups have sometimes created severe barriers to entry in a given trade—the building trades, to cite just one example. Those who were able to get unionized jobs in the building trades benefited; others did not.
- For years, the American automobile industry successfully lobbied to have Congress and the president restrict imports of Japanese automobiles to protect American manufacturing interests. The same scenario has occurred at various times with respect to steel products, citizen-band radios, chrome, and cheeses. While American companies producing these products benefited from restrictions on imports, the end result for you, as a consumer, is that you have to pay higher prices for cars, steel products, and so on because of less competition from imports.
- Public education interest groups have lobbied for benefits for teachers and the American public school system that employs them, yet these groups may also have restricted educational choices. Most families in America face a monopoly situation with respect to K through 12 (kindergarten through high

school) schooling. That is to say, unless they have the resources to send their children to private schools, they must accept the public school that is closest to their house.

- Consumer groups have successfully lobbied for improved auto safety. As a result, cars now have padded dashboards, shoulder harnesses, air bags, high-impact bumpers, and the like. At the same time, these safety measures have driven up the prices of the cars we drive.

Taking Action

An obvious way to get involved in politics is to join an interest group whose goals you endorse, including one of the organizations on your campus. You can find lists of interest groups operating at the local, state, and national levels by simply going to a search engine online, such as Yahoo!, and keying in the words "interest groups." If you have a particular interest or goal that you would like to promote, consider forming your own group, as a group of Iowa students did when they formed a group called Students Toward Environmental Protection. In the photo alongside, Terri Legueri, a student of Grinnell College in Iowa, holds a protest sign during a rally held by the group in 2002. The students wanted Iowa's lawmakers to issue tougher regulations governing factory farms and to expand the state's bottle deposit requirements. (AP Photo/ Charlie Neibergall)

Key Terms

direct technique 138

free rider problem 132

indirect technique 141

interest group 131

labor force 136

lobbying 138

lobbyist 138

patron 132

pluralist theory 133

political action
    committee (PAC) 141

public-interest group 134

rating system 142

trade organization 135

Chapter Summary

1 An interest group is an organization of people sharing common objectives who actively attempt to influence government policymakers through direct and indirect methods. Interest groups differ from political parties in that interest groups pursue specialized interests, are tightly organized, and do not compete for public office, as parties do.

2 Interest groups (1) help bridge the gap between citizens and government; (2) help raise public awareness and inspire action on various issues; (3) often provide public officials with specialized and detailed information, which helps officials to make informed public-policy choices; and (4) help to ensure that public officials are carrying out their duties responsibly. Pluralist theory explains American politics as a contest among various interest groups that compete at all levels of government to gain benefits for their members. Concerns over the potential harm that can be caused by interest groups, or factions, date back to the beginning of the nation.

3 The most common interest groups are private groups that seek government policies that will benefit (or at least, not harm) their members' interests. Many major interest groups are concerned about issues relating to the following areas or groups of persons:

business, labor, agriculture, consumers, senior citizens, the environment, and professionals.

4 Direct techniques used by interest groups include lobbying efforts and providing election support, particularly through the use of political action committees (PACs). Indirect techniques include advertising and other promotional efforts, mobilizing constituents, bringing lawsuits, and organizing demonstrations and protests. Interest group contributions for "issue advocacy" present a particularly thorny challenge because free speech issues are necessarily involved.

5 Interest group representatives serve as information sources for members of Congress. Government policymakers, in turn, often serve as political consultants or lobbyists for interest groups on leaving government office.

6 The Federal Regulation of Lobbying Act of 1946 attempted to regulate the activities of lobbyists, but it contained many loopholes. Lobbyists were able to continue influencing legislation with little government oversight or disclosure of their activities. In 1995, the Lobbying Disclosure Act created stricter definitions of who is a lobbyist, forcing many more lobbyists to register and report their activities to Congress.

RESOURCES FOR FURTHER STUDY

Selected Readings

Biersack, Robert, ed. *After the Revolution: PACs, Lobbies, and the Republican Congress.* New York: Allyn & Bacon, 1999. This collection of essays examines the way in which special interests worked after the Republicans became the dominant party in Congress in 1995.

Cigler, Allan J., and Burdett A. Loomis, eds. *Interest Group Politics,* 6th ed. Washington, D.C.: CQ Press, 2002. This sixth edition contains many new essays, including examinations of religious activists, environmental groups, and consumer groups. The editors assert that a new era of interest group politics is emerging.

Hernson, Paul S., Ronald G. Shaiko, and Clyde Wilcox, eds. *The Interest Group Connection: Electioneering, Lobbying, and*

Policymaking, 2d ed. New York: Chatham House Publishers, 2003. This collection of new essays from leading scholars examines the theory and the reality of interest groups' influence on public policymaking.

Putnam, Robert D. *Bowling Alone: The Collapse and Revival of American Community.* New York: Simon & Schuster, 2000. The author, a professor of public policy at Harvard University, argues that Americans are now less connected to their families, communities, and the republic itself. The author has numerous statistics showing declining participation in everything from interest groups to bowling leagues and family picnics. He also proposes some solutions.

InfoTrac Citations

Using your InfoTrac password, access the InfoTrac database at **http://infotrac.thomsonlearning.com**. Once at the site, you can do "key word" searches to locate the following articles, each of which deals with a topic covered in this chapter. The key words to use in your search are indicated in parentheses.

- "Easy Shot—The NRA v. National Security" (National Rifle Association)

- "Follow the Money: Hard Money. Soft Money. Lobbying money. Which Buys the Most Influence in Washington?

FORTUNE's Power 25 Survey Attempts an Answer and Ranks the Top Lobbying Groups" (Lobbying Influence)

- "Issue Advocacy: Reaching Outside the Base: How the Nova Scotia Nurses' Union Geared Its Message to Conservative Voters and Won—Big Time" (Issue Advocacy)

- "Understanding the Lobbying Disclosure Act" (Federal Regulation of Lobbying Act)

Politics on the Web

To find particular interest groups online, a good point of departure is the Internet Public Library Association, which provides links to hundreds of professional and trade associations. Go to **http://www.ipl.org/ref/AON**

- The Institute for Global Communications offers a host of lobbying and public-interest activities. Its home page can be accessed at
http://www.igc.apc.org

- You can access the National Rifle Association online at
http://www.nra.org

- The AARP's Web site can be found at
http://www.aarp.org

- To learn about the activities of the National Education Association, go to
http://nea.org

- You can find information on environmental issues and the activities of the National Resource Defense Council at
http://www.nrdc.org

Web Resources on Your CD-ROM

On your CD-ROM, you will find Web resources, news articles, Internet activities, and video clips related to the topics in this chapter. Resources related to this chapter include the following:

- **Values Inventory**—Political Ideology: Gun Control.
- **Why Does It Matter?**—Visit Web Sites for and against Gun Control.
- **Updates**—Keep up with the issues in this chapter!
- **Web Resources**—Internet Activities: Original Intent and the Purpose of the Second Amendment; Milestones in Federal Gun Control Legislation.
- **Where Do You Stand?**—Dialogue: Do We Need an Armed Citizenry?
- **Comparative Politics**—Britain's Trade Union Congress.
- **Videos**—Gun Control.
- **NewsEdge**—Visit this global resource for current events related to this chapter.

chapter 7
political parties

CHAPTER OBJECTIVES

After reading this chapter, you should be able to . . .

▶ Explain what a political party is and how parties function in American politics and government.

▶ Summarize the origins and development of the two-party system in the United States.

▶ Indicate some of the reasons why the two-party system has endured.

▶ Describe the different types of third parties and how they function in the American political system.

▶ Discuss the structure of American political parties.

151

Should We Have a System of Proportional Representation?

In the United States, we have a two-party system. Although third parties field candidates during elections, the two major parties have garnered 90 percent of the popular vote since the 1880s. As you will read in this chapter, our electoral system dictates that third parties share almost none of the fruits of their electoral success. For example, even though nearly 20 million people voted for Ross Perot for president in 1992—19 percent of the vote—he did not receive a single vote in the electoral college, nor was he offered any post in the winning candidate's administration. In contrast, many other democracies around the world have a multiparty system in which more than two political parties compete for electoral offices; after elections, they share political power in proportion to the number of votes they received.

Proportional representation creates a legislature that represents the overall distribution of public support for every political party. This means that even minority parties, which received a small percentage of the vote, are rewarded with at least a few seats in the legislature and often some administrative posts in government. Proponents of this system argue that only when the full diversity of opinion within a country is represented can the government's decisions be regarded as legitimate. Others argue that such a system creates a fragmented government that is weak and unstable.

Our System Should Reward Third-Party Success

America today is a modern, complex society with a multitude of interests. Some argue that rather than having only two groups, Democrats and Republicans, in Congress, we should have three, four, five, or even a dozen groups represented, through proportional representation. No party would have exclusive control of the government. Instead, the different parties would have to form coalitions to obtain a majority vote to get legislation passed.

Currently, the United States has a plurality system in which the winner takes all. If one party's candidate receives 45 percent of the vote, and two other parties' candidates receive 42 and 13 percent, respectively, the party with 45 percent wins all. In a proportional system, each party submits its list of candidates, and the party that wins 45 percent of the vote receives 45 percent of the seats for its candidates on the list. Significantly, the parties that received 42 and 13 percent get seats also.

Those in favor of proportional representation argue that the diverse interests of Americans would have a better chance of being represented in Congress if we had such a system. This contention is bolstered by research results reported by G. Bingham Powell of Yale University.[1] Based on a study of 150 democratic elections in twenty democracies over a period of twenty-five years, Powell found that, overall, citizens' interests were better represented under a multiparty system with proportional representation than under a two-party system.

The Current System Is Strong and Stable

Few Americans have ever considered an alternative to our two-party system. Supporters of the status quo—the two-party system—argue that third parties continue to be relevant by forcing the two major parties to consider the platforms offered by third-party candidates. Furthermore, neither the Republicans nor the Democrats represent a uniform set of beliefs. Each party incorporates a broad spectrum of opinions. One political commentator argues that there are currently at least six Democratic parties in the House of Representatives—including the Hispanic caucus, the black caucus, the "new Democrats," and the progressive labor caucus, among others.[2] Thus, the current system allows for a broad array of opinions to be heard at the highest levels of power.

Besides, America is so diverse, and includes so many groups and interests, that a multiparty system would be unwieldy. How would our president be able to get any legislation passed? He or she would have to build a coalition of several parties. Every time one party pulled out of the coalition, the proposed legislation would fail. We would end up with a powerless president and a powerless Congress.

Where Do You Stand?

1. If we had a multiparty system, what type of party would you want created to coincide with your interests?

2. Do you believe that our "winner-take-all" system works better than a proportional representation system might work? Why or why not?

Interacting with Your CD-ROM Resources

Use your CD-ROM to access a values inventory, participation exercises, resources on the Web, and video clips. Important resources related to this feature include:

- **Values Inventory**—Political Ideology: Proportional Representation.
- **Where Do You Stand?**—Dialogue: Should We Have a Proportional System of Representation?
- **Web Resources**—Internet Activities: A Political Quiz on Proportional Representation; The Case for Proportional Representation.

INTRODUCTION

Some Americans believe that an electoral system that rewards third-party electoral success would be ideal for the United States. Currently, however, such a system remains just that—an ideal. The two major political parties have a long history in this country, and traditionalists are not convinced that the Republican and Democratic parties will be replaced in the future by an alternative party system.

A **political party** can be defined as a group of individuals *outside the government* who organize to win elections, operate the government, and determine policy. Political parties were an unforeseen development in American political history. The founders defined many other important institutions, such as the presidency and Congress, and described their functions in the Constitution. Political parties, however, are not even mentioned in the Constitution. In fact, the founders decried factions and parties. Thomas Jefferson probably best expressed the founders' antiparty sentiments when he declared, "If I could not go to heaven but with a party, I would not go there at all."[3]

If the founders did not want political parties, who was supposed to organize political campaigns and mobilize supporters of political candidates? Clearly, there was a practical need for some kind of organizing group to form a link between citizens and their government. Even our early national leaders, for all their antiparty feelings, realized this: several of them were active in establishing or organizing the first political parties.

Political parties continue to serve as major vehicles for citizen participation in our political system. It is hard to imagine democracy without political parties. Political parties provide a way for the public to choose who will serve in government and which policies will be carried out. Even citizens who do not identify with any political party or who choose not to participate in elections are affected by party activities and influence on government.

POLITICAL PARTY A group of individuals outside the government who organize to win elections, operate the government, and determine policy.

America's Two-Party System

In the United States, we have a **two-party system.** This means that two major parties—the Democrats and the Republicans—dominate national politics. Why has the two-party system become so firmly entrenched in the United States? According to some scholars, the first major political division in this country—between the Federalists and the Anti-Federalists—established a precedent that continued over time and ultimately resulted in the domination of the two-party system. Today, both parties—the Republican Party and the Democratic Party—tend to be moderate, middle-of-the-road parties built on compromise. The parties' similarities have often led to criticism; their sternest critics call them "tweedledee" and "tweedledum."[4] (We discuss the policy positions of the two parties in more detail later in this chapter.)

Recent polling data indicate that a sizable number of American voters (about 40 percent) feel that the two-party system does not address issues that are important to them or represent their views; 67 percent say they would like to see a strong third party run candidates for president, Congress, and state and local offices.[5] Yet the two-party system continues to thrive. A number of factors help to explain this phenomenon.

TWO-PARTY SYSTEM A political system in which two strong and established parties compete for political offices.

The Self-Perpetuation of the Two-Party System

One of the major reasons for the perpetuation of the two-party system is simply that there is no alternative. Minor parties, called **third parties,**[6] traditionally have found it extremely difficult to compete with the major parties for votes. The reasons for this are multifold, including election laws and institutional barriers.

THIRD PARTY In the United States, any party other than one of the two major parties (Republican and Democratic) is considered a minor party, or third party.

Election Laws Favoring Two Parties
American election laws tend to favor the major parties. In many states, for example, the established major parties need relatively few signatures to place their candidates on the ballot, whereas a third party must get many more signatures. The criterion is often based on the total party vote in the last election, which penalizes a new party competing for the first time.

The rules governing campaign financing also favor the major parties. As you will read in Chapter 9, both major parties receive federal funds for campaign expenses and for their national conventions. Third parties, in contrast, receive federal funds only if they garner 5 percent of the vote and then only *after* the election.

Institutional Barriers to a Multiparty System   As mentioned in this chapter's opening *America at Odds* feature, the structure of our institutions—from single-member congressional districts to the winner-take-all electoral system—prevents third parties from enjoying electoral success. One of the major institutional barriers is the winner-take-all feature of the electoral college system for electing the president (discussed in more detail in Chapter 9). In a winner-take-all system, the winner of a state's popular vote gets all of that state's electoral votes. Thus, third-party candidates have little incentive to run for president because they are unlikely to get enough popular votes to receive any state's electoral votes. (Two states—Maine and Nebraska—allocate their electoral votes proportionately, as discussed in Chapter 9.)

Another institutional barrier to a multiparty system is the single-member district. Currently, all federal and most state legislative districts are single-member districts—voters elect one member from their district to the House of Representatives and to their state legislature.[7] In most European countries, by contrast, districts are drawn as multimember districts and are represented by multiple elected officials from different parties, according to the proportion of the vote their party received, as you read in the opening *America at Odds* feature.

Finally, third parties find it difficult to break through in an electoral system that perpetuates their own failure: because third parties normally do not win elections, Americans tend not to vote for them or to contribute to their campaigns, so they do not win elections—and so on. As long as Americans hold to the perception that third parties can never win big in an election, the current two-party system is likely to persist. (For more on whether third parties could win big elections despite these institutional barriers, see this chapter's *Perception versus Reality* feature.)

AMERICA at odds

Should Third-Party Candidates Debate?

Only twice since 1960, when the first presidential debate was held on television, have American TV viewers and radio listeners been able to hear the voice of a third-party candidate. The first third-party candidate to participate in a debate was John Anderson in 1980, and the second was H. Ross Perot in 1992. In 1996, the Commission for Presidential Debates (CPD) chose not to allow any third-party candidates on the air because they did not have a "realistic" chance of succeeding at the polls.[8] In the 2000 elections, third-party candidates were again excluded from the debates. Under the CPD's criteria for participating in the 2000 debates, only candidates who had a level of support of at least 15 percent of the national electorate could participate.

Critics of these developments point out that the founders had strong feelings about the right of people to govern themselves through free elections. And free elections mean little if minor-party candidates do not have realistic access to public forums, such as televised debates. Furthermore, the CPD is not a government organization but a nonprofit corporation consisting of three Republicans and three Democrats and co-chaired by former heads of the Republican National Committee and Democratic National Committee. Small wonder, say these critics, that third-party candidates are excluded from the debates.

Supporters of the CPD's position point out that opening up the presidential and vice presidential debates to third-party candidates could lead to chaos. Where would you draw the line? Should all third-party candidates be allowed to participate, even those who have virtually no electoral support? It is essential to establish some kind of standards for deciding who can and who cannot participate. Furthermore, third parties have always been an unpredictable element in American politics. Allowing parties that have little national support to participate in the debates would only lead to political confusion.

perception versus REALITY

Third Parties Have Little Influence on Elections

Although the two major parties dominate the political process in the United States, in every election a few minor parties run candidates for federal, state, and local offices. These candidates attract little attention from the media, the major-party candidates, and most voters.

THE PERCEPTION

The perception is that minor parties have little influence on elections. Indeed, most voters consider a vote for a minor-party candidate to be a wasted vote. Few minor-party candidates have ever won an election, and none has won the presidency since Abraham Lincoln, the candidate for the new Republican Party in 1860. A few third-party candidates for president have won electoral votes in modern times: George Wallace, running for the American Independent Party in 1968, won forty-six electoral votes; Strom Thurmond, running for the States' Rights Party in 1948, won thirty-nine electoral votes. Neither of these candidates came close to winning the election, however.

Typically, third parties run in elections to influence the electorate, rather than to win the election. They can bring substantial pressure to bear on the major parties. For example, in 2000, Ralph Nader made it clear that he was running as the Green Party's candidate to show Americans how a third party might offer alternatives to the present two-party system. Nader admitted that his intention was not to win the election—which he knew was a virtual impossibility—but to establish a progressive political reform movement that would monitor the activities of politicians in Washington, D.C.

THE REALITY

The reality is that minor-party candidates have influenced the outcomes in a number of elections, including the 2000 presidential elections. If Nader had not run in 2000, George W. Bush would probably not be president now. Nader's popular votes in Florida or New Hampshire, for example, most likely tipped the balance in favor of Bush. In exit polls, half of Nader voters said they would have voted for Al Gore if Nader had not been running. Without Nader in the race, it is likely that Gore would have won either Florida or New Hampshire, or both, thus giving the electoral vote victory and the presidency to Al Gore. Similarly, Ross Perot's run in the 1992 election, in which he won 19 percent of the vote nationwide, may have helped Bill Clinton win that year.

Green Party presidential candidate Ralph Nader speaks at the National Press Club on on the night of the 2000 presidential election. (Ira Wyman/CORBIS Sygma)

One of the great surprises of the 1998 elections was the stunning victory of Jesse Ventura, a candidate running for governor in Minnesota on the Reform Party ticket (he subsequently left the Reform Party). No one expected the former professional wrestler to defeat his respected Democratic and Republican opponents. Ventura's campaign galvanized younger voters, who appeared at the polls in record numbers on election day. Ventura continued to influence political debate after his win, including naming a third-party member, Dean Barkley, in 2002 to serve the last two months of the late Paul Wellstone's U.S. Senate term.

Despite Ventura's win of a governorship, few third-party candidates have served as much more than the "spoiler" in big races. Nonetheless, sometimes the spoiler can have a lasting impact on the politics of the country.

What's Your Opinion?

Do you think Ralph Nader should have stepped aside in 2000 rather than serve as the spoiler of Al Gore's presidential chances? Do you think another third-party candidate could win an important office, as Jesse Ventura did in Minnesota?

Components of the Two Major American Parties

The two major American political parties are sometimes described as three-dimensional entities. This is because each party consists of three components: (1) the party in the electorate, (2) the party organization, and (3) the party in government.

The Party in the Electorate
The party in the **electorate** is the largest component, consisting of all of those people who describe themselves as Democrats or Republicans. There are no dues, no membership cards, and no obligatory duties. Members of the party in

ELECTORATE All of the citizens eligible to vote in a given election.

the electorate never need to work on a campaign or attend a party meeting. In most states, they may register as Democrats or Republicans, but registration is not legally binding and can be changed at will.

The Party Organization   Each major party has a national organization with national, state, and local offices. As will be discussed later in this chapter, the party organizations are made up of several levels of people who maintain the party's strength between elections, make its rules, raise money, organize conventions, help with elections, and recruit candidates.

The Party in Government   The party in government consists of all of the candidates who have won elections and now hold public office. Even though members of Congress, state legislators, presidents, and all other officeholders almost always run for office as either Democrats or Republicans, the individual candidates do not always agree on government policy. The party in government helps to organize the government's agenda by coaxing and convincing its own party members to vote for its policies. If the party is to translate its promises into public policies, the job must be done by the party in government.

Where the Parties Stand on the Issues

PARTY PLATFORM The document drawn up by each party at its national convention that outlines the policies and positions of the party.

Each of the two major political parties, as well as most of the minor parties, develops a **party platform,** or declaration of beliefs. The platform represents the official party position on various issues, although neither all party members nor all candidates running on the party's ticket share these positions exactly. The major parties usually revise their platforms every four years, at the party's national convention held to nominate a presidential and vice presidential candidate. A new party agenda is also usually announced every two years as a new session of Congress gets under way. The party agendas of the Democrats and Republicans for the 108th Congress are shown in Table 7–1.

Party labels do not necessarily tell you what candidates are going to do when they take office, however. For example, although the Democratic Party is generally known as the party

TABLE 7–1

Agendas of the Democratic and Republican Parties for the 108th Congress

DEMOCRATIC AGENDA	REPUBLICAN AGENDA
Homeland Security—To address existing vulnerabilities in our homeland security and authorize grants for first responders and state and local governments.	**Economic Growth**—To provide immediate job growth while laying the groundwork for long-term economic prosperity; to rally the stock market and energize the economy.
Medicare Prescription Drug Benefits—To create a voluntary comprehensive outpatient drug benefit for all Medicare beneficiaries.	**Federal Budget**—To craft a budget that funds important priorities such as homeland security, defense, health care, and other national needs.
Education Reform—To provide full funding for the No Child Left Behind Act of 2002. To fully fund Head Start programs.	**National Security**—To fund the ongoing war on terrorism, including military efforts.
Pension Protection—To help American families prepare for retirement; to provide participants with better investment education, information, and advice.	**Welfare Reform**—To extend welfare reform, strengthen work requirements, and promote healthy marriages and abstinence programs.
Health-Care Reform—To expand health coverage, improve the quality of care, and enact a Patients' Bill of Rights.	**Education Reform**—To monitor implementation of the No Child Left Behind Act of 2002.
Civil Rights—To expand hate crimes protections and strengthen the enforcement of existing civil rights laws.	**Tax Relief**—To make permanent the tax relief of 2001, including repeal of the marriage penalty and the death tax.
Environment—To address global climate change and reduce greenhouse gas emissions.	**Medicare Prescription Drug Benefits**—To provide prescription drug coverage for seniors.
Veterans Benefits—To address health-care and death benefits concerns of veterans.	**Energy Policy**—To decrease dependence on foreign oil, promote conservation measures, and create jobs.
Minimum Wage—To raise the minimum wage by $1.50.	**Bankruptcy Reform**—To pass bankruptcy reform legislation and restore consumer confidence in the financial markets.
Crime—To protect Americans from crime and terrorism, assist victims, and improve the administration of justice.	**Liability Reform**—To limit frivolous lawsuits that hurt the economy.

SOURCES: Democratic Policy Committee, January 7, 2003; Representative Deborah Pryce, Chair, Republican Conference, U.S. House of Representatives, January 7, 2003.

of the "little people" and generally favors social legislation to help the underclass in society, it was a Democratic president, Bill Clinton, who signed a major welfare reform bill in 1996 forcing many welfare recipients off the welfare rolls. The Democrats are also known to side with labor unions, yet President Clinton approved the North American Free Trade Agreement, despite bitter public denunciations by most of the nation's unions.

Republicans have often been known to oppose social legislation and welfare and to emphasize self-reliance, yet in an "Open Letter" that appeared in *USA Today* in 1999, Republicans Dennis Hastert (Speaker of the House of Representatives) and Trent Lott (then Senate majority leader) stated that it was time to "move on" to an agenda that would save Social Security, improve education, and ease the tax burden on "working people."[9] Thus, it may be that, as one veteran of American politics has stated, solutions to political issues are found not on the sides of the political spectrum but in the "sensible center."[10]

Events may dramatically alter the agendas of the two political parties. The terrorist attacks of September 11, 2001, thrust national security to the front of the political agendas of the two parties and played an important role in the outcome of the 2002 congressional elections, as discussed in this chapter's *The Politics of Homeland Security* feature.

The POLITICS of HOMELAND SECURITY

Security versus the Economy in the 2002 Elections

The entire House of Representatives and a third of the Senate face elections every two years. Every four years, these elections coincide with a presidential election, as they did in 2000. When congressional elections occur in the middle of a president's term, they are called midterm elections. In 2002, the midterm elections took on unusual significance, in part because the country faced the combined crises of a war on terrorism and a stagnating economy.

These elections were also significant because George W. Bush had assumed office after one of the most contested presidential elections in history. In 2002, he was seeking a more decisive victory for his party. Bush took an active role in the midterm elections, campaigning on behalf of Republican candidates in many close races across the country. How Republicans fared in the elections would necessarily reflect on the president's leadership in the war and on the economy.

AMERICANS TRUST REPUBLICANS ON HOMELAND SECURITY

According to a CNN/*USA Today*/Gallup poll, an overwhelming majority of Americans in 2002 thought Republicans would do a better job than Democrats in dealing with terrorism and defense issues.[11] On the issue of terrorism, 61 percent of respondents said that the Republican Party would do a better job, while only 23 percent said that Democrats would. On military and defense issues, Americans trust the Republican Party by 65 percent, compared to 24 percent for Democrats. In the same poll, Democrats enjoyed a distinct advantage on the issues of prescription drugs for older Americans and a patients' bill of rights.

Republicans capitalized on this perception in the 2002 elections. Repeatedly, President Bush and Republican candidates attacked Democrats on their commitment to homeland security, focused the attention of the nation on a potential war with Iraq, and, in the end, won a decisive, if narrow, victory. As one political analyst commented after the elections, "[I]f the

American people don't trust you on security, it doesn't matter what you say about prescription drugs."[12]

AMERICANS WORRY ABOUT THE ECONOMY, BUT NOT ENOUGH

Nearly coinciding with George W. Bush's inauguration as president in January 2001, the American economy entered a recession, which was deepened by the terrorist attacks of September 11. Although many forecasters predicted a short-lived economic downturn, the stock market remained in decline throughout 2002. Corporate scandals, such as the bankruptcies of Enron and WorldCom, also increased Americans' sense of economic insecurity leading up to the 2002 elections. Americans repeatedly listed the weak economy as an important issue in 2002, but Democrats were never able to capitalize on voters' concerns.

One reason may be that economic woes are difficult to politicize. For example, Americans do not like to see a politician get excited about another layoff announcement. Jenny Backus, a spokeswoman for the Democratic Congressional Campaign Committee, pointed out in August 2002, "What you don't want to do is capitalize on people's misery. We are not counting on hard times."[13] Democrats focused on particular economic issues on which they *disagreed* with Republicans, such as tax breaks for the wealthy, privatizing Social Security, or lowering trade barriers for foreign goods. But these issues simply did not "get out the vote" the way fears of terrorism and potential war with Iraq did in 2002.

Interestingly, after the elections, topping the list of each party's agenda for the new session of Congress was the issue on which it was considered weak: homeland security for the Democrats, and the economy for the Republicans (see Table 7–1).

Are We Safer?

Which party do you trust to do a better job on issues relating to terrorism and homeland security? Why?

President Bush shakes hands with Secretary of Homeland Security Tom Ridge during a welcome ceremony held on February 28, 2003, for the employees of the new agency. The president's decisive response to the terrorist attacks of September 11, 2001, including the creation of a new cabinet department, strengthened support for his administration—and no doubt helped to secure votes for Republican congressional candidates in the 2002 elections. (Reuters NewMedia Inc./CORBIS)

Party Affiliation

What does it mean to belong to a political party? In many European countries, being a party member means that you actually join a political party. You get a membership card to carry around in your wallet, you pay dues, and you vote to select your local and national party leaders. In the United States, becoming a member of a political party is far less involved. To be a member of a political party, an American citizen has only to think of herself or himself as a Democrat or a Republican (or a member of a third party, such as the Green Party, the Libertarian Party, or the American Independent Party). Members of parties do not have to pay dues, work for the party, or attend party meetings. Nor must they support the party platform.[14]

PARTY IDENTIFIER A person who identifies himself or herself as being a member of a particular political party.

PARTY ELITE A loose-knit group of party activists who organize and oversee party functions and planning during and between campaigns.

Generally, the party in the electorate consists of **party identifiers** (those who identify themselves as being a member of one of the parties) and the **party elite**, active party members who choose to work for the party and even become candidates for office. Political parties need year-round support from the latter group to survive. During election campaigns in particular, candidates depend on active party members or volunteers to mail literature, answer phones, conduct door-to-door canvasses, organize speeches and appearances, and, of course, donate money. Between elections, parties also need active members to plan the upcoming elections, organize fund-raisers, and stay in touch with party leaders in other communities to keep the party strong. Generally, the major functions of American political parties are carried out by the party elite, a small, relatively loose-knit group of party activists.

AMERICA at odds

Do Americans Trust the Major Parties?

For some time, a number of scholars and commentators have argued that the major parties are declining in strength. As evidence of this, they point to the rise in the number of independent voters over the last fifty years. As further evidence, they claim that voters' preference for divided government in recent years means that Americans have lost confidence in both parties—they trust neither party enough to want it to govern.

As you can see in Figure 7–1, the number of independent voters has indeed increased significantly. Yet much evidence also indicates that the parties are still strong. According to political scientist Larry Bartels, partisan loyalties have actually had a greater impact on voting behavior in recent presidential elections than in the past.[15] Furthermore, a closer

FIGURE 7-1
Party Identification in Presidential Election Years

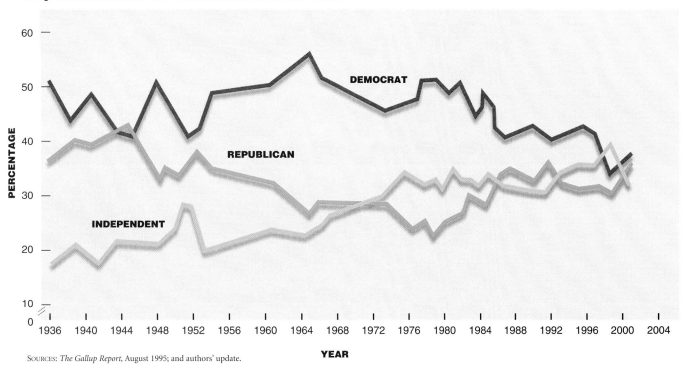

SOURCES: *The Gallup Report,* August 1995; and authors' update.

look at those who identify themselves as independents shows that a good portion of them "lean" toward one party or the other and often vote Democratic or Republican.

Certainly, there is evidence that Americans prefer divided government—that is, a government in which the legislative branch is controlled by one major party and the executive branch by another. Indeed, the 2000 elections gave divided government new meaning. The presidential elections were closer than they had been in a century. Do such close election outcomes represent a vote of no confidence in both parties? Yes, say some. Others, however, note that both parties have moved toward the political center in their attempt to capture votes. The election outcomes can be interpreted as a signal of the voters' approval of centrist policies.

Why People Join Political Parties

Generally, in the United States people belong to a political party because they agree with many of its main ideas and support some of its candidates. In a few countries, such as the People's Republic of China, people belong to a political party because they are required to do so to get ahead in life, regardless of whether they agree with the party's ideas and candidates.

People join political parties for a multitude of reasons. One reason is that people wish to express their **solidarity,** or mutual agreement, with the views of friends, loved ones, and other like-minded people. People also join parties because they enjoy the excitement of politics. In addition, many believe they will benefit materially from joining a party, through better employment or personal career advancement. The traditional institution of **patronage**—rewarding the party faithful with government jobs or contracts—lives on, even though it has been limited to prevent abuses.[16] Finally, some join political parties because they wish to actively promote a set of ideals and principles that they feel are important to American politics and society.

Generally, people join political parties because of their overall agreement with what the party stands for. Thus, when interviewed, people may make the following remarks when asked why they support the Democratic Party: "It seems that the economy is better when the Democrats are in

SOLIDARITY Mutual agreement with others in a particular group.

PATRONAGE A system of rewarding the party faithful and workers with government jobs or contracts.

control." "The Democrats are for the working people." People might say about the Republican Party: "The Republicans help small businesses more than the Democrats." "The Republicans deal better with foreign policy issues."

Demographic Factors and Party Identification

Regardless of how accurate or inaccurate these stereotypes are, individuals with similar characteristics do tend to align themselves more often with one or the other major party. Factors such as race, age, income, education, and marital status all influence party identification.

Generally, slightly more men than women identify with the Republican Party, while more women than men identify themselves as Democrats. While slightly more whites identify with the Republican Party, people in the other categories (nonwhite, black, and Hispanic) overwhelmingly classify themselves as Democrats. As to age, the most notable differences in party preferences are found in those over age sixty-five: a significantly larger number of people in this group identify themselves as Democrats than as Republicans. As mentioned, other factors, such as income, religion, and marital status, also seem to influence party preference.

Although there is clearly a link between these factors and party preference, each party encompasses diverse interests and activities. Both political parties welcome various groups and strive to attract as many members as possible.

What Do Political Parties Do?

As noted earlier, the Constitution does not mention political parties. Historically, though, political parties have played a vital role in our democratic system. Their main function has been to link the people's policy preferences to actual government policies. Political parties also perform many other functions.

Selecting Candidates

One of the most important functions of the two political parties is to recruit and nominate candidates for political office. This function simplifies voting choices for the electorate. Political parties take the large number of people who want to run for office and narrow the field to one candidate. They accomplish this by the use of the **primary,** which is a preliminary election to choose a party's final candidate. It is much easier for voters to choose between two candidates who have been selected by established political parties than to choose among many candidates.

PRIMARY A preliminary election held for the purpose of choosing a party's final candidate.

Informing the Public

Political parties help educate the public about currently important political issues. In recent years, these issues have included defense and environmental policies, our tax system, welfare reform, crime, education, and Social Security. Each party presents its view of these issues through television announcements, newspaper articles or ads, campaign speeches, rallies, debates, and pamphlets. These activities help citizens learn about the issues, consider proposed solutions, and form opinions.

Through these activities, political parties also help to stimulate citizens' interest and participation in public affairs. They seek people to work at party headquarters or to help with door-to-door canvasses, which involve distributing campaign literature and asking people to vote for the party's candidate. Political parties also ask volunteers to work at polling places where people cast their votes during elections and to drive voters to the polling places. Through such pursuits, citizens can participate in the political process.

Coordinating Policymaking

In our complex government, parties are essential for coordinating policy among the various branches of the government. The political party is usually the major institution through which the executive and legislative branches cooperate with each other. Each president, cabinet head,

Drawing by Dana Fradon; © 1987 The New Yorker Magazine, Inc.

"My God! I went to sleep a Democrat and I've awakened a Republican."

and congressperson is normally a member of the Democratic or the Republican Party. The party with fewer members in the legislature is the **minority party.** The party with the most members is the **majority party.** The president works through party leaders in Congress to promote the administration's legislative program. Parties also act as the glue of our federal structure by connecting the various levels of government with a common bond. (For a more detailed discussion of the role played by political parties in Congress, see Chapter 11.)

Checking the Power of the Party in Government

The party that does not control Congress or a state legislature, or the presidency or a state governorship, also plays a vital function in American politics. The "out party" acts as a watchdog and keeps an eye on the activities of the party in power. The out party thus provides a check on the activities of the party in government. Such monitoring by the loyal opposition encourages the party in power to heed the public's wishes and to remain responsive.

Balancing Competing Interests

Political parties are often described as vast umbrellas under which Americans with diverse interests can gather. Political parties are essentially **coalitions**—individuals and groups with a variety of interests and opinions who join together to support the party's platform, or parts of it.

The Republican Party, for example, includes a number of groups with many different views on the issue of abortion. The role of party leaders in this situation is to adopt a broad enough view on the issue so that the various groups will not be alienated. In this way, different groups can hold their individual views and still come together under the umbrella of the Republican Party. Leaders of both the Democratic Party and the Republican Party modify contending views and arrange compromises among different groups. In so doing, the parties help to unify, rather than divide, their members.

Running Campaigns

Through their national, state, and local organizations, parties coordinate campaigns. Political parties take care of a large number of small and routine tasks that are essential to the smooth functioning of the electoral process. They work at getting party members registered and at conducting drives for new voters. They sometimes staff the polling places.

MINORITY PARTY The political party that has fewer members in the legislature than does the opposing party.

MAJORITY PARTY The political party that has more members in the legislature than does the opposing party.

COALITION An alliance of individuals or groups with a variety of interests and opinions who join together to support all or part of a political party's platform.

A Short History of American Political Parties

Political parties have been a part of American politics since the early years of our nation. Throughout the course of our history, several parties have formed, and some have disappeared. Even today, although we have only two major political parties, numerous other parties are also contending for power, as will be discussed later in this chapter.

The First Political Parties

The founders reacted negatively to the idea of political parties because they thought the power struggles that would occur between small economic and political groups would eventually topple the balanced democracy they wanted to create. Nonetheless, two major political factions—the Federalists and Anti-Federalists—were formed even before the Constitution was ratified. Remember from Chapter 2 that the Federalists pushed for the ratification of the Constitution because they wanted a stronger national government than the one that had existed under the Articles of Confederation. The Anti-Federalists argued against ratification. They supported states' rights and feared a too-powerful central government.

These two national factions continued, in somewhat altered form, after the Constitution was ratified. Alexander Hamilton, the first secretary of the Treasury, became the leader of the Federalist Party, which supported a strong central government that would encourage the development of commerce and manufacturing. The Federalists generally thought that a democracy should be ruled by its wealthiest and best-educated citizens. Opponents of the Federalists and Hamilton's policies referred to themselves not as Anti-Federalists, but as Republicans. Today, they are often referred to as Jeffersonian Republicans to distinguish this group from the later Republican Party. The Jeffersonian Republicans were more sympathetic to the "common man" and favored a more limited role for government. They believed that the nation's welfare would be best served if the states had more power than the central government. In their view, Congress should dominate the government, and government policies should help the nation's shopkeepers, farmers, and laborers.

From 1796 to 1860

The nation's first two parties clashed openly in the elections of 1796, in which John Adams, the Federalists' candidate to succeed Washington as president, defeated Thomas Jefferson. Over the next four years, Jefferson and James Madison worked to extend the influence of the Democratic Republican Party. In the presidential elections of 1800 and 1804, Jefferson won

In 1796, John Adams (left), the Federalists' candidate to succeed Washington as president, defeated Thomas Jefferson. (Library of Congress)

the presidency under the Democratic Republican banner. His party also won control of Congress. The Federalists never returned to power and thus became the first (but not the last) American party to go out of existence. (See the time line of American political parties in Figure 7–2.)

The Democratic Republicans dominated American politics for the next twenty years. Jefferson was succeeded in the White House by two other Democratic Republicans—James Madison and James Monroe. In the mid-1820s, however, the Democratic Republicans split into two groups. Andrew Jackson, who was elected president in 1828, aligned himself with the group that called themselves the Democrats. The Democrats were mostly small farmers and debtors. The other group, the National Republicans (later the Whig Party), was led by the well-known John Quincy Adams and Henry Clay, and the great orator Daniel Webster. It was a coalition of bankers, businesspersons, and southern planters.

As the Whigs and Democrats competed for the White House throughout the 1840s and 1850s, the two-party system as we know it today emerged. Both parties were large, with well-known leaders and supporters across the nation. They both had grassroots organizations of party workers committed to winning as many political offices (at all levels of government) for

FIGURE 7–2
A Time Line of U.S. Political Parties

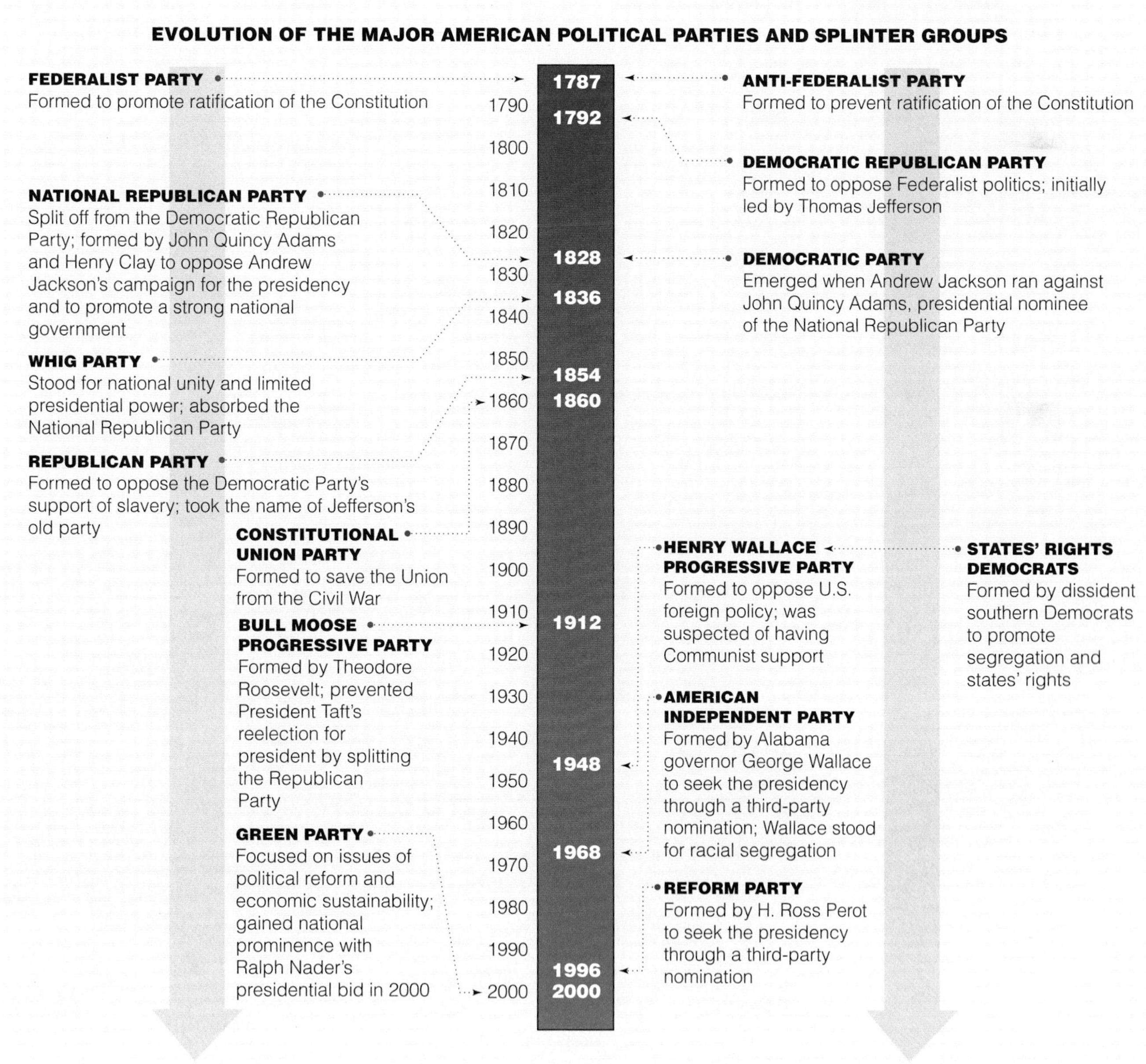

EVOLUTION OF THE MAJOR AMERICAN POLITICAL PARTIES AND SPLINTER GROUPS

FEDERALIST PARTY
Formed to promote ratification of the Constitution

ANTI-FEDERALIST PARTY
Formed to prevent ratification of the Constitution

DEMOCRATIC REPUBLICAN PARTY
Formed to oppose Federalist politics; initially led by Thomas Jefferson

NATIONAL REPUBLICAN PARTY
Split off from the Democratic Republican Party; formed by John Quincy Adams and Henry Clay to oppose Andrew Jackson's campaign for the presidency and to promote a strong national government

DEMOCRATIC PARTY
Emerged when Andrew Jackson ran against John Quincy Adams, presidential nominee of the National Republican Party

WHIG PARTY
Stood for national unity and limited presidential power; absorbed the National Republican Party

REPUBLICAN PARTY
Formed to oppose the Democratic Party's support of slavery; took the name of Jefferson's old party

CONSTITUTIONAL UNION PARTY
Formed to save the Union from the Civil War

HENRY WALLACE PROGRESSIVE PARTY
Formed to oppose U.S. foreign policy; was suspected of having Communist support

STATES' RIGHTS DEMOCRATS
Formed by dissident southern Democrats to promote segregation and states' rights

BULL MOOSE PROGRESSIVE PARTY
Formed by Theodore Roosevelt; prevented President Taft's reelection for president by splitting the Republican Party

AMERICAN INDEPENDENT PARTY
Formed by Alabama governor George Wallace to seek the presidency through a third-party nomination; Wallace stood for racial segregation

GREEN PARTY
Focused on issues of political reform and economic sustainability; gained national prominence with Ralph Nader's presidential bid in 2000

REFORM PARTY
Formed by H. Ross Perot to seek the presidency through a third-party nomination

Timeline dates: 1787, 1790, 1792, 1800, 1810, 1820, 1828, 1830, 1836, 1840, 1850, 1854, 1860, 1870, 1880, 1890, 1900, 1910, 1912, 1920, 1930, 1940, 1948, 1950, 1960, 1968, 1970, 1980, 1990, 1996, 2000

Andrew Jackson (1767–1845) was the greatest military hero of his time and became associated with increased popular participation in government. The National Republican Party, a split-off from the Democratic Republican Party, was formed by John Q. Adams and Henry Clay to oppose Jackson's 1828 campaign for the presidency. Jackson won the election, nonetheless. (Library of Congress)

REALIGNING ELECTION An election in which the popular support for and relative strength of the parties shift as the parties are reestablished with different coalitions of supporters.

Chief Justice Charles Evans Hughes administering the oath of office to Franklin Delano Roosevelt on the east portico of the U.S. Capitol, March 4, 1933. (Library of Congress)

the party as possible. Both the Whigs and the Democrats remained vague on the issue of slavery, and the Democrats were divided into northern and southern camps. By the mid-1850s, the Whig coalition fell apart, and most Whigs were absorbed into the new Republican Party, which opposed the extension of slavery into new territories. Campaigning on this platform, the Republicans succeeded in electing Abraham Lincoln as the first Republican president in 1860.

From the Civil War to the Great Depression

By the end of the Civil War in 1865, the Republicans and the Democrats were the most prominent political parties. From the election of Abraham Lincoln in 1860 until the election of Franklin Roosevelt in 1932, the Republican Party, sometimes referred to as the Grand Old Party, or the GOP, remained the majority party in national politics, winning all but four presidential elections.

After the Great Depression

The social and economic impact of the Great Depression of the 1930s destroyed the majority support that the Republicans had enjoyed for so long and contributed to a realignment in the two-party system. In a **realigning election,** the popular support for and relative strength of the parties shift. As a result, the minority (opposition) party may emerge as the majority party. (A realigning election can also reestablish the majority party in power, albeit with a different coalition of supporters.) The landmark realigning election of 1932 brought Franklin Delano Roosevelt to the presidency and the Democrats back to power at the national level. Realigning elections also occurred in 1860, 1896, and 1968.

Roosevelt was reelected to the presidency in 1936, 1940, and 1944. When he died in office in 1945, his vice president, Harry Truman, assumed the presidential office. Truman ran for the presidency in 1948 and won the election. A Republican candidate, Dwight D. Eisenhower, won the presidential elections of 1952 and 1956. From 1960 through 1968, the Democrats, led by John F. Kennedy and Lyndon B. Johnson, respectively, held power. The Republicans came back into power in 1968 and, except for Jimmy Carter's one term (1977–1981), retained the presidency until Bill Clinton was elected in 1992. The Republicans regained the presidency in 2001, when George W. Bush became president.

In Congress, the Democrats were the dominant party from the Great Depression until 1994, when the Republicans gained control of both houses. They have held control of Congress ever since, except for two years when the Democrats controlled the Senate by one vote.

Third Parties and American Politics

Throughout American history, smaller minor parties, or third parties, have competed for power in the nation's two-party system. Indeed, as mentioned earlier, third parties have been represented in most of our national elections. Although third parties have found it difficult—if not impossible—to gain credibility within the two-party–dominated American system, they play an important role in our political life.

The Many Kinds of Third Parties

Third parties are as varied as the causes they represent, but all of these parties have one thing in common: their members and leaders want to challenge the major parties because they believe that certain needs and values are not being properly addressed. Third parties name candidates who propose to remedy the situation.

Some third parties have tried to appeal to the entire nation; others have focused on particular regions of the country, states, or local areas. Most third parties have been short-lived. A few, however, including the Socialist Labor Party (founded in 1891) and the Socialist Party (founded in 1901) lasted for a long time. The number and variety of third parties make them difficult to classify, but most fall into one of the general categories discussed in the following subsections.

Issue-Oriented Parties
An issue-oriented third party is formed to promote a particular cause or timely issue. For example, the Free Soil Party was organized in 1848 to oppose the expansion of slavery into the western territories. The Prohibition Party was formed in 1869 to advocate prohibiting the use and manufacture of alcoholic beverages. Most issue-oriented parties fade into history as the issue that brought them into existence fades from public attention, is taken up by a major party, or is resolved.

Some issue-oriented parties endure, however, when they expand their focus beyond a single area of concern. For example, the Green Party USA (the Green Party) was founded in 1972 to raise awareness of environmental issues, but it is no longer a single-issue party. Ralph Nader, the presidential candidate for the Green Party in 2000, campaigned against alleged corporate greed and the major parties' ostensible indifference to a number of issues, including universal health insurance, child poverty, the excesses of globalism, and the failure of the drug war. (For a discussion of the Green Party in the United States and Germany, see this chapter's *Comparative Politics* feature on the following page.)

IDEOLOGY A set of beliefs about human nature, social inequality, and government institutions that form the basis of a political or economic system.

Ideological Parties
As will be discussed in Chapter 8, an **ideology** is a comprehensive set of beliefs about human nature and government institutions. An ideological party supports a particular set of beliefs or political doctrine. For example, a party such as the Socialist Workers Party may believe that our free enterprise system should be replaced by one in which government or workers own all of the factories in the economy. The party's members may feel that competition should be replaced by cooperation and social responsibility so as to achieve an equitable distribution of income. In contrast, an ideological party such as the Libertarian Party may oppose virtually all forms of government interference with personal liberties and private enterprise.

When Theodore Roosevelt did not receive the Republican Party's presidential nomination in 1912, he created the Bull Moose Party (also called the Progressive Party) to promote his platform. (Library of Congress)

Splinter or Personality Parties
A splinter party develops out of a split within a major party. Often this split involves the formation of a party to elect a specific person. For example, when Theodore Roosevelt did not receive the Republican Party's nomination for president in 1912, he created the Bull Moose Party (also called the Progressive Party) to promote his platform. From the Democrats have come Henry Wallace's Progressive Party and the States' Rights (Dixiecrat) Party, both formed in 1948. In 1968, the American Independent Party was formed to support George Wallace's campaign for president.

Most splinter parties have been formed around a leader with a strong personality, which is why they are sometimes called personality parties. When that person steps aside, the party usually collapses. A good example of a personality party is the Reform Party, which was formed in 1996 mainly to provide a campaign vehicle for H. Ross Perot.

comparative politics

The German Greens

Although the Green Party in the United States has only recently attracted national media attention, the Greens have been politically active in Europe for more than two decades. The German Green Party, known as *die Grünen,* was founded in 1979 when more than two hundred environmentalist groups merged to support limits on nuclear energy. They expanded their platform in the 1980s to include demilitarizing Europe and dismantling the North Atlantic Treaty Organization (NATO). In 1983, they won 5.6 percent of the vote, which, in Germany's system of proportional representation, was enough to gain seats in the Bundestag, Germany's legislature.

The German Greens have had to contend with ideological splits within the party. Under the leadership of Joschka Fischer, the German Greens moved more to the center in German politics. In 1998, the Greens won enough votes to be invited to form a coalition government with the Social Democrats. Fischer became Germany's foreign minister, a notion that is unthinkable in the "winner-take-all" system in the United States. In the September 2002 election in Germany, the Greens garnered 8.6 percent of the vote, which translated into 55 seats in the 603-seat Bundestag.

In the United States, a few Green candidates for state offices in 2002 garnered as much as 35 percent of the vote, but that did not win them any seats in their state legislatures. The Green candidate for governor of Maine won 9.3 percent of the vote but was not asked to be part of the new governor's administration. Because Germany has a system of proportional representation, the Greens can win seats in government with a showing of as little as 5 percent at the polls. For the U.S. Green Party, 5 percent for Ralph Nader in 2000 would have resulted in a share of federal campaign funds in 2004, but nothing more.

Foreign Minister Joschka Fischer, the top candidate of the German Green Party, waves to supporters after a speech during a campaign rally in Frankfurt, Germany, in September 2002. (AP Photo/Bernd Kammerer)

For Critical Analysis

Aside from the system of proportional representation in Germany, do you think there are other explanations for why the Green Party has been so much more successful there, and in other European countries, than it has been in the United States?

The Effect of Third Parties on American Politics

Although most Americans do not support third parties or vote for their candidates, third parties have influenced American politics in several ways, some of which we examine here.

Third Parties Bring Issues to the Public's Attention Third parties have brought many political issues to the public's attention. They have exposed and focused on unpopular or highly debated issues that major parties have preferred to ignore. Third parties are in a position to take bold stands on issues that are avoided by major parties because third parties are not trying to be all things to all people. Progressive social reforms such as the minimum wage, women's right to vote, railroad and banking legislation, and old-age pensions were first proposed by third parties. The Free Soilers of the 1850s, for example, were the first true antislavery party, and the Populists and Progressives put many social reforms on the political agenda.

Some people have argued that third parties are often the unsung heroes of American politics, bringing new issues to the forefront of public debate. Some of the ideas proposed by third parties were never accepted, while others were taken up by the major parties as they became more popular.

Third Parties Can Affect the Vote Third parties can influence not only voter turnout but also election outcomes. As you read in the *Perception versus Reality* feature on page 155, third parties have occasionally taken victory from one major party and given it to another, thus playing the "spoiler" role.

For example, in 1912, when the Progressive Party split off from the Republican Party, the result was three major contenders for the presidency: Woodrow Wilson, the Democratic candidate; William Howard Taft, the regular Republican candidate; and Theodore Roosevelt, the Progressive candidate. The presence of the Progressive Party "spoiled" the Republicans' chances for victory and gave the election to Wilson, the Democrat. Without Roosevelt's third party, Taft might have won. Similarly, many commentators contended that Ralph Nader "spoiled" the chances of Democratic candidate Al Gore in the 2000 elections, because many of those who voted for Nader would have voted Democratic had Nader not been a candidate. In fact, to minimize Nader's impact on the vote for Gore, some "vote swapping" was done via the Internet. Voters in states that were solidly in the Gore camp reportedly agreed to vote for Nader, and, in exchange, Nader supporters in closely contested states agreed to cast their votes for Gore.

A significant showing by a minor party also reduces an incumbent party's chances of winning the election, as you can see in Figure 7–3. In 1992, for example, third-party candidate H. Ross Perot captured about 19 percent of the vote. Had those votes been distributed between the candidates of the major parties, incumbent George Bush and candidate Bill Clinton, the outcome of the election might have been different.

Third Parties Provide a Voice for Dissatisfied Americans
Third parties also provide a voice for voters who are frustrated with and alienated from the Republican and Democratic parties. Americans who are unhappy with the two major political parties can still participate in American politics through third parties that reflect their opinions on political issues. Certainly, young Minnesota voters turned out in record numbers during the 1998 elections to vote for Jesse Ventura, a Reform Party candidate for governor in that state. Similarly, Ralph Nader was able to engage young Americans who might never have gone to the polls in 2000 if he had not been a candidate.

One of the most surprising results of the 1998 elections was Jesse Ventura's victory in the Minnesota gubernatorial race. Few thought that Reform Party candidate Ventura (a former professional wrestler known as Jesse "The Body," who was dubbed Jesse "The Mind" during the campaign) had even a slim chance to win the governorship. (Andy King/CORBIS Sygma)

FIGURE 7-3

The Effect of Third Parties on Vote Distribution

In eight presidential elections, a third party's candidate received more than 10 percent of the popular vote—in six of those elections, the incumbent party lost. As shown here, only in 1856 and 1924 did the incumbent party manage to hold on to the White House in the face of a significant third-party showing.

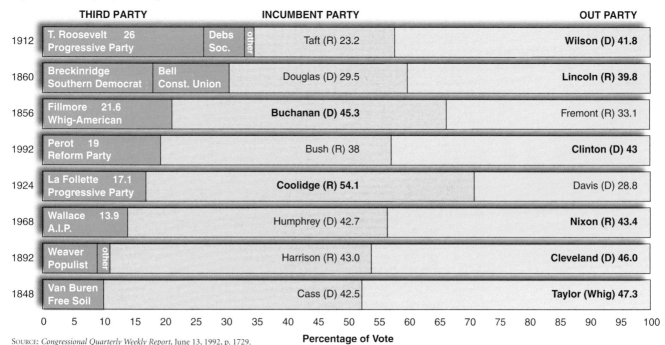

	THIRD PARTY	INCUMBENT PARTY	OUT PARTY
1912	T. Roosevelt 26 Progressive Party / Debs Soc. / other	Taft (R) 23.2	Wilson (D) 41.8
1860	Breckinridge Southern Democrat / Bell Const. Union	Douglas (D) 29.5	Lincoln (R) 39.8
1856	Fillmore 21.6 Whig-American	Buchanan (D) 45.3	Fremont (R) 33.1
1992	Perot 19 Reform Party	Bush (R) 38	Clinton (D) 43
1924	La Follette 17.1 Progressive Party	Coolidge (R) 54.1	Davis (D) 28.8
1968	Wallace 13.9 A.I.P.	Humphrey (D) 42.7	Nixon (R) 43.4
1892	Weaver Populist / other	Harrison (R) 43.0	Cleveland (D) 46.0
1848	Van Buren Free Soil	Cass (D) 42.5	Taylor (Whig) 47.3

0 5 10 15 20 25 30 35 40 45 50 55 60 65 70 75 80 85 90 95 100

Percentage of Vote

SOURCE: *Congressional Quarterly Weekly Report*, June 13, 1992, p. 1729.

State and local parties help their candidates run for office. These 2002 campaign signs in Franklin, Tennessee, are typical. (AP Photo/ Mark Humphrey)

How American Political Parties Are Structured

In theory, each of the major American political parties has a standard, pyramid-shaped organization (see Figure 7–4). This theoretical structure is much like that of a large company, in which the bosses are at the top and the employees are at various lower levels.

Actually, neither major party is a closely knit or highly organized structure. Both parties are fragmented and *decentralized*, which means there is no central power with a direct chain of command. If there were, the national chairperson of the party, along with the national committee, could simply dictate how the organization would be run, just as if it were Microsoft or General Electric. In reality, state party organizations are all very different and are only loosely tied to the party's national structure. Local party organizations are often quite independent from the state organization. There is no single individual or group who gives

FIGURE 7–4

The Theoretical Structure of the American Political Party

The relationship between state and local parties varies from state to state. Further, some state parties resist national party policies.

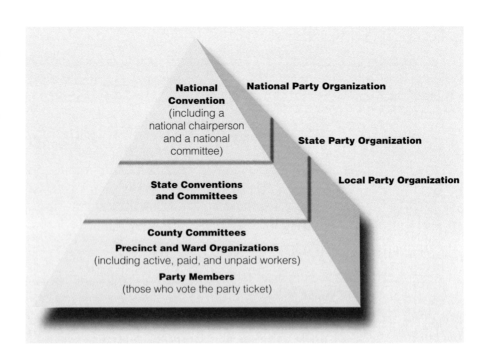

orders to all party members. Instead, a number of personalities, frequently at odds with one another, form loosely identifiable leadership groups.

State and Local Party Organizations

In both the Democratic and Republican parties, state and local party organizations are separate from the national party organizations. Most state and local parties work closely with their national organizations only during major elections.

State Organizations

The powers and duties of state party organizations differ from state to state. In general, the state party organization is built around a central committee and a chairperson. The committee works to raise funds, recruit new party members, maintain a strong party organization, and help members running for state offices.

The state chairperson is usually a powerful party member chosen by the committee. In some cases, however, the chairperson is selected by the governor or a senator from that state.

Local Organizations

Local party organizations differ greatly, but generally there is a party unit for each district in which elective offices are to be filled. These districts include congressional and legislative districts, counties, cities and towns, wards, and precincts.

A **ward** is a political division or district within a city. A **precinct** can be either a political district within a city, such as a block or a neighborhood, or a portion of a rural county. The local, grassroots foundations of politics are formed within voting precincts. Polling places are located within the precincts. Political parties elect or appoint precinct captains or chairpersons who organize the precinct, assist new members, register voters, and take care of party business.

WARD A local unit of a political party's organization, consisting of a division or district within a city.

PRECINCT A political district within a city (such as a block or a neighborhood) or a portion of a rural county; the smallest voting district at the local level.

The National Party Organization

On the national level, the party's presidential candidate is considered to be the leader of the party. In some cases, well-known members of Congress are viewed as national party leaders. In addition to the party leaders, the structure of both parties includes four major elements: the national convention, the national committee, the national chairperson, and the congressional campaign committees.

The National Convention

Most of the public attention that the party receives comes at the **national convention,** which is held every four years during the summer before the presidential election. The news media always cover these conventions, and as a result, they have become quite extravagant. They are often described as the party's national voice and are usually held in major cities.

The national conventions are attended by delegates chosen by the states in various ways. The delegates' most important job is to choose the party's presidential and vice presidential candidates, who together make up the **party ticket.** The delegates also write the party platform, which, as mentioned, sets forth the party's positions on national issues. Essentially, through its platform, the party promises to initiate certain policies if it wins the presidency. Despite the widespread perception that, once in office, candidates can and do ignore these promises, in fact, many of them become law.[17]

NATIONAL CONVENTION The meeting held by each major party every four years to select presidential and vice presidential candidates, to write a party platform, and to conduct other party business.

PARTY TICKET A list of a political party's candidates for various offices.

The National Committee

Each state elects a number of delegates to the **national party committee.** The Republican National Committee and the Democratic National Committee direct the business of their respective parties during the four years between national conventions. The committees' most important duties, however, are to organize the next national convention and to plan how to obtain a party victory in the next presidential election.

NATIONAL PARTY COMMITTEE The political party leaders who direct party business during the four years between the national party conventions, organize the next national convention, and plan how to obtain a party victory in the next presidential election.

The National Chairperson

The party's national committee elects a **national party chairperson** to serve as administrative head of the national party. The chairperson is chosen by the party's presidential candidate at a meeting of the national committee right after the

NATIONAL PARTY CHAIRPERSON An individual who serves as a political party's administrative head at the national level and directs the work of the party's national committee.

Every four years, each major party holds a national convention to nominate the party's presidential and vice presidential candidates. In 2000, the Republican National Convention was held in Philadelphia, and the Democratic National Convention was held in Los Angeles. The first Democratic National Convention was held in 1832 in Baltimore, where it was held every four years thereafter through 1852. The first Republican National Convention was held in 1856 in Philadelphia. Chicago has hosted more national party conventions than any other city. (Left: AP Photo/Laura Rach; Right: AP Photo/Ed Reinke)

national convention.[18] The main duty of the national chairperson is to direct the work of the national committee from party headquarters in Washington, D.C. The chairperson is involved in raising funds, providing for publicity, promoting party unity, recruiting new voters, and other activities. In presidential election years, the chairperson's attention is focused on the national convention and the presidential campaign.

The Congressional Campaign Committee   Each party has a campaign committee, made up of senators and representatives, in each chamber of Congress. Members are chosen by their colleagues and serve for two-year terms. The committees work to help reelect party members to Congress.

Political Parties and Your Everyday Life

In the past, the activities of political parties often had a very direct effect on citizens' everyday lives. In the 1930s, for example, strong party machines dominated local politics in many large cities. In some cities, such as Chicago, the party machine was almost omnipresent. Had you been living in such a city, the party machine would have affected your everyday life. Party machines then bestowed government contracts on loyal supporters. The machines often helped the poor and the unfortunate with gifts of food and clothing (particularly before an election).

Today, there are no real party machines. Nonetheless, political parties do affect your everyday life, if more indirectly. Consider that whichever party has the most members in Congress dominates that institution. Congressional leaders and committee chairs come from the dominant political party. Thus, a particular political party's success can often lead to new laws and regulations that affect your daily life. You may have to pay higher or lower taxes, face more or fewer employment opportunities, or experience changes in the social environment around you. Suppose, for example, that you live in a city with a relatively high and rising crime rate. If a political party that wants to spend more govern-ment resources on crime reduction wins a majority in Congress, your everyday life could be significantly affected.

Similarly, political parties play important roles in state legislatures and governorships. A state legislature controlled by Democrats will create and implement different policies than a legislature controlled by Republicans, and vice versa. These policies could affect the amount of tuition you pay, the amount of state taxes that are withheld from your paycheck, the speed limit on your state's highways, the job opportunities available to you, and so on.

Taking Action

Getting involved in political parties is as simple as going to the polls and casting your vote for the candidate of one of the major parties—or of a third party. If you want to go a step further, you can attend a speech given by a political candidate or even volunteer to assist political parties or specific candidates' campaign activities. In the photo shown here, students at the University of California at Davis took action by attending a campaign speech given by Peter Camejo, the Green Party gubernatorial candidate, prior to the 2002 elections. For a third party candidate, Camejo made a strong showing during the campaigns, although he lost the election. (AP Photo/Steve Yeater)

Key Terms

Chapter Summary

1 A political party is a group of individuals outside the government who organize to win elections, to operate the government, and to determine policy.

2 In the United States, we have a two-party system in which two major parties, the Democrats and the Republicans, vie for control of the government. The two-party system has become entrenched in the United States for several reasons, including election laws and institutional barriers, which make it difficult for third parties to compete successfully against the major parties.

3 Each of the two major parties consists of three components: the party in the electorate, the party organization, and the party in government. Generally, the party organization takes positions on issues facing the nation and outlines them in the party platform. The party in government will attempt to enact policies consistent with the party platform, although this is not mandatory for candidates once they take office.

4 A large number of party members, known as party identifiers, are not actively involved in party politics. A smaller group of actively involved party members, the party elite, carry out the major functions of the party. People join political parties for a variety of reasons, including the desire to express their solidarity with the views of others; to benefit materially from party membership; and to promote political ideas and principles.

5 Political parties link the people's policy preferences to actual government policies, select candidates to run for political office, inform the public about important political issues, coordinate policymaking among the various branches and levels of government, check the power of the party in government (a function of the "out party"), balance competing interests and effect compromises, and run campaigns.

6 In the early years of the nation, the Federalists and the Democratic Republicans vied for power and laid the groundwork for our two-party system. Since 1860, the Democrats and Republicans have been the major parties controlling American government.

7 There are many different kinds of minor parties, or third parties. Some are issue oriented while others are based on ideology. Some third parties form as splinter parties as a result of a split within a major party. Third parties bring political issues to the public's attention, alter election outcomes by gaining votes that would otherwise go to one of the major parties, and provide a voice for dissatisfied voters.

8 In theory, both of the major political parties have a pyramid-shaped organization, with the national committee and national chairperson at the top of the organization and the local party units at the bottom. In practice, the parties are decentralized, and the state and local party organizations work closely with the national organization only during major elections.

9 At the national level, the most public event is the party's national convention, which is held every four years. Delegates from each state choose the party's presidential and vice presidential candidates and write the party platform.

RESOURCES FOR FURTHER STUDY

Selected Readings

Black, Earl, and Merle Black. *The Rise of Southern Republicans.* Cambridge, Mass.: Belknap Press of Harvard University Press, 2002. The authors study the transformation in southern politics since the 1960s. The conservative wing of the Democratic Party had held power in the South since Reconstruction. The election of Ronald Reagan as president in 1980, however, contributed to a political shift in the South and the rise of the Republican Party as representing white southern interests.

Cohen, Jeffrey E., Richard Fleisher, and Paul Kantor, eds. *American Political Parties: Decline or Resurgence?* Washington, D.C.: CQ Press, 2001. This collection of essays examines the role of political parties in democratic governance, as well as recent trends in political partisanship, campaign finance, and party realignments.

Disch, Lisa Jane. *The Tyranny of the Two-Party System.* New York: Columbia University Press, 2002. The author argues that neither the Constitution nor the winner-take-all system need create a two-party system as we know it. Furthermore, the present system impairs democracy. She argues in favor of a system of "electoral fusion," popular in the nineteenth century, in which candidates run on the ballots of both the established party and a third party.

Frymer, Paul. *Uneasy Alliances: Race and Party Competition in America.* Ewing, N.J.: Princeton University Press, 1999. The author, a political scientist at the University of California at Los Angeles, examines the relationship between the two major political parties and African Americans. He concludes that two-party competition for white voters has the effect of excluding African Americans and other minorities from participation in the political process.

Green, John C., and Paul S. Herrnson, eds. *Responsible Partisanship? The Evolution of American Political Parties since 1950.* Lawrence, Kan.: University Press of Kansas, 2003. This collection of articles examines the role of political parties in government and in the electorate, as well as trends in voting behavior and party identification. It focuses on recent changes in laws governing parties and party finance.

InfoTrac Citations

Using your InfoTrac password, access the InfoTrac database at **http://infotrac.thomsonlearning.com**. Once at the site, you can do "key word" searches to locate the following articles, each of which deals with a topic covered in this chapter. The key words to use in your search are indicated in parentheses.

- "On the Road with Ralph Nader" (Green Party Nader)

- "The Continuing Judicial Assault on Patronage" (Patronage City)

- "Mushy Moderates; Budget Politics" (Republican Party)

- "Let's Take Back the Debates!" (Presidential Debates Third Parties)

Politics on the Web

For a list of political sites available on the Internet, sorted by country and with links to parties, organizations, and governments throughout the world, go to **http://www.agora.stm.it/politic/home.htm**

- The Democratic Party is online at **http://www.democrats.org**

- The Republican National Committee is at **http://www.rnc.org**

- The Libertarian Party has a Web site at **http://www.lp.org**

- The Socialist Party's Web site can be accessed at **http://sp-usa.org**

- The Green Party's Web site can be accessed by going to **http://www.greenparty.org**

- For information on the Reform Party, go to its Web site at **http://www.reformparty.org**

Web Resources on Your CD-ROM

On your CD-ROM, you will find Web resources, news articles, Internet activities, and video clips related to the topics in this chapter. Resources related to this chapter include the following:
- **Values Inventory**—Political Ideology: Proportional Representation.
- **Why Does It Matter?**—Contact the Local Chapter of Your Chosen Political Party.
- **Updates**—Keep Up with the Issues in This Chapter!
- **Web Resources**—Internet Activities: A Political Quiz on Proportional Representation; The Case for Proportional Representation.
- **Where Do You Stand?**—Dialogue: Should We Have a Proportional System of Representation?
- **Comparative Politics**—Germany's Green Party.
- **Video**—Conventions.
- **NewsEdge**—Visit This Global Resource for Current Events Related to This Chapter.

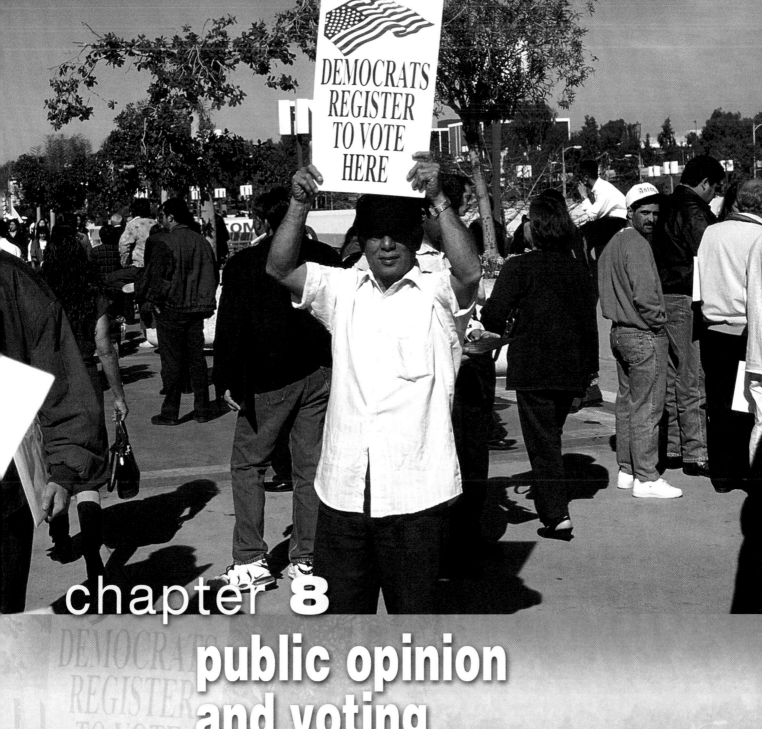

chapter 8

public opinion and voting

CHAPTER OBJECTIVES

After reading this chapter, you should be able to . . .

Explain what public opinion is and how it is measured.

Describe the political socialization process.

Summarize the history of polling in the United States, and explain how polls are conducted, and how they are used in the political process.

Indicate some of the factors that affect voter turnout.

Discuss the different factors that affect voter choices and the various ideologies that comprise the American political spectrum.

175

Is Political Polling Good for Democracy?

Data culled from public opinion polls are used by a variety of groups in America and for a variety of purposes. During political campaigns, opinion polls provide candidates with feedback on how well their images or stances on particular issues meet with public approval. Politicians in office often use surveys to learn the public's views on particular issues. Today, polls are part of our political life and are taken daily on virtually every imaginable issue or topic.

One of the issues over which Americans are at odds is whether our elected representatives should let public opinion dictate government policy. Some believe that government officials should listen closely to the people when forming policy. Others contend that public officials should use their own judgment and that letting public opinion determine policy issues would be bad for democracy.

Elected Officials Should Follow the Will of the People

Many Americans believe that our government representatives, when creating policies, should be guided by the public's views on the issues at hand. If members of Congress have to decide whether to declare war, for example, they should survey the public to see what the people want. After all, a democracy is, at least in theory, a government by the people. Indeed, according to Thomas Jefferson, "The will of the people is the only legitimate foundation of any government." Polls are powerful tools for soliciting information and obtaining feedback from the people. Why, then, shouldn't policymakers solicit feedback, in the form of political polls, from Americans before making important decisions?

This group also points out that the polls themselves indicate that Americans want to participate in policymaking. According to one poll, 94 percent of the respondents believed that the views of the majority of Americans should have a great deal or a fair amount of influence on the decisions of officials in Washington, D.C. More than half of the respondents thought that elected officials should even go against their own knowledge and judgment in favor of what the majority wants.[1]

Clearly, a direct democracy—a type of democracy in which the people participate directly (see Chapter 1)—is unthinkable in a country as large as the United States. Yet polls offer Americans the opportunity to communicate more directly with the president and members of Congress. Our elected representatives should use opinion polls to ensure that their decisions are consistent with the will of the citizenry.

Elected Officials Should Use Their Own Judgment

Other groups contend that elected officials should ignore public opinion polls—for a number of reasons. For one thing, when voters in a district elect a person to represent them in government, they expect that person to have some moral backbone and to make reasonable and sound judgments. They don't want a representative who blindly follows public opinion when making decisions. Clearly, public opinion is not always right or in the interests of the nation. At one time, for example, polls showed that a majority of Americans supported racial segregation. Was segregation therefore a reasonable policy?

Consider also that people responding to questions in opinion polls often have little time to dwell on the questions. Thus, their responses can hardly reflect thoughtful, considered judgments. As one political scientist noted, "Modern polling can give us back only what citizens know the moment the phone rings."[2] Additionally, poll respondents often lack information on particular issues. To base policy decisions on the snap judgments of uninformed respondents would be a mistake.

There is another reason why polls should not drive policy decision making. Simply put, policy choices involve risks and consequences that are not addressed in polls. Any sound decision-making process requires careful evaluation of those risks and consequences. Opinion polls simply do not allow for this type of deliberation.

Where Do You Stand?

1. In your opinion, to what extent should government officials be guided by public opinion polls when forming policy?

2. "Polls are unlikely to be improved enough to help with policy choices." Do you agree with this statement? Why or why not?

Interacting with Your CD-ROM Resources

Use your CD-ROM to access resources on the Web, simulations, participation exercises, and video clips. Important resources related to this chapter include:

- **Values Inventory**—Political Ideology: Political Polling, Good for Democracy?
- **Where Do You Stand?**—Dialogue: Is Political Polling Good for Democracy?
- **Web Resources**—Internet Activities: Using the Internet for Election Forecasting; How to Analyze a Poll.

INTRODUCTION

Many Americans are concerned about the low number of citizens who have turned out to vote during recent elections. After all, if people do not vote, how can their opinions affect public policy? In a democracy, at a minimum, members of the public must form opinions and openly express them to their elected public officials. Only when the opinions of Americans are communicated effectively to elected representatives can those opinions form the basis of government action. As President Franklin D. Roosevelt once said, "A government can be no better than the public opinion that sustains it."

What exactly is "public opinion"? How do we form our opinions on political issues? How can public opinion be measured accurately? What factors affect voter participation? Researchers and scholars have addressed these questions time and again. They are important questions because the backbone of our democracy has always been civic participation—taking part in the political life of the country. Civic participation means many things, but perhaps the most important way that Americans participate in their democracy is through voting—expressing their opinions in the polling places.

What Is Public Opinion?

People hold opinions—sometimes very strong ones—about a variety of issues, ranging from the ethics of capital punishment to the latest trends in fashion. In this chapter, however, we are concerned with only a portion of those opinions. For our purposes here, we define **public opinion** as the views of the citizenry on a particular issue. Public opinion is the sum total of a complex collection of opinions held by many people on issues in the public arena, such as taxes, health care, Social Security, clean-air legislation, unemployment, and so on.

When you hear a news report or read a magazine article stating that "a significant number of Americans" feel a certain way about an issue, you are probably hearing that a particular opinion is held by a large enough number of people to make government officials turn their heads and listen. For example, in 2000, as public opinion surveys showed that Americans were becoming increasingly concerned about education, many politicians, including the two presidential candidates, began taking strong public stances on this issue.

PUBLIC OPINION The views of the citizenry about politics, public issues, and public policies; a complex collection of opinions held by many people on issues in the public arena.

An NBC pollster conducts an interview. Public opinion polls allow us to measure public opinion on a given issue at a given point in time. (Billy E. Barnes/PhotoEdit)

Political socialization starts at a very young age, usually within the family unit. Children also learn about politics and government through such school activities as reciting the Pledge of Allegiance and displaying the American flag. (Mary Kate Denny/PhotoEdit)

POLITICAL SOCIALIZATION A learning process through which most people acquire their political attitudes, opinions, beliefs, and knowledge.

AGENTS OF POLITICAL SOCIALIZATION People and institutions that influence the political views of others.

How Do People Form Political Opinions?

When asked, most Americans are willing to express an opinion on political issues. Not one of us, however, was born with such opinions. Most people acquire their political attitudes, opinions, beliefs, and knowledge through a complex learning process called **political socialization.** This process begins early in childhood and continues throughout the person's life.

Most political socialization is informal, and it usually begins during early childhood, when the dominant influence on a child is the family. Although parents normally do not sit down and say to their children, "Let us explain to you the virtues of becoming a Democrat," their children nevertheless come to know the parents' feelings, beliefs, and attitudes. The strong early influence of the family later gives way to the multiple influences of school, peers, television, co-workers, and other groups. People and institutions that influence the political views of others are called **agents of political socialization.**

The Importance of Family

As just suggested, most parents or guardians do not deliberately set out to form their children's political ideas and beliefs. They are usually more concerned with the moral, religious, and ethical values of their offspring. Yet a child first sees the political world through the eyes of his or her family, which is perhaps the most important force in political socialization. Children do not "learn" political attitudes the same way they learn to master in-line skating. Rather, they learn by hearing their parents' everyday conversations and stories about politicians and issues and by observing their parents' actions. They also learn from watching and listening to their siblings, as well as from the kinds of situations in which their parents place them.

The family's influence is strongest when children clearly perceive their parents' attitudes. For example, in one study, more high school students could identify their parents' political party affiliation than their parents' other attitudes or beliefs. In many situations, the political party of the parents becomes the political party of the children, particularly if both parents belong to the same party.

The Schools and Educational Attainment

Education also strongly influences an individual's political attitudes. From their earliest days in school, children learn about the American political system. They say the Pledge of Allegiance and sing patriotic songs. They celebrate national holidays, such as Presidents' Day and Veterans Day, and learn about the history and symbols associated with them. In the upper grades, young people acquire more knowledge about government and democratic procedures through civics classes and through student government and various clubs. They also learn citizenship skills through school rules and regulations. Generally, those with more education have more knowledge about politics and policy than those with less education. The level of education also influences a person's political values, as will be discussed later in this chapter.

Although the schools have always been important agents of political socialization, many Americans today feel that our schools are not fulfilling this mission. Too many students are graduating from high school with too little knowledge of the American system of government (including the U.S. Constitution—see this chapter's *Perception versus Reality* feature for details). Indeed, in 2000, a majority of Americans ranked education at the top of the list of America's most important problems.

The Media

The **media**—newspapers, magazines, television, radio, and the Internet—also have an impact on political socialization. The most influential of these media is, of course, television. Children in the elementary grades spend an average of thirty-two hours per week watching television—more time than they spend in academic classes. Television does not necessarily decrease the level of information about politics. It is the leading source of political and public affairs information for most people.

Students learn about the political process early on when they participate in class elections. (Michael Newman/PhotoEdit)

MEDIA Newspapers, magazines, television, radio, the Internet, and any other printed or electronic means of communication.

What Do Americans Really Know about the U.S. Constitution?

To be sure, virtually all Americans know that the Constitution is important. But how much do they *really* know about that document? Here, perception and reality differ.

THE PERCEPTION

According to a poll taken by the National Constitution Center, 91 percent of Americans say that the Constitution is important to them, 88 percent are proud of the Constitution, and 77 percent believe that the Constitution matters in their everyday lives. When asked how much they knew about the Constitution, a majority (70 percent) felt that they knew some, quite a bit, or a great deal. The remaining 30 percent claimed to know very little.

THE REALITY

In reality, the majority of those polled in the survey knew very little about the Constitution and the government structure it established. Consider the following findings:

‣ More than half of the respondents did not know the number of senators in Congress (one respondent thought there were seven).

‣ Only 6 percent could name the rights that are guaranteed by the First Amendment.

‣ Over 60 percent could not name all three branches of the federal government (33 percent did not know that there were three branches).

‣ About 35 percent believed that the Constitution mandates English as this country's official language.

‣ Close to 80 percent did not know how many amendments have been added to the Constitution.

‣ Almost 85 percent believed that the Constitution states that "all men are created equal" (thus confusing the Constitution with the Declaration of Independence).

‣ One-third did not know that the first ten amendments are called the Bill of Rights (one respondent thought that they were called the Pledge of Allegiance).

A handful of respondents had various other misconceptions—that the Constitution was written in France, for example, or that only the rights of judges and lawyers are protected by the Constitution.

Significantly, about 90 percent of the respondents had at least a high school education, and 30 percent were college graduates. Moreover, 84 percent felt that if our government system is to work as intended, citizens must be active and informed.

In the early years of this nation, Supreme Court chief justice John Marshall stated, "The people make the Constitution, and the people can unmake it. It is the creature of their own will, and lives only by their will." The question is, can the Constitution live if citizens are unfamiliar with its provisions?

What's Your Opinion?

Should Americans be required to complete an American Government class before being allowed to vote?

Some contend that the media's role in shaping public opinion is increasing to the point at which the media are as influential as the family, particularly among high school students. For example, in her analysis of the media's role in American politics, media scholar Doris A. Graber points out that high school students, when asked where they obtain the information on which they base their attitudes, mention the mass media far more than their families, friends, and teachers.[3]

Other studies have shown that the media's influence on people's opinions may not be as great as was once thought. Generally, people watch television and read articles with preconceived ideas about the issues. These preconceived ideas act as a kind of perceptual screen that blocks out information that is not consistent with those ideas. For example, if you are already firmly convinced that daily meditation is beneficial for your health, you probably will not change your mind if you watch a TV show that asserts that those who meditate live no longer on average than people who do not. Generally, the media tend to wield the most influence over the views of persons who have not yet formed opinions about certain issues or political candidates. (See Chapter 10 for a more detailed discussion of the media's role in American politics.)

Opinion Leaders

Every state or community has well-known citizens who are able to influence the opinions of their fellow citizens. These people may be public officials, religious leaders, teachers, or celebrities. They are the people to whom others listen and from whom others draw ideas and convictions about various issues of public concern. These opinion leaders play a significant role in the formation of public opinion. Martin Luther King, Jr. (1929–1968), for example, was a powerful opinion leader during the civil rights movement.

Opinion leaders often include politicians. Certainly, Americans' attitudes are influenced by the public statements of important government leaders such as the president or secretary of state. Sometimes, however, opinion leaders can fall from grace when they express views radically different from what most Americans believe. For example, in 2002 Senate Republican leader Trent Lott (R., Miss.) expressed an opinion that seemed to approve of America's history of racial segregation. Within two weeks, public disapproval of this opinion forced Lott to resign from his position in the Republican Party leadership, although he continued to serve out his term as senator.

President Bush gestures as he addresses a gathering of religious and charitable leaders on December 12, 2002, in Philadelphia. During his remarks, Bush stated that then Senate Republican leader Trent Lott's comments about the segregated past were "offensive." (AP Photo/George Widman)

Major Life Events

Often, the political attitudes of an entire generation of Americans are influenced by a major event. For example, the Great Depression (1929–1939), the most severe economic depression in modern U.S. history, persuaded many Americans who lived through it that the federal government should step in when the economy is in decline. Many observers then felt that increased federal spending and explicit job-creation programs contributed to the economic recovery. The generation that lived through World War II (1941–1945) tends to believe American intervention in foreign affairs is good. In contrast, the generation that came of age during the Vietnam War (1963–1973) is more skeptical of American interventionism. A national tragedy, such as the terrorist attacks of September 11, 2001, is also likely to influence the political attitudes of a generation of Americans, though in what way is as yet difficult to predict.

Peer Groups

Once children enter school, the views of friends begin to influence their attitudes and beliefs. From junior high school on, the **peer group**—friends, classmates, co-workers, club members, or church group members—becomes a significant factor in the political socialization process. Most of this socialization occurs when the peer group is actively involved in political activities. For example, your political beliefs might be influenced by a peer group with which you are working on a common political cause, such as preventing the clear-cutting of old-growth forests or saving an endangered species. Your political beliefs probably would not be as strongly influenced by peers with whom you snowboard regularly or attend concerts.

Some Americans worry that peer influence, particularly at the high school level, may be a negative agent in the political socialization process because of the increasing hostility among teens to traditional American values and political culture. For example, a recent poll indicates that 35 percent of teens believe that they are under a "great deal" or "some" pressure from their peers to "break the rules." Additionally, 48 percent of teens say they "like to live dangerously"; 48 percent say they like to "shock people"; and 54 percent say that one usually cannot trust people who are in power.[4]

Polls also indicate that a significant number of high school students blame peer influence for the "bad things" that are happening in America, such as school killings. In a survey taken of views on the high school killings in Littleton, Colorado, for example, about 40 percent of the teen-age respondents placed the blame on peer influence, and only 4 percent thought that parents or family were responsible for the violence. (Interestingly, 45 percent of the adults surveyed in the same poll felt that the responsibility for the shootings lay with the parents and family, and none of the parents considered peer influence to be a cause.[5])

PEER GROUP Associates, often those close in age to oneself; may include friends, classmates, co-workers, club members, or church group members. Peer group influence is a significant factor in the political socialization process.

Economic Status and Occupation

A person's economic status may influence her or his political views. For example, poorer people are more likely to favor government assistance programs than wealthier people are. On an issue such as abortion, lower-income people are more likely to be conservative—that is, to be against abortion—than are higher-income groups (of course, there are many exceptions). In general, people in lower economic classes tend to identify with and vote for the Democratic Party.

Where a person works will also affect her or his opinion. Individuals who spend a great deal of time working together tend to be influenced by their co-workers. For example, labor union members working together for a company will tend to have similar political opinions, at least on the issue of government involvement in labor. Individuals working for a nonprofit agency that depends on government funds will tend to support government spending in that area. Business

In general, people in lower economic classes tend to identify with and vote for the Democratic Party. Here, a group of Iowa citizens demonstrate in downtown Des Moines, Iowa, on April 2, 2003, to protest Bush's tax cuts. (AP Photo/Alex Dorgan-Ross)

managers are more likely to favor tax laws favorable to businesses than are people who work in factories. People who work in factories are more likely to favor a government-sponsored, nationwide health-care program than are business executives.

Measuring Public Opinion

If public opinion is to affect public policy, then public officials must be made aware of it. They must know which issues are of current concern to Americans and how strongly people feel about those issues. They must also know when public opinion changes. Of course, public officials most commonly learn about public opinion through election results, personal contacts, interest groups, and media reports. The only relatively precise way to measure public opinion, however, is through the use of public opinion polls.

A **public opinion poll** is a numerical survey of the public's opinion on a particular topic at a particular moment. The results of opinion polls are most often cast in terms of percentages: 62 percent feel this way, 27 percent do not, and 11 percent have no opinion. Of course, a poll cannot survey the entire U.S. population. Therefore, public opinion pollsters have devised scientific polling techniques for measuring public opinion through the use of **samples**—groups of people who are typical of the general population.

PUBLIC OPINION POLL A numerical survey of the public's opinion on a particular topic at a particular moment.

SAMPLE In the context of opinion polling, a group of people selected to represent the population being studied.

Early Polling Efforts

Since the 1800s, magazines and newspapers have often spiced up their articles by conducting **straw polls,** or mail surveys, of readers' opinions. Straw polls try to read the public's collective mind by simply asking a large number of people the same question. Today, many newspapers and magazines still run "mail-in" polls. Increasingly, though, straw polls make use of telephone technology—encouraging people to call "900" numbers, for example—or the Internet. Visitors to a Web page can instantly register their opinion on an issue with the click of a mouse. The problem with straw polls is that the opinions expressed usually represent only a small subgroup of the population, or a **biased sample.** A survey of readers of the *Wall Street Journal* will likely produce different results than a survey of readers of the *Reader's Digest.*

The most famous of all straw-polling errors was committed by the *Literary Digest* in 1936 when it tried to predict the presidential election outcome. The *Digest* had accurately predicted the winning candidates in several earlier presidential elections, but in 1936 the *Digest* predicted that Alfred Landon would easily defeat incumbent Franklin D. Roosevelt. Instead, Roosevelt won by a landslide. The editors of the *Digest* had sent mail-in cards to citizens whose names appeared in telephone directories, to its own subscribers, and to automobile owners—in all, to a staggering 2,376,000 people. In the mid-Depression year of 1936, however, people who owned a car or a telephone or who subscribed to the *Digest* were certainly not representative of the majority of Americans. The vast majority of Americans were on the opposite end of the socioeconomic ladder. Despite the enormous number of people surveyed, the sample was unrepresentative and consequently inaccurate.

STRAW POLL A nonscientific poll; a poll in which there is no way to ensure that the opinions expressed are representative of the larger population.

BIASED SAMPLE A poll sample that does not accurately represent the population.

Several newcomers to the public opinion poll industry, however, did predict Roosevelt's landslide victory. These organizations are still at the forefront of the polling industry today: the Gallup Poll, started by George Gallup; and Roper Associates, founded by Elmo Roper and now known as the Roper Center.

Gallup Poll—Secret Ballot of October 29, 1944. (© Bettmann/CORBIS)

GALLUP POLL—SECRET BALLOT

Please Do Not Sign Your Name

• • •

Mark ☒ before the man you prefer for President.

☐ **Dewey**   ☐ **Roosevelt**

☐ **Thomas**

Polling Today

As you read in the opening *America at Odds* feature, polling is used extensively by political candidates and policymakers today. Politicians and the news media generally place a great deal of faith in the accuracy of poll results. Polls can be remarkably accurate when they are conducted properly. In the last thirteen presidential elections, Gallup polls conducted early in September predicted the eventual winners in ten of the thirteen races. Even polls taken several months in advance have been able to predict the eventual winner quite well. This success is largely the result of careful sampling techniques.

Sampling   Today, most Gallup polls sample between 1,500 and 2,000 people. How can interviewing such a small sample possibly indicate what millions of voters think? Clearly, to be representative of all the voters in the population, a sample must consist of a group of people who are typical of the general population. If the sample is properly selected, the opinions of those in the sample will be representative of the opinions held by the population as a whole. If the sample is not properly chosen, then the results of the poll may not reflect the ideas of the general population.

The most important principle in sampling is randomness. A **random sample** means that each person within the entire population being polled has an equal chance of being chosen. For example, if a poll is trying to measure how women feel about an issue, the sample should include respondents from all groups within the female population in proportion to their percentage of the entire population. A properly drawn random sample, for example, would include appropriate numbers of women in terms of age, racial and ethnic characteristics, occupation, and so on.

RANDOM SAMPLE In the context of opinion polling, a sample in which each person within the entire population being polled has an equal chance of being chosen.

Bias   In addition to trying to secure a random sample, poll takers also want to assure that there is no bias in their polling questions. How a question is phrased can significantly affect how people answer it. For example, consider a question about whether high-speed connections to the Internet should be added to the school library's computer center. One way to survey opinions on this issue is simply to ask, "Do you believe that the school district should provide high-speed connections to the Internet?" Another way to ask the same question is, "Are you willing to pay higher property taxes so that the school district can have high-speed connections to the Internet?" Undoubtedly, the poll results will differ depending on how the question is phrased.

Polling questions also sometimes reduce complex issues to questions that call for simply "yes" or "no" answers. For example, a survey question might ask respondents whether they favor giving aid to foreign countries. A respondent's opinion on the issue might vary, depending on the recipient country or the purpose and type of the aid. The poll would nonetheless force the respondent to give a "yes" or "no" answer that does not necessarily reflect his or her true opinion.

Respondents to such questions sometimes answer " I don't know" or "I don't have enough information to answer," even when the poll does not offer such answers. For example, a study of how polling is conducted on the complex issue of school vouchers (see Chapter 4 for more on this issue) found that about 4 percent volunteered the answer "don't know" when asked if they favored or opposed vouchers. When respondents were offered the option of answering "I haven't heard or read enough to answer," however, the proportion choosing that answer jumped to 33 percent.[6]

Reliability of Polls   In addition to potential bias, poll takers must also be concerned about the general reliability of their polls. Those interviewed may be influenced by the interviewer's personality or tone of voice. They may answer without having any information on the issue, or they may give the answer that they think will please the interviewer. Additionally, any opinion poll contains a **sampling error,** which is the difference between what the sample results show and what the true results would have been had everybody in the relevant population been interviewed.

SAMPLING ERROR In the context of opinion polling, the difference between what the sample results show and what the true results would have been had everybody in the relevant population been interviewed.

Opinion polls of voter preferences cannot reflect rapid shifts in public opinion unless they are taken frequently. During the 2000 presidential election, the media reported extensively on the many polls conducted, with seemingly wild discrepancies. A *Newsweek* poll in mid-September 2000 reported that Al Gore led George W. Bush by a fourteen-point margin. One week later, another *Newsweek* poll found that Gore's lead had been reduced to a margin of just two points. Gallup polls taken during the same period showed Gore leading one day and then, a few days later, showed Bush ahead in the race. Some commentators concluded that the wide swings in the polls simply reflected the fact that many voters—about 30 percent of the

Alabama governor Don Siegelman fills out an exit poll questionnaire after casting his vote in November 2000. During the 2000 elections, miscalls of the Florida vote based on exit polling data ignited a controversy over the use of such polls. (AP Photo/ Dave Martin)

PUSH POLL A campaign tactic used to feed false or misleading information to potential voters, under the guise of taking an opinion poll, with the intent to "push" voters away from one candidate and toward another.

electorate, most of them independents—had not made up their minds. Thus, their opinions were quite volatile, changing from one poll to the next.

Exit Polls   The reliability of polls was also called into question by the use of exit polls in the 2000 election. The Voter News Service (VNS)—a consortium of news networks—conducted polls of people exiting voting booths on election day. These exit polls were used by the news networks to predict the winner of the Florida race—and they were wrong, not just once, but twice. First, they claimed that the Florida vote had gone to Gore. Then, a few hours later, they said it had gone to Bush. Finally, they said the Florida race was too close to call.

These miscalls of the election outcome in Florida caused substantial confusion—and frustration—for the candidates as well as for the voters. They also led to a significant debate over exit polls: Should exit polls be banned, even though they provide valuable information on voter behavior and preferences?

One noticeable difference in the media coverage of the 2002 congressional elections was the lack of exit polls. On election day in 2002, the VNS announced that it would not release exit poll data, stating that it was "not satisfied with the accuracy" of its exit polls. Media outlets were forced to rely more heavily on returns from state election officials, and many close elections were not called until very late that night. In January 2003, the VNS went out of business.

Misuse of Polls   Today, a frequently heard complaint is that, instead of measuring public opinion, polls can end up creating it. For example, to gain popularity, a candidate might claim that all the polls show that he is ahead in the race. People who want to support the winning candidate (rather than the candidate of their choice) may support this candidate despite their true feelings. This is often called the "bandwagon" effect. Presidential approval ratings lend themselves to the bandwagon effect. For more on these types of polls, see this chapter's *The Politics of Homeland Security* feature.

The media also sometimes misuse polls. Many journalists take the easy route during campaigns and base their political coverage almost exclusively on poll findings, with no mention of the chance for bias or the margin of error in the poll. A useful checklist for evaluating the quality of opinion polls is presented in Table 8–1. An increasingly common misuse of polls by politicians is the **push poll,** discussed next. The checklist in Table 8–1 can also help you distinguish between a poll conducted by a legitimate polling organization and a push poll conducted by a political campaign.

TABLE 8–1
Checklist for Evaluating Public Opinion Polls

Because public opinion polls are so widely used by the media and policymakers, and their reliability is so often called into question, several organization have issued guidelines for evaluating polls. Below is a list of questions that you can ask to evaluate the quality and reliability of a poll.

1. Who conducted the poll, and who sponsored or paid for it?

2. How many people were interviewed for the survey, and what part of the population did they represent (for example, registered voters, likely voters, persons over age eighteen)?

3. How were these people chosen (how random was the sample)?

4. How were respondents contacted and interviewed (by telephone, by mail-in survey)?

5. Who should have been interviewed but was not (what was the "nonresponse" rate—people who should have been part of the random sample but who refused to be interviewed, do not have telephones, or do not have listed telephone numbers, for example)?

6. What is the margin of error for the poll (the acceptable margin of error for national polls is usually plus or minus 4 percent)?

7. What questions did the poll ask?

8. In what order were the questions asked?

9. When was the poll conducted?

10. What other polls were conducted on this topic, and do they report similar findings?

The POLITICS of HOMELAND SECURITY

The "Perpetual War Campaign"

Pollsters routinely conduct surveys to gauge a sitting president's popularity among the public. How has President George W. Bush fared in this respect? When he first took office, some doubted that he would be a very popular president. After all, he had not won the popular vote in the 2000 presidential elections. Furthermore, although the Republicans held a slim majority in the House of Representatives, until 2002 the Senate was controlled by the opposition party—the Democrats.

Then came the terrorist attacks of September 11, 2001. The Bush administration declared a "war on terrorism" and provided the leadership the nation sought. Working closely with Congress, the president took steps to devise and implement homeland security strategies. He also launched a military attack against Afghanistan to replace the terrorist-friendly Taliban regime and to destroy al Qaeda terrorist camps. As a result of these actions, President Bush's approval ratings soared. Indeed, they climbed to 90 percent, the highest ratings ever reported in the history of the Gallup poll.

WAR AND PRESIDENTIAL APPROVAL RATINGS

Traditionally, presidents have had widespread public support during times of war or national crises. During such periods, Americans tend to show their patriotism, put aside their political and ideological differences, and stand behind the nation's leader. This support typically has a short life, however. Once the national emergency is over, presidential ratings usually drop considerably.

Consider the first Gulf War in 1991. When Iraq invaded Kuwait, President George H. W. Bush sent U.S. troops to Saudi Arabia to thwart Saddam Hussein's aggression. Bush's approval ratings jumped significantly, ultimately reaching 89 percent. Within a year, however, his ratings fell to 50 percent, and the voters did not reelect him in 1992.

The younger Bush seemed to be suffering a similar fate by the spring of 2002, when his ratings began to drop. Bush's continued emphasis on the war on terrorism and the "national emergency" posed by terrorist threats, however, convinced the public that we remained a nation at war. The administration began to talk about a "preemptive" war against Iraq to quell the threat posed by that nation and its leader, Saddam Hussein. By the spring of 2003, when the second Gulf War was under way, Bush's approval ratings again climbed—to over 70 percent.

A WAR WITH NO END IN SIGHT

The war on terrorism is unlike any previous war in several respects. For one thing, it is a somewhat elusive war. As Robert Reich, former secretary of labor during the Clinton administration, put it, America's goal of "rooting out terrorism on a global level" is not only "breathtaking in scope" but also vague. Who, exactly, are our enemies? Immediately after 9/11, the enemies appeared to be terrorists and countries that harbored them. Prior to the second Gulf War in 2003, however, President Bush

A Marine with the First Marine Division mans a post on a street in the center of Baghdad. Behind the Marine sit the remains of an icon of the fallen Iraqi regime, the pedestal from which a giant Saddam Hussein statue was pulled down by Iraqi citizens and Marines. The First Marine Division and other elements of the First Marine Expeditionary Force secured the capital city less than three weeks into Operation Iraqi Freedom. (U.S. Marine photo by Sergeant Joseph R. Chenelly)

made it clear that our enemies also included any nation caught producing weapons of mass destruction that could be used "to terrorize nations," including the United States.

Even more notable is the fact that there is no obvious end to this war, which Reich has labeled a "permanent war."[7] In 2001, President Bush stated that the war against Afghanistan was "just the beginning" of the war on terrorism. Then came Iraq. What nations might be targeted next for regime change, by military force if need be? At what point can our leaders declare that this war has ended?

Scholars of American government, including Norman Ornstein, have often spoken of the "permanent political campaign." Prior to elections, candidates campaign for office; following elections, incumbents spend a major portion of their time campaigning to retain their offices.[8] Some observers contend that President George W. Bush's permanent political campaign consists of a "permanent war campaign." He has crafted his political image as a wartime president and will likely continue to foster that image through the 2004 elections.

Are We Safer?

During wartime, it is difficult to criticize a sitting president's policies or motives without sounding unpatriotic. How might the lack of any widespread criticism of President Bush's policies

AMERICA at odds

Defining a Push Poll

A relatively recent tactic in political campaigns is to ask "fake" polling questions that are actually designed to "push" voters toward one candidate or another. The use of *push polls* has become so prevalent today that many states are taking steps to ban them. The problem with trying to ban push polls, or even to report accurately on which candidates are using them, is that defining a push poll can be difficult.

The National Council on Public Polls describes push polls as outright political manipulation, the spreading of rumors and lies by one candidate about another. For example, a push poll might ask, "Do you believe the rumor that Candidate A misused campaign funds to pay for a family vacation?" Push pollsters usually do not give their name or identify the poll's sponsor. The interviews last less than a minute, whereas legitimate pollsters typically interview a respondent for five to thirty minutes. Based on these characteristics, it can sometimes be easy to distinguish a push poll from a legitimate poll conducted by a respected research organization.

Some researchers argue that identifying a push poll is not that easy, however. Political analyst Charlie Cook points out that "there are legitimate polls that can ask push questions, which test potential arguments against a rival to ascertain how effective those arguments might be in future advertising. . . . These are not only legitimate tools of survey research, but any political pollster who did not use them would be doing his or her clients a real disservice."[9] Distinguishing between push polls and push questions, then, is sometimes difficult—which is usually the intent of the push pollsters. A candidate does not want to be accused of conducting push polls because the public considers them a "dirty trick" and may turn against the candidate who uses them. In several recent campaigns, candidates have accused each other of conducting push polls—accusations that could not always be proved or disproved. The result has been an increase in public cynicism about opinion polls and the political process in general.

Factors Affecting Voter Turnout

The increasing public cynicism about the political process just described is one factor affecting voter turnout. In the past, legal restrictions, based on income, gender, race, and other factors, limited the number of people who could vote. Today, those restrictions have virtually disappeared, yet voter turnout has remained at the 50 percent level in the last several presidential elections, as you can see in Figure 8–1. Why, when the right to vote is available to more Americans than ever, do so few people choose to exercise that right?

FIGURE 8–1
Voter Turnout since 1964

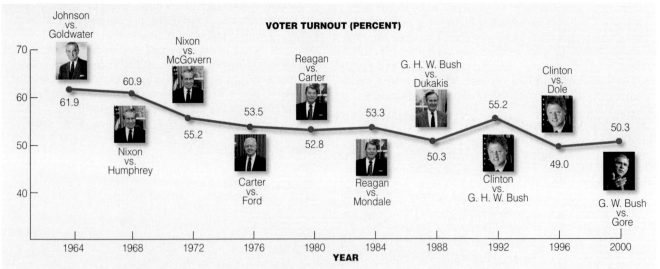

VOTER TURNOUT (PERCENT)

SOURCES: *Statistical Abstract of the United Staters*, various issues; the Committee for the Study of the American Electorate; and authors' udpate.

The Legal Right to Vote

In the United States today, all citizens who are at least eighteen years of age have the right to vote. This was not always true, however. Recall from Chapter 5 that restrictions on *suffrage,* the legal right to vote, have existed since the founding of our nation. Expanding the right to vote has been an important part of the gradual democratization of the American electoral process. Table 8–2 summarizes the major amendments, Supreme Court decisions, and laws that extended the right to vote to various American groups.

Historical Restrictions on Voting

Those who drafted the Constitution left the power to set suffrage qualifications to the individual states. Most states limited suffrage to adult white males who owned property, but these restrictions were challenged early on in the history of the republic. By 1810, religious restrictions on the right to vote were abolished in all states, and property ownership and tax-payment requirements gradually began to disappear as well. By 1850, all white males were allowed to vote. Restrictions based on race and gender continued, however.

The Fifteenth Amendment, ratified in 1870, guaranteed suffrage to African American males. Yet, for most of the next century, African Americans were effectively denied the ability

An African American does his part to "get out the vote" prior to an election. African Americans faced significant restrictions on voting until the 1950s and 1960s, when new laws and policies helped to end both formal and informal barriers to voting for this group. Today, although voter turnout among African Americans is increasing, they remain underrepresented at the polls. (Bob Daemmrich/Sygma/CORBIS)

TABLE 8-2

Extension of the Right to Vote

YEAR	ACTION	IMPACT
1870	Fifteenth Amendment	Discrimination based on race outlawed.
1920	Nineteenth Amendment	Discrimination based on gender outlawed.
1924	Congressional act	All Native Americans given citizenship.
1944	*Smith v. Allwright*	Supreme Court prohibits white primary.
1957	Civil Rights Act of 1957	Justice Department can sue to protect voting rights in various states.
1960	Civil Rights Act of 1960	Courts authorized to appoint referees to assist voter-registration procedures.
1961	Twenty-third Amendment	Residents of District of Columbia given right to vote for president and vice president.
1964	Twenty-fourth Amendment	Poll tax in national elections outlawed.
1965	Voting Rights Act of 1965	Literacy tests prohibited; federal voter registrars authorized in seven southern states.
1970	Voting Rights Act Amendments of 1970	Voting age for federal elections reduced to eighteen years; maximum thirty-day residency requirement for presidential elections; state literacy tests abolished.
1971	Twenty-sixth Amendment	Minimum voting age reduced to eighteen for all elections.
1975	Voting Rights Act Amendments of 1975	Federal voter registrars authorized in ten more states; bilingual ballots to be used in certain circumstances.
1982	Voting Rights Act Amendments of 1982	Extended provisions of Voting Rights Act amendments of 1970 and 1975; allows private parties to sue for violations.

Civil rights protesters, led by Martin Luther King, Jr., march on the road from Selma to Montgomery, Alabama, in March 1965. During the five-day, fifty-mile march, federal troops were stationed every one hundred yards along the route to protect the marchers from violent attacks by segregationists. (AP Photo/Matt Heron/Smithsonian)

LITERACY TEST A test given to voters to ensure that they could read and write and thus evaluate political information; a technique used in many southern states to restrict African American participation in elections.

POLL TAX A fee of several dollars that had to be paid in order to vote; a device used in some southern states to prevent African Americans from voting.

GRANDFATHER CLAUSE A clause in a state law that restricted the franchise to those whose grandfathers had voted; one of the techniques used in the South to prevent African Americans from exercising their right to vote.

to exercise their voting rights. Using methods ranging from mob violence to economic restrictions, groups of white southerners kept black Americans from voting. Some states required those who wished to vote to pass **literacy tests** and to answer complicated questions about government and history before they could register to vote. These tests, however, were not evenly applied to whites and African Americans. The **poll tax,** a fee of several dollars, was another device used to prevent African Americans from voting. At the time, this tax was a sizable burden, not only for most blacks but also for immigrants, small farmers, and the poor generally. Another popular restriction was the **grandfather clause,** which restricted the franchise to those whose grandfathers had voted.

Voting Rights Today   Today, these devices for restricting voting rights are explicitly outlawed by constitutional amendments and by the Voting Rights Act of 1965, as discussed in Chapter 5. Furthermore, the Nineteenth Amendment gave women the right to vote in 1920. In 1971, the Twenty-sixth Amendment reduced the voting age to eighteen.

Some restrictions on voting rights still exist. Every state except North Dakota requires voters to register with the appropriate state or local officials before voting. In the past, many states expected people to appear in person at an official building during normal working hours to register. In 1993, however, Congress passed the National Voter Registration Act (often referred

Suffragists protesting at the White House circa 1910. (Corbis)

A voter in Georgia, right, learns how to use a touch-screen voting machine. For the November 2002 elections, Georgia implemented the $54 million makeover of the state election system, and voters in all 159 counties cast their votes on the touch-screen devices. (AP Photo/Gregory Smith)

to as the Motor Voter Law), which made registration easier. The act requires states to provide all eligible citizens with the opportunity to register to vote when they apply for or renew a driver's license. The law also requires that states allow mail-in registration, with forms given out at certain public-assistance agencies. Since the law took effect on January 1, 1995, it has facilitated millions of registrations.

Residency requirements are also usually imposed for voting. Since 1972, no state can impose a residency requirement of more than thirty days. Twenty-five states require that length of time, while the other twenty-five states require fewer or no days. Another voting requirement is citizenship. Aliens may not vote in any public election held anywhere in the United States. Most states also do not permit prison inmates, mentally ill people, convicted felons, or election-law violators to vote.

Who Actually Votes

Just because an individual is eligible to vote does not necessarily mean that the person will actually go to the polls on election day and vote. Why do some eligible voters go to the polls while others do not? Although nobody can answer this question with absolute conviction, certain factors, including those discussed here, appear to affect voter turnout.

Educational Attainment, Income Level, and Age   Among the factors affecting voter turnout, education appears to be the most important. The more education a person has, the more likely it is that she or he will be a regular voter. People who graduated from high school vote more regularly than those who dropped out, and college graduates vote more often than high school graduates. Differences in income also lead to differences in voter turnout. Wealthy people tend to be overrepresented among regular voters.

Generally, older voters turn out to vote more regularly than younger voters do, although participation tends to decline among the most elderly. Participation likely increases with age because older people tend to be more settled, are already registered, and have had more experience with voting.

Minority Status   Racial and ethnic minorities traditionally have been underrepresented among the ranks of voters. In several recent elections, however, participation by these groups, particularly African Americans and Hispanics, has increased.

Turnout among both African Americans and Hispanics rose significantly in the 1996 elections, but it did not show a further increase in 2000. African American turnout in 2000 held steady at 10 percent of overall turnout, which is identical to the 1996 percentage. Turnout among Hispanics, who constituted 6 percent of the voting electorate in 1996, even decreased somewhat in the 2000 election—to 4 percent. Of course, in absolute terms, the number of Hispanics in the United States has increased. In the years between 1996 and 2000, the majority of newly naturalized citizens in the United States were of Hispanic origin.

AMERICA at odds

Is Low Voter Turnout Really a Problem?

For many, low voter turnout means one thing: a drifting away from a true democracy. After all, they argue, voting is the cornerstone of democracy. The fewer people who vote, the less democratic our government. Furthermore, when fewer people vote, special interest groups have an easier time getting their candidates elected and their agendas passed. What we see is a dominance of the "intensely interested," says Curtis Gans of the Nonpartisan Committee for the Study of the American Electorate. The most motivated voters are those on the political extremes.[10] As long as voter turnout remains low, government policy will continue to steer benefits to the more vocal, better organized, and wealthier groups in our society at the expense of other deserving groups.

Others believe that low voter turnout is not a significant problem. Indeed, these observers argue that low voter turnouts essentially mean that the political situation and system are all right and that there is no need to go to the polls to "change things." Those unconcerned about voter apathy also point out that voting is voluntary. Whatever Americans choose to do is, by definition, acceptable because they are exercising their right to do as they wish. Is that not the essence of a democracy? Would it not be antithetical to our democratic principles to coerce people to vote and perform their "civic duties"?

An issue often left out of the debate over voter turnout is the reliability of the statistics. The category "voting-age population" is calculated by the U.S. Census Bureau. The category excludes military personnel and eligible voters living abroad but includes legal and illegal aliens, those in mental institutions, and convicted felons. Thus, the voting-age population may actually be larger than the population of voting-age individuals eligible to vote.[11]

The question, then, is whether voter turnout is so low as to jeopardize our democracy. Americans remain at odds over this important issue.

Why People Vote as They Do

What prompts some citizens to vote Republican and others to vote Democratic? What persuades voters to choose certain kinds of candidates? Clearly, more is involved than measuring one's own position against the candidates' positions and then voting accordingly. Voters choose candidates for many reasons, some of which are explored here. These questions cannot be answered with absolute certainty, but because of the technology of opinion polling, researchers have collected more information on voting than on any other form of political participation in the United States. These data shed some light on why people decide to vote for particular candidates.

Party Identification

Many voters have a standing allegiance to a political party, or a party identification, although the proportion of the population that does so is shrinking. For established voters, party identification is one of the most important and lasting predictors of how a person will vote. Party identification is an emotional attachment to a party that is influenced by family, age, peer groups, and other factors that play a role in the political socialization process discussed earlier.

Increasingly, there are indications that party identification has lost some of its impact. As we saw in Chapter 7, a growing number of voters now call themselves independents. Despite this label, though, many independents actually do support one or the other of the two major parties quite regularly. Figure 8–2 shows how those who identified themselves as Democrats, Republicans, and independents voted in the 2000 presidential elections.

Perception of the Candidates

Voters' choices also depend on their image of the candidates. Voters often base their decisions more on their *impressions* of the candidates than on the candidates' *actual* qualifications.

To some extent, voter attitudes toward candidates are based on emotions rather than on any judgment about experience or policy. In 2000, for example, voters' decisions in the presidential elections were largely guided by their perceptions of which candidate they could trust to behave with some integrity when in office. The scandals of the Clinton years (1993–2001) certainly had an impact on the voters. In fact, the 2000 exit polls indicated that two out of ten voters voted against Vice President Al Gore not necessarily because they supported George W. Bush, but because they wanted to express their opposition to President Clinton and his administration. Exit polls also showed that honesty ranked as the single most important trait that the voters were seeking in the next president.

Policy Choices

When people vote for candidates who share their positions on particular issues, they are engaging in policy voting. If a candidate for senator in your state opposes gun control laws, for example, and you decide to vote for her for that reason, you have engaged in policy voting.

Historically, economic issues have had the strongest influence on voters' choices. When the economy is doing well, it is very difficult for a challenger, particularly at the presidential level, to defeat the incumbent. In contrast, when the country is experiencing increasing inflation, rising unemployment, or high interest rates, the incumbent will likely be at a disadvantage. Studies of how economic conditions affect voting choices differ in their conclusions, however. Some studies indicate that people vote on the basis of their personal economic well-being, whereas other studies seem to show that people vote on the basis of the nation's overall economic health.

FIGURE 8–2

Party Identification and Voting Behavior in the 2000 Presidential Elections

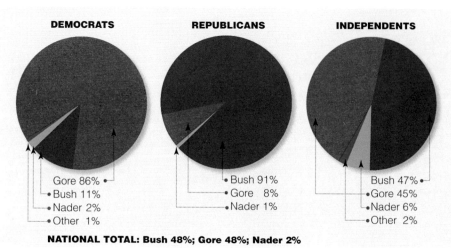

DEMOCRATS

Gore 86%
Bush 11%
Nader 2%
Other 1%

REPUBLICANS

Bush 91%
Gore 8%
Nader 1%

INDEPENDENTS

Bush 47%
Gore 45%
Nader 6%
Other 2%

NATIONAL TOTAL: Bush 48%; Gore 48%; Nader 2%

Source: *The New York Times*, November 12, 2000, Section 4, p. 4.

Some of the most heated debates in American political campaigns involve social issues, such as abortion, gay and lesbian rights, the death penalty, and religion in the schools. In general, presidential candidates prefer to avoid taking a definite stand on these types of issues, because voters who have strong opinions about such issues are likely to be offended if a candidate does not share their views.

Socioeconomic Factors

Some of the factors that influence how people vote can be described as socioeconomic. These factors include a person's educational attainment, income level, age, gender, religion, and geographic location. Some of these factors have to do with the families and circumstances into which individuals are born; others have to do with choices made later in life. Figure 8–3 shows how various groups voted in the 2000 presidential elections.

Educational Attainment   As a general rule, people with more education are more likely to vote Republican, although at the upper levels of educational attainment this pattern breaks down. Typically, those with less education are more inclined to vote for the Democratic nominee.

Occupation and Income Level   Professionals and businesspersons tend to vote Republican. Manual laborers, factory workers, and especially union members are more likely to vote Democratic. In the past, the higher the income, the more likely it was that a person would vote Republican. Conversely, a much larger percentage of low-income individuals voted Democratic. But this pattern is also breaking down, and there are no hard and fast rules. Some very poor individuals are devoted Republicans, just as some extremely wealthy persons are supporters of the Democratic Party.

Age   Although one might think that a person's chronological age would determine political preferences, apparently age does not matter very much. Some differences can be identified, however: young adults tend to be more liberal than older Americans on most issues, and young adults tend to hold more progressive views than older persons on such issues as racial and gender equality.

Although older Americans tend to be somewhat more conservative than younger groups, their greater conservatism may be explained simply by the fact that individuals maintain the values they learn when they first became politically aware. Forty years later, those values may be considered relatively conservative. Additionally, people's attitudes are sometimes shaped by the

Generally, older Americans turn out to vote in far greater numbers than do younger Americans. Here, elderly residents of the Mary Immaculate residential community vote in a function room located near the lobby of the retirement home in Lawrence, Massachusetts, in November 2000. A strong voter turnout was expected at the site, whose residents are mostly retired widows. (AP Photo/Charles Krupa)

FIGURE 8-3

Voting by Groups in the 2000 Presidential Elections

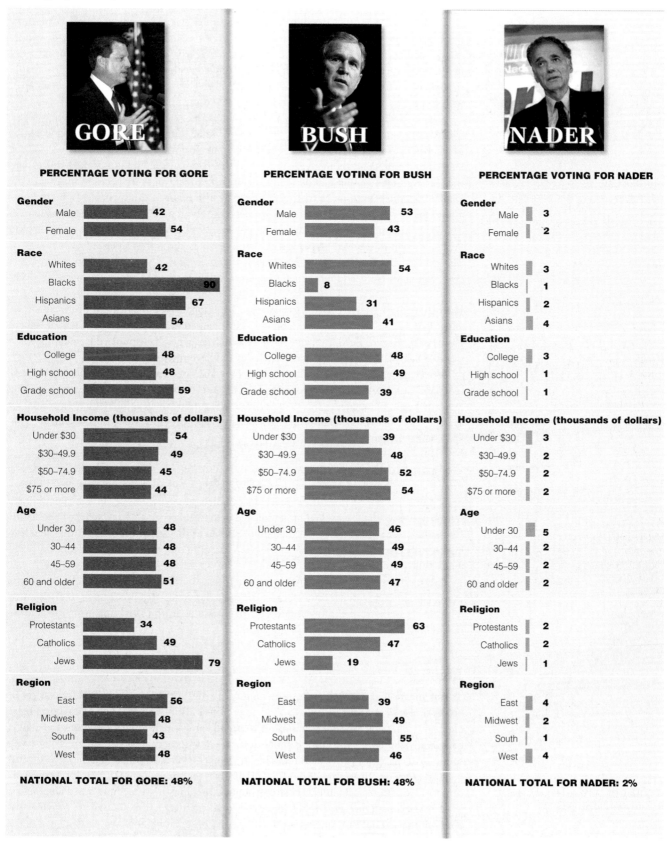

	PERCENTAGE VOTING FOR GORE	PERCENTAGE VOTING FOR BUSH	PERCENTAGE VOTING FOR NADER
Gender			
Male	42	53	3
Female	54	43	2
Race			
Whites	42	54	3
Blacks	90	8	1
Hispanics	67	31	2
Asians	54	41	4
Education			
College	48	48	3
High school	48	49	1
Grade school	59	39	1
Household Income (thousands of dollars)			
Under $30	54	39	3
$30–49.9	49	48	2
$50–74.9	45	52	2
$75 or more	44	54	2
Age			
Under 30	48	46	5
30–44	48	49	2
45–59	48	49	2
60 and older	51	47	2
Religion			
Protestants	34	63	2
Catholics	49	47	2
Jews	79	19	1
Region			
East	56	39	4
Midwest	48	49	2
South	43	55	1
West	48	46	4
NATIONAL TOTAL	**FOR GORE: 48%**	**FOR BUSH: 48%**	**FOR NADER: 2%**

SOURCE: *The New York Times,* November 12, 2000, Section 4, p. 4.

events that unfolded as they grew up. Individuals who grew up during an era of Democratic Party dominance will likely remain Democrats throughout their lives. The same will hold true for those who grew up during an era of Republican Party dominance.

In elections from 1952 through 1980, voters under the age of thirty clearly favored the Democratic presidential candidates. This trend reversed itself in 1984 when voters under thirty voted heavily for Ronald Reagan. George H. W. Bush maintained that support in 1988. In 1992, however, Bill Clinton won back the young voters by 10 percentage points, a margin that expanded to 20 percentage points in 1996. In 2000, the youth vote was fairly evenly split, with 48 percent voting for Al Gore and 46 percent voting for George W. Bush.

Gender

GENDER GAP A term used to describe the difference between the percentage of votes cast for a particular candidate by women and the percentage of votes cast for the same candidate by men.

Until relatively recently, there seemed to be no fixed pattern of voter preferences by gender in presidential elections. One year, more women than men would vote for the Democratic candidate; another year, more men than women would do so. Some political analysts believe that a **gender gap** became a major determinant of voter decision making in the 1980 presidential elections. In that year, Ronald Reagan outdrew Jimmy Carter by 16 percentage points among male voters, whereas women gave about an equal number of votes to each candidate. Although the gender gap has varied since 1980, it reappeared in force in 1996, when President Clinton received 54 percent of women's votes and only 43 percent of men's votes. The gender gap was also significant in 2000, with more women (54 percent) than men (42 percent) voting for Gore, and more men (53 percent) than women (43 percent) voting for Bush.

Religion and Ethnic Background

Traditionally, the majority of Protestants have voted Republican, while Catholics and Jews have tended to be Democrats. Voters of Italian, Irish, Polish, Eastern European, and Slavic descent have generally supported Democrats, while those of British, Scandinavian, and French descent have voted Republican.

African Americans vote principally for Democrats. They have given the Democratic presidential candidate a clear majority of their votes in every election since 1952, although this majority began to weaken in the 1980s. Democratic presidential candidates have received, on average, more than 80 percent of the African American vote since 1956. In 2000, the percentage reached 90 percent.

Geographic Region

SOLID SOUTH A term used to describe the tendency of the southern states to vote Democratic after the Civil War.

Where a voter lives also influences his or her preferences. For more than one hundred years after the Civil War, most white southerners, regardless of background or socioeconomic status, were Democrats. In large part, this is because the Republicans were in power when the Civil War broke out, and many southerners thus blamed the Republicans for that conflict and its results for the South. Known as the **Solid South,** this strong coalition has recently crumbled in the presidential elections, although the rural vote in the South still tends to be Democratic.

Although the Solid South is no more, it appears that something like a Solid Northeast may be emerging, with a strong Democratic majority. Republicans continue to draw much of their strength from the mountain and plains states in the West and from rural areas throughout the country (except in the South).

Ideology

IDEOLOGUE An individual who holds very strong political opinions.

As was mentioned in Chapter 7, some political parties form to support a particular set of beliefs or political doctrine, called an ideology. Voters also sometimes adhere to a particular ideology. Generally, Americans fall into two broad camps with respect to political ideology: conservatives and liberals. The meanings of these terms have changed over the years and will continue to change as political attitudes and ideologies evolve. We know that they fall within a political spectrum that ranges from the far left (extremely liberal) to the far right (extremely conservative). People who hold very strong political opinions are sometimes called **ideologues.** Most Americans, however, are not interested in all political issues and have a mixed set of opinions that do not fit neatly under the liberal or conservative label.

Figure 8–4 illustrates the spectrum of political attitudes and its relationship to the two major American political parties—Democrats and Republicans. As you can see, those with

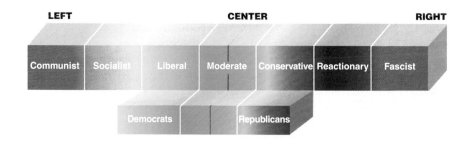

FIGURE 8-4
The Political Spectrum

liberal views tend to identify with and vote for the Democratic Party, whereas those with conservative views tend to identify with and vote for the Republican Party.

Liberalism   Liberals usually believe in such ideals as constitutionally guaranteed civil liberties, political equality, free political competition, and separation of church and state. Modern **liberalism** generally supports the notion that the national government should take an active role in solving the nation's domestic problems. Further, today's liberals feel that the national government must look out for the interests of the individual against the majority. They generally support social-welfare programs that assist the poor and the disadvantaged.

There is a close relationship between those holding liberal views and those identifying themselves politically as Democrats. Keep in mind, though, that not all Democrats share all of the liberal views just discussed. Rather, those with liberal views simply tend to find that on the whole the Democratic Party's positions on issues are more acceptable than those of the Republican Party. Ideology, therefore, is not a perfect indicator of how someone will vote.

Conservatism   Conservatives, as the term implies, seek to conserve tradition and the ways of the past. **Conservatism,** as a political philosophy, thus defends traditional institutions and practices. It places a high value on the principles of community, continuity, law and order, and—in some countries—the preservation of rule by the privileged classes. In the United States, today's conservatives seek to preserve such traditions as states' rights, family values, individual initiative, and free enterprise. They want to minimize government interference in the business affairs of the nation. They believe that the federal government is already too big and should not be expanded further. Indeed, many conservatives believe that the share of annual national income going to government should fall from the current 40 percent to a much lower proportion.

In terms of party affiliation and voting, conservatives tend to identify with the Republican Party. Again, however, you need to be careful about associating the term *conservative* with the Republican Party. Republicans do not constitute a cohesive group that is consistently in favor of a fixed array of political, social, and economic policy prescriptions.

The Political Center   People whose views fall in the middle of the political spectrum are generally called **moderates.** Moderates rarely classify themselves as either liberal or conservative, and they may vote for either Republicans or Democrats. Many moderates do not belong to either major political party and often describe themselves as independents (see Chapter 7).

The Extreme Left and Right   On both ends of the political spectrum are those who espouse radical views. The **radical left** consists of those who would like significant changes to the political order, usually to promote egalitarianism. Often, members of the radical left do not wish to work within the established political processes to reach their goals. They may even accept or advocate the use of violence or overthrowing the government in order to obtain those goals. Socialists believe in equality and, usually, active government involvement in the economy to bring about this goal. Communists believe in total equality and base their beliefs on the political philosophy of Karl Marx (1818–1883).

The **radical right** includes reactionaries, those who wish to turn the clock back to some previous era when there weren't, for example, so many civil rights for the nation's minorities

LIBERALISM A set of political beliefs that includes the advocacy of active government, including government intervention to improve the welfare of individuals and to protect civil rights.

CONSERVATISM A set of beliefs that includes a limited role for the national government in helping individuals, support for traditional values and lifestyles, and a cautious response to change.

MODERATE With regard to political views, a person whose views fall in the middle of the political spectrum.

RADICAL LEFT Persons on the extreme left side of the political spectrum who would like to significantly change the political order, usually to promote egalitarianism.

RADICAL RIGHT Persons on the extreme right side of the political spectrum. The radical right includes reactionaries (who would like to return to the values and social systems of some previous era) and libertarians (who believe in no regulation of the economy and individual behavior, except for defense and law enforcement).

and women. Reactionaries strongly oppose liberal and progressive politics and resist political and social change. Like those on the radical left, members of the radical right may even advocate the use of violence to achieve their goals. A less extreme right-wing ideology is libertarianism. Libertarians believe in virtually total political and economic liberty for individuals and no government regulation of the economy and individual behavior (except for defense and law enforcement).

Ideology as an Indicator of Voting Behavior   A significant percentage of Americans today identify themselves as moderates. Recent polls indicate that 41 percent of Americans consider themselves to be moderates, 18 percent consider themselves liberals, and 41 percent identify themselves as conservatives. Additionally—and somewhat surprisingly—most Americans do not see a relationship between today's issues and political ideology. For example, polling data show that only a small fraction—about 2 percent—of Americans identify either side of the abortion debate with conservatism or liberalism.

For some Americans, then, where they fall in the political spectrum is a strong indicator of how they will vote: liberals vote for Democrats, Greens, or other liberal candidates, and conservatives vote for Republicans, Libertarians, or other conservative candidates. The large numbers of Americans who fall in the political center do not adhere strictly to an ideology. In most elections, the candidates compete aggressively for these voters because they know their "base"—on the left or right—is secure.

In 1949, historian Arthur Schlesinger, Jr., described the position between the political extremes as the **vital center.** The center is vital because, without it, reaching the compromises that are necessary to a political system's continuity may be difficult, if not impossible. As we have already mentioned, voter apathy and low voter turnout are found most commonly among those in the center. That means that the most motivated voters are the "ideologically zealous."[12] The declining number of political moderates in Congress in the mid-1990s seemed to be proof of this trend. President George W. Bush has looked to the vital center for support on many of his policies, but, as you will read in the next chapter, he cannot afford to alienate his base of support on the right as he approaches a reelection campaign in 2004.

VITAL CENTER The center of the political spectrum, or those who hold moderate political views. The center is vital because, without it, it may be difficult, if not impossible, to reach the compromises that are necessary to a political system's continuity.

why does it MATTER?

Voting and Your Everyday Life

For many of you, voting is a civic duty that you must undertake to be a responsible citizen. For others, voting seems to be a waste of time. After all, how much can one vote more or less really matter? Moreover, even if a vote would make a difference, does it matter who is in office?

On both counts, such a cavalier attitude toward voting is misguided. Each vote does count, particularly given the closeness of elections throughout our history. The congressional and presidential elections in 2000 proved that point. The presidency was decided by just several hundred votes in the state of Florida. Several senatorial elections were also decided by very narrow margins, such as the one in Washington State between Maria Cantwell and Slade Gorton.

What a Difference a President Makes

Think about some of the political issues that affect you on a personal level.

- If you are living in a town that depends on logging or mining, if a president declares the surrounding region a national monument and thus out of bounds for such activities, your pocketbook may be affected.
- If you are working, you pay income taxes. In the 2000 campaign, Al Gore proposed a relatively weak tax-reduction program. George W. Bush proposed a more aggressive one and succeeded in putting it into effect in his first year in office. Your after-tax income, and thus your standard of living, was directly affected by this tax cut and will continue to be affected by each and every presidential election.
- Most of us rely on the government to assure that our drinking water and the waterways where we go fishing, boating, or swimming are safe and free of toxic pollution. Vice President Al Gore was well known for his commitment to environmental issues and public health protections. In contrast, George W. Bush was known during the 2000 campaign to favor industry over environmentalists on some issues. In 2002, President Bush's administration proposed a new rule that could allow unlimited amounts of raw animal waste from factory farms to

flow into waterways. If you use or live near waterways that could be polluted, you may be directly affected by the president's regulations.

Taking Action

One of the lessons Americans learned from the 2000 elections is that every vote counts. The 2002 congressional elections reaffirmed this fact. A House seat in Colorado was decided by only 121 votes. The Democrats lost control of the U.S. Senate by just 20,000 votes in two states: Missouri and New Hampshire. Despite these extremely close elections, voter turnout is at record lows. Nationwide, only 76 percent of eligible voters register, and only about 51 percent actually vote. Those numbers are even lower for young voters: only about 45 percent of eligible voters between the ages of 18 and 24 years register, and only about 32 percent vote.

Many groups focus on registration and "get out the vote" efforts targeted at young voters. For example, "Rock the Vote" was formed for the purpose of getting young people involved in political issues. The organization holds concerts and sponsors other activities to "get out the youth vote" prior to elections. In the photo below, two volunteers register Michael Pitts (center) to vote during a "Rock the Vote" concert in Fresno, California, prior to the 2002 elections. (AP Photo/The Fresno Bee, Tomas Ovalle)

Key Terms

agents of political socialization 178

biased sample 182

conservatism 195

gender gap 194

grandfather clause 188

ideologue 194

liberalism 195

literacy test 188

media 179

moderate 195

peer group 181

political socialization 178

poll tax 188

public opinion 177

public opinion poll 182

push poll 184

radical left 195

radical right 195

random sample 183

sample 182

sampling error 183

Solid South 194

straw poll 182

vital center 196

Chapter Summary

1 Public opinion is the views of the citizenry about politics, public issues, and public policies. Most people acquire their political views through a complex learning process called political socialization, which begins early in a person's childhood and continues throughout that person's life.

2 A public opinion poll is a numerical survey of the public's opinion on a particular topic at a particular moment. To achieve the most accurate results possible, pollsters use random samples, in which each person within the entire population being polled has an equal chance of being chosen. Nonetheless, there are many problems with polls.

3 One of the major problems with polls today is the way they are used by politicians and the media. The media frequently neglect to inform the public about a poll's possible bias or margin of error. Politicians use push polls as a campaign tactic to "push" voters toward one candidate and away from another. The public today tends to regard poll taking and poll results with some cynicism.

4 In the early days of this nation, an important factor affecting voter turnout was, of course, the existence of numerous restrictions on voting. These restrictions were based on property, race, gender, religious beliefs, and payment of taxes. Over time, these restrictions were removed (refer back to Table 8–2 on page 187).

5 Currently, there are still some voting restrictions in the form of registration, residency, and citizenship requirements. Even those who meet these requirements do not always turn out at the polls, however. Although the reasons why some people vote and others do not cannot be known with certainty, indications are that voter turnout is affected by specific factors, including educational attainment, income level, age, and minority status.

6 The following factors all influence voters' preferences: party identification, perception of the candidates, policy choices, socioeconomic factors, and ideology. An individual may adhere to a particular ideology, such as liberalism or conservatism, that influences how he or she will vote. Many Americans today consider themselves moderates, however, and candidates compete aggressively for their votes.

RESOURCES FOR FURTHER STUDY

Selected Readings

Alvarez, R. Michael, and John Brehm. *Hard Choices, Easy Answers: Values, Information, and American Public Opinion.* Princeton, N.J.: Princeton University Press, 2002. The authors examine the process of opinion polling in the United States. In particular, they examine how such factors as a respondent's political knowledge and psychological predisposition affect survey responses. They conclude that most often respondents are simply uncertain about how their personal values translate into political opinions.

Baradat, Leon P. *Political Ideologies,* 8th ed. Upper Saddle River, N.J.: Prentice Hall, 2002. Now in its eighth edition, this book gives a broad but clear overview of political ideologies and how they change over time. It is an excellent introduction to the spectrum of political attitudes that have shaped world politics.

Jacobs, Lawrence R., and Robert Y. Shapiro. *Politicians Don't Pander: Political Manipulation and the Loss of Democratic Responsiveness.* Chicago: University of Chicago Press, 2000. The authors exam-ine how and to what degree politicians use public opinion polls when making policy decisions. They conclude that, in fact, politicians generally do not "pander" to public opinion. They make decisions based largely on their own belief but then use polls to determine how to "sell" their policies to the public.

Ornstein, Norman, and Thomas E. Mann, eds. *The Permanent Campaign and Its Future.* Washington, D.C.: American Enterprise Institute; Brookings Institution, 2000. This book examines how political campaigns have become an ongoing process of public relations events. Even after a successful election, office-holders look ahead to the next election, gauging and even manipulating public opinion rather than governing.

InfoTrac Citations

Using your InfoTrac password, access the InfoTrac database at http://infotrac.thomsonlearning.com. Once at the site, you can do "key word" searches to locate the following articles, each of which deals with a topic covered in this chapter. The key words to use in your search are indicated in parentheses.

- "The Last Straw Poll: Seven Things from Campaign 2000 to Eliminate" (Last Straw Poll)

- "When Should You Take a Poll?" (Media Influence Campaigns)

- "The Second Battle for Woman Suffrage: Alabama White Women, the Poll Tax, and V. O. Key's Master Narrative of Southern Politics" (Poll Tax Women)

- "Democratic Lead (Now Only Three Points) in Party Identification Has Declined to a New Low, Says The Harris Poll; Self-Identified Conservatives Now Outnumber Liberals 2-to-1 but Still Trail Moderates" (Party Identification)

Politics on the Web

Recent polls conducted and analyzed by the Roper Center for Public Opinion Research can be found at http://www.ropercenter.uconn.edu

- According to its home page, the mission of the National Election Studies (NES) "is to produce high-quality data on voting, public opinion, and political participation that serves the research needs of social scientists, teachers, students, and policymakers concerned with understanding the theoretical and empirical foundations of mass politics in a democratic society." The NES is a good source of information on public opinion. To reach this site, go to http://www.umich.edu/~nes

- At the Gallup organization's Web site, you can find the results of recent polls as well as an archive of past polls and information on how polls are conducted. Go to

http://www.gallup.com

- You can find further links to poll data and other sources on public opinion at the following site: http://www.publicagenda.org

- The Polling Report Web site provides polling results on a number of issues, organized by topics. The site is easy to use and up to date. Go to http://www.pollingreport.com

- The PBS Democracy Project provides some good tips on how to analyze a poll at the following Web page: http://www.pbs.org/democracy/readbetweenthelines/poll.html

Web Resources on Your CD-ROM

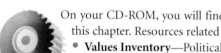

On your CD-ROM, you will find Web resources, news articles, Internet activities, and video clips related to the topics in this chapter. Resources related to this chapter include the following:
- **Values Inventory**—Political Ideology: Political Polling, Good for Democracy?
- **Why Does It Matter?**—Conduct a Poll.
- **Updates**—Keep up with the issues in this chapter!
- **Web Resources**—Internet Activities: Using the Internet for Election Forecasting; How to Analyze a Poll.
- **Where Do You Stand?**—Dialogue: Is Political Polling Good for Democracy?
- **Comparative Politics**—Voter Turnout.
- **Video**—Problems with Polls; Collecting Data.
- **NewsEdge**—Visit this global resource for current events related to this chapter.

chapter 9
campaigns and elections

CHAPTER OBJECTIVES

After reading this chapter, you should be able to . . .

▷ Discuss how candidates are nominated.

▷ Indicate what is involved in launching a political campaign today.

▷ Describe the structure and functions of a campaign organization.

▷ Summarize the laws that regulate campaign financing and the role of money in modern political campaigns.

▷ Explain how elections are held and how the electoral college functions in presidential elections.

Should We Eliminate the Electoral College?

The electoral college has been around as long as the Constitution. Today, the presidential candidate who wins the most popular votes in a state receives all of that state's electoral votes (except in Maine and Nebraska, where electoral votes are awarded proportionately). The candidate who wins a majority of the electoral votes—270 out of the 538 electoral votes—becomes president. The candidate's running mate becomes vice president.

A proposal to eliminate the electoral college was first introduced in Congress in 1797. Over the past two hundred years, there have been more than one thousand proposals in Congress to eliminate or reform the electoral college.

It's Time to Let the People Decide— Abolish the Electoral College

The electoral college, according to its opponents, is an eighteenth-century anachronism. Small and midsize states have a louder voice in selecting a president than they should. Take an example: the twenty-two smallest states together have a smaller population than California has, yet they have nearly twice as many electoral votes.

In any event, a person who has not won the most votes at the polls should not occupy the White House. Anyone who loses the popular contest but wins the presidency due to a majority of electoral votes—as George W. Bush did in 2000—will find it difficult to govern effectively.

Furthermore, the electoral college concept misleads the voters. Before the 2000 elections, how many voters really understood that they were *not* casting their votes directly for a presidential candidate but were voting for a slate of electors instead? To eliminate such confusion in the future, we must eliminate the electoral college.

At the very least, argue the electoral college's detractors, the states could abandon their "winner-take-all" system of awarding electoral votes. The Constitution specifically allows the states to decide how to allocate electoral votes. Maine and Nebraska award electoral votes by congressional district—the winner of each district gets one electoral vote—and then award two "at-large" electoral votes to the winner of the state's popular vote. Thus, electoral votes are allocated more in proportion to the popular vote in those states.

Keep the Status Quo— There Is a Reason behind It

Supporters of the electoral college point to our federal system of government created by the Constitution. The states play an important role in our federal system, and these states, including small states, have rights. The Constitution provides that each state, regardless of size, can send two senators to Congress. The number of each state's electoral votes is determined by the number of that state's representatives in Congress, including senators. The electoral college system is thus weighted in favor of the small states and guarantees that their wishes cannot be ignored.

If we eliminated the electoral college, presidential candidates could even more easily ignore the small states. Because the candidates do not have unlimited budgets or time, they would probably not bother to campaign in the smaller states but would concentrate their efforts on states with large populations.

According to Alan Natapoff of the Massachusetts Institute of Technology, the electoral college offers yet another benefit: the current state-by-state, winner-take-all system makes close elections more likely. Candidates have to appeal for every vote, so each voter's influence increases. According to Natapoff, the electoral college system forces candidates to reach beyond their core constituencies to other interest groups and organizations.[1]

Finally, argue some constitutional scholars, the small states will never ratify a constitutional amendment abolishing the electoral college. The system is here to stay, and the best we can do is better educate voters on how it works.

Where Do You Stand?

1. Does it really matter that a candidate who loses the popular vote may nonetheless become president because of the electoral college? Why or why not?

2. Do you have less respect for a president who was elected without winning the most popular votes? If so, why? If not, why not?

Interacting with Your CD-ROM Resources

Use your CD-ROM to access resources on the Web, simulations, participation exercises, and video clips. Important resources related to this chapter include:

■ **Values Inventory**—Political Ideology: Should We Eliminate the Electoral College?
■ **Where Do You Stand?**—Dialogue: Should We Abandon the Electoral College?
■ **Web Resources**—Internet Activities: In Defense of the Electoral College; A Detailed Analysis of How the Electoral College Works.

INTRODUCTION

Electoral college voting is the final step in a long process in which candidates compete to become the president of this nation. During elections, other candidates also struggle to become representatives of the people—in Congress or in state offices. The population of the United States is now close to 285 million. Clearly, all voting-age citizens cannot gather in one place to make laws and run the government. We have to choose representatives to govern the nation and act on behalf of our interests. We accomplish this through popular elections.

Campaigning for election has become an arduous task for every politician. As you will see in this chapter, American campaigns are long, complicated, and very expensive undertakings. They can also be wearing on the citizens who are not running for office. Yet they are an important component of our political process because it is through campaigns that citizens learn about the candidates and decide how they will cast their votes.

How We Nominate Candidates

The first step on the long road to winning an election is the nomination process. Nominations narrow the field of possible candidates and limit each political party's choice to one person. In the past, self-nomination was the most common way to become a candidate, and this method is still used in small towns and rural sections of the country. A self-proclaimed candidate usually files a petition to be listed on the ballot. Each state has laws that specify how many signatures a candidate must obtain to show that he or she has some public support. An alternative is to be a write-in candidate—voters write the candidate's name on the ballot on election day.

Serious candidates for most offices are rarely nominated in these ways, however. As you read in Chapter 7, most candidates for high office are nominated by a political party and receive considerable support from party activists throughout their campaigns.

Party Control over Nominations

George Washington was essentially unopposed in the first election in 1789—no other candidate was seriously considered in any state. But many of the Constitution's framers wondered how candidates would be nominated after Washington. Most envisioned that candidates would simply "stand" for election, rather than actively run for office. Instead of shaking hands and making speeches, they would stay on their farms and wait for the people's call, as Washington did. Some framers believed that the electors of the electoral college would put forward candidates' names.

By the end of Washington's eight years in office, however, political divisions among the nation's leaders had solidified into political parties, the Federalists and the Democratic Republicans (see Chapter 7). Party leaders recognized that the ability to choose nominees was essential to their political power. Beginning in 1797, they began to hold congressional conferences, later called **caucuses**,[2] to nominate candidates in secret. The voters at large played no part in choosing nominees.

By the presidential race of 1824, the caucus method of nomination had become a controversial issue. Andrew Jackson and other presidential candidates who felt that the caucus was undemocratic derisively referred to the system as "King Caucus." Faced with rising opposition, party leaders were forced to find other methods of nominating candidates. As the caucus system faded away in presidential politics, its use diminished at the state and local levels as well.

The Party Nominating Convention

As the use of the caucus method diminished around the country, it was replaced in many states by party conventions. A **nominating convention** is an official meeting of a political party to choose its candidates and to select **delegates**—persons sent to a higher-level party

CAUCUS A meeting held by party leaders to choose political candidates. The caucus system of nominating candidates was eventually replaced by nominating conventions and, later, by direct primaries.

NOMINATING CONVENTION An official meeting of a political party to choose its candidates. Nominating conventions at the state and local levels also select delegates to represent the people of their geographic areas at a higher-level party convention.

DELEGATE A person selected to represent the people of one geographic area at a party convention.

convention to represent the people of one geographic area. For example, delegates at a local party convention would nominate candidates for local office and would also choose delegates to represent the party at the state convention. By 1840, the convention system had become the most common way of nominating candidates for government offices at every level.

Little by little, criticism of the corruption in nominating conventions at the state level caused state legislatures to disband most of them. They are still used in some states, including Connecticut, Delaware, Michigan, and Utah, to nominate candidates for some state offices. At the national level, the convention is still used to select presidential and vice presidential candidates.

The Direct Primary and Loss of Party Control

DIRECT PRIMARY An election held within each of the two major parties—Democratic and Republican—to choose the party's candidates for the general election.

In most states, direct primaries gradually replaced nominating conventions. A **direct primary** is an election held within each of the two major parties—Democratic and Republican—to pick its candidates for the general election. This is the method most commonly used today to nominate candidates for office.

Most states require the major parties to use a primary to choose their candidates for the U.S. Senate and the House, for the governorship and all other state offices, and for most local offices as well. A few states, however, use different combinations of nominating conventions and primaries to pick candidates for the top offices. Although the primaries are *party* nominating elections, they are closely regulated by the states. The states set the dates and conduct the primaries. The states also provide polling places, election officials, registration lists, and ballots, in addition to counting the votes.

The advent of the direct primary has meant some loss of party control over the nominating process. As you will read shortly, state laws have created different types of primaries across the country, though they generally fall into two broad categories: closed primaries and open primaries. Open primaries allow voters to vote for a party's candidates even if they do not belong to that party. As open primaries have become more common, the nominating process has become less party centered and more candidate centered.

CLOSED PRIMARY A primary in which only party members can vote to choose that party's candidates.

Closed Primaries

In a **closed primary,** only party members can vote to choose that party's candidates, and they may vote only in the primary of their own party. Thus, only registered Democrats can vote in the Democratic primary to select candidates of the Democratic Party. Only registered Republicans can vote for the Republican candidates. A person usually

These boxes are full of voter information booklets that were prepared for the March 5, 2002, Los Angeles County primary election. There were several hundred different versions of the pamphlet, which was used by voters in different parties and geographic areas. (AP Photo/Reed Saxon)

establishes party membership when she or he registers to vote. Some states have a *semiclosed* primary, which allows voters to register with a party or change their party affiliations on election day. Regular party workers favor the closed primary because it promotes party loyalty. Independent voters oppose it because it excludes them from the nominating process.

Open Primaries

An **open primary** is a direct primary in which voters can vote for a party's candidates regardless of whether they belong to the party. In most open primaries, all voters receive both a Republican ballot and a Democratic ballot. Voters then choose either the Democratic or the Republican ballot in the privacy of the voting booth. In a *semiopen* primary, voters request the ballot for the party of their choice.

OPEN PRIMARY A primary in which voters can vote for a party's candidates regardless of whether they belong to the party.

Blanket and Nonpartisan Primaries

Some states have a "wide-open" primary, or **blanket primary,** in which each voter receives a single ballot listing each party's candidates for each nomination. Voters may choose candidates from different parties. Thus, for example, a voter might choose a Democratic candidate for governor but a Republican candidate for senator, or vice versa.

BLANKET PRIMARY A "wide-open" primary in which each voter receives a single ballot listing each party's candidates for each nomination.

Washington adopted the blanket primary in 1935, and for many years it was the only state to have one. More recently, this form of primary was adopted in Alaska and then, by a 1996 ballot initiative, in California. These states are in the process of devising a different type of primary to use in future elections, however, due to a recent United States Supreme Court ruling. Political parties in California had challenged the 1996 law in court, arguing that the law violated the parties' First Amendment rights of association. In June 2000, the Supreme Court ruled in favor of the political parties,[3] thus invalidating the California blanket primary. In 2002, however, a federal court ruling allowed the state of Washington to continue holding its blanket primaries. Alaska recently enacted legislation that adopted the open primary model.

Louisiana is unique in that all candidates run in the same, nonpartisan primary election. Figure 9–1 shows which states have closed (or semiclosed), open (or semiopen), blanket, or nonpartisan primaries.

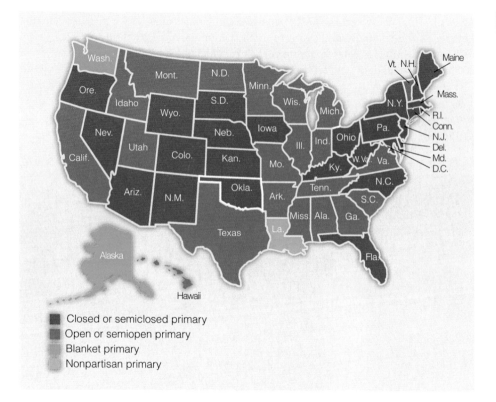

FIGURE 9-1
Types of Direct Primaries

■ Closed or semiclosed primary
■ Open or semiopen primary
■ Blanket primary
■ Nonpartisan primary

Nominating Presidential Candidates

In some respects, being nominated for president is more difficult than being elected. The nominating process narrows a very large number of hopefuls down to a single candidate from each party. Choosing a presidential candidate is unlike nominating candidates for any other office. One reason for this is that the nomination process combines several different methods.

Presidential Primaries
The majority of the states hold presidential primaries, beginning early in the election year. For a candidate, a good showing in the early primaries results in plenty of media attention as television networks and newspaper reporters play up the results. Subsequent state primaries tend to serve as contests to eliminate unlikely candidates.

State legislatures and state parties make the laws that determine how the primaries are set up, who may enter them, and who may vote in them. Several different methods of voting are used in presidential primaries. In some states, for example, primary voters only select delegates to a party's national convention and do not know which candidates the delegates intend to vote for at the convention. In other states, the voters cast ballots for candidates, and the delegates must vote for the winning candidate at the national convention.

In some states, delegates to the national convention are chosen through caucuses or conventions instead of through presidential primaries. Iowa, for example, holds caucuses to choose delegates to local conventions. These delegates, in turn, choose those who will attend the state and national conventions. Other states use a combination of caucuses and primaries.

Primaries—The Rush to Be First
In an effort to make their primaries prominent in the media and influential in the political process, many states have moved the date of their primary to earlier in the year. This "front-loading" of the primaries started after the 1968 Democratic National Convention in Chicago, which appeared to be ruled by a few groups. Then, in 1988, southern states created "Super Tuesday" by holding most of their primaries on the same day in early March. Recently, many states in the Midwest, New England, and the Pacific West (including California) have moved their primaries to an earlier date, too. If this trend continues, we may eventually have a one-day national primary.

The practice of front-loading primaries gained a momentum of its own in the last decade. The states with later primary dates found that most nominations were decided early in the season, leaving their voters out of the action. As more states moved their primary dates up, however, the more important the early primaries became. Sometimes, the political parties try to manipulate primary dates to maximize their candidates' media attention. For example, in 2000 several Republican state primaries were held between the New Hampshire primary and "Super Tuesday," a period when no Democratic events were held. The Republican candidates consequently dominated the news during that time. The order and timing of primary dates also influence the candidates' fund-raising.

Democratic candidate Al Gore and Republican candidate Senator John McCain of Arizona at work in New Hampshire several months before the February 2000 primary election in that state. Traditionally, a candidate who had a successful showing in the New Hampshire primary had time to obtain enough financial backing to continue in the race, become known to the voters through political advertising, and so on. Today, given the shortened primary season, a successful showing in New Hampshire is less significant than it once was. (Left: AP Photo/Jim Cole; Right: AP Photo/Stephan Sevoia)

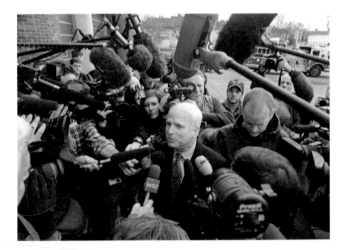

Some Americans worry that with a shortened primary season, long-shot candidates will no longer be able to propel themselves into serious contention by doing well in small, early-voting states, such as New Hampshire or Iowa. Traditionally, for example, a candidate who had a successful showing in the New Hampshire primary had time to obtain enough financial backing to continue in the race. The candidate also had time to become known to the voters through political advertising, TV appearances, and campaign speeches along the campaign trail. With the shortened primary season, the winners will be those candidates who can start their fund-raising early and load up on national TV spots. The fear is that an accelerated schedule of presidential primaries will likely favor the richest candidates.

National Party Conventions　　Born in the 1830s, the American national political convention is unique in Western democracies. Elsewhere, candidates for prime minister or chancellor are chosen within the confines of party councils. That is actually the way the framers wanted it done—the Constitution does not mention a nominating convention. Indeed, Thomas Jefferson loathed the idea. He feared that if the presidential race became a popularity contest, it would develop into "mobocracy."

The 2000 Republican National Convention, held in Philadelphia July 31–August 3, 2000. (AP Photo/ Ron Edmonds)

The 2000 Democratic National Convention, held in Los Angeles August 14–17, 2000. (AP Photo/ Ron Edmonds)

At one time, the conventions were indeed giant free-for-alls. It wasn't clear who the winning presidential and vice presidential candidates would be until the delegates voted. As more states opted to hold primaries in which candidates ran and delegates were selected, the drama of national conventions diminished. Today, the conventions have been described as giant pep rallies. Nonetheless, each convention's task remains a serious one. In late summer or early fall, two to three thousand delegates gather at each convention to represent the wishes of the voters and political leaders of their home states. They adopt the official party platform and declare their support for the party's presidential and vice presidential candidates.

CREDENTIALS COMMITTEE A committee of each national political party that evaluates the claims of national party convention delegates to be the legitimate representatives of their states.

On the first day of the convention, delegates hear the reports of the **Credentials Committee,** which inspects each prospective delegate's claim to be seated as a legitimate representative of her or his state. When the eligibility of delegates is in question, the committee decides who will be seated. In the evening, there is usually a keynote speaker to whip up enthusiasm among the delegates. The second day includes committee reports and debates on the party platform. The third day is devoted to nominations and voting. Balloting begins with an alphabetical roll call in which states and territories announce their votes. By midnight, the convention's real work is over and the presidential candidate has been selected. The vice presidential nomination and the acceptance speeches occupy the fourth day.

During the 2000 conventions, many Americans complained that the conventions had become little more than giant infomercials. Convention activities were highly staged events. Even so-called impromptu moments seem to have been well prepared. Furthermore, the major news networks have cut their convention coverage dramatically since the 1980s. In view of these developments, some Americans question whether the conventions serve any purpose at all.

AMERICA at odds

Do National Conventions Serve Any Purpose Today?

The budget for the Democratic National Convention in 2004, which will be held in Boston's Fleet Center, is expected to exceed $49 million—including $400,000 for balloons and ticker tape and $231,000 for janitors to sweep it up afterward.[4] But for what purpose? Forty-five percent of Americans reported that they watched little or none of the television coverage of either party's convention in 2000.[5] Do the conventions even merit significant TV coverage?

Yes, according to political commentator George F. Will. Will argues that a well-scripted political convention is "the meticulous expression of the party's thinking" and an important part of the process of persuading voters to support the party's candidates.[6] Tom Johnson, chair of CNN, makes a similar argument. Johnson contends that even though the conventions are largely contrived, they offer a valuable perspective on the parties, the policies they represent, and their candidates—all important information for the voters. Furthermore, consider what is at stake in selecting a president. The winner will have the power to launch nuclear weapons, make decisions that influence war and peace, and shape policy through presidential appointments, such as to the Supreme Court.[7]

Others argue that the conventions today are simply fund-raising stunts, giving the major political parties a chance to reward contributors and ask for more money. Interest groups—corporations and lobbyists—are the first ones asked to pay the high price tag of the convention. Interest groups thus increase their access to the candidates and their influence on the party's platform. Everything that goes on at the conventions is considered "party building" and is therefore exempt from campaign-financing regulations (these regulations will be discussed shortly). With the 2004 conventions, the question of whether national party conventions serve any meaningful purpose for voters will likely be raised again.

The Modern Political Campaign

Once nominated, candidates focus on their campaigns. The term *campaign* originated in the military context. Generals mounted campaigns, using their scarce resources (soldiers and materials) to achieve military objectives. Using the term in a political context is apt. In a political campaign, candidates also use scarce resources (time and money) in an attempt to defeat their adversaries in the battle to win votes.

To run a successful campaign, the candidate's campaign staff must be able to raise funds for the effort, get media coverage, produce and pay for political ads, schedule the candidate's time effectively with constituent groups and potential supporters, convey the candidate's position on the issues, conduct research on the opposing candidate, and get the voters to go to the polls. When party identification was stronger and TV campaigning was still in its infancy, a strong party organization on the local, state, or national level could furnish most of the services and expertise that the candidate needed. Less effort was spent on advertising a single candidate's position and character because the party label communicated that information to many of the voters.

Today, party labels are no longer as important as they once were. In part, this is because fewer people identify with the major parties, as evidenced by the rising number of independent voters (see Chapter 7). Instead of relying so extensively on political parties, candidates now turn to professionals to manage their campaigns.

The Professional Campaign Organization

With the rise of candidate-centered campaigns in the past two decades, the role of the political party in managing campaigns has declined. Professional **political consultants** now manage nearly all aspects of a presidential candidate's campaign, and most candidates for governor, the House, and the Senate also rely on consultants. Political consultants generally specialize in a particular area of the campaign, such as researching the opposition, conducting polls, developing the candidate's advertising, or organizing "get out the vote" efforts. Nonetheless, most candidates have a campaign manager who coordinates and plans the

POLITICAL CONSULTANT A professional political adviser who, for a large fee, works on an area of a candidate's campaign. Political consultants include campaign managers, pollsters, media advisers, and "get out the vote" organizers.

President Bush walks with his long-time political consultant and senior adviser Karl Rove, left, on March 1, 2002, as they leave the White House. (AP Photo/Ron Edmonds)

CAMPAIGN STRATEGY The comprehensive plan for winning an election developed by a candidate and his or her advisers. The strategy includes the candidate's position on issues, slogan, advertising plan, press events, personal appearances, and other aspects of the campaign.

campaign strategy. Figure 9–2 shows a typical presidential campaign organization. As this figure also indicates, the political party continues to play an important role in recruiting volunteers and getting out the vote.

A major development in contemporary American politics is the focus on reaching voters through effective use of the media, particularly television. (For example, examine the types of campaign ads aired during the 2002 Georgia Senate race, discussed in this chapter's *The Politics of Homeland Security* feature.) At least half of the budget for a major political campaign is consumed by television advertising. The media consultant is therefore a pivotal member of the campaign staff. The nature of political advertising is discussed in more detail in Chapter 10. How candidates obtain the money needed to pay for advertising, consultants, and other campaign costs is discussed next.

What It Costs to Win

The modern political campaign is an expensive undertaking. Huge sums must be spent for professional campaign managers and consultants, television and radio ads, the printing of campaign literature, travel, office rent, equipment, and other necessities. To get an idea of the cost of waging a campaign for Congress today, consider that the average winning House campaign in 2002 cost $840,000. The average winning Senate campaign cost much more—on average, $7.2 million.

FIGURE 9–2

A Typical Presidential Campaign Organization

Most aspects of a candidate's campaign are managed by professional political consultants, as this figure illustrates.

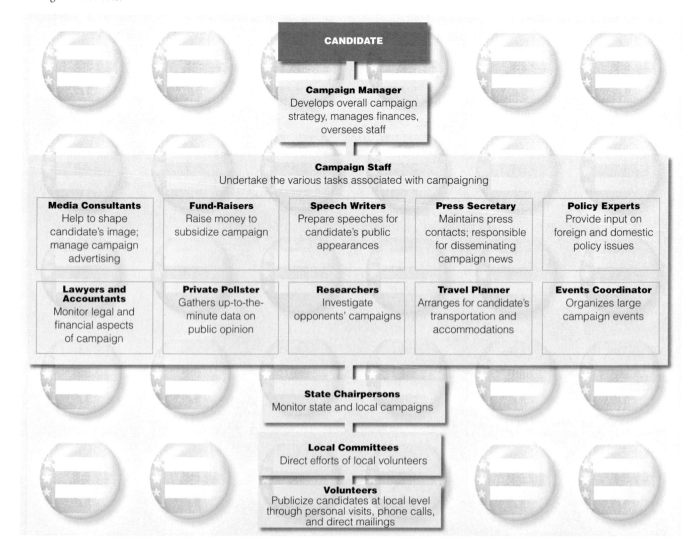

CANDIDATE

Campaign Manager
Develops overall campaign strategy, manages finances, oversees staff

Campaign Staff
Undertake the various tasks associated with campaigning

Media Consultants Help to shape candidate's image; manage campaign advertising	**Fund-Raisers** Raise money to subsidize campaign	**Speech Writers** Prepare speeches for candidate's public appearances	**Press Secretary** Maintains press contacts; responsible for disseminating campaign news	**Policy Experts** Provide input on foreign and domestic policy issues
Lawyers and Accountants Monitor legal and financial aspects of campaign	**Private Pollster** Gathers up-to-the-minute data on public opinion	**Researchers** Investigate opponents' campaigns	**Travel Planner** Arranges for candidate's transportation and accommodations	**Events Coordinator** Organizes large campaign events

State Chairpersons
Monitor state and local campaigns

Local Committees
Direct efforts of local volunteers

Volunteers
Publicize candidates at local level through personal visits, phone calls, and direct mailings

The POLITICS of HOMELAND SECURITY

Terrorist Attacks and Attack Ads

The midterm elections in 2002 were the first major elections since the terrorist attacks of September 11, 2001. Although he wasn't running for reelection himself, President George W. Bush made the war on terrorism a major campaign issue. He also personally campaigned on behalf of many Republican candidates.

A CLOSE RACE TURNED UGLY

A key Republican goal in 2002 was to retake the Senate. Democrats held the Senate by a margin of 51 to 49, and Republicans saw Senator Max Cleland, the Democratic incumbent in Georgia, as vulnerable. Nonetheless, as election day neared, Cleland held a slight lead over his opponent, Republican Saxby Chambliss, a member of the House of Representatives who was challenging Cleland for the Senate seat. Not surprisingly in such a close race, both campaigns turned to *attack ads*, which, as you will read in Chapter 10, are ads that attack the character of an opposing candidate. What is surprising in the Georgia race, however, is that Cleland, a Vietnam veteran who lost both legs and an arm in the war, was attacked as weak on national security.

In October 2002, Chambliss began running ads that accused Cleland of blocking President Bush's bill to create the Department of Homeland Security. Chambliss's campaign managers even used images of Osama bin Laden and Saddam Hussein in ads attacking Cleland's voting record. The reality was that Cleland supported the Democrats' alternative homeland security bill, but this distinction was difficult to communicate in thirty-second television ads. Cleland enlisted the help of fellow Georgia Senator Zell Miller to answer the attacks with ads of his own. In one, Miller stated, "It's disgraceful for anybody to question Max Cleland's commitment to our national security. Max Cleland is my hero."

EVEN SEPTEMBER 11 VICTIMS WEIGHED IN

Families of those killed in the September 11 terrorist attacks formed interest groups following the attacks to lobby the government on issues ranging from victim compensation to safety codes for skyscrapers. They have also gotten into the campaign business. On October 30, 2002, a coalition of September 11 family groups ran ads in several Georgia newspapers attacking Saxby Chambliss for opposing, as chairman of the House Subcommittee on Terrorism and Homeland Security, the creation of an independent commission to study intelligence mistakes before the attacks. In an "Open Letter to Saxby Chambliss from 9/11 Families," four September 11 family groups argued that "the independent commission [is] vitally needed in the war on terrorism. . . . We want to prevent other families from suffering the loss our families have had to endure. We ask you to set politics aside and act in the best interests of the nation."[8]

Although the newspaper ads received some attention from the national media, they did little to influence the election. Chambliss defeated Cleland and helped the Republicans take control of the Senate. Most commentators agreed that Chambliss's attack ads severely eroded Cleland's support in the weeks before the election.

Are We Safer?

Neither Democrats nor Republicans can afford to appear "weak" on homeland security because they would then be vulnerable to campaign attack ads that resonate with voters. How do you think this political fact might influence the war on terrorism?

Presidential campaigns are even more costly. In 1992, Americans were stunned to learn that about $550 million had been spent in the presidential campaigns. In 1996, presidential campaign expenditures rose even higher, to about $600 million. In 2000, they climbed to $800 million, making the 2000 presidential campaigns the most expensive in history.

Clearly, money matters in determining success at the polls. In the 2002 elections, for example, candidates who outspent their opponents generally emerged victorious in the House and Senate races.[9]

The connection between money and campaigns gives rise to some of the most difficult challenges in American politics. The biggest fear is that campaign contributors may be able to influence people running for office by giving large gifts or loans. Another possibility is that some special interest groups will try to buy favored treatment from those who are elected to office. In an attempt to prevent these abuses, the government regulates campaign financing.

The Federal Election Campaign Act (FECA)

Congress passed the Federal Election Campaign Act (FECA) of 1971[10] in an effort to curb irregularities and abuses in the ways political campaigns were financed. The 1971 act placed no limit on overall spending but restricted the amount that could be spent on mass media advertising, including television. It limited the amount that candidates and their families could contribute to their own campaigns and required disclosure of all contributions and expenditures in excess of $100. In principle, the 1971 act limited the role of labor unions and corporations in political campaigns. Also in 1971, Congress passed a law that provided for a $1 checkoff on federal income tax returns for general campaign funds to be used by major-party presidential candidates. This law was first applied in the 1976 campaign. (Since then, the amount of the checkoff has been raised to $3.)

Amendments in 1974   The 1971 act did not go far enough, however. Amendments to the act passed in 1974 essentially did the following:

- *Created the Federal Election Commission (FEC) to administer and enforce the act's provisions.*
- *Provided public financing for presidential primaries and general elections.* Presidential candidates who raise some money on their own in at least twenty states can get funds from the U.S. Treasury to help pay for primary campaigns. For the general election campaign, presidential candidates receive federal funding for almost all of their expenses if they are willing to accept campaign-spending limits.
- *Limited presidential campaign spending.* Any candidate accepting federal support must agree to limit expenditures to amounts set by federal law.
- *Required disclosure.* Candidates must file periodic reports with the FEC that list who contributed to the campaign and how the money was spent.
- *Limited contributions.* Individuals can contribute up to $1,000 to each candidate in each federal election or primary. The total limit for any individual in one year is $25,000. Groups can contribute a maximum of $5,000 to a candidate in any election.

Buckley v. Valeo   In a significant 1976 case, *Buckley v. Valeo*,[11] the Supreme Court declared unconstitutional the provision in the 1971 act that limited the amount each individual could spend on his or her own campaign. The Court held that a "candidate, no less than any other person, has a First Amendment right to engage in the discussion of public issues and vigorously and tirelessly to advocate his own election."

The Rise of PACs   The FECA allows corporations, labor unions, and special interest groups to set up *political action committees* (PACs) to raise money for candidates. For a PAC to be legitimate, the money must be raised from at least fifty volunteer donors and must be given to at least five candidates in the national elections. PACs can contribute up to $5,000 per candidate in each election, but there is no limit on the total amount of PAC contributions during an election cycle. As discussed in Chapter 6, the number of PACs has grown significantly since the 1970s, as have their campaign contributions. In the 2002 election cycle, about 36 percent of campaign funds spent on House races came from PACs.[12]

Skirting the Campaign-Financing Rules

The money spent on campaigns has been rising steadily for decades. Spending during the 2000 campaigns, though, marked a major leap—it was about twice what it had been in 1996. In all, candidates spent an estimated $3 billion on presidential and congressional races and $1 billion or more on state contests. Where does all this money come from? The answer is that individuals and corporations have found **loopholes**—legal ways of evading certain legal requirements—in the federal laws limiting campaign contributions.

LOOPHOLE A legal way of evading a certain legal requirement.

Soft Money   The biggest loophole in the FECA and its amendments was that they did not prohibit individuals or corporations from contributing to political *parties*. Many contributors would make donations to the national parties to cover the costs of such activities as registering voters, printing brochures and fliers, advertising in the media (which often means running candidate-oriented ads), campaigns to "get out the vote," and fund-raising events.

Contributions to political parties, instead of to particular candidates, are referred to as **soft money** because, as one observer said, they are "so squishy." Although soft money clearly was used to support the candidates, it was difficult to track exactly where the money was going.

Although this loophole had existed since the passage of a 1979 amendment to the federal election laws, it was little known or used until the 1990s (see Figure 9–3). By 2000, though, the use of soft money had become standard operating procedure, and the parties raised nearly $463 million through soft money contributions. Soft dollars became the main source of campaign money in the presidential race, far outpacing PAC contributions and federal campaign funds. In both 1996 and 2000, the political parties and their interest group allies went to great lengths to skirt the laws that were put on the books in the 1970s.

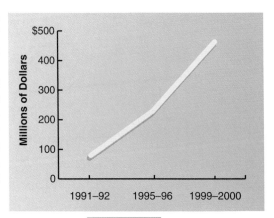

FIGURE 9-3
The Growth in Soft Money Contributions

Independent Expenditures   Another major loophole in campaign-financing laws was that they did not prohibit corporations, labor unions, and special interest groups from making **independent expenditures** in an election campaign. Independent expenditures, as the term implies, are expenditures for activities that are independent from (not coordinated with) those of the candidate or a political party. In other words, as we discussed in Chapter 6, interest groups can wage their own "issue" campaigns as long as they do not go so far as to say "Vote for Candidate X." The problem is, where do you draw the line between advocating a position on a particular issue, such as abortion (which a group has a right to do under the First Amendment's guarantee of freedom of speech), and contributing to the campaign of a candidate who endorses that position?

In addressing this thorny issue, the United States Supreme Court has developed two determinative tests. Under the first test, a group's speech is a campaign "expenditure" only if it explicitly calls for the election of a particular candidate. Using this test, the courts repeatedly have held that interest groups have the right to advocate their positions. For example, the Christian Coalition has the right to publish voter guides informing voters of candidates' positions. The second test applies when a group or organization has made expenditures explicitly for the purpose of endorsing a candidate. Such expenditures are permissible unless they were made in "coordination" with a campaign. According to the Supreme Court, an issue-oriented group has a First Amendment right to advocate the election of its preferred candidates as long as it acts independently.

In 1996, the Supreme Court held that these guidelines apply to expenditures by political parties as well. Parties may spend money on behalf of candidates if they do so independently—that is, if they do not let the candidates know how, when, or for what the money was spent.[13] As critics of this decision have pointed out, parties generally work closely with candidates, so establishing the "independence" of such expenditures is problematic.

SOFT MONEY Campaign contributions that are made to political parties, instead of to particular candidates.

INDEPENDENT EXPENDITURE An expenditure for activities that are independent from (not coordinated with) those of a political candidate or a political party.

The Bipartisan Campaign Reform Act of 2002

Demand for further campaign-finance reform had been growing for several years, but in 2000 a Republican presidential candidate, John McCain, made it one of the cornerstones of his campaign. McCain competed aggressively against George W. Bush in the Republican presidential primaries, and his continued popularity after he lost the Republican nomination forced Congress to address the issue in 2001. A series of corporate scandals, including the bankruptcies of Enron and WorldCom, both of which had been large campaign contributors, also kept campaign-finance reform in the public eye.

Forcing incumbent political leaders to address campaign-finance reform is one of the most difficult tasks in government. Most elected officials came to power under the existing laws. They recognize that setting tighter limits and closing loopholes could hurt their reelection bids in the future. Nonetheless, in 2002, Congress passed and the president signed the Bipartisan Campaign Reform Act.

Changes under the New Law   The most significant change imposed by the 2002 law was to ban the large, unlimited contributions to national political parties known as soft

Campaign-finance reform proponent Senator John McCain, (R., Ariz.), speaks at a rally on Capitol Hill on March 20, 2002, following a cloture vote on campaign-finance reform. (AP Photo/Dennis Cook)

money. The law also regulates the use of campaign ads paid for by interest groups. Such issue advocacy is now prohibited within thirty days of a primary election or sixty days of a general election.

The 2002 act increased the amount an individual can contribute to a federal candidate from $1,000 to $2,000. The amount that an individual can give to all federal candidates was raised from $25,000 per year to $95,000 over a two-year election cycle. Individuals can still contribute to state and local parties, so long as the contributions do not exceed $10,000 per year per individual. The new law went into effect on November 6, 2002.

Constitutional Challenges to the New Law

Soon after the 2002 act was passed, several groups filed lawsuits challenging the constitutionality of its provisions. Supporters of the restrictions on campaign ads by special interest groups argue that the large amounts of funds spent on these ads create an appearance of corruption in the political process. In contrast, an attorney for the National Rifle Association (NRA), one of the plaintiffs claiming that the provision unconstitutionally restricts free speech, argues that because the NRA represents "millions of Americans speaking in unison . . . [it] is not a *corruption* of the democratic political process; it *is* the democratic political process."[14]

Those who drafted the law anticipated the constitutional challenges and included a provision in the law to expedite the legal process. The lawsuits go first to a three-judge panel of the U.S. District Court for the District of Columbia and then directly to the United States Supreme Court. Free speech issues will probably dominate the court debate.

Campaign Contributions and Policy Decisions

Considering the passion on both sides of the debate about campaign-finance reform, one might wonder how much campaign contributions actually influence policy decisions. Table 9–1 lists the top twenty industries and other groups contributing to both parties in the 2002 election cycle. These contributors must want something in return for their dollars, but what, exactly, does the money buy? Do these donations influence government policymaking?

Clearly, there is no reason to conclude that a member of Congress who received X dollars from certain groups while campaigning for Congress will vote differently on policy issues than she or he would otherwise vote. After all, many groups make contributions not so much to influence a candidate's views as to ensure that a candidate whose views the group supports will win the elections.

Many groups routinely donate to candidates from both parties so that, regardless of who wins, the groups will have access to the officeholder. Note that some of the groups listed in Table 9–1 contributed to both parties. Not surprisingly, campaign contributors find it much easier than other constituents to get in to see politicians or get them to return phone calls. Because politicians are more likely to be influenced by those with whom they have personal contacts, access is important for those who want to influence policymaking. The real question is whether money also buys votes.

TABLE 9-1

Top Industries and Other Groups Contributing Funds in the 2002 Election Cycle

This table lists the top twenty contributors during the 2002 election cycle.

RANK	INDUSTRY/GROUP	AMOUNT	TO DEMOCRATS	TO REPUBLICANS
1	Lawyers/Law Firms	$87,535,952	74%	26%
2	Retired	$73,702,456	37%	63%
3	Real Estate	$55,467,560	49%	51%
4	Securities/Invest.	$53,525,303	48%	52%
5	TV/Movies/Music	$46,094,726	83%	17%
6	Health Professionals	$36,685,402	38%	62%
7	Insurance	$34,342,171	30%	70%
8	Leadership PACs	$29,304,867	43%	57%
9	Pharm./Health Prod.	$24,935,877	24%	75%
10	Public-Sector Unions	$24,394,109	93%	6%
11	Computer Equip./Svcs.	$23,791,324	49%	51%
12	Oil & Gas	$22,667,199	20%	80%
13	Business Services	$20,137,740	45%	54%
14	Electric Utilities	$19,370,827	33%	67%
15	Bldg. Trade Unions	$18,873,390	92%	8%
16	Commercial Banks	$18,723,997	36%	63%
17	Industrial Unions	$17,374,078	99%	1%
18	Misc. Mfg./Distrib.	$16,982,910	24%	76%
19	General Contractors	$15,523,880	30%	70%
20	Telephone Utilities	$13,924,394	40%	60%

SOURCE: Center for Responsive Politics, 2003.

AMERICA at odds

Does Money Buy Votes?

Several "watchdog" groups are devoted to discovering whether campaign contributions directly affect how legislators vote. The Center for Responsive Politics (**http://www.opensecrets.org**) is one such group. In a special section of its Web site entitled "Tracking the Payback," the center examines key legislation before Congress, the groups and industries that stand to benefit from it, the congressional committees overseeing it, and the campaign contributors to those committees' members. The Center focuses primarily on research and statistics rather than conclusions, however.

Charles Lewis, a former journalist, concludes that Congress has been "bought" by special interests. He supports his conclusions with hundreds of examples, from gun control legislation to prescription drug laws.[15] Another journalist, Jeffrey H. Birnbaum, opens his recent book with the following statement: "Almost everyone who works in official Washington eventually has what can be described as the Moment: that instant when they finally realize that money plays too big a role in politics, way too big." Birnbaum then explains how money is the grease that keeps the wheels of D.C. politics in motion. The relationship between campaign donors and politicians, says Birnbaum, is part of "a deeply ingrained system that's as difficult to fix as it is horrific to behold."[16]

Political scientists and academicians tend to make fewer generalizations, however. Political scientist Jeff Fox points out that, by and large, members of Congress vote along party lines. Additionally, public opinion plays an important role in many policy debates, and few politicians will defy public opinion and lose potential voters to accommodate a campaign donor's wishes. Also, politicians often receive donations from different groups, making it difficult to please all groups if their wishes happen to conflict. According to Fox, money is most likely to influence policymaking decisions when the public is inattentive to an issue, when there is little competition from opposing groups, when the politician personally benefits from a contribution, and in some other particular circumstances. Generally, while not discounting the importance of money in the nation's capital, Fox believes that votes are influenced by contributions far less often than Americans think.[17]

How We Elect Candidates

The drama surrounding the 2000 presidential elections probably caused Americans to learn more than they ever wanted to know about the election process in this country. The focus on the Florida vote taught citizens about the significance of balloting procedures, types of voting equipment, county election boards, state election laws, and state officials in the elective process. Even the courts became involved, and ultimately the Supreme Court cast the deciding "vote" on who would be our next president. (Foreigners were also engaged in the events taking place in the United States—see this chapter's *Comparative Politics* feature for details.)

Types of Elections

GENERAL ELECTION A regularly scheduled election to elect the U.S. president, vice president, and senators and representatives in Congress; general elections are held in even-numbered years on the first Tuesday after the first Monday in November.

The ultimate goal of the political campaign and the associated fund-raising efforts is, of course, winning the election. The most familiar kind of election is the **general election**, which is a regularly scheduled election held in even-numbered years on the first Tuesday after the first Monday in November. During general elections, the voters decide who will be the U.S. president, vice president, and senators and representatives in Congress. The president and vice president are elected every four years, senators every six years, and representatives every two years. General elections are also held to choose state and local government officials, often at the same time as those for national offices. A **special election** is held at the state or local level when the voters must decide an issue before the next general election or when vacancies occur by reason of death or resignation.

SPECIAL ELECTION An election that is held at the state or local level when the voters must decide an issue before the next general election or when vacancies occur by reason of death or resignation.

Types of Ballots

AUSTRALIAN BALLOT A secret ballot that is prepared, distributed, and counted by government officials at public expense; used by all states in the United States since 1888.

Since 1888, all states in the United States have used the **Australian ballot**—a secret ballot that is prepared, distributed, and counted by government officials at public expense. Two variations of the Australian ballot are used today. Most states use the **party-column ballot** (also called the Indiana ballot), which lists all of a party's candidates together in a single column under the party label. In some states, the party-column ballot allows voters to vote for all of a party's candidates for local, state, and national offices by making a single "X" or pulling a single lever. The major parties favor this ballot form because it encourages straight-ticket voting.

PARTY-COLUMN BALLOT A ballot (also called the Indiana ballot) that lists all of a party's candidates under the party label; voters can vote for all of a party's candidates for local, state, and national offices by making a single "X" or pulling a single lever.

Other states use the **office-block ballot**, which lists together all of the candidates for each office. Politicians tend to dislike the office-block ballot because it places more emphasis on the office than on the party and thus encourages split-ticket voting.

OFFICE-BLOCK BALLOT A ballot that lists together all of the candidates for each office.

Conducting Elections and Counting the Votes

Recall from Chapter 8 that local units of government, such as cities, are divided into smaller voting districts, or precincts. State laws usually restrict the size of precincts, and local officials set their boundaries. Within each precinct, voters cast their ballots at one polling place.

POLL WATCHER A representative from one of the two major political parties who is allowed to monitor a polling place to make sure that the election is run fairly and to avoid fraud.

A precinct election board supervises the polling place and the voting process in each precinct. The board sets hours for the polls to be open according to the laws of the state and sees that ballots or voting machines are available. In most states, the board provides the list of registered voters and makes certain that only qualified voters cast ballots in that precinct. When the polls close, the board counts the votes and reports the results, usually to the county clerk or the board of elections. Representatives from each party, called **poll watchers**, are allowed at each polling place to make sure the election is run fairly and to avoid fraud.

Elections in Great Britain

Understandably, the foreign media had some fun with the American 2000 presidential elections. After all, here was the leading democratic nation of the world tied up in electoral knots. Why didn't the candidate who won the most popular votes become president? What is this electoral college? Where is it? British journalists, in particular, had a field day. Yet do the British have a better system?[18]

In a way, it is hard to compare British and U.S. elections because of the different government structures. Britain is a constitutional monarchy. There, a hereditary, unelected monarch (the queen) is the head of state and fills a largely ceremonial role. The real head of government is the prime minister, who is the leader of the party in power in Parliament. In the United States, in contrast, these roles are combined—the president is both head of state and chief executive.

BRITISH ELECTIONS

In British elections, which are held at intervals of not more than five years, the people do not vote directly for the prime minister but for members of Parliament. Actually, they vote for members of the House of Commons, the lower chamber of Parliament (the upper chamber, the House of Lords, is not elective; it also has relatively few powers). As in the United States, the elections are party based. Whichever party wins the most seats in Parliament is the controlling party, and that party's leader normally becomes the prime minister.

The candidate who wins the most votes in a district, even if only by a very small margin, becomes the representative for the entire district. Thus, it is possible—and has happened on occasion—that the party winning the most popular votes will not end up with the most seats in Parliament. This is similar to the situation that occurs in the United States when a presidential candidate wins most of the popular votes but does not gain the majority of the electoral college votes.

NO AUTOMATIC RECOUNTS OR DELAYS

Although there are some similarities, U.S. and British elections also have some significant differences. Unlike the United States, Britain has no laws calling for automatic recounts when the vote is close, nor can a candidate demand a recount. Whether a

Britain's prime minister Tony Blair and his wife, Cherie, leave a polling station close to his official Downing Street residence after casting their votes on May 2, 2002, in the local council elections. Some 22 million people across the country were entitled to vote in what was the biggest test of public opinion since Blair's general election landslide in 2001. (AP Photo/Stefan Rousseau, POOL)

recount will be conducted is left to the discretion of the local "returning officer" in charge of the voting. If a losing candidate believes that voting fraud or serious irregularities occurred, however, she or he can take that claim to court. If the claim is proved, there are two options: the elections can be ruled invalid and new elections held; or the candidate who won as a result of the vote fraud can be disqualified and replaced in Parliament by the candidate who came in second.

In the 2000 elections in the United States, delays in tallying the votes occurred in several states while waiting for absentee ballots to arrive. In Britain, people are allowed to send absentee ballots, but the ballots must arrive on election day. British law also allows persons who are unable to go to the polls on election day to appoint a proxy to vote in their stead.

For Critical Analysis

Should the states in this country require that all absentee ballots be returned by election day?

Presidential Elections and the Electoral College

As you read in the chapter-opening *America at Odds* feature, when voters vote for president and vice president, they are not voting directly for the candidates. Instead, they are voting for **electors** who will cast their ballots in the **electoral college.** The electors are selected during each presidential election year by the states' political parties, subject to the laws of the state. Each state has as many electoral votes as it has U.S. senators and representatives (see Figure 9–4 on the next page). In addition, there are three electors from the District of Columbia. The

ELECTOR A member of the electoral college.

ELECTORAL COLLEGE The group of electors who are selected by the voters in each state to officially elect the president and vice president. The number of electors in each state is equal to the number of that state's representatives in both chambers of Congress.

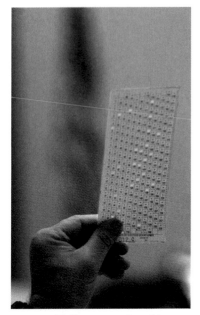

Contested ballots are reviewed in Florida after the November 2000 elections. (Left: Amy E. Conn/AP Photo; Right: Victor R. Caivano/AP Photo)

WINNER-TAKE-ALL SYSTEM A term used to describe the system used in most states of awarding all of the state's electoral votes to the candidate who receives the largest popular vote in that state.

electoral college system is a **winner-take-all system,** in which the candidate who receives the largest popular vote in a state is credited with all that state's electoral votes. The only exceptions are Maine and Nebraska, as discussed in the chapter-opening feature.

Electoral College Voting In December, after the general election, electors (either Democrats or Republicans, depending on which candidate won the state's popular vote) meet in their state capitals to cast their votes for president and vice president. When the Constitution was drafted, the framers intended for the electors to use their own discretion in deciding who would make the best president. Today, however, the electors usually vote for the candidates who won popular support in their states. The electoral college ballots are then sent to the Senate, which counts and certifies them before a joint session of Congress held early in January. The candidates who receive a majority of the electoral votes are officially declared president and vice president. To be elected, a candidate must receive more than half of the 538

FIGURE 9–4

Electoral Votes in the 2000 Presidential Elections

This distorted map shows the relative weight of the states with respect to the number of electoral votes each state cast in the 2000 presidential elections. Not surprisingly, during presidential campaigns, the candidates try to maximize their chances at winning the elections by making frequent appearances in California, New York, Texas, Florida, and other states that have large numbers of electoral votes.

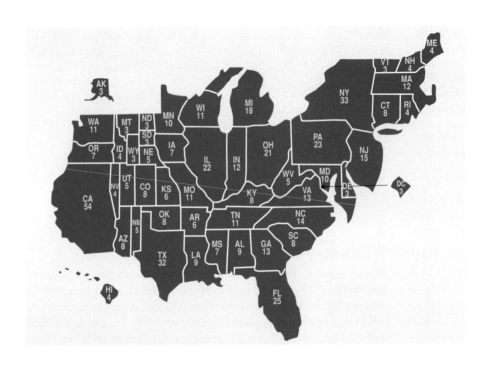

Protesters hold signs and flags in front of the U.S. Supreme Court on December 11, 2000. The Court was about to hear arguments on an appeal by Republican candidate George W. Bush to stop the hand recount of presidential ballots in Florida. (AP Photo/Steve Helber)

electoral votes available. Thus, a candidate needs 270 votes to win. If no candidate gets an electoral college majority (which has happened twice—in 1800 and 1824), the House of Representatives votes on the candidates, with each state delegation casting only a single vote. The vice president is then chosen by the Senate, with each senator casting one vote.

Was the 2000 Election an Anomaly?
The events surrounding the 2000 presidential election are still fresh in the minds of some Americans. It was the first time since 1888 that the electoral college system gave Americans a president who had not won the popular vote.[19] The events of the election will undoubtedly be recounted in history books, but was it an anomaly? Can we expect the winner of the popular vote also to win the electoral vote for the next 112 years? Or will presidential elections continue to be close in the near future, even as close as the 2000 election?

In 2000, Vice President Al Gore won the popular vote by 540,000 votes. Nonetheless, on election night, the outcome in Florida, which would have given Gore the winning votes in the electoral college, was deemed "too close to call." Initially, George W. Bush was leading Al Gore by only 1,700 votes, out of 6 million cast in that state. An initial recount in Florida reduced Bush's lead to just over 300 votes. Controversy erupted over the types of ballots used, however, and some counties in Florida began recounting ballots by hand. This was the issue that ultimately came before the United States Supreme Court: Did manual recounts of some ballots but not others violate the Constitution's equal protection clause? On December 12, five weeks after the election, the Supreme Court finally ruled against the manual recounts. The final vote tally in Florida gave Bush a 537-vote lead, all of Florida's twenty-five electoral votes, and the presidency.[20]

Other recent presidential elections have been extremely close. In 1960, John F. Kennedy defeated Richard Nixon by less than 120,000 votes, out of 70 million cast, although Kennedy had a sizable victory in the electoral college. In 1968, a shift of only 60,000 votes to third-party candidate George C. Wallace would have thrown the race into the House of Representatives. Again in 1976, a shift of only a few thousand votes would have produced an electoral victory for Gerald Ford despite a popular vote win for Jimmy Carter.

Future Elections Are Not Easy to Predict
Some scholars have suggested that we simply know too little about elections to make any predictions about the future. Polls are not as accurate as we hope. Voters are not as predictable as we think. Finally, variables such as third-party candidates and voter turnout will continue to affect future elections.

Campaigns and Your Everyday Life

Campaigns certainly do affect your everyday life whenever election time comes around. In the months before an election, it seems that everywhere you look, you see signs urging voters to select one candidate or another. When you turn on the TV, you hear campaign ads praising the virtues of one of the candidates or lamenting the shortcomings of his or her opponent. News channels have an ongoing stream of announcements about the candidates' issue positions or about which candidate is ahead in the race. If you open a newspaper or go to a news Web site, you are bombarded with campaign news. You may even get phone calls asking you to vote for a particular candidate.

To be sure, this barrage of campaign information can affect your everyday life, but campaigns are important to you for another reason as well: they offer you the chance to become familiar with the candidates for office. You learn about their personalities, their views on issues, and the promises they make. During campaigns, you have an opportunity to compare the contestants for office and, ultimately, decide how you will cast your vote.

Campaigns are important to your everyday life for another reason: the winning candidates will hold government offices. Winning congressional candidates may pass new laws or change old ones, and you may or may not benefit from the results. The winning candidate in the presidential campaigns will have significant influence over what laws and policies will be adopted in the future—and many of these may directly affect your life. (For some examples, refer back to the *Why Does It Matter?* feature in Chapter 8.)

Taking Action

As you have read in this chapter, many groups have worked toward reforming the way campaign funds are raised and spent in politics

today. One nonprofit, nonpartisan, grassroots organization that lobbies for campaign-finance reform is Common Cause. In the photo below, Elena Nunez, a participant in Colorado Common Cause's effort to reform campaign financing, holds up a mock-up of a TV remote control with a large mute button at a news conference. Nunez is asking voters to "mute" attack ads directed against a Colorado initiative to amend the state constitution to limit campaign financing and set contribution limits. (AP Photo/ Ed Andrieski)

Key Terms

Australian ballot 216

blanket primary 205

campaign strategy 210

caucus 203

closed primary 204

Credentials Committee 208

delegate 203

direct primary 204

elector 217

electoral college 217

general election 216

independent expenditure 213

loophole 212

nominating convention 203

office-block ballot 216

open primary 205

party-column ballot 216

political consultant 209

poll watcher 216

soft money 213

special election 216

winner-take-all system 218

Chapter Summary

1 Today, candidates are nominated for political offices by either a state caucus system (in a few states) or by a direct primary. The direct primary is a statewide election held within each party to pick its candidates for the general election.

2 The majority of the states hold presidential primaries to elect delegates to the parties' national conventions. The primary campaign recently has been shortened to the first few months of the year. In late summer or early fall, each political party holds a national convention during which the convention delegates, among other things, adopt the official party platform and decide who will be the party's presidential and vice presidential candidates.

3 American political campaigns are lengthy and extremely expensive. In recent years, they have become more candidate centered than party centered in response to technological innovations and declining party identification among the voters. Candidates rely less on the party and more on paid professional campaign managers and political consultants.

4 The amount of money spent in financing campaigns has increased dramatically in the last two elections. Federal legislation instituted major reforms in the 1970s by limiting spending and contributions, but the parties have skirted the federal campaign regulations. In 2002, Congress passed the Bipartisan Campaign Reform Act, which aims to curb the use of soft money and independent expenditures in elections.

5 General elections are regularly scheduled elections held in even-numbered years on the first Tuesday after the first Monday in November. During general elections, the voters decide who will be the U.S. president, vice president, and senators and representatives in Congress. State general elections, which may occur at the same time, are held to elect state and local government officials. Since 1888, all states in the United States have used the Australian ballot—a secret ballot that is prepared, distributed, and counted by government officials at public expense.

6 Elections are held in voting precincts (districts within each local government unit). Precinct officials supervise the polling place and the voting process. Poll watchers from each of the two major parties typically monitor the polling place as well to ensure that the election is conducted fairly and to prevent voting fraud.

7 In the presidential elections, citizens do not vote directly for the president and vice president; instead, they vote for electors who will cast their ballots in the electoral college. Each state has as many electoral votes as it has U.S. senators and representatives; there are also three electors from the District of Columbia. The electoral college is a winner-take-all system because, in nearly all states, the candidate who receives the largest popular vote in a state takes all of that state's electoral votes.

RESOURCES FOR FURTHER STUDY

Selected Readings

Abramson, Paul R., John H. Aldrich, and David W. Rohde. *Change and Continuity in the 2000 and 2002 Elections.* Washington, D.C.: CQ Press, 2003. This book offers a thorough analysis and comparison of the 2000 presidential elections and the 2002 midterm elections.

Burton, Michael J., and Daniel M. Shea. *Campaign Mode: Strategy, Leadership, and Successful Elections.* Lanham, Md.: Rowman & Littlefield, 2002. The authors, both of whom have served as political consultants to major political candidates, offer first-hand observations on campaign strategy and what they call the "campaign mode"—a state of mind in which strategic thinking is combined with political ambition.

Moore, James C., and Wayne Slater. *Bush's Brain: How Karl Rove Made George W. Bush President.* New York: John Wiley & Sons, 2003. The authors take a close-up look at President George W. Bush's long-time political consultant, Karl Rove.

Sabato, Larry J., ed. *Overtime! The Election 2000 Thriller.* Reading, Mass.: Addison Wesley Longman, 2001. This collection of essays is an excellent source for contemporary accounts of the drama accompanying the 2000 elections.

 ## InfoTrac Citations

Using your InfoTrac password, access the InfoTrac database at **http://infotrac.thomsonlearning.com**. Once at the site, you can do "key word" searches to locate the following articles, each of which deals with a topic covered in this chapter. The key words to use in your search are indicated in parentheses.

- "A Functional Analysis of Congressional Television Spots, 1986–2000" (Media Influence Campaigns)

- " 'In Presidential Politics . . . You Win from the Middle': Political Consultant Who Cut His Teeth in Louisiana Helped Bush Capture the White House" (Political Consultant Bush)

- "La Donna Is Catastrophe: Gore's Ghastly Brazile" (Campaign Manager Gore)

- "Wife's Fortune Poses Campaign-Spending Question for Kerry" (Campaign Spending Kerry)

Politics on the Web

You can find out exactly what the letter of the law is with respect to campaign financing by accessing the Federal Election Commission's Web site. The commission has provided an online "Citizen's Guide" that spells out exactly what is and is not legal. You can also download actual data on campaign donations from the site. Go to
http://www.fec.gov

• If you want to look at the data available from the Federal Election Commission in a more user-friendly way, you can access the following nonpartisan independent site that allows you to type in an elected official's name and receive large amounts of information on contributions to that official. Go to:
http://www.FECInfo.com

• Another excellent source for information on campaign financing, including who's contributing what amounts to which candidates, is the Center for Responsive Politics. You can access its Web site at
http://www.opensecrets.org

• Common Cause offers similar information on its Web site at
http://www.commoncause.org

• A site that offers information on campaign financing, as well as voting, can be accessed at
http://www.vote-smart.org

Web Resources on Your CD-ROM

On your CD-ROM, you will find Web resources, news articles, Internet activities, and video clips related to the topics in this chapter. Resources related to this chapter include the following:
  • **Values Inventory**—Political Ideology: Should We Eliminate the Electoral College?
  • **Why Does It Matter?**—Establish Your Views on the Electoral College.
  • **Updates**—Keep up with the issues in this chapter!
• **Web Resources**—Internet Activities: In Defense of the Electoral College; A Detailed Analysis of How the Electoral College Works.
• **Where Do You Stand?**—Dialogue: Should We Abandon the Electoral College?
• **Comparative Politics**—Campaigns and Elections in the United Kingdom.
• **Video**—Soft Money; 1876 and 2000; Presidential Elections; Electoral College.
• **NewsEdge**—Visit this global resource for current events related to this chapter.

chapter 10
politics and the media

CHAPTER OBJECTIVES

After reading this chapter, you should be able to . . .

▶ Explain the role of a free press in a democracy.

▶ Define the different types of media and indicate which one is the primary news source for most Americans.

▶ Summarize how television influences the conduct of political campaigns.

▶ Describe types of media bias and explain how such bias affects the political process.

▶ Describe the extent to which the Internet is reshaping political campaigns.

What Is the Media's Role in Wartime?

Not surprisingly, Americans were glued to their television sets and radios on September 11, 2001, to learn about the events unfolding in New York, Washington, D.C., and Pennsylvania. Americans continued to stay tuned in during the weeks following the terrorist attacks. According to the Pew Research Center, in mid-October 2001, 78 percent of those surveyed reported that they were still paying "very close" attention to news about the attacks—compared to only 58 percent who said the same a month after the Oklahoma City bombing in 1995. Perhaps even more striking is that Americans reported a greater interest in all news stories following the terrorist attacks. Forty-eight percent said they followed all news stories "very closely" after September 11—compared to only 23 percent who said the same throughout the 1990s. Such a high level of interest in the news was unprecedented in the history of the Pew Research Center's polls.[1]

Such intense public interest in the news about the terrorist attacks, the investigation of the perpetrators, and the ensuing war on terrorism gives the media tremendous influence over public opinion. Americans view these events through the media's "lens"—seeing and hearing what the media choose to report. Many observers have criticized the way the news about the attacks and the war on terrorism has been conveyed. Some have even argued that the reporting has been more "patriotic" than factual. In a time of national crisis and war, what is the role of the media?

What Americans Did Not Hear

The American press tends to temper its coverage when civilian deaths are involved. Compared to coverage in the foreign press, the American press showed few graphic scenes of the dead and dying on September 11. Details of civilian casualties from American bombing campaigns in Afghanistan were also limited. For example, in December 2001, some U.S. bombs aimed at an al Qaeda stronghold in Afghanistan went astray and destroyed a village. The *New York Times* reported simply that bombs "also hit civilian targets." The *Independent* of London, by contrast, gave a detailed account of the freshly dug graves at the village, the blasted houses and rubble, and, rather sarcastically, the report from the U.S. Defense Department that the bombing had never happened.[2]

A study by the Project for Excellence in Journalism found that the American press rarely dissented from the Bush administration's viewpoint on the terrorist attacks. In the three months after the September 11 attacks, the study found that no more than 10 percent of news stories could be perceived as critical of the official U.S. point of view.[3] The public clearly approved of this pro-American reporting. In November 2001, 77 percent of those surveyed rated the media's performance as "excellent" or "good." Sixty-nine percent of Americans said they thought news organizations should "stand up for America."[4]

Guidelines for War Reporting

Only relatively recently have foreign correspondents been able to report from "behind enemy lines." American reporters were not stationed in Berlin during World War II, but they were in Baghdad during the First Gulf War (1990–1991). This change in war reporting has forced reporters to ask, in the words of historian and journalist Harold Evans, "Is the first duty of the correspondent to truth or to his country?"[5] Reporters may learn details about military strategy, civilian casualties, or "friendly fire" incidents that could aid the enemy or hinder the allies. Should they report this information?

By the same token, should the media report stories critical of the president in a time of war? Most Americans approve of some military censorship to protect national security. They also believe, however, that the press should report all points of view, including those critical of the United States, and that reporters should investigate stories fully themselves rather than trust government or military officials. Clearly, the role of the media in time of war is an issue that Americans will continue to debate as the war on terrorism continues.

Where Do You Stand?

1. Do you think the American media should criticize the president in time of war?

2. To what extent do you think the military should censor the press regarding matters of national security?

Interacting with Your CD-ROM Resources

Use your CD-ROM to access resources on the Web, simulations, participation exercises, and video clips. Important resources related to this feature include:

■ **Values Inventory**—Political Ideology: What Is the Media's Role in Wartime?
■ **Where Do You Stand?**—Dialogue: What's the Media's Role during Wartime?
■ **Web Resources**—Internet Activities: Media Portrayal of Combat in the Gulf War; A New Professionalism in War Reporting.

INTRODUCTION

The debate over the media's role in war reporting underscores the importance of the media in American politics. Strictly defined, the term *media* means communication channels. It is the plural form of *medium of communication.* In this strict sense, any method used by people to communicate—including the telephone—is a communication medium. In this chapter, though, we look at the **mass media**—channels through which people can communicate to mass audiences. These channels include the **print media** (newspapers and magazines) and the **electronic media** (radio, television, and, to an increasing extent, the Internet).

The media are a dominant presence in our lives largely because they provide entertainment. Americans today enjoy more leisure time than at any time in history, and we fill it up with books, movies, and television—a huge amount of television. But the media play a vital role in our political lives as well. The media have a wide-ranging influence on American politics, particularly during campaigns and elections. Politicians and political candidates have learned—often the hard way—that positive media exposure and news coverage are essential to winning votes.

MASS MEDIA Communication channels, such as newspapers and radio and television broadcasts, through which people can communicate to mass audiences.

PRINT MEDIA Communication channels that consist of printed materials, such as newspapers and magazines.

ELECTRONIC MEDIA Communication channels that involve electronic transmissions, such as radio, television, and, to an extent, the Internet.

The Role of the Media in a Democracy

As you read in Chapter 4, one of the most important civil liberties protected in the Bill of Rights is freedom of the press. Like free speech, a free press is considered a vital tool of the democratic process. If people are to cast informed votes, they must have access to a forum in which they can discuss public affairs fully and assess the conduct and competency of their officials. The media provide this forum.

The framers knew firsthand the power of mass media. In the 1700s, political ideas were disseminated through newspapers and pamphlets, which could be no less powerful than radio and television are today. Thomas Paine's *Common Sense* was a fifty-page pamphlet that could

In the spring of 2003, the media focused on the war with Iraq. Here, New York governor George Pataki, right, and Mayor Michael Bloomberg, center, discuss the war on a TV news program hosted by John Gambling. A news report of the war in Iraq plays on a television in the background. (AP Photo/Ed Bailey, Pool)

Thomas Paine (Library of Congress)

be printed and distributed quickly and cheaply. It sold 500,000 copies (the equivalent of about 8 or 9 million copies with today's population) in a few months and helped to persuade the colonial masses of the need for independence from England. The *Federalist Papers,* which argued in favor of the U.S. Constitution, were first published in New York newspapers, as were many of the arguments of the Anti-Federalists.

The exact nature of the media's influence on the political process today is difficult to characterize. Clearly, what the media say and do has an impact on what Americans think about political issues. But just as clearly, the media also *reflect* what Americans think about politics. Some scholars argue that the media is the fourth "check" in our political system—checking and balancing the power of the president, the Congress, and the courts. The power of the media today is enormous, but how the media use their power is an issue about which Americans are often at odds.

The Agenda-Setting Function of the Media

One of the criticisms often levied against the media is that they play too large a role in determining the issues, events, and personalities that are in the public eye. When people hear the evening's top news stories, they usually assume automatically that these stories concern the most important issues facing the nation. In actuality, the media decide the relative importance of issues by publicizing some issues and ignoring others, and by giving some stories high priority and others low priority. By helping to determine what people will talk and think about, the media set the *political agenda*—the issues that politicians will address. In other words, to borrow from Bernard Cohen's classic statement on the media and public opinion, the media may not be successful in telling people what to think, but they are "stunningly successful in telling their audience what to think about."[6]

For example, television played a significant role in shaping public opinion concerning the Vietnam War (1964–1975), which has been called the first "television war." Part of the public opposition to the war in the late 1960s came about as a result of the daily portrayal of the war's horrors on TV news programs. Film footage and narrative accounts of the destruction, death, and suffering in Vietnam brought the war into living rooms across the United States. (Today, the "saturation coverage" on television of potential terrorist threats may also influence how Americans react to those threats. For a discussion of this issue, see this chapter's *The Politics of Homeland Security* feature.)

Beginning with the Vietnam War, the media have brought close-up war coverage into the living rooms of virtually all Americans. Here, Stuart Williams, a retired banker, keeps up with TV reports on the 2003 war in Iraq at his home in Boulder, Colorado. Williams suffered post-traumatic stress as a result of being held, along with his wife, for three months by Iraq as civilian "human shields" during the first Gulf War in 1991. (AP Photo/Ed Andrieski)

The POLITICS of HOMELAND SECURITY

Saturation News Coverage

Cable television, the Internet, and the competitive nature of news coverage today have created what many media observers have dubbed "saturation news coverage." CNN, MSNBC, CNBC, the Fox News Network, and many other channels have news coverage twenty-four hours a day, and the traditional networks will break into any regularly scheduled program to bring you "breaking news." As you read in this chapter's opening *America at Odds* feature, the public followed news coverage of the terrorist attacks on September 11, 2001, very closely. Since September 11, news about terrorist threats and the war on terrorism—including the war against Afghanistan in late 2001 and the invasion of Iraq in early 2003—has continued to dominate the news networks.

HIGH ALERT

In February 2003, the Department of Homeland Security (DHS) raised the color-coded "national threat level" to orange, or "high," meaning that the United States faced a high risk of terrorist attack. According to the Web site of the DHS, "Recent intelligence reports, corroborated through multiple intelligence sources, suggest an increased likelihood that the al Qaeda terrorist network may attempt to attack Americans in the United States or abroad."

The news media gave this story saturation coverage, including interviews with local police chiefs, customs officials, and airport security guards. Reporters speculated about chemical attacks, biological attacks, and dirty bombs. But few could suggest specific actions that Americans could take to protect themselves.

"THREAT FATIGUE"

Some Americans followed the news of the heightened terror alert carefully and canceled travel plans, chose not to use city subways, or stocked up on ready-to-eat meals. Others paid little attention to the alerts. In the year following the September 11 attacks, the federal government had issued similar warnings that it had "credible evidence" of threats against the Statue of Liberty and the Brooklyn Bridge in New York and the Golden Gate Bridge in San Francisco. Yet in that first year after 9/11, except for isolated incidents against Americans abroad, no terrorist strikes occurred.

In February 2003, *Washington Post* columnist Marc Fisher wrote that his son had asked him, "Daddy, why do they keep that sign on TV that says 'Terror Alert HIGH'?" Fisher replied, "To make us so nervous that we'll come back to their channel to

Jerome Johnson of Vienna, Virginia, a suburb of Washington, stocks up on home-protection supplies, including plastic sheeting and duct tape, at his local Home Depot on February 12, 2003. America's terror alerts have led some people to buy wood stoves, drums to collect rainwater, duct tape, and plastic sheeting in preparation for a possible terrorist attack. (AP Photo/Adele Starr)

see what's happened, so they can make more money."[7] Such cynical observations reveal an unintended consequence of the media's saturation coverage: threat fatigue. Americans may simply tire of hearing about threats that don't materialize and ignore the dangers altogether.

Are We Safer?

Do you think that with saturation news coverage Americans will become so accustomed to the threat of terrorism that they will fail to recognize the real dangers terrorists present?

The degree to which the media influence public opinion is not always clear, however. As you read in Chapter 8, some studies show that people filter the information they receive from the media through their own preconceived ideas about issues. Scholars who try to analyze the relationship between American politics and the media inevitably confront the chicken-and-egg conundrum: Do the media cause the public to hold certain views, or do the media merely reflect views that are formed independently of the media's influence?

The Medium Does Affect the Message

Of all the media, television has the greatest impact. Television reaches into almost every home in the United States. Virtually all homes have televisions. Even outside their homes, Americans can watch television—in airports, shopping malls, bowling lanes, golf clubhouses, and dentists' offices. Today, television is the primary news source for more than 65 percent of Americans. Figure 10–1 shows the clear prominence of television among the media.

As you will read shortly, politicians take maximum advantage of the power and influence of television. But does the television medium alter the presentation of political information in any way? If you compare the coverage given to an important political issue by the print media and by the TV networks, you will note some striking differences. For one thing, the print media (particularly leading newspapers such as the *Washington Post,* the *New York Times,* and the *Wall Street Journal*) treat an important issue in much more detail. In addition to news stories based on reporters' research, you will find editorials taking positions on the issue and arguments supporting those positions. Television news, in contrast, is often criticized as being too brief and too superficial.

Time Constraints   The medium of television necessarily imposes constraints, particularly with respect to time, on how political issues are presented. News stories must be reported quickly, in only a few minutes or occasionally in only a **sound bite,** a brief comment lasting for just a few seconds that captures a thought or a perspective and has an immediate impact on the viewers.

A Visual Medium   Television reporting also relies extensively on visual elements, rather than words, to capture the viewers' attention. Inevitably, the photos or videos selected to depict a particular political event have exaggerated importance. The visual aspect of television contributes to its power, but it also creates a potential bias. Those watching the news presentation do not know what portions of a video being shown have been deleted, what other photos may have been taken, or whether other records of the event exist. This kind of "selection bias" will be discussed in more detail later in this chapter.

Television Is "Big Business"   Today's TV networks compete aggressively with each other to air "breaking news" and to produce quality news programs. Competition in the television industry understandably has had an effect on how the news is presented. To make profits,

SOUND BITE   In televised news reporting, a brief comment, lasting for only a few seconds, that captures a thought or a perspective and has an immediate impact on the viewers.

FIGURE 10–1

Media Usage by Consumers, 1984 to 2002

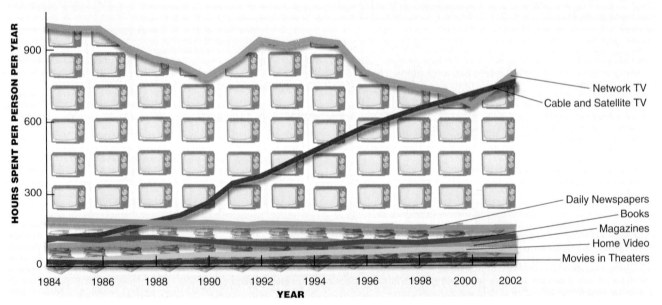

SOURCE: U.S. Department of Commerce, *Statistical Abstract of the United States, 2002* (Washington, D.C.: U.S. Government Printing Office, 2002), p. 698; and authors' update.

or even stay in business, TV stations need viewers. And to attract viewers, the news industry has turned to "infotainment"—programs that inform and entertain at the same time. Slick sets, attractive reporters, and animated graphics that dance across the television screen are now commonplace on most news programs, particularly on the cable news channels.

TV networks also compete with each other for advertising income. Although the media in the United States are among the freest in the world, they nonetheless remain vulnerable to the influence of the political bias of their advertising sponsors on their programming.

The Candidates and Television

Given the TV-saturated environment in which we live, it should come as no surprise that candidates spend a great deal of time—and money—obtaining TV coverage through political ads, debates, and general news coverage. Candidates and their campaign managers realize that the time and money are well spent because television has an important impact on the way people see the candidates, understand the issues, and cast their votes.

Political Advertising

Today, televised **political advertising** consumes at least half of the total budget for a major political campaign. In the 2000 election cycle, $665 million was spent for political advertising on broadcast TV. As you can see in Figure 10–2, this is more than twice the amount spent in the 1992 election cycle. In the 2002 election cycle, the amount of funds spent on television advertising topped $1 billion for the first time.

The Emergence of Televised Political Advertising
Political advertising first appeared on television during the 1952 presidential campaign. At that time, there were only about 15 million television sets; today, there are well over 100 million. Initially, political TV commercials were more or less like any other type of advertising. Instead of focusing on the positive qualities of a product, thirty-second or sixty-second ads focused on the positive

FIGURE 10-2
Political Ad Spending on Broadcast TV, 1992–2002
As you can see in this figure, spending for political advertising has increased steadily over the last five elections.

SOURCE: Television Bureau of Advertising, as presented in Lorraine Woellert and Tom Lowry, "A Political Nightmare: Not Enough Airtime," *Business Week*, November 23, 2000, p. 111; and authors' update.

POLITICAL ADVERTISING Advertising undertaken by or on behalf of a political candidate to familiarize voters with the candidate and his or her views on campaign issues.

This is a video image of Democratic presidential candidate Vice President Al Gore from a Democratic National Committee television campaign commercial entitled "Starts-Generic," which was released on June 27, 2000. The Democratic Party aired a series of positive ads that starred the vice president. Each ad flashed "The Gore Plan" across the screen as specific points were mentioned. (AP Photo/Democratic National Committee)

Republican presidential candidate George W. Bush is greeted by senior citizens in the first Republican National Committee television commercial of 2000, released on June 10, 2000. The sixty-second ad explained the essence of Bush's plans for Social Security, one of the sharpest points of disagreement between Bush and Vice President Gore. (AP/Republican National Committee)

© The Cartoon Bank. Used with permission.

*"The thing to do now, Senator, is to
hit back with some negative advertising of our own."*

NEGATIVE POLITICAL ADVERTISING
Political advertising undertaken for the
purpose of discrediting an opposing
candidate in the eyes of the voters; attack
ads and issue ads are forms of negative
political advertising.

ATTACK AD A negative political
advertisement that attacks the character of
an opposing candidate.

ISSUE AD A negative political
advertisement that focuses on flaws in an
opposing candidate's position on a
particular issue.

qualities of a political candidate. Within the decade, however, **negative political advertising**
began to appear in the TV medium.

Negative Political Ads   Despite the barrage of criticism levied against the candidates'
use of negative political ads during recent election cycles, such ads are not new. Indeed, **attack
ads**—advertising that attacks the character of an opposing candidate—have a long tradition
in this country. In 1800, an article in the *Federalist Gazette of the United State*s described
Thomas Jefferson as having a "weakness of nerves, want of fortitude, and total imbecility of
character."

Candidates also use **issue ads**—ads that focus on flaws in the opponents' positions on
issues. For example, in the 2000 presidential campaigns, rarely did the candidates attack each
other personally. Rather, they leveled criticisms at each other's stated positions on various
issues, such as education and Social Security, and previous actions with respect to those issues.
Candidates also try to undermine their opponents' credibility by pointing to discrepancies
between what the opponents say in their campaign speeches and their political records, such
as voting records, which are available to the public and thus can easily be verified. As noted in
Chapters 6 and 9, issue ads are also used by interest groups to gather support for candidates
who endorse the groups' causes.

Issue ads can be even more devastating than personal attacks—as Barry Goldwater learned
in 1964 when his opponent in the presidential race, President Lyndon Johnson, aired the
"daisy girl" ad. This ad, which set new boundaries for political advertising, showed a little girl
standing quietly in a field of daisies. She held a daisy and pulled off the petals, counting to herself. Suddenly, a deep voice was heard counting: "10, 9, 8, 7, 6 . . . ." When the countdown hit
zero, the unmistakable mushroom cloud of an atomic bomb filled the screen. Then President
Johnson's voice was heard saying, "These are the stakes: to make a world in which all of God's

The "daisy" commercial (left) was used
by President Lyndon B. Johnson in 1964.
A remake (right) targeted Gore in the
2000 election. The ad contended that
because the Clinton/Gore administration
"sold" the nation's security "to
Communist Red China in exchange for
campaign contributions," China has "the
ability to threaten our homes with long-
range nuclear warheads." It then showed
a girl, counting down as she plucked
daisy petals. Her counting was then
replaced by a countdown of a missile,
which was followed by a nuclear bomb
explosion. "Don't take a chance. Please
vote Republican" then appeared on the
screen. (Left: Doyle, Dane, and Bernbach;
Right: Aretino Industries/ABC News)

The 1960 presidential debate between Republican Vice President Richard M. Nixon (left) and Senator John F. Kennedy, the Democratic presidential nominee (right), was viewed by many as helping Kennedy win at the polls. (AP Photo/Ron Edmonds)

children can live, or to go into the dark. We must either love each other or we must die." A message on the screen then read: "Vote for President Johnson on November 3." The implication, of course, was that Goldwater would lead the country into a nuclear war.[8]

Television Debates

Televised debates have been a feature of presidential campaigns since 1960, when presidential candidates Republican Richard M. Nixon and Democrat John F. Kennedy squared off in the first great TV debate. Television debates provide an opportunity for voters to find out how candidates differ on issues. They also allow candidates to capitalize on the power of television to improve their image or point out the failings of their opponents.

The presidential debates of 1992 included a third-party candidate, H. Ross Perot, along with the candidates from the two major parties, Republican George H. W. Bush, the incumbent president, and Democrat Bill Clinton. In 1996, two third-party candidates, H. Ross Perot and John Hagelin, sought to participate in the TV debates but were prevented from doing so by the Commission for Presidential Debates.[9]

In 2000, the commission similarly excluded Ralph Nader and Pat Buchanan from the debates. (For a further discussion of third-party candidates and presidential debates, see Chapter 7.) In 2000, there were three presidential debates between George W. Bush and Al Gore, each using a different format, and one vice presidential debate between their respective running mates, Dick Cheney and Joe Lieberman. During the debates, the candidates had to respond to some hard, pointed questions, such as questions about their views on abortion and gay and lesbian rights.

Many contend that the presidential debates offer a significant opportunity for voters to assess the personalities and issue positions of the candidates. Thus, the debates help to shape the outcome of the election. Others doubt that these televised debates—or the "spins" put on them by political commentators immediately after they are over—have ever been taken very seriously by voters.

Republican presidential candidate Texas governor George W. Bush and Democratic presidential candidate Vice President Al Gore engage in a presidential debate prior to the 2000 elections. (AP Photo/Ron Edmonds)

News Coverage

Whereas political ads are expensive, coverage by the news media is free. Accordingly, the candidates try to take advantage of the media's interest in campaigns to increase the quantity and quality of news coverage. This is not always easy. Generally, the media devote the lion's share of their coverage to polls showing who is ahead in the race.

During his 2000 presidential campaign, after children at the YMCA Family Center in Raytown, Missouri, asked Democratic presidential candidate Vice President Al Gore what those big black things were, Gore pulled down a television news crew's boom microphone for them to get a closer look. (AP Photo/Stephan Savoia)

Texas governor and presidential candidate George W. Bush stands with his hand over his heart while reciting the Pledge of Allegiance with students from the Woodbury Elementary School in Bedford, New Hampshire, in the fall of 1999. (Charles Krupa/AP Photo)

MANAGED NEWS COVERAGE News coverage that is manipulated (managed) by a campaign manager or political consultant to gain media exposure for a political candidate.

SPIN DOCTOR A political candidate's press adviser who tries to convince reporters to give a story or event concerning the candidate a particular "spin" (interpretation, or slant).

SPIN A reporter's slant on, or interpretation of, a particular event or action.

In recent years, candidates' campaign managers and political consultants have shown increasing sophistication in creating newsworthy events for journalists and TV camera crews to cover, an effort commonly referred to as **managed news coverage.** As one scholar points out, "To keep a favorable image of their candidates in front of the public, campaign managers arrange newsworthy events to familiarize potential voters with their candidates' best aspects."[10]

Besides becoming aware of how camera angles and lighting affect a candidate's appearance, the political consultant plans political events to accommodate the press. The campaign staff attempts to make what the candidate is doing appear interesting. The staff also knows that journalists and political reporters compete for stories and that they can be manipulated by granting favors, such as an exclusive personal interview with the candidate. Each candidate's press advisers, often called **spin doctors,** also try to convince reporters to give the story or event a **spin,** or interpretation, that is favorable to the candidate.

AMERICA at odds

Who Are the Real "Winners" in Expensive Campaigns?

In Chapter 9, we discussed the recent efforts to limit the amount of funds raised and spent in political campaigns. Campaign-finance reformers have had to fight incumbent politicians who see themselves as the beneficiaries of the old laws. But the other "winners" in expensive political campaigns are TV stations.

Indeed, the National Association of Broadcasters spends millions of dollars (in 2000, over $30 million) on lobbying efforts to squelch reform that would allow free political TV airtime. On average, a candidate has to pay about $3,000 to purchase a thirty-second spot for a political ad. For an ad broadcast during a popular show with high viewer ratings, the price goes up—to $5,000 or more. A local TV station can make even more from campaign ads for ballot initiatives than from candidate ads. For example, in 2002, local television and radio stations in Arizona made an estimated $30 million from a flurry of last-minute ads for ballot initiatives in that state.[11] The campaigns have only so many days until the election, and the stations have only so many advertising spots to sell, so the price of each spot goes up with the demand.

The public has decried the negative, tasteless, and relentless political ads that appear every campaign season. Americans generally blame the politicians, their media consultants, and the system of campaign financing. Reformers have focused on how much money candidates can raise from individuals and groups. Yet limits on contributions do little to reform the system when broadcasters continue to charge top dollar to air campaign ads. The law of the free market dictates that broadcasters will continue to air these ads as long as political campaigns pay for them.

Talk Radio—The Wild West of the Media

Ever since Franklin D. Roosevelt held his first "fireside chats" on radio, politicians have realized the power of radio. Today, talk radio is a political force to be reckoned with. In 1988, there were 200 talk-show radio stations. Today, there are over 1,200, and that number is growing. The most recent estimates are that one in six Americans listens to talk radio regularly.

Talk radio is sometimes characterized as the Wild West of the media. Journalistic conventions do not exist. Political ranting and raving are common. Many popular talk shows do seem to have a conservative bent, but their supporters argue that talk radio has been a good way to counter the liberal bias in the print and TV media (we discuss bias in the media in the following section).

Some people are uneasy because talk shows empower fringe groups, perhaps magnifying their rage. Clearly, a talk show is not necessarily a democratic forum in which all views are aired. Talk-show hosts such as Rush Limbaugh do not attempt to hide their political biases; if anything, they exaggerate them for effect. Supporters of the sometimes outrageous, sometimes reactionary remarks broadcast during talk-radio shows reply that such shows are simply a response to consumer demand. Furthermore, those who think that talk radio is good for the country argue that talk shows, taken together, provide a great populist forum for political debate. They maintain that in a sense, talk radio has become an equalizer because it is relatively inexpensive to start up a rival talk show.

Those who claim that talk-show hosts go too far in their rantings and ravings ultimately have to deal with the constitutional issue of free speech. After all, as First Amendment scholars point out, there is little the government can do about the forces that shape the media. The courts have

President Franklin D. Roosevelt (1933–1945) was the first president to use radio broadcasts to send messages to the American people. Roosevelt gave twenty-eight "fireside chats," the first of which—on the bank crisis—was transmitted on March 12, 1933. It lasted for thirteen minutes and forty-two seconds. He transmitted his last fireside chat on Monday, June 12, 1944. (Library of Congress)

Conservative talk-show host Rush Limbaugh puffs on his cigar while waiting to tee off at the Pebble Beach Golf Links. Limbaugh began hosting his nationally syndicated show in 1988, and today it is the highest-rated national radio talk show in America. (AP Photo/Eric Risberg)

always protected freedom of expression to the fullest extent possible, although, for many reasons, the government has been able to exercise some control over the electronic media—see the discussion of freedom of the press in Chapter 4.

The Question of Media Bias

Since the media first appeared on the American political landscape, they have been criticized by one group or another as being biased. The many studies that have been undertaken on the subject of media bias, however, have reached different conclusions.

Studies on Media Bias

For years, conservatives have contended that there is a liberal bias in the media. Indeed, some evidence seems to support this. For example, in a significant study conducted in the 1980s, the researchers found that the media producers, editors, and reporters (the "media elite") showed a notably liberal bias in their news coverage.[12] Surveys over the past three decades have also consistently shown that national, Washington-based reporters are more likely to describe themselves as liberals than conservatives. Surveys also show that a majority of these reporters have voted Democratic for quite some time.

Yet other research data suggest that even if reporters hold liberal views, these views are not reflected in their reporting. Based on an analysis of media coverage of presidential campaigns, Kathleen Hall Jamieson, director of the Annenberg Public Policy Center at the University of Pennsylvania, concludes that there is no systematic liberal, Democratic bias in news coverage.[13] A poll of the voters on the question of media bias during the 2000 presidential campaigns revealed that 57 percent of those surveyed thought that the media "often" let political views influence coverage. Yet, overall, the voters believed that the media had been fair to both presidential candidates.[14]

Calvin Exoo, in his study of the media and politics, suggests that journalists have neither a liberal nor a conservative bias. Rather, they are constrained by both the pro-American bias of media ownership and the journalists' own code of objectivity. Most are more interested in improving their career prospects than in discussing public policies.[15] Other scholars, including political scientist Thomas Patterson, agree that news reporting is largely apolitical. Media bias exists, but it is toward bad news and cynicism and is not partisan in nature.

The Bias against Losers

Kathleen Hall Jamieson believes that media bias plays a significant role in shaping presidential campaigns and elections, but she argues that it is not a partisan bias. Rather, it is a bias against losers. A candidate who falls behind in the race is immediately labeled a "loser," making it even more difficult for the candidate to regain favor in the voters' eyes.[16] The 2000 campaigns provided many examples of this phenomenon. During the summer months, when Al Gore was lagging behind George W. Bush, the media talked about Gore's failure to gain "traction," his failure to reach the voters, and his seemingly wooden personality. Bush, in contrast, was described as warm and easygoing. In the fall, when polls showed Gore pulling ahead, suddenly Bush received the "loser" treatment—Americans heard about his difficulty pronouncing certain words, such as *nuclear,* and other trivial matters, not about his plans for tax cuts, educational reforms, and so on.

Jamieson argues that the media use the winner-loser paradigm to describe events throughout the campaigns. Even a presidential debate is regarded as a "sporting match" that results in a winner and a loser. Before the 2000 debates, reporters focused on what each candidate had to do to "win" the debate. When the debate was over, reporters immediately speculated about who had "won" as they waited for postdebate polls to answer that question. According to Jamieson, this approach "squanders the opportunity to reinforce learning." The debates are an important source of political information for the voters, and this fact is eclipsed by the media's win-lose focus.

"Selection Bias"

As mentioned earlier, television is big business, and maximizing profits from advertising is a major consideration in what television stations choose to air. After all, a station or network that incurs losses will eventually go bankrupt. The expansion of the media universe to include cable channels and the Internet has also increased the competition among news sources. As a result, news directors select programming they believe will attract the largest audiences and garner the highest advertising revenues. Furthermore, most Americans have a remote control in hand while watching TV and quickly click to another channel if they lose interest in one particular station's programming.[17] Consequently, even when an in-depth political discussion is available on television, viewership may be abysmal.

Self-Censorship   In 2000, the Pew Research Center released a survey that studied how journalists choose news stories and why they pursue some stories but not others. More than half of the journalists surveyed reported that they sometimes avoid newsworthy stories because their audiences might find them too complex or dull.[18] Roughly the same number said that newsworthy stories are "often or sometimes ignored" to protect the corporate interests of the news organization. The pressure to avoid a story is sometimes subtle, however. The journalists in the survey reported that they choose not to pursue a story when they "get signals" or "anticipate negative responses" from superiors in their news organization. In general, the journalists surveyed were pessimistic about their profession, with a majority saying that the media do only a "fair" job of telling the public what it wants and needs to know.[19]

TV News Magazines and Commentary   In the battle to increase ratings and decrease costs, many news directors have opted to use the TV "news magazine" format. These programs, such as *The O'Reilly Factor* on Fox and *Larry King Live* on CNN, are popular with viewers and relatively inexpensive to produce. Journalists themselves lament the effect that these programs are having on the delivery of the news.

In another cost-cutting measure, news networks have reduced the number of news correspondents. As a result, talk *about* news is replacing news—viewers receive commentary rather than information. Every viewpoint gets aired, whether or not there is research to back it up. Some media researchers believe that what we are now hearing and viewing is simply cocktail party conversation that is falsely labeled journalism.

A Changing News Culture   A large majority of news professionals also believe that the culture of news is changing. The traditional respect for facts and factual verification is giving way to a news culture characterized by argument, opinion, haste, and news as entertainment. According to the survey, 69 percent of journalists believe that the distinction between reporting and commentary has been seriously eroded.

The American public agrees with journalists that news coverage is less accurate today than it was in the past. According to a Gallup poll conducted in December 2000, 65 percent of the respondents thought that news stories and reports were "often inaccurate."[20] In a similar poll conducted in 1985, only 34 percent of the respondents thought that news stories and reports were "often inaccurate."

Racial Bias in the Media?

Another type of media bias that recent studies have identified is racial bias. As you read in Chapter 5, Americans and political leaders are concerned about the practice of "racial profiling" by law enforcement officers. Racial profiling is a denigrating form of discrimination that occurs when, for example, a police officer pulls over a disproportionate number of drivers from a particular minority group. In recent years, some researchers have noticed another, far more subtle type of discrimination based on skin color: racial profiling in the media.

News Reporting on Crime and Drugs   In 2000, political scientists Franklin Gilliam and Shanto Iyengar published the results of a study they had conducted on the effects of news reporting on attitudes toward African Americans.[21] These scholars found that stories about crime dominate local news programming because crime stories satisfy viewers' demands for "action news." The prevalence of this kind of reporting, they claim, has led to a crime narrative ("script") that includes two core elements: (1) crime is violent, and (2) perpetrators of crime are nonwhite males. This crime script has a significant impact on the viewing public because local television news is the public's primary source of information on public affairs.

Gilliam and Iyengar's central finding was that the racial element of the crime script promotes negative attitudes about African Americans among white viewers (but not among African American viewers). One result is increased support among the public for more punitive approaches to crime.

Larry King, host of CNN's *Larry King Live,* addresses a question to Republican presidential candidates Senator John McCain of Arizona, left, Alan Keyes, center, and Governor George W. Bush of Texas prior to the 2000 presidential elections. The Republican presidential debate was carried on the King show. (AP Photo/ Eric Draper, Pool)

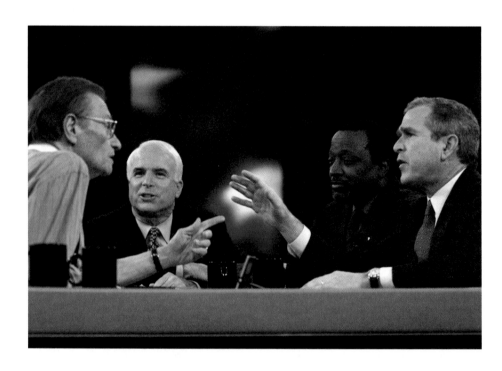

Some scholars contend that the media also create misperceptions about drug users. A medical study on the effects of U.S. drug policy showed that the majority of Americans have little firsthand experience with the problems associated with drug use. What they know about this issue comes largely from the news media, particularly television. That Americans are getting the wrong picture is confirmed by another study of drug policy conducted by a prominent group of physicians, the Physician Leadership on National Drug Policy (PLNDP). The PLNDP found that more than half of those who admit to using cocaine and heroin are white and that over 67 percent of regular marijuana users are white; less than 17 percent are African Americans.[22]

"Racializing" Welfare   Yale University political scientist Martin Gilens contends that racial profiling in the media has also promoted negative attitudes toward welfare. Based on a detailed analysis of surveys and other sources, Gilens believes that TV programs and news magazines misrepresent the racial composition of America's poor people by calling up old stereotypes—such as African Americans as "lazy"—when visually portraying poverty. Gilens concludes that this "racialization" of welfare is responsible for a contradictory belief held by many Americans: welfare should be ended, and at the same time, the government should be spending more to help poor people trying to support themselves.[23]

Media Blackface   According to Mikal Muharrar, the problem of racial profiling can best be understood as the "politically acceptable and very American practice of defining a social problem in 'blackface'—that is, in racial terms—through indirect association." Issues defined in blackface, he contends, include the black drug dealer, the black criminal, and the lazy black welfare recipient. Defining issues in this way allows "the issue—be it crime, welfare, drug abuse, or what have you—[to be] seen by many as a real issue that is only *coincidentally* about race." This is brilliant, he claims, because the media can thus deny responsibility for any punitive public policies that result from such media profiles.[24]

Political News on the Web

The Internet has become, in a very brief span of time, a significant medium for the delivery of political news. Today, at least two-thirds of Americans have Internet access. If you count those who have access outside their homes, such as at school or work, an even higher number of Americans are Internet users. Around 50,000 more Americans are connected to the Internet each day. About two-thirds of Internet users now consider the Internet to be an important source of news.[25]

Certainly, news now abounds on the Web. Virtually every major news provider, both print and broadcast, has deployed a Web site. Although there are a few Internet-only news outlets, most news sites on the Web are maintained by already well-established newspapers, magazines, and TV broadcasters. Has the growth of the Internet as a source for news been responsible for a decline in the use of traditional news sources? For a discussion of this question, see this chapter's *Perception versus Reality* feature on the next page.

Tabloid Journalism on the Internet

Matt Drudge, creator of the Web's *Drudge Report,* has become widely known for his tabloid-type journalism. Critics refer to him as a "cybergossip" who is not all that concerned about distinguishing between fact and fiction in his "news" reports. For example, in January 1998, he "reported" that President Bill Clinton had had an affair with White House intern Monica Lewinsky. The allegation was unsubstantiated and apparently had been taken from a *Newsweek* article that was never printed. Nonetheless, it set the media wheels in motion. Within

Matt Drudge carries a laptop computer as he walks up the stairs in Los Angeles. The *Drudge Report,* the daily barrage of breaking news, gossip, and politics that he e-mails to some 65,000 subscribers, is hotter than hot. (AP Photo/Michael Caulfield)

Does Online Information Mean the Death of Traditional News?

News on the Web is, in fact, itself news. Numerous articles appear in the traditional press discussing how much news is being transmitted on the Internet.

THE PERCEPTION

A broad sampling of traditional news articles about online information sources gives the impression that people are turning to their information appliance—the personal computer—when they need news. Because this perception is becoming increasingly widespread, the traditional news media, including TV networks, are devoting substantial resources to establish a "presence" on the Internet.

THE REALITY

Clearly, the number of Americans who go online to obtain news is rising rapidly. Recent studies suggest, though, that those who obtain news online are also those who view news programs on TV and read daily newspapers. In other words, there is no evidence that going online for news leads to less reading or viewing of more traditional news sources. In fact, one recent survey indicated that Internet users and nonusers alike ranked printed books and magazines higher than television as important news sources.[26]

What's Your Opinion?

Do you believe that the Internet will ever replace traditional news sources (TV broadcasts, newspapers, and news magazines)?

---

days, the *Washington Post* had investigated the allegation and published an article based on documented facts. The other major media quickly followed suit, and the details of the "Lewinsky scandal" unfolded before the American public.

In one sense, what happened here was not really new. After all, printed tabloids have often been the first to mention breaking scandals or other news items, which then find their way into the more "respectable" news media. What is striking about the events following the *Drudge Report*'s story about Monica Lewinsky is how quickly the story was investigated and reported on by the leading print and electronic news sources. Indeed, some journalists claim that the Internet has not only increased the amount of tabloid "reporting" but has also accelerated the pace of publication. Thus, online tabloids could dramatically increase the potential impact of tabloid journalism on mainstream journalism. Indeed, Drudge himself has become somewhat mainstream. He has a radio show that is carried on some of the biggest stations in the country.

The accelerated pace of publication has also had another effect: an increased pressure on news publishers to compete for top stories within a short period. Even respected, mainstream news organizations have occasionally posted inaccurate stories on their Web sites.[27]

"Narrowcasting" the News

Technology is quickening the pace at which the "one size fits all" news standard is being replaced by highly specialized "packets." The Internet is the ultimate vehicle for what is known as "narrowcasting"—tailoring media programming to the specialized tastes and preferences of targeted audiences. If you are interested in UFOs, you can direct the Internet to give you just news on UFOs.

The latest in news systems further enhances the narrowcasting of news. Using so-called **push technology,** Web users can totally customize their daily supply of information. The best-known providers of this type of service are CNN/PointCast Network and Infogate. You decide which type of news you want, and the provider will "push" this news through your Internet hookup. How do you decide what type of news you really want? You first select one of the thousand or more search engines available. Then you start "surfing" the Web to find the sites that you like most. Then you tell the "push" software which sites to go to and how many times a day. One of the problems with such narrowcasting is that users do not get different views on a particular subject.

PUSH TECHNOLOGY Software that enables Internet users to customize the type of information they receive from Web sources. The information is "pushed" to the user automatically as it is put on the Web.

Cyberspace and Political Campaigns

Today's political parties and candidates not only realize the benefits of using computers and computer databases to communicate with voters but also understand that the Internet can be used to conduct online campaigns and raise funds. Voters also are increasingly using the Web to access information about parties and candidates, promote political goals, and obtain political news.

In a sense, the use of the Internet is the least costly way for candidates to contact, recruit, and mobilize supporters, as well as disseminate information on their positions on issues. In effect, the Internet can replace brochures, letters, and position papers. Individual voters or political-party supporters can use the Internet to avoid having to go to special meetings or to a campaign site to do volunteer work or obtain information on a candidate's position.

That the Internet is now a viable medium for communicating political information and interacting with voters was made clear in the 2000 presidential election cycle. According to a postelection Pew Research Center survey, 18 percent of Americans said that they went online for election news, up from 4 percent who did so in the 1996 campaign. Nearly seven in ten of this group went online to seek information on the candidates' positions. Moreover, 43 percent of this group claimed that the information they found online affected their voting decisions.[28]

Online Fund-Raising

Today's political candidates are realizing that the Internet can be an effective—and inexpensive—way to raise campaign funds. The leading candidates in the 2000 presidential race all engaged in online fund-raising, as did the national committees of the Republican and Democratic parties.

Fund-raising on the Internet by presidential candidates began in earnest after the Federal Election Commission decided, in June 1999, that the federal government could distribute

During the 1999–2000 election cycle, the Web was widely used by the political parties and candidates as a campaign vehicle.

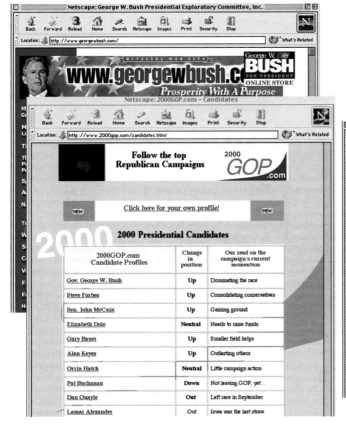

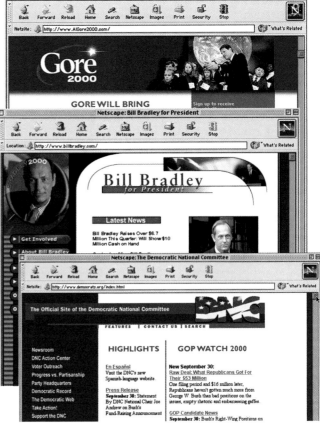

matching funds for credit-card donations received by candidates via the Internet. By the end of the following month, Democratic presidential contender Bill Bradley had already garnered $312,000 in online contributions; Democrat Al Gore and Republican George W. Bush had received $70,000 and $41,572, respectively; and the Republican National Committee had raised $200,000 from donations made online. Republican senator John McCain's prowess in garnering support via the Web was widely noted in the media. During the night hours following his victory in the New Hampshire presidential primary, he raised $300,000 and enlisted 4,000 new volunteers through his Web site. By the end of the week, these totals had climbed to $2 million and 22,000 volunteers, respectively. The success of fund-raising via the Internet, and particularly the ability of candidates to extend their appeals to "low-dollar" donors online, led one campaign analyst to conclude that the Internet is "the ultimate grassroots fund-raising mechanism."[29]

Of course, voters can also go online to find out who is contributing to which candidates. In addition to the Federal Election Commission's online database of campaign contributors, numerous public-interest Web sites can be accessed by voters interested in learning where the money is coming from. Common Cause, the Center for Responsive Politics, and Vote Smart are just a few of the Web sites that offer this information (for the Web sites of these organizations, see the *Politics on the Web* feature at the end of Chapter 9).

The Rise of the Internet Campaign Strategist

Increasingly, candidates are facing the need for professionals who can create well-designed, informative, and user-friendly campaign Web sites to attract viewers, hold their attention, manage their e-mail, and track credit-card contributions from supporters. Enter the Internet campaign strategist—a professional consultant who manages a candidate's Web site.

For example, Democratic presidential candidate Bill Bradley hired Lynn Reed (who ran the Clinton/Gore Web site in 1996) to manage his Web site for the 2000 campaign. For a monthly consulting fee of $4,000, Reed agreed to screen position papers and other campaign materials before they were posted on the site, offer suggestions on how to make the site easier to navigate, handle incoming e-mail and credit-card campaign contributions, and generally integrate the Web site into the overall campaign strategy developed by Bradley's political advisers.[30]

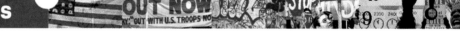

AMERICA at odds

Will the Internet Change Political Campaigning as We Know It?

Although some observers claim that Internet use will fundamentally change the way political candidates conduct their campaigns, others are not so sure. For one thing, to reach out to large numbers of voters, candidates need a mass medium, such as television, and the Internet is not that kind of medium—at least, not yet. Certainly, Democratic candidate Bill Bradley was aware of the Internet's limited reach when he announced his candidacy on his Web site in 1999. Before he made the announcement, he had his campaign staff call reporters from the major media to alert them to go online to see the announcement.

Notably, for all the publicity given to Internet fund-raising during the 2000 campaigns, a Gallup poll found that only 1 percent of those with Internet access have ever donated funds to a campaign online. And although a growing number of Americans are accessing the Internet to find information on the candidates, that number remains small. Indeed, perhaps the most significant use of the Web during a political campaign occurred not in the United States but in South Korea—see this chapter's *Comparative Politics* for details.

Additionally, many candidates' Web sites were not all that user friendly. According to Alex Zoghlin, the founder of a Web site development and strategy company, even John

comparative politics

Cyber Activism in South Korea

With nearly 60 percent of South Korea's citizens online, cyberspace has become a forum where South Koreans commonly address a broad range of issues. It is estimated that South Koreans spend more time in front of their computers than watching television.[31]

WAGING CYBER WAR AGAINST CORRUPT CANDIDATES

In January 2000, nearly six hundred civic groups in South Korea pledged to oust that country's most corrupt politicians from the National Assembly. And so they did—by using the Internet. The activists created a special Web site for campaigning against the reelection of sixty-seven members of the National Assembly in the April 2000 elections. These members, the site proclaimed, were "unfit" to hold office, and page after page of information on each candidate explained why. Data obtained from South Korea's National Elections Commission showed that 15 percent of the candidates had serious criminal records, and many others had committed such criminal offenses as tax evasion or draft dodging. This cyber revolt against corruption, hailed as the first

of its kind, was successful: fifty-eight of the sixty-seven candidates lost, including some candidates with powerful political connections.[32]

FREE SPEECH GOES NUCLEAR

Cyber activism has been on the rise since 2000. South Korean groups now have Web sites and cyber forums that address such issues as North-South reunification, the U.S. military presence in South Korea, and the nuclear threat from North Korea. In a country that is largely unaccustomed to democracy, the Internet has become a unique forum for free speech.

In October 2002, North Korea revealed that it was restarting its program to develop nuclear weapons. The announcement threw relations among North Korea, South Korea, and the United States into turmoil. Not surprisingly, South Koreans turned to the Internet to discuss the evolving global situation.

For Critical Analysis

What factors do you think influence whether the Internet can become a useful forum for political dissent in a nation?

McCain's Web site was difficult to navigate. The iconography changed from page to page and confused viewers, and the links sometimes failed to work.[33] Coverage of national convention news on the parties' Web sites was faulty and delayed. In sum, although the Internet may eventually transform political campaigning, it will probably not do so for some years to come.

why does it MATTER?

Politics, the Media, and Your Everyday Life

The relationship between politics and the media influences your everyday life no matter who you are. Why? The reason is that, especially during elections, the media present political stories, issues, and debates virtually every day twenty-four hours a day.

The point is that you will never be able to avoid political information. No matter what magazine or newspaper you read, you cannot avoid the political discussions that are regular features in the print media. If you watch the news on TV, there are political stories every single day. If you listen to commercial FM or AM radio, you will hear political news at least once an hour. During campaigns, you will hear paid political announcements on a regular basis.

Because political news dominates much of the media, you have three choices: (1) you can simply "tune out" the political information you encounter; (2) you can "stay tuned," but assimilate the information superficially because you are not very knowledgeable about politics; or (3) you can fully enjoy and utilize all of the political information to which you are exposed by gaining a better, deeper, and more analytical understanding of American politics and government.

It will always be part of your life. Therefore, simply for your own enjoyment, you have an incentive to gain a better grasp of politics.

Taking Action

Remember, too, that you can use the media to express your views—by writing letters to newspapers editors or calling a radio

talk show, for example. Radio talk-show hosts routinely invite listeners to call their stations and share their thoughts on political issues. Additionally, many political leaders have call-in radio shows during which voters can ask questions or voice their concerns on specific topics. The photo below shows Donald DiFrancesco answering a New Jersey resident's question on a radio program. DiFrancesco was acting governor of New Jersey during 2001 and 2002. (AP Photo/Daniel Hulshizer)

Key Terms

attack ad 230

electronic media 225

issue ad 230

managed news coverage 232

mass media 225

negative political
    advertising 230

political advertising 229

print media 225

push technology 238

sound bite 228

spin 232

spin doctor 232

Chapter Summary

1 The mass media include the print media (newspapers and magazines) and electronic media (radio, television, and the Web). The media have long played a vital role in the democratic process, both reflecting and influencing what Americans think about politics. The media can also influence what issues are on the political agenda.

2 Television is the primary news source for most Americans, but the limitations of the TV medium significantly affect the scope and depth of news coverage. Candidates for political office spend a great deal of time and money obtaining TV exposure through political ads, debates, and general news coverage. Candidates and their political consultants have become increasingly sophisticated in creating newsworthy events for the media to cover.

3 Talk radio has been characterized as the Wild West of the media, where the usual journalistic conventions do not apply. Political ranting and raving are common.

4 The media are frequently accused of bias toward one group or another. Studies have examined whether the media show a liberal bias, commercial bias, or racial bias. The expanding media universe, which now includes cable news channels twenty-four hours a day and the Internet, has changed the nature of news coverage.

5 An increasing number of Americans are turning to Web sites for political news. Virtually all major newspapers and magazines now have online versions, and the major TV news sources also have Web sites.

6 The Internet provides an inexpensive way for candidates to contact, recruit, and mobilize supporters; to disseminate information on the issues; and to raise funds. A problem with using the Internet for campaigning is that it cannot yet reach mass audiences, as TV can. Voters can go to various Web sites to learn who is contributing to a particular candidate's campaign.

RESOURCES FOR FURTHER STUDY

Selected Readings

Croteau, David, and William Hoynes. *Media/Society: Industries, Images, and Audiences.* Thousand Oaks, Calif.: Pine Forge Press, 2002. This insightful exploration of the media from their beginnings to the leap into cyberspace shows the complex interactions between the media and society, and emphasizes how economics drives news coverage.

Graber, Doris A. *Media Power in Politics.* Washington, D.C.: CQ Press, 2000. The essays in this collection explore how the mass media can shape political agendas and, in so doing, profoundly change American politics.

Herman, Edward S., and Noam Chomsky. *Manufacturing Consent: The Political Economy of the Mass Media.* New York: Pantheon Books, 2002. The authors argue that media bias inevitably results from such factors as media ownership and advertising.

NBC, Marc Robinson, Tom Brokaw, *et al. Brought to You in Living Color: Seventy-Five Years of Great Moments in Television and Radio from NBC.* New York: John Wiley & Sons, 2002. This book offers not only an impressive history of NBC but also numerous insights into network programming and entertainment spanning much of the past century.

 ## InfoTrac Citations

Using your InfoTrac password, access the InfoTrac database at **http://infotrac.thomsonlearning.com**. Once at the site, you can do "key word" searches to locate the following articles, each of which deals with a topic covered in this chapter. The key words to use in your search are indicated in parentheses.

- "Packaging the President: what the public sees of the nation's chief executive is carefully manipulated by the spin doctors at the White House" (Spin Doctors)

- "'Fair'? R-i-i-ght—Fox News Channel's Bias Is Clear" (Fox News Bias)

- "Lament of the Liberals" (Media Bias)

- "The Drudge Report Has Nothing on These Guys: Political Commentary Is Just a Click Away" (Drudge Report)

Politics on the Web

Literally thousands of news sources, including newspapers, news magazines, and television and radio stations, are now online. Total News Now offers a directory of more than a thousand news sources, including Fox News, MSNBC, CBS, ABC, and *USA Today*. To find Total News Now, go to

http://totalnews.com

- Another site for news sources is the Ultimate Collection of News Links. This site provides links to more than six thousand news sources, ranging from daily newspapers to business magazines and subject-specific weekly or monthly publications. You can access this site at

  http://pppp.net/links/news/NA.html

- If you are interested in news stories covered by ABC, CBS, and NBC television since 1968, you can find abstracts of these stories at Vanderbilt University's Television News Archive, which is online at

  http://tvnews.vanderbilt.edu

- To find out what newspapers are online and whether your own local paper may be on the Web, you can access Newspapers Online at

  http://www.newspapers.com

- The Claremont Institute is an interactive community that aims to bring Internet users together with public-policy organizations under "the broad umbrella of 'conservative' thoughts, ideas, and actions." It can be found at

  http://www.townhall.com

- The Polling Report Web site provides polling results on a number of issues, organized by topics. The site is easy to use and up to date. Go to

  http://www.pollingreport.com

- The PBS Democracy Project provides some good tips on how to analyze a poll at the following Web page:

  http://www.pbs.org/democracy/
  readbetweenthelines/poll.html

Web Resources on Your CD-ROM

On your CD-ROM, you will find Web resources, news articles, Internet activities, and video clips related to the topics in this chapter. Resources related to this chapter include the following:

- **Values Inventory**—Political Ideology: What Is the Media's Role in Wartime?
- **Why Does It Matter?**—Write a Letter to an Editor with Your Feelings about the President.
- **Updates**—Keep up with the issues in this chapter!
- **Web Resources**—Internet Activities: Media Portrayal of Combat in the Gulf War; A New Professionalism in War Reporting.
- **Where Do You Stand?**—Dialogue: What's the Media's Role during Wartime?
- **Comparative Politics**—Internet Censorship in China.
- **Video**—Internet Voting.
- **NewsEdge**—Visit this global resource for current events related to this chapter.

chapter **11**

congress

245

Does Congress Have to Look like America to Represent It?

The 108th Congress that began its term in January 2003 is, as Congress has always been, a predominantly white male institution. Of the 535 members of Congress (435 in the House and 100 in the Senate), 14 percent are women, 7 percent are African American, and 4 percent are Hispanic. In contrast, in the general population of the United States, 51 percent are women, 12.5 percent are Hispanic, and 12.1 percent are African American. Clearly, in terms of race and gender, Congress does not look like America. Does this matter?

In 1776, John Adams wrote of representative assemblies, "[They] should be in miniature an exact portrait of the people at large." James Wilson repeated the sentiment at the Constitutional Convention in 1787 when he said, "The legislature ought to be the most exact transcript of the whole society, . . . the faithful echo of the voices of the people." The theory of representation to which the founders subscribed dictates that the competing interests in society should be represented in Congress. Are race and gender among these "interests"? Can a man represent a woman's interests? Can a white person represent the interests of African Americans?

Demographic Balance Matters

Demographic balance in Congress matters because the experiences of different groups can lead to different perceptions, interests, and desires. Female legislators might be more interested in or sensitive to women's health issues or sexual harassment, for example. African Americans or Hispanics in Congress may be more concerned about the erosion of civil liberties than other members of Congress are. Can the interests of all Americans be adequately represented by white men?

Furthermore, about 30 percent of the members of Congress are millionaires, compared to only 1 percent of Americans. Most members of the House and Senate are lawyers. A large number also have significant investments in U.S. corporations. Trent Franks (R., Ariz.), a freshman congressman, is the owner of Liberty Petroleum Corporation. He took a pay cut when he came to the House of Representatives, where the annual salary is only $154,000. Of course, this is a very comfortable salary when compared to the median household income in the United States of about $42,000 per year.

The notion that our legislators should mirror their constituents in terms of race or gender, or even income or age, is called "descriptive representation" by political scientists. It has sometimes been dismissed by those outside academia as mere "political correctness" rather than genuine political reform. Still, proponents argue that descriptive representation is vital to overcoming the political marginalization of minorities and women in our society.

Legislators Are the Trustees of Society

No one disputes that a member of Congress has an obligation to his or her constituents. Less clear is the extent to which broad national interests should play a role in congressional representation. The "trustee" view of representation holds that legislators should act as the trustees of the broad interests of the entire society. If legislators believe that a national need outweighs the narrow interests of their constituents, they should vote their conscience. If legislators are trustees, then there is no reason why white males cannot represent the interests of women and minorities as well as any other group of legislators. For example, for decades, Ted Kennedy (D., Mass.), a white senator, has been well known for championing the cause of civil rights in Congress.

As you will read later in this chapter, one of the objections to racial gerrymandering—in which congressional districts are redrawn to maximize the number of minority group members within district boundaries—is that it assumes that people of a particular race, merely because of their race, think alike. Opponents of "descriptive representation" argue that there is no reason to assume that a black member of Congress can represent the interests of black people better than a white member of Congress. African Americans hold a broad range of views on the issues facing our nation, as do women, Hispanics, and Asians. As long as our views are represented, it does not matter whether our race or gender is represented.

Where Do You Stand?

1. Do you think that Congress needs to look like America to represent it?

2. Do you feel that your views are adequately represented in Congress now?

Interacting with Your CD-ROM Resources

Use your CD-ROM to access resources on the Web, simulations, participation exercises, and video clips. Important resources related to this feature include:

- **Values Inventory**—Political Ideology: Does Congress Have to Look like America to Represent It?
- **Where Do You Stand?**—Dialogue: Does Congress Have to Look like America to Represent It?
- **Web Resources**—Internet Activities: Congressional Demographics; The Congressional Hispanic Caucus.

INTRODUCTION

Congress is the lawmaking branch of government. When someone says, "There ought to be a law," at the federal level it is Congress that will make that law. The framers had a strong suspicion of a powerful executive authority. Consequently, they made Congress—not the executive branch (the presidency)—the central institution of American government. Yet, as noted in Chapter 2, the founders created a system of checks and balances to ensure that no branch of the federal government, including Congress, could exercise too much power.

Many Americans view Congress as a largely faceless, anonymous legislative body that is quite distant and removed from their everyday lives. Yet as you read in the chapter-opening feature, the people you elect to Congress represent and advocate your interests at the very highest level of power. Furthermore, the laws created by the men and women in the U.S. Congress affect the daily lives of every American in one way or another. Getting to know your congressional representatives and how they are voting in Congress on issues that concern you is an important step toward becoming an informed voter.

The Structure and Make-Up of Congress

The framers agreed that the Congress should be the "first branch of the government," as James Madison said, but they did not agree on its organization. Ultimately, they decided on a bicameral legislature—a Congress consisting of two chambers. This was part of the Great Compromise, which you read about in Chapter 2. The framers favored a bicameral legislature so that the two chambers, the House and the Senate, might serve as checks on each other's power and activity. The House was to represent the people as a whole, or the majority. The Senate was to represent the states and would protect the interests of small states by giving them the same number of senators (two per state) as the larger states. (For a discussion of the differences between the U.S. Congress and the British Parliament, see this chapter's *Comparative Politics* feature.)

comparative politics

How the British Parliament Differs from the U.S. Congress

The framers of the U.S. Constitution, for the most part, were used to the British form of government in which the central institution is the national legislature, known as Parliament. Like our own Congress, Parliament is a bicameral body: it is made up of the House of Commons and the House of Lords. Unlike Congress, however, the British Parliament (as in all parliamentary systems) is based on the *fusion* of powers rather than the *separation* of powers. It manages both the legislative and the executive powers of the nation. Parliament's legislative powers include passing and changing laws; its executive powers include choosing the prime minister, who is the leader of the majority party in the House of Commons, and the cabinet (the heads of executive agencies) that will serve the prime minister.

THE HOUSE OF COMMONS

The House of Commons is the legislative branch and currently consists of 659 elected officials. This lower house, known as "the Commons," is the more powerful of the two houses. Its members, known as Members of Parliament, or MPs, are popularly elected from geographic districts. Any MP is allowed to introduce legislation, but most measures are introduced by the government, which is made up of the prime minister and the cabinet collectively. The bill is then debated and sent to one of the eight standing committees that review bills and prepare them for final consideration by the full chamber. Unlike congressional committees, which specialize in areas such as agriculture or the armed forces, committees in the House of Commons are general committees that consider bills on a wide variety of subjects.

THE HOUSE OF LORDS

The upper chamber of Parliament is known as the House of Lords. In the past, the House of Lords included 750 hereditary peers (members of the nobility who became so by birth) with such titles as *baron, viscount, earl,* and *duke*. Due to recent reforms, only 92 hereditary peers now sit in the House of Lords. The other members of the House of Lords include 544 persons who are appointed as peers for life by the queen and 26 bishops of the Church of England.

The House of Lords was once a powerful branch of the British government, but today it has little real authority over legislation. If the House of Lords defeats a bill passed in the Commons, the Commons need only pass it a second time in the next session to make the bill become law. The House of Lords may amend legislation, but any changes it makes can be canceled by the Commons.

For Critical Analysis

What is one of the key differences between the upper chamber of the British Parliament and the U.S. Senate?

Bengie Regensberg, the Democratic candidate for state House of Representatives District 68, speaks to Sandra Sandoval about the drought in Dilia, New Mexico, prior to the 2000 elections. Much of District 68 is rural, populated with constituents concerned about farming and ranching issues along with future economic development. (AP Photo/ Tony Talbot)

Apportionment of House Seats

APPORTIONMENT The distribution of House seats among the states on the basis of their respective populations.

The Constitution provides for the **apportionment** (distribution) of House seats among the states on the basis of their respective populations. States with larger populations, such as California, have many more representatives than states with smaller populations, such as Wyoming. California, for example, currently has fifty-three representatives in the House; Wyoming has only one.

Every ten years, House seats are reapportioned based on the outcome of the decennial (ten-year) census conducted by the U.S. Census Bureau. Figure 11–1 indicates the states that gained and lost seats based on population changes noted in the 2000 census. This redistribution of seats took effect with the 108th Congress elected in 2002.

FIGURE 11–1

Reapportionment of House Seats following the 2000 Census

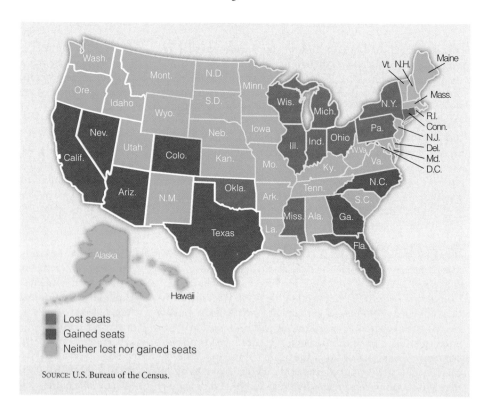

SOURCE: U.S. Bureau of the Census.

Each state is guaranteed at least one seat, no matter what its population. Today, seven states have only one representative.[1] The District of Columbia, American Samoa, Guam, and the U.S. Virgin Islands all send nonvoting delegates to the House. Puerto Rico, a self-governing possession of the United States, is represented by a nonvoting resident commissioner.

Congressional Districts

Whereas senators are elected to represent all of the people in the state, representatives are elected by the voters of a particular area known as a **congressional district.** The Constitution makes no provisions for congressional districts, and in the early 1800s each state was given the right to decide whether to have districts at all. Most states set up single-member districts, in which voters in each district elected one of the state's representatives. In states that chose not to have districts, representatives were chosen at large, from the state as a whole. In 1842, however, Congress passed an act that required all states to send representatives to Congress from single-member districts, as you read in Chapter 7.

In the early 1900s, the number of House members increased as the population expanded. In 1929, however, a federal law fixed House membership at 435 members. Today, the 435 members of the House are chosen by the voters in 435 separate congressional districts across the country. If a state's population allows it to have only one representative, as is the situation in a few states, the entire state is one congressional district. In contrast, states with large populations have numerous districts. California, for example, because its population entitles it to send fifty-three representatives to the House, has fifty-three congressional districts.

The lines of the congressional districts are drawn by the authority of state legislatures. States must meet certain requirements, though, in drawing district boundaries. To ensure equal representation in the House, districts must contain, as nearly as possible, an equal number of people. Additionally, each district must have contiguous boundaries and must be "geographically compact."

The Requirement of Equal Representation
If congressional districts are not made up of equal populations, the value of people's votes is not the same. In the past, state legislatures often used this knowledge to their advantage. For example, traditionally, many state legislatures were controlled by rural areas. By drawing districts that were not equal in population, rural leaders attempted to curb the number of representatives from growing urban centers. At one point in the 1960s, in many states the largest district had twice the population of the smallest district. In effect, this meant that a person's vote in the largest district had only half the value of a person's vote in the smallest district.

For some time, the Supreme Court refused to address this problem. In 1962, however, in *Baker v. Carr,*[2] the Court ruled that the Tennessee state legislature's **malapportionment** was an issue that could be heard in the federal courts because it affected the constitutional requirement of equal protection under the law. Two years later, in *Wesberry v. Sanders,*[3] the Supreme Court held that congressional districts must have equal populations. This principle has come to be known as the **"one person, one vote" rule.** In other words, one person's vote has to count as much as another's vote.

Gerrymandering
Although the Supreme Court, in the 1960s, established the requirement that congressional districts must be equal in population, it continued to be silent on the issue of gerrymandered districts. **Gerrymandering** occurs when a district's boundaries are drawn to maximize the influence of a certain group or political party. This can be done by drawing the boundaries in such a way as to include as many of the political party's voters as possible. In another form of gerrymandering, the lines are drawn so that the opponent's supporters are spread across two or more districts, thus diluting the opponent's strength. (The term *gerrymandering* was originally used in reference to the tactics of Elbridge Gerry, governor of Massachusetts, in drawing district lines prior to the 1812 election—see Figure 11–2 on page 250.)

CONGRESSIONAL DISTRICT The geographic area that is served by one representative in Congress.

MALAPPORTIONMENT A condition that results when, based on population and representation, the voting power of citizens in one district becomes more influential than the voting power of citizens in another district.

"ONE PERSON, ONE VOTE" RULE A rule, or principle, requiring that congressional districts must have equal populations so that one person's vote counts as much as another's vote.

GERRYMANDERING The drawing of a legislative district's boundaries in such a way as to maximize the influence of a certain group or political party.

Elbridge Gerry, governor of Massachusetts 1810–1812. (Library of Congress)

FIGURE 11-2
The First "Gerrymander"

Prior to the 1812 elections, the Massachusetts legislature divided up Essex County in a way that favored Governor Elbridge Gerry's party; the result was a district that looked like a salamander. A newspaper editor of the time referred to it as a "gerrymander," and the name stuck. (Library of Congress)

Although there have been constitutional challenges to political gerrymandering,[4] the practice continues. It was certainly evident following the 2000 census. Sophisticated computer programs can now analyze the partisan leanings of individual neighborhoods and city blocks. District lines are drawn to "pack" the opposing party's voters into the smallest number of districts or "crack" the opposing party's voters into several different districts. "Packing and cracking" makes congressional races less competitive and helps to ensure that incumbents will be reelected (the power of incumbency will be discussed in more detail shortly).

Although political gerrymandering has a long history in this country, racial gerrymandering is a relatively new phenomenon. In the early 1990s, the U.S. Department of Justice instructed state legislatures to draw district lines to maximize the voting power of minority groups. As a result, several so-called **minority-majority districts** were created, many of which took on bizarre shapes. For example, North Carolina's newly drawn Twelfth Congressional District was 165 miles long—a narrow strip that, for the most part, followed Interstate 85. Georgia's new Eleventh District stretched from Atlanta to the Atlantic, splitting eight counties and five municipalities. The practice of racial gerrymandering has generated heated argument on both sides of the issue.

MINORITY-MAJORITY DISTRICT A district whose boundaries are drawn so as to maximize the voting power of minority groups.

AMERICA at odds

Racial Gerrymandering

Some groups contend that minority-majority districts are necessary to ensure equal representation of minority groups, as mandated by the Voting Rights Act of 1965. They further contend that these districts have been instrumental in increasing the number of African Americans holding political office. Furthermore, argue supporters, minority-majority districts are not racially segregated but rather are among the most racially integrated districts in the country. Minority-majority districts in the South contain, on average, 45 percent nonblack voters, whereas before 1990 redistricting plans in the South created segregated, white-majority districts.[5]

Opponents of racial gerrymandering argue that such race-based districting is unconstitutional because it violates the equal protection clause. Furthermore, opponents point to a basic flaw in the underlying rationale for such a practice: racial gerrymandering assumes that people of a particular race, merely because of their race, think alike, share the same political interests, and will prefer the same candidates at the polls. In a series of cases in the 1990s, the Supreme Court agreed and held that when race is the dominant factor in the drawing of congressional district lines, the districts are unconstitutional and must be redrawn.[6]

In 2001, however, the Supreme Court issued a ruling that seemed—at least to some observers—to be out of step with its earlier rulings. North Carolina's Twelfth District, which had been redrawn in 1997, was again challenged in court as unconstitutional, and a lower court agreed. When the case reached the Supreme Court, however, the justices concluded that there was insufficient evidence that race had been the dominant factor in redrawing the district's boundaries.[7] Clearly, the controversy over racial gerrymandering will continue for some time to come.

Congressional Elections

The U.S. Constitution requires that congressional representatives be elected every second year by popular vote. Senators are elected every six years, also (since the ratification of the Seventeenth Amendment) by popular vote. Under Article I, Section 4, of the Constitution, state legislatures control the "Times, Places and Manner of holding Elections for Senators and Representatives." Congress, however, "may at any time by Law make or alter such Regulations." As you read in Chapter 9, control over the process of nominating congressional candidates has shifted from party conventions to direct primaries in which the party identifiers in the electorate select the candidates who will carry that party's endorsement into the actual election.[8]

Who Can Be a Member of Congress?

The Constitution sets forth only a few qualifications that those running for Congress must meet. To be a member of the House, a person must be a citizen of the United States for at least seven years prior to his or her election, a legal resident of the state from which he or she is to be elected, and at least twenty-five years of age. To be elected to the Senate, a person must be a citizen for at least nine years, a legal resident of the state from which she or he is to be elected, and at least thirty years of age. The Supreme Court has ruled that neither the Congress nor the states can add to these three qualifications.[9]

Once elected to Congress, a senator or representative receives an annual salary from the government. He or she also enjoys certain perks and privileges. Additionally, if a member of Congress wants to run for reelection in the next congressional elections, that person's chances are greatly enhanced by the power that incumbency brings to a reelection campaign.

The Power of Incumbency

The power of incumbency has long been noted in American politics. Today, incumbents win so often and by such large margins that political scientist Ross K. Baker has compared our electoral system to a kind of "hereditary entitlement."[10] As you can see in Table 11–1 on the following page, most incumbents in Congress are reelected at election time.

Incumbent politicians enjoy several advantages over their opponents. A key advantage is their fund-raising ability. Most incumbent members of Congress have a much larger network of contacts, donors, and lobbyists than their opponents. Incumbents raise, on average, twice as much in campaign funds as their challengers. Other advantages that incumbents can put to work at election time include:

TABLE 11-1
The Power of Incumbency

	PRESIDENTIAL-YEAR ELECTIONS						MIDTERM ELECTIONS						
	1980	1984	1988	1992	1996	2000	1978	1982	1986	1990	1994	1998	2002
House													
Number of incumbent candidates	398	411	409	368	384	403	382	393	394	406	387	402	393
Reelected	361	392	402	325	361	394	358	354	385	390	349	395	383
Percentage of total	90.7	95.4	98.3	88.3	94.0	97.8	93.7	90.1	97.7	96.0	90.2	98.3	97.5
Defeated	37	19	7	43	23	9	24	39	9	16	38	7	10
Senate													
Number of incumbent candidates	29	29	27	28	21	29	25	30	28	32	26	29	28
Reelected	16	26	23	23	19	23	15	28	21	31	24	26	24
Percentage of total	55.2	89.6	85.2	82.1	90.5	79.3	60.0	93.3	75.0	96.9	92.3	89.7	85.7
Defeated	13	3	4	5	2	6	10	2	7	1	2	3	4

SOURCES: Norman Ornstein, Thomas E. Mann, and Michael J. Malbin, *Vital Statistics on Congress, 2001–2002* (Washington, D.C.: The AEI Press, 2002); and authors' updates.

- *Congressional franking privileges*—members of Congress can mail newsletters and other correspondence to their constituents at the taxpayer's expense.
- *Professional staffs*—members have large administrative staffs both in Washington, D.C., and in their home districts.
- *Lawmaking power*—members of Congress can back legislation that will benefit their states or districts, and then campaign on that legislative record in the next election.
- *Access to the media*—because they are elected officials, members have many opportunities to stage events for the press and thereby obtain free publicity.
- *Name recognition*—incumbent members are far better known to the voters than challengers are.

Critics of the advantage enjoyed by incumbents argue that it reduces the competition necessary for a healthy democracy. It also suppresses voter turnout. Voters are less likely to turn out when an incumbent candidate is virtually guaranteed reelection. The solution often proposed to eliminate the power of incumbency is term limits. Persuading incumbent politicians to vote for term limits, however, is nearly impossible.

Congressional Terms and Term Limits

As you read earlier, members of the House of Representatives serve two-year terms, and senators serve six-year terms. This means that every two years, we hold congressional elections: the entire House of Representatives and a third of the Senate are up for election. In January of every odd-numbered year, a "new" Congress convenes (of course, two-thirds of the senators are not new, and most incumbents are reelected, so they are not new to Congress, either). Each Congress has been numbered consecutively, dating back to 1789. The Congress that convened in 2003 is the 108th.

Each congressional term is divided into two regular sessions, or meetings—one for each year. Until about 1940, Congress remained in session for only four or five months, but the complicated rush of legislation and increased demand for services from the public in recent years have forced Congress to remain in session through most of each year.[11] Both chambers, however, schedule short recesses, or breaks, for holidays and vacations. The president may call a *special session* during a recess, but because Congress now meets on nearly a year-round basis, such sessions are rare.

As you will read in Chapter 12, the president can serve for no more than two terms in office, thanks to the Twenty-second Amendment. There is no limit on the number of terms a

Term limits have stirred controversy at all levels of government. Here, Maryland politician Robin Ficker expresses his views on term limits from atop a stepladder during rush-hour traffic in Bethesda, Maryland. A "Yes" vote on Question C, a question on the ballot for an upcoming election, would establish term limits for certain county officeholders. (AP Photo/Leslie E. Kossaff)

senator or representative can serve, however. Indeed, Strom Thurmond (R., S.C.) served eight terms in the U.S. Senate, from 1955 until he retired, at the age of one hundred, in 2003. Efforts to pass a constitutional amendment that would impose term limits on members of Congress have had little success. Most recently, the House of Representatives failed to pass a term-limits constitutional amendment in 1995. Nonetheless, the notion of imposing congressional term limits remains an important—and controversial—issue.

AMERICA at odds

Are Term Limits the Cure for Congressional Careerism?

In contrast to congressional representatives and senators in the past, today's legislators often view holding congressional office as a career in itself. As a result, the argument goes, our political leaders make decisions less on the basis of any perceived national interest than on how their decisions will affect their chances for reelection. One of the arguments in favor of term limits is that they would remove the element of careerism from politics. Term limits would allow legislators to exercise independent judgment, and Congress could assume the role of a deliberative body whose foremost concern is to maintain a carefully crafted balance of power among competing interests.

Although polls show that a majority of Americans support term limits, it may be difficult—if not impossible—to enact them. Incumbents, once in power, rarely vote to force themselves out. In the years when the Democrats controlled Congress, they tended to oppose term limits, and the Republicans favored them. Since 1994, when the Republicans came to power, Republican members have been abandoning the push for term limits.

Indeed, several members of Congress who pledged voluntarily to serve no more than two or three terms have reneged on their promises.

There is another explanation for the weakening support for term limits among many Republicans, however. David Broder, columnist for the *Washington Post,* argues that there is "an acknowledgment on the part of Republicans that running government is a serious business where experience counts."[12] Members of Congress who oppose term limits may simply be acknowledging that governing this country is a task best left to experienced politicians.

Congressional Leadership

How each chamber of Congress is organized is largely a function of the two major political parties. The majority party in each chamber chooses the major officers of that chamber, controls debate on the floor, selects all committee chairpersons, and has a majority on all committees.

House Leadership

Both the House and the Senate have systems of leadership. Before Congress begins work, members of each party in each chamber meet to choose their leaders. The Constitution provides for the presiding officers of the House and Senate; Congress may choose what other leaders it feels it needs.

SPEAKER OF THE HOUSE The presiding officer in the House of Representatives. The Speaker has traditionally been a long-time member of the majority party and is often the most powerful and influential member of the House.

Speaker of the House   Chief among the leaders in the House of Representatives is the **Speaker of the House.** This office is mandated by the Constitution and is filled by a vote taken at the beginning of each congressional term. The Speaker has traditionally been a long-time member of the majority party who has risen in rank and influence through years of service in the House. The candidate for Speaker is selected by the majority-party caucus; the House as a whole then approves the selection.

Republican Dennis Hastert became Speaker of the House in 1999. The Speaker holds a substantial amount of power. Here, he administers the oath to members of the 108th Congress on January 7, 2003, on the floor of the U.S. House of Representatives. (AP Photo/Joe Marquette)

As the presiding officer of the House and the leader of the majority party, the Speaker has a great deal of power. In the nineteenth century, the Speaker had even more power and was known as the "king of the congressional mountain." Speakers known by such names as "Uncle Joe Cannon" and "Czar Reed" ruled the House with almost exclusive power. A revolt in 1910 reduced the Speaker's powers and gave some of those powers to various committees. Today, the Speaker still has many important powers, including the following:

- The Speaker has substantial control over what bills get assigned to which committees.
- The Speaker presides over the sessions of the House, recognizing or ignoring members who wish to speak.
- The Speaker votes in the event of a tie, interprets and applies House rules, rules on points of order (questions about procedures asked by members), puts questions to a vote, and interprets the outcome of most of the votes taken.
- The Speaker plays a major role in making important committee assignments, which all members desire.
- The Speaker schedules bills for action.

The Speaker may choose whether to vote on any measure. If the Speaker chooses to vote, he appoints a temporary presiding officer (called a Speaker *pro tempore*), who then occupies the Speaker's chair. Under the House rules, the only time the Speaker *must* vote is to break a tie, because otherwise a tie automatically defeats a bill. The Speaker does not often vote, but by choosing to vote in some cases, the Speaker can actually cause a tie and defeat a proposal that is unpopular with the majority party.

Majority Leader

The **majority leader** of the House is elected by the caucus of party members to act as spokesperson for the party and to keep the party together. The majority leader's job is to help plan the party's legislative program, organize other party members to support legislation favored by the party, and make sure the chairpersons on the many committees finish work on bills that are important to the party. The House majority leader makes speeches on important bills, stating the majority party's position.

Minority Leader

The House **minority leader** is the leader of the minority party. Although not as powerful as the majority leader, the minority leader has similar responsibilities. The primary duty of the minority leader is to maintain cohesion within the party. The

MAJORITY LEADER The party leader elected by the majority party in the House or in the Senate.

MINORITY LEADER The party leader elected by the minority party in the House or in the Senate.

The current House minority leader is Nancy Pelosi (D., Calif.), shown on the left. The current House majority leader is Tom DeLay (R., Tex.), shown on the right. (Left: AP/Eric Risberg; Right: AP/*The Facts,* Eric Lyle Kayne)

minority leader persuades influential members of the party to follow its position and organizes fellow party members in criticism of the majority party's policies and programs.

Whips The leadership of each party includes assistants to the majority and minority leaders known as **whips.** Whips originated in the British House of Commons, where they were named after the "whipper in," the rider who keeps the hounds together in a fox hunt. The term was applied to assistant party leaders because of the pressure that they place on party members to follow the party's positions. Whips try to determine how each member is going to vote on certain issues and then advise the party leaders on the strength of party support. Whips also try to see that members are present when important votes are to be taken and that they vote with the party leadership. For example, if the Republican Party strongly supports a tax-cut bill, the Republican Party whip might meet with other Republican Party members in the House to try to persuade them to vote with the party.

Senate Leadership

The Constitution makes the vice president of the United States the president of the Senate. As presiding officer, the vice president may call on members to speak and put questions to a vote. The vice president is not an elected member of the Senate, however, and may not take part in Senate debates. The vice president may cast a vote in the Senate only in the event of a tie. In the past, the vice president had little influence in the Senate and was rarely even present. In view of today's closely divided Senate, if President George W. Bush's policies are to become law, Vice President Dick Cheney may occasionally need to break tie votes in the Senate.

President *Pro Tempore* Because vice presidents are rarely available to preside over the Senate, senators elect another presiding officer, the president *pro tempore* ("pro tem"), who serves in the absence of the vice president. The president pro tem is elected by the whole Senate and is ordinarily the member of the majority party with the longest continuous term of service in the Senate. In the absence of both the president pro tem and the vice president, a temporary presiding officer is selected from the ranks of the Senate, usually a junior member of the majority party.

Party Leaders The real power in the Senate is held by the majority leader, the minority leader, and their whips. The majority leader is the most powerful individual and chief spokesperson of the majority party. The majority leader directs the legislative program and

WHIP A member of Congress who assists the majority or minority leader in the House or in the Senate in managing the party's legislative preferences.

Bill Frist (R., Tenn.), left, is the Senate majority leader, and Tom Daschle (D., S. Dak.), right, is the Senate minority leader. (Left: AP/Doug Mills, File; Right: AP Photo/Dennis Cook)

party strategy. The minority leader commands the minority party's opposition to the policies of the majority party and directs the legislative strategy of the minority party.

Congressional Committees

Thousands of bills are introduced during every session of Congress, and no single member can possibly be adequately informed on all the issues that arise. The committee system is a way to provide for specialization, or a division of the legislative labor. Members of a committee can concentrate on just one area or topic—such as agriculture or transportation—and develop sufficient expertise to draft appropriate legislation when needed. The flow of legislation through both the House and the Senate is determined largely by the speed with which the members of these committees act on bills and resolutions. The permanent and most powerful committees of Congress are called **standing committees;** their names are listed in Table 11–2.

Before any bill can be considered by the entire House or Senate, it must be approved by a majority vote in the standing committee to which it was assigned. As mentioned, standing committees are controlled by the majority party in each chamber. Committee membership is generally divided between the parties according to the number of members in each chamber. Most House and Senate committees are also divided into **subcommittees,** which have limited areas of jurisdiction. Today, there are more than two hundred subcommittees. There are also other types of committees in Congress. Special, or select, committees, which may be either permanent or temporary, are formed to study specific problems or issues. Joint committees are formed by the concurrent action of both chambers of Congress and consist of members from each chamber. Joint committees have dealt with the economy, taxation, and the Library of Congress. There are also conference committees, which include members from both the House and the Senate. They are formed for the purpose of achieving agreement between the House and the Senate on the exact wording of legislative acts when the two chambers pass legislative proposals in different forms. No bill can be sent to the White House to be signed into law unless it first passes both chambers in identical form.

STANDING COMMITTEE A permanent committee in Congress that deals with legislation concerning a particular area, such as agriculture or foreign relations.

SUBCOMMITTEE A division of a larger committee that deals with a particular part of the committee's policy area. Most of the standing committees in Congress have several subcommittees.

TABLE 11–2

Standing Committees in the 108th Congress, 2003–2005

HOUSE COMMITTEES	SENATE COMMITTEES
Agriculture	Agriculture, Nutrition, and Forestry
Appropriations	Appropriations
Armed Services	Armed Services
Budget	Banking, Housing, and Urban Affairs
Education and the Workforce	Budget
Energy and Commerce	Commerce, Science, and Transportation
Financial Services	Energy and Natural Resources
Government Reform	Environment and Public Works
House Administration	Finance
International Relations	Foreign Relations
Judiciary	Governmental Affairs
Resources	Health, Education, Labor, and Pensions
Rules	Judiciary
Science	Rules and Administration
Small Business	Small Business and Entrepreneurship
Standards of Official Conduct	Veterans' Affairs
Transportation and Infrastructure	
Veterans' Affairs	
Ways and Means	

Senators Hillary Rodham Clinton,
(D., N.Y.) and Joseph Lieberman
(D., Conn.), both members of the
Senate Subcommittee on Clean Air,
Wetlands, and Climate Change, listen
to testimony at a hearing. The hearing
was held on February 11, 2002, to
examine the possible health hazards
stemming from the fires and dusts at
the World Trade Center terrorist
attacks site. The senators heard expert
testimony on disaster management,
health monitoring, and the effects of
pollution on residents and rescue
workers. (AP Photo/Jeff Zelevansky)

Most of the actual work of legislating is performed by the committees and subcommittees
(the "little legislatures"[13]) within Congress. In creating or amending laws, committee members work closely with relevant interest groups and administrative agency personnel. (For
more details on the interaction among these groups, see the discussion of "iron triangles" in
Chapter 13.)

A Congress Divided

In recent years, power in Congress has been almost evenly divided between Republicans and
Democrats. Although the Democrats controlled Congress for nearly forty years, from 1955
until 1994, since then the Republicans have held a slim majority. The 2000 elections returned
a majority of Republicans to the House of Representatives. In the Senate, however, there were
initially fifty Republicans and fifty Democrats. In May 2001, that situation changed when
Senator James Jeffords of Vermont announced that he was leaving the Republican Party and
becoming an independent. Jeffords also declared that he would sit with the Democratic
Caucus for party organizational purposes, thus giving the Democrats control of the Senate.

The evenly divided Senate and the bitter presidential election in 2000 caused many to wonder whether partisanship would prevail in Congress. In fact, on some issues, the Democratic
Senate and the Republican White House were not able to work together. Filling vacant federal
judgeships proved to be one of the most contentious political issues facing President George
W. Bush (see Chapter 14 for more on the federal judiciary). In several instances during the
107th (2001–2003) Congress, the Senate Judiciary Committee voted along partisan lines to
defeat the president's nominees.

The 2002 congressional elections gave the Republicans a slight majority in the Senate. From
the beginning, however, the Republican leadership stumbled. Trent Lott (R., Miss.), who was
poised to return as Senate majority leader, was forced to step down from his leadership post
after he made comments that were perceived to be racist at a private party and the comments
were made public. For their part, many Democrats, reflecting on their party's losses in 2002,
concluded that their party lacked strong leadership and vision. Some pledged to take stronger
stands on certain issues, such as the economy and President Bush's tax plan, which could
mean more partisanship.

The Differences between the House and the Senate

The major differences between the House and the Senate are listed in Table 11–3. To understand what goes on in the chambers of Congress, we need to look at the effects of bicameralism. Each chamber of Congress has developed certain distinct features.

Size Matters

Obviously, with 435 members, the House cannot operate the same way that the Senate can with only 100 members. (There are also nonvoting delegates from the District of Columbia, Guam, American Samoa, Puerto Rico, and the U.S. Virgin Islands in the House.) With its larger size, the House needs both more rules and more formal rules; otherwise no work would ever get done. The most obvious formal rules that are required have to do with debate on the floor.

The Senate normally permits extended debate on all issues that arise before it. In contrast, the House uses an elaborate system: the House **Rules Committee** normally proposes time limitations on debate for any bill, which are accepted or modified by the House. Despite its greater size, as a consequence of its stricter time limits on debate, the House is often able to act on legislation more quickly than the Senate.

In the Senate, Debate Can Just Keep Going and Going

At one time, both the House and the Senate allowed unlimited debates, but the House ended this practice in 1811. In the Senate, the tradition of unlimited debate, called **filibustering**, dates back to 1790 and continues today. The longest filibuster was waged by Senator Strom Thurmond of South Carolina, who held forth on the Senate floor for twenty-four hours and eighteen minutes in an attempt to thwart the passage of the 1957 Civil Rights Act.

Today, under Senate Rule 22, debate may be ended by invoking **cloture**—a method of closing debate and bringing the matter under consideration to a vote in the Senate. Sixteen senators must sign a petition requesting cloture, and then, after two days have elapsed, three-fifths of the entire membership must vote for cloture. Once cloture is invoked, each senator may speak on a bill for no more than one hour before a vote is taken. Additionally, a final vote must take place within one hundred hours after cloture has been invoked.

RULES COMMITTEE A standing committee in the House of Representatives that provides special rules governing how particular bills will be considered and debated by the House. The Rules Committee normally proposes time limitations on debate for any bill, which are accepted or modified by the House.

FILIBUSTERING The Senate tradition of unlimited debate, undertaken for the purpose of preventing action on a bill.

CLOTURE A method of ending debate in the Senate and bringing the matter under consideration to a vote by the entire chamber.

TABLE 11–3

Major Differences between the House and the Senate

HOUSE*	SENATE*
Members chosen from local districts	Members chosen from an entire state
Two-year term	Six-year term
Originally elected by voters	Originally (until 1913) elected by state legislatures
May impeach (accuse, indict) federal officials	May convict federal officials of impeachable offenses
Larger (435 voting members)	Smaller (100 members)
More formal rules	Fewer rules and restrictions
Debate limited	Debate extended
Floor action controlled	Unanimous consent rules
Less prestige and less individual notice	More prestige and media attention
Originates bills for raising revenues	Power of "advice and consent" on presidential appointments and treaties
Local or narrow leadership	National leadership

*Some of these differences, such as term of office, are provided for in the Constitution, while others, such as debate rules, are not.

The Senate Wins the Prestige Race, Hands Down

Because of the large number of representatives, few can garner the prestige that a senator enjoys. Senators have relatively little difficulty in gaining access to the media. Members of the House, who run for reelection every two years, have to survive many reelection campaigns before they can obtain recognition for their activities. Usually, a representative has to become an important committee leader before she or he can enjoy the consistent attention of the national news media.

The Legislative Process

Look at Figure 11–3, which shows the basic elements of the process through which a bill becomes law at the national level. Not all of the complexities of the process are shown, to be sure. For example, the schematic does not indicate the extensive lobbying and media politics that are often involved in the legislative process. There is also no mention of the informal negotiations and "horse trading" that go on to get a bill passed.

The basic steps in the process are as follows:

1. *Introduction of legislation.* Most bills are proposed by the executive branch, although individual members of Congress or its staff can come up with ideas for new legislation; so, too, can private citizens or lobbying groups. Only a member of Congress can formally introduce legislation, however. In reality, an increasing number of bills are proposed, developed, and often written by the White House or an executive agency. Then a "friendly" senator or representative introduces the bill in Congress. Such bills are rarely ignored entirely, although they are often amended or defeated.

2. *Referral to committees.* As soon as a bill is introduced and assigned a number, it is sent to the appropriate standing committee. In the House, the Speaker assigns the bill to the appropriate committee. In the Senate, the presiding officer assigns bills to the proper committees. For example, a farm bill in the House would be sent to the Agriculture Committee; a gun control bill would be sent to the Judiciary Committee. A committee chairperson will typically send the bill on to a subcommittee. For example, a Senate bill concerning additional involvement in NATO in Europe would be sent to the Senate Foreign Relations Subcommittee on European Affairs. Alternatively, the chairperson may decide to put the bill aside and ignore it. Most bills that are pigeonholed in this manner receive no further action.

   If a bill is not pigeonholed, committee staff members go to work researching the bill. The committee may hold public hearings during which people who support or oppose the bill may express their views. Committees also have the power to order witnesses to testify at public hearings. Witnesses may be executive agency officials, experts on the subject, or representatives of interest groups concerned about the bill.

   The subcommittee must meet to approve the bill as it is, add new amendments, or draft a new bill. This meeting is known as the **markup session.** If members cannot agree on changes, a vote is taken. When a subcommittee completes its work, the bill goes to the full standing committee, which then meets for its own markup session. The committee may hold its own hearings, amend the subcommittee's version, or simply approve the subcommittee's recommendations.

3. *Reports on a bill.* Finally, the committee will report the bill back to the full chamber. It can report the bill favorably, report the bill with amendments, or report a newly written bill. It can also report a bill unfavorably, but usually such a bill will have been pigeonholed earlier instead. Along with the bill, the committee will send to the House or Senate a written report that explains the committee's actions, describes the bill, lists the major changes made by the committee, and gives opinions on the bill.

4. *The Rules Committee and scheduling.* Scheduling is an extremely important part of getting a bill enacted into law. A bill must be put on a calendar. Typically, the House Rules Committee plays a major role in the scheduling process. This committee, along with the House leaders, regulates the flow of the bills through the House. The Rules Committee will also specify the amount of time to be spent on debate and whether amendments can be made by a floor vote.

MARKUP SESSION A meeting held by a congressional committee or subcommittee to approve, amend, or redraft a bill.

FIGURE 11-3

How a Bill Becomes a Law

This illustration shows the most typical way in which proposed legislation is enacted into law. The process is illustrated with two hypothetical bills, House bill No. 100 (HR 100) and Senate bill No. 200 (S 200). Bills must be passed by both chambers in identical form before they can be sent to the president. The path of HR 100 is traced by an orange line, and that of S 200 by a purple line. In practice, most bills begin as similar proposals in both chambers.

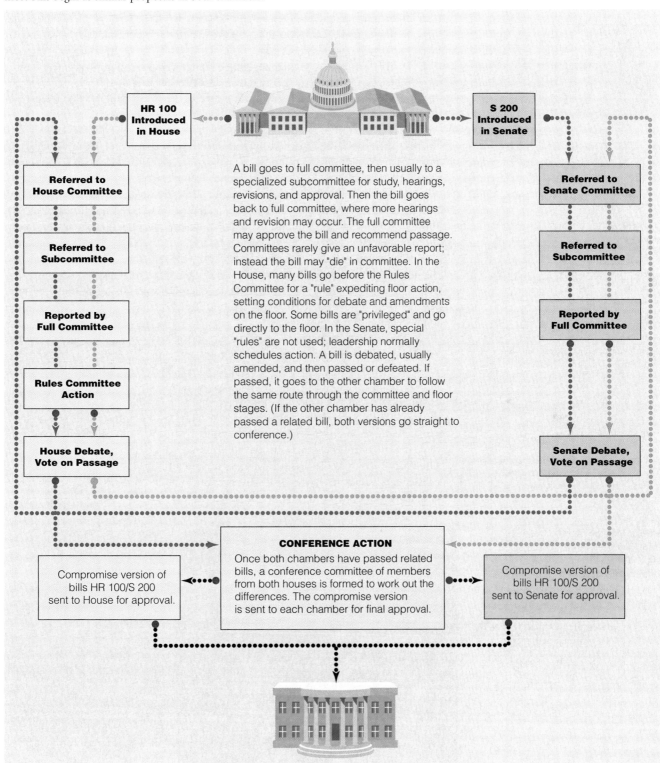

HR 100 Introduced in House

Referred to House Committee

Referred to Subcommittee

Reported by Full Committee

Rules Committee Action

House Debate, Vote on Passage

S 200 Introduced in Senate

Referred to Senate Committee

Referred to Subcommittee

Reported by Full Committee

Senate Debate, Vote on Passage

A bill goes to full committee, then usually to a specialized subcommittee for study, hearings, revisions, and approval. Then the bill goes back to full committee, where more hearings and revision may occur. The full committee may approve the bill and recommend passage. Committees rarely give an unfavorable report; instead the bill may "die" in committee. In the House, many bills go before the Rules Committee for a "rule" expediting floor action, setting conditions for debate and amendments on the floor. Some bills are "privileged" and go directly to the floor. In the Senate, special "rules" are not used; leadership normally schedules action. A bill is debated, usually amended, and then passed or defeated. If passed, it goes to the other chamber to follow the same route through the committee and floor stages. (If the other chamber has already passed a related bill, both versions go straight to conference.)

CONFERENCE ACTION

Once both chambers have passed related bills, a conference committee of members from both houses is formed to work out the differences. The compromise version is sent to each chamber for final approval.

Compromise version of bills HR 100/S 200 sent to House for approval.

Compromise version of bills HR 100/S 200 sent to Senate for approval.

A compromise bill approved by both chambers is sent to the president, who can sign it, veto it, or let it become law without the president's signature. Congress may override a veto by a two-thirds majority vote in each chamber.

In the Senate, a few leading members control the flow of bills. The Senate brings a bill to the floor by "unanimous consent," a motion by which all members present on the floor set aside the formal Senate rules and consider a bill. In contrast to the procedure in the House, individual senators have the power to disrupt work on legislation.

5. *Floor debate.* Because of its large size, the House imposes severe limits on floor debate. The Speaker recognizes those who may speak and can force any member who does not "stick to the subject" to give up the floor. Normally, the chairperson of the standing committee reporting the bill will take charge of the session during which it is debated. You can often watch such debates on C-SPAN.

   Only on rare occasions does a floor debate change anybody's mind. The written record of the floor debate completes the legislative history of the proposed bill in the event that the courts have to interpret it later on. Floor debates also give the full House or Senate the opportunity to consider amendments to the original version of the bill.

6. *Vote.* In both the House and the Senate, the members present generally vote for or against the bill. There are several methods of voting, including voice votes, standing votes, and recorded votes (also called roll-call votes). Since 1973, the House has had electronic voting. The Senate does not have electronic voting, however.

7. *Conference committee.* To become a law, a bill must be passed in identical form by both chambers. When the two chambers pass separate versions of the same bill, the measure is turned over to a special committee called a **conference committee**—a temporary committee with members from the two chambers.

   Most members of the committee are drawn from the standing committees that handled the bill in both chambers. In theory, the conference committee can consider only those points in a bill on which the two chambers disagree; no proposals are supposed to be added. In reality, however, the conference committee sometimes makes important changes in the bill or adds new provisions.

   Once the conference committee members agree on the final compromise bill, a **conference report** is submitted to each house. The bill must be accepted or rejected by both houses as it was written by the committee, with no further amendments made. If the bill is approved by both chambers, it is ready for action by the president.

8. *Presidential action.* All bills passed by Congress have to be submitted to the president for approval. The president has ten days to decide whether to sign the bill or veto it. If the president does nothing, the bill goes into effect unless Congress has adjourned before the ten-day period expires. In that case, the bill dies in what is called a **pocket veto.**

9. *Overriding a veto.* If the president decides to veto a bill, Congress can still get the bill enacted into law. With a two-thirds majority vote in both chambers, Congress can override the president's veto.

CONFERENCE COMMITTEE A temporary committee that is formed when the two chambers of Congress pass separate versions of the same bill. The conference committee, which consists of members from both the House and the Senate, works out a compromise form of the bill.

CONFERENCE REPORT A report submitted by a congressional conference committee after it has drafted a single version of a bill.

POCKET VETO A special type of veto power used by the chief executive after the legislature has adjourned. Bills that are not signed by the president die after a specified period of time and must be reintroduced if Congress wishes to reconsider them.

House Speaker Dennis Hastert of Illinois, center, points to a mock coffin filled with tax regulations at a Capitol Hill news conference where Hastert and other lawmakers urged Congress to override President Clinton's veto of a bill that would have eliminated the so-called "Death Tax." A congressional attempt to override the veto failed. (AP Photo/Dennis Cook)

Investigation and Oversight

Steps 8 and 9 of the legislative process just described illustrate the integral role that both the executive and the legislative branches play in making laws. The relationship between Congress and the president is at the core of our system of government, although, to be sure, the judicial branch plays a vital role as well (see Chapter 14). One of the most important functions of Congress is its oversight of the executive branch and its many federal departments and agencies. The executive bureaucracy, which includes the president's cabinet departments, wields tremendous power, as you will read in Chapters 12 and 13. Congress can rein in that power by choosing not to provide the funds necessary for the bureaucracy to function (the budgeting process is discussed later in this chapter).

The Investigative Function

Congress also has the authority to investigate the actions of the executive branch, the need for certain legislation, and even the actions of its own members. The Congressional Research Service and the Congressional Budget Office, for example, both provide members of Congress with vital information about policies and economic projections. The numerous congressional committees and subcommittees regularly hold hearings to investigate the actions of the executive branch. Congressional committees receive opinions, reports, and assessments on a broad range of issues, from the state of the world economy to the loss of the space shuttle *Columbia* in 2003.

Impeachment Power

Congress also has the power to impeach and remove from office the president, vice president, and other "civil officers," such as federal judges. To impeach means to accuse or charge a public official with improper conduct in office. The House of Representatives is vested with this power and has exercised it twice against the president; the House voted to impeach Andrew Johnson in 1868 and Bill Clinton in 1998. After a vote to impeach in the full House, the president is then tried in the Senate. If convicted by a two-thirds vote, the president is removed from office. Both Johnson and Clinton were acquitted by the Senate. A vote to impeach President Richard Nixon was pending before the full House of Representatives in 1974 when Nixon chose to resign. Nixon is the only president ever to resign from office.

Congress can also take action to remove other officials. The House of Representatives voted to impeach Judge Alcee Hastings in 1988, and the Senate removed him from the bench (he was later elected to the House in 1992). Only one United States Supreme Court justice has ever been impeached; the House impeached Samuel Chase in 1804, although he was later acquitted by the Senate.

The House Judiciary Committee, shown here, approved three articles of impeachment against President Richard M. Nixon in late July 1974. The articles charged Nixon with obstruction of justice, abuse of power, and contempt of Congress. Nixon resigned on August 9, 1974, before the full House of Representatives voted on the articles. (AP Photo)

Sandra Day O'Connor waves as she arrives in Washington, D.C., in September 1981, shortly after her nomination to the United States Supreme Court was confirmed by the Senate. O'Connor was the first woman to be appointed to the nation's highest court. (AP Photo/ Scott Applewhite)

Senate Confirmation

Article II, Section 2, of the Constitution states that the president may appoint ambassadors, justices of the Supreme Court, and other officers of the United States "with the Advice and Consent of the Senate." The Constitution leaves the precise nature of how the Senate will give this "advice and consent" up to the lawmakers. In practice, the Senate confirms the president's nominees for the Supreme Court, other federal judgeships, and the president's top-level advisers. Nominees appear first before the appropriate Senate committee—the Judiciary Committee for federal judges, or the Foreign Relations Committee for ambassadors, for example. If the individual committee approves of the nominee, the full Senate will vote on the nomination.

As you will read further in Chapters 12 and 14, Senate confirmation hearings have been very politicized at times. Judicial appointments often receive the most intense scrutiny by the Senate because the judges serve on the bench for life. The president has a somewhat freer hand with cabinet appointments because the heads of executive departments are expected to be fiercely loyal to the president. Nonetheless, Senate confirmation remains an important check on the president's power. We discuss the relationship between Congress and the president in more detail in Chapter 12.

The Budgeting Process

The Constitution makes it very clear that Congress has the power of the purse. Only Congress can impose taxes, and only Congress can authorize expenditures. To be sure, the president submits a budget, but all final decisions are up to Congress.

The congressional budget is, of course, one of the most important determinants of what policies will or will not be implemented. For example, the president might order executive agencies under presidential control to undertake specific programs, but these orders are meaningless if there is no money to pay for their execution. It is Congress, after all, that has the power of the "purse strings," and this power is significant. Congress can easily nullify a

President George W. Bush speaks to reporters during a bipartisan budget meeting with members of Congress. Congress's power to control the "purse strings" of government is one of its most significant powers. (AP Photo/Ron Edmonds)

president's ambitious program by simply refusing to allocate the necessary funds to executive agencies to implement it.

Thus, although the congressional budgeting process may seem abstract and unimportant to our everyday lives, it is in fact relevant. Also, tracking the various legislative acts and the amendments that are "tacked on" to various budget bills that are sure to pass can be an informative experience for any American concerned about how government policies are established and implemented.

Authorization and Appropriation

The budgeting process involves a two-part procedure. **Authorization** is the first part. It involves the creation of the legal basis for government programs. In this phase, Congress passes authorization bills outlining the rules governing the expenditure of funds. Limits may be placed on how much money can be spent and for what period of time.

Appropriation is the second part of the budgeting process. In this phase, Congress determines how many dollars will actually be spent in a given year on a particular set of government activities. Appropriations must never exceed the authorized amounts, but they can be less. (How "real" are the dollar amounts in the federal budget? Congressional accounting practices are examined in this chapter's *Perception versus Reality* feature.)

AUTHORIZATION A part of the congressional budgeting process that involves the creation of the legal basis for government programs.

APPROPRIATION A part of the congressional budgeting process that involves determining how many dollars will be spent in a given year on a particular set of government activities.

perception versus REALITY

Accounting Standards at the U.S. Congress

In the early 2000s, a series of corporate bankruptcies uncovered "accounting irregularities" at several U.S. corporations. The president and Congress promised to improve federal oversight of corporate accounting practices. The Financial Accounting Standards Board and the Securities and Exchange Commission both took steps to prevent practices such as inflating revenues or hiding debt from shareholders and the public. But could similar practices be used by the U.S. Congress, the guardian of the federal budget?

THE PERCEPTION
Every year Congress and the president wrangle over the particulars of the federal budget. Some years, they actually fail to agree—in 1995, the federal government partially shut down because Democrats and Republicans could not agree on a budget. Americans recognize that partisanship and politicking are part of the budgeting process. They also largely understand that budget projections may be unreliable. Government officials admit that five- and ten-year projections may be off by as much as $1 trillion. For example, a predicted surplus of $281 billion in 2008 could turn into a deficit of $661 billion.[14]

When it comes to the actual dollar amounts in the current budget, however, the public generally regards them as "real" numbers that would hold up to scrutiny by an accountant. Americans assume that when Congress says that it spent so many dollars on a particular program in a given year, those dollars were actually spent on that program during that year.

THE REALITY
In reality, however, our elected representatives regularly "fudge" the actual numbers, as well as the projections. When members of Congress expressed outrage and righteous indignation about the bankruptcies of Enron and WorldCom, Congress itself was engaging in similar misrepresentations.

"Congress routinely commits financial flim-flam that would land CEOs in jail," argues Jonathan Karl, a reporter for CNN.[15] For example, the federal government conducts a census every ten years, as mandated by the Constitution. In 2000, however, Congress voted to classify the census, for budgeting purposes, as an "emergency." This maneuver shifted $4.5 billion from the government's operating budget to an emergency spending bill and helped Congress claim that it was meeting self-imposed spending limits. Congress can also shift federal pay periods by a few days to alter a particular year's budget outlook. In fiscal year 2001, Congress used this trick with the military payroll, shifting $2.3 billion from the 2001 budget to 2002. Furthermore, Congress regularly "borrows" from the so-called Medicare and Social Security trust funds. Congress uses this money to pay operating expenses without reflecting this "debt" in the federal budget. The head of the General Accounting Office, David Walker, has admitted, "You won't find shown as a liability the amount that the U.S. government owes to the trust funds of Social Security and Medicare."[16]

Both parties have used these accounting practices for decades. David Stockman, budget director under President Ronald Reagan, admitted in 1985, "We have increasingly resorted to squaring the circle with accounting gimmicks, evasions, half-truths, and downright dishonesty in our budget numbers."[17]

What's Your Opinion?
After the large corporate bankruptcies in the early 2000s, Congress passed tougher penalties for some types of accounting fraud, including sentences of twenty years in prison. Should Congress be held accountable for using similar accounting practices, and if so, how?

ENTITLEMENT PROGRAM A government program (such as Social Security) that allows, or entitles, a certain class of people (such as the elderly) to receive special benefits. Entitlement programs operate under open-ended budget authorizations that, in effect, place no limits on how much can be spent.

FISCAL YEAR A twelve-month period that is established for bookkeeping or accounting purposes. The government's fiscal year runs from October 1 through September 30.

FIRST BUDGET RESOLUTION A budget resolution, which is supposed to be passed in May, that sets overall revenue goals and spending targets for the next fiscal year, which begins on October 1.

SECOND BUDGET RESOLUTION A budget resolution, which is supposed to be passed in September, that sets "binding" limits on taxes and spending for the next fiscal year.

CONTINUING RESOLUTION A temporary resolution passed by Congress when an appropriations bill has not been decided by the beginning of the new fiscal year.

Many **entitlement programs** operate under open-ended authorizations that, in effect, place no limits on how much can be spent. The government is obligated to provide benefits, such as Social Security benefits, veterans' benefits, and the like, to persons who qualify under entitlement laws. The remaining federal programs are subject to discretionary spending and can be altered at will by Congress. National defense is the most important item in the discretionary-spending part of the budget.

The Actual Budgeting Process

Look at Figure 11–4, which is a schematic outlining the lengthy budgeting process. The process runs from January, when the president submits a proposed federal budget for the next **fiscal year,** to the start of that fiscal year on October 1. In actuality, about eighteen months prior to October 1, the executive agencies submit their requests to the Office of Management and Budget (OMB), and the OMB outlines a proposed budget. If the president approves it, the budget is officially submitted to Congress.

The legislative budgeting process comprises eight to nine months before the start of the fiscal year. The **first budget resolution** is supposed to be passed in May. It sets overall revenue goals and spending targets and, by definition, the size of the federal budget deficit or surplus. The **second budget resolution,** which sets "binding" limits on taxes and spending, is supposed to be passed in September, prior to the beginning of the fiscal year on October 1. Whenever Congress is unable to pass a complete budget by October 1, it passes **continuing resolutions,** which enable the executive agencies to keep on doing whatever they were doing the previous year with the same amount of funding. Even continuing resolutions have not always been passed on time.

The budget process involves making predictions about the state of the U.S. economy for years to come. This process is necessarily very imprecise. Since 1996, both Congress and the president have attempted to make ten-year projections for income (from taxes) and spending, but no one can know what the financial picture of the United States will look like in ten years.[18] The work force could grow or shrink, which would drastically alter government revenue from taxes. Any number of emergencies could arise that would require increased government spending—from going to war against terrorists to inoculating federal employees against smallpox. How the government goes about planning for and funding such contingencies is discussed in this chapter's *The Politics of Homeland Security* feature.

FIGURE 11–4
The Budgeting Process

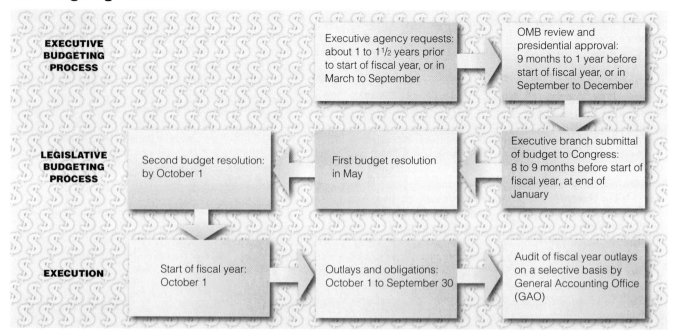

EXECUTIVE BUDGETING PROCESS

Executive agency requests: about 1 to 1½ years prior to start of fiscal year, or in March to September

OMB review and presidential approval: 9 months to 1 year before start of fiscal year, or in September to December

LEGISLATIVE BUDGETING PROCESS

Second budget resolution: by October 1

First budget resolution in May

Executive branch submittal of budget to Congress: 8 to 9 months before start of fiscal year, at end of January

EXECUTION

Start of fiscal year: October 1

Outlays and obligations: October 1 to September 30

Audit of fiscal year outlays on a selective basis by General Accounting Office (GAO)

The POLITICS of HOMELAND SECURITY

Is the Big Spending Really to Fight Terrorists?

The Congressional Budget Office predicted that the government would run a deficit (in which the government spends more than it raises in revenues in a particular year) of $200 billion to $300 billion in fiscal year 2003. Nonetheless, on February 13, 2003, Congress passed an omnibus discretionary spending package for $397 billion. President Bush commended the bill's passage, stating, "This budget will provide valuable resources for priorities such as homeland security, military operations, and education." One could reasonably (but incorrectly) argue that since September 11, 2001, the federal government has had to spend more on antiterrorism measures, which have increased spending and driven up the federal deficit. Of the $397 billion of discretionary funds appropriated in February 2003, however, only 6 percent was related to homeland security.

Government Printing Office employees stand behind copies of President Bush's 2004 fiscal year federal budget on February 3, 2003. President Bush had sent Congress a $2.23 trillion spending plan that would accelerate tax cuts to bolster the weak economy, overhaul some of the government's biggest social programs, and shower billions of additional dollars on defense and homeland security. (AP Photo/ Susan Walsh)

IT ISN'T ALL DUE TO SEPTEMBER 11

Spending on homeland security and national defense has been a small blip on the radar screen of total increases in federal spending in the past eight years. Roughly $30 billion was spent on homeland security and national defense programs in the months following September 11. Of this amount, $10 billion went to fighting in Afghanistan and about $20 billion to improving transportation security and rebuilding New York City. But in fiscal year 2002, Congress voted an additional $90 billion of new discretionary spending, only a small amount of which was related to increased security either at home or abroad. This spending included funds for medical research and highway construction.[19]

What has been true, and will continue to be true into the foreseeable future, is that numerous expenditures that have absolutely nothing to do with countering terrorism will be approved in the name of the fight against terrorism. Consider the latest set of "gifts" to agribusiness, a brazen example of how old-fashioned special interest subsidies can be hidden under the cover of the war on terrorism. Since 1978, farmers have received subsidies of over $300 billion from the federal government. With the Farm Security and Rural Investment Act of 2002, new subsidies, combined with existing federal subsidies, will cost American taxpayers about $180 billion over ten years. An attempt was made to link the 2002 farm bill to national security needs by, among other things, including the word *security* in the act's title, but few observers were convinced that the bill had much to do with national security (see Chapter 13 for a further discussion of this legislation).

THE NEW DEPARTMENT OF HOMELAND SECURITY

When President Bush proposed the new Department of Homeland Security (DHS), he argued that it would not make government larger. In principle, the DHS has simply combined twenty-two agencies and 170,000 workers to create a more efficient way to protect Americans at home. Realize, though, that this department is the most massive new bureaucracy since the Department of Defense (DOD) was created in 1947. The likeli-

hood of the DHS remaining even close to its original size is small. Many DHS activities, like DOD activities, are secret. This reduces the chances that spending on them will be carefully scrutinized. Furthermore, DHS activities, like DOD activities, are complex and far-reaching. It is easy to claim—and difficult to refute—that a cut in spending on one project will have spillover effects that will irreparably damage many other projects.

The result with the DOD is a budget that seems immune to shrinkage. And, of course, plenty of private-sector firms have an incentive to keep that budget big because they are doing business with the department. Hence, they lobby for additional funding so that they, too, can get some of those extra federal dollars. It is likely that these types of incentives will work their magic with the new DHS budget. Indeed, since the DHS asked private corporations to make proposals about new technologies to fight terrorism, some 1,500 companies have pitched their ideas. Again, it is easy to imagine spending on projects barely related to homeland security.

Are We Safer?

Few government agencies achieve the most efficient spending as they try to fulfill the nation's goals. Can homeland security be undertaken only by government? To what extent can the private sector help protect Americans from terrorist acts?

why does it MATTER?

Congress and Your Everyday Life

It is almost a cliché to say that Congress affects your everyday life. After all, Congress has passed laws that affect virtually every aspect of your everyday life, from establishing safety standards for your job to declaring when daylight-saving time starts and ends to deciding whether there should be a military draft. Perhaps more important, Congress decides how much the federal government will spend each year. But how much the federal government will spend is also tied to possibly the most important congressional action with respect to your everyday life: how the federal government taxes you.

Federal Income Taxes—They Haven't Always Been There

If we were writing this text in 1900, we would have nothing to say about Congress and income taxes. Not until February 3, 1913, when the Sixteenth Amendment to the Constitution was ratified, did Congress actually start to require U.S. residents to pay federal income taxes. That amendment reads:

> The Congress shall have power to lay and collect taxes on incomes, from whatever source derived, without apportionment among the several States, and without regard to any census or enumeration.

Today, about 22 percent of all total national income each year goes to the federal government as taxes. This is the highest percentage in the history of the United States, matching the level reached during World War II. Because you can spend only the income left after you pay taxes, the level at which Congress chooses to tax you is indeed important to your everyday life.

Taking Action

Several individuals and groups have tried since 1913 to reform or eliminate the income tax system in the United States. Other individuals and groups take action in response to state or local tax proposals. For example, in the photo above, David Orr, right, and Forrest Perry both supported a proposed Tennessee state tax reform. They made up their own radio station in Nashville to mock local radio personalities who were opposed to the reform. Lining the street nearby are other supporters of the tax reform. (AP Photo/John Russell)

Key Terms

apportionment 248	continuing resolution 266	malapportionment 249	Rules Committee 259
appropriation 265	entitlement program 266	markup session 260	second budget resolution 266
authorization 265	filibustering 259	minority leader 255	Speaker of the House 254
cloture 259	first budget resolution 266	minority-majority district 250	standing committee 257
conference committee 262	fiscal year 266	"one person, one vote"	subcommittee 257
conference report 262	gerrymandering 249	rule 249	whip 256
congressional district 249	majority leader 255	pocket veto 262	

Chapter Summary

1 The U.S. Constitution established a bicameral legislature—a Congress consisting of two chambers, the House and the Senate.

2 Each representative to the House is elected by voters in a specific area, or congressional district. The lines of congressional districts are drawn by the authority of state legislatures, and in the past, districts of unequal population and the practice of gerrymandering (drawing district lines to maximize the control of a particular party or group) were common. Over time, as a result of Supreme Court decisions, state legislatures were required to ensure that voting districts had equal populations.

3 The U.S. Constitution requires that congressional representatives be elected every second year by popular vote. Senators are elected every six years, also (since the ratification of the Seventeenth Amendment) by popular vote. State legislatures control the times, places, and manner of holding congressional elections.

4 Only a few qualifications—relating to citizenship, residency, and age—must be met to be a member of Congress. Nonetheless, incumbent legislators have proved to have an advantage over their opponents at reelection time. Americans have been at odds over congressional "careerism" and the issue of term limits.

5 The majority party in each chamber of Congress chooses the major officers of that chamber, controls debate on the floor, selects committee chairpersons, and has a majority on all committees. The Speaker of the House is the chief leader in the House of Representatives. Other significant leaders in the House are the majority leader, the minority leader, and the whips.

6 The Constitution makes the vice president the president of the Senate, but in practice the vice president is rarely present in the Senate. The president "pro tem" (*pro tempore*), an alternate presiding officer elected by the senators, serves in the absence of the vice president. The real power in the Senate is held by the majority leader, the minority leader, and their respective whips.

7 Most of the actual work of Congress is handled by committees and subcommittees. The permanent and most powerful committees are called standing committees. Before any bill can be considered by the entire House or Senate, it must be approved by a majority vote in the standing committee to which it was assigned.

8 Many of the differences between the House and the Senate are due to their different sizes. With its larger size, the House requires more formal rules, particularly with respect to debate on the floor. In the House, the Rules Committee places time limitations on debate for most bills. In the Senate, in contrast, the tradition of unlimited debate, or filibustering, continues. Members of the Senate generally enjoy more prestige due to their positions than do members of the House.

9 There are several steps in the legislative process—the process by which a bill becomes a law. To become law, a bill must be passed in identical form by both chambers. If the bill is approved by both houses, it is submitted to the president, who can sign the bill, veto it, or do nothing (in which case the bill becomes law within ten days unless Congress adjourns before that ten-day period expires, effecting a pocket veto).

10 Congress is charged with certain powers to oversee and investigate other branches of government, including the executive and judicial branches. The House of Representatives has the power to impeach the president, vice president, and federal judges. The Senate can refuse to confirm certain officers of government, including the president's cabinet members and Supreme Court justices. Congress can also refuse to fund certain government programs.

11 The Constitution provides that only Congress can impose taxes and authorize expenditures. The congressional budgeting process involves authorization and appropriation. Whenever Congress is unable to pass a complete budget by the beginning of the new fiscal year on October 1, it operates on the basis of continuing resolutions, which enable the executive agencies to keep on doing whatever they were doing the previous year with the same amount of funding.

RESOURCES FOR FURTHER STUDY

Selected Readings

Jacobson, Gary C. *The Politics of Congressional Elections,* 5th ed. New York: Longman Publishers, 2001. Now in its fifth edition, this book provides a comprehensive view of congressional elections, including gerrymandering, the incumbency factor, fund-raising, and campaign strategy. It also provides an excellent general overview of congressional and national politics.

Oleszek, Walter J. *Congressional Procedures and the Policy Process,* 5th ed. Washington, D.C.: CQ Press, 2001. This book provides a comprehensive overview of how Congress functions, including House and Senate rules, the budgeting process, new developments in how the two chambers resolve differences, and new trends in legislative oversight. It has even been assigned to new congressional staff members.

Rosenthal, Cindy Simon, ed. *Women Transforming Congress (Congressional Studies Series,* Vol. 4). Norman, Okla.: University of Oklahoma Press, 2003. Written by leading scholars, as well as by women in politics, the essays in this book follow women on the campaign trail, in committee rooms, in floor debate, and in policy deliberations to examine how women have transformed the predominantly male institution of Congress.

Schickler, Eric. *Disjointed Pluralism: Institutional Innovation and the Development of the U.S. Congress.* Princeton, N.J.: Princeton University Press, 2001. The author examines how the institution of Congress has changed over time by analyzing leadership, committee, and procedural restructuring across the twentieth century. The book is an important study in American political development.

InfoTrac Citations

Using your InfoTrac password, access the InfoTrac database at http://infotrac.thomsonlearning.com. Once at the site, you can do "key word" searches to locate the following articles, each of which deals with a topic covered in this chapter. The key words to use in your search are indicated in parentheses.

- "Segregation Forever? Where the GOP and the Black Caucus Link Arms" (Gerrymandering Segregation)

- "What Trent Meant . . . And the Real Secret in Strom Thurmond's Past" (Trent Lott Thurmond)

- Democrats Threaten Filibuster against Estrada" (Filibuster Estrada)

- "The Law—The 'Protective Return' Pocket Veto: Presidential Aggrandizement of Constitutional Power" (Pocket Veto)

Politics on the Web

There is an abundance of online information relating to Congress and congressional activities. The THOMAS site (named for Thomas Jefferson), maintained by the Library of Congress, provides a record of all bills introduced into Congress, information about each member of Congress and how he or she voted on specific bills, and other data. Go to http://thomas.loc.gov

- GPO Access on the Web offers information on Congress in session, bills pending and passed, and a history of the bills at http://thorplus.lib.purdue.edu:80/gpo

- To learn more about how a bill becomes a law, go to http://www.vote-smart.org

  Click on "Vote Smart Classroom," select "An Introduction to the U.S. Government," and then choose "How a Bill Becomes a Law."

- You can find e-mail addresses and home pages for members of the House of Representatives at http://www.house.gov

- For e-mail addresses and home pages for members of the Senate, go to http://www.senate.gov

Web Resources on Your CD-ROM

On your CD-ROM, you will find Web resources, news articles, Internet activities, and video clips related to the topics in this chapter. Resources related to this chapter include the following:

- **Values Inventory**—Political Ideology: Does Congress Have to Look like America to Represent It?
- **Updates**—Keep up with the issues in this chapter!
- **Why Does It Matter?**—Discuss Members of Congress on Usenet.
- **Web Resources**—Internet Activities: Congressional Demographics; The Congressional Hispanic Caucus.
- **Where Do You Stand?**— Dialogue: Does Congress Have to Look Like America to Represent It?
- **Comparative Politics**—The European Parliament and the European Union.
- **Video**—Campaign Costs.
- **NewsEdge**—Visit this global resource for current events related to this chapter.

chapter 12
the presidency

CHAPTER OBJECTIVES

After reading this chapter, you should be able to . . .

▸ List the constitutional requirements for becoming president.

▸ Explain the roles that a president performs while in office.

▸ Indicate the scope of presidential powers.

▸ Describe key areas where Congress and the president have advantages in their institutional relationship.

▸ Discuss the role of cabinet members in presidential administrations.

271

Should Presidents Be Able to Go to War on Their Own?

When the framers wrote the provisions for the office of the presidency, they did so with George Washington in mind. He was the general who had led the colonies to victory in the Revolutionary War, and he had the respect and admiration of the nation. His ability to lead the armed forces as "commander in chief" was unquestioned, and so the framers gave the president that explicit authority.

As commander in chief, the president has the power to defend the nation and to repel sudden attacks by foreign powers. In an offensive war, however, only Congress has the constitutional authority to declare war. Congress has declared war against other nations, but not since 1941 when it declared war on Japan. The United Nations (UN) charter, which the United States signed in 1945, makes war illegal except in cases of self-defense—when the president can act without Congress. This has led some scholars to argue that Congress's authority to "declare war" is meaningless today. So, should presidents be able to commit U.S. troops to war on their own?

Presidents Must Have a Free Hand to Act

The War Powers Resolution of 1973, discussed in more detail later in this chapter, requires the president to inform Congress within forty-eight hours after American forces have been deployed. The resolution, therefore, gives the president the opportunity to act first and ask Congress later. When a president acts, as commander in chief, to place troops in harm's way, Congress cannot simply reverse the order and bring them home. Even debating the issue could undermine the troops' effectiveness and destroy troop morale.

Furthermore, those who favor giving the president a free hand point out that, in modern warfare, the enemy is likely to exploit congressional indecision over troop deployments. For example, in October 2002, Congress passed a resolution authorizing President George W. Bush to use military force against Iraq if the latter did not comply with the UN's demand to disarm. By March 2003, however, many of the signers of that resolution had changed their minds and publicly said that President Bush should wait for the UN to authorize an offensive attack against Iraq.

Congress's commitment to a military campaign could easily weaken in the face of a terrorist attack on U.S. troops overseas or decreasing support from U.S. allies. Presidents, in contrast, have demonstrated the ability to harden themselves against such blows to the national will. As political scientist Harold Laski once wrote, "Great power makes great leadership possible." The president's war powers today are tremendous, and presidents will rise to the occasion and exhibit great leadership.

Congress Must Check the President's War Powers

The framers recognized that Congress's size and complex decision-making processes would make it a more deliberative and divided institution than the presidency. They expected Congress to hold public debates about the most monumental choice of any nation: whether or not to go to war. Even among scholars today who believe that the president should have expansive war powers, some make a distinction between air strikes and ground troops. When thousands of American men and women are asked to risk their lives in a ground assault, these scholars say, the decision should be debated in Congress first.

Even if Congress is not asked for a declaration of war, it has other means to check the president's war powers, and it should use them. First, Congress can deny the president the funds to wage war. Second, Congress can use its persuasive powers to rein in the president, sway public opinion, and limit the length and breadth of a war.

Some scholars argue that if fulfilling U.S. treaty obligations involves committing U.S. troops, the president can do so without authorization from Congress. Others dismiss this argument. In fact, in 1995 the Senate passed a unanimous resolution that holds that a UN Security Council resolution is not a substitute for congressional authorization of military action. The Supreme Court has also upheld this view: although a treaty obligation is a legal commitment, Congress can compel the president to violate it.[1]

Where Do You Stand?

1. Do you think that presidents should have the right to go to war on their own, without seeking authorization from Congress?

2. Do you think that some aspects of modern warfare require more independent action by the president than the framers of the Constitution envisioned when they gave the power to declare war to Congress alone?

Interacting with Your CD-ROM Resources

Use your CD-ROM to access resources on the Web, simulations, participation exercises, and video clips. Important resources related to this feature include:

- **Values Inventory**—Political Ideology: Presidential War Powers.
- **Where Do You Stand?**—Dialogue: Should Presidents Be Able to Declare War on Their Own?
- **Web Resources**—Internet Activities: One Congressperson's View against the Iraq War.

INTRODUCTION

Former president Lyndon Johnson (1963–1969) stated in his autobiography[2] that "[o]f all the 1,886 nights I was President, there were not many when I got to sleep before 1 or 2 A.M., and there were few mornings when I didn't wake up by 6 or 6:30." President Harry Truman (1945–1953) once observed that no one can really understand what it is like to be president: there is no end to "the chain of responsibility that binds him," and he is "never allowed to forget that he is president." These responsibilities are, for the most part, unremitting. Unlike Congress, the president never adjourns.

Given the demands of the presidency, why would anyone seek the office? In part, the motivation is related to very special perks associated with the presidency. The president enjoys, among other things, the use of the White House. The White House has 132 rooms located on 18.3 acres of land in the heart of the nation's capital. At the White House, the president in residence has a staff of more than eighty persons, including chefs, gardeners, maids, butlers, and a personal tailor. Amenities also include a tennis court, a swimming pool, bowling lanes, and a private movie theater. Additionally, the president has at his disposal a fleet of automobiles, helicopters, and jets (including *Air Force One,* which costs $30,000 an hour to run). For relaxation, the presidential family can go to Camp David, a resort hideaway in the Catoctin Mountains of Maryland. Other perks include free dental and medical care.

These amenities are part of the motivation for wanting to be president of the United States. A greater motivation, though, is that the presidency is at the apex of the political ladder. It is the most powerful and influential political office that any one individual can hold. Presidents can help to shape not only domestic policy but also global developments. With the demise of the Soviet Union and its satellite Communist countries in the early 1990s, the president of the United States is regarded by many as the leader of the most powerful nation on earth. The president heads the greatest military force anywhere. It is not surprising, therefore, that many Americans aspire to attain this office.

Who Can Become President?

The notion that anybody can become president of this country has always been a part of the great American dream. Certainly, the requirements for becoming president set forth in Article II, Section 1, of the Constitution are not difficult to meet:

> No Person except a natural born Citizen, or a Citizen of the United States, at the time of the Adoption of this Constitution, shall be eligible to the Office of President; neither shall any Person be eligible to that Office who shall not have attained to the Age of thirty-five Years, and been fourteen Years a Resident within the United States.

It is true that modern presidents have included a haberdasher (Harry Truman), a peanut farmer (Jimmy Carter), and an actor (Ronald Reagan), although all of these men also had significant political experience before assuming the presidency. If you look at Appendix E, though, you will see that the most common previous occupation of U.S. presidents has been the legal profession. Out of forty-three presidents, twenty-six have been lawyers, and many presidents have been wealthy. Additionally, although the Constitution states that anyone who is thirty-five years of age or older can become president, the average age at inauguration has been fifty-four. The youngest person elected president was John F. Kennedy (1961–1963), who assumed the presidency at the age of forty-three (the youngest person to hold the office was Theodore Roosevelt, who was forty-two when he became president after the assassination of William McKinley); the oldest was Ronald Reagan (1981–1989), who was sixty-nine years old when he became president.

To date, all U.S. presidents have been male, white, and (with the exception of John F. Kennedy, who was a Roman Catholic) from the Protestant tradition. Polls indicate, though, that many Americans expect to see a woman or an African American assume the office in the not-too-distant future. According to one survey, 54 percent of respondents expect to live to see a woman elected to the presidency, and 75 percent expect to see an African American elected as president.[3]

Harry Truman became president after the death of Franklin D. Roosevelt on April 12, 1945. At the beginning of Truman's life, he certainly did not appear destined to become a great political leader. His background was modest. The young Truman never went to college. He failed as a farmer, a concert pianist, and a businessman—both as a haberdasher and as an entrepreneur in oil drilling. Nonetheless, his political acumen led to his reelection in 1948. Some have remarked that Truman was living proof that "anyone can become president." (All photos from Truman Presidential Museum and Library)

Franklin D. Roosevelt once said, "The presidency is not merely an administrative office. That is the least of it. It is preeminently a place of moral leadership."[4] Although "character" is not among the constitutional requirements for becoming president, presidents, as the nation's leaders, are expected to perform their duties with integrity. Because the president wields so much power, many Americans expect the person in office to demonstrate a high degree of moral rectitude, honesty, and trustworthiness.

AMERICA at odds

Presidential Character—Does It Matter?

During the administration of President Bill Clinton (1993–2001), much was said about morality and presidential leadership. Some people suggested that the media delved too deeply into Clinton's moral character, subjecting him to greater scrutiny than earlier presidents had experienced. Others argued that a president's performance as the nation's leader is inextricably connected to character. Clearly, there is a distinction between a political *office*, such as the office of the presidency, and the *person* who holds that office, just as there is a distinction between *official* conduct and *private* conduct. Yet can the personal and official elements of any political office ever be totally separated?

Some claim that personal ethics and official conduct can be compartmentalized—a president's private morality and activities should matter little to the public, as long as they do not affect official decisions. During the impeachment hearings against President Clinton in 1998, conservative Republicans attempted to rally like-minded, morally upright Americans against Clinton's alleged sexual relationship with White House intern Monica Lewinsky. Clinton was impeached by the House, but later acquitted by the Senate. During the entire proceedings, his moral character was attacked repeatedly. But public opinion polls taken during that time showed that many Americans were not really very concerned about the president's behavior in his private life.

According to at least one scholar, however, people should be concerned. University of Texas professor Marvin Olasky claims that "a study of presidential history shows a link between lying about adultery and lying about other matters."[5] He cites several examples

The Senate is shown in session in this video image, taken during a brief session in which the senators unanimously approved the procedures to be followed during President Clinton's impeachment trial in January 1999. The overlay on the video image shows the vote count. (AP Photo/APTN)

of past presidents who, following sexual affairs and their cover-ups, found it easier to break faith with others, including the American people, in their official conduct. Olasky concludes that journalists and voters should closely scrutinize the sexual allegations made about presidential candidates, as well as the private ethical standards and conduct of presidents. To do otherwise would be negligent.

The President's Many Roles

As will be discussed shortly, the president has the authority to exercise a variety of powers; some of these are explicitly outlined in the Constitution, and some are simply required by the office—such as the power to persuade. In the course of exercising these powers, the president assumes various roles. For example, as commander in chief of the armed services, the president can exercise significant military powers. Which roles a president plays successfully usually depends on what is happening domestically and internationally, as well as on the president's personality. Some presidents, including Bill Clinton during his first term, have shown much more interest in domestic policy than in foreign policy. Others, such as George H. W. Bush (1989–1993), were more interested in foreign affairs than in domestic policies.

Table 12–1 on the following page summarizes the major roles of the president. An important role is, of course, that of chief executive. Other roles include those of commander in chief, chief of state, chief diplomat, chief legislator, and political party leader.

President George W. Bush, right, speaks to his staff inside the private dining room at the White House prior to his address to the nation on September 11, 2001. (AP Photo/The White House, Paul Morse, HO)

TABLE 12–1
The Roles of the President

ROLE	DESCRIPTION	SPECIFIC FUNCTIONS
Chief executive	Enforces laws and federal court decisions, along with treaties signed by the United States	■ Can appoint, with Senate approval, and remove high-ranking officers of the federal government ■ Can grant reprieves, pardons, and amnesty ■ Can handle national emergencies during peacetime, such as riots or natural disasters
Commander in chief	Leads the nation's armed forces	■ Can commit troops for up to ninety days in response to a military threat (War Powers Resolution) ■ Can make secret agreements with other countries ■ Can set up military governments in conquered lands ■ Can end fighting by calling a cease-fire (armistice)
Chief of state	Performs certain ceremonial functions as personal symbol of the nation	■ Decorates war heroes ■ Dedicates parks and post offices ■ Throws out first baseball of baseball season ■ Lights national Christmas tree
Chief diplomat	Directs U.S. foreign policy and is the nation's most important representative in dealing with foreign countries	■ Can negotiate and sign treaties with other nations, with Senate approval ■ Can make pacts (executive agreements) with other heads of state, without Senate approval ■ Can accept the legal existence of another country's government (power of recognition) ■ Receives foreign chiefs of state
Chief legislator	Informs Congress about the condition of the country and recommends legislative measures	■ Proposes legislative program to Congress in traditional State of the Union address ■ Suggests budget to Congress and submits annual economic report ■ Can veto a bill passed by Congress ■ Can call special sessions of Congress
Political party leader	Heads political party	■ Chooses a vice president ■ Makes several thousand top government appointments, often to party faithful (patronage) ■ Tries to execute the party's platform ■ May attend party fund-raisers ■ May help reelect party members running for office as mayors, governors, or members of Congress

Chief Executive

According to Article II of the Constitution,

> The executive Power shall be vested in a President of the United States of America. . . . [H]e may require the Opinion, in writing, of the principal Officer in each of the executive Departments, upon any Subject relating to the Duties of their respective Offices . . . and he shall nominate, and by and with the Advice and Consent of the Senate, shall appoint . . . Officers of the United States . . . . [H]e shall take Care that the Laws be faithfully executed.

CHIEF EXECUTIVE The head of the executive branch of government. In the United States, the president is the head of the executive branch of the federal government.

This constitutional provision makes the president of the United States the nation's **chief executive,** or the head of the executive branch of the federal government. When the framers created the office of the president, they created a uniquely American institution. Nowhere else in the world at that time was there a democratically elected chief executive. The executive branch is also unique among the branches of government because it is headed by a single individual—the president.

Commander in Chief

The Constitution states that the president "shall be Commander in Chief of the Army and Navy of the United States, and of the Militia of the several States, when called into the actual

Unlike many of the men who preceded him in the presidential office, President George W. Bush has publicly emphasized his role as commander in chief. Here, the president shakes hands with a group of Weapons Ordinance Mates in May 2003 on the deck of the aircraft carrier USS *Abraham Lincoln* as it steams toward San Diego. (AP Photo/Damian Dovarganes)

Service of the United States." As **commander in chief** of the nation's armed forces, the president exercises tremendous power.

As you read in the chapter-opening *America at Odds* feature, under the Constitution, war powers are divided between Congress and the president. Congress was given the power to declare war and the power to raise and maintain the country's armed forces. The president, as commander in chief, was given the power to deploy the armed forces. The president's role as commander in chief has evolved over the last century. We examine this shared power between the president and Congress in more detail later in this chapter.

COMMANDER IN CHIEF The supreme commander of the military forces of the United States.

Chief of State

Traditionally, a country's monarch has played the role of chief of state—the country's representative to the rest of the world. The United States, of course, has no king or queen to act as **chief of state.** Thus, the president of the United States fulfills this role. The president engages in many symbolic or ceremonial activities, such as throwing out the first baseball to open the baseball season and turning on the lights of the national Christmas tree. The president also

CHIEF OF STATE The person who serves as the ceremonial head of a country's government and represents that country to the rest of the world.

President Woodrow Wilson throwing out the first ball on the opening day of the baseball season in 1916. (National Photo Company Collection/Library of Congress)

comparative politics

Having a Separate Chief of State

In the seven Western European countries headed by royalty, the monarch is considered the chief of state and plays a ceremonial role. In the United Kingdom, for example, Queen Elizabeth represents the state at ceremonial occasions, such as the opening of sessions of Parliament, the christening of ships, and receptions for foreign ambassadors.

In the monarchies of the Netherlands and Norway, the king or queen initiates the process of forming a government after national elections by determining which parties can combine to rule in a coalition. This process really depends on the results of the election and the desires of the political parties—yet the monarch must certify the results.

The majority of European states are not monarchies, but they nonetheless split the duties of government between a

Queen Elizabeth II (Official photograph by John Swannell)

prime minister and a president. In Switzerland, for example, the president is elected indirectly by the legislature and assumes purely ceremonial duties.

Throughout Western Europe, the pattern is the same: presidents have ceremonial powers only. The single exception to this rule occurs in France, which has a presidential system in which the head of state has real political power, particularly in foreign affairs.

For Critical Analysis

What are the benefits of having a single person perform only chief-of-state activities? Are there any benefits to the American system, in which the duties of chief executive and chief of state are combined?

---

decorates war heroes, dedicates parks and post offices, receives visiting chiefs of state at the White House, and goes on official state visits to other countries.

Some argue that presidents should not perform such ceremonial functions because they take time that the president should be spending on "real work." (See this chapter's *Comparative Politics* feature for more information on how other countries handle this issue.)

Chief Diplomat

DIPLOMAT In regard to international relations, a person who represents one country in dealing with representatives of another country.
CHIEF DIPLOMAT The role of the president in recognizing and interacting with foreign governments.

A **diplomat** is a person who represents one country in dealing with representatives of another country. In the United States, the president is the nation's **chief diplomat.** The Constitution did not explicitly reserve this role to the president, but since the beginning of this nation, presidents have assumed the role based on their explicit constitutional powers to recognize foreign governments and, with the advice and consent of the Senate, to appoint ambassadors and make treaties. As chief diplomat, the president directs the foreign policy of the United States and is its most important representative.

Chief Legislator

Nowhere in the Constitution do the words *chief legislator* appear. The Constitution, however, does require that the president "from time to time give to the Congress Information of the State of the Union, and recommend to their Consideration such Measures as he shall judge necessary and expedient." The president has, in fact, become a major player in shaping the congressional agenda—the set of measures that actually get discussed and acted on. This was not always the case. In the nineteenth century, some presidents preferred to let Congress lead the way in proposing and implementing policy. Since the administration of Theodore Roosevelt (1901–1909), however, presidents have taken an activist approach. Presidents are now expected to develop a legislative program and propose a budget to Congress every year. This shared power often puts Congress and the president at odds—as you will read shortly.

Party Leader

The president of the United States is also the leader of his or her political party. The Constitution, of course, does not mention this role because, in the eyes of the founders, presidents (and other political representatives) were not to be influenced by "factional" (partisan) interests.

As party leader, the president exercises substantial powers. For example, the president chooses the chairperson of the party's national committee. The president can also exert political power within the party by using presidential appointment and removal powers. Naturally, presidents are beholden to the party members who put them in office, and usually they indulge in the practice of patronage—appointing individuals to government or public jobs—to reward those who helped them win the presidential contest. The president may also reward party members with fund-raising assistance (campaign financing is discussed in Chapter 9). The president is, in a sense, "fund-raiser in chief" for his or her party. Understandably, the use of patronage within the party system gives the president singular powers.

The President's Constitutional Powers

As you have read, the constitutional source for the president's authority is found in Article II of the Constitution, which states, "The executive Power shall be vested in a President of the United States of America." The Constitution then sets forth the president's relatively limited constitutional responsibilities. Just how much power should be entrusted to the president was debated at length by the framers of the Constitution. On the one hand, they did not want a king. On the other hand, they believed that a strong executive was necessary if the republic was to survive. The result of their debates was an executive who was granted enough powers in the Constitution to balance those of Congress.[6]

Article II grants the president broad but vaguely described powers. From the very beginning, there were different views as to what exactly the "executive Power" clause enabled the president to do. Nonetheless, Sections 2 and 3 of Article II list the following specific presidential powers:

- To serve as commander in chief of the armed forces and the state militias.
- To appoint, with the Senate's consent, the heads of the executive departments, ambassadors, justices of the Supreme Court, and other top officials.
- To grant reprieves and pardons, except in cases of impeachment.
- To make treaties, with the advice and consent of the Senate.
- To deliver the annual State of the Union address to Congress and to send other messages to Congress from time to time.
- To call either house or both houses of Congress into special sessions.
- To receive ambassadors and other representatives from foreign countries.
- To commission all officers of the United States.
- To ensure that the laws passed by Congress "be faithfully executed."

In addition, Article I, Section 7, gives the president the power to veto legislation. We discuss some of these powers in more detail below. As you will see, many of these powers are balanced by the powers of Congress. We address the complex relationship between the president and Congress in a later section of this chapter.

Proposal and Ratification of Treaties

A **treaty** is a formal agreement between two or more sovereign states. The president has the sole power to negotiate and sign treaties with other countries. The Senate, however, must approve the treaty by a two-thirds vote of the members present before it becomes effective. If the treaty is approved by the Senate and signed by the president, it becomes law.

Presidents have not always succeeded in winning the Senate's approval for treaties. Woodrow Wilson (1913–1921) lost his effort to persuade the Senate to approve the Treaty of Versailles,[7] the peace treaty that ended World War I in 1918. Among other things, the treaty would have made the United States a member of the League of Nations. In contrast, Jimmy Carter (1977–1981) convinced the Senate to approve a treaty returning the

TREATY A formal agreement between the governments of two or more countries.

As party leader, the president can influence election outcomes by assisting party members in their campaigns for Congress. Here, President George W. Bush speaks to supporters at a $1,000-a-plate fund-raiser held in Denver for congressional csandidate Bob Beauprez (R., Colo.) prior to the 2002 elections. (AP Photo)

One of the significant powers of the president is the power to negotiate and sign treaties. Here, President Jimmy Carter, left, and other officials watch as Panama's president, General Omar Torrijos, signs the Panama Canal Treaty on September 7, 1977. (AP Photo)

Panama Canal to Panama by the year 2000 (over such objections as that of Senator S. I. Hayakawa, a Republican from California, who said, "We stole it fair and square"). The treaty was approved by a margin of a single vote.

The Power to Grant Reprieves and Pardons

The president's power to grant a pardon serves as a check on judicial power. A pardon is a release from punishment or the legal consequences of a crime; it restores a person to the full rights and privileges of citizenship. The president can grant a pardon for any federal offense, except in cases of impeachment. One of the most controversial pardons was that granted by President Gerald Ford (1974–1977) to former President Richard Nixon (1969–1974) after the Watergate affair, before any formal charges were brought in court. Sometimes pardons are granted to a class of individuals, as a general amnesty. For example, President Jimmy Carter granted amnesty to approximately 10,000 people who had resisted the draft during the war in Vietnam.

President Gerald Ford reads a proclamation in the White House on September 9, 1974, granting former president Richard Nixon "a full, free and absolute pardon" for all "offenses against the United States" during the period of his presidency. (AP Photo)

The President's Veto Power

As noted in Chapter 11, the president can **veto** a bill passed by Congress. Congress can over-ride the veto with a two-thirds vote by the members present in each chamber. The result of an overridden veto is that the bill becomes law against the wishes of the president. If the president does not send a bill back to Congress after ten congressional working days, the bill becomes law without the president's signature. If the president refuses to sign the bill and Congress adjourns within ten working days after the bill has been submitted to the president, the bill is killed for that session of Congress. As mentioned in Chapter 11, this is called a *pocket veto*.

Presidents used the veto power sparingly until the administration of Andrew Johnson (1865–1869). Johnson vetoed twenty-one bills, and his successor, Ulysses Grant (1869–1877), vetoed forty-five. Franklin D. Roosevelt (1933–1945) vetoed more bills by far than any of his predecessors or successors in the presidency. During his administration, there were 372 regular vetoes, 9 of which were overridden by Congress, and 263 pocket vetoes. By the end of his presidency in 2001, President Clinton had vetoed thirty-seven bills.

Many presidents have complained that they cannot control "pork-barrel" legislation—federal expenditures tacked on to bills to "bring home the bacon" to a particular congressional member's district. For example, expenditures on a specific sports stadium might be added to a bill involving crime. The reason is simple: without a line-item veto (the ability to veto just one item in a bill), to eliminate the "pork" in proposed legislation, the president would have to veto the entire bill—and that might not be feasible politically. Congress passed and President Clinton signed a line-item veto bill in 1996. The Supreme Court concluded in 1998 that it was unconstitutional, however.[8]

The President's Inherent Powers

In addition to the powers explicitly granted by the Constitution, the president also has inherent powers—powers that are necessary to carry out the specific responsibilities of the president as set forth in the Constitution. The presidency is, of course, an institution of government, but it is also an institution that consists, at any one moment in time, of one individual. That means that the lines between the presidential office and the person who holds that office often become blurred. Certain presidential powers that are today considered part of the rights of the office were simply assumed by strong presidents to be inherent powers of the presidency, and their successors then continued to exercise these powers.

VETO A Latin word meaning "I forbid"; the refusal by an official, such as the president of the United States or a state governor, to sign a bill into law.

President Bill Clinton used line-item veto powers to eliminate thirty-eight construction projects worth $287 million from the military construction bill during a ceremony in the Oval Office in the fall of 1997. "The use of the line-item veto saves taxpayers nearly $290 million and makes clear the old rules have in fact changed," Clinton declared during the ceremony. The line-item veto legislation, passed in 1996, was declared unconstitutional by the U.S. Supreme Court in 1998. (AP Photo/Greg Gibson)

President Woodrow Wilson clearly indicated this interplay between presidential personality and presidential powers in the following statement:

> The President is at liberty, both in law and conscience to be as big a man as he can. His capacity will set the limit; and if Congress be overborne by him, it will be no fault of the makers of the Constitution— it will be from no lack of constitutional powers on his part, but only because the President has the nation behind him, and Congress has not.[9]

In other words, because the Constitution is vague as to the actual carrying out of presidential powers, presidents are left to define the limits of their authority—subject, of course, to the other branches of government.

As you will read in this chapter, Congress has sometimes allowed the president to exercise certain powers and has sometimes limited presidential powers. Additionally, the Supreme Court, as the head of the judicial branch of the government and the final arbiter of the Constitution, can check the president's powers. The Court, through its power of judicial review, can determine whether the president, by taking a certain action, has exceeded the powers granted by the Constitution.

The Expansion of Presidential Powers

The Constitution defines presidential powers in very general language, and even the founders were uncertain just how the president would perform the various roles. Only experience would tell. Thus, over the past two centuries, the powers of the president have been defined and expanded by the personalities and policies of various White House occupants.

For example, George Washington removed officials from office, interpreting the constitutional power to appoint officials as implying a power to remove them as well.[10] He established the practice of meeting regularly with the heads of the three departments that then existed and of turning to them for political advice. He set a precedent of the president acting as chief legislator by submitting proposed legislation to Congress. Abraham Lincoln (1861–1865), confronting the problems of the Civil War during the 1860s, took several important actions while Congress was not in session. He suspended certain constitutional liberties, spent funds that Congress had not appropriated, blockaded southern ports, and banned "treasonable correspondence" from the U.S. mails. All of these actions were carried out in the name of his

As commander in chief, George Washington used troops to put down a rebellion in Pennsylvania, and as chief diplomat, he made foreign policy without consulting Congress. This latter action laid the groundwork for the president's active role in the area of foreign policy. (Library of Congress)

By the time Abraham Lincoln gave his Inauguration Day speech, seven southern states had already seceded from the Union. Four more states seceded after he issued a summons to the militia. In 1863, during the Civil War, Lincoln issued the Emancipation Proclamation. Some scholars believe that his skillful and vigorous handling of the Civil War increased the power and prestige of the presidency. (Library of Congress)

When Franklin D. Roosevelt assumed the presidency in 1933, he launched his "Hundred Days" of legislation to counter the effects of the Great Depression. Roosevelt's administration not only extended the role of the national government in regulating the nation's economic life but also further increased the power of the president. (Library of Congress)

power as commander in chief and his constitutional responsibility to "take Care that the Laws be faithfully executed."

Other presidents, including Thomas Jefferson, Andrew Jackson, Woodrow Wilson, and Franklin D. Roosevelt, have also greatly expanded the powers of the president. The power of the president continues to evolve, depending on the person holding the office, the relative power of Congress, and events at home and abroad.

The Expansion of the President's Legislative Powers

Congress has come to expect the president to develop a legislative program. From time to time the president submits special messages on certain subjects. These messages call on Congress to enact laws that the president thinks are necessary. The president also works closely with members of Congress to persuade them to support particular programs. The president writes, telephones, and meets with various congressional leaders to discuss pending bills. The president also sends aides to lobby on Capitol Hill. One study of the legislative process found that "no other single actor in the political system has quite the capability of the president to set agendas in given policy areas." As one lobbyist told a researcher, "Obviously, when a president sends up a bill [to Congress], it takes first place in the queue. All other bills take second place."

The Power to Persuade   The president's political skills and ability to persuade others play a large role in determining the administration's success. According to Richard Neustadt, in his classic work entitled *Presidential Power,* "Presidential power is the power to persuade."[11] For all of the resources at the president's disposal, the president still must rely on the cooperation of others if the administration's goals are to be accomplished. After three years in office, President Harry Truman made this remark about the powers of the president:

> The president may have a great many powers given to him in the Constitution and may have certain powers under certain laws which are given to him by the Congress of the United States; but the principal power that the president has is to bring people in and try to persuade them to do what they ought to do without persuasion. That's what the powers of the president amount to.[12]

Persuasive powers are particularly important when divided government exists. If a president from one political party faces a Congress dominated by the other party, the president must overcome more opposition than usual to get legislation passed. For example, when George W. Bush assumed the presidency in 2001, he faced an almost evenly divided Congress. During his first year in office, his ability to win congressional support for his agenda depended largely on his persuasive powers.

Going Public   The president may also use a strategy known as "going public"[13]—that is, using press conferences, public appearances, and televised events to arouse public opinion in favor of certain legislative programs. The public may then pressure legislators to support the administration's programs. A president who has the support of the public can wield significant persuasive powers over Congress. Presidents who are voted into office through "landslide" elections have increased bargaining power because of their widespread popularity (but see this chapter's *Perception versus Reality* feature on the following page). Those with less popular support have less bargaining leverage.

The Power to Influence the Economy   Some of the greatest expansion of presidential power occurred during Franklin D. Roosevelt's administration. Roosevelt claimed the presidential power to regulate the economy during the Great Depression in the 1930s. Since that time, Americans have expected the president to be actively involved in economic matters and social programs. Today, Congress annually receives from the president a suggested budget and the *Economic Report of the President*. The budget message suggests what amounts of money the government will need for its programs. The *Economic Report of the President* talks about the state of the nation's economy and recommends ways to improve it.

President Bush promotes his economic stimulus agenda during remarks at the Society for Human Resource Management in Alexandria, Virginia, in February 2003. By promoting their legislative programs directly to the public, presidents can bring pressure to bear on Congress to pass the legislation. (AP Photo/ J. Scott Applewhite)

Presidents and the "Popular Vote"

Every four years, American citizens go to the polls to cast their votes for the presidential candidate of their choice. Some presidential contests are very close, such as the 2000 race between Al Gore and George W. Bush. Others are less so, such as the one between Lyndon Johnson and Barry Goldwater in 1964. When a presidential candidate wins the race by a wide margin, we may hear the election referred to as a *landslide election* or a *landslide victory* for the winning candidate.

THE PERCEPTION

The traditional perception has been that, in general, our presidents are elected by a majority of eligible American voters. As the people's choice, the president is beholden to the wishes of the broad American electorate that voted him into office. A president who has been swept into office in a so-called landslide election may claim to have received a "mandate from the people" to govern the nation. A president may assert that a certain policy or program he endorsed in campaign speeches is backed by popular support simply because he was elected to office by a majority of the voters.

THE REALITY

In reality, the "popular vote" is not all that popular, in the sense of representing the wishes of a majority of American citizens

who are eligible to vote. In fact, the president of the United States has never received the votes of a majority of all adults of voting age. Lyndon Johnson, in 1964, came the closest of any president in history to gaining the votes of a majority of the voting-age public, and even he gained the votes of less than 40 percent of those who were old enough to cast a ballot.

Of course, the highly contested race between Bush and Gore ended up giving Americans a strange new view of how we elect our presidents. Al Gore won the popular vote by over 500,000 votes, but Bush was elected because he won the electoral vote. In any event, neither candidate won a significant number of states by more than 20 percent of the popular vote. Bush won twenty such states, but most of them were small except for Texas. Gore won four such states, but two of them—New York and Massachusetts—had large populations.

It is useful to keep these figures in mind whenever a president claims to have received a mandate from the people. The truth is, no president has ever been elected with sufficient popular backing to make this a serious claim.

What's Your Opinion?

Does it matter whether a presidential candidate, once elected, received a relatively high (or low) percentage of the popular votes cast?

The Legislative Success of Various Presidents   Look at Figure 12–1, which shows the success record of presidents in getting their legislation passed. Success is defined as how often the president won his way on roll-call votes on which he took a clear position. As you can see, typically a president's success record is very high when he first takes office and then gradually declines. This is sometimes attributed to the president's "honeymoon period," when the Congress may be most likely to work with the president to achieve his legislative agenda. The media often put a great deal of emphasis on the president's success during his "first hundred days" in office. Ironically, this is also the period when the president is least experienced in the "ways" of the White House, particularly if the president was a Washington outsider, such as a state governor, before becoming president.

The Increasing Use of Executive Orders

EXECUTIVE ORDER A presidential order to carry out a policy or policies described in a law passed by Congress.

As the nation's chief executive, the president is considered to have the inherent power to issue **executive orders,** which are presidential orders to carry out policies described in laws that have been passed by Congress. These orders have the force of law. Presidents have issued executive orders for a variety of purposes, including to establish procedures for appointing non-career administrators, restructure the White House bureaucracy, ration consumer goods and administer wage and price controls under emergency conditions, classify government information as secret, implement affirmative action policies, and regulate the export of certain items. Presidents issue executive orders frequently, sometimes as many as one hundred a year.

Evolving Presidential Power in Foreign Affairs

As you read in the chapter-opening *America at Odds* feature, the precise extent of the president's power in foreign affairs is constantly evolving. The president is commander in chief and chief diplomat, but only Congress has the power to formally declare war, and the Senate must ratify any treaty that the president has negotiated with other nations. George Washington laid

FIGURE 12–1
Presidential Success Record

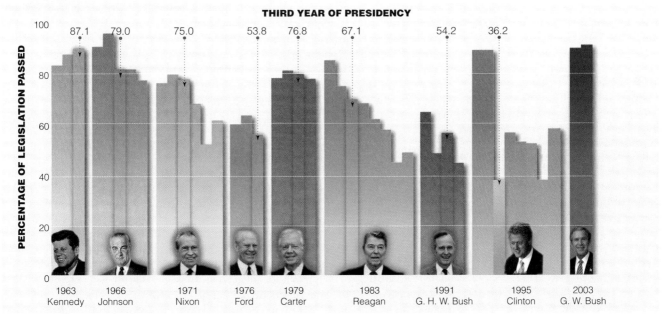

THIRD YEAR OF PRESIDENCY

| | 87.1 | 79.0 | 75.0 | 53.8 | 76.8 | 67.1 | 54.2 | 36.2 |

| 1963 Kennedy | 1966 Johnson | 1971 Nixon | 1976 Ford | 1979 Carter | 1983 Reagan | 1991 G. H. W. Bush | 1995 Clinton | 2003 G. W. Bush |

SOURCE: *CQ Weekly Report*, various issues.

the groundwork for our long history of the president's active role in foreign policy. For example, when war broke out between Britain and France in 1793, Washington chose to disregard a treaty of alliance with France and to pursue a course of strict neutrality. Since that time, presidents have taken military actions and made foreign policy on many occasions without consulting Congress.

The Power to Make Executive Agreements
Presidential power in foreign affairs is enhanced by the ability to make **executive agreements,** which are pacts between the president and other heads of state. Executive agreements do not require Senate approval (even though Congress may refuse to appropriate the necessary funds to carry out the agreements), but they have the same legal status as treaties.

Presidents form executive agreements for a wide range of purposes. Some involve routine matters, such as promises of trade or assistance to other countries. Others concern matters of great importance. In 1940, for example, President Franklin D. Roosevelt formed an important executive agreement with Prime Minister Winston Churchill of Great Britain. The agreement provided that the United States would lend American destroyers to Britain to help protect that nation's land and shipping during World War II. In return, the British allowed the United States to use military and naval bases on British territories in the Western Hemisphere.

To prevent presidential abuse of the power to make executive agreements, Congress passed a law in 1972 that requires the president to inform Congress within sixty days of making any executive agreement. The law did not limit the president's power to make executive agreements, however, and they continue to be used far more than treaties in making foreign policy.

Presidential Military Actions
As you have read, the Constitution gives Congress the power to declare war. Consider, however, that although Congress has declared war only five times in this nation's history,[14] the United States has engaged in more than two hundred activities involving the armed services. Before the United States entered World War II in 1941, Franklin D.

EXECUTIVE AGREEMENT A binding international agreement, or pact, that is made between the president and another head of state and that does not require Senate approval.

Franklin D. Roosevelt and Winston Churchill discuss matters relating to World War II aboard a British battleship in August 1941. (Bettmann/CORBIS)

Roosevelt ordered the Navy to "shoot on sight" any German submarine that appeared in the Western Hemisphere security zone. Without a congressional declaration of war, President Truman sent U.S. armed forces to Korea in 1950, thus involving American troops in the conflict between North and South Korea.

The United States also entered the Vietnam War (1964–1975) without a congressional declaration, and President Lyndon Johnson personally selected targets and ordered bombing missions during that war. President Nixon personally made the decision to invade Cambodia in 1970. President Reagan sent troops to Lebanon and Grenada in 1983 and ordered American fighter planes to attack Libya in 1986 in retaliation for terrorist attacks on American citizens. No congressional vote was taken before President George H. W. Bush sent troops into Panama in 1989. Bush did, however, obtain congressional approval to use American troops to force Iraq to withdraw from Kuwait in 1991. President Clinton made the decision to send troops to Haiti in 1994 and to Bosnia in 1995, and to bomb Iraq in 1998. In 1999, he also decided to send U.S. forces, under the command of NATO (the North Atlantic Treaty Organization), to bomb Yugoslavia.

The War Powers Resolution

As commander in chief, the president can respond quickly to a military threat without waiting for congressional action. This power to commit troops and to involve the nation in a war upset many members of Congress as the undeclared war in Vietnam dragged on for years into the 1970s. Criticism of the president's role in Vietnam led to the passage of the War Powers Resolution of 1973, which limits the president's war-making powers. The law, which was passed over Nixon's veto, requires the president to notify Congress within forty-eight hours of deploying troops. It also prevents the president from sending troops abroad for more than sixty days (or ninety days, if more time is needed for a successful withdrawal). If Congress does not authorize a longer period, the troops must be removed.

The War on Terrorism

President George W. Bush did not obtain a declaration of war from Congress for the war against terrorism that began on September 11, 2001. Instead, Congress invoked the War Powers Resolution and passed a joint resolution authorizing the president to use "all necessary and appropriate force against those nations, organizations, or persons he determines planned, authorized, committed, or aided the terrorist attacks that occurred on September 11, 2001." The resolution set no date for Bush to halt military operations, and, as a consequence, the president has invoked certain emergency wartime measures. For example, through executive order the president created military tribunals for trying terrorist suspects.

President Bush speaks at the U.S. Coast Guard installation in Philadelphia in March 2003. Bush, linking war in Iraq to his global antiterrorism campaign, warned that Saddam Hussein or his terrorist allies might try to strike America in retaliation for the U.S.–led fighting. (AP Photo/Pablo Martinez Monsivais)

The president has also held American citizens as "enemy combatants," denying them access to their attorneys (see Chapter 5 for a discussion of this issue).

Nuclear Weapons   As commander in chief, the president has been responsible, since 1945, for the most difficult of all military decisions—if and when to use nuclear weapons. In 1945, Harry Truman made the awesome decision to drop atomic bombs on the Japanese cities of Hiroshima and Nagasaki. "The final decision," he said, "on where and when to use the atomic bomb was up to me. Let there be no mistake about it." Today, the president travels at all times with the "football"—the briefcase containing the codes used to launch a nuclear attack.

Congressional and Presidential Relations

Despite the seemingly immense powers at the president's disposal, the president is limited in what he or she can accomplish, or even attempt. In our system of checks and balances, the president must share some powers with the legislative and judicial branches of government. And the president's power is checked not only by these institutions, but also by the media, public opinion, and the voters. The founders hoped that this system of shared power would lessen the chance of tyranny. The consequence, however, has sometimes been an inability by the president to exercise decisive leadership. Secretary of Defense William Cohen once said about the American system of checks and balances, "The difficulty with this diffusion of power . . . is that everyone is in check, but no one is in charge."[15]

Some scholars believe the relationship between Congress and the president is the most important one in the American system of government.[16] Congress has the upper hand in relation to the president in some distinct areas, primarily in passing legislation. In some other areas, though, particularly in foreign affairs, the president can exert tremendous power that Congress is virtually unable to check.

Advantage: Congress

Congress has the advantage over the president in the areas of legislative authorization, the regulation of foreign and interstate commerce, and some budgetary matters. Of course, as you have already read, the president today proposes a legislative agenda and a budget to Congress every year. Nonetheless, only Congress has the power to pass the legislation and appropriate

President Bush is surrounded by members of Congress in April 2001, in the Rose Garden of the White House. Bush invited the lawmakers to the White House for a luncheon to mark the president's first one hundred days in office and to promote bipartisanship. (AP Photo/Ron Edmonds)

the funds. The most the president can do constitutionally is veto an entire bill if it contains something that the president does not like.

As you have read, presidential popularity is considered to be a source of power for the president in relation to Congress. Presidents spend a great deal of time courting public opinion, eyeing the "presidential approval ratings," and meeting with the press. Much of this activity is for the purpose of gaining leverage with Congress. The president can put all of his or her persuasive powers to work in achieving a legislative agenda, but Congress retains the ultimate lawmaking authority.

Divided Government   When government is divided—with at least one house of Congress controlled by a different party than the White House—the president can have difficulty getting a legislative agenda to the floor for a vote. President Bill Clinton found this to be the case after the congressional elections of 1994 brought Republicans to power in Congress. Clinton's success rate in implementing his legislative agenda dropped to only 36.2 percent in 1995, after a high of 86.4 the previous year (see Figure 12–1 on page 285).

Different Constituencies   Congress and the president have different constituencies, and this fact influences their relationship. Members of Congress represent a state or a local district, and this gives them a particularly regional focus. As we discussed in Chapter 11, members of Congress like to have legislative successes of their own to bring home to their constituents—military bases that remain open, public works projects that create jobs, or trade rules that benefit a big, local employer. Ideally, the president's focus should be on the nation as a whole: national defense, homeland security, the national economy. At times, this can put the president at odds even with members of his or her own party in Congress.

Furthermore, members of Congress and the president face different election cycles (every two years in the House, every six years in the Senate, and every four years for the president), and the president is limited to two terms in office. Consequently, the president and Congress sometimes feel a different sense of urgency about implementing legislation. For example, the president often feels the need to demonstrate legislative success during the first year in office, when the excitement over the election is still fresh in the minds of politicians and the public.

Advantage: The President

The president has the advantage over Congress in dealing with a national crisis, in setting foreign policy, and in influencing public opinion. In times of crisis, the presidency is arguably the most crucial institution in government because, when necessary, the president can act quickly, speak with one voice, and represent the nation to the world. George W. Bush's presidency was unquestionably changed by the terrorist attacks of September 11, 2001. He represented the United States as it was under attack from foreign enemies and reeling from shock and horror. The president swiftly announced his resolve to respond to the terrorist attacks. No member of Congress could wield the kind of personal power that accrues to a president in a time of national crisis. (See this chapter's *The Politics of Homeland Security* feature for more on presidential power during national emergencies.)

The framers of the Constitution recognized the need for individual leadership in foreign affairs. They gave the president the power to negotiate treaties and lead the armed forces. Some scholars have argued that recent presidents have abused the powers of the presidency by committing U.S. troops to undeclared wars and by negotiating secret agreements without consulting Congress. For example, Arthur M. Schlesinger, Jr., wrote in 1972 of an "imperial presidency," referring in particular to the extensive war powers used by Lyndon Johnson and Richard Nixon in conducting the Vietnam War. For example, in 1970 Nixon ordered secret bombing raids of Cambodia and Laos, Vietnam's neighbors, thereby expanding the war.

Others have argued that there is an unwritten "doctrine of necessity" under which presidential powers can and should be expanded during a crisis. When this has happened in the past, however, Congress has always retaken some control when the crisis was over, in a natural process of institutional give-and-take.

The POLITICS of HOMELAND SECURITY

Presidential Power in a Time of Crisis

Thomas E. Cronin, in his work on the American presidency, points out that there are cycles in politics over which the president has little control. Yet these cycles influence presidential power. "There are times when, and conditions under which, presidents are afforded considerable leverage and power. There are also times when presidents are kept on a short leash."[17] When George W. Bush became president, many observers assumed that he would be one of those presidents who are granted limited power to influence the domestic agenda or foreign policy. September 11, 2001, changed that perception entirely. In some circles, Bush is now regarded as one of the most powerful presidents in decades.

LEADERSHIP STYLE

George W. Bush became president under inauspicious circumstances: he lost the popular vote to his opponent, Al Gore, and he won the electoral college only after the Supreme Court intervened in the ballot counting in Florida. Even after the leap in Bush's approval ratings after September 11, 2001, from 51 percent the week before the attacks to 90 percent two weeks after the attacks, there were doubts about his leadership. Many in the news media suggested that he was not prepared for the task of leading the nation to war. Bush came to the presidency with little experience in foreign policy. He prefers to delegate the more mundane aspects of the day-to-day operations of his office. Some scholars have pointed out that he does not possess a "deliberative" leadership style and lacks an understanding of the broader implications of his decisions.[18]

SOURCES OF BUSH'S POWER

Despite these shortcomings, Bush has proved to be confident, outgoing, and adept at rallying public support. By taking an active role in the congressional elections of 2002, he managed to secure something of the "mandate" he lacked after his own election in 2000. Bush campaigned aggressively for Republican candidates in forty states, making the congressional elections about national issues such as homeland security and a potential war in Iraq. Republicans regained control of the Senate and increased their majority in the House.

The unexpected success on Election Day 2002 is just one source of Bush's power. Earlier that same year, he persuaded Congress to vote overwhelmingly in favor of a war in Iraq if Iraqi President Saddam Hussein failed to appropriately disarm. Then he achieved a resounding success at the United Nations by securing a unanimous vote from the Security Council to challenge Saddam Hussein and reinstate weapons inspections. As columnist James Klurfeld pointed out at the end of 2002, Bush "has support to start a war against Iraq any time he wants, . . . and at a time when there is no challenger to United States military power."[19]

In early 2003, Bush faced increasingly vocal opposition to war in Iraq from the public and some members of Congress, as well as challenges from France and Germany to his policy in Iraq. In March 2003, however, Bush opted to invade Iraq despite this opposition.

President Bush talks with Senate Majority Leader Tom Daschle (D., S.Dak.), left, as Vice President Dick Cheney and Speaker of the House of Representatives Dennis Hastert (R., Ill.), second from the left, join in during a meeting with congressional leaders in the White House Oval Office in September 2002. (AP Photo/Doug Mills)

President Bush addressing the United Nations General Assembly on September 12. (UN/DPI Photo #UNE 563/Mark Garten)

Are We Safer?

Do you think that the president should be given emergency powers in a time of crisis, even if this risks upsetting the system of checks and balances established by the Constitution?

AMERICA at odds

Executive Privilege

As you read in Chapter 11, Congress has the authority to investigate and oversee the activities of other branches of government. Nonetheless, both Congress and the public have accepted that a certain degree of secrecy by the executive branch is necessary to protect national security. Some presidents have claimed an inherent executive power to withhold information from, or to refuse to appear before, Congress or the courts. This is called **executive privilege,** and it has been invoked by presidents from George Washington to George W. Bush.

One of the problems with executive privilege is that it has been used for more purposes than simply to safeguard national security secrets. President Nixon invoked executive privilege in an attempt to avoid handing over taped White House conversations to Congress during the **Watergate scandal.** President Clinton invoked the privilege in an attempt to keep details of his sexual relationship with Monica Lewinsky a secret. President George W. Bush claimed executive privilege to keep Tom Ridge, when he was director of the Office of Homeland Security, from testifying before Congress. Some scholars have argued that invoking executive privilege has impeded legitimate congressional investigations and that Congress should pass a law to ban its use or that the Supreme Court should find it unconstitutional.

Others disagree. Particularly since the war on terrorism began, the Bush administration has maintained that it has been compelled—for our own safety— to keep more information secret than ever before. Information about homeland security measures and protection of vital infrastructure, such as nuclear power facilities, has been kept secret. Attorney General John Ashcroft has instructed federal agencies to remove previously public information from Web sites. Even some ardent advocates of government openness agree that in the war on terrorism, some openness must yield to security concerns.[20]

EXECUTIVE PRIVILEGE An inherent executive power claimed by presidents to withhold information from, or to refuse to appear before, Congress or the courts. The president can also accord the privilege to other executive officials.

WATERGATE SCANDAL A scandal involving an illegal break-in at the Democratic National Committee offices in 1972 by members of President Nixon's reelection campaign staff. Before Congress could vote to impeach Nixon for his participation in covering up the break-in, Nixon resigned from the presidency.

The Organization of the Executive Branch

In the early days of this nation, presidents answered their own mail, as George Washington did. Only in 1857 did Congress authorize a private secretary for the president, to be paid by the federal government. Even Woodrow Wilson typed most of his correspondence, although by that time several secretaries were assigned to the president. When Franklin D. Roosevelt became president in 1933, the entire staff consisted of thirty-seven employees. Only after Roosevelt's New Deal and World War II did the presidential staff become a sizable organization.

The President's Cabinet

The Constitution does not specifically mention presidential assistants and advisers. The Constitution states only that the president "may require the Opinion, in writing, of the principal Officer in each of the executive Departments." Since the time of our first president, presidents have had an advisory group, or **cabinet,** to turn to for counsel. Originally, the cabinet consisted of only four officials—the secretaries of state, treasury, and war and the attorney general. Today, the cabinet includes fourteen secretaries and the attorney general (see Table 12–2 for the names of today's cabinet members).

Because the Constitution does not require the president to consult with the cabinet, its use is purely discretionary. Some presidents have relied on the counsel of their cabinets. Other presidents solicited the opinions of their cabinets and then did what they wanted to do anyway. After a cabinet meeting in which a vote was seven nays against his one aye, President Lincoln supposedly said, "Seven nays and one aye, the ayes have it."[21] Still other presidents have sought counsel from so-called **kitchen cabinets.** A kitchen cabinet is a very informal group of persons, such as Ronald Reagan's trusted California coterie, to whom the president

CABINET An advisory group selected by the president to assist with decision making. Traditionally, the cabinet has consisted of the heads of the executive departments and other officers whom the president may choose to appoint.

KITCHEN CABINET The name given to a president's unofficial advisers. The term was coined during Andrew Jackson's presidency.

TABLE 12-2

The Cabinet as of 2003

AGRICULTURE
Ann Veneman

HEALTH AND
HUMAN SERVICES
Tommy Thompson

LABOR
Elaine Chao

COMMERCE
Donald Evans

HOMELAND SECURITY
Tom Ridge

STATE
Colin Powell

DEFENSE
Donald Rumsfeld

HOUSING AND URBAN
DEVELOPMENT
Mel Martinez

TRANSPORTATION
Norman Mineta

EDUCATION
Rod Paige

INTERIOR
Gale Norton

TREASURY
John Snow

ENERGY
Spencer Abraham

JUSTICE
John Ashcroft

VETERANS AFFAIRS
Anthony Principi

turns for advice. The term *kitchen cabinet* originated during the presidency of Andrew Jackson, who relied on the counsel of close friends who often met with him in the kitchen of the White House.

In general, few presidents have relied heavily on the advice of the formal cabinet, and often presidents meet with their cabinet heads only reluctantly. To a certain extent, the growth of other components of the executive branch has rendered the formal cabinet less significant as an advisory board to the president. Additionally, the department heads are at times more responsive to the wishes of their own staffs or to their own political ambitions than they are to the president. They may be more concerned with obtaining resources for their departments than with helping presidents achieve their goals. As a result, there is often a conflict of interest between presidents and their cabinet members. It is likely that formal cabinet meetings are held more out of respect for the cabinet tradition than for their problem-solving value.

The Executive Office of the President

In 1939, President Franklin D. Roosevelt set up the **Executive Office of the President (EOP)** to cope with the increased responsibilities brought on by the Great Depression. Since then, the EOP has grown significantly to accommodate the expansive role played by the national government, including the executive branch, in the nation's economic and social life.

The EOP is made up of the top advisers and assistants who help the president carry out

EXECUTIVE OFFICE OF THE PRESIDENT (EOP) A group of staff agencies that assist the president in carrying out major duties. Franklin D. Roosevelt established the EOP in 1939 to cope with the increased responsibilities brought on by the Great Depression.

major duties. Over the years, the EOP has changed according to the needs and leadership style of each president. It has become an increasingly influential and important part of the executive branch. Table 12–3 lists the various offices within the EOP. We look at some of the key offices of the EOP in the following subsections.

The White House Office

WHITE HOUSE OFFICE The personal office of the president. White House Office personnel handle the president's political needs and manage the media.

CHIEF OF STAFF The person who directs the operations of the White House Office and who advises the president on important matters.

PRESS SECRETARY A member of the White House staff who holds news conferences for reporters and makes public statements for the president.

Of all of the executive staff agencies, the **White House Office** has the most direct contact with the president. The White House Office is headed by the **chief of staff,** who advises the president on important matters and directs the operations of the presidential staff. The chief of staff, who is often a close, personal friend of the president, has been one of the most influential of the presidential aides in recent years. A number of other top officials, assistants, and special assistants to the president also aid him in such areas as national security, the economy, and political affairs. A **press secretary** meets with reporters and makes public statements for the president. The counsel to the president serves as the White House lawyer and handles the president's legal matters. The White House staff also includes speechwriters, researchers, the president's physician, the director of the staff for the First Lady, and a correspondence secretary. Altogether, the White House Office has more than four hundred employees.

The White House staff has several duties. First, the staff investigates and analyzes problems that require the president's attention. Staff members who are specialists in certain areas, such as diplomatic relations or foreign trade, gather information for the president and suggest solutions. White House staff members also screen the questions, issues, and problems that people present to the president, so matters that can be handled by other officials do not reach the president's desk. Additionally, the staff provides public relations support. For example, the press staff handles the president's relations with the White House press corps and schedules news conferences. Finally, the White House staff ensures that the president's initiatives are effectively transmitted to the relevant government personnel. Several staff members are usually assigned to work directly with members of Congress for this purpose.

The Office of Management and Budget

OFFICE OF MANAGEMENT AND BUDGET (OMB) An agency in the Executive Office of the President that assists the president in preparing and supervising the administration of the federal budget.

The **Office of Management and Budget (OMB)** was originally the Bureau of the Budget. Under recent presidents, the OMB has become an important and influential unit of the Executive Office of the President. The main function of the OMB is to assist the president in preparing the proposed annual budget, which the president must submit to Congress in January of each year (see Chapter 11 for details on

TABLE 12-3
The Executive Office of the President

DEPARTMENT	YEAR ESTABLISHED
White House Office	1939
Office of the Vice President of the United States	1939
Council of Economic Advisers	1946
National Security Council	1947
Office of the U.S. Trade Representative	1963
Council on Environmental Quality	1969
Office of Management and Budget	1970
Office of Science and Technology Policy	1976
Office of Administration	1977
Office of Policy Development	1977
—Domestic Policy Council	1993
—National Economic Council	1993
Office of National Drug Control Policy	1989

SOURCE: *United States Government Manual, 2000/01* (Washington, D.C.: U.S. Government Printing Office, 2000).

preparing the annual budget). The federal budget lists the revenues and expenditures expected for the coming year. It indicates which programs the federal government will pay for and how much they will cost. Thus, the budget is an annual statement of the public policies of the United States translated into dollars and cents. Making changes in the budget is a key way for presidents to try to influence the direction and policies of the federal government.

The president appoints the director of the OMB with the consent of the Senate. The director of the OMB has become at least as important as the cabinet members and is often included in cabinet meetings. She or he oversees the OMB's work and argues the administration's position before Congress. The director also lobbies members of Congress to support the president's budget or to accept key features of it. Once the budget is approved by Congress, the OMB has the responsibility of putting it into practice. The OMB oversees the execution of the budget, checking the federal agencies to ensure that they use funds efficiently.

Beyond its budget duties, the OMB also reviews new bills prepared by the executive branch. It checks all legislative matters to be certain that they agree with the president's own position.

The Council of Economic Advisers

The Employment Act of 1946 established a **Council of Economic Advisers (CEA)**, consisting of three members, to advise the president on economic matters. For the most part, the function of the CEA has been to prepare the annual economic report to Congress. Each of the three members is appointed by the president and can be removed at will.

COUNCIL OF ECONOMIC ADVISERS (CEA) A three-member council created in 1946 to advise the president on economic matters.

The National Security Council

The **National Security Council (NSC)** was established in 1947 to manage the defense and foreign policy of the United States. Its members are the president, the vice president, and the secretaries of state and defense; it also has several informal advisers. The NSC is the president's link to his key foreign and military advisers. The president's special assistant for national security affairs heads the NSC staff.

NATIONAL SECURITY COUNCIL (NSC) A council that advises the president on domestic and foreign matters concerning the safety and defense of the nation; established in 1947.

President George W. Bush addresses the media at the Pentagon on September 17, 2001, following a meeting with his national security team and leaders of the National Guard and Reserve forces. Seated at the table with Bush, from left to right, are Deputy Secretary of Defense Paul Wolfowitz, National Security Adviser Condoleezza Rice, and Secretary of Defense Donald H. Rumsfeld. (Department of Defense photo by R. D. Ward)

The Vice Presidency and Presidential Succession

As a rule, presidential nominees choose running mates who balance the ticket or whose appointment rewards or appeases party factions. For example, a presidential candidate from the South may solicit a running mate from the West. President Clinton ignored this tradition when he selected Senator Al Gore of Tennessee as his running mate in 1992 and in 1996. Gore, close in age and ideology to Clinton, also came from the mid-South. Despite these similarities, Clinton gained two advantages by choosing Gore: Gore's appeal to environmentalists and Gore's compatibility with Clinton.

George W. Bush picked Dick Cheney, a well-known Republican with extensive political experience in Washington, D.C. Among other things, Cheney had held the post of secretary of defense in the administration of Bush's father (1989–1993). The appointment of Cheney helped Bush gather support from those who thought his lack of national political experience and familiarity with Washington politics would be a handicap.

The Role of Vice Presidents

Vice presidents play a unique role in the American political system. On the one hand, they are usually regarded as appendages to the presidency and can wield little power on their own. For much of our history, the vice president has had almost no responsibilities. (In recent years, however, vice presidents, including Al Gore and Dick Cheney, have been important presidential advisers.) On the other hand, the vice president is in a position to become the nation's chief executive should the president die, be impeached, or resign the presidential office. Eight vice presidents have become president because of the death of the president.

Presidential Succession

One of the questions left unanswered by the Constitution is what the vice president should do if the president becomes incapable of carrying out necessary duties while in office. The Twenty-fifth Amendment to the Constitution, ratified in 1967, filled this gap. The amendment states that when the president believes that he is incapable of performing the duties of office, he must inform Congress in writing of this fact. Then the vice president serves as acting president until the president can resume his normal duties. For example, President George W. Bush invoked the Twenty-fifth Amendment in 2002 before undergoing a colonoscopy.

Vice President Dick Cheney greets people during a visit to an Operation Enduring Freedom base in the Middle East on March 17, 2003. (Air Force Photo by Senior Airman Danielle Upton)

TABLE 12-4

The Line of Succession to the U.S. Presidency

1. Vice president
2. Speaker of the House of Representatives
3. President pro tem of the Senate
4. Secretary of the Department of State
5. Secretary of the Department of the Treasury
6. Secretary of the Department of Defense
7. Attorney general
8. Secretary of the Department of the Interior
9. Secretary of the Department of Agriculture
10. Secretary of the Department of Commerce
11. Secretary of the Department of Labor
12. Secretary of the Department of Health and Human Services
13. Secretary of the Department of Housing and Urban Development
14. Secretary of the Department of Transportation
15. Secretary of the Department of Energy
16. Secretary of the Department of Education
17. Secretary of the Department of Veterans Affairs
18. Secretary of the Department of Homeland Security

When the president is unable to communicate, a majority of the cabinet, including the vice president, can declare that fact to Congress. Then the vice president serves as acting president until the president resumes normal duties. If a dispute arises over the return of the president's ability to discharge the normal functions of the presidential office, a two-thirds vote of Congress is required to decide whether the vice president shall remain acting president or whether the president shall resume these duties.

The Twenty-fifth Amendment also addresses the question of how the president should fill a vacant vice presidency. Section 2 of the amendment states, "Whenever there is a vacancy in the office of the Vice President, the President shall nominate a Vice President who shall take office upon confirmation by a majority vote of both Houses of Congress."

In 1973, Gerald R. Ford became the first appointed vice president of the United States after Spiro Agnew was forced to resign. One year later, President Richard Nixon resigned, and Ford advanced to the office of president. President Ford named Nelson Rockefeller as his vice president. For the first time in U.S. history, neither the president nor the vice president was elected to his position.

What if both the president and the vice president die, resign, or are disabled? According to the Succession Act of 1947, then the Speaker of the House of Representatives will act as president on his resignation as Speaker and as representative. If the Speaker is unavailable, next in line is the president pro tem of the Senate, followed by members of the president's cabinet in the order of the creation of their departments (see Table 12–4).

The Presidency and Your Everyday Life

Certainly, the presidency affects your everyday life in the sense that the media treat you to a daily dose of every activity the president engages in, whether it be taking a jog, acquiring a new dog, or attending church. Everyone accepts the daily entertainment value of examining the current president through a microscope. More important to your daily life, though, are the vast powers the president can wield. As one example, the president's ability, through executive order, to declare large areas of American land as national monuments can affect your life.

Executive Orders and More

Presidential executive orders, because the president is our chief executive, have the force of law. In principle, executive orders are issued to carry out policies that have been described in laws that

have been passed by Congress. In reality, some presidents have used executive orders extensively, perhaps even illegally. In 1971, for example, President Richard M. Nixon issued an executive order establishing wage and price controls for the entire United States. The effect on each American's everyday life was profound. The order led to shortages of gasoline and a number of other problems in the marketplace. In all, by the time George W. Bush assumed the presidency, his forty-two predecessors in that office had issued 13,500 executive orders.

In addition to issuing executive orders, presidents can affect your everyday life in other ways. For example, the president proposes most major legislation, even though all legislation must be introduced by members of Congress. Had President Bill Clinton's proposed overhaul of our nation's health-care system been successful in the last decade, your everyday life with respect to medical care would have been dramatically changed. Although Congress decides how much is actually spent, it is now the president's Office of Management and Budget that prepares the budget each year.

Taking Action

If you believe that the president now in office should (or should not) take a particular action, you can get involved. One way to do this is by contacting your political representatives to voice your views. For example, in early 2003, supporters of the "Win Without War" campaign organized a "virtual" march on Washington. The actors shown in the photo to the left (including Tyne Daly in the foreground) contacted participants in the campaign and asked them all to phone, fax, or e-mail their representatives in Congress about their opposition to a war with Iraq. (AP Photo/Nick Ut)

Key Terms

cabinet 290

chief diplomat 278

chief executive 276

chief of staff 292

chief of state 277

commander in chief 277

Council of Economic
  Advisers (CEA) 293

diplomat 278

executive agreement 285

Executive Office of the
  President (EOP) 291

executive order 284

executive privilege 290

kitchen cabinet 291

National Security
  Council (NSC) 293

Office of Management and
  Budget (OMB) 292

press secretary 292

treaty 279

veto 280

Watergate scandal 290

White House Office 292

Chapter Summary

1 The Constitution sets forth relatively few requirements for becoming president. To be eligible for the presidency, a person must be a natural-born citizen, at least thirty-five years of age, and a U.S. resident for fourteen years. Most presidents have been well educated, and many have been wealthy. The average age of presidents at the time of their inauguration has been fifty-four. To date, all U.S. presidents have been male, white, and (with the exception of John F. Kennedy, who was a Roman Catholic) from the Protestant tradition.

2 Article II of the Constitution makes the president the nation's chief executive, commander in chief, and chief of state. Over time, the president has also assumed other roles, such as chief diplomat and chief legislator. The president is also the leader of his or her political party.

3 The Constitution gives the president explicit powers, such as the power to propose and ratify treaties, to grant reprieves and pardons, and to veto acts of Congress. Over time, the scope of the president's power has expanded beyond these explicit powers. For example, the president also has certain inherent powers—powers necessary to fulfill the presidential responsibilities explicitly mentioned in the Constitution. The president's powers to persuade and to conduct foreign affairs are also significant.

4 The relationship between the president and Congress is arguably one of the most important institutional relationships in American government. Congress has the advantage in this relationship in certain areas, such as legislative authorization, the regulation of foreign and interstate commerce, and some budgetary matters. The president has the advantage in other areas, such as in dealing with a national crisis, setting foreign policy, and influencing public opinion.

5 The cabinet—advisers to the president—consists of the heads of the fifteen executive departments. Some presidents have preferred to rely on the counsel of close friends and associates (sometimes called a "kitchen cabinet").

6 The president also receives advice from the members of the Executive Office of the President (including the White House Office, the Office of Management and Budget, the Council of Economic Advisers, and the National Security Council).

7 The vice president is next in line for the presidency if the president should die, be impeached, resign from office, or become incapacitated. The Twenty-fifth Amendment sets out procedures to be followed in the event the president becomes incapacitated. The Succession Act of 1947 established the line of succession to the presidency in the event that both the president and the vice president die or become unable to fulfill their responsibilities (see Table 12–4 on page 295).

RESOURCES FOR FURTHER STUDY

Selected Readings

Barber, James David. *Presidential Character: Predicting Performance in the White House,* 4th ed. Englewood Cliffs, N.J.: Prentice Hall, 1992. Now in its fourth edition, this book is a classic study of political psychology. Barber identifies four presidential personality types and argues that one can use these types to predict how presidential candidates will perform once in office.

Cronin, Thomas E., and Michael A. Genovese. *The Paradoxes of the American Presidency.* New York: Oxford University Press, 1998. This book examines the unique paradox in American government of *democratic leadership*—the vesting in one person of power that, by definition, is held by the people. It is an excellent examination of the vagaries of presidential power.

Ellis, Richard J. *Founding the American Presidency.* Lanham, Md.: Rowman & Littlefield, 1999. This book examines the issues most heatedly debated by the Constitution's framers and includes selections from the Constitutional Convention and the later debates over ratification of the Constitution.

Frum, David. *The Right Man: The Surprise Presidency of George W. Bush.* New York: Random House, 2003. This book offers an insider's view of the presidency of George W. Bush. David Frum served as White House speechwriter during Bush's first year in office. He provides both humorous anecdotes and a serious view of the president during the crisis of September 11, 2001.

Thurber, James A., ed. *Rivals for Power: Presidential-Congressional Relations,* 2d ed. Lanham, Md.: Rowman & Littlefield, 2002. Legal scholars, political scientists, former White House staff, and former members of Congress all contribute to this examination of the rivalry between the president and Congress.

InfoTrac Citations

Using your InfoTrac password, access the InfoTrac database at **http://infotrac.thomsonlearning.com**. Once at the site, you can do "key word" searches to locate the following articles, each of which deals with a topic covered in this chapter. The key words to use in your search are indicated in parentheses.

- "The Executive Power over Foreign Affairs" (Explicit Constitutional Powers)

- "Bully Pulpit: George W. Bush's Religious Rhetoric" (Inherent Powers)

- "When Is a War Not a War? The U.S. Constitution Gives Congress the Power to 'Declare War,'" but Modern Presidents Have Dispensed with the Formalities" (War Powers Resolution)

- "Transcript of President Bush Press Conference October 11" (Press Conference Bush)

Politics on the Web

The White House home page offers links to numerous sources of information on the presidency. You can access this site at
http://www.whitehouse.gov

- The Library of Congress's White House page is another useful site that offers links to information related to the presidency. Go to
http://lcweb.loc.gov/global/executive/fed.html

- If you are interested in reading the inaugural addresses of American presidents from George Washington to George W. Bush, go to
http://www.bartleby.com/124

In addition to the full text of the inaugural addresses, this site provides biographical information on the presidents and a picture of each president.

- If you would like to research documents and academic resources concerning the presidency, a good Internet site to consult is that provided by Texas A&M University at
http://www.tamu.edu/whitehouse

Web Resources on Your CD-ROM

On your CD-ROM, you will find Web resources, news articles, Internet activities, and video clips related to the topics in this chapter. Resources related to this chapter include the following:

- **Values Inventory**—Political Ideology: Presidential War Powers.
- **Why Does It Matter?**—Tell the President How You Feel about an Issue.
- **Updates**—Keep up with the issues in this chapter!
- **Web Resources**—Internet Activities: One Congressperson's View against the Iraq War.
- **Where Do You Stand?**—Dialogue: Should Presidents Be Able to Declare War on Their Own?
- **Comparative Politics**—Britain's Tony Blair and the War in Iraq, 2003.
- **Video**—Great Presidents.
- **NewsEdge**—Visit this global resource for current events related to this chapter.

chapter 13
the bureaucracy

CHAPTER OBJECTIVES

After reading this chapter, you should be able to . . .

Describe the size and functions of the U.S. bureaucracy.

Discuss the structure and basic components of the federal bureaucracy.

Indicate when the federal civil service was established and explain how bureaucrats get their jobs.

Explain how regulatory agencies make rules and the significance of agencies' rulemaking powers for American government.

Identify the key players in "iron triangles" and explain how they affect policymaking in government.

Should the Federal Bureaucracy Be Privatized?

The president of the United States, as the head of the executive branch, is the nation's chief administrator. Helping the president are the fifteen cabinet departments, hundreds of federal agencies, and some 2.6 million federal employees in the executive branch. This is what is meant by the federal bureaucracy. The cost of maintaining this bureaucracy is staggering—as you will read in this chapter.

To curb costs and increase efficiency, governments around the world have been experimenting with privatizing certain services traditionally performed by government. Privatization involves contracting with firms or individuals in the private sector to perform specific types of government services. Within the United States, state and local governments have privatized many of their services. To a limited extent, the federal government has also privatized some of its work. President George W. Bush has announced plans to go further in this direction and privatize some 850,000 federal jobs in the near future. Of course, certain types of government work that are inherently governmental in nature, such as intelligence gathering, cannot be contracted out to the private sector.

Is privatization the solution to the problems of bureaucratic waste and inflexibility? Americans are at odds over this issue. While some say yes, others are not so sure.

We Should Create a "Market-Based" Government

Those in favor of privatization argue that the private sector would deliver services more efficiently and at lower cost. Private organizations that submit bids for government work must find ways to lower the cost of providing the services if they are to compete successfully with other bidders. Thus, if government programs were turned over to the marketplace, the inefficiencies characteristic of government-run operations would disappear.

Consider just one example—the National Railroad Passenger Corporation (Amtrak). Although its passengers pay a higher fare per mile than the average airline or bus passenger, Amtrak has trouble meeting its operating costs. Indeed, keeping Amtrak afloat has cost the taxpayers more than $25 billion since its creation in 1970.[1] Proponents of privatization claim that if Amtrak were privatized, Americans would have better rail service at lower cost.

Some have suggested a type of privatization called "managed competition," in which government agencies compete with private organizations for the job of providing specific services. If a government agency can perform the work at a lower cost, then the agency will retain the job. Forcing the bureaucracy to compete with the private sector could help to create a more efficient government.

We Should Not Put Government Services Up for Sale

Other Americans are less optimistic about the outcome of privatizing the work of the bureaucracy. Among the strongest opponents of privatization are the labor unions that protect the rights of government workers. For example, the American Federation of State, County, and Municipal Employees (AFSCME) contends not only that the benefits of contracting out government services are elusive but also that employee welfare would suffer—because employees in the private sector usually have fewer rights than government employees enjoy.

The AFSCME also points out that when state and local governments have experimented with privatization, the public sector has frequently outperformed the private sector. Furthermore, contracting out has led to some giant boondoggles. In New Jersey, for example, a privately run vehicle inspection program cost taxpayers $247 million more than it would have cost if run by the state.[2]

Generally, those who oppose privatization believe that the quality of government services deteriorates when profit making becomes a factor in the delivery of services. Additionally, the private sector is less sensitive to the needs of minority and disadvantaged groups than government agencies traditionally have been. Finally, this group feels that the expertise of government bureaucrats is especially necessary today, when we face the threat of terrorist attacks and need to respond effectively.

Where Do You Stand?

1. In your opinion, which kinds of government work could be handled just as well, if not better, by the private sector? Why?

2. The argument for privatization is based on the idea that competition for government work will increase efficiency and lower costs. Do you agree? Why or why not?

Interacting with Your CD-ROM Resources

Use your CD-ROM to access resources on the Web, simulations, participation exercises, and video clips. Important resources related to this feature include:

- **Values Inventory**—Political Ideology: Should the Federal Bureaucracy Be Privatized?
- **Where Do You Stand?**—Dialogue: Should the Federal Bureaucracy Be Privatized?
- **Web Resources**—Internet Activities: Privatization in Indianapolis; The Possible Abolition of Amtrak.

INTRODUCTION

Did you eat breakfast this morning? If you did, **bureaucrats**—individuals who work in the offices of government—had a lot to do with that breakfast. If you had bacon, the meat was inspected by federal agents. If you drank milk, the price was affected by rules and regulations of the Department of Agriculture. If you looked at a cereal box, you saw fine print about minerals and vitamins, which was the result of regulations made by several other federal agencies, including the Food and Drug Administration. If you ate leftover pizza for breakfast, bureaucrats made sure that the kitchen of the pizza house was sanitary and safe and that the employees who put together (and perhaps delivered) the pizza were protected against discrimination in the workplace.

Today, the word *bureaucracy* often evokes a negative reaction. For some, it conjures up visions of depersonalized automatons performing their chores without any sensitivity toward the needs of those they serve. For others, it is synonymous with government "red tape." A **bureaucracy,** however, is simply a large, complex administrative organization that is structured hierarchically in a pyramid-like fashion.[3] Government bureaucrats carry out the policies of elected government officials. Bureaucrats deliver our mail, clean our streets, teach in our public schools, and run our national parks. Life as we know it would be impossible without government bureaucrats to keep our governments—federal, state, and local—in operation.

Some critics think that the bureaucracy has grown too big and is too costly to maintain. For some, privatization of the federal bureaucracy, or at least a sizable chunk of it, is one way to downsize the bureaucracy and save taxpayers' dollars—an issue discussed in this chapter's opening *America at Odds* feature. Before we examine the growth of the bureaucracy, though, we need first to look at its nature.

The Nature and Size of the Bureaucracy

The concept of a bureaucracy is not confined to the federal government. Any large-scale organization has to have a bureaucracy. In each bureaucracy, everybody (except the head of the bureaucracy) reports to at least one other person. For the federal government, the head of

BUREAUCRAT An individual who works in a bureaucracy; as generally used, the term refers to a government employee.

BUREAUCRACY A large, complex, hierarchically structured administrative organization that carries out specific functions.

The government, through its bureaucracy, extensively regulates American social and economic life. Here, employees of the Environmental Protection Agency run tests at a toxic waste clean-up site in Denver. (A. Ramey/PhotoEdit)

the bureaucracy is the president of the United States, and the bureaucracy is part of the executive branch.[4]

A bureaucratic form of organization allows each person to concentrate on her or his area of knowledge and expertise. In your college or university, for example, you do not expect the basketball coach to solve the problems of the finance department. The reason the bureaucracy exists is that Congress, over time, has delegated certain tasks to specialists. For example, in 1914, Congress passed the Federal Trade Commission Act, which established the Federal Trade Commission to regulate deceptive and unfair trade practices. Those appointed to the commission were specialists in this area. Similarly, in 1972, Congress passed the Consumer Product Safety Act, which established the Consumer Product Safety Commission to investigate the safety of consumer products placed on the market. The commission is one of many federal administrative agencies.

Another key aspect of any bureaucracy is that the power to act resides in the *position* rather than in the *person*. In your college or university, the person who is currently president has more or less the same authority as any previous president. Additionally, bureaucracies usually entail standard operating procedures—directives on what procedures should be followed in specific circumstances. Bureaucracies normally also have a merit system, meaning that people are hired and promoted on the basis of demonstrated skills and achievements.

The Growth of Bureaucracy

The federal government that existed in 1789 was small. It had three departments, each with only a few employees: (1) the Department of State (nine employees); (2) the Department of War (two employees); and (3) the Department of the Treasury (thirty-nine employees). By 1798, the federal bureaucracy was still quite small. The secretary of state had seven clerks. His total expenditures on stationery and printing amounted to $500, or about $6,100 in 2003 dollars. The Department of War spent, on average, a grand total of $1.4 million each year, or about $17.1 million in 2003 dollars.

Times have changed. Figure 13–1 shows the growth in the number of government employees since 1975. Most growth has been at the state and local levels. All in all, the three levels of government employ about 15 percent of the civilian labor force. Currently, more Americans are employed by government (at all three levels) than by the entire manufacturing sector of the U.S. economy.

During election campaigns, politicians throughout the nation claim they will "cut big government and red tape" and "get rid of overlapping and wasteful bureaucracies." For the last several decades, virtually every president has campaigned on a platform calling for a reduction in the size of the federal bureaucracy. Yet at the same time, candidates promise to establish programs that require new employees—even if they are "consultants" who are not officially counted as part of the bureaucracy.

FIGURE 13–1

Government Employment at Federal, State, and Local Levels

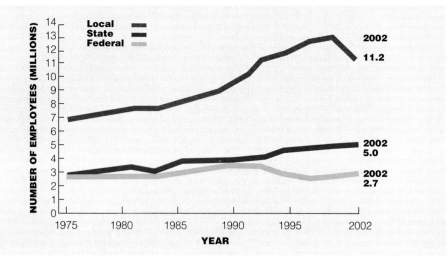

Source: U.S. Department of Commerce, Bureau of the Census, 2003.

The Costs of Maintaining the Government

The costs of maintaining the government are high and growing. In 1929, government at all levels accounted for about 8.5 percent of the total national income in the United States. Today, that figure approaches 30 percent of the nation's gross domestic product. The average citizen pays a similar portion of his or her income to federal, state, and local governments. You do this by paying income taxes, sales taxes, property taxes, and many other types of taxes and fees. To fully understand the amount of money spent by federal, state, and local governments each year, consider that the same sum of money could be used to purchase all of the farmland in the United States plus all of the assets of the one hundred largest American corporations.

The government is costly, to be sure, but it also provides numerous services for Americans. Cutting back on the size of government inevitably means a reduction in those services.

How the Federal Bureaucracy Is Organized

A complete organization chart of the federal government would cover an entire wall. A simplified version is provided in Figure 13–2. The executive branch consists of a number of bureaucracies that provide services to Congress, to the federal courts, and to the president

FIGURE 13-2

The Organization of the Federal Government

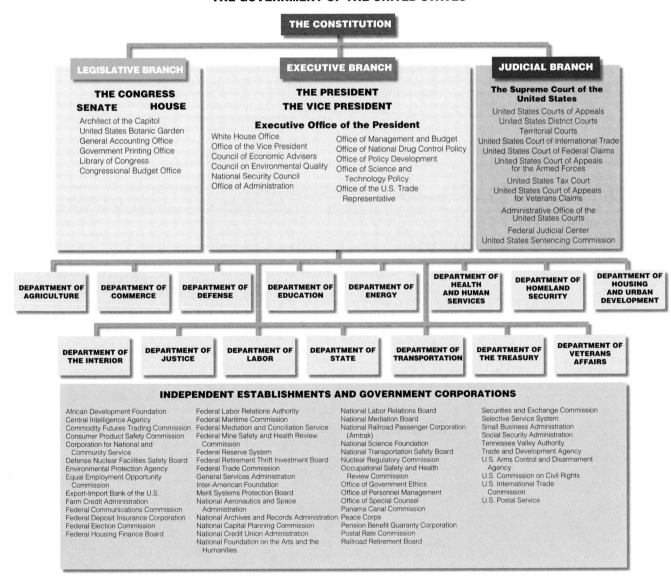

THE GOVERNMENT OF THE UNITED STATES

THE CONSTITUTION

LEGISLATIVE BRANCH

THE CONGRESS
SENATE   HOUSE

Architect of the Capitol
United States Botanic Garden
General Accounting Office
Government Printing Office
Library of Congress
Congressional Budget Office

EXECUTIVE BRANCH

THE PRESIDENT
THE VICE PRESIDENT

Executive Office of the President

White House Office
Office of the Vice President
Council of Economic Advisers
Council on Environmental Quality
National Security Council
Office of Administration

Office of Management and Budget
Office of National Drug Control Policy
Office of Policy Development
Office of Science and
  Technology Policy
Office of the U.S. Trade
  Representative

JUDICIAL BRANCH

The Supreme Court of the United States

United States Courts of Appeals
United States District Courts
Territorial Courts
United States Court of International Trade
United States Court of Federal Claims
United States Court of Appeals
  for the Armed Forces
United States Tax Court
United States Court of Appeals
  for Veterans Claims
Administrative Office of the
  United States Courts
Federal Judicial Center
United States Sentencing Commission

| DEPARTMENT OF AGRICULTURE | DEPARTMENT OF COMMERCE | DEPARTMENT OF DEFENSE | DEPARTMENT OF EDUCATION | DEPARTMENT OF ENERGY | DEPARTMENT OF HEALTH AND HUMAN SERVICES | DEPARTMENT OF HOMELAND SECURITY | DEPARTMENT OF HOUSING AND URBAN DEVELOPMENT |

| DEPARTMENT OF THE INTERIOR | DEPARTMENT OF JUSTICE | DEPARTMENT OF LABOR | DEPARTMENT OF STATE | DEPARTMENT OF TRANSPORTATION | DEPARTMENT OF THE TREASURY | DEPARTMENT OF VETERANS AFFAIRS |

INDEPENDENT ESTABLISHMENTS AND GOVERNMENT CORPORATIONS

African Development Foundation
Central Intelligence Agency
Commodity Futures Trading Commission
Consumer Product Safety Commission
Corporation for National and
  Community Service
Defense Nuclear Facilities Safety Board
Environmental Protection Agency
Equal Employment Opportunity
  Commission
Export-Import Bank of the U.S.
Farm Credit Administration
Federal Communications Commission
Federal Deposit Insurance Corporation
Federal Election Commission
Federal Housing Finance Board

Federal Labor Relations Authority
Federal Maritime Commission
Federal Mediation and Conciliation Service
Federal Mine Safety and Health Review
  Commission
Federal Reserve System
Federal Retirement Thrift Investment Board
Federal Trade Commission
General Services Administration
Inter-American Foundation
Merit Systems Protection Board
National Aeronautics and Space
  Administration
National Archives and Records Administration
National Capital Planning Commission
National Credit Union Administration
National Foundation on the Arts and the
  Humanities

National Labor Relations Board
National Mediation Board
National Railroad Passenger Corporation
  (Amtrak)
National Science Foundation
National Transportation Safety Board
Nuclear Regulatory Commission
Occupational Safety and Health
  Review Commission
Office of Government Ethics
Office of Personnel Management
Office of Special Counsel
Panama Canal Commission
Peace Corps
Pension Benefit Guaranty Corporation
Postal Rate Commission
Railroad Retirement Board

Securities and Exchange Commission
Selective Service System
Small Business Administration
Social Security Administration
Tennessee Valley Authority
Trade and Development Agency
U.S. Arms Control and Disarmament
  Agency
U.S. Commission on Civil Rights
U.S. International Trade
  Commission
U.S. Postal Service

SOURCE: *United States Government Manual, 2002/03* (Washington, D.C.: U.S. Government Printing Office, 2002), p. 21.

Every day, hundreds of thousands of government employees report to work at various federal buildings across the country. In spite of recent attempts to downsize the bureaucracy, the total number of people working for all levels of government continues to rise. (Mark Richards/PhotoEdit)

directly. (For a comparison of the organization of the U.S. bureaucracy with that of other countries, see this chapter's *Comparative Politics* feature.)

The executive branch of the federal government includes four major types of structures:

- Executive departments.
- Independent regulatory agencies.
- Independent executive agencies.
- Government corporations.

Each type of structure has its own relationship to the president and its own internal workings.

comparative politics

The U.S. Bureaucracy Really Is Special

Americans like to think that they are different, and with respect to the federal bureaucracy, they have a lot of facts to back them up. Consider that in the United States, the federal bureaucracy is controlled by several institutions. The president and Congress can exercise control over any agency. If you ever get appointed to a senior position in the federal bureaucracy, you will have to deal with two masters: the one who appointed you (the executive branch) and the one who pays you (Congress). Several congressional committees or subcommittees may also be able to nose around in your affairs.

Not so in Great Britain. In that country and in most parliamentary systems, the prime minister controls the cabinet ministers (the equivalent of our "secretaries") who appoint the bureaucrats. Most British and French bureaucrats, for example, have little or nothing to do with Parliament. Rather, they take orders only from the ministers in charge of their departments.

Because the U.S. political system is federal, as opposed to unitary (see Chapter 3), most agencies in the federal bureaucracy have counterparts at the state or local level. The federal agencies often work together with state and local agencies in performing certain government functions. Consider the Department of Health and Human Services. It is involved with numerous state and local government agencies, and it often reimburses state and local governments for money spent on health care for the nation's underclass. The Department of Labor provides funds to state and local agencies to help pay for job-training programs.

In contrast, in any unitary system, by definition the number of subnational agencies is very limited. Local governments in France at the *département* (a unit of government somewhat like our county) and municipal levels have almost no control over housing, education, or health and employment programs. Those programs are all run by the central government.

For Critical Analysis

Would a bureaucracy in a unitary system be more "efficient" than a bureaucracy in a federal system, such as the United States? Would a unitary or a federal system promote more responsiveness to citizens' needs?

President Bush stands in front of the new employees of the Department of Homeland Security. The federal government marked a historic day on March 1, 2003, when over 170,000 employees from more than twenty different agencies officially became part of the new cabinet department. (AP Photo/Rick Bowmer)

The Executive Departments

You were introduced to the various executive departments in Chapter 12, when you read about how the president works with the cabinet and other close advisers. The fifteen executive departments (also referred to as cabinet departments), which are directly accountable to the president, are the major service organizations of the federal government. They are responsible for performing government functions, such as training troops (Department of Defense), printing money (Department of the Treasury), and enforcing federal laws setting minimum safety and health standards for workers (Department of Labor).

Each department was created by Congress as the perceived need for it arose, and each department manages a specific policy area. In 2002, for example, Congress created the Department of Homeland Security to deal with the threat of terrorism. Following the terrorist attacks of September 11, 2001, President George W. Bush established a special office, called the Office of Homeland Security, within the Executive Office of the President. Because of the importance of this policy area, Bush soon agreed that Congress should create a new cabinet department to combine the expertise of groups that previously had been scattered among several departments and agencies. The creation of the new cabinet department elevated the status of homeland security to a major administrative level in the executive branch of the federal government.

The head of each department is known as the secretary, except for the Department of Justice, which is headed by the attorney general. Each department head is appointed by the president and confirmed by the Senate. Table 13–1 on the next two pages provides an overview of each of the departments within the executive branch.

A Typical Departmental Structure

Cabinet departments consist of the various heads of the department (the secretary of the department, deputy secretary, undersecretaries, and so on), plus a number of agencies. For example, the National Park Service is an agency within the Department of the Interior. The Drug Enforcement Administration is an agency within the Department of Justice.

TABLE 13-1

Executive Departments

DEPARTMENT (Year Established)		PRINCIPAL DUTIES	SELECTED SUBAGENCIES
State (1789)		Negotiates treaties; develops our foreign policy; protects citizens abroad.	Passport Agency; Bureau of Diplomatic Security; Foreign Service; Bureau of Human Rights and Humanitarian Affairs; Bureau of Consular Affairs.
Treasury (1789)		Pays all federal bills; borrows money; collects federal taxes; mints coins and prints paper currency; supervises national banks.	Internal Revenue Service; U.S. Mint.
Interior (1849)		Supervises federally owned lands and parks; operates federal hydroelectric power facilities; supervises Native American affairs.	U.S. Fish and Wildlife Service; National Park Service; Bureau of Indian Affairs; Bureau of Land Management.
Justice (1870)		Furnishes legal advice to the president; enforces federal criminal laws; supervises the federal corrections system (prisons).	Federal Bureau of Investigation; Drug Enforcement Administration; Bureau of Prisons; U.S. Marshals Service.
Agriculture (1889)		Provides assistance to farmers and ranchers; conducts research to improve agricultural activity and to prevent plant disease; works to protect forests from fires and disease.	Soil Conservation Service; Agricultural Research Service; Food and Safety Inspection Service; Federal Crop Insurance Corporation; Farmers Home Administration.
Commerce (1903)		Grants patents and trademarks; conducts national census; monitors the weather; protects the interests of businesses.	Bureau of the Census; Bureau of Economic Analysis; Minority Business Development Agency; Patent and Trademark Office; National Oceanic and Atmospheric Administration.
Labor (1913)		Administers federal labor laws; promotes the interests of workers.	Occupational Safety and Health Administration; Bureau of Labor Statistics; Employment Standards Administration; Office of Labor-Management Standards.

TABLE 13-1

Executive Departments (Continued)

DEPARTMENT (Year Established)	PRINCIPAL DUTIES	SELECTED SUBAGENCIES
Defense (1949)*	Manages the armed forces (Army, Navy, Air Force, Marines); operates military bases.	National Security Agency; Joint Chiefs of Staff; Departments of the Air Force, Navy, Army.
Health and Human Services (1979)†	Promotes public health; enforces pure food and drug laws; is involved in health-related research.	Food and Drug Administration; Public Health Service, including the Centers for Disease Control; Administration for Children and Families; Health Care Financing Administration.
Housing and Urban Development (1965)	Concerned with the nation's housing needs; develops and rehabilitates urban communities; promotes improvements in city streets and parks.	Office of Block Grant Assistance; Emergency Shelter Grants Program; Office of Urban Development Action Grants; Office of Fair Housing and Equal Opportunity.
Transportation (1967)	Finances improvements in mass transit; develops and administers programs for highways, railroads, and aviation.	Federal Aviation Administration; Federal Highway Administration; National Highway Traffic Safety Administration; Federal Transit Administration.
Energy (1977)	Involved in conservation of energy and resources; analyzes energy data; conducts research and development.	Office of Civilian Radioactive Waste Management; Office of Nuclear Energy; Energy Information Administration.
Education (1979)†	Coordinates federal programs and policies for education; administers aid to education; promotes educational research.	Office of Special Education and Rehabilitation Services; Office of Elementary and Secondary Education; Office of Postsecondary Education; Office of Vocational and Adult Education.
Veterans Affairs (1989)	Promotes the welfare of veterans of the U.S. armed forces.	Veterans Health Administration; Veterans Benefits Administration; National Cemetery System.
Homeland Security (2002)	Works to prevent terrorist attacks within the United States, reduce America's vulnerability to terrorism, and minimize the damage from potential attacks and natural disasters.	U.S. Customs Service; Bureau of Citizenship and Immigration Services; Bureau of Immigration and Customs Enforcement; Bureau of Customs and Border Patrol; U.S. Coast Guard; Secret Service; Federal Emergency Management Agency.

* Formed from the Department of War (1789) and the Department of the Navy (1798).
† Formed from the Department of Health, Education, and Welfare (1953).

Although there are organizational differences among the departments, each department generally follows a typical bureaucratic structure. The Department of Agriculture provides a model for how an executive department is organized (see Figure 13–3).

One aspect of the secretary of agriculture's job is to carry out the president's agricultural policies. Another aspect, however, is to promote and protect the department. The secretary spends time ensuring that Congress allocates enough money for the department to work effectively. The secretary also makes sure that constituents, or the people the department serves—usually owners of major farming corporations—are happy. In general, the secretary tries to maintain or improve the status of the department with respect to all of the other departments and units of the federal bureaucracy.

The secretary of agriculture is assisted by a deputy secretary and several assistant secretaries and undersecretaries, all of whom are nominated by the president and put into office with Senate approval. The secretary and each assistant secretary have staff who help with all sorts of jobs, such as hiring new people and generating positive public relations for the Department of Agriculture.

FIGURE 13–3

The Organization of the Department of Agriculture

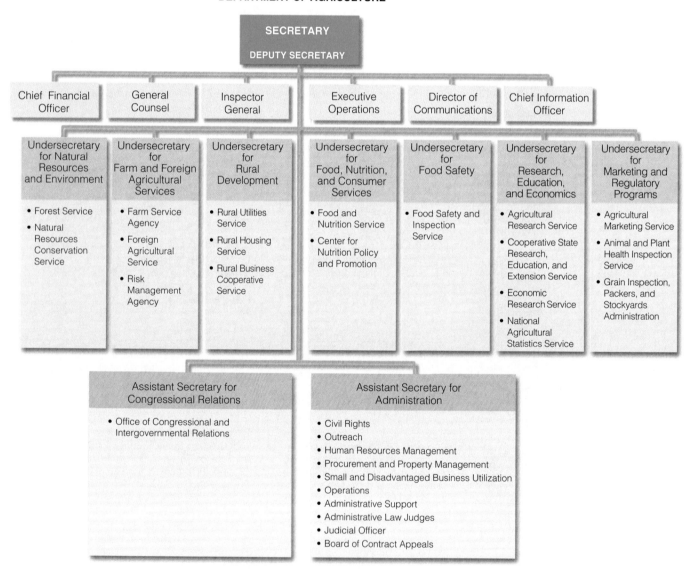

SOURCE: *United States Government Manual, 2002/03* (Washington, D.C.: U.S. Government Printing Office, 2002), p. 108.

Independent Executive Agencies

Independent executive agencies are federal bureaucratic organizations that have a single function. They are independent in the sense that they are not located within a department; rather, independent executive agency heads report directly to the president who has appointed them. A new federal independent executive agency can be created only through joint cooperation between the president and Congress.

Prior to the twentieth century, the federal government did almost all of its work through the executive departments. In the twentieth century, in contrast, presidents asked for certain executive agencies to be kept separate, or independent, from existing departments. Today, there are more than two hundred independent executive agencies.

Sometimes, agencies are kept independent because of the sensitive nature of their functions; at other times, Congress has created independent agencies to protect them from **partisan politics**—politics in support of a particular party. The Civil Rights Commission, which was created in 1957, is a case in point. Congress wanted to protect the work of the Civil Rights Commission from the influences not only of its own political interest groups but also of the president. The Central Intelligence Agency (CIA), which was formed in 1947, is another good example. Both Congress and the president know that the intelligence activities of the CIA could be abused if it were not independent. Finally, the General Services Administration (GSA) was created as an independent executive agency in 1949 to monitor federal government spending. To perform its function of overseeing congressional spending, it has to be an independent agency.

Among the more than two hundred independent executive agencies, a few stand out in importance either because of the mission they were established to accomplish or because of their large size. We list some of the most important independent executive agencies in Table 13–2.

INDEPENDENT EXECUTIVE AGENCY
A federal agency that is not located within a cabinet department.

PARTISAN POLITICS Political actions or decisions that benefit a particular party.

Independent Regulatory Agencies

Independent regulatory agencies are responsible for a specific type of public policy. Their function is to create and implement rules that regulate private activity and protect the public interest in a particular sector of the economy. They are sometimes called the "alphabet soup" of government, because most such agencies are known in Washington by their initials.

One of the earliest independent regulatory agencies was the Interstate Commerce Commission (ICC), established in 1887. (This agency was abolished in 1995.) After the ICC was formed, other agencies were created to regulate aviation (the Civil Aeronautics Board, or CAB, which was abolished in 1985), communication (the Federal Communications

INDEPENDENT REGULATORY AGENCY A federal organization that is responsible for creating and implementing rules that regulate private activity and protect the public interest in a particular sector of the economy.

TABLE 13–2

Selected Independent Executive Agencies

NAME	DATE FORMED	PRINCIPAL DUTIES
Central Intelligence Agency (CIA)	1947	Gathers and analyzes political and military information about foreign countries so that the United States can improve its own political and military status; conducts covert activities outside the United States.
General Services Administration (GSA)	1949	Purchases and manages all property of the federal government; acts as the business arm of the federal government, overseeing federal government spending projects; discovers overcharges in government programs.
National Science Foundation (NSF)	1950	Promotes scientific research; provides grants to all levels of schools for instructional programs in the sciences.
Small Business Administration (SBA)	1953	Promotes the interests of small businesses; provides low-cost loans and management information to small businesses.
National Aeronautics and Space Administration (NASA)	1958	Responsible for U.S. space program, including building, testing, and operating space vehicles.

Commission, or FCC), the stock market (the Securities and Exchange Commission, or SEC), and many other areas of business. Table 13–3 lists some major independent regulatory agencies.

Government Corporations

GOVERNMENT CORPORATION An agency of the government that is run as a business enterprise. Such agencies engage in primarily commercial activities, produce revenues, and require greater flexibility than that permitted in most government agencies.

The newest form of federal bureaucratic organization is the **government corporation,** a business that is owned by the government. Government corporations are not exactly like corporations in which you buy stock, become a shareholder, and share in the profits by collecting dividends. The U.S. Postal Service is a government corporation, but it does not sell shares. If a government corporation loses money in the course of doing business, it is not shareholders who foot the bill but taxpayers.

Government corporations are like private corporations in that they provide a service that could be handled by the private sector. They are also like private corporations in that they charge for their services, though sometimes they charge less than what a consumer would pay for similar services provided by private-sector corporations. Table 13–4 lists some of the major government corporations.

How Bureaucrats Get Their Jobs

As already noted, federal bureaucrats holding top-level positions are appointed by the president and confirmed by the Senate. These bureaucrats include department and agency heads, their deputy and assistant secretaries, and so on. The list of positions that are filled by appointments is published after each presidential election in a document called *Policy and Supporting Positions.* The booklet is more commonly known as the "Plum Book," because the eight thousand jobs it summarizes are known as "political plums." Normally, these jobs go to those who supported the winning presidential candidate—in other words, the patronage system is alive and well.[5]

CIVIL SERVICE Employees of the civil government, or civil servants.

The rank-and-file bureaucrats—the rest of the federal bureaucracy—are part of the **civil service** (employees of the civil government, or civil servants). They obtain their jobs through the Office of Personnel Management (OPM), an agency established by the Civil Service Reform Act of 1978. The OPM recruits, interviews, and tests potential government workers

TABLE 13-3
Selected Independent Regulatory Agencies

NAME	DATE FORMED	PRINCIPAL DUTIES
Federal Reserve System Board of Governors (Fed)	1913	Determines policy with respect to interest rates, credit availability, and the money supply.
Federal Trade Commission (FTC)	1914	Works to prevent businesses from engaging in unfair trade practices and to stop the formation of monopolies in the business sector; protects consumers' rights.
Securities and Exchange Commission (SEC)	1934	Regulates the nation's stock exchanges, where shares of stocks are bought and sold; requires full disclosure of the financial profiles of companies that wish to sell stocks and bonds to the public.
Federal Communications Commission (FCC)	1934	Regulates all communications by telegraph, cable, telephone, radio, and television.
National Labor Relations Board (NLRB)	1935	Protects employees' rights to join unions and to bargain collectively with employers; attempts to prevent unfair labor practices by both employers and unions.
Equal Employment Opportunity Commission (EEOC)	1964	Works to eliminate discrimination that is based on religion, gender, race, color, national origin, age, or disability; examines claims of discrimination.
Environmental Protection Agency (EPA)	1970	Undertakes programs aimed at reducing air and water pollution; works with state and local agencies to help fight environmental hazards.
Nuclear Regulatory Commission (NRC)	1974	Ensures that electricity-generating nuclear reactors in the United States are built and operated safely; regularly inspects operations of such reactors.

and determines who should be hired. The OPM makes recommendations to the individual agencies as to which persons meet the standards (typically, the top three applicants for a position), and the agencies generally decide whom to hire. The 1978 act also created the Merit Systems Protection Board (MSPB) to oversee promotions, employees' rights, and other employment matters. The MSPB evaluates charges of wrongdoing, hears employee appeals from agency decisions, and can order corrective action against agencies and employees.

The idea that the civil service should be based on a merit system dates back more than a century. The Civil Service Reform Act of 1883 established the principle of government employment on the basis of merit through open, competitive examinations. Initially, only about 10 percent of federal employees were covered by the merit system. Today, more than 90 percent of the federal civil service is recruited on the basis of merit.

Regulatory Agencies: Are They the Fourth Branch of Government?

In Chapter 2, we considered the system of checks and balances among the three branches of the U.S. government—executive, legislative, and judicial. Recent history, however, shows that it may be time to regard the regulatory agencies as a fourth branch of the government. Although the U.S. Constitution does not mention regulatory agencies, they can and do make **legislative rules** that are as legally binding as laws passed by Congress. With such powers, this administrative branch has an influence on the nation's businesses that rivals that of the president, Congress, and the courts. Indeed, most Americans do not realize how much of our "law" is created by regulatory agencies, as we indicate in this chapter's *Perception versus Reality* feature on the next page.

Regulatory agencies have been on the American political scene since the nineteenth century, but their golden age came during the regulatory explosion of the 1960s and 1970s. Congress itself could not have overseen the actual implementation of all of the laws that it was enacting at the time to control pollution and deal with other social problems. It therefore chose (and still chooses) to delegate to administrative agencies the tasks involved in implementing its laws. By delegating some of its authority to an administrative agency, Congress may indirectly monitor a particular area in which it has passed legislation without becoming bogged down in the details relating to the enforcement of that legislation—details that are

The Web site maintained by the Office of Personnel Management provides employment information.

LEGISLATIVE RULE An administrative agency rule that carries the same weight as a statute enacted by a legislature.

TABLE 13–4
Selected Government Corporations

NAME	DATE FORMED	PRINCIPAL DUTIES
Tennessee Valley Authority (TVA)	1933	Operates a Tennessee River control system and generates power for a seven-state region and for U.S. aeronautics and space programs; promotes the economic development of the Tennessee Valley region; controls floods and promotes the navigability of the Tennessee River.
Federal Deposit Insurance Corporation (FDIC)	1933	Insures individuals' bank deposits up to $100,000; oversees the business activities of banks.
Export/Import Bank of the United States (Ex/Im Bank)	1933	Promotes American-made goods abroad; grants loans to foreign purchasers of American products.
National Railroad Passenger Corporation (Amtrak)	1970	Provides a national and intercity rail passenger service network; controls over 23,000 miles of track with about 505 stations.
U.S. Postal Service (formed from the Post Office Department [although not a cabinet department until later, the Post Office itself is older than the Constitution])	1971	Delivers mail throughout the United States and its territories; is the largest government corporation.

perception versus REALITY

Who Makes the Law?

The Constitution is clear. In Article I, Section 1, it states as follows:

All legislative Powers herein granted shall be vested in a Congress of the United States, ...

Further, the Constitution, in Article II, Section 3, indicates that the president "shall take Care that the Laws be faithfully executed."

THE PERCEPTION

Not surprisingly, most Americans assume that Congress makes the laws at the federal level because the Constitution authorized only Congress to do so. Indeed, all federal statutes must be enacted by Congress. Americans normally also assume that the regulatory agencies simply administer the laws' provisions—no more, no less. That perception is simple and straightforward—but incomplete.

THE REALITY

Through their rulemaking functions, regulatory agencies staffed by bureaucrats, not Congress, make much of the "law" in the United States. Some even claim that administrative agency rulemaking has created a "new executive state," in which the execu-

tive branch has assumed functions that the founders intended Congress to have.[6]

Indeed, much of the body of environmental law consists of regulations issued by the Environmental Protection Agency. And some federal agencies have even levied taxes, which is a power that supposedly only Congress can exercise. For example, the Federal Communications Commission has imposed a tax on long-distance telephone services to help fund the provision of Internet services to schools.

State agencies have also established much of the law governing states. Consider just one state—Oregon. The Oregon Health Plan pays for physician-assisted suicide as a result of an agency rule, not legislation passed by state legislators. Development on Oregon beaches is restricted by rule, not legislation. Logging on private land is regulated by rule. The way books are chosen for public and school libraries is decided by rule. Library Internet access policies are decided by rule.

In short, Congress and the state legislatures do not make all of the laws in our land.

What's Your Opinion?

Why would Congress willingly give up its legislative powers to administrative agencies?

often best left to specialists. In recent years, the government has been hiring increasing numbers of specialists to oversee its regulatory work.

Agency Creation

ENABLING LEGISLATION A law enacted by a legislature to establish an administrative agency. Enabling legislation normally specifies the name, purpose, composition, and powers of the agency being created.

To create an administrative agency, Congress passes **enabling legislation,** which specifies the name, purpose, composition, and powers of the agency being created. The Federal Trade Commission (FTC), for example, was created in 1914 by the Federal Trade Commission Act, as mentioned earlier. The act prohibits unfair and deceptive trade practices. The act also describes the procedures that the agency must follow to charge persons or organizations with violations of the act, and it provides for judicial review of agency orders.

Other portions of the act grant the agency powers to "make rules and regulations for the purpose of carrying out the Act," to conduct investigations of business practices, to obtain reports on business practices from interstate corporations, to investigate possible violations of federal antitrust statutes, to publish findings of its investigations, and to recommend new legislation. The act also empowers the FTC to hold trial-like hearings and to **adjudicate** (formally resolve) certain kinds of trade disputes that involve FTC regulations or federal antitrust laws. When adjudication takes place, within the FTC or any other regulatory agency, an administrative law judge (ALJ) conducts the hearing and, after weighing the evidence presented, issues an *order.* Unless it is overturned on appeal, the ALJ's order becomes final.

ADJUDICATE To render a judicial decision. In regard to administrative law, the process in which an administrative law judge hears and decides issues that arise when an agency charges a person or firm with violating a law or regulation enforced by the agency.

Enabling legislation makes the regulatory agency a potent organization. For example, the Securities and Exchange Commission (SEC) imposes rules regarding the disclosures a company must make to those who purchase its stock. Under its enforcement authority, the SEC also investigates and prosecutes alleged violations of these regulations. Finally, the SEC sits as judge and jury in deciding whether its rules have been violated and, if so, what punishment should be imposed on the offender (although the judgment may be appealed to a federal court).

Rulemaking

A major function of a regulatory agency is **rulemaking**—the formulation of new regulations. The power that an agency has to make rules is conferred on it by Congress in the agency's enabling legislation. For example, the Occupational Safety and Health Administration (OSHA) was authorized by the Occupational Safety and Health Act of 1970 to develop and issue rules governing safety in the workplace. Under this authority, OSHA has issued various safety standards. For example, OSHA deemed it in the public interest to issue a rule regulating the health-care industry to prevent the spread of certain diseases, including acquired immune deficiency syndrome (AIDS). The rule specified various standards—on how contaminated instruments should be handled, for instance—with which employers in that industry must comply. Agencies cannot just make a rule at any time they wish, however. Rather, they must follow certain procedural requirements, particularly those set forth in the Administrative Procedure Act of 1946.

Agencies must also make sure that their rules are based on substantial evidence and are not "arbitrary and capricious." Therefore, prior to proposing a new rule, an agency may engage in extensive investigation (through research, on-site inspections of the affected industry, surveys, and so on) to obtain data on the problem to be addressed by the rule. Based on this information, the agency may undertake a cost-benefit analysis of a new rule to determine whether its benefits outweigh its costs. For example, when issuing new rules governing electrical equipment, OSHA predicted that they would cost business $21.7 billion annually but would save 60 lives and eliminate 1,600 worker injuries a year. The agency also estimated that its safety equipment regulations for manufacturing workers would cost $52.4 billion, save 4 lives, and prevent 712,000 lost workdays because of injuries each year.

Don't get the idea that rulemaking is isolated from politics. Indeed, as you will read shortly, bureaucrats work closely with members of Congress as well as interest groups when making rules.

RULEMAKING The process undertaken by an administrative agency when formally proposing, evaluating, and adopting a new regulation.

AMERICA at odds

Should Agencies Give More Weight to Compliance Costs?

As already mentioned, the number of regulatory rules generated by federal agencies has climbed steadily over the years, as have the costs of administering those rules. Not surprisingly, the costs of complying with agency rules have also risen. For every dollar spent on regulation, the public now spends $45 in compliance costs—twice as much as twenty-five years ago. According to one author, the total cost of compliance with regulatory rules today is close to $1 trillion, which equates to one-tenth of the U.S. economy.[7]

Should federal agencies give more weight to compliance costs when issuing new regulatory rules? Consider just one example. In 1996, the Environmental Protection Agency (EPA) issued new rules establishing more rigorous standards for particulate matter and ozone. (Ozone, which is the basic ingredient of smog, is formed when sunlight combines with pollutants from cars and other sources.) Business groups estimated that the cost of complying with these new rules could amount to over $100 billion per year. Should the EPA have been required to take these costs into account when issuing the new rules?

Some Americans, and particularly businesses, believe that agencies should not have such a free hand in devising rules that are extremely costly to implement. Others contend that agencies should not be concerned with compliance costs but should focus only on fulfilling their regulatory purpose. For the EPA, this means preserving and improving the quality of our environmental resources, such as air and water, and protecting against the adverse effects of pollution. Indeed, the EPA pointed out that the rules would save 15,000 lives. But even if that were true, does it justify issuing regulations that businesses believe will cost $100 billion to implement? Given that the EPA values a human life at $5 million, the agency felt that its rules were more than justified. Yet what if compliance costs were not just $100 billion but $200 billion, or $300 billion, or even higher? Where do you draw the line?[8]

Policymaking and the Iron Triangle

NEUTRAL COMPETENCY The application of technical skills to jobs without regard to political issues.

Federal bureaucrats are expected to exhibit **neutral competency,** which means that they are supposed to apply their technical skills to their jobs without regard to political issues. In principle, they should not be swayed by the thought of personal or political gain. In reality, each independent agency and each executive department is interested in its own survival and expansion. Each is constantly battling the others for a larger share of the budget. All agencies and departments wish to retain or expand their functions and staffs; to do this, they must gain the goodwill of both the White House and Congress.

Although administrative agencies of the federal government are prohibited from directly lobbying Congress, departments and agencies have developed techniques to help them gain congressional support. Each organization maintains a congressional information office, which specializes in helping members of Congress by supplying any requested information and solving casework problems. For example, if a member of the House of Representatives receives a complaint from a constituent that his Social Security checks are not arriving on time, that member of Congress may go to the Social Security Administration and ask that something be done. Typically, requests from members of Congress receive immediate attention.

IRON TRIANGLE A three-way alliance among legislators, bureaucrats, and interest groups to make or preserve policies that benefit their respective interests.

Analysts have determined that one way to understand the bureaucracy's role in policymaking is to examine the **iron triangle,** which is the three-way alliance among legislators (members of Congress), bureaucrats, and interest groups. (Iron triangles are also referred to as subgovernments, policy communities, or issue networks.) Presumably, the laws that are passed and the policies that are established benefit the interests of all three sides of the iron triangle.

Agriculture as an Example

Consider the bureaucracy within the Department of Agriculture. It consists of about 100,000 individuals working directly for the federal government and thousands of other individuals who work indirectly for the department as contractors, subcontractors, or consultants. Now consider that various interest groups or client groups are concerned with what certain bureaus or agencies in the Agriculture Department do for agribusinesses. Some of these groups are the American Farm Bureau Federation, the National Cattleman's Association, the National Milk Producers Association, the Corn Growers Association, and the Citrus Growers Association.

Finally, take a close look at Congress and you will see that two major committees are concerned with agriculture: the House Committee on Agriculture and the Senate Committee on Agriculture, Nutrition, and Forestry. Each committee has several specialized subcommittees. The triangle is an alliance of bureaucrats, interest groups, and legislators who cooperate to create mutually beneficial regulations or legislation. Iron triangles, or policy communities, are well established in almost every part of the bureaucracy.

Congress's Role

The secretary of agriculture is nominated by the president (and confirmed by the Senate) and is the head of the Department of Agriculture. But that secretary cannot even buy a desk lamp if Congress does not approve the appropriations for the department's budget. Within Congress, the responsibility for considering the Department of Agriculture's request for funding belongs first to the House and Senate appropriations committees and then to the agriculture subcommittees under them. The members of those subcommittees, most of whom represent agricultural states, have been around a long time and have their own ideas about what is appropriate for the Agriculture Department's budget. They carefully scrutinize the ideas of the president and the secretary of agriculture.

The Influence of Interest Groups

Finally, the various interest groups—including producers of farm chemicals and farm machinery, agricultural cooperatives, grain dealers, and exporters—have vested interests in whatever the Department of Agriculture does and in whatever Congress lets the department do. Those interests are well represented by the lobbyists who crowd the halls of Congress. Many lobbyists have been working for agricultural interest groups for decades. They know the congressional committee members and Agriculture Department staff extremely well and routinely meet with them.

The Success of the Iron Triangle in Agriculture

For whatever reason, our nation's farmers have benefited greatly from the iron triangle in agriculture. Indeed, according to the Organization for Economic Cooperation and Development, U.S. taxpayers paid more than $400 billion to farmers between 1986 and 1985.[9] In 1996, Congress decided to change course and passed the Freedom to Farm Act. The purpose of the legislation was to gradually wean farmers from subsidies and let the market dictate prices for farm goods.

In 2002, however, as mentioned in Chapter 11, Congress passed the Farm Security and Rural Investment Act. The act called for an 80 percent increase in agricultural subsidies (guaranteeing prices for certain agricultural products), for a total handout to farmers of up to $190 billion over a ten-year period. The bill even included *new* subsidies for some products, including milk, peanuts, lentils, chickpeas, honey, wool, and mohair.

AMERICA at odds

Why Did Congress Pass the 2002 Farm Legislation?

The 2002 farm bill generated a flurry of controversy among Americans and drew sharp criticism from foreigners as well. Some referred to the bill as a "low point" in the Bush administration. Others wondered where the "adult supervision" was when this bill was passed. These critics pointed out that it was no accident that the bill was passed just months before the 2002 elections, when incumbents in Congress were campaigning for reelection. After all, the bill gave billions of dollars to farm states that were congressional battlegrounds in the 2002 campaigns. It was also no coincidence, say these critics, that the lawmakers in Congress who negotiated the final version of the bill were from Iowa and Texas, the states that saw the greatest increases in subsidies.

Supporters of the bill, including a majority in Congress, believed that the subsidies were necessary to enable American farmers to compete in the international marketplace with farmers from other countries that have such subsidies, such as the nations of the European Union. President Bush, in defending the bill's passage, also stressed that the bill provided an important safety net for farmers and that "the success of America's farmers and ranchers is essential to the success of the American economy." Furthermore, said the president, "American farm and ranch families embody some of the best values of our nation: hard work and risk-taking, love of the land and love of our country."[10]

The problem, according to the bill's critics, is that the bulk of this flood of subsidies goes to the wealthiest 10 percent of the nation's agricultural producers. Are these agribusinesses more representative of the nation's values than workers in urban areas? And why should Americans have to pay for overproduction in the agricultural sector with their tax dollars? Furthermore, by encouraging American exports and depressing global prices, the bill makes it impossible for poorer developing nations to compete in the international market.

President Bush talks with Representative Eva Clayton (D., N.C.), right, as he signs a ten-year, $190 billion farm bill on May 13, 2002. The bill expanded subsidies to growers, and even some fellow Republicans called the measure a budget-busting step backward in agriculture planning. (AP Photo/ Ron Edmonds)

Curbing Waste and Improving Efficiency

There is no doubt that our bureaucracy is costly. There is also little doubt that at times it can be wasteful and inefficient. Each year it is possible to cull through the budgets of the various federal agencies and discover quite outrageous examples of government waste. Here are some recent ones:

- More than $11 million paid to psychics by the Pentagon and the Central Intelligence Agency to discover whether the psychics would offer insights about foreign threats to the United States.
- Payments of more than $20 million a year to thousands of prison inmates through the Social Security Administration's Supplemental Income Program.
- A total of $10 million per year paid by the Department of Energy to its employees to encourage them to lose weight.
- More than $30 million paid over two years by the Internal Revenue Service to tax filers claiming nonexistent slavery tax credits.
- A total of $1.1 million spent for a program that informed tenants of public housing about the types of gemstones, incense, and clothing colors that would best improve their self-esteem.

According to researcher Robert Tollison, "You could multiply the famous examples by a factor of one-thousand and still not cover the wasteful and redundant government programs."[11]

The government has made several attempts to reduce waste, inefficiency, and wrongdoing. For example, over the years both the federal government and state governments have passed laws requiring more openness in government (see this chapter's *The Politics of Homeland Security* feature for a discussion of how this trend is currently being reversed). Further attempts at bureaucratic reform have included, among other things, encouraging government employees to report to appropriate government officials any waste and wrongdoing that they observe.

The POLITICS of HOMELAND SECURITY

Security versus Government in the Sunshine

The past four decades saw a trend toward more openness in government. The theory was that because Americans pay for the government, they own it—and they have a right to know what the government is doing with the taxpayers' dollars.

In response to pressure for more government openness and disclosure, Congress passed the Freedom of Information Act in 1966. This act required federal agencies to disclose any information in agency files, with some exceptions, to any persons requesting it. Since the 1970s, "sunshine laws," which require government meetings to be open to the public, have been enacted at all levels of American government. During the Clinton administration (1993–2001), Americans gained even greater access to government information as federal and state agencies went online.

9/11 AND ITS AFTERMATH

The trend toward greater openness in government came to an abrupt halt on September 11, 2001. In the wake of the terrorist attacks on the World Trade Center and the Pentagon, the government began tightening its grip on information. In the months following the attacks, hundreds of thousands of documents were removed from government Web sites. No longer can the public access plans of nuclear power plants, descriptions of airline security violations, or maps of pipeline routes. Certain documents, such as reports detailing consequences of industrial accidents at chemical plants, can be viewed only under government supervision. Agencies were instructed to be more cautious about releasing information in their files and were given new guidelines on what should be considered public information.

State and local agencies followed the federal government's lead. Some states barred access to such information as emergency preparedness evacuation plans. Others established commissions or panels whose activities are exempt from state sunshine laws. State agency heads in many areas were given the authority to withhold any information that might be useful to terrorists, including drawings of schools, public utilities, and certain buildings.

HOW FAR SHOULD WE GO?

In the burst of patriotic fervor that followed the terrorist attacks of 9/11, few Americans, including members of Congress, voiced any objections to these restrictions. After all, it is not unusual for governments to increase secrecy during times of crisis. But as the war on terrorism continues—with seemingly no end in sight—many Americans have become worried about the secrecy surrounding the Bush administration. Is the public being denied access to too much information, including information that is only indirectly related to security needs?

Certainly, some government information and activities should be kept secret. No one claims, for example, that presidential conversations with cabinet members or other advisers concerning national security should be disclosed to the public. And clearly some revision of disclosure policies was necessary after 9/11. Yet is it necessary to withhold information about the arrest and detainment of suspected terrorists, including who they are, where they are, and why they have been arrested? Is it necessary to advise federal agencies to lean toward withholding information whenever possible, as Attorney General John Ashcroft has asked federal agencies to do?

According to Morton Halperin, who served in three earlier presidential administrations, the Bush administration is characterized by "more secrecy and commitment to secrecy than in any administration in the whole post–World War II period."[12] The consequences of this secrecy for the nation are yet to be seen. Some worry that it will lead to less government accountability and a public that is not sufficiently informed to engage in meaningful debate.

Are We Safer?

Generally, this concern over government secrecy is one aspect of a dilemma facing Americans that has been touched on throughout this text: How should national security be balanced against citizens' rights? With respect to information disclosure, do you think that sacrificing citizens' rights to live in an open society is too high a price to pay for national security?

Helping Out the Whistleblowers

The term **whistleblower,** as applied to the federal bureaucracy, has a special meaning: it is someone who blows the whistle, or reports, on gross governmental inefficiency, illegal action, or other wrongdoing. Federal employees are often reluctant to blow the whistle on their superiors, however, for fear of reprisals.

To encourage federal employees to report government wrongdoing, Congress has passed laws to protect whistleblowers. The 1978 Civil Service Reform Act included some protection for whistleblowers by prohibiting reprisals against whistleblowers by their superiors. The act also set up the Merit Systems Protection Board as part of this protection. The Whistle-Blower Protection Act of 1989 provided further protection for whistleblowers. That act authorized the Office of Special Counsel (OSC), an independent agency, to investigate complaints of

WHISTLEBLOWER In the context of government employment, someone who "blows the whistle" on (reports to authorities) gross governmental inefficiency, illegal action, or other wrongdoing.

Coleen Rowley, an agent for the Federal Bureau of Investigation (FBI), testifies before the Senate Judiciary Committee on June 6, 2002. The committee was investigating oversight on counterterrorism. Rowley had earlier accused FBI headquarters of putting roadblocks in the way of Minneapolis field agents during an investigation of a terrorist suspect. (AP Photo/Joe Marquette)

reprisals against whistleblowers. Many federal agencies also have toll-free hotlines that employees can use to anonymously report bureaucratic waste and inappropriate behavior.

In spite of these laws, there is little evidence that whistleblowers are adequately protected against retaliation. According to a study conducted by the General Accounting Office, 41 percent of the whistleblowers who turned to the OSC for protection during a recent three-year period reported that they were no longer employed by the agencies on which they blew the whistle. Many other federal employees who have blown the whistle say that they would not do so again because it was so difficult to get help, and even when they did, the experience was a stressful ordeal. Creating more effective protection for whistleblowers remains an ongoing goal of the government. The basic problem, though, is that most organizations, including federal government agencies, do not like to have their wrongdoings and failings exposed, especially by insiders.

Improving Efficiency and Getting Results

The Government Performance and Results Act, which went into effect in 1997, has forced the federal government to change the way it does business. In pilot programs throughout the federal government, agencies are experiencing a three-year shakedown. Since 1997, virtually every agency (except for the intelligence agencies) has had to describe its new goals and a method for evaluating how well those goals are met. A results-oriented goal of an agency could be as broad as lowering the number of highway traffic deaths or as narrow as trying to reduce the number of times an agency's phone rings before it is answered.

As one example, consider the National Oceanic and Atmospheric Adminstration. It improved the effectiveness of its short-term forecasting services, particularly in issuing warnings of tornadoes. The warning time has increased from seven to nine minutes. This may seem insignificant, but it provides additional critical time for those in the path of a tornado.

President George W. Bush's "performance-based budgeting" further extends this idea of focusing on results. Performance-based budgeting is designed to increase overall agency performance and accountability by linking the funding of federal agencies to their actual performance. Numerous federal programs now have to meet specific performance criteria. If they do, they will receive more funds. If they do not, their funding will be reduced or removed entirely. To determine the extent to which performance criteria have been met, the Office of Management and Budget now "grades" each agency on how well it manages its operations, and these grades are considered during the budgeting process.

Another Approach—Pay-for-Performance Plans

For some time, the private sector has used pay-for-performance plans as a means to increase employee productivity and efficiency. About one-third of the major firms in this country use some kind of alternative pay system such as team-based pay, skill-based pay, profit-sharing plans, or individual bonuses. In contrast, workers for the federal government traditionally have received fixed salaries; and promotions, salary increases, and the like are given on the basis of seniority, not output.

The federal government has also been experimenting with pay-for-performance systems. For example, the U.S. Postal Service has implemented an Economic Value Added program, which ties bonuses to performance. As part of a five-year test of a new pay system, three thousand scientists working in Air Force laboratories are getting salaries based on actual results. Also, the Department of Veterans Affairs has launched a skill-based pay project at its New York regional office.

Many hope that by offering such incentives, the government will be able to compete more effectively with the private sector for skilled and talented employees. Additionally, according to some, pay-for-performance plans will go a long way toward countering the entitlement mentality that has traditionally characterized employment within the bureaucracy.

Privatization

Another alternative for reforming the federal bureaucracy is **privatization,** which means turning over certain types of government work to the private sector. As you read in this chapter's opening *America at Odds* feature, privatization can take place by contracting out (outsourcing) work to the private sector or by "managed competition" in which the task of providing public services is opened up to competition. In managed competition, both the relevant government agency and private firms can compete for the work. Vouchers are another way in which certain services traditionally provided by government, such as education, can be provided on the open market. The government pays for the vouchers, but the services are provided by the private sector.

PRIVATIZATION The transfer of the task of providing services traditionally provided by government to the private sector.

State and local governments have been experimenting with privatization for some time. Virtually all of the states have privatized at least a few of their services, and some states, including California, Colorado, and Florida, have privatized over one hundred tasks formerly undertaken by government. In Scottsdale, Arizona, the city contracts for fire protection. In Baltimore, Maryland, nine of the city's schools are outsourced to private entities. In other cities, services ranging from janitorial work to recreational facilities are handled by the private sector.

As mentioned earlier, the Bush administration intends to follow the states' lead and privatize work now undertaken by some 850,000 federal workers. Whether airport traffic control, military support services, and a host of other federal services should also be privatized is

Jerry Jordan, left, vice president, and Ted Kirsch, president, both of the Philadelphia Federation of Teachers, speak at a Philadelphia news conference in April 2002. The two were speaking against the privatization of Philadelphia schools. The framework for Philadelphia's ambitious school privatization is set, but numerous details remain to be decided. (AP Photo/Dan Loh)

currently being debated in think tanks and, to some extent, by policymakers. One issue that has been of foremost concern to Americans is whether Social Security should be partially privatized.

Is It Possible to Reform the Bureaucracy?

Some claim that the bureaucracy is so massive, unwieldy, and self-perpetuating that it is impossible to reform. Attempts at reform, including those just discussed, can, at most, barely touch the surface of the problem.

In large part, this is because the positions over which the president has direct or indirect control, through the appointment process, amount to less than 1 percent of the 2.6 million civilian employees who work for the executive branch. The bureaucracy is also deeply entrenched and is often characterized by inertia and by slow-moving responses to demands for change. As Laurence J. Peter, of "Peter Principle" fame, once said, a "bureaucracy defends the status quo long past the time when the quo has lost its status." It should come as no surprise, then, that virtually every president in modern times has found it difficult to exercise much control over the bureaucracy.

Complicating the problem is the fact that political appointees often know little about the work of the agency to which they are appointed and are rarely trained specifically in the areas that they supervise. Typically, they must look for assistance to the rank-and-file staff, whose jobs do not come and go with each administration. Furthermore, federal employees have significant rights. Once a federal worker is hired, firing him or her is extremely difficult, regardless of job performance. Similarly, once a federal agency is created, it takes on a life of its own and tends to become permanent. Indeed, President Ronald Reagan (1981–1989) once commented that "a government bureau is the nearest thing to eternal life we'll ever see on this earth."[13]

why does it MATTER?

The Federal Bureaucracy and Your Everyday Life

Taken as a whole, the spending and actions of bureaucrats affect just about everything you can or cannot do. Just consider some of the fifteen executive departments and how their actions affect your everyday life. The Department of Transportation develops and administers programs for the highways on which you travel. The Department of Agriculture provides assistance to farmers, affecting the prices that you pay for food. The Department of Treasury includes the U.S. Mint, which determines the kinds of money you use in your daily activities. The Department of Homeland Security coordinates efforts to protect your safety in the event of terrorist attacks.

Taking Action

Although this chapter's focus is on the federal bureaucracy, realize that all levels of government require bureaucracies to implement their goals. In virtually every community, however, there are needs that government agencies cannot meet. Often, agencies simply lack the funds to hire more personnel or to provide assistance to those in need. To help address these needs, many Americans do volunteer work. If you want to take action in this way, check with your local government offices and find out which agencies or

offices have volunteer programs. In the photo shown here, volunteers are answering "hot lines" that teenagers can call when they need help. Many volunteers at such "hot line" services have found this type of work especially rewarding. (AP Photo/Lennox McLendon)

Key Terms

adjudicate 312

bureaucracy 301

bureaucrat 301

civil service 310

enabling legislation 312

government corporation 310

independent executive
agency 309

independent regulatory
agency 309

iron triangle 314

legislative rule 311

neutral competency 314

partisan politics 309

privatization 319

rulemaking 313

whistleblower 317

Chapter Summary

1 A bureaucracy is a large, complex administrative organization that is structured hierarchically in a pyramid-like fashion. The federal bureaucracy is an administrative organization that carries out the policies of elected government officials.

2 In 1789, the federal bureaucracy had only about fifty civilian employees. Today, the federal government has about 2.7 million employees. Together, the three levels of government employ about 15 percent of the civilian labor force.

3 There are four major types of bureaucratic structures within the executive branch of the federal government. These structures include executive departments, independent executive agencies, independent regulatory agencies, and government corporations.

4 Bureaucrats holding the top positions in the federal government are appointed by the president and confirmed by the Senate. Rank-and-file employees obtain their jobs through the Office of Personnel Management (OPM), which was created by the Civil Service Reform Act of 1978. The 1978 act also created the Merit Systems Protection Board to protect employees' rights. The civil service is based on the merit system, which was initiated in 1883 by the Civil Service Reform Act of that year.

5 Administrative agencies are sometimes regarded as the fourth branch of government because of the powers they wield. They can make legislative rules that are as legally binding as the laws passed by Congress.

6 Iron triangles, or policy communities, are at work throughout the bureaucracy. An iron triangle consists of legislators, bureaucrats, and interest groups that work together to create mutually beneficial legislation in a specific policy area, such as agriculture.

7 Over the years, Congress has made several attempts to curb bureaucratic waste and inefficiency by creating protections for whistleblowers and providing incentives to federal workers to improve their efficiency. The need to reform the bureaucracy is widely recognized, but some claim that it may be impossible to do so effectively.

RESOURCES FOR FURTHER STUDY

Selected Readings

Behn, Robert D. *Rethinking Democratic Accountability.* Washington, D.C.: The Brookings Institution, 2001. The author looks closely at an ongoing question: How can the American bureaucracy be made more accountable to society?

Gronlund, Ake, ed. *Electronic Government: Design, Applications, and Management.* Hershey, Pa.: Idea Group Publishing, 2002. This collection of essays focuses on how electronic government might make government services better and more effective while at the same time including citizens in democratic processes.

Light, Paul C. *Government's Greatest Achievements: From Civil Rights to Homeland Security.* Washington, D.C.: The Brookings Institution, 2002. At a time when the U.S. government and bureaucracy are increasingly targeted for criticism, this book reminds us of the government's many achievements over the past half-century.

Savas, Emanuel S. *Privatization and Public-Private Partnerships.* Chatham, N.J.: Chatham House, 2000. Although the author believes that privatization and competition in the provision of government services can only help governments, he also explores some of the arguments against privatization.

InfoTrac Citations

Using your InfoTrac password, access the InfoTrac database at **http://infotrac.thomsonlearning.com**. Once at the site, you can do "key word" searches to locate the following articles, each of which deals with a topic covered in this chapter. The key words to use in your search are indicated in parentheses.

- "Youth Employment—Keep Summertime Hiring Legal" (Department of Labor)

- "Closed Doors: The Ashcroft Justice Department's Aversion to Open Government Is Bad Enough at Present, but Potentially Even More Harmful as Precedent" (Department of Justice Ashcroft)

- "New Department of Homeland Security to Include Most Immigration Functions" (Civil Service Homeland Security)

- "Whistleblower Files Lawsuit against Former Employer Carnival Cruise Lines" (Whistleblower Lawsuit)

Politics on the Web

For information on the government, including the Web sites for federal agencies, go to the federal government's "gateway" Web site at
http://www.firstgov.gov

- The Web site of the Office of Management and Budget offers information ranging from new developments in administrative policy to the costs of the bureaucracy to paperwork-reduction efforts. You can access the OMB directly at
http://www.whitehouse.gov/omb

- To learn more about the mission of the General Services Administration (GSA) and its role in managing the federal bureaucracy, go to
http://www.gsa.gov

- Federal World is a government site that contains links to numerous federal agencies and government information. You can find this site at
http://www.fedworld.gov

- If you want to get an idea of what federal agencies are putting on the Web, you can go to the Department of Commerce's Web site at
http://www.doc.gov

- The *Federal Register* is the official publication for executive-branch documents. This publication, which includes the orders, notices, and rules of all federal administrative agencies, is online at
http://www.access.gpo.gov/su_docs/regulatory.html

- The *United States Government Manual* contains information on the functions, organization, and administrators of every federal department. You can now access the most recent edition of the manual online at
http://www.access.gpo.gov/nara/nara001.html

Web Resources on Your CD-ROM

On your CD-ROM, you will find Web resources, news articles, Internet activities, and video clips related to the topics in this chapter. Resources related to this chapter include the following:

- **Values Inventory**—Political Ideology: Should the Federal Bureaucracy Be Privatized?
- **Why Does It Matter?**—Interact with a Bureaucracy of Your Choice.
- **Updates**—Keep up with the issues in this chapter!
- **Web Resources**—Internet Activities: Privatization in Indianapolis; The Possible Abolition of Amtrak.
- **Where Do You Stand?**—Dialogue: Should the Federal Bureaucracy Be Privatized?
- **Comparative Politics**—The German Chancellor and the Bureaucracy.
- **Video**—Bureaucratic Rulemaking.
- **NewsEdge**—Visit this global resource for current events related to this chapter.

chapter **14**
the judiciary

CHAPTER OBJECTIVES

After reading this chapter, you should be able to . . .

- Summarize the origins of the American legal system and the basic sources of American law.

- Delineate the structure of the federal court system.

- Indicate how federal judges are appointed.

- Explain how the federal courts make policy.

- Describe the role of ideology and judicial philosophies in judicial decision making.

323

Supreme Court Appointees: Does Partisanship Matter?

Normally, the United States Supreme Court is not an issue in presidential campaigns. In 2000, however, the Supreme Court was an issue. Although the candidates rarely referred to the Court during the campaign, scholars and news commentators did. They pointed out that several of the justices on the Court are nearing retirement. If one or more of the justices were to retire in the four years following the elections, whoever became president would have the opportunity to appoint their replacements—and thus "make a difference" in national politics for many years to come.

By 2003, George W. Bush had not had the opportunity to appoint new justices to the high court. But suppose that he does appoint one or more new justices to the Supreme Court during his tenure as president. Are the conservative or liberal leanings of Supreme Court nominees really as significant as they are often made out to be? Some say that the ideology of Supreme Court nominees does matter. Others are not so sure.

The Ideology of Supreme Court Nominees Does Matter

Those who argue that the ideology of Supreme Court nominees does matter believe that the next set of Supreme Court justices will be critical. Suppose, for example, that Justice John Paul Stevens, a staunch liberal on the Court, retires and Bush appoints as his replacement a justice with strongly conservative views. This would move the Court even further to the right ideologically. We would have a strongly conservative Court making the final decisions on constitutional questions affecting our rights. The Court could decide on the constitutionality of new or old laws relating to abortion, gun control, affirmative action, gay rights, states' rights versus federal regulatory powers, and the separation of church and state, particularly with respect to public aid to religious schools and school prayer.

The current Supreme Court is split on these and other important issues of our time. The next one or two Supreme Court justices will make a difference. Ideology does matter.

Ideology Will Not Matter All That Much

Others argue that one factor looms large in the debate over judicial appointments, and that factor is the Senate. A president can *nominate* a justice to the Court, but the Senate must *confirm* the nomination. In other words, without the Senate's approval, no justice can sit on the high court.

Even though the Republicans now control the Senate, the confirmation of a president's judicial appointee is never a fore-

gone conclusion. Furthermore, history tells us that justices do not always conform to the wishes of their nominating presidents once they are on the bench.

Consider just one example. Republican president George H. W. Bush (1989–1993) appointed David Souter to the Court with the expectation that Souter would take a conservative approach on the bench. Souter has, however, been a leading counterforce to the Court's conservatives—more evidence that justices can confound the expectations of the presidents who appoint them.

Finally, some scholars argue that the partisan labels *liberal* and *conservative* do not adequately describe the range of views on today's Supreme Court. These scholars note that the current dividing lines on the Court have less to do with partisanship than with other issues. An important division on the Court currently has to do with the justices' perception of how the Court should approach its work. Should the Court, when making a decision, take a "legalistic" approach and establish "rules" for the lower courts to follow based on the text of a law, tradition, and case precedents? Or should the Court take a more "pragmatic" approach and establish flexible "standards" to guide the lower courts based on the context and purpose of a law? Neither approach in this debate, which is sometimes referred to as a debate over text versus context, carries an ideological guarantee with respect to the outcome of a specific case. In other words, in one case a legalistic approach may result in an opinion that many would perceive as "liberal." In another case, the same approach may result in an opinion that could be viewed as "conservative."

Where Do You Stand?

1. The debate over partisanship and Supreme Court nominations assumes that a justice's personal ideological preferences and philosophical leanings will affect his or her judicial decision making. Do you agree with this assumption? Is it possible for a justice to separate his or her personal philosophical and ideological convictions from the judicial decision-making process?

2. When interpreting a law—such as the Constitution or a statute—and applying it to a specific case, should Supreme Court justices take into account such factors as why the law was created, the circumstances that existed at the time of its creation, and whether those circumstances have changed? Why or why not?

Interacting with Your CD-ROM Resources

Use your CD-ROM to access resources on the Web, simulations, participation exercises, and video clips. Important resources related to this feature include:

- **Values Inventory**—Political Ideology: Supreme Court Nominees—Does Partisanship Matter?
- **Where Do You Stand?**—Dialogue: Does Ideology Matter in the Appointment of Supreme Court Justices?
- **Web Resources**—Internet Activities: Frequently Asked Questions about Supreme Court Nominees/ Appointments; Justice Antonin Scalia.

INTRODUCTION

When the United States Supreme Court renders an opinion on how the Constitution is to be interpreted, it is, necessarily, making policy on a national level. The exercise of policymaking powers always generates controversy, and this is certainly true with respect to today's Court, as you read in the chapter-opening feature. To understand the nature of this controversy, however, you need to first understand how the **judiciary** (the courts) functions in this country. We begin by looking at the origins and sources of American law. We then examine the federal (national) court system, at the apex of which is the United States Supreme Court.

JUDICIARY The courts; one of the three branches of the federal government in the United States.

The Origins and Sources of American Law

The American colonists brought with them the legal system that had developed in England over hundreds of years. Thus, to understand how the American legal system operates, we need to go back in time to the early English courts and the traditions they established.

The Common Law Tradition

After the Normans conquered England in 1066, William the Conqueror and his successors began the process of unifying the country under their rule. One of the means they used to this end was the establishment of the "king's courts," or *curiae regis*. Before the Norman Conquest, disputes had been settled according to the local legal customs and traditions in various regions of the country. The law developed in the king's courts applied to the country as a whole. What evolved in these courts was the beginning of the **common law**—a body of general rules prescribing social conduct that was applied throughout the entire English realm.

COMMON LAW The body of law developed from judicial decisions in English and U.S. courts, not attributable to a legislature.

PRECEDENT A court decision that furnishes an example or authority for deciding subsequent cases involving identical or similar facts and legal issues.

STARE DECISIS A common law doctrine under which judges normally are obligated to follow the precedents established by prior court decisions.

The Rule of Precedent   The early English courts developed the common law rules from the principles underlying judges' decisions in actual legal controversies. Judges attempted to be consistent, and whenever possible, they based their decisions on the principles applied in earlier cases. They sought to decide similar cases in a similar way and considered new cases with care, because they knew that their decisions would make new law. Each interpretation became part of the law on the subject and served as a legal **precedent**—that is, a decision that furnished an example or authority for deciding subsequent cases involving similar legal principles or facts.

The practice of deciding new cases with reference to former decisions, or precedents, eventually became a cornerstone of the English and American judicial systems. The practice forms a doctrine called ***stare decisis***[1] ("to stand on decided cases"). Under this doctrine, judges are obligated to follow the precedents established in their jurisdictions. For example, if the Supreme Court of Georgia holds that a state law requiring political candidates to pass drug tests is unconstitutional, that decision will control the outcome of future cases on that issue brought before the state courts in Georgia. Similarly, a decision on a given issue by the United States Supreme Court (the nation's highest court) is binding on all inferior courts. For example, if the Georgia case on drug testing is appealed to the Supreme Court and the Court agrees that the Georgia law is unconstitutional, the high court's ruling will be binding on *all* courts in the United States. In other words, similar drug-testing laws in other states would be invalid and unenforceable.

A fourteenth-century depiction of the Battle of Hastings. In the lower right, William the Conqueror is shown killing the English King Harold. (Smithsonian Photo)

Departures from Precedent   Sometimes a court will depart from the rule of precedent if it decides that a precedent is simply incorrect or that technological or social changes have rendered the precedent inapplicable. Cases that overturn precedent often receive a great deal of publicity. For example, in 1954, in *Brown v. Board of Education of Topeka*,[2] the United States Supreme Court expressly overturned precedent when it concluded that separate educational facilities for African Americans, which had been upheld as constitutional in numerous prior cases under the "separate-but-equal" doctrine[3] (see Chapter 5), were inherently unequal and violated the equal protection clause. The Supreme Court's departure from precedent in *Brown* received a tremendous amount of publicity as people began to realize the political and social ramifications of this change in the law.

Sources of American Law

In any governmental system, the primary function of the courts is to interpret and apply the law. In the United States, the courts interpret and apply numerous sources of law when deciding cases. We look here only at the **primary sources of law**—that is, sources that *establish* the law—and the relative priority of these sources when particular laws come into conflict.

Constitutional Law

PRIMARY SOURCE OF LAW A source of law that establishes the law. Primary sources of law include constitutions, statutes, administrative agency rules and regulations, and decisions rendered by the courts.

CONSTITUTIONAL LAW Law based on the U.S. Constitution and the constitutions of the various states.

Constitutional Law   The U.S. government and each of the fifty states have separate written constitutions that set forth the general organization, powers, and limits of their respective governments. **Constitutional law** consists of the rights and duties set forth in these constitutions.

The U.S. Constitution is the supreme law of the land. As such, it is the basis of all law in the United States. Any law that violates the Constitution is invalid and unenforceable. Because of its paramount importance in the American legal system, the complete text of the U.S. Constitution is found in Appendix A.

The Tenth Amendment to the U.S. Constitution reserves to the states and to the people all powers not granted to the federal government. Each state in the union has its own constitution. Unless they conflict with the U.S. Constitution or a federal law, state constitutions are supreme within the borders of their respective states.

STATUTORY LAW The body of law enacted by legislatures (as opposed to constitutional law, administrative law, or case law).

Statutory Law   Statutes enacted by legislative bodies at any level of government make up another source of law, which is generally referred to as **statutory law.** Federal statutes—laws enacted by the U.S. Congress—apply to all of the states. State statutes—laws enacted by state legislatures—apply only within the state that enacted the law. Any state statute that conflicts with the U.S. Constitution, with federal laws enacted by Congress, or with the state's constitution will be deemed invalid and will not be enforced. Statutory law also includes the ordinances (such as local zoning or housing-construction laws) passed by cities and counties, none of which can violate the U.S. Constitution, the relevant state constitution, or any existing federal or state laws.

ADMINISTRATIVE LAW The body of law created by administrative agencies (in the form of rules, regulations, orders, and decisions) in order to carry out their duties and responsibilities.

Administrative Law   Another important source of American law consists of **administrative law**—the rules, orders, and decisions of administrative agencies. As you read in Chapter 13, at the federal level, Congress creates executive agencies, such as the Food and Drug Administration or the Environmental Protection Agency, to perform specific functions. Typically, when Congress establishes an agency, it authorizes the agency to create rules that have the force of law and to enforce those rules by bringing legal actions against violators. Rules issued by various government agencies now affect virtually every aspect of our economy. For example, almost all of a business's operations, including the firm's capital structure and financing, its hiring and firing procedures, its relations with employees and unions, and the way it manufactures and markets its products, are subject to government regulation.

Government agencies exist at the state and local levels as well. Commonly, state agencies are created that parallel federal agencies. Just as federal statutes take precedence over conflicting state statutes, federal agency regulations take precedence over conflicting state regulations.

CASE LAW The rules of law announced in court decisions. Case law includes the aggregate of reported cases that interpret judicial precedents, statutes, regulations, and constitutional provisions.

Case Law   As is evident from the discussion of the common law tradition, another basic source of American law consists of the rules of law announced in court decisions, or **case law.** These rules of law include interpretations of constitutional provisions, of statutes enacted by legislatures, and of regulations issued by administrative agencies. Thus, even though a legislature passes a law to govern a certain area, how that law is interpreted and applied depends on the courts. The importance of case law, or judge-made law, is one of the distinguishing characteristics of the common law tradition. (See this chapter's *Comparative Politics* feature for a discussion of another type of legal system that is used in many other countries.)

Legal Systems of the World

Legal systems, of course, vary from country to country, because each country's law reflects the interests, customs, activities, and values that are unique to that nation's culture. Even though the laws and legal systems of various countries differ substantially, broad similarities do exist.

TWO TYPES OF LEGAL SYSTEMS

Basically, there are two types of legal systems in today's world. One is the common law system of England and the United States, which we have already discussed. The other type of system is based on Roman civil law, or "code law." The term *civil law*, as used here, refers not to civil as opposed to criminal law but to codified law—an ordered grouping of legal principles enacted into law by a legislature or governing body. In a *civil law system*, the primary source of law is a statutory code, and case precedents are not judicially binding, as they normally are in a common law system. Although judges in a civil law system commonly refer to previous decisions as sources of legal guidance, they are not bound by precedent; in other words, the doctrine of *stare decisis* does not apply.

Generally, those countries that were once colonies of Great Britain retained their English common law heritage after they achieved their independence. Similarly, the civil law system, which is followed in most of the continental European countries, was retained in the Latin American, African, and Asian countries that were once colonies of the continental European nations. Japan and South Africa also have civil law systems, and ingredients of the civil law system are found in the Islamic

courts of predominantly Muslim countries. In the United States, the state of Louisiana, because of its historical ties to France, has in part a civil law system. The legal systems of Puerto Rico, Québec, and Scotland are similarly characterized as having elements of the civil law system.

LEGAL SYSTEMS COMPARED

Common law and civil law systems are not wholly distinct. For example, although the United States has a common law system, crimes are defined by statute as in civil law systems. Civil law systems may also allow considerable room for judges to develop law. There is also some variation within common law and civil law systems. The judges of different common law nations have produced differing common law principles. Although the United States and India both derived their legal traditions from England, the common law principles governing certain areas of the law vary in some respects between the two countries.

Similarly, the laws of nations that have civil law systems differ considerably. For example, the French code tends to set forth general principles of law, while the German code is far more specific and runs to thousands of sections. In some Middle Eastern countries, codes are grounded in the religious law of Islam. The religious basis of these codes makes them far more difficult to alter.

For Critical Analysis

Would the judicial branch exercise more power and influence in a common law system than in a civil law system? Why or why not?

Civil Law and Criminal Law

All of the sources of law just discussed can be classified in other ways as well. One of the most significant classification systems divides all law into two categories: civil law and criminal law. **Civil law** spells out the duties that individuals in society owe to other persons or to their governments, excluding the duty not to commit crimes. Typically, in a civil case, a private party sues another private party (although the government can also sue a party for a civil law violation). The object of a civil lawsuit is to make the defendant—the person being sued—comply with a legal duty (such as a contractual promise) or pay money damages for failing to comply with that duty.

Criminal law, in contrast, has to do with wrongs committed against the public as a whole. Criminal acts are prohibited by local, state, or federal government statutes. Thus, criminal defendants are prosecuted by public officials, such as a district attorney (D.A.), on behalf of the government, not by their victims or other private parties. In a criminal case, the government seeks to impose a penalty (a fine and/or imprisonment) on a person who has violated a criminal law. When someone robs a convenience store, that person has committed a crime and, if caught and proved guilty, will normally be in prison for some period of time.

CIVIL LAW The branch of law that spells out the duties that individuals in society owe to other persons or to their governments, excluding the duty not to commit crimes.

CRIMINAL LAW The branch of law that defines and governs actions that constitute crimes. Generally, criminal law has to do with wrongful actions committed against society for which society demands redress.

Basic Judicial Requirements

A court cannot decide just any issue at any time. Before any court can hear and decide a case, specific requirements must be met. To a certain extent, these requirements act as restraints on the judiciary because they limit the types of cases that courts can hear and decide. Courts also have procedural requirements that frame the judicial process.

JURISDICTION The authority of a court to hear and decide a particular case.

TRIAL COURT A court in which trials are held and testimony taken.

FEDERAL QUESTION A question that pertains to the U.S. Constitution, acts of Congress, or treaties. A federal question provides a basis for federal court jurisdiction.

DIVERSITY OF CITIZENSHIP A basis for federal court jurisdiction over a lawsuit that arises when (1) the parties in the lawsuit live in different states or when one of the parties is a foreign government or a foreign citizen, and (2) the amount in controversy is more than $75,000.

STANDING TO SUE The requirement that an individual must have a sufficient stake in a controversy before he or she can bring a lawsuit. The party bringing the suit must demonstrate that he or she has either been harmed or been threatened with a harm.

Jurisdiction

In Latin, *juris* means "law," and *diction* means "to speak." Thus, **jurisdiction** literally refers to the power "to speak the law." Jurisdiction applies either to the geographic area in which a court has the right and power to decide cases, or to the right and power of a court to decide matters concerning certain persons, property, or subject matter. Before any court can hear a case, it must have jurisdiction over the person against whom the suit is brought, the property involved in the suit, and the subject matter.

A state trial court (a **trial court** is, as the term implies, a court in which a trial is held and testimony taken), for example, usually has jurisdictional authority over the residents of a particular area of the state, such as a county or district. A state's highest court (often called the state supreme court)[4] has jurisdictional authority over all residents within the state. In some cases, if an individual has committed an offense such as injuring someone in an automobile accident or selling defective goods within the state, the court can exercise jurisdiction even if the individual is a resident of another state. State courts can also exercise jurisdiction over people who do business within the state. A New York company that distributes its products in California, for example, can be sued by a California resident in a California state court.

Because the federal (national) government is a government of limited powers, the jurisdiction of the federal courts is limited. Article III, Section 2, of the Constitution states that the federal courts can exercise jurisdiction over all cases "arising under this Constitution, the Laws of the United States, and Treaties made, or which shall be made, under their Authority." Whenever a case involves a claim based, at least in part, on the U.S. Constitution, a treaty, or a federal law, a federal question arises. Any lawsuit involving a **federal question** can originate in a federal court.

Federal courts can also exercise jurisdiction over cases involving **diversity of citizenship.** Such cases may arise when the parties in a lawsuit live in different states or when one of the parties is a foreign government or a foreign citizen. Before a federal court can take jurisdiction in a diversity case, the amount in controversy must be more than $75,000.

Standing to Sue

To bring a lawsuit before a court, a person must have **standing to sue,** or a sufficient "stake" in the matter to justify bringing a suit. Thus, the party bringing the suit must have suffered a harm or been threatened with a harm by the action at issue, and the issue

Most cases start in some type of trial court, where testimony is taken and other evidence evaluated. Trial courts exist in all of the fifty state court systems. In the federal court system, trial courts are called district courts. (Dennis MacDonald/PhotoEdit)

must be justiciable. A **justiciable**[5] **controversy** is one that is real and substantial, as opposed to hypothetical or academic.

The requirement of standing clearly limits the issues that can be decided by the courts. For example, suppose that an environmental interest group sues a company for polluting a local stream in violation of federal law. Even if the company is, in fact, violating federal law, the group cannot sue the firm unless it can produce evidence that its members have actually been harmed, or are about to be harmed, by the polluting activity.

Consider another example. After Congress passed the Line Item Veto Act of 1996 (see Chapter 12), six members of Congress brought a suit challenging the constitutionality of the act. They contended that the act gave the president powers that were intended for Congress, thus diluting their votes. When the case reached the Supreme Court, the Court did not even reach the constitutionality issue. Why not? In the eyes of the Court, the challengers had not met the threshold requirement of standing. According to the Court, the injury they asserted was "wholly abstract" and would remain so until the president actually used the line-item veto.[6] (In a case brought after the president had used the line-item veto, the Supreme Court did address the constitutionality of the issue. As noted in Chapter 12, the Court invalidated the act because it provided for procedures that are not authorized by the Constitution.)

Court Procedures   Both the federal and the state courts have established procedural rules that apply in all cases. These procedures are designed to protect the rights and interests of the parties, ensure that the litigation proceeds in a fair and orderly manner, and identify the issues that must be decided by the court—thus saving court time and costs. Different procedural rules apply in criminal and civil cases. Generally, criminal procedural rules attempt to ensure that defendants are not deprived of their constitutional rights.

Parties involved in civil or criminal cases must comply with court procedural rules or risk being held in contempt of court. A party who is held in contempt of court can be fined, taken into custody, or both. A court must take care to ensure that the parties—and the court itself—comply with procedural requirements. Procedural errors often serve as grounds for a mistrial or for appealing the court's decision to a higher tribunal.

The Federal Court System

The federal court system is a three-tiered model consisting of U.S. district courts (trial courts), U.S. courts of appeals, and the United States Supreme Court. Figure 14–1 shows the organization of the federal court system.

JUSTICIABLE CONTROVERSY A controversy that is not hypothetical or academic but real and substantial; a requirement that must be satisfied before a court will hear a case.

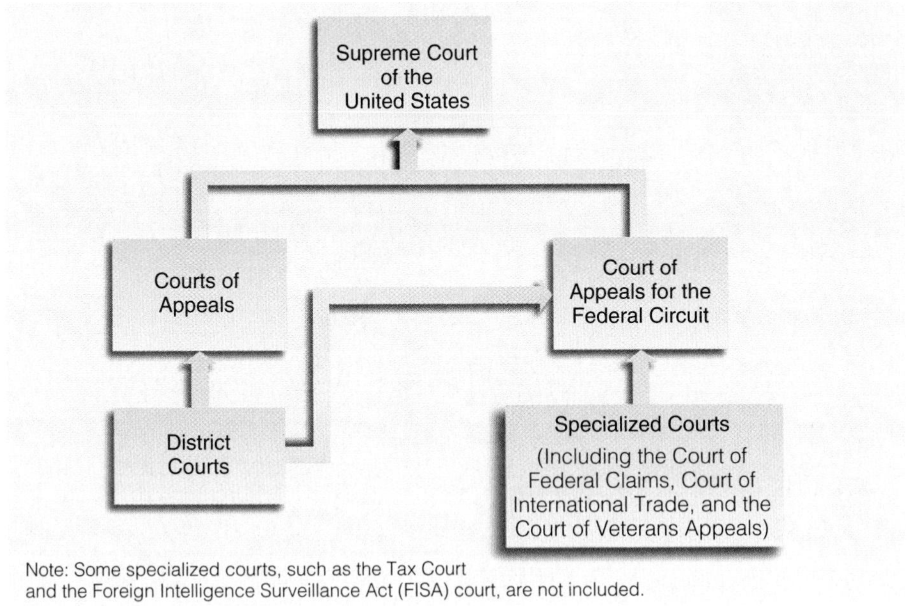

FIGURE 14–1

The Organization of the Federal Court System

Note: Some specialized courts, such as the Tax Court and the Foreign Intelligence Surveillance Act (FISA) court, are not included.

Bear in mind that the federal courts constitute only one of the fifty-two court systems in the United States. Each of the fifty states has its own court system, as does the District of Columbia. No two state court systems are exactly the same, but generally each state has different levels, or tiers, of courts, just as the federal system does. Generally, state courts deal with questions of state law, and the decisions of a state's highest court on matters of state law are normally final. If a federal question is involved, however, a decision of a state supreme court may be appealed to the United States Supreme Court. (For a discussion of another federal court, see this chapter's *The Politics of Homeland Security* feature.)

U.S. District Courts

On the lowest tier of the federal court system are the U.S. district courts, or federal trial courts. These are the courts in which cases involving federal laws begin, and the cases are decided by a judge or a jury (if it is a jury trial). There is at least one federal district court in every state, and there is one in the District of Columbia. The number of judicial districts varies over time, primarily owing to population changes and corresponding caseloads. Currently, there are ninety-four judicial districts; Figure 14–2 shows their geographic boundaries. The federal system also includes other trial courts, such as the Court of International Trade and others shown in Figure 14–1. These courts have limited, or specialized, subject-matter jurisdiction; that is, they can exercise authority only over certain subjects.

U.S. Courts of Appeals

On the middle tier of the federal court system are the U.S. courts of appeals. Courts of appeals, or **appellate courts,** do not hear evidence or testimony. Rather, an appellate court

APPELLATE COURT A court having appellate jurisdiction that normally does not hear evidence or testimony but reviews the transcript of the trial court's proceedings, other records relating to the case, and the attorneys' respective arguments as to why the trial court's decision should or should not stand.

FIGURE 14–2

U.S. Courts of Appeals and U.S. District Courts

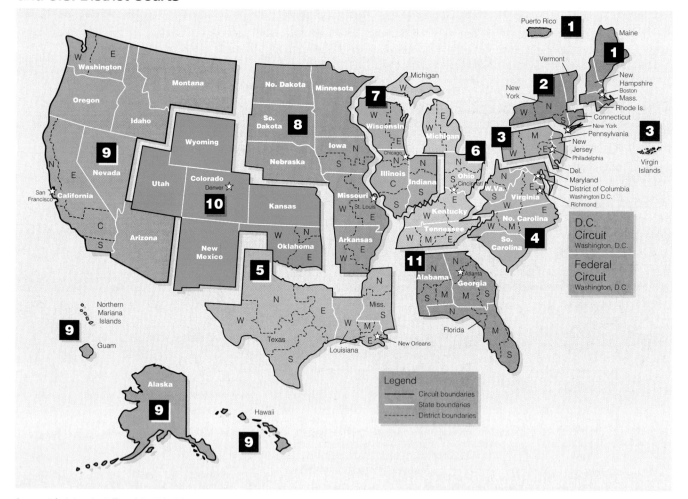

SOURCE: Administrative Office of the United States Courts.

The POLITICS of HOMELAND SECURITY

Expanding the Secret Spy Court

At one time, England had a special king's court that convened in a room in Westminster Palace. The court, which was created in 1487, became known as the "Star Chamber" because the ceiling of the room in which the court met was decorated with stars. Initially, the purpose of the court was to hear cases that lay outside the scope of the common law. In its later years, it evolved into a court in which the political opponents of the king were prosecuted. The proceedings of the Star Chamber were secret, there were no juries, and the procedures used resembled an inquisition. The court was abolished in 1641, but its name survives as a symbol of arbitrariness, oppression, and a basic disregard of civil rights.

In August 2002, news articles appeared in the media about a U.S. court that, like the Star Chamber, conducts its sessions in secret. Prior to the publication of these articles, most Americans had never heard of this court, which is known as the FISA court because it was created by the Foreign Intelligence Surveillance Act (FISA) of 1978. The FISA was intended to provide oversight to government surveillance, which previously could be undertaken directly by the Federal Bureau of Investigation (FBI) or the Department of Justice (DOJ).

Attorney General John Ashcroft, center, discusses the ultrasecret Foreign Intelligence Surveillance Act court. Ashcroft believes there are adequate safeguards to ensure that the government does not overstep its bounds gathering information. (AP Photo/Joe Marquette)

THE WORK OF THE FISA COURT

The FISA court was established to review requests from the DOJ for warrants permitting the government to wiretap the communications of foreign agents operating on U.S. soil. In 1994, by a presidential executive order, the FISA court was authorized to permit warrants for physical searches, as well as electronic surveillance. Under the FISA, warrants could be issued only when the primary purpose of the warrant was to collect information about foreign intelligence.

Obtaining intelligence information through surveillance is one thing. Obtaining evidence to use in a criminal prosecution is quite another. The FISA initially permitted only the former. In 2001, however, Congress passed the USA Patriot Act, which, among other things, amended the FISA. In the interests of preventing and containing terrorism, the act authorized the FISA court to approve search warrants not just for the purpose of obtaining foreign intelligence but for any "significant purpose." In effect, the amendments mean that warrants can now be issued to gather evidence that can be used in criminal prosecutions against anyone in the United States suspected of terrorist affiliations or activities.

SECRET PROCEEDINGS

The proceedings of the FISA court are not open to the public, nor are the records of the court's proceedings public records, as the records of other courts are. The court consists of a panel of eleven U.S. district court judges who are appointed by the chief justice of the United States. The judges meet a few days a month in a heavily guarded, windowless room in the basement of the Justice Department. During its sessions, the court evaluates and approves requests for search warrants. Unlike regular courts, the FISA court does not require a finding of probable cause that a crime has been committed before it will issue a warrant.

By 2003, the court had denied only one of the estimated 7,500 to 10,000 applications for warrants that have been submitted. In

May 2002, the court denied an application on the ground that the FBI and the DOJ had supplied the court with inaccurate information in more than seventy-five applications for search warrants during the previous two years. In its ruling, the court also objected to a Justice Department proposal that criminal prosecutors be given routine access to intelligence gathered by the FBI, instead of having to obtain the court's permission before doing so. In November 2002, however, a FISA appellate panel overturned the ruling and held in favor of the DOJ.[7]

AN AMERICAN STAR CHAMBER?

As mentioned, few Americans had heard of the FISA court until August 2002, when stories about the court's May 2002 decision appeared in the media. The Senate Judiciary Committee, which was reviewing requests by the Justice Department for broader investigative powers, had access to the court opinion and released the information to the public. The publication of the May 2002 FISA ruling was an exception, however. Normally, the public has no way of knowing what takes place in the FISA court. Because FISA court records are closed to the public, no one can find out who has been targeted by the government for surveillance, and why.

Since its beginning, the FISA court has been viewed warily by civil rights groups for these reasons. Now, with the expansion of the court's powers, civil libertarians and others are wondering if we are witnessing the evolution of another Star Chamber. As they point out, evidence obtained through FISA–authorized secret surveillance can now be used in criminal prosecutions against U.S. citizens.

Are We Safer?

Will authorizing the FISA court to allow surveillance targeted not just at foreign agents but also at U.S. citizens make us safer? Or, in the long run, will these actions curb rights and liberties that protect us against government oppression?

reviews the transcript of the trial court's proceedings, other records relating to the case, and the attorneys' respective arguments as to why the trial court's decision should or should not stand. In contrast to a trial court, where normally a single judge presides, an appellate court consists of a panel of three or more judges. The task of the appellate court is to determine whether the trial court erred in applying the law to the facts and issues involved in a particular case.

There are thirteen U.S. courts of appeals in the United States. The courts of appeals for twelve of the circuits, including the Court of Appeals for the D.C. Circuit, hear appeals from the U.S. district courts located within their respective judicial circuits (see Figure 14–2 on page 330). Appeals from decisions made by federal administrative agencies, such as the Federal Trade Commission, may also be made to the U.S. courts of appeals. The Court of Appeals for the Federal Circuit has national jurisdiction over certain types of cases, such as those concerning patent law and some claims against the national government.

The decisions of the federal appellate courts may be appealed to the United States Supreme Court. If a decision is not appealed, or if the high court declines to review the case, the appellate court's decision is final.

The United States Supreme Court

The highest level of the three-tiered model of the federal court system is the United States Supreme Court. According to Article III of the U.S. Constitution, there is only one national Supreme Court. Congress is empowered to create additional ("inferior") courts as it deems necessary. The inferior courts that Congress has created include the second tier in our model—the U.S. courts of appeals—as well as the district courts and any other courts of limited, or specialized, jurisdiction.

The United States Supreme Court consists of nine justices—a chief justice and eight associate justices—although that number is not mandated by the Constitution. The Supreme Court has original, or trial, jurisdiction only in rare instances (set forth in Article III, Section 2). In other words, only rarely does a case originate at the Supreme Court level. Most of the Court's work is as an appellate court. The Supreme Court has appellate authority over cases decided by the U.S. courts of appeals, as well as over some cases decided in the state courts when federal questions are at issue.

WRIT OF *CERTIORARI* An order from a higher court asking a lower court for the record of a case.

The Writ of *Certiorari*   To bring a case before the Supreme Court, a party may request that the Court issue a **writ of *certiorari*,**[8] popularly called "cert.," which is an order that the

This is a photo of the Supreme Court chamber. In 1935, the Court moved from its quarters in the Capitol building to its own building, constructed with white Vermont marble. No television cameras have been allowed inside the Supreme Court chamber during the presentation of an actual case. (Paul Conklin/PhotoEdit)

Supreme Court issues to a lower court requesting the latter to send it the record of the case in question. Parties can petition the Supreme Court to issue a writ of *certiorari*, but whether the Court will do so is entirely within its discretion. The Court will not issue a writ unless at least four of the nine justices approve. In no instance is the Court required to issue a writ of *certiorari*.[9]

Most petitions for writs of *certiorari* are denied. A denial is not a decision on the merits of a case, nor does it indicate that the Court agrees with a lower court's opinion. Furthermore, the denial of a writ has no value as a precedent. A denial simply means that the decision of the lower court remains the law within that court's jurisdiction.

Which Cases Reach the Supreme Court?

There is no absolute right to appeal to the United States Supreme Court. Although thousands of cases are filed with the Supreme Court each year, on average the Court hears fewer than one hundred. As Figure 14–3 shows, the number of cases heard by the Court each year has declined significantly since the 1980s. In large part, this is due to the Court's raising of its standards for accepting cases in recent years.

Typically, the petitions granted by the Court involve cases that raise important policy issues that need to be addressed. In recent years, for example, the Court has heard cases involving such pressing issues as whether school vouchers allowing public funds to be used for tuition at religious schools violate the establishment clause, whether carpal tunnel syndrome should be considered a disability under the Americans with Disabilities Act of 1990, and whether various laws enacted to curb online obscenity and pornography violate the First Amendment's guarantee of free speech. Also, if the lower courts have rendered conflicting opinions on an important issue, the Supreme Court may review a case involving that issue to define the law on the matter. For example, in 2002 the Court agreed to review two cases raising the issue of whether affirmative action programs (see Chapter 5) violate the equal protection clause of the Constitution. Different federal appellate courts had reached conflicting opinions on this issue.

Supreme Court Opinions

Like all appellate courts, the United States Supreme Court normally does not hear any evidence. The Court's decision in a particular case is based on the written record of the case and the written arguments (legal briefs) that the attorneys submit. The attorneys also present **oral arguments**—arguments presented in person rather than on paper—to the Court, after which the justices discuss the case in **conference.** The conference is strictly private—only the justices are allowed in the room.

When the Court has reached a decision, the chief justice, if in the majority, assigns the task of writing the Court's **opinion** to one of the justices. When the chief justice is not in the majority, the most senior justice voting with the majority assigns the writing of the Court's opinion. The opinion outlines the reasons for the Court's decision, the rules of law that apply, and the judgment.

Often, one or more justices who agree with the Court's decision may do so for different reasons than those outlined in the majority opinion. These justices may write **concurring opinions,** setting forth their own legal reasoning on the issue. Frequently, one or more justices

ORAL ARGUMENT An argument presented to a judge in person by an attorney on behalf of his or her client.

CONFERENCE In regard to the Supreme Court, a private meeting of the justices in which they present their arguments with respect to a case under consideration.

OPINION A written statement by a court expressing the reasons for its decision in a case.

CONCURRING OPINION A statement written by a judge or justice who agrees (concurs) with the court's decision, but for reasons different from those in the majority opinion.

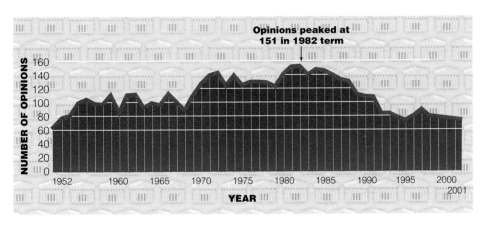

FIGURE 14–3

The Number of Supreme Court Opinions

During the 1952 term (the term beginning in October 1952 and ending in June 1953), the Supreme Court issued 65 written opinions. The number of opinions peaked at 151 in the 1982 term and has been declining more or less steadily ever since. During the 2001 term (ending in June 2002), the Court issued 79 written opinions.

DISSENTING OPINION A written opinion by a judge or justice who disagrees with the majority opinion.

disagree with the Court's conclusion. These justices may write **dissenting opinions,** outlining the reasons why they feel the majority erred in arriving at its decision. Although a dissenting opinion does not affect the outcome of the case before the Court, it may be important later. In a subsequent case concerning the same issue, a jurist or attorney may use the legal reasoning in the dissenting opinion as the basis for an argument to reverse the previous decision and establish a new precedent.

Federal Judicial Appointments

Unlike state court judges, who are often elected, all federal judges are appointed. Article II, Section 2, of the Constitution authorizes the president to appoint the justices of the Supreme Court with the advice and consent of the Senate. Laws enacted by Congress provide that the same procedure be used for appointing judges to the lower federal courts as well.

Federal judges receive lifetime appointments (because under Article III of the Constitution they "hold their Offices during good Behaviour"). Federal judges may be removed from office through the impeachment process, but such proceedings are extremely rare and are usually undertaken only if a judge engages in blatantly illegal conduct, such as bribery. In the history of this nation, only thirteen federal judges have been impeached, seven of whom were removed from office. Normally, federal judges serve until they resign, retire, or die.

Although the Constitution sets no specific qualifications for those who serve on the Supreme Court, all who have done so share one characteristic: all have been attorneys. The backgrounds of the Supreme Court justices have been far from typical of the characteristics of the American public as a whole. Table 14–1 summarizes the backgrounds of all of the 108 Supreme Court justices to 2003.

TABLE 14-1

Background of Supreme Court Justices to 2003

	NUMBER OF JUSTICES (108 = Total)
Occupational Position before Appointment	
Private legal practice	25
State judgeship	21
Federal judgeship	28
U.S. attorney general	7
Deputy or assistant U.S. attorney general	2
U.S. solicitor general	2
U.S. senator	6
U.S. representative	2
State governor	3
Federal executive post	9
Other	3
Religious Background	
Protestant	83
Roman Catholic	11
Jewish	6
Unitarian	7
No religious affiliation	1
Age on Appointment	
Under 40	5
41–50	31
51–60	58
61–70	14
Political Party Affiliation	
Federalist (to 1835)	13
Jeffersonian Republican (to 1828)	7
Whig (to 1861)	1
Democrat	44
Republican	42
Independent	1
Educational Background	
College graduate	92
Not a college graduate	16
Gender	
Male	106
Female	2
Race	
Caucasian	106
African American	2

SOURCES: Congressional Quarterly, *Congressional Quarterly's Guide to the U.S. Supreme Court* (Washington, D.C.: Congressional Quarterly Press, 1997); and authors' update.

The Nomination Process

The president receives suggestions and recommendations as to potential nominees for Supreme Court positions from various sources, including the Justice Department, senators, other judges, the candidates themselves, state political leaders, bar associations, and other interest groups. After selecting a nominee, the president submits her or his name to the Senate for approval. The Senate Judiciary Committee then holds hearings and makes its recommendation to the Senate, where it takes a majority vote to confirm the nomination.

When appointing judges to the district courts (and, to a lesser extent, the courts of appeals), the usual practice is to let the senator or senators of the president's political party from the state in which there is a vacancy recommend nominees to the presidential administration.

It should come as no surprise that partisanship plays a significant role in the president's selection of nominees to the federal bench, particularly to the Supreme Court, the crown jewel of the federal judiciary. Traditionally, presidents have attempted to strengthen their legacies by appointing federal judges with similar political and philosophical views. (For a further discussion of judicial appointments and presidential legacies, see this chapter's *Perception versus Reality* feature.) In the history of the Supreme Court, fewer than 13 percent of the justices nominated by a president have been from an opposing political party.

Confirmation or Rejection by the Senate

The president's nominations are not always confirmed. In fact, almost 20 percent of presidential nominations for the Supreme Court have been either rejected or not acted on by the Senate. The process of nominating and confirming federal judges, especially Supreme Court justices, often involves political debate and controversy. Many bitter battles over Supreme Court appointments have ensued when the Senate and the president have disagreed on political issues.

From 1893 until 1968, the Senate rejected only three Court nominees. From 1968 through 1986, however, two presidential nominees to the highest court were rejected, and two more nominations, both by President Ronald Reagan, failed in 1987. First, the Senate rejected Robert Bork, who faced sometimes hostile questioning about his views of the Constitution during the confirmation hearings. Next, Reagan nominated Douglas Ginsburg, who

perception versus REALITY

Judicial Appointments and Presidential Legacies

It is not unusual for a U.S. president to want to create a legacy—a long-lasting imprint on American politics. In principle, a sitting president can make a mark on the future by appointing (always with the consent of the Senate) federal court judges who share the president's political philosophy. Every year, there are numerous vacancies within the federal judiciary, and occasionally a vacancy occurs on the Supreme Court.

THE PERCEPTION

It is commonly perceived that a president will naturally nominate federal judges who share the president's political and philosophical views. Certainly, this was a widely shared assumption when Bill Clinton became president in 1992. Prior to his election, Clinton campaigned in favor of what are generally considered liberal causes—abortion rights, gay rights, and more aggressive enforcement of environmental laws. He also promised to appoint more minorities and women to federal court benches. Consequently, the public's initial perception of Clinton was that he was going to appoint liberal-leaning individuals to the federal judiciary.

THE REALITY

In reality, presidential appointments do not always fulfill the expectations of the president's party. Certainly, this was true with respect to Clinton's appointments. To be sure, during his first years in office, Clinton appointed more women and minorities to the federal bench than his predecessors had. Nonetheless, Clinton spurned activists and ideologues in his court appointments, choosing instead cautious moderates, such

as respected state jurists and partners in large law firms. Prospective nominees were never asked their views on abortion, and even some pro-lifers were appointed. His Supreme Court nominees—Ruth Bader Ginsburg and Stephen Breyer—were clear moderates who were easily confirmed. Indeed, the moderation and compromise that marked the Clinton administration's judicial appointments caused some Democrats to view the Clinton years as a lost opportunity to pursue a liberal policy agenda.

Keep in mind that often an important consideration in nominating a particular judicial candidate to a federal court bench is whether the candidate will likely be confirmed by the Senate. This is especially true when the president's party is not in control of the Senate. After the 1994 elections, Clinton, faced a Republican-controlled Senate. Thus, if he had nominated judges with more liberal and activist views, they might not have been confirmed by the Senate. Similarly, when President George H. W. Bush appointed David Souter to the Supreme Court in 1990, the Democrats controlled Congress. One of the reasons that Bush selected Souter was his sparse track record as a jurist—there was little for the Senate to oppose during the confirmation process.

What's Your Opinion?

What are some of the pros and cons of the constitutional requirement that the Senate confirm presidential appointments to the federal judiciary? Would the nation be better off if the Constitution were amended to drop this requirement? Why or why not?

The Senate has the ultimate say over who becomes a justice of the United States Supreme Court. Here, Ruth Bader Ginsburg faces questioning by members of the Senate Judiciary Committee. On August 10, 1993, she became the 107th justice of the Supreme Court—and one of the only two women ever to be appointed to that tribunal. (Rob Crandall/Stock Boston)

ultimately withdrew his nomination when the press leaked information about his alleged use of marijuana during the 1970s. Finally, the Senate approved Reagan's third choice, Anthony Kennedy. Although both of President George H. W. Bush's nominees to the Supreme Court—David Souter and Clarence Thomas—were confirmed by the Senate, Thomas's nomination aroused considerable controversy. Thomas's confirmation hearings were extremely volatile and received widespread publicity on national television. The nation watched as Anita Hill, a former aide, leveled charges of sexual harassment at Thomas.

In 1993, President Bill Clinton had little trouble gaining approval for his nominee to fill the seat left vacant by Justice Byron White. Ruth Bader Ginsburg became the second female Supreme Court justice, the first being Sandra Day O'Connor, who was appointed by President Reagan in 1981. When Justice Harry Blackmun retired in 1994, Clinton nominated Stephen Breyer to fill Blackmun's seat. Breyer was confirmed without significant opposition.

Judicial Appointments and the Bush Administration

As discussed in the chapter-opening *America at Odds* feature, prior to the 2000 presidential elections there was much conjecture about how the elections might affect the federal judiciary. As we said previously, however, as of 2003 no Supreme Court justice has left the bench of the high court, nor has any announced an intention to do so. Thus, President George W. Bush has not had an opportunity to nominate a new Supreme Court justice.

There are numerous vacancies to be filled on the lower courts, however, including vacancies on the benches of the thirteen U.S. courts of appeals. Recall that these courts of appeals, or federal appellate courts, occupy the level just below the Supreme Court in the federal court system. Also recall that decisions rendered by these courts are final unless overturned by the Supreme Court. Given that the Supreme Court issues opinions in fewer than one hundred cases a year, the decisions of the federal appellate courts have a wide-reaching impact on American society. For example, a decision interpreting the federal Constitution by the U.S. Court of Appeals for the Ninth Circuit, if not overruled by the Supreme Court, establishes a precedent that will be followed in the states of Washington, Oregon, California, Arizona, Nevada, Idaho, Montana, Alaska, and Hawaii.

President Bush meets with Judge Charles Pickering, left. Pickering was one of thirty judicial nominees who failed to win Senate confirmation while the Democrats controlled that chamber during the 107th Congress. After Bush renominated Pickering to the U.S. Court of Appeals for the Fifth Circuit in January 2003, Senate Democrats vowed to block his confirmation. (AP Photo/Ron Edmonds)

In January 2003, when the Republicans took control of the Senate, 25 of the 179 seats on the U.S. courts of appeals were vacant. Republican appointees already held the majority in seven of the thirteen federal appellate courts, and they will probably become more dominant as vacancies are filled. Although the Democrats have been able to block the confirmation of some of Bush's nominees, few doubt that the impact of a Republican president and Senate, acting together, will result in an even more conservative federal judiciary.

The Courts as Policymakers

In a common law system, such as that of the United States, judges and justices play a major role in government. In part, this is because of the doctrine of *stare decisis,* which theoretically obligates judges to follow precedents. Additionally, unlike judges in some other countries, U.S. judges have the power to decide on the constitutionality of laws or actions undertaken by the other branches of government.

Clearly, the function of the courts is to interpret and apply the law, not to make law—that is the function of the legislative branch of government. Yet judges can and do "make law"; indeed, they cannot avoid making law in some cases because the law does not always provide clear answers to questions that come before the courts. Constitutional and statutory provisions and other legal rules tend to be expressed in general terms, and the courts must decide how those general provisions and rules apply to specific cases.

Consider the Americans with Disabilities Act of 1990. The act requires employers to reasonably accommodate the needs of employees with disabilities. But the act does not say exactly what employers must do to "reasonably accommodate" such persons. Thus, the courts must decide, on a case-by-case basis, what this phrase means. Additionally, in some cases there is no relevant law or precedent to follow. In recent years, for example, courts have been struggling with new kinds of legal issues stemming from new communications technology, including the Internet. Until legislative bodies establish laws governing these issues, it is up to the courts to fashion the law that will apply—and thus make policy.

The Impact of Court Decisions

As already mentioned, how the courts interpret particular laws can have a widespread impact on society. For example, in 1996, in *Hopwood v. State of Texas,*[10] the U.S. Court of Appeals for the Fifth Circuit held that an affirmative action program implemented by the University of Texas School of Law in Austin was unconstitutional. The program allowed admissions officials to take race and other factors into consideration when determining which students would be admitted. The court stated that the program violated the equal protection clause because it discriminated in favor of minority applicants. The court's decision in *Hopwood* set a precedent for all federal courts within the Fifth Circuit's jurisdiction (which covers Texas, Louisiana, and Mississippi). Thus, whenever similar affirmative action programs in those states are challenged, the federal courts hearing the cases must apply the law as interpreted by the Court of Appeals for the Fifth Circuit.

Decisions rendered by the United States Supreme Court, of course, have an even broader impact on American society, because all courts in the nation are obligated to follow precedents set by the high court. Thus, when the Supreme Court interprets laws, it establishes national policy. If the Court deems that a law passed by Congress or a state legislature violates the Constitution, for example, that law will be void and unenforceable in any court within the United States. The power of the courts to declare laws or actions of the other two branches unconstitutional is known as **judicial review,** a topic to which we now turn.

JUDICIAL REVIEW The power of the courts to decide on the constitutionality of legislative enactments and of actions taken by the executive branch.

The Power of Judicial Review

The Constitution does not actually mention judicial review. Rather, the Supreme Court claimed the power for itself in *Marbury v. Madison.*[11] In that case, which was decided by the

John Marshall (1755–1835) served as chief justice of the Supreme Court from 1801 to 1835. (Library of Congress)

Court in 1803, Chief Justice John Marshall held that a provision of a 1789 law affecting the Supreme Court's jurisdiction violated the Constitution and was thus void. Marshall declared, "It is emphatically the province and duty of the judicial department [the courts] to say what the law is. . . . If two laws conflict with each other, the courts must decide on the operation of each. . . . So if a law be in opposition to the constitution . . . the court must determine which of these conflicting rules governs the case. This is the very essence of judicial duty."

Although the Constitution did not explicitly provide for judicial review, most constitutional scholars believe that the framers intended that the federal courts should have this power. In *Federalist Paper* No. 78, Alexander Hamilton clearly espoused the doctrine of judicial review. Hamilton stressed the importance of the "complete independence" of federal judges and their special duty to "invalidate all acts contrary to the manifest tenor of the Constitution." Without judicial review by impartial courts, there would be nothing to ensure that the other branches of government stayed within constitutional limits when exercising their powers, and "all the reservations of particular rights or privileges would amount to nothing." Chief Justice Marshall shared Hamilton's views and adopted Hamilton's reasoning in *Marbury v. Madison.*

AMERICA at odds

Should the Federal Courts Second-Guess Congress?

Not surprisingly, the power of judicial review—the courts' most significant policymaking tool—has led to controversy. After all, this power, in effect, allows unelected federal judges to invalidate laws enacted by the elected members of Congress.

Some contend that our elected representatives in Congress, and not the federal courts, should have the final say on whether a particular law is consistent with the Constitution. A number of scholars and many other Americans believe that the framers never intended the judiciary to have extensive policymaking powers, including the power of judicial review. They point out that the Constitution does not specifically mention the power of judicial review. Rather, the Court claimed this power for itself in 1803, in its decision in *Marbury v. Madison,* as just discussed. They emphasize that some of the framers, including James Madison and Thomas Jefferson, felt that giving the judiciary too much power could be dangerous. Indeed, Madison, in his *Federalist* essays, argued that combining judicial power with executive and legislative authority was the "very definition of tyranny."

Others maintain that if the courts did not possess this power and if Congress alone had the power to decide whether a law was consistent with the Constitution, Americans would be at the mercy of congressional majorities. To be sure, Congress is the voice of the people—but not *all* of the people. If a congressional majority decides to pass a law infringing on the rights of the minority, what is to stop Congress from doing so? Without the courts and their power of judicial review, the "tyranny of the majority" feared by the nation's founders could result.

Judicial Activism versus Judicial Restraint

As already noted, making policy is not the primary function of the federal courts. Yet it is unavoidable that courts do, in fact, influence or even establish policy when they interpret and apply the law. Further, the power of judicial review gives the courts, and particularly the Supreme Court, an important policymaking tool. When the Supreme Court upholds or invalidates a state or federal statute, the consequences for the nation can be profound.

One issue that is often debated is how the federal courts should wield their policymaking power, particularly the power of judicial review. Often, this debate is couched in terms of judicial activism versus judicial restraint.

Activist versus Restraintist Justices

Although the terms *judicial activism* and *judicial restraint* lack any precise meaning, generally an activist judge or justice believes that the courts should actively use their powers to check the actions of the legislative and executive branches to ensure that they do not exceed their authority. A restraintist judge or justice, in contrast, generally assumes that the courts should defer to the decisions of the legislative and executive branches, because members of Congress and the president are elected by the people whereas federal court judges are not. In other words, the courts should not thwart the implementation of legislative acts unless they are clearly unconstitutional.

Chief Justice Earl Warren (1897–1974) presided over the U.S. Supreme Court from 1953 to 1969. The Warren Court played a significant role in furthering the civil rights of African Americans and other minorities. (Library of Congress)

Judicial Activism/Restraint and Political Ideology

One of the Supreme Court's most activist eras occurred during the period from 1953 to 1969 under the leadership of Chief Justice Earl Warren. The Warren Court propelled the civil rights movement forward by holding, among other things, that laws permitting racial segregation violated the equal protection clause (see Chapter 5).

Because of the activism of the Warren Court, the term *judicial activism* has often been linked with liberalism. Indeed, many liberals are in favor of an activist federal judiciary because they believe that the judiciary can "right" the "wrongs" that result from unfair laws or from "antiquated" legislation at the state and local levels. Neither judicial activism nor judicial restraint is necessarily linked to a particular political ideology, however. In fact, many observers now claim that the Supreme Court is actively pursuing a conservative agenda.

Ideology and the Courts

The policymaking role of the courts gives rise to an important question: To what extent do ideology and personal policy preferences affect judicial decision making? Numerous scholars have attempted to answer this question, especially with respect to Supreme Court justices.

Ideology and Supreme Court Decisions

In one study, judicial scholars Jeffrey Segal and Harold Spaeth concluded that "the Supreme Court decides disputes in light of the facts of the case vis-à-vis the ideological attitudes and values of the justices. Simply put, Rehnquist votes the way he does because he is extremely conservative."[12] The authors maintain that the Supreme Court justices base their decisions on policy preferences simply because they are free to do so—they are not accountable to the electorate because they are not elected to their positions. The desire to attain higher office is also not a factor in the Court's decision making because the justices are at the apex of the judicial career ladder.

Few doubt that ideology affects judicial decision making, although, of course, other factors play a role as well. Different courts (such as a trial court and an appellate court) can look at the same case and draw different conclusions as to what law is applicable and how it should be applied. Certainly, there are numerous examples of how ideology affects Supreme Court decisions. As new justices replace old ones and new ideological alignments are formed, the Court's decisions are affected. Yet many scholars argue that there is no real evidence indicating that personal preferences influence Supreme Court decisions to an *unacceptable* extent.

Keep in mind that judicial decision making, particularly at the Supreme Court level, can be very complex. When deciding cases, the Supreme Court often must consider any number of sources, including constitutions, statutes, and administrative agency regulations—as well as cases interpreting relevant portions of those sources. At times, the Court also takes public opinion into account when deciding an issue—although whether the Court should give significant weight to public opinion is subject to controversy.

AMERICA at odds

Should the Supreme Court Look to Public Opinion?

Daryl Renard Atkins was sentenced to death after he was convicted of carjacking and killing an airman in Virginia to get money for beer. One test showed that Atkins had an IQ of 59. In 2002, the U.S. Supreme Court held that executing a mentally retarded person would violate the Eighth Amendment, which prohibits "cruel and unusual punishment." (AP Photo/Daily Press, Joe Fudge)

If the public holds strong views on an issue and the Supreme Court renders a decision that is contrary to those views, the decision may be difficult to enforce. After all, the Court has no enforcement powers but must rely on government officials to enforce its rulings. But should the Court ever reach out to public opinion for guidance when making decisions? The Court's decision in *Atkins v. Virginia*,[13] a case decided in 2002, launched a controversy over just this issue.

In the *Atkins* case, the Supreme Court held that executing a convicted murderer who was mentally retarded would violate the Eighth Amendment's prohibition against "cruel and unusual punishment." In reaching its decision, the Court noted that over the past thirteen years, eighteen of the thirty-eight states that allow capital punishment have decided to exempt mentally retarded persons from execution. Also, public opinion polls show that most Americans feel that the execution of mentally retarded persons is cruel and wrong, a sentiment expressed by large numbers of psychiatric professionals and religious groups as well. In sum, concluded the Court, "it is fair to say that a national consensus has developed" against such executions.

Some critics complained that the decision was based less on legal precedent than on trends as evidenced by state actions, professional and religious groups, public opinion polls, and even foreign countries. Two justices dissented from the Court's majority opinion, contending that the majority were swayed by personal preferences: "Seldom has an opinion of this Court rested so obviously upon nothing but the personal views of the members." Others, however, believed that the Court was right to consider public opinion because the meaning of the Eighth Amendment can only be drawn from evolving standards of decency. After all, at one time it was not considered cruel or unusual punishment to lock someone in the stocks on the public square or to execute rapists.

The Ideological Complexion of the Rehnquist Court

In contrast to the liberal Supreme Court under Earl Warren (1953–1969) and to a lesser extent under Warren Burger (1969–1986), today's Court is generally conservative. Three of the justices (William Rehnquist, Antonin Scalia, and Clarence Thomas) are notably rightist in their views. Four of the justices (John Paul Stevens, David Souter, Ruth Bader Ginsburg, and Stephen Breyer) hold liberal-to-moderate views. Sandra Day O'Connor and Anthony Kennedy tend to hold the middle ground, and when the Court is sharply divided on an issue, theirs are often the swing votes. The ideological alignments vary, however, depending on the nature of the case before the Court.

The Court began its rightward shift after President Ronald Reagan (1981–1989) appointed conservative William Rehnquist as chief justice in 1986, and the Court moved further to the right as other conservative appointments to the bench were made by Reagan and George H. W. Bush (1989–1993).

As mentioned in the chapter-opening *America at Odds* feature, however, it would be a mistake to look at the judicial philosophy of today's Supreme Court solely in terms of the political ideologies of liberalism and conservatism. In fact, some Supreme Court scholars have suggested that the justices' judicial philosophies with respect to how the law should be interpreted and their perception of the Supreme Court's role in the federal judiciary are more important in understanding why they decide as they do.

Strict versus Broad Construction

Legal scholars have often used the terms *strict* and *broad* construction to describe how judges and justices interpret the law. Generally, strict constructionists look to the letter of the law as written when trying to decipher its meaning, whereas broad constructionists look more to the purpose and context of the law. Strict constructionists believe that the letter of the law should guide the courts' decisions. Broad constructionists believe that the law is an evolving set of standards and is not fixed in concrete. The Constitution, for example, is a "living Constitution," not a dead document. Generally, broad constructionists are more willing to "read between the lines" of a law to serve what they perceive to be the law's intent and purpose.

The Rehnquist Court. In the top row, from left to right, are Ruth Bader Ginsburg, David Souter, Clarence Thomas, and Stephen Breyer. In the bottom row, from left to right, are Antonin Scalia, John Paul Stevens, Chief Justice William Rehnquist, Sandra Day O'Connor, and Anthony Kennedy. (Getty News Images)

Strict construction of the law is often linked with conservative views, and broad construction with liberal views. The conservative justices on today's Supreme Court are often labeled strict constructionists. Justice Antonin Scalia, one of the Court's most conservative justices, gives some insights into a strict constructionist's approach to the law in his book, *A Matter of Interpretation*.[14] According to Scalia, constitutional principles are fixed, not evolving: "The Constitution that I interpret and apply is not living, but dead." He further states, "Our first responsibility is not to make sense of the law—our first responsibility is to follow the text of the law."

The Role of the Supreme Court

How justices view the role of the Supreme Court in the federal judiciary also affects their decision making. Two of the Court's justices—Antonin Scalia and Stephen Breyer—have made public their different visions of the Court's role. For Justice Scalia, a conservative voice on the Court, the Court should establish clear rules for the lower courts to follow when they apply the law. For Justice Breyer, who holds moderate-to-liberal views, the Court's role should be to establish flexible standards for the lower courts to apply on a case-by-case basis. This rules-versus-standards debate is reflected in the justices' opinions.

In one case, for example, Breyer, who wrote the majority opinion, concluded that a seniority system in the workplace should "ordinarily" take priority over a disabled worker's right to "reasonable accommodation" under the Americans with Disabilities Act of 1990 (ADA)—see Chapter 5. Yet, stated Breyer, there might be special circumstances that would make a disabled worker's reassignment to another position "reasonable" even though an employee with more seniority also had a right to the position. In other words, Breyer left the door open for the lower courts to deal with the question on a case-by-case basis, in light of the surrounding circumstances. Justice Scalia, in his dissent, concluded that a seniority system should always prevail. Saying that it should "ordinarily" prevail did not give any clear guidance to the lower courts and turned the "reasonable accommodation" provision in the ADA into a "standardless grab bag."[15]

These two positions reflect totally different concepts of the Court's role. For Scalia, it would be irresponsible to leave the law in such an indeterminate state. Therefore, the justices must provide strong guidance for the lower courts. For Breyer, an absolutist approach is unworkable. In a "participatory democracy," claims Breyer, the Court should not stand in the way of a new understanding of the law that "bubbles up from below."[16]

The Supreme Court and States' Rights

Liberals have long worried that the Rehnquist Court's conservative reading of the Constitution is eroding too many rights. Today, however, another worry has surfaced: Is the Supreme Court going too far in the direction of states' rights?

The Court's "States' Rights Agenda"

Clearly, the Rehnquist Court is noticeably at odds with the Supreme Courts of yesteryear on the issue of states' rights. In a landmark case decided in 1995, *United States v. Lopez*,[17] the Court held that Congress had exceeded its constitutional authority under the commerce clause when it passed the Gun-Free School Zones Act in 1990. This was the first time in sixty years that the Supreme Court had limited the national government's regulatory authority under the commerce clause.

In several subsequent cases, the Court similarly placed limits on Congress's powers and upheld states' rights. As discussed in Chapter 3, the Court has held that state employees cannot sue

State and local governments may pass laws requiring gun-free zones around school districts. When the federal government passed such a law, however, the U.S. Supreme Court held that Congress had exceeded its constitutional authority under the commerce clause. This Supreme Court decision, rendered in 1995, marked the first time in sixty years that the Court had limited the federal government's regulatory authority under the commerce clause. (Copyright © Rudi Von Briel/Photo Edit)

their state employers, in either state or federal courts, for violations of federal laws prohibiting age-based and disability-based discrimination. The Court's reasoning is that the Eleventh Amendment to the Constitution renders states, as sovereign entities, immune from such suits. In effect, this means that federal laws establishing and protecting civil rights are not being applied to a wide group of citizens—state employees.

Many have criticized this "states' rights agenda" of the Supreme Court as being inconsistent with the federal structure of the nation as designed by the founders. According to some scholars, these decisions are also at odds with the Constitution.

Beyond Strict Construction? As already noted, many of the justices on today's Court are considered to be strict constructionists. Yet some scholars believe that the Court has gone beyond strict constructionism in its reading of the Constitution. Consider, for example, the cases just mentioned relating to state sovereign immunity from lawsuits based on federal claims. The decisions in these cases rest on the Court's interpretation of the Eleventh Amendment.

Now consider the complete text of that amendment:

> The Judicial power of the United States shall not be construed to extend to any suit in law or equity, commenced or prosecuted against one of the United States by Citizens of another State, or by Citizens or Subjects of any Foreign State.

Clearly, a literal reading of this amendment could not possibly have served as a basis for the Court's decisions in these cases. The cases do not involve citizens suing the government of *another* state; nor do they involve suits brought by foreigners against a state government. Rather, they involve citizens suing their own state government. Nonetheless, through the Court's interpretation of the amendment over the years, the end result is that citizens of a state cannot sue their state government in a federal court *or* a state court for claims based on federal law. The Court has even held that states are immune from proceedings brought before federal administrative agencies,[18] which, as part of the executive branch, do not involve the "Judicial power" addressed in the Eleventh Amendment.

Is the Supreme Court Redesigning the Federal Structure? According to John T. Noonan, Jr., a federal appellate court judge, the connection between state sovereignty and the Eleventh Amendment "is imaginary." At one time, he states, the same justices making these states' rights decisions believed that the Court's decisions in constitutional matters had to be faithful to the text of the Constitution. Now, however, the Court has turned away from strict constructionism and toward what he calls "a more adventurous reading of the Constitution."[19]

Noonan's views are not those of a flaming liberal criticizing the conservative direction of today's high court. In fact, Noonan was appointed to his post by a conservative president—Ronald Reagan. Nor is Noonan alone in his concern over the Court's position on states' rights. Other scholars have also criticized the Court for attempting to redesign the federal structure of the nation. Although Alexander Hamilton regarded the judiciary (the Supreme Court) as the "least dangerous" branch of government, some of today's critics have begun to regard it as the "most dangerous" branch. As one observer commented, "For several years now judicial conservatives have been marching to a new and very different drummer, but to date only a tiny, mostly academic cadre of astute Court watchers has grasped the content and the implications of the Supreme Court majority's agenda."[20]

The Case for the Courts

The federal courts have often come under attack, particularly in the last decade or so, for many reasons. This should come as no surprise in view of the policymaking power of the courts. Because of our common law tradition, the federal judiciary in the United States has always played a far more significant role in politics and government than do the judiciaries in countries that do not have a common law system. After all, just one Supreme Court decision can establish what national policy will be on such issues as abortion, racial segregation, or online pornography.

Certainly, policymaking by unelected judges and justices on the federal courts has serious implications in a democracy. Some contend that making policy from the bench has upset the balance of powers envisioned by the framers of the Constitution. They cite Thomas Jefferson, who once said, "It is a very dangerous doctrine to consider the judges as the ultimate arbiters of all constitutional questions." This group believes that we should rein in the power of the federal courts, and particularly judicial activism. Indeed, in the mid-1990s, when the Republicans took control of Congress, a number of bills proposing strategies to restrain the power of the federal judiciary were introduced in Congress. Among other things, it was proposed that Congress, not the Supreme Court, have the ultimate say in determining the meaning of the Constitution.

Others argue that a strong case can be made for leaving the courts alone. For one thing, there are already sufficient checks on the courts, some of which we look at next. For another, Americans traditionally have held the federal courts, and particularly the Supreme Court, in high regard.

Judicial Traditions and Doctrines

One check on the courts is judicial restraint. Supreme Court justices traditionally have exercised a great deal of self-restraint. Justices sometimes admit to making decisions that fly in the face of their personal values and policy preferences, simply because they feel obligated to do so in view of existing law. Self-restraint is also mandated by various judicially established traditions and doctrines, including the doctrine of *stare decisis*, which theoretically obligates the Supreme Court to follow its own precedents. Furthermore, the Supreme Court will not hear a meritless appeal just so it can rule on the issue. Finally, more often than not, the justices narrow their rulings to focus on just one aspect of an issue, even though there may be nothing to stop them from broadening their focus and thus widening the impact of their decisions.

Other Checks

The judiciary is subject to other checks as well. Courts may make rulings, but they cannot force federal and state legislatures to appropriate the funds necessary to carry out those rulings. For example, if the Supreme Court decides that prison conditions must be improved, a legislature has to find the funds to carry out the ruling. Additionally, legislatures can rewrite (amend) old laws or pass new ones to negate courts' rulings. This may happen when a court interprets a statute in a way that Congress had not intended. Congress may also propose amendments to the Constitution to reverse Supreme Court rulings, and Congress has the authority to limit or otherwise alter the jurisdiction of the lower federal courts. Finally, although it is most unlikely, Congress could even change the number of justices on the Supreme Court, in an attempt to change the ideological balance on the Court.

The Public's Regard for the Supreme Court

As mentioned, some have proposed that Congress, not the Supreme Court, be the final arbiter of the Constitution. In debates on this topic, one factor is often overlooked: the American public's high regard for the Supreme Court and the federal courts generally. The Court continues to be respected as a fair arbiter of conflicting interests and the protector of constitutional rights and liberties. Even when the Court issued its decision to halt the manual recount of votes in Florida following the 2000 elections, Americans respected the Court's decision-making authority—even though many disagreed with the Court's decision. Polls continue to show that Americans place more trust and confidence in the Supreme Court than they do in Congress. In the eyes of many Americans, the Supreme Court stands in sharp contrast to a Congress that seems incapable of rising above the partisan bickering of Washington politics.

why does it MATTER?

The Judiciary and Your Everyday Life

"The Judicial Department comes home in its effects to every man's fireside: it passes on his property, his reputation, his life, his all." So stated John Marshall, chief justice of the United States Supreme Court from 1801 to 1835. If you reflect a moment on these words, you will realize their truth. A single Supreme Court decision can affect the lives of millions of Americans. Consider just a few examples:

- In 1942, the Supreme Court held that wheat produced by an individual farmer for consumption on his own farm was subject to federal regulation, even though the commerce clause of the Constitution states that the national government can regulate only *interstate* commerce. The Court's reasoning was ingenious: when farmers consume their own wheat, less wheat is put into the interstate marketplace; therefore, the farmer's home consumption affects the overall price of wheat in the nation. This decision was one of a number of decisions that upheld Congress's authority to regulate commercial activities—even activities occurring solely within state borders. As a result, today the federal government regulates virtually every aspect of business life in this country. Thus, we now have minimum-wage laws, uniform workplace standards, and literally thousands of other federal regulations.
- In 1954, the Supreme Court held that state laws upholding racial segregation in public schools violated the Fourteenth Amendment to the Constitution and were thus invalid. This decision has affected the lives of millions of Americans.
- Beginning in 1978, the Supreme Court has also upheld the constitutionality of many affirmative action programs designed to "level the playing field" for African Americans, other minorities, and women—groups that had become disadvantaged due to past discriminatory treatment. Although affirmative action has come under attack in the last decade, these programs continue to exist and affect how businesses hire and fire employees, how universities make admissions decisions, and how government agencies decide who should benefit from government contracts.
- In 1973, the Supreme Court held that the constitutional right to privacy included the right to have an abortion. This controversial decision has also affected the lives of millions of Americans.
- Over time, the Supreme Court has issued many decisions concerning the rights of accused persons. If you are ever stopped by a police officer, you will be entitled to exercise these rights. You do not have to worry about being thrown into jail arbitrarily or about not being able to have legal assistance when you need it.

Taking Action

In this chapter, you have learned about the role played by the judiciary in our system of government. If you feel strongly about a particular judicial nominee, contact the U.S. senators from your state and voice your opinion. To get a better understanding of court procedures, consider visiting your local county court when a trial is in session (check with the clerk of the court before entering the trial room, though). If you have an opportunity to participate in a mock trial at your school, consider doing so. In the photo above, a College of William and Mary law student stands at podium, left, and makes opening remarks to a jury during a mock trial of a terrorist. The mock trial relied heavily on computer technology and the Internet to bring together the witnesses, lawyers, judge, and jury. (AP Photo/Gary C. Knapp)

Key Terms

administrative law 326	constitutional law 326	jurisdiction 328	*stare decisis* 325
appellate court 330	criminal law 327	justiciable controversy 329	statutory law 326
case law 326	dissenting opinion 334	opinion 333	trial court 328
civil law 327	diversity of citizenship 328	oral argument 333	writ of *certiorari* 332
common law 325	federal question 328	precedent 325	
concurring opinion 333	judicial review 337	primary source of law 326	
conference 333	judiciary 325	standing to sue 328	

Chapter Summary

1 The American legal system is an offshoot of the common law tradition that developed in England over hundreds of years. The cornerstone of the English and American legal systems is the doctrine of *stare decisis,* which theoretically obligates judges to follow precedents (previous court decisions in their jurisdiction) when interpreting the law.

2 Primary sources of American law include constitutional law, statutory law, administrative law, and case law. Law can also be classified in other ways. An important classification divides all law into civil law or criminal law.

3 Certain judicial requirements limit the types of cases courts can hear and decide. Before a court can hear a case, it must have jurisdiction over the person against whom the case is brought, the property involved, and the subject matter. The party bringing the case must also have standing to sue—that is, the party must have a definable stake in the controversy at hand and the issue must be real and definite, not hypothetical or abstract. Additionally, both the federal and state courts have established procedural rules that apply in judicial proceedings.

4 The federal court system is a three-tiered model consisting of U.S. district (trial) courts, U.S. courts of appeals, and the United States Supreme Court. There is no absolute right of appeal to the Supreme Court.

5 All federal judges are appointed by the president and confirmed by the Senate. Presidents have attempted to strengthen their legacies by appointing federal judges with similar political, ideological, and philosophical views.

6 Judges play an important policymaking role in the United States because of our common law system, the doctrine of *stare decisis,* and the power of judicial review. Judges can decide on the constitutionality of laws or actions undertaken by the other branches of government. The extent to which ideology affects judicial decision making in the federal courts has led to substantial controversy because federal judges are appointed and are not accountable to the electorate.

7 Judicial activism has also led to controversy. Activist judges believe that the courts should actively check the actions of the other two branches of government to ensure that they do not exceed their authority. Restraintist judges tend to show more deference to the decisions of the other branches because they are elected by the people whereas federal judges are not. Although activism is often associated with the liberalism of the Warren Court, today judicial activism is increasingly associated with conservative judges.

8 The extent to which ideology affects the Supreme Court's decision making has often been explored, with differing conclusions. Some scholars have recently suggested that other factors—such as how the justices interpret the law or their perception of the role of the Supreme Court in the federal judiciary—may be more important than conservative or liberal political ideology in understanding why the justices decide as they do.

9 One of the issues that concerns Americans today is the rightward direction of the Supreme Court with respect to states' rights. Some observers contend that the Court's "states' rights agenda" is inconsistent with the federal structure as established by the Constitution.

10 Although the courts are often criticized for allowing personal preferences and philosophies to influence their decision making, in fact there are many checks on the courts. The courts are restrained by judicial traditions and doctrines, their lack of enforcement powers, and potential congressional actions in response to court decisions.

RESOURCES FOR FURTHER STUDY

Selected Readings

Bugliosi, Vincent. *The Betrayal of America: How the Supreme Court Undermined the Constitution and Chose Our President.* New York: Thunder's Mouth Press, 2001. The author offers a critical appraisal of the role of the Supreme Court in deciding the outcome of the 2000 elections in the *Bush v. Gore* decision.

Finkelman, Paul, and Melvin I. Urofsky. *Landmark Decisions of the United States Supreme Court.* Washington, D.C.: CQ Press, 2002. The authors look at more than a thousand landmark Supreme Court cases and their impact on American democracy and society.

Noonan, John T., Jr. *Narrowing the Nation's Power: The Supreme Court Sides with the States.* Berkeley: University of California Press, 2002. The author, a federal appellate court judge, offers a critical look at the Supreme Court's position on states' rights, which he feels is threatening our democracy.

Raskin, Jamin B. *We the Students: Supreme Court Cases for and about Students,* 2d ed. Washington, D.C.: CQ Press, 2003. The author, using an interactive approach, focuses on a number of Supreme Court cases dealing with issues of high interest to students.

InfoTrac Citations

Using your InfoTrac password, access the InfoTrac database at http://infotrac.thomsonlearning.com. Once at the site, you can do "key word" searches to locate the following articles, each of which deals with a topic covered in this chapter. The key words to use in your search are indicated in parentheses.

- "Common Law Torts: The Latest in Employment Lawsuits" (Common Law)

- "Pledging a Fight: Court Ruling on Pledge Incites Debate" (9th Circuit Pledge)

- "Circuit Breaker: If You're Worried about Conservative Control of the Federal Judiciary, Watch the District of Columbia" (Appellate Courts)

- "Houston Attorney Thought to Be High on List of Possible Supreme Court Nominees" (Supreme Court Nominees)

Politics on the Web

An excellent Web site for information on the justices of the United States Supreme Court is http://oyez.nwu.edu

This site offers biographies of the justices, links to opinions they have written, and, for justices who have served after 1920, video and audio materials. Oral arguments before the Supreme Court are also posted on this site.

- Another helpful Web site is http://supct.law.cornell.edu/supct

This is the index of the United States Supreme Court. It has recent Court decisions by year and name of party, and it also has selected historic decisions rendered by the Court.

- The Supreme Court makes its opinions available online at its official Web site. Go to http://supremecourtus.gov

- FindLaw offers a free searchable database of Supreme Court decisions since 1907 at http://www.findlaw.com

- Increasingly, decisions of the state courts are also becoming available online. You can search through the texts of state cases that are on the Internet, as well as federal cases and state and federal laws, by accessing WashLaw at http://www.washlaw.edu

- To learn more about the federal court system, go to http://www.uscourts.gov

This is the home page for the federal courts. Among other things, you can follow the "path" a case takes as it moves through the federal court system.

Web Resources on Your CD-ROM

On your CD-ROM, you will find Web resources, news articles, Internet activities, and video clips related to the topics in this chapter. Resources related to this chapter include the following:

- **Values Inventory**—Political Ideology: Supreme Court Nominees—Does Partisanship Matter?
- **Why Does It Matter?**—Sit in on a Jury Trial.
- **Updates**—Keep up with the issues in this chapter!
- **Web Resources**—Internet Activities: Frequently Asked Questions about Supreme Court Nominees/Appointments; Justice Antonin Scalia.
- **Where Do You Stand?**—Dialogue: Does Ideology Matter in the Appointment of Supreme Court Justices?
- **Comparative Politics**—Islamic Law.
- **Video**—Judicial Selection; Bork; Legislative Checks on Judiciary.
- **NewsEdge**—Visit this global resource for current events related to this chapter.

chapter 15

domestic policy

CHAPTER OBJECTIVES

After reading this chapter, you should be able to . . .

Explain what domestic policy is and what policy areas fall in this category.

Summarize the steps in the policymaking process.

Discuss this nation's social-welfare policy and the programs it includes.

Evaluate the nation's policies on crime and drugs.

Describe the two major areas of economic policymaking.

349

Is Capital Punishment Cruel and Unusual?

In 2000, Governor George Ryan of Illinois became the darling of the anti–death penalty movement. Horrified that thirteen people on the state's death row had been proved innocent, Ryan placed a moratorium on executions in Illinois until the system could be "fixed." Then, in 2003, hours before his term of office ended, Ryan commuted the death sentences of all 167 inmates on the state's death row to life in prison without parole. Death penalty opponents hailed the actions as the first steps toward reforming or even repealing a process that they believe is seriously flawed. Supporters of capital punishment criticized Ryan for arbitrarily discontinuing a practice favored by a majority of citizens in Illinois. Indeed, about 64 percent of U.S. residents support the death penalty.

As you read in Chapter 4, the Constitution prohibits cruel and unusual punishments. The United States Supreme Court has held that the question of whether an execution is "cruel and unusual" is determined by the "changing norms and standards of society."[1] Thus, almost by definition, the Court is bound to current social norms when deciding death penalty cases. Should the fact that most Americans support capital punishment be the deciding factor in determining whether it violates the Constitution?

The Death Penalty Maintains Order and Fairness

Former assistant U.S. attorney and novelist Scott Turow believes that the real reason most Americans support the death penalty is that it seems to restore "moral order." That is, some crimes are so horrible that executing the person responsible seems to be the only fitting response. The criminal justice system would not be "just" if it treated murder like any other crime. In some states, for instance, a third offense can land a convict in prison for twenty-five or fifty years. The Supreme Court ruled in 2003 that sentencing a defendant to prison for fifty years for the theft of nine videotapes—because it was the defendant's third offense—did not constitute cruel and unusual punishment.[2] Why, then, should someone who commits murder be given the same or even a less severe punishment than someone who steals a few videotapes or a car stereo?

Capital punishment is also central to the victim's rights movement. The strongest condemnation of Governor Ryan's decision to commute all death sentences came from the victims' loved ones. The victim's rights movement is premised on the idea that society owes more than just a seat at a trial to those who have experienced the trauma of a murdered family member or friend. Victims' families often speak of the sense of "closure" that a murderer's execution brings.

The Death Penalty Is Administered Arbitrarily and Unfairly

A driving force behind Governor Ryan's decision to suspend executions was the evidence of false confessions, purported police torture, refusal to test DNA evidence, and other misconduct committed in the pursuit of convictions. The increased participation of victims' families and friends in the prosecutorial process has only increased the public pressure on police officers, prosecutors, and judges to solve violent crimes.

Furthermore, many capital defendants are provided with inexperienced or seemingly incompetent counsel by the state, which greatly increases the chances that they will be found guilty. The location of the trial also affects the chances that a defendant will receive a death sentence. While Texas executed thirty-three convicts in 2002, twelve states do not apply the death penalty under any circumstances.

Finally, race appears to play a role in the likelihood that the death penalty will be imposed. One recent study found that the presence of five or more white men on the jury greatly increased the possibility of a death sentence. Evidence also shows that the death penalty is significantly more likely to be imposed in cases involving black defendants and white victims than in cases involving white defendants and black victims or defendants and victims of the same race. Clearly, argue death penalty opponents, the system of capital punishment is cruel and unusual when it depends so heavily on such random characteristics as the skill of the lawyer, the place of the crime, the race of the jury, or the race of the victim.

Where Do You Stand?

1. Do you think that the death penalty deters people from committing violent crimes?

2. Do you think that the wishes of the victim's family and friends should carry any weight in determining how a convict is punished?

Interacting with Your CD-ROM Resources

Use your CD-ROM to access resources on the Web, simulations, participation exercises, and video clips. Important resources related to this feature include:

- **Values Inventory**—Political Ideology: Is Capital Punishment Cruel and Unusual?
- **Where Do You Stand?**—Dialogue: Is Capital Punishment Cruel and Unusual?
- **Web Resources**—Internet Activities: The Case against the Death Penalty; Support for the Death Penalty.

INTRODUCTION

Developing policies to fight crime and to sentence the perpetrators is one of the most difficult tasks that lawmakers face. Policymakers need to determine what types of punishment will deter future crimes, and to what extent criminals can be rehabilitated and released from prison. They must also decide how much to spend on efforts to fight crime. How are these decisions made? Who are the major participants in the decision-making process?

To learn the answers to these and similar questions, you need to delve into the politics of policymaking. As stated in Chapter 1, policy, or public policy, can be defined as a government plan or course of action taken in response to a political issue or to enhance the social or political well-being of society. Public policy is the end result of the policymaking process, which will be described shortly. **Domestic policy**, in contrast to foreign policy, consists of public policy concerning issues *within* a national unit.

In this chapter, after discussing how policy is made through the policymaking process, we look at several aspects of domestic policy, including social-welfare policy, crime policy, and economic policy. Bear in mind that although the focus here is on policy and policymaking at the national level, state and local governments also engage in policymaking and establish policies to achieve goals relating to activities within their boundaries.

DOMESTIC POLICY Public policy concerning issues within a national unit, such as national policy concerning welfare or crime.

The Policymaking Process

The Welfare Reform Act (the popular name for the 1996 Personal Responsibility and Work Opportunity Reconciliation Act) marked a major change in this nation's welfare policy. This law did not appear out of nowhere. First, the problem addressed by the new law had to become part of the political agenda—that is, be defined as a political issue to be resolved by government action. Furthermore, once the issue got on the political agenda, proposed solutions to the problem had to be formulated and then adopted. Agenda setting, policy formulation, and policy adoption are all parts of the **policymaking process.** The process does not end there, however. Once the law is passed, it has to be implemented and then evaluated.

Each phase of the policymaking process involves interactions among various individuals and groups. The president and members of Congress are obviously important participants in the process. Remember from Chapter 6 that interest groups play a key role in politics. Groups

POLICYMAKING PROCESS The procedures involved in getting an issue on the political agenda; formulating, adopting, and implementing a policy with regard to the issue; and then evaluating the results of the policy.

In August 1996, President Clinton signed the Welfare Reform Act into law. In so doing, he fulfilled a promise that he made during his 1992 campaign to "change welfare as we know it." (Stephen Jaffee/Reuters)

that may be affected adversely by a new policy will try to convince Congress not to adopt the policy. Groups that will benefit by a new policy will exert whatever influence they can on Congress to do the opposite. Congressional committees and subcommittees may investigate the problem to be addressed by the policy and, in so doing, solicit input from members of a certain group or industry.

Generally, the participants in policymaking and the nature of the debates involved depend on the particular policy being proposed, formed, or implemented. Whatever the policy, however, debate over its pros and cons usually occurs during each stage of the policymaking process.

Agenda Setting

AGENDA SETTING The first stage of the policymaking process, which consists of getting an issue on the political agenda to be addressed by Congress.

The first stage of the policymaking process, often called **agenda setting** or *agenda building*, consists of getting an issue on the political agenda. A problem in society can become a political issue to be addressed by the government in a number of different ways. An event or series of events, such as an unusual number of airplane crashes, may lead to the perception that airline travel is unsafe and that the government should take action to rectify the problem. Dramatic increases in crime rates may make crime reduction a priority on the national political agenda. Sometimes, the social or economic effects of a national calamity, such as the Great Depression of the 1930s or the terrorist attacks of September 2001, create a need for government action. (For a discussion of policymaking during a time of crisis, see this chapter's *The Politics of Homeland Security* feature.)

The ideology of the dominant party in government may also have an influence on agenda setting. Republicans tend to favor turning more responsibilities over to state and local governments. Therefore, a Republican-controlled government is more likely to pursue legislation, such as the welfare reform legislation passed in 1996, that gives state and local governments more responsibilities over an area formerly controlled by the national government.

Policy Formulation and Adoption

The second stage in the policymaking process involves the formulation and adoption of specific plans for achieving a particular goal, such as welfare reform. The president, members of Congress, administrative agencies, and interest group leaders typically are the key participants in developing proposed legislation. Remember from Chapter 13 that iron triangles—alliances consisting of congressional committee members, interest group leaders, and bureaucrats in administrative agencies—work together in forming mutually beneficial policies. To a certain extent, the courts also establish policies when they interpret statutes passed by legislative bodies or make decisions concerning disputes not yet addressed by any law, such as disputes involving new technology (see Chapter 14).

Note that some issues may get on the political agenda but never proceed beyond that stage of the policymaking process. Usually, this happens when it is impossible to achieve a consensus over what policy should be adopted. Welfare reform had been on the political agenda for years, for example, but a new welfare policy was not developed and formally proposed until the Republican sweep of Congress in 1994. Even then, the president and Congress were unable to reach a consensus on the bill's specific provisions until 1996.

Policy Implementation

Because of our federal system, the implementation of national policies necessarily requires the cooperation of the federal government and the various state and local governments. For example, the 1996 Welfare Reform Act required the states to develop plans for implementing the new welfare policy within their borders. The federal government, though, retained some authority over the welfare system by providing that state welfare plans had to be certified, or approved, by the federal government. Successful implementation also usually requires the support of groups outside the government. For example, the work requirements of the new welfare policy meant that the business sector would also play a key role in the policy's implementation.

The POLITICS of HOMELAND SECURITY

Policymaking in a Time of Crisis

Following the terrorist attacks of September 11, 2001, policymakers in Washington, D.C., took immediate action to address the crisis. President George W. Bush took a number of steps to reduce the threat of terrorism. Among other things, he declared a war on terrorism that strongly altered both domestic policy and foreign policy in the following months and years. The president also worked closely with Congress to address specific needs of the nation.

POST-9/11 POLICYMAKING

Within a matter of weeks, Congress passed, and the president signed, new legislation addressing specific needs of the nation. Among other things, Congress passed an aviation security bill that made airport security a federal responsibility. One of the most controversial bills passed during this time was the USA Patriot Act, which, as you have read elsewhere in this text, gave sweeping new surveillance powers to the federal government.

As noted elsewhere in this chapter, policy formulation and adoption involves not only the executive branch and Congress, but also interest groups having a stake in the outcome of the process. Even in the shadow of the 9/11 tragedy, lobbyists were hard at work protecting their interests in the halls of Congress. Consider the effect of lobbying by the airline industry.

The airline industry was, of course, particularly hard hit by the terrorist attacks. Steep losses were incurred due to airport shutdowns immediately following the 9/11 attacks and a significant decline in travel generally. Congress acted quickly to bail the airlines out of their financial crisis. Within two weeks after 9/11, Congress passed the Air Transportation Safety and System Stabilization Act. The act provided for payments of up to $5 billion to compensate the airlines for their losses, as well as federal loans of up to $10 billion to help them weather the crisis. The new law also provided protection to the airlines against liability for losses due to acts of terrorism by expanding federally guaranteed aviation insurance.

President Bush signed the USA Patriot Act on October 26, 2001. The law gave law enforcement personnel unprecedented authority to search homes and business records secretly and to eavesdrop on telephone and computer conversations. (AP Photo/Doug Mills)

A QUESTION OF TIMING

Some contend that Congress acted too hastily in addressing various needs stemming from the national crisis. Consider the airline bailout bill. Some critics claimed that the airlines themselves were responsible for the crisis, at least in part. After all, to save on costs, the airlines had cut back on several expenses prior to 9/11, include those relating to passenger screening and airport security generally. Why did Congress conclude that the nation's taxpayers should have to foot the bill to keep those airlines in business? Even if some of the airlines had to declare bankruptcy, the end result would likely have been that the airlines would be sold to other, stronger companies that could make ends meet without federal assistance.

Consider another example—the USA Patriot Act. This statute, which is 342 pages long, made changes to over fifteen different federal laws. While some of the act's provisions, such as providing relief for victims of 9/11, seemed appropriate,

other provisions have generated considerable controversy. Civil rights proponents have pointed out that the government already had most of the tools it needs to investigate and detect terrorist conspiracies and prosecute terrorists. The Electronic Frontier Foundation (EFF), a group concerned with protecting privacy rights in cyberspace, has been a particularly vocal critic of the additional online surveillance powers granted to the federal government by the act. According to the EFF, the legislation demanded far more deliberation than it was given by Congress, which enacted the law only five weeks after 9/11. Instead, to rush the bill through, Congress suspended normal committee and hearing processes and other procedures, such as interagency review.

Are We Safer?

Should Congress act with great deliberation when policymaking, even in times of national emergency? Or is it better to deal with the emergency by quickly passing new laws to address specific needs that appear on the policymaking agenda?

Policy implementation also involves agencies in the executive branch (see Chapter 13). Once Congress establishes a policy by enacting legislation, the executive branch, through its agencies, enforces the new policy. The courts are also involved in policy implementation, because the legislation and administrative regulations enunciating the new policy must be interpreted and applied to specific situations by the courts.

Policy Evaluation

The final stage of policymaking involves evaluating the success of a policy during and following its implementation. Once a policy has been implemented, groups both inside and outside the government evaluate the policy. Congress may hold hearings to obtain feedback from different groups on how a statute or regulation has affected those groups. Scholars and scientists may conduct studies to determine whether a particular law, such as an environmental law designed to reduce air pollution, has actually achieved the desired result—less air pollution. Sometimes, feedback obtained in these or other ways indicates that a policy has failed, and a new policy-making process may be undertaken to modify the policy or create a more effective one.

The Welfare Reform Act of 1996 was passed due to a perceived failure of the existing welfare policy to achieve its goal of improving the plight of the poor. Over time, as the states continued to implement their programs, data were gathered and analyzed to accurately determine the policy's effectiveness in reducing poverty. Since 1996, welfare reform has been studied and evaluated. In 2003, Congress passed a welfare reform reauthorization bill that essentially endorsed the provisions of the 1996 act, with some modifications. We will look at some of the specific provisions and consequences of welfare reform later in this chapter.

Social-Welfare Policy

Social-welfare policy consists of all government actions that are undertaken to give assistance to specific groups, such as the aged, the ill, and the poor. Social-welfare policy is the government's response to the decision made by the American people, through their elected representatives, that everyone in the nation should be provided with a certain minimum level of income. Social-welfare policy is often implemented through **income redistribution**—income

SOCIAL-WELFARE POLICY All government actions that are undertaken to give assistance to specific groups, such as the aged, the ill, and the poor.

INCOME REDISTRIBUTION The transfer of income from one group to another; income is taken from some people through taxation and given to others.

One of the goals of the Welfare Reform Act of 1996 was to get people off welfare and into productive jobs. The new welfare policy was remarkably successful. In the years since 1996, welfare caseloads have been cut in half. Here, Pam Johnson sits at her desk at the welfare office in Ava, Missouri. Johnson was a welfare recipient who worked her way off welfare and into a full-time job at the welfare office. (AP Photo/John S. Stewart)

Medicare and Social Security are often described as "sacred cows" because members of Congress rarely feel that they can attack these programs if they want to be reelected. Not surprisingly, outlays for Medicare and Social Security continue to rise. Today, Social Security and Medicare combined account for one of every three dollars spent at the federal level. In spite of such real increases, senior citizens resist any threatened reduction in the rate of growth of their benefits. (Mark Richards/PhotoEdit)

is taken from some people through taxation and given to others. Government programs that redistribute income fall into two areas: social insurance programs (such as Social Security and Medicare) and public-assistance programs, often called welfare.

Social Security and Medicare

A major aspect of income redistribution in the United States involves the Social Security system. Social Security includes what has been called old-age, survivors', and disability insurance (OASDI). This is essentially a program of compulsory saving financed from payroll taxes levied on both employers and employees. Workers pay for Social Security while working and receive the benefits later, usually after retirement. When the insured worker dies, benefits accrue to the survivors, including the spouse and children. Special benefits provide for disabled workers. Over 90 percent of all employed persons in the United States are covered by OASDI.

Medicare, launched in 1965, is a social-insurance program under which the federal government pays for part of the cost of medical care for retired persons or persons with disabilities who are covered by Social Security. Like the Social Security program, Medicare is financed by payroll taxes on employers and employees.

Problems with the Social Security System   Social Security was originally designed as a social-insurance program that workers paid for themselves and that provided benefits that were determined by the size of a worker's past contributions. Today, Social Security is not really an insurance program because people are not guaranteed that the benefits they receive will be in line with the contributions they have made. The benefits are legislated by Congress, and there is no guarantee that Congress will continue to legislate the same amount of benefits in the future as it does today. Congress could (and probably will have to) legislate for lower real levels of benefits instead of higher ones. In essence, Social Security is an intergenerational income transfer that is only vaguely related to past earnings. It transfers income from Americans who work—younger and middle-aged individuals—to older, retired persons who do not work.

A key problem with the Social Security system is that the number of people who are working relative to the number of people who are retiring is declining. This means that workers will have to pay more of their income in Social Security taxes to pay for the retirement benefits of older, retired workers. Today, Social Security benefits cost about 15 percent of all taxable payroll income in the economy. By the year 2025, this figure is projected to rise to almost 23 percent. In today's dollars, that amounts to more than a trillion dollars of additional taxes annually. Clearly, increasing or even maintaining the current level of Social Security benefits will create a financial strain for the government (that is, all taxpayers). For a comparison of the U.S. problem with Social Security with similar problems in other countries, see this chapter's *Comparative Politics* feature.

Should We Privatize Social Security?　　One proposed reform of the Social Security system that has been the center of debate in recent years is privatization. If Social Security were privatized, individuals would have a choice: they could stay with the current government-financed system, or they could place the funds that they would otherwise pay in Social Security taxes in private pension plans. In the 2000 presidential elections, candidate George W. Bush proposed that workers be allowed to invest a portion of their payroll tax contributions in a government-approved investment fund. Polls taken during the 2000 election cycle showed that 57 percent of voters supported this plan. Several successful congressional candidates in 2002 also supported voluntary individual retirement accounts for younger workers.

　　The implicit rate of return on Social Security contributions has dropped steadily over the years (the system started in 1937). It was 135 percent in 1940, but today it is only 2 percent and will soon become negative. Many economists argue that long-term sound investments will yield a far greater rate of return than what Americans receive from Social Security.

　　One problem with such a reform is that *current* retirees might see an erosion of their benefits. Up until now, they have received relatively high implicit returns on their contributions,

comparative politics

If You Think We Have a Social Security Problem, Consider Europe

Worries about Social Security and its future in the United States seem like child's play to those who are dealing with Europe's Social Security problem. Look at Table 15–1 to see what the state-funded pension liabilities are in selected countries.

　　The situation in the United States looks pretty good in comparison. Consider that in Europe, most pensions are 100 percent government paid. In contrast, in the United States we have relatively wide-ranging private pension plans funded either by companies or by individuals, or by both. In essence, for many—if not most—Americans, Social Security payments are supplementary retirement income, rather than the sole source of pension funds available on retirement. In Europe, the situation is different.

　　Consider France. In that country, over 99 percent of all pension payments are paid directly out of government (that is, taxpayer-financed) funds. The mandatory retirement age for the majority of workers in France is sixty. For some workers, including train conductors, truck drivers, and subway and bus drivers working in Paris, the mandatory retirement age is fifty-five or lower. Most individuals receiving government retirement funds are not allowed to work. Currently, 10 percent of annual national income goes to pension payments.

　　Moreover, France and the rest of Europe have even worse demographics than the United States with respect to the declining number of working individuals for every retired person. Consequently, over the next thirty years European countries must decide how to handle this challenge.

For Critical Analysis

Why do you think it is often illegal to work while receiving government-paid pensions in Europe?

TABLE 15–1

How the United States Stacks Up Relative to Other Countries with Respect to Pension (Social Security) Liabilities

COUNTRY	NET PENSION LIABILITIES AS A PERCENTAGE OF GROSS DOMESTIC PRODUCT (GDP)
United States	66
Germany	160
Belgium	165
United Kingdom	186
France	216
Japan	218
Italy	233
Canada	250

SOURCE: Organization of Economic Cooperation and Development.

During a news conference held just before the 2002 elections, New Jersey Democratic Senator Frank Lautenberg cast his shadow on a pledge he signed not to privatize Social Security. Whether Social Security should be partially privatized has been a topic of debate in recent years. (AP Photo/Daniel Hulshizer)

and they continue to receive cost-of-living increases. There is another problem: If we allow individuals to have control over how their Social Security contributions are invested, what happens if they make bad choices? During the 1990s, investing in the stock market yielded a very high rate of return. But that has not always been the case. In some periods in U.S. history, stock market investments have turned out very poorly, as they have since 2001. The government may end up with a worse welfare problem if it allows individuals to decide how to invest their Social Security contributions. Not every American is a sophisticated investor.

Supplemental Security Income (SSI)

Many people who are poor but do not qualify for Social Security benefits are assisted through other programs. The federally financed and administered Supplemental Security Income (SSI) program was instituted in 1974. The purpose of SSI is to establish a nationwide minimum income for the aged, the blind, and the disabled. SSI has become one of the fastest-growing transfer programs in the United States: in 1974, less than $8 billion was spent; the estimate for 2004 is over $28 billion. Americans currently eligible for SSI include children and individuals claiming mental disabilities, including drug addicts and alcoholics.

Temporary Assistance to Needy Families

Traditionally, the basic welfare program in the United States was known as Aid to Families with Dependent Children (AFDC), a state-administered program financed in part by federal grants. The program was designed to provide aid to families in which dependent children did not have the financial support of the father because of desertion, disability, or death. Under the AFDC program, the federal government largely set the requirements that had to be met before a welfare applicant could receive welfare payments.

The 1996 Welfare Reform Act replaced the AFDC program with a system that gives the states more discretion in establishing welfare rules and in managing the welfare program. Under the new welfare system, the federal government turns over to the states, in the form of "block" (lump-sum) grants, funds targeted for Temporary Assistance to Needy Families. Essentially, these block grants represent the funds that would otherwise have gone to the AFDC program. Unlike the AFDC program, in which the federal government paid for any increased welfare spending, the new system requires the states to pay any additional costs incurred in providing welfare assistance to the poor.

Goals of the Welfare Reform Act

One of the goals of the 1996 act was to get individuals off welfare and into productive jobs. To this end, the act requires the states to limit welfare assistance to two years. After two years, welfare recipients may continue receiving benefits but only if they are are working, either in public-service jobs or in the private sector. The act limits lifetime welfare benefits to five years (but states may provide for a shorter period— or even a longer period, if they finance the additional costs).

Another key provision of the 1996 Welfare Reform Act allows states to deny welfare benefits to unmarried teen-age mothers. Under the AFDC program, if an unwed mother had insufficient income to support a child, she could obtain welfare payments for that purpose. If the mother had another child, her welfare payments increased. Because the mother could be assured of welfare assistance, she had little incentive to get a job. After all, the income that the mother earned from a job (after taxes and paying for day-care, transportation, and other job-associated costs) often amounted to only a little more than she received from the government—without having to work. The 1996 act attempted to overcome this problem by discouraging illegitimate births. Not only does the act allow the states to deny welfare assistance to unwed teenage mothers, it also provides that "bonus payments" will be given to states that reduce illegitimate births among welfare mothers.

Much of domestic government spending is on some form of welfare payments. Here, a single parent applies for infant care and infant food assistance in California. When other programs are added, aggregate welfare expenses doubled from 1988 to 1998. In 1993, for the first time in American history, aggregate government welfare payments exceeded the total expenditures for national defense. (PhotoEdit)

Measuring the Success of Welfare Reform   Six years after the implementation of the 1996 Welfare Reform Act, many have concluded that the reform was a stunning success. President George W. Bush summed up this view when he made the following announcement:

> [W]elfare reform is a true success story. Since the passage of the bill in 1996, welfare caseloads have dropped more than 50 percent. . . . We're helping people become independent people, so they can realize their full human potential.[3]

Welfare caseloads have indeed decreased and are at their lowest level in over thirty years. The most rapid declines, however, took place in the first two years of welfare reform. Since then, the reduction in welfare caseloads has either slowed or stopped. Since 1998, for example, Wisconsin has not reduced its welfare rolls at all, and New Mexico and Indiana have seen their welfare rolls increase slightly. Moreover, at least two-thirds of former welfare recipients remain dependent on some form of government assistance. Thus, some observers conclude that, contrary to popular belief, former welfare recipients are not achieving self-sufficiency and independence from the government.

How about life after welfare? The majority of individuals and families who leave the welfare rolls find low-wage employment. As just mentioned, they rely heavily on supplemental government benefits to survive. Additionally, they frequently return to the welfare rolls. Not surprisingly, statistics on poverty in America show that the poor are simply "treading water." For example, as you can see in Figure 15–1, overall there has not been any significant change in the poverty rate. The percentage of people below the poverty line in America has hovered between 10 and 15 percent since the early 1970s. Today, one in five American children lives in poverty—twice the rate in Western Europe. One in four African American families is poor, as are nearly 40 percent of African American children. In particular, millions of women with children seem to be "falling through the cracks."

Food Stamps

Food stamps are government-issued coupons that can be used to purchase food. The food stamp program was established in 1964, mainly to shore up the nation's agricultural sector by increasing demand for food through retail channels. In 1964, some 367,000 Americans were receiving food stamps. By 2003, that number had climbed to more than 23 million. The annual cost of the program jumped from $860,000 to an estimated $28 billion over the same period. Thus, the food stamp program has become a major part of the welfare system in the United States. The program has also become a method of promoting better nutrition among the poor.

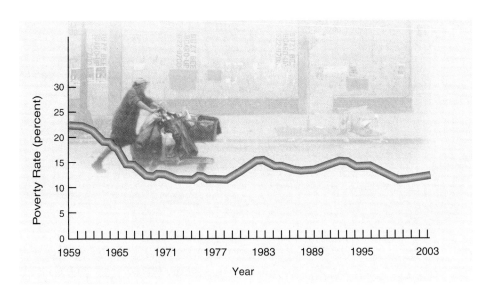

FIGURE 15–1

The Poverty Rate

This figure shows that since the 1970s the poverty rate has remained relatively stable, notwithstanding the very large increases in welfare spending.

The Earned Income Tax Credit (EITC) Program

In 1975, the Earned Income Tax Credit (EITC) program was created to provide rebates of Social Security taxes to low-income workers. Over one-fifth of all tax returns claim an EITC. In some states, such as Mississippi, as well as the District of Columbia, nearly half of all families are eligible for the EITC.

The program has been controversial because, although the program was intended to help full-time workers, many part-time workers benefit from it. The General Accounting Office (GAO) estimates that the average EITC recipient works 1,300 hours annually, compared to a normal work year of 2,000 hours. Additionally, according to the GAO, the program has not had any significant effect on the poverty rate.

AMERICA at odds

What Should Be Done about the Homeless Population?

The existence of a homeless population in the United States, one of the most economically developed countries in the world, is—at least for many Americans—inexplicable. Although no one knows for sure how many Americans are homeless, it is estimated that as many as 600,000 people sleep in homeless shelters every night. Others find refuge with families or friends, and still others sleep on the streets. Should the government be doing more to help this group of Americans?

Some Americans believe that the government should do more. They claim that the cost of housing in the United States is so high that some people have no choice but to be "homeless." More federal and state funds should be allocated to providing low-income ("affordable") housing to serve the needs of people who cannot afford the exorbitant housing costs in many of today's cities. In addition, this group argues that cities should *not* be allowed to criminalize homelessness by prohibiting sleeping on sidewalks or in public parks. In 2002, Santa Monica, California, went so far as to make it illegal to hand out free meals to the homeless in some areas of the city.[4] Clearly, these types of laws do not solve the problem of homelessness but simply "pass the buck" by forcing the homeless to migrate to other cities.

A homeless man sleeps in a public park. How to deal with the problem of homelessness is a difficult question facing the nation's policymakers. (U.S. Census Bureau)

Other Americans take a different view, arguing that more low-income housing and homeless shelters do not address the complex causes of homelessness. Many, perhaps one-third, of the homeless suffer from mental problems, and at least one-half of the homeless are addicted to alcohol or other drugs. Rather than spend resources providing for more shelters and rehabilitation programs, society should focus its attention on the roots of these problems: broken homes and inadequate education.

Policies on Crime and Drugs

It is the subject we all love to hate—crime and illegal drugs. Traditionally, crime was under the purview of state governments, but increasingly it has been placed on the national agenda. Crime committed by career criminals or related to drug trafficking is especially likely to be viewed as a problem for the national government to solve. Moreover, the national government received broad new authority to investigate crime as a result of the USA Patriot Act and other antiterrorism laws passed in 2001.

Worries about crime are certainly not new in this nation. In fact, according to some criminologists, crime was probably as common in the mid-1700s as it is now. In the mid-1800s, citizens in some cities reported a notable increase in criminal activities. In 1910, one author stated that crime was "increasing steadily" and "threatening to bankrupt the Nation." In the 1920s, racial violence and labor union battles led to a sharp increase in social violence and crime. From the 1930s to the 1960s, the United States experienced stable or slightly declining overall crime rates, but during the 1960s and subsequent decades, the crime rate rose dramatically. It climbed from fewer than 2,000 crimes per 100,000 inhabitants in 1960 to nearly 6,000 crimes per 100,000 inhabitants in 1991. Since then, we have seen a decline in the overall crime rate as well as in the violent crime rate (which peaked in 1994).

Even though crime rates have been declining for years, polls show that many Americans believe that crime is on the increase. This is especially true with respect to crime by juveniles, including school crimes. See this chapter's *Perception versus Reality* feature on the next page for a discussion of this issue.

What Does Crime Cost Us?

Look at Table 15–2 on page 363. There you see that the cost of crime in the United States involves more than just the value of stolen goods. In fact, property loss is only about 10 percent of the total cost of crime. The other costs are (1) what we spend on the criminal justice system, including prison construction and maintenance; (2) private protection in the form of security systems, alarms, sensors, and so on; (3) urban decay; (4) destroyed lives; and (5) medical care.

One cost that is sure to rise is the cost of building and maintaining prisons. In 2000, the Department of Justice reported that the total U.S. prison and jail population exceeded two million—more than twice what it was a decade earlier. As the number of incarcerations in the United States increases, so does the cost of building and operating prisons and jails. Each week, an estimated 1,500 new prison beds are needed. When operational costs are included and construction costs are spread over the life of a facility, the cost of sentencing one person to one year in jail or prison now averages between $30,000 and $42,000. In all, the annual nationwide cost of building, maintaining, and operating prisons is about $40 billion today.

No matter how many prisons are built, they will continue to be overcrowded as long as we maintain the same legislation with respect to psychoactive drugs. The reason is that of the more than one million people arrested each year, the majority are arrested for drug offenses. Given that from 20 to 40 million Americans violate one or more drug laws each year, the potential "supply" of prisoners seems virtually without limit.

The War on Drugs

Despite the billions of dollars spent on enforcing existing drug laws, drug abuse continues to be a serious problem. Consider that since 1980, the number of people incarcerated for violating drug laws has grown from 50,000 to over 450,000. In fact, the majority of inmates in today's prisons are not violent offenders but drug users who violated one or another drug law.

A number of Americans believe that, by relying on incarceration as a "solution" to the drug problem, the war on drugs has made matters worse, not better, for American society.[5] Certainly, it has been responsible for prison overcrowding and the consequent need to spend more tax dollars on prison construction and maintenance. It also does little, if anything, to mitigate the harms suffered by drug users and those around them.

What we need, claims this group, is a more pragmatic approach to the drug problem. Federal drug policy should focus less on trying to eradicate illegal drug use and more on drug rehabilitation programs, ranging from prison rehabilitation programs to special **drug courts** that permit nonviolent drug abusers to undergo treatment as an alternative to serving time. The first drug court was established in Florida in 1989. Today, there are over three hundred such courts nationwide. A number of studies have indicated that rehabilitation programs monitored by drug courts are effective in reducing drug abuse.

Another group of Americans, including many Republicans in Congress, argue that what we need is more spending on drug enforcement rather than treatment. In fact, according to recent public opinion surveys, the majority of Americans believe that tougher criminal penalties provide the best "solution" to the drug problem.

DRUG COURT A court in which persons convicted of violating certain drug laws are ordered to undergo treatment in a rehabilitation program as an alternative to serving time in a jail or prison.

perception versus REALITY

Crime in the Schools

Whenever some crazed teenager or group of teens opens fire on classmates, teachers, and administrators, the world gets another dose of what appears to be a frightening reality—violence is increasing in America's schools.

THE PERCEPTION

All it takes is a few nightly news stories showing young bodies being wheeled out of schools on gurneys to convince the world that violence in our schools is increasing. Certainly, it is shocking when a couple of adolescents open fire in a school with semiautomatic weapons. It is shocking when a sixteen-year-old in Pearl, Mississippi, stabs his mother to death and then shoots two classmates to death and wounds several others. When adolescents are depicted on the evening news, it is often in the context of violence, particularly at schools.

THE REALITY

In fact, according to the Justice Department's Bureau of Justice Statistics and the Department of Education's National Center for Education Statistics, crime in the nation's schools has been decreasing since 1993. Victimization rates at schools have dropped from 48 crimes per 1,000 students to 43 crimes per 1,000 students. The fact is, only one-half of 1 percent of juveniles are arrested for violent crime in any given year today. School shootings are still extremely rare; they are not on the increase. In the 1992–1993 school year, there were fifty-five school-associated violent deaths. In the 2001–2002 school year, there were only four.[6]

Indeed, adolescents are not really killing other adolescents at an increasing rate. They rarely kill one another. Less than 3 per-

cent of homicides in the United States involve an individual under the age of eighteen killing another person under eighteen.

Nevertheless, Americans believe that juveniles are responsible for 43 percent of all homicides. In fact, they are responsible for only 9 percent. The *Wall Street Journal* took a poll a few years ago. Seventy-one percent of respondents believed that a killing was likely in their schools. In reality, the chances of that happening are one in a million.

Perhaps as a result of a misguided perception about school violence, we are in an era of zero tolerance. Authorities seize not only weapons and illegal drugs at school, but also nail clippers, asthma inhalers, and headgear. Even though less than 1 percent of all violent incidents involving teen-agers occur on school grounds, authorities believe that zero tolerance is necessary. As a consequence, a large number of innocent schoolchildren are being accused of violating the rules. Sometimes, accusations border on the bizarre. In one case, a six-year-old was apprehended for bringing a "weapon" to school. The weapon was a plastic knife given to him by his grandmother so that he could spread peanut butter on his sandwich. A middle schooler who shared her asthma inhaler with a friend who experienced a wheezing attack on a school bus was suspended for drug trafficking. An eighth grader who made a joke about a high school massacre spent twenty-six days on home confinement.

What's Your Opinion?
Do zero-tolerance policies cause more harm than they prevent?

TABLE 15-2

The Total Yearly Cost of Crime in the United States

EXPENDITURE	EXPLANATION	TOTAL COST (PER YEAR)
Criminal justice	Spending on police, courts, and prisons at the federal, state, and local levels.	$100 billion
Private protection	Spending on private guards, security systems, alarms, and so on.	$70 billion
Urban decay	The cost of lost jobs and fleeing residents because of excessive crime in inner cities.	$50 billion
Property loss	The value of stolen goods and vandalized buildings.	$50 billion
Destroyed lives	The economic value of lost lives (death) and broken lives as a result of robberies, rapes, and other crimes.	$175 billion
Medical care	The cost of treating victims.	$10 billion
TOTAL		**$455 billion**

SOURCES: Federal Bureau of Investigation; *Business Week*, various issues.

Money totaling $1 million in cash lies stacked and bagged after a drug bust by the Federal Bureau of Investigation. Also seized in the operation were 1,600 pounds of marijuana. The war on drugs costs the federal government billions of dollars each year. (AP Photo/Chris Gardner)

Economic Policy

Economic policy consists of all actions taken by the government to smooth out the ups and downs in the nation's overall business activity. Economic policy is solely the responsibility of the national government.

ECONOMIC POLICY All actions taken by the national government to smooth out the ups and downs in the nation's overall business activity.

MONETARY POLICY Actions taken by the Federal Reserve Board to change the amount of money in circulation so as to affect interest rates, credit markets, the rate of inflation, the rate of economic growth, and unemployment.

One of the tools used in this process is **monetary policy,** which involves changing the amount of money in circulation so as to affect interest rates, credit markets, the rate of inflation, the rate of economic growth, and unemployment. Monetary policy is not specifically under the direct control of Congress and the president, because it is determined by the Federal Reserve System, an independent regulatory agency. As discussed in Chapter 13, independent regulatory agencies are not directly controlled by either Congress or the president. Thus, monetary policy is not established through the policymaking process outlined earlier in this chapter.

FISCAL POLICY The use of changes in government expenditures and taxes to alter national economic variables, such as the unemployment rate and price stability.

The national government also controls **fiscal policy,** which is the use of changes in government expenditures and taxes to alter national economic variables. These variables include the rate of unemployment, the level of interest rates, the rate of inflation, and the rate of economic growth.

In this section we look briefly at the politics of monetary and fiscal policy, as well as the federal tax system and the issue of deficit spending.

Monetary Policy

As mentioned, monetary policymaking is under the authority of the Federal Reserve System (the Fed), which was established by Congress as the nation's central banking system in 1913. The Fed is governed by a board of seven governors, including the very powerful chairperson. The president appoints the members of the board of governors, and the Senate must approve the nominations. Members of the board serve for fourteen-year terms. Although the Fed's board of governors acts independently, the Fed has, on occasion, yielded to presidential pressure, and the Fed's chairperson must follow a congressional resolution requiring the chairperson to report monetary targets over each six-month period. Nevertheless, to date, the Fed has remained one of the truly independent sources of economic power in the government.

FEDERAL OPEN MARKET COMMITTEE (FOMC) The most important body within the Federal Reserve System; the FOMC decides how monetary policy should be carried out by the Federal Reserve.

EASY-MONEY POLICY A monetary policy that involves stimulating the economy by expanding the rate of growth of the money supply. An easy-money policy supposedly will lead to lower interest rates and induce consumers to spend more and producers to invest more.

STAGFLATION A condition that occurs when both inflation and unemployment are rising.

Easy Money and Stagflation   The Fed and its **Federal Open Market Committee (FOMC)** make decisions about monetary policy several times each year. In theory, monetary policy is relatively straightforward. In periods of recession and high unemployment, we should pursue an **easy-money policy** to stimulate the economy by expanding the rate of growth of the money supply. An easy-money policy supposedly will lead to lower interest rates and induce consumers to spend more and producers to invest more. In periods of rising inflation, the Fed does the reverse: it reduces the rate of growth in the amount of money in circulation. This policy should cause interest rates to rise, thus inducing consumers to spend less and businesses to invest less. In theory, this sounds quite simple; the reality, however, is not simple at all. During periods of **stagflation**—rising inflation *and* rising unemployment—an expansionary monetary policy (increasing or expanding the rate of growth of the money supply) will lead to even more inflation.

Riding against the Wind   The economy goes through business cycles involving recessions (when unemployment is high) and boom times (when unemployment is low and the economy is in a period of growth). Monetary policy, in principle, should be countercyclical. The Fed should thus "ride against the wind" and create policies that go counter to business activity. Economic researchers have concluded, however, that, on average, the Fed's policy has been procyclical from the beginning. That is, by the time the Fed increased the money supply, it was time to decrease it; and by the time the Fed began to reduce the rate of growth in the amount of money in circulation, it was time to start increasing it.

These coordination difficulties are caused by the length of time it takes for a change in monetary policy to become effective. There is usually a lag of about fourteen months between the time the economy slows down (or speeds up) and the time the economy begins to feel the effects of a policy change. Therefore, by the time a change in policy becomes effective, a different policy may be needed. Perhaps the Fed's most devastating blunder occurred during the 1930s. Many economists believe that what would have been a severe recession became the Great Depression because the Fed's policy resulted in about a one-third decrease in the money supply.

Fiscal Policy

The principle underlying fiscal policy, like that underlying monetary policy, is relatively simple: when unemployment is rising and the economy is going into a recession, fiscal policy should stimulate economic activity by increasing government spending, decreasing taxes, or both. When unemployment is decreasing and prices are rising (leading to inflation), fiscal policy should curb economic activity by reducing government spending, increasing taxes, or both. This particular view of fiscal policy is an outgrowth of the economic theories of the British economist John Maynard Keynes (1883–1943). Keynes's theories were the result of his study of the Great Depression of the 1930s.

Keynesian economics suggests that the forces of supply and demand operate too slowly in recessions, and therefore the government should undertake actions to stimulate the economy during such periods. Keynesian economists maintain that the Great Depression resulted from a serious imbalance in the economy. The public was saving more than usual, and businesses were investing less than usual. According to Keynesian theory, at the beginning of the depression, the government should have filled the gap that was created when businesses began limiting their investments. The government could have done so by increasing government spending or cutting taxes.

One of the problems with fiscal policy is that typically a lag exists between the government's decision to institute fiscal policy and the actual implementation of that policy. This is because the power to create fiscal policy does not rest with one individual or institution. Even if the president wants to institute a new fiscal policy, he is only one of many participants in the fiscal policymaking process. The president, with the aid of the director of the Office of Management and Budget, the secretary of the Treasury Department, and the Council of Economic Advisers, designs a desired mix of taxes and government expenditures. But they can only *recommend* this mix. It is up to Congress, with the help of many committees (such as the House Ways and Means Committee, the Senate Finance Committee, and the Senate Budget Committee), to enact the legislation necessary to implement fiscal policy.

As chairperson of the Federal Reserve Board, Alan Greenspan holds one of the nation's (and world's) most powerful positions. Here, he appears before the House Financial Services Committee on April 30, 2003. (AP Photo/Dennis Cook)

KEYNESIAN ECONOMICS An economic theory proposed by British economist John Maynard Keynes that is typically associated with the use of fiscal policy to alter national economic variables. Keynesian economics gained prominence during the Great Depression of the 1930s.

ACTION-REACTION SYNDROME For every government action, there will be a reaction by the public. The government then takes a further action to counter the public's reaction—and the cycle begins again.

The Federal Tax System   The government raises money to pay its expenses in two ways: through taxes levied on business and personal income and through borrowing. In 1960, individuals paid 52 percent of total federal tax revenues. By 2003, this proportion was more than 80 percent (adding income taxes and Social Security payments together).

The Action-Reaction Syndrome   An examination of the Internal Revenue Code shows that it consists of thousands of pages, thousands of sections, and thousands of subsections. In other words, our tax system is not simple. Part of the reason for this is that tax policy has always been plagued by the **action-reaction syndrome,** a term describing the following phenomenon: *for every government action, there will be a reaction by the public.* Eventually,

In the early months of President George W. Bush's administration, Republicans and Democrats hotly debated Bush's proposed tax-cut bill. In the photo on the left, Bush makes a pitch for tax cuts before business leaders at the U.S. Chamber of Commerce. In the photo on the right, Tom Daschle (D., S.Dak.) displays at a news conference a list of Democrat-sponsored amendments to the proposed bill that were "killed" by the Senate. (Left: AP Photo/Ron Edmonds; Right: AP Photo/ Dennis Cook)

the government will react with another action, and the public will follow with further reaction. The ongoing action-reaction cycle is clearly operative in policymaking with respect to taxes.

Tax Loopholes   Generally, the action-reaction syndrome means that the higher the tax rate—the action on the part of the government—the greater the public's reaction to that tax rate. Individuals and corporations facing high tax rates will react by making concerted attempts to get Congress to add various loopholes to the tax law that will allow them to reduce their taxable incomes.

When the Internal Revenue Code imposed very high tax rates on high incomes, it also provided for more loopholes. These loopholes enabled many wealthy individuals to decrease their tax bills significantly. For example, special tax provisions allowed investors in oil and gas wells to reduce their taxable income. Additional loopholes permitted individuals to shift income from one year to the next—which meant that they could postpone the payment of their taxes for one year. Still more loopholes let U.S. citizens form corporations outside the United States in order to avoid some taxes completely.

Will We Ever Have a Truly Simple Tax System?   The Tax Reform Act of 1986 was intended to lower taxes and simplify the tax code—and it did just that for most taxpayers. A few years later, however, large federal deficits forced Congress to choose between cutting spending and raising taxes, and Congress opted to do the latter. Tax increases occurred under the administrations of both George H. W. Bush (1989–1993) and Bill Clinton (1993–2001). In fact, the tax rate for the highest income bracket rose from 28 percent in 1986 to 39.6 percent in 1993. Thus, the effective highest marginal tax rate increased by over 40 percent.

In response to this sharp increase in taxes, those who were affected lobbied Congress to legislate special exceptions and loopholes so that the full impact of the rate increase would not be felt by the wealthiest and most powerful Americans. As a result, the tax code is more complicated than it was before the 1986 Tax Reform Act.

In 1997, lawmakers again talked about simplifying the tax rules. Nevertheless, the tax bill that was signed into law that year made the tax rules even more complicated. It added new forms to fill out, new instructions to decipher, and over eight hundred pages to the Internal Revenue Code. In 2002 and 2003, some advisers to George W. Bush suggested that the administration try again to simplify the tax code. When Bush proposed a second tax-cut package, however, he included a proposal to eliminate most taxes on dividends from investments in corporate stock that was not particularly simple. Today, the tax code is more complicated than ever.

AMERICA at odds

Do All Americans Pay Their Fair Share in Taxes?

The American income tax system is progressive—meaning that as you earn more income, you pay a higher and higher tax rate on the additional income earned. Today, Americans who earn up to $27,000 have an average federal tax rate of 14 percent. Americans who earn more than $373,000 have an average federal tax rate of 28 percent.[7] About 13 percent of American workers earn so little that they have no income tax liability at all. Many Americans argue that this is a fair system—those who can pay more should, while those who earn the least need to keep as much of what they earn as possible. Others argue that this system is inherently unfair and politically dangerous—those who pay little or nothing in taxes have no reason to care about tax policy or about the costs of running the government.

In 2001, the richest 1 percent of taxpayers paid 25 percent of all taxes, while the poorest 60 percent of Americans paid only 14 percent of taxes. The top 50 percent of income earners pay 96 percent of all federal income taxes. Robert Samuelson, a contributing editor for *Newsweek,* argues that such a steeply progressive tax system is politically corrupting and economically destructive. "Overtaxing the rich poses dangers. It encourages self-serving and cynical politics. Government is tempted to tax the few and distribute to the many without considering the consequences."[8]

In 2003, as Congress and the president debated tax cuts that would benefit the wealthy, some Americans accused the president of "buying votes," arguing that the wealthy make large campaign contributions and turn out to vote far more than the poor. Not so, argue those who favor a less progressive tax system. If the rich are so politically powerful, why haven't they succeeded in reducing their tax burden already? Even after the president's tax cuts, the wealthy still pay most of the taxes. Rather, argues this group, tax policies over the years have favored the middle- and lower-income brackets far more than the rich through expanded personal exemptions and standard deductions, and with tax credits for child care and education. Indeed, the complex and confusing tax system may guarantee only one thing: that Americans will never agree on who pays their fair share.

The Public Debt

When the government spends more than it receives, it has to finance this shortfall. Typically, it borrows. The U.S. Treasury sells IOUs on behalf of the U.S. government. They are called U.S. Treasury bills or bonds. The sale of these bonds to corporations, private individuals, pension plans, foreign governments, foreign companies, and foreign individuals is big business. After all, except for a few years in the late 1990s and early 2000s, federal government expenditures have exceeded federal government revenues virtually every year for many decades. The deficit reached a peak in 1982 when it amounted to almost 6 percent of annual total national income.

Every time there is a federal government deficit, there is an increase in the total accumulated **public debt** (also called the national debt), which is defined as the total value of all outstanding federal government borrowing. If the existing public debt is $5 trillion and the government runs a deficit of $100 billion, then at the end of the year the public debt is $5.1 trillion. Table 15–3 shows what has happened to the net public debt over time.

PUBLIC DEBT The total amount of money that the national government owes as a result of borrowing; also called the national debt.

TABLE 15-3
The Public Debt

YEAR	NET PUBLIC DEBT (BILLIONS OF CURRENT DOLLARS)
1940	42.7
1945	235.2
1950	219.0
1955	226.6
1960	237.2
1965	261.6
1970	284.9
1975	396.9
1980	709.3
1985	1,499.4
1990	2,410.4
1995	3,603.3
1999	3,632.9
2000	3,448.6
2001	3,200.3
2002	3,528.7
2003	3,878.7
2004	4,254.5*

*Estimate.

SOURCES: U.S. Department of the Treasury and Office of Management and Budget; 2004 data are estimated.

We often hear about the burden of the public debt. Some even maintain that the government will eventually go bankrupt. As long as the government can collect taxes to pay for interest on its public debt, however, that will never happen. What happens instead is that when Treasury bonds come due, they are simply "rolled over," or refinanced. That is, if a $1 million Treasury bond comes due today and is cashed in, the U.S. Treasury pays it off with the money it gets from selling another $1 million bond.

The interest on these bonds is paid by federal taxes. Even though most of the interest is being paid to American citizens, the more the federal government borrows to meet these payments, the greater the percentage of its budget that is committed to making interest payments. This reduces the government's ability to supply money for needed community services, such as transportation, education, and housing programs.

why does it MATTER?

Domestic Policy and Your Everyday Life

A number of domestic policy issues affect your everyday life—crime, drug policy, labor legislation, and even monetary policy.

When a Dollar Is Not Really a Dollar

To a large extent, all U.S. monetary policy is carried out by the U.S. Federal Reserve System, and, more particularly, by its board of governors and its chairperson. Although the media covering business activities often have a lot to say about the actions of the Federal Reserve, the Fed, as it is normally called, is usually not a household discussion topic. It should be, though. The Fed determines to a large extent the overall price level and thus how much you pay for the things you buy every day. If the Fed carries out an easy monetary policy by lowering interest rates and causing an increase in the money supply in circulation, inflation may result, meaning that the average of all prices will rise. If the inflation rate is 10 percent in one year, by the end of that year your dollar will buy 10 percent less in terms of real goods and services.

The domestic policymaking of the Fed may also affect the interest rate at which you finance your first home. It may affect how much it costs per month to borrow to buy a car. It can even affect what you end up paying in interest charges on a student loan. The fact is, monetary policy is the most pervasive domestic policy in which the federal government can engage. As long as we use money to buy things, monetary policy will affect our everyday lives.

Taking Action

If you are concerned about the Fed's monetary policy, you need to learn more about it. You might take a first step in this direction by reading through a comic book titled *The Story of Monetary Policy,* which was published by the Federal Reserve. In this twenty-three page publication, which explains monetary economics to high school and college students, the usually austere economists of the Fed did not hesitate to make fun of themselves occasionally. (AP Photo/file)

Key Terms

action-reaction syndrome 366

agenda setting 352

domestic policy 351

drug court 362

easy-money policy 364

economic policy 364

Federal Open Market
   Committee (FOMC) 364

fiscal policy 364

income redistribution 354

Keynesian economics 365

monetary policy 364

policymaking process 351

public debt 367

social-welfare policy 354

stagflation 364

Chapter Summary

1 Public policy can be defined as a government plan or course of action taken in response to a political issue or to enhance the social or political well-being of society. Domestic policy consists of public policy concerning issues within a national unit. Domestic policies are formed through a policymaking process involving several steps, or phases: agenda setting, policy formulation and adoption, policy implementation, and policy evaluation.

2 Social-welfare policy consists of all government actions that are undertaken to give assistance to specific groups, such as the aged, the ill, and the poor. Social-welfare policy is implemented primarily through income redistribution—income is taken from some people through taxation and given to others.

3 The Social Security program provides old-age, survivors', and disability insurance (OASDI) to retired workers who have made Social Security contributions while working. Today, Social Security is essentially an intergenerational income transfer in which the income paid by younger Americans who work is transferred to older, retired persons who do not work. Americans continue to debate whether the Social Security system is viable and how it might be reformed.

4 Major public-assistance programs designed to help the poor include Supplemental Security Income (SSI), Temporary Assistance to Needy Families (the basic welfare program), food stamps, and the Earned Income Tax Credit (EITC) program. The Welfare Reform Act of 1996 turned over significant welfare-management responsibilities to state governments.

5 Monetary policy is the use of changes in the amount of money in circulation to affect interest rates, credit markets, the rate of inflation, the rate of economic growth, and unemployment. Monetary policy is made by the Federal Reserve System (the Fed).

6 Fiscal policy is the use of changes in government expenditures and taxes to alter national economic variables, including the rate of unemployment, the level of interest rates, the rate of inflation, and the rate of economic growth.

7 The government raises revenues to pay its expenses by levying taxes on business and personal income or through borrowing. Individual income taxes constitute an increasing percentage of federal revenue. When federal government expenditures exceed federal government revenues, we experience an increasing public (national) debt.

RESOURCES FOR FURTHER STUDY

Selected Readings

Brill, Steven. *After: How America Confronted the September 12 Era.* New York: Simon & Schuster, 2003. The author looks at how various interest groups, key politicians and policymakers, and others responded to the terrorist attacks of September 11, 2001.

Ehrenreich, Barbara. *Nickel and Dimed: On (Not) Getting By in America.* New York: Owl Books, 2002. An acclaimed journalist takes on a variety of low-wage jobs to explore the living conditions of the "working poor," including those who are just coming off the welfare rolls. She concludes that even at wages slightly above the minimum, it is impossible to live at even a basic level of decency.

Phillips, Kevin. *Wealth and Democracy: A Political History of the American Rich.* New York: Broadway Books, 2003. The author explores the influence of money on government and policymaking, concluding that politics is now a hostage of money to a greater degree than ever before.

President's Council of Economic Advisers. *Economic Report of the President.* Washington, D.C.: U.S. Government Printing Office, published annually. This report contains extensive information on economic developments in the United States and on current monetary and fiscal policy.

InfoTrac Citations

Using your InfoTrac password, access the InfoTrac database at **http://infotrac.thomsonlearning.com**. Once at the site, you can do "key word" searches to locate the following articles, each of which deals with a topic covered in this chapter. The key words to use in your search are indicated in parentheses.

- "The Key to Welfare Reform Is Postsecondary Education" (Welfare Reform Education)

- "War on Drugs: U.S. Has No 'Exit Strategy'" (War On Drugs U.S.)

- "HHS Releases Comprehensive Plan to End Chronic Homelessness" (Homelessness)

- "Some Legislators, GOP, Democrats, Fear Bush's Proposed Tax Breaks Too Costly" (Bush Tax Breaks)

Politics on the Web

A wealth of data on everything that has to do with crime, including public attitudes, can be found on the interactive Web site offered by the Bureau of Justice Statistics and called the Source Book of Criminal Justice Statistics. You can access this site at **http://www.albany.edu/sourcebook**

- The national debt is a hot topic at the end of each federal fiscal year (October), as well as when national elections come around. The debt is the sum over time of each year's deficit. This URL will acquaint you with the size of the national debt: **http://www.census.gov/statab/www/brief.html**

This site will give you "USA Statistics in Brief." If you can't get to it in this way, start with the U.S. Census Bureau's home page at **http://www.census.gov**

Click on "Subjects A to Z." Then click on "S" in the alphabetic lineup and then on "Statistical Abstract."

- If you are interested in reading an Economic Report of the President, go to **http://www.gpo.access.gov/index.html**

- Information on federal departments and agencies can be obtained at **http://www.firstgov.gov**

Web Resources on Your CD-ROM

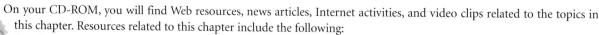

On your CD-ROM, you will find Web resources, news articles, Internet activities, and video clips related to the topics in this chapter. Resources related to this chapter include the following:
- **Values Inventory**—Political Ideology: Is Capital Punishment Cruel and Unusual?
- **Why Does It Matter?**—Select and Investigate an Interest Group with Ties to Domestic Policy.
- **Updates**—Keep up with the issues in this chapter!
- **Web Resources**—Internet Activities: The Case against the Death Penalty; Support for the Death Penalty.
- **Where Do You Stand?**—Dialogue: Is Capital Punishment Cruel and Unusual?
- **Comparative Politics**—Government Policies toward Drug Users in Europe.
- **Video**—Domestic Policy Regulations.
- **NewsEdge**—Visit this global resource for current events related to this chapter.

chapter **16**
foreign policy

CHAPTER OBJECTIVES

After reading this chapter, you should be able to . . .

Explain what is meant by the term *foreign policy.*

Discuss how U.S. foreign policy is made and identify the key players in this process.

Summarize the history of American foreign policy through the years.

Describe the types of terrorist threats that Americans face and the foreign policy challenges presented by the war on terrorism.

Discuss some of the actions taken by the United States to curb the threat of nuclear, biological, and chemical warfare.

Summarize the arguments for and against continued U.S. support of the United Nations.

371

Should the United States Be the Global Cop?

Since the collapse of the Soviet Union in 1991, the United States has been the sole military superpower. As we have pointed out many times before, the United States has also been a target of terrorist attacks, in 1993 at the World Trade Center in New York, in 1998 at its embassies in Kenya and Tanzania, in Yemen in 2000, and, of course, on September 11, 2001. Even before September 11, some Americans contended that the United States has moral and ethical responsibilities to the rest of the world to defend freedom and to promote democracy. Since September 11, the need to defend Americans against potential terrorist attacks has increased the demand that the United States play the role of global cop. Others suggest that the United States should simply mind its own business: let the rest of the world solve its own problems and avoid foreign "entanglements" that make Americans vulnerable to terrorist attack.

The United States Must Be Vigilant

In the weeks preceding the U.S. invasion of Iraq, Americans debated the risks of overthrowing Saddam Hussein versus the risks of letting him stay in power. Some groups argued that if the United States allowed Hussein to remain in power, concealing his alleged stockpiles of chemical and biological weapons, and presumably pursuing a nuclear weapons program, the consequences would be disastrous for the United States and for the world. As President George W. Bush said in his speech of March 17, 2003, "Responding to such enemies only after they have struck first is not self-defense, it is suicide."

Furthermore, those in favor of U.S. activism in foreign affairs argue that the United States should intervene when human rights are being violated. Only the United States has the military might to intervene successfully. When we have failed to act in cases of ethnic violence and humanitarian catastrophe in the past, thousands, if not millions, have died. Look at what happened when the United States stood back and watched Hutu extremists slaughter hundreds of thousands of Tutsi in Rwanda in 1994. In contrast, when the United States invaded Afghanistan in 2001, the oppressive Taliban regime was driven from power and a new government began to rebuild the country.

Many areas in the world, including parts of Africa and the Middle East, will never see stability unless the United States becomes the world's police officer. The United Nations and the Red Cross can provide humanitarian relief, but without concerted military and political pressure for solutions, relief alone can do very little.

Defend the Homeland, but Stay Out of Global "Hot Spots"

Those who favor a more isolationist foreign policy believe that the United States should keep its troops at home. So many ethnic battles are occurring at any one time throughout the world that it is impossible for the United States to act as the world's global cop. The United Nations is the institution that should address the world's minor ethnic flare-ups and humanitarian crises. Even a superpower cannot handle all of the world's "hot spots."

Besides, as Professor M. T. Owens of the Naval War College points out, "imperial policing" carries a price tag, including terrorist attacks against U.S. citizens and U.S. property worldwide.[1] The terrorist attacks of September 11, 2001, were motivated in part by the continued U.S. troop presence in Saudi Arabia since the first Gulf War (1990–1991), something Muslim extremists find abominable. During the first two years after September 11, terrorists were able to hit U.S. targets overseas, including the murder of a U.S. diplomat in Jordan and sniper attacks on U.S. soldiers in Kuwait. Owens contends that policing the world will become even more costly because of such terrorist threats and actions. The more deeply we become involved in world affairs, the more difficult will be the task of protecting American citizens and property abroad.

Finally, the U.S. government has an obligation to defend the homeland. The best way to do this is to refrain from offending other nations or groups. Yet, since the collapse of the Berlin Wall in 1989, the United States has been dispatching troops with greater frequency than during the Cold War. The interventions in Somalia (1994), Haiti (1994), and Kosovo (1999) had nothing to do with U.S. national security.

Where Do You Stand?

1. What guidelines should be used to determine when the United States has the right to intervene in the affairs of another nation?

2. Do you think terrorist attacks are more likely when the United States intervenes in the affairs of another nation?

Interacting with Your CD-ROM Resources

Use your CD-ROM to access resources on the Web, simulations, participation exercises, and video clips. Important resources related to this feature include:

- **Values Inventory**—Political Ideology: Should the United States Be the Global Cop?
- **Where Do You Stand?**—Dialogue: Should the United States Be the Global Cop?
- **Web Resources**—Internet Activities: The U.S., Iraq, and the World Policeman Role; Support for U.S. Unilateralism.

INTRODUCTION

The idea that the United States has a moral responsibility toward the people of other nations is not new. Indeed, it has been one of the great shaping forces of this country's relations with other nations since at least the mid-1800s. The westward expansion of the United States—and the conquest of some 75,000 Spanish-speaking people and 150,000 Native Americans in the process—created a need for a rationale that could justify such expansion and conquest. In 1845, news reporter John O'Sullivan provided one. He stated that it was the "manifest destiny" of the United States "to overspread the continent allotted by Providence for the free development of our yearly multiplying millions."[2] O'Sullivan contended that Americans had a God-given right to extend—by force, if necessary—the benefits of American democracy to less civilized and more backward peoples, meaning, more specifically, Mexicans and Native Americans.

The concept of manifest destiny provided an ideology for continued U.S. expansion in the Western Hemisphere. As the United States grew into a world superpower in the twentieth century, the concept of manifest destiny was left behind. The idea that the United States has a responsibility toward others in the world, however, continues to be reflected in U.S. foreign policy. **Foreign policy** is a systematic and general plan that guides a country's attitudes and actions toward the rest of the world. Foreign policy includes all of the economic, military, commercial, and diplomatic positions and actions that a nation takes in its relationships with other countries. Although foreign policy seems quite removed from the concerns of everyday life, it can and does have a significant impact on the day-to-day lives of Americans.

FOREIGN POLICY A systematic and general plan that guides a country's attitudes and actions toward the rest of the world. Foreign policy includes all of the economic, military, commercial, and diplomatic positions and actions that a nation takes in its relationships with other countries.

Who Makes U.S. Foreign Policy?

The framers of the Constitution envisioned that the president and Congress would cooperate in developing American foreign policy. The Constitution did not spell out exactly how this was to be done, however. As commander in chief, the president has assumed much of the decision-making power in the area of foreign policy. Nonetheless, members of Congress, a number of officials, and a vast national security bureaucracy help to shape the president's decisions and to limit the president's powers.

The President's Role

Article II, Section 2, of the Constitution names the president commander in chief of the armed forces. As commander in chief, the president oversees the military and guides defense policies. Starting with Abraham Lincoln, presidents have interpreted this role broadly and

Secretary of Defense Donald H. Rumsfeld escorts President George W. Bush from the Pentagon. The president, as commander in chief of the armed forces, oversees the military and guides defense policies. (Department of Defense/Helene C. Stikkel)

have sent American troops, ships, and weapons to trouble spots at home and around the world. The Constitution also authorizes the president to make treaties, which must be approved by two-thirds of the Senate. In addition, the president is empowered to form executive agreements—pacts between the president and the heads of other nations. Executive agreements do not require Senate approval. Furthermore, the president's foreign policy responsibilities take on special significance because the president has ultimate control over the use of nuclear weapons.

As head of state, the president also influences foreign policymaking. As the symbolic head of our government, the president represents the United States to the rest of the world. When a serious foreign policy issue or international question arises, the nation expects the president to make a formal statement on the matter.

The Cabinet

All members of the president's cabinet concern themselves with international problems and recommend policies to deal with them. As U.S. power in the world has increased and as economic factors have become increasingly important, the Departments of Commerce, Agriculture, Treasury, and Energy have become more involved in foreign policy decisions. The secretary of state and the secretary of defense, however, are the only cabinet members who concern themselves with foreign policy matters on a full-time basis.

The Department of State
The Department of State is, in principle, the government agency most directly involved in foreign policy. The department maintains diplomatic relations with nearly two hundred independent nations around the globe, as well as with the United Nations and other multilateral organizations, such as the Organization of American States. Most U.S. relations with other countries are maintained through embassies, consulates, and other U.S. offices around the world.

As the head of the State Department, the secretary of state has traditionally played a key role in foreign policymaking, and many presidents have relied heavily on the advice of their secretaries of state. Since the end of World War II, though, the preeminence of the State Department in foreign policy has declined dramatically.

The Department of Defense
The Department of Defense is the principal executive department that establishes and carries out defense policy and protects our national security. The secretary of defense advises the president on all aspects of U.S. military and defense pol-

The Pentagon in Arlington, Virginia, houses the U.S. Department of Defense. The Pentagon was completed on January 15, 1943. At that time, it was the world's largest office building. It has 6.5 million square feet of floor space, 17 miles of corridors, and 7,748 windows. (Department of Defense/Master Sgt. Ken Hammond, U.S. Air Force)

icy, supervises all of the military activities of the U.S. government, and works to see that the decisions of the president as commander in chief are carried out. The secretary advises and informs the president on the nation's military forces, weapons, and bases and works closely with the U.S. military, especially the Joint Chiefs of Staff, in gathering and studying defense information.

The Joint Chiefs of Staff include the chief of staff of the Army, the chief of staff of the Air Force, the chief of naval operations, and the commandant of the Marine Corps. The chairperson of the Joint Chiefs of Staff is appointed by the president for a four-year term. The joint chiefs serve as the key military advisers to the president, the secretary of defense, and the National Security Council. They are responsible for handing down the president's orders to the nation's military units, preparing strategic plans, and recommending military actions. They also propose military budgets, new weapons systems, and military regulations.

Other Agencies

Several other government agencies are also involved in the foreign relations of the United States. The Arms Control Disarmament Agency was formed in 1961 to study and develop policies to deal with the nuclear arms race. The United States Information Agency works to strengthen communications and understanding between the United States and other nations. It is best known for running Voice of America, a round-the-clock radio program that is broadcast in approximately forty different languages. The Agency for International Development gives financial and technical help to other countries. The Peace Corps sends American volunteers to work on development and education projects in other countries. Two key agencies in the area of foreign policy are the National Security Council and the Central Intelligence Agency.

The National Security Council   The National Security Council (NSC) was established by the National Security Act of 1947. Its official function is "to advise the president with respect to the integration of domestic, foreign, and military policies relating to national security." The formal members of the NSC include the president, the vice president, the secretary of state, and the secretary of defense, but meetings are often attended by the chairperson of the Joint Chiefs of Staff, the director of the Central Intelligence Agency, and representatives from other departments. The assistant for national security affairs, who is a member of the president's White House staff, is the director of the NSC. The assistant informs the president, coordinates advice and information on foreign policy, and serves as a liaison with other officials.

President Bush meets with his National Security Council in the Situation Room of the White House, October 12, 2001, to discuss national security issues after a fourth case of anthrax exposure was discovered. (Reuters/White House/Eric Draper © Reuters NewMedia Inc./ CORBIS)

The NSC and its members can be as important and powerful as the president wants them to be. Some presidents have made frequent use of the NSC, whereas others have convened it infrequently. Similarly, the importance of the role played by the assistant for national security affairs in shaping foreign policy can vary significantly, depending on the administration.

The Central Intelligence Agency   The Central Intelligence Agency (CIA) was created after World War II to coordinate American intelligence activities abroad. The CIA provides the president and his advisers with up-to-date information about the political, military, and economic activities of foreign governments. The CIA gathers much of its intelligence from overt sources, such as foreign radio broadcasts and newspapers, people who travel abroad, and satellite photographs. Other information is gathered from covert activities, such as its own secret investigations into the economic or political affairs of other nations. The CIA has tended to operate autonomously, and the nature of its work, methods, and operating funds is kept secret.

Congress's Powers

Although the executive branch takes the lead in foreign policy matters, Congress also has some power over foreign policy. Remember that Congress alone has the power to declare war. It also has the power to appropriate funds to build new weapons systems, to equip U.S. armed forces, and for foreign aid. The Senate has the power to approve or reject treaties and the appointment of ambassadors.

In 1973, Congress passed the War Powers Resolution, which limits the president's use of troops in military action without congressional approval. Presidents since then, however, have not interpreted the resolution to mean that Congress must be consulted before military action is taken. On several occasions, presidents have ordered military action and then informed Congress after the fact.

Several congressional committees are directly concerned with foreign affairs. The most important are the Armed Services Committee and the International Relations Committee in the House and the Armed Services Committee and the Foreign Relations Committee in the Senate. Other congressional committees deal with matters such as oil, agriculture, and imports that indirectly influence foreign policy.

A Short History of American Foreign Policy

Although many U.S. foreign policy initiatives have been rooted in moral idealism, a primary consideration in U.S. foreign policy has always been national security—the protection of the independence and political integrity of the nation. Over the years, the United States has attempted to preserve its national security in many ways. These ways have changed over time and are not always internally consistent. This is because foreign policymaking, like domestic policymaking, reflects the influence of various political groups in the United States. These groups—including the voting public, interest groups, Congress, and the president and relevant agencies of the executive branch—are often at odds over what the U.S. position should be in regard to particular foreign policy issues.

Isolationism

The nation's founders and the early presidents believed that avoiding political involvement with other nations—**isolationism**—was the best way to protect American interests. The colonies were certainly not yet strong enough to directly influence European developments. As president of the new nation, George Washington did little in terms of foreign policy. Indeed, in his farewell address in 1797, he urged Americans to "steer clear of permanent alliances with any portion of the foreign world." During the 1700s and 1800s, the United States generally stayed out of conflicts and political issues elsewhere.

ISOLATIONISM A political policy of noninvolvement in world affairs.

James Monroe served two terms as president, beginning in 1817 and leaving office in 1825. (Library of Congress)

In 1823, President James Monroe proclaimed what became known as the **Monroe Doctrine.** In his message to Congress in December 1823, Monroe made it clear that the United States would not tolerate foreign intervention in the Western Hemisphere. In return, promised Monroe, the United States would stay out of European affairs. The Monroe Doctrine buttressed the policy of isolationism toward Europe.

MONROE DOCTRINE A U.S. policy, announced in 1823 by President James Monroe, that the United States would not tolerate foreign intervention in the Western Hemisphere, and in return, the United States would stay out of European affairs.

The Beginning of Interventionism

Isolationism gradually became interventionism as the United States began to trade more with Japan, China, and other Asian countries and as it expanded westward across the North American continent. As a result of its westward expansion, the United States found itself in conflict with Mexico, France, Spain, and Great Britain. The first true step toward **interventionism** (direct involvement in foreign affairs) occurred with the Spanish-American War of 1898. The United States fought to free Cuba from Spanish rule. Spain lost and subsequently ceded control of several of its possessions, including Guam, Puerto Rico, and the Philippines, to the United States. The United States acquired a **colonial empire** and was acknowledged as a world power.

INTERVENTIONISM Direct involvement by one country in another country's affairs.

The growth of the United States as an industrial economy also confirmed its position as a world power. For example, American textile manufacturers were particularly interested in China as a market for America's cheap cotton exports. The so-called open-door policy toward China was a statement of principles initiated by the United States in 1899 that Western nations would respect each other's equal trading privileges in China. Furthermore, in the early 1900s, President Theodore Roosevelt proposed that the United States could invade Latin America when it was necessary to guarantee political or economic stability.

COLONIAL EMPIRE A group of colonized nations that are under the rule of a single imperial power.

The World Wars

When World War I broke out in 1914, President Woodrow Wilson initially proclaimed a policy of **neutrality**—the United States would not take sides in the conflict. The United States did not enter the war until 1917, after U.S. ships in international waters were attacked by German submarines that were blockading Britain. After World War I ended in 1918, the United States returned to a policy of isolationism. We refused to join the League of Nations, an international body intended to resolve peacefully any future conflicts between nations.

NEUTRALITY A position of not being aligned with either side in a dispute or conflict, such as a war.

The battleship USS *Arizona* belches smoke as it topples over into the sea during the Japanese surprise attack on Pearl Harbor, Hawaii, on December 7, 1941. The attack, which left 2,343 Americans dead and 916 missing, forced America out of its policy of isolationism. President Franklin D. Roosevelt announced that it was "a date which will live in infamy," and Congress declared war on Japan on December 8. (National Archives)

Isolationism was relatively short-lived, however, lasting only until the Japanese attacked Pearl Harbor in 1941. The United States joined the Allies—Australia, Great Britain, Canada, China, France, and the Soviet Union—that fought the Axis nations of Germany, Italy, and Japan. One of the most significant foreign policy actions during World War II was the dropping of atomic bombs on the Japanese cities of Hiroshima and Nagasaki.

The Cold War

After World War II ended in 1945, the wartime alliance between the United States and the Soviet Union began to deteriorate quickly. The Soviet Union opposed American political and economic values. Many Americans thought that the Soviet Union and the spread of communism posed a major threat to democracy. After the war ended, one after another, the countries of Eastern Europe—Hungary, Poland, Bulgaria, Romania, and Czechoslovakia—fell under Soviet domination, forming what became known as the **Communist bloc.**

COMMUNIST BLOC The group of Eastern European nations that fell under the control of the Soviet Union following World War II.

The Iron Curtain   Britain's Prime Minister Winston Churchill established the tone for a new relationship between the Soviet Union and the Western allies in his famous "iron curtain" speech in Fulton, Missouri, on March 5, 1946:

> An iron curtain has descended across the Continent. Behind that line all are subject in one form or another, not only to Soviet influence but to a very high . . . measure of control from Moscow.

The reference to an **iron curtain** described the political boundaries between the democratic countries in Western Europe and the Soviet-controlled Communist countries in Eastern Europe.

IRON CURTAIN A phrase coined by Winston Churchill to describe the political boundaries between the democratic countries in Europe and the Soviet-controlled Communist countries in Eastern Europe.

The Marshall Plan and the Policy of Containment   In 1947, after Great Britain announced that it was withdrawing economic and military aid from Greece and Turkey and it appeared that communists, backed by the Soviets, would take over those areas, President Harry Truman took action. He convinced Congress to appropriate $400 million in aid for those countries to prevent the spread of communism.[3] The Truman administration also instituted a policy of economic assistance to war-torn Europe, called the **Marshall Plan** after George Marshall, who was then the U.S. secretary of state. During the next five years,

MARSHALL PLAN A plan providing for U.S. economic assistance to European nations following World War II to help those nations recover from the war; the plan was named after George C. Marshall, secretary of state from 1947 to 1949.

President Harry Truman, Secretary of State George C. Marshall, Paul G. Hoffman, and W. Averell Harriman discuss Western European affairs at a conference in the president's office in November 1948. (Truman Presidential Museum and Library)

Congress appropriated $17 billion for aid to sixteen European countries. By 1952, the nations of Western Europe, with U.S. help, had indeed recovered and were again prospering.

These actions marked the beginning of a policy of **containment**—a policy designed to contain the spread of communism by offering threatened nations U.S. military and economic aid.[4] To make the policy of containment effective, the United States initiated a policy of **collective security** involving the formation of mutual defense alliances with other nations. In 1949, by the North Atlantic Treaty, the United States, Canada, and ten European nations formed a military alliance—the North Atlantic Treaty Organization (NATO)—and declared that an attack on any member of the alliance would be considered an attack against all members. President Truman stationed four American army divisions in Europe as the nucleus of the NATO armed forces. Truman also pledged military aid to any European nation threatened by communist expansion.

Thus, by 1949, almost all illusions of friendship between the Soviet Union and the Western allies had disappeared. The United States became the leader of the **Western bloc** of democratic nations that included France, Great Britain, Australia, Canada, Japan, the Philippines, and other countries in Western Europe and Latin America. The tensions between the Soviet Union and the United States became known as the **Cold War,** a war of words, warnings, and ideologies that lasted from the late 1940s through the early 1990s. The term *iron curtain,* from Winston Churchill's speech in 1946, became even more appropriate in 1961, when the Soviets insisted that Berlin be split by the Berlin Wall, which separated East Berlin from West Berlin.

Although the Cold War was mainly a war of words and belief systems, the wars in Korea (1950–1953) and Vietnam (1964–1975) are examples of confrontations that grew out of the efforts to contain communism.

The Arms Race and Deterrence   The tensions induced by the Cold War led both the Soviet Union and the United States to try to surpass each other militarily. They began competing for more and better weapons, particularly nuclear weapons, with greater destructive power. This phenomenon, which was commonly known as the arms race, was supported by a policy of **deterrence**—of rendering ourselves and our allies so strong militarily that our very strength would deter (stop or discourage) any attack on us. Deterrence is essentially a policy of "building weapons for peace." Out of deterrence came the theory of **mutually assured destruction (MAD),** which held that if the forces of both nations were equally capable of destroying each other, neither would take a chance on war.

The End of the Cold War

In 1962, the United States and the Soviet Union came close to a nuclear confrontation in what became known as the **Cuban missile crisis.** The United States learned that the Soviet Union had placed nuclear weapons on the island of Cuba, ninety miles from the coast of Florida. The crisis was defused diplomatically: a U.S. naval blockade of Cuba convinced the Soviet Union to agree to remove the missiles. The United States also agreed to remove some of its missiles near the Soviet border in Turkey. Both sides recognized that a direct nuclear confrontation between the two superpowers was unthinkable. (Later, after the collapse of the Soviet Union, formerly secret Soviet government documents confirmed that Cuba's dictator, Fidel Castro, had requested that the Soviets launch a nuclear attack on Miami.)

CONTAINMENT A U.S. policy designed to contain the spread of communism by offering military and economic aid to threatened nations.

COLLECTIVE SECURITY A national defense and security policy that involved the formation of mutual defense alliances, such as the North Atlantic Treaty Organization, with other nations.

WESTERN BLOC The democratic nations that emerged victorious after World War II, led by the United States.

COLD WAR The war of words, warnings, and ideologies between the Soviet Union and the United States that lasted from the late 1940s through the early 1990s.

DETERRENCE A policy of building up military strength for the purpose of discouraging (deterring) military attacks by other nations; the policy of "building weapons for peace" that supported the arms race between the United States and the Soviet Union during the Cold War.

MUTUALLY ASSURED DESTRUCTION (MAD) A phrase referring to the assumption, on which the policy of deterrence was based, that if the forces of two nations are equally capable of destroying each other, neither will take a chance on war.

CUBAN MISSILE CRISIS A nuclear stand-off that occurred in 1962 when the United States learned that the Soviet Union had placed nuclear warheads in Cuba, an island ninety miles off the U.S. coast. The crisis was defused diplomatically, but it is generally considered the closest the two Cold War superpowers came to a nuclear confrontation.

The Cuban missile crisis brought the United States to the brink of war with the Soviet Union in 1962. Here, President John F. Kennedy, right, is shown with Soviet Foreign Minister Andrei Gromyko. Kennedy warned Gromyko that the "gravest consequences" would follow if Soviet offensive weapons were introduced into Cuba. (Library of Congress)

The statue of Vladimir Lenin is taken down in the Latvian town of Jurnala in August 1991. Anti-Communist feelings swept across the Soviet Union, including the Baltic states of Estonia, Latvia, and Lithuania, in the fall of 1991. By the end of the year, the Soviet Union ceased to exist. (AP Photo)

DÉTENTE A French word meaning a relaxation of tensions. Détente characterized the relationship between the United States and the Soviet Union in the 1970s, as the two Cold War rivals attempted to pursue cooperative dealings and arms control.

Détente and Arms Control

In 1969, the United States and the Soviet Union began negotiations on a treaty to limit the number of antiballistic missiles (ABMs) and offensive missiles that each country could develop and deploy. In 1972, both sides signed the Strategic Arms Limitation Treaty (SALT I), which marked the beginning of a period of **détente,** a French word that means relaxation of tensions. The two nations also engaged in scientific and cultural exchanges.

In 1983, President Ronald Reagan (1981–1989) nearly reignited the arms race by proposing a missile defense system, known as the strategic defense initiative (SDI, or "Star Wars"). Nonetheless, Reagan and Soviet leader Mikhail Gorbachev pursued arms control agreements, as did Reagan's successor, President George H. W. Bush (1989–1993).

The Dissolution of the Soviet Union

In the late 1980s, the political situation inside the Soviet Union began to change rapidly. Mikhail Gorbachev had initiated an effort to democratize the Soviet political system and decentralize the economy. The reforms quickly spread to other countries behind the iron curtain. In 1989, the Berlin Wall, constructed nearly thirty years earlier, was torn down, and East and West Germany were united.

In August 1991, a number of disgruntled Communist Party leaders, who wanted to curb the movement toward greater autonomy in the republics within the Soviet Union, illegally seized control of the Soviet central government. Russian citizens rose up in revolt and defied those leaders. The democratically elected president of the Russian republic (the largest republic in the Soviet Union), Boris Yeltsin, openly defied the military troops in Moscow. The attempted coup was overthrown after three days. Over the next several weeks, the Communist Party in the Soviet Union lost virtually all of its power. Most of the fifteen republics constituting the Soviet Union declared their independence, and by the end of the year, the Union of Soviet Socialist Republics (USSR) no longer existed.

Post–Cold War Foreign Policy

The demise of the Soviet Union altered the framework and goals of U.S. foreign policy. During the Cold War, the moral underpinnings of American foreign policy were clear to all— the United States was the defender of the "free world" against the Soviet aggressor. When the Cold War ended, U.S. foreign policymakers were forced, for the first time in decades, to rethink the nation's foreign policy goals and adapt them to a world arena in which, at least for a time, the United States was the only remaining superpower.

As you read in the chapter-opening *America at Odds* feature, U.S. foreign policymakers have struggled since the end of the Cold War to determine the degree of intervention that is appropriate and prudent for the U.S. military. Should we intervene in a humanitarian crisis, such as a famine? Should the U.S. military participate in peacekeeping missions, such as after civil or ethnic strife in other countries? Americans have faced these questions in Somalia, Bosnia, Kosovo, and Rwanda. Yet no overriding framework emerged in U.S. foreign policy until September 11, 2001. Since that date, our goal has been to capture and punish the terrorists who planned and perpetrated that act and to prevent future terrorist attacks against Americans, even if that means "regime change," which was one of the goals of the second Gulf War against Iraq in 2003.

The War on Terrorism

One of the most troubling challenges to governments around the world is how to control terrorism. Terrorism is defined as the use of staged violence, often against civilians, to achieve

A plane approaches New York's World Trade Center moments before it struck the second tower, as seen from downtown Brooklyn on September 11, 2001. In an unprecedented show of terrorist horror, the 110-story towers collapsed in a shower of rubble and dust after two hijacked airliners carrying scores of passengers slammed into them. (AP Photo/ William Kratzke)

political goals. International terrorism has occurred in virtually every region of the world. The most devastating terrorist attack in U.S. history occurred on September 11, 2001, when terrorists used hijacked airliners as missiles to bring down the World Trade Center towers in New York City and to destroy part of the Pentagon building in Washington, D.C. A fourth airplane crashed in a Pennsylvania field after the hijackers were overtaken by the passengers. It was believed that this airliner was to be used to destroy the White House or the capitol building in Washington, D.C. In all, three thousand innocent civilians were killed as a result of these terrorist acts.

Terrorist attacks have occurred with increasing frequency during the past three decades. Other examples of terrorist acts include the Palestinian attacks on Israeli Olympic athletes in Munich in 1972; a number of hijackings of commercial airliners in the 1970s and 1980s; the Libyan suitcase bombing of an American airliner over Lockerbie, Scotland, in 1988; the bombing of the World Trade Center in New York in 1993; the bombing of an American military barracks in Saudi Arabia in 1996; the bombing of two U.S. embassies in Africa in 1998; and the bombing of the USS *Cole* in a Yemeni port in 2000. What motivates terrorists to act, and what can be done to stop them?

Local or Regional Terrorism

Some terrorist acts have been committed by extremists who are motivated by the desire to obtain freedom from a nation or government that they regard as an oppressor. Terrorists have sometimes acted to disrupt peace talks. In Israel, for example, numerous suicide bombings by Palestinians against Israeli civilians have successfully stalled efforts to forge a lasting peace between Israel and the Palestinians. Terrorist acts by rebels and separatist groups have also been used to demand peace negotiations. In 2002, for example, Chechen separatists seized control of a theater in Moscow, holding 800 theatergoers hostage for three days. The terrorists demanded that Russia negotiate a stop to the armed conflict in the breakaway republic of Chechnya. The crisis ended when Russian police pumped poison gas into the theater, killing all the terrorists and 117 hostages.

The United States has also been the victim of homegrown terrorists. The bombing of the Oklahoma City federal building in 1995 was the act of vengeful extremists in the United States who claimed to fear an oppressive federal government. Although Timothy McVeigh and Terry Nichols, who were convicted of the crime, were not directly connected to a particular political group, they expressed views characteristic of the extreme right-wing militia movement in the United States.

State-Sponsored Terrorism

Some terrorist attacks have been planned and sponsored by governments. For example, the bombing of Pan Am Flight 103, which exploded over Lockerbie, Scotland, in 1988 killing all 259 on board and 11 people on the ground, was later proved to be the work of an intelligence officer working for Libya. The United Nations imposed economic sanctions against Libya in an effort to force Libyan dictator Muammar Qaddafi to extradite those who were suspected of being responsible for the bombing. More than a decade after the bombing, Libya agreed to hand the men over for trial, and one of them was found guilty and sentenced to twenty years in prison.

The case of Pan Am Flight 103 illustrates the difficulty in punishing the perpetrators of state-sponsored terrorism. The victim country must first prove who the terrorists were and for whom they were working. Then it must decide what type of retribution is warranted. Today, the U.S. State Department lists Iran, Syria, Libya, Cuba, North Korea, and Sudan as state sponsors of international terrorism. Does a state-sponsored terrorist act warrant war? What if, as in the case of Iraq, the state is suspected of possessing weapons of mass destruction that it could pass on to terrorists? (We discuss the case of the war in Iraq later in this chapter.) What if, as in the case of Afghanistan in 2001, the state is accused of aiding and protecting a foreign terrorist network?

Foreign Terrorist Networks

A relatively new phenomenon in the late 1990s and early 2000s has been the emergence of nonstate terrorist networks, such as al Qaeda. Al Qaeda is the nongovernmental, quasi-hierarchical, terrorist organization that planned and carried out the terrorist attacks of September 11, 2001. It receives its inspiration and much of its funding from the Saudi dissident Osama bin Laden. It operates in "cells," however, so that often one cell of the organization will not know what the other cells are planning. Throughout the 1990s, al Qaeda conducted training camps in the mountains of Afghanistan, which was ruled by an ultraconservative religious faction known as the Taliban. After their training, al Qaeda operatives dispersed into small units across the globe, connected by e-mail and the Internet.

Before September 11, the U.S. government had monitored the activities and movements of several al Qaeda operatives and had connected the terrorist attacks on two U.S. embassies in Africa and the bombing of the USS *Cole* to al Qaeda. In 1998, President Bill Clinton ordered the bombing of terrorist camps in Afghanistan in retaliation for the embassy bombings, but

U.S. troops board a plane at Pope Air Force Base in North Carolina on February 13, 2003. The troops were being sent to Kuwait to join thousands of other troops in preparation for a possible war with Iraq. (AP Photo/Bob Jordan)

with little effect. Al Qaeda cells continued to operate largely unimpeded until the terrorist attacks of September 11.

Again, the case of al Qaeda illustrates the difficulties of combating terrorism. How can a traditional government, even with overwhelming military power, contain a global terrorist network in which the enemy is scattered across the globe working in isolated groups?

Unilateralism and Multilateralism in the War on Terrorism

In September 2002, President George W. Bush articulated what has become known as the "Bush Doctrine":

> We will . . . [defend] the United States, the American people, and our interests at home and abroad by identifying and destroying the threat before it reaches our borders. While the United States will constantly strive to enlist the support of the international community, we will not hesitate to act alone, if necessary, to exercise our right of self-defense by acting preemptively against such terrorists, to prevent them from doing harm against our people and our country.[5]

President Bush clearly expressed U.S. willingness for **unilateral** action in the war on terrorism. In the war against al Qaeda and the Taliban in Afghanistan in 2001 and 2002, the United States assembled a broad **coalition** of support from other countries. As the United States turned its attention to Iraq in 2002 and 2003, however, American allies in Europe and elsewhere were markedly less supportive.

Some national security experts agree that the war on terrorism, perhaps more than any conventional war, requires **multilateral** cooperation. To contain and capture terrorists, governments must share intelligence and law enforcement efforts. Most al Qaeda operatives captured outside Afghanistan were caught because of information sharing and law enforcement cooperation among countries—including our traditional allies such as Britain, France, and Germany, as well as other nations such as Pakistan, Yemen, and Syria. Can the Bush Doctrine of unilateral action be sustained in the war on terrorism?

UNILATERAL In international relations, action that involves or affects only one side in a conflict or that is taken by only one nation.

COALITION An alliance of nations to undertake a foreign policy action, particularly military action. A coalition is often a temporary alliance that dissolves after the action is concluded.

MULTILATERAL Involving more than one side or nation.

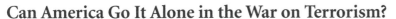

AMERICA at odds

Can America Go It Alone in the War on Terrorism?

As you read earlier, U.S. foreign policy was founded on the notion that we would avoid international "entanglements." Since World War II, however, we have been deeply committed to international alliances such as NATO and the United Nations. Some scholars

President Bush answers a question during a news conference held on March 6, 2003, to prepare the nation for the possibility of war. The president said that the United States will drive Saddam Hussein from power if it comes to war in Iraq, with or without support from France, Germany, and other skeptical allies. (AP Photo/Lawrence Jackson)

argue that notwithstanding these alliances, essentially it has been the overwhelming military superiority of the United States that has assured peace in the world.

For example, military historian Victor Davis Hanson has pointed out that in all of the major crises in modern times, American military power has been essential. The United States played a pivotal role in driving back the totalitarian regimes of Germany, Italy, and Japan in World War II, and we alone stopped the spread of Soviet communism after the war ended. Today, the United States must not hesitate to use its power unilaterally to combat terrorism or whenever circumstances demand.[6] To assure that not only America but also the world is free from the fear of terrorism, the United States must destroy the dictatorships that harbor terrorists and replace them with democracies.

Others argue that such international alliances as the United Nations and NATO are largely responsible for the relative peace that the world has enjoyed for over fifty years. When the world's powers act jointly through the United Nations, their actions are vested with an authority and legitimacy that increases the likelihood that countries will cooperate. Furthermore, it is simply not practical for the United States to act alone. Clearly, we need other nations to share their airspace and intelligence efforts, at the very least. Even the conservative think tank Project for a New American Century concluded, in its analysis of U.S. defense strategy, that the United States cannot defend its national interests from inside "fortress America."[7] We must have troops, aircraft, and ships stationed overseas, and this necessitates alliances, treaties, and multilateral cooperation.

Weapons Proliferation in an Unstable World

The Cold War may be over, but the threat of nuclear warfare—which formed the backdrop of foreign policy during the Cold War—has by no means disappeared. The existence of nuclear weapons in Russia and in other countries around the world continues to challenge U.S. foreign policymakers. Concerns about nuclear proliferation mounted in 1998 when India and Pakistan detonated nuclear devices within a few weeks of each other—events that took U.S. intelligence agencies by surprise. Increasingly, American officials have focused on the threat of an attack by a rogue nation or a terrorist group that possesses **weapons of mass destruction (WMDs).**

WEAPONS OF MASS DESTRUCTION (WMDs) Nuclear, chemical, and biological weapons that can inflict massive civilian casualties and pose long-term health dangers to human beings.

Senate Foreign Relations Committee Chairman Senator Richard Lugar (R., Ind.), left, accompanied by former Senator Sam Nunn (D., Ga.), center, and Matthew Bunn, right, lead author of a Harvard study on "Controlling Nuclear Warheads and Materials," gestures during a news conference held in Washington on March 12, 2003, to discuss the report. The possibility that terrorists might detonate a nuclear bomb in a major city "is real and urgent," stated the report, but although the government is spending $1 billion a year to reduce such a threat, it is not addressing it seriously enough. (AP Photo/Linda Spillers)

Russia's Current Nuclear Arsenal

Russia, the strongest of the fifteen republics that formerly constituted the Soviet Union, still has nearly six thousand nuclear warheads, according to the Monterey Institute's Center for Nonproliferation Studies. Such warheads could be delivered by land-based missiles, dropped from planes, or launched from submarines. Under a bilateral agreement, no Russian missiles are targeted at the United States. Experts say, however, that Russia could reprogram its missiles within minutes.

Russia, no matter how strapped for funds, wants to maintain its nuclear arsenal as a "badge" of first-class military status. For some time, Western analysts have debated the dangers posed by Russia's aging strategic missile forces. Even inside Russia, scientists have expressed concern over the potential for nuclear accidents involving nuclear-tipped rockets. Russia has begun to modernize some of its nuclear arsenal and missiles to avert such dangers.

More worrisome, perhaps, is Russia's current economic and political instability. Many Russian troops remain unpaid and desperate. The chief of one Russian nuclear lab even committed suicide because its research was so curtailed by lack of funds. In the United States, defense policymakers fear that a dissatisfied Russian officer could launch a nuclear strike or, alternatively, sell a nuclear warhead or key substance to a terrorist organization or rogue state. Small amounts of nuclear material have already turned up on the black market worldwide. Their source? Russia.

North Korea's Nuclear Program

Beginning in the 1950s, after the armistice that ended the Korean civil war, North Korean scientists studied nuclear technology in the Soviet Union. In 1959, North Korea and the Soviet Union signed a nuclear cooperation treaty in which the Soviets agreed to provide technical assistance to establish a nuclear research center in North Korea. North Korea built the center in 1964 and later expanded it to include a large plutonium reprocessing plant.

Despite its ongoing pursuit of nuclear technology and the development of nuclear energy facilities, North Korea signed the Treaty on the Non-Proliferation of Nuclear Weapons (NPT)

U.S. Secretary of State Colin Powell, left, meets with Chinese president Jiang Zemin in Beijing's Great Hall of the People on February 24, 2003. Powell said that China is eager to play a positive role in helping to resolve the developing crisis over North Korea's nuclear weapons programs. (AP Photo/Greg Baker)

in 1985 and submitted to weapons inspections by the International Atomic Energy Agency (IAEA) in 1992. Throughout the 1990s, however, there were discrepancies between North Korean declarations and IAEA inspection findings. In 2002, U.S. intelligence discovered that North Korea had been receiving materials from Pakistan for a highly enriched uranium production facility. Later that year, North Korea openly lifted the freeze on its plutonium-based nuclear weapons program and expelled the IAEA inspectors.

Furthermore, North Korea also has an extensive missile technology program. North Korea has exported missiles, missile components, and technology to Egypt, Iran, Libya, Pakistan, Syria, and Yemen. It has a program to develop a missile with intercontinental range, although it has not been flight-tested. North Korea has test-fired medium-range missiles over Japan into the Pacific Ocean.

North Korea's dictator, Kim Jong Il, has remained openly hostile to the United States. He once stated that he would only consider direct talks with the United States about his nuclear program. Secretary of State Colin Powell indicated on numerous occasions that any talks with North Korea must also include nearby countries. The Bush administration rejected any offers by Kim Jong Il to halt his weapons program in return for economic aid from the United States.

Iraq: A Crisis for the Global Community

On March 20, 2003, the global standoff with Iraqi president Saddam Hussein erupted into war. In the decade following the first Gulf War in 1991, Hussein had repeatedly defied United Nations (UN) resolutions and threatened Iraq's neighbors in the Persian Gulf. The broad coalition of nations that drove Iraqi forces from Kuwait in 1991 to thwart Hussein's attempt to take over that nation had stopped short of sending troops to Baghdad to unseat Hussein. The official cease-fire that ended the first Gulf War required that Iraq submit to inspections of its research facilities for chemical, biological, and nuclear weapons. In 1998, however, Iraq refused to let the inspections continue. This action represented a major challenge to the weapons inspection regime favored by the UN to halt weapons proliferation.

The UN had also imposed economic sanctions on Iraq until the weapons inspectors finished their job. Because many European and Middle Eastern countries decried the sanctions as overly harsh on the Iraqi people, the UN attempted to revise the sanctions with a so-called oil-for-food program. Iraq continued to reject UN weapons inspection proposals, however. Between the end of the first Gulf War and 2003, Saddam Hussein violated seventeen separate UN resolutions and used much of the oil-for-food revenues to build massive palaces.

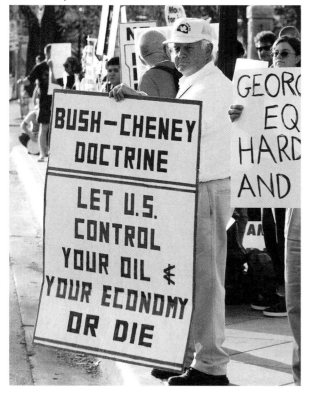

Individuals gather outside the Texas capitol in Austin, Texas, on March 21, 2003, to protest President Bush's decision to go to war with Iraq. (AP Photo/Harry Cabluck)

A Policy of "Regime Change"   After the terrorist attacks of September 11, 2001, the United States took a leadership role in denouncing regimes that support terrorists. In his State of the Union address in January 2002, President Bush included Iraq in what he deemed an "axis of evil"—regimes that sponsor terror and seek to develop weapons of mass destruction. Although Bush included North Korea and Iran on the same list, the focus of American foreign policymakers throughout 2002 was "regime change" in Iraq. In October 2002, Bush justified the U.S. policy of removing Saddam Hussein from power:

[There is] a grave threat to peace. . . . The threat comes from Iraq. It arises directly from the Iraqi regime's own actions—its history of aggression, and its drive toward an arsenal of terror. . . . Iraq's weapons of mass destruction are controlled by a murderous tyrant who has already used chemical weapons to kill thousands of people. This same tyrant has tried to dominate the Middle East, has invaded and brutally occupied a small neighbor, has struck other nations without warning, and holds an unrelenting hostility toward the United States.[8]

Shortly thereafter, Congress authorized President Bush to use force to disarm Iraq if necessary, and the UN Security Council unanimously adopted a resolution outlining an enhanced inspection regime for Iraq's disarmament. Iraq agreed to cooperate with inspectors, but continued to deny that it had any weapons of mass destruction.

The Failure of Diplomacy   Diplomatic efforts to disarm Iraq began to fail in February 2003. Although the United States and Britain presented their own evidence to the UN that Iraq was continuing to develop weapons of mass destruction, UN weapons inspectors claimed that they could not confirm this evidence. In fact, the inspectors followed up on some U.S. intelligence reports of Iraqi mobile bioweapons labs and underground storage facilities, but they found no evidence that either existed in Iraq.[9]

Although public opinion in the United States strongly favored seeking an additional resolution from the UN on the use of military force in Iraq, there was simply not enough support. France, China, and Russia, all permanent members of the UN Security Council, vowed to block any new U.S. resolution. In particular, France's president, Jacques Chirac, stated that he would veto any resolution that would lead to war. On March 16, 2003, President Bush met with foreign leaders who still supported using force to compel Iraq's disarmament, including British Prime Minister Tony Blair. On March 17, Bush gave Saddam Hussein an ultimatum: leave Iraq within forty-eight hours or face war. Hussein remained defiant.

The Second Gulf War—the Invasion of Iraq   On March 20, U.S. and British forces entered Iraq from Kuwait. President Bush secured the support of at least thirty nations (the "coalition of the willing"), but most of the world's nations and peoples opposed the attack. In the following days, U.S. forces seized the highway to Baghdad and advanced rapidly, taking the Baghdad airport on April 4 and the rest of the city in the next five days. On April 6, the British entered the southern metropolis of Basra. Kurdish rebels seized the northern cities of Kirkuk and Mosul on April 10 and 11. By April 14, the war was effectively over. Saddam Hussein's fate was not known, but it was thought that he could have died in a bombardment on April 7.

The United States and Britain deployed about half as many troops in this war as they did in the first Gulf War. Still, Iraqi military units crumbled quickly under air and land attacks. Coalition casualties were light. Several surprises greeted the coalition. Saddam Hussein's Baath Party turned out to have more of an independent life than western observers had assumed, and Baath loyalists intimidated most Iraqis into passivity throughout the war. With the fall of the regime, massive looting and disorder broke out across the country—also an unexpected development. The relatively small number of coalition troops was unable to restore order immediately.

The war's end provoked many debates in the international community about the role of the UN in Iraqi reconstruction. In the United States, an important issue was how quickly power could be handed over to new local authorities in Iraq. After the war, the United States began searching Iraq for weapons of mass destruction.

Arms Control Treaties: Do They Work?

For decades, the diplomatic solution to arms control has been treaties. The United States has been a signatory to a number of weapons treaties, including the Nuclear Test-Ban Treaty, signed in 1963, and the Treaty on the Non-Proliferation of Nuclear Weapons mentioned earlier, signed in 1968.

In recent years, however, doubts have surfaced as to the efficacy of signing arms control treaties. In 1999, the U.S. Senate refused to ratify the Comprehensive Nuclear Test Ban Treaty, which prohibits all nuclear test explosions worldwide. In 2001, President George W. Bush unilaterally pulled out of the 1972 Anti-Ballistic Missile Treaty, which had been part of the SALT I agreement with the former Soviet Union. In a statement in December 2001, Bush explained that the thirty-year-old treaty "hinders our government's ability to develop ways to protect our people from future terrorist or rogue state missile attacks."[10] What is the role of arms control treaties in the war on terrorism, and can treaties really prevent the spread of weapons of mass destruction?

Treaties with the Former Soviet Union

Efforts to end the arms race with the Soviet Union continued even after the collapse of that government in 1991. In 1992, the United States signed the Strategic Arms Reduction Treaty (START I) with four former Soviet republics—Russia, Ukraine, Belarus, and Kazakhstan—to reduce the number of long-range nuclear weapons to about 6,500 each by 2001. A second treaty (START II), signed in 1993, called for these arsenals to be reduced even further—to approximately 3,500 each by 2003. The treaties obligate the two nations to exchange "memorandums of understanding" twice yearly, accounting for their destruction of these weapons. According to a Russian memorandum declassified in 2002, the total number of Russian warheads stands at 5,858, down from about 10,000 in 1992.[11]

Despite the apparent progress, a problem is inherent in the START process. Even though the United States has given the former Soviet Union hundreds of millions of dollars to dismantle parts of the former Soviet arsenal, Russia has resisted U.S. inspection. Therefore, the United States has not been able to monitor what Russian authorities have done with their nuclear warheads. In addition, START II does not cover nonstrategic nuclear weapons.

Biological Weapons Treaties

Biological warfare materials and chemical weapons are considered the poor country's nuclear bombs. While treaties to stop the spread of nuclear weapons have made the headlines, what to do about biological and chemical weapons has generated less concern. Yet, according to Dr. Donald Henderson, director of the Center for Civilian Biodefense Studies at Johns Hopkins University, biological terrorism is much more threatening than explosive or chemical terrorism. Smallpox and anthrax toxins can spread like wildfire, with fatality rates near 80 to 90 percent.[12]

In 1972, more than 130 nations ratified the Biological and Toxins Weapons Convention (BWC), which specifically prohibits the development and production of biological weapons. The treaty outlines no method for monitoring compliance with its provisions, however. Throughout the 1990s, BWC member-states attempted to negotiate a system of compliance. In July 2001, the United States rejected such efforts as ineffective and harmful to U.S. interests. The United States also announced that it would oppose further discussions on amending the BWC until 2006.

By the mid-1990s, at least twenty countries had undertaken military research programs that resulted in the development of biological weapons.[13] Before launching the second Gulf War, the United States presented evidence that Iraq had stockpiled biological warfare agents, including tens of thousands of liters of deadly botulinum and anthrax cultures. Even in the United States, domestic terrorists have been able to obtain cultures of anthrax bacteria and the bacteria that cause bubonic plague. In 2001, unknown terrorists mailed anthrax, in a powder form, to congressional offices and media outlets in the United States, causing the deaths of five people. The terrorists were never caught.

Chemical Weapons Treaties

The Chemical Weapons Convention (CWC), a treaty ratified by the United States in 1997, was intended to abolish all chemical weapons worldwide. According to its critics, however, loopholes and weak enforcement mechanisms may render the CWC less effective than desirable. Specifically, these critics believe that Russia will continue to develop new chemical weapons. Many senators have expressed concern, but the United States does not have the capability to verify other countries' compliance with the CWC. Moreover, according to a national intelligence estimate, the production of new classes of chemical weapons would be difficult to detect and confirm even through a CWC–sponsored investigation.

Iraq is not a signatory of the CWC. It made substantial use of chemical weapons during the Iran-Iraq War (1980–1988) and, in 1988, mounted a massive chemical attack against the Kurdish town of

U.S. ambassador and chief negotiator Donald A. Mahley addresses a group of representatives from nations that signed the Biological Weapons Convention in a session held on July 25, 2001. The United States rejected efforts to negotiate a system of compliance with the terms of the convention, or treaty, having concluded that the efforts were ineffective and harmful to U.S. interests. (AP Photo/Donald Stampfli)

Halabja, killing 5,000 civilians. Under the cease-fire agreement that ended the first Gulf War in 1991, Iraq declared to UN weapons inspectors that it possessed large chemical weapons stockpiles. By mid-1995, inspectors had largely destroyed Iraq's chemical stocks and munitions. Nonetheless, before the start of the second Gulf War in 2003, the United States accused Iraq of secretly storing chemical weapons agents and of rebuilding much of its chemical weapons production infrastructure.

From the start of the second Gulf War in March 2003, U.S. inspectors began a new search for weapons of mass destruction in Iraq. No "smoking gun" turned up during the first month after the war, but the United States remained confident that the search would be successful eventually. "We'll find them, and it's just going to be a matter of time to do so," President Bush said in May.

Members of a mobile exploration team examine a suspected mobile biological weapons facility that was recovered by U.S. forces in northern Iraq in late April 2003. (Department of Defense)

Too Little, Too Late   According to some critics, the U.S. response to the threat of biological and chemical warfare has been too little, too late. While the threat of biological and chemical warfare has increased, the United States has spent very little for research on detection devices, antidotes to germ agents, and protective suits. Because vaccine development takes from ten to twenty years, the United States is not in a position to protect its troops against biowarfare agents, particularly those that have been genetically engineered recently.

Given the relative ineffectiveness of treaties to halt the proliferation of weapons of mass destruction, what can the United States do to protect itself from a nuclear, biological, or chemical weapons attack? In 2003, President Bush made **preemptive war** a key element in the defense of the United States from these weapons. (For a discussion of the policy of preemptive war, see this chapter's *The Politics of Homeland Security* feature on the next page.)

PREEMPTIVE WAR A strategy of striking against an enemy before the enemy is able to launch an attack. It characterizes the foreign policy of the George W. Bush administration in the war on terrorism.

China—The Next Superpower?

China, even more than the former Soviet Union, has the potential to become a genuinely great power. After all, it is a country with a great culture, a great people, and, increasingly, a great economy. Given its impressive record of economic growth and its definite desire to become a superpower, China just may succeed in becoming a superpower in the twenty-first century.

During the late 1990s, Jiang Zemin, the president of China, flew to India to mend fences with an old adversary, went to Pakistan to renew an old friendship, and saw European officials on a regular basis. More important, China undertook civilian and military cooperation in the nuclear arena with Pakistan. The United States has complained vociferously about such nuclear cooperation. China's answer has been, "Mind your own business." The Chinese have also been caught selling sophisticated weapons systems and nuclear technology to Iran and perhaps to other countries. Although China has stated on several occasions that it has not done so and has promised not to do so in the future, the U.S. intelligence community believes that China is still supplying such weapons.

Critics of the Clinton administration (1993–2001) argued that it overlooked virtually everything negative that Beijing did. Those who regularly visit China contend that its leaders have one goal—to overtake the preeminence of the United States in the world arena. Foreign policy observers are worried that the United States will end up with a bipolar relationship similar to its relationship with the Soviet Union after World War II. Unlike the Soviet Union, however, China does not have dreams of territorial conquests (except for Taiwan). That means that relations between the United States and China will be much more multifaceted than relations between the United States and the Soviet Union were. China clearly needs the United States. A third of its exports go to the United States (with only 2 percent of American exports going to China).

Freer World Trade and the WTO

One of the long-term policy goals of the United States and many other nations has been to ease restrictions on international trade. Indeed, multilateral efforts toward creating freer

Does the Threat of Terrorism Justify Preemptive War?

As you have read throughout this chapter, the terrorist attacks of September 11, 2001, placed U.S. foreign policymakers on a new war footing. The old Cold War policies of containment and deterrence needed to be revised to apply to foreign terrorist networks rather than a communist superpower. The notion that had sustained U.S. foreign policy for decades—that the United States would never launch a "first strike" against the Soviet Union—seemed to some to be irrelevant in the war on terrorism. A new policy emerged, that of preemptive war.

The idea of a preemptive strike against Saddam Hussein is not new. In January 1998, eighteen policy analysts sent an open letter to President Bill Clinton arguing that the containment of Iraq was a failure and that removing Saddam Hussein from power should be the aim of U.S. foreign policy.[14] Among the eighteen signers were individuals who became members of the Bush administration: Secretary of Defense Donald Rumsfeld, Deputy Secretary of Defense Paul Wolfowitz, and Deputy Secretary of State Richard Armitage. But, as one senior administration official told the *New York Times*, "Without September 11, we never would have been able to put Iraq at the top of our agenda. It was only then that this president was willing to worry about the unthinkable—that the next attack could be with weapons of mass destruction supplied by Saddam Hussein."[15]

PREEMPTION AND WEAPONS PROLIFERATION

The United Nations Charter allows a country to act in self-defense. In the war on terrorism, many U.S. policymakers today have concluded that this should include *anticipatory* self-defense. For example, in 1962 the United States acted preemptively in the Cuban missile crisis by imposing a naval blockade of Cuba. Israel acted preemptively in 1967 when it attacked Egypt, Syria, and Jordan. Before that war began, Israel's neighbors had amassed troops on its borders, leading Israel to conclude that an attack was imminent. In 2003, many officials in the United States, Britain, Spain, Italy, Australia, and elsewhere saw the threat by Saddam Hussein as clearly "imminent."

Even when the threat of attack is not imminent, however, preemption may be desirable because the style of deterrence used in the Cold War will not work against madmen. If terrorist groups are bent on the destruction of the United States, no degree of political pressure or economic sanctions will deter them.

PREEMPTION POSES A MORAL DILEMMA

Thomas Jefferson once said of the United States, "We love and we value peace; we know its blessings from experience."[16] Attacking a nation without clear evidence that it is about to attack us is not consistent with American values of peace, freedom, and justice. In September 2002, as Congress prepared to debate authorizing military force against Iraq, Representative Ron Paul (R., Tex.) clearly outlined the moral dilemma presented by preemptive war:

> Naked aggression is the province of dictators and rogue states. This is the danger of a new "preemptive first strike" doctrine. America is the most moral nation on earth, founded on moral principles, and we must apply moral principles when deciding to use military force.[17]

Moreover, when we engage in a preemptive attack, such action is illegal under the United Nations Charter, which we agreed to follow as a UN member. We thus risk alienating many of our allies, who see our action as a violation of international law.

Are We Safer?

Do you think that pursuing a policy of preemptive war against "rogue" nations will help prevent terrorists from obtaining and using weapons of mass destruction?

MOST-FAVORED-NATION (MFN) STATUS A status granted by a clause in an international treaty. Generally, most-favored-nation clauses are designed to establish equality of international treatment. For example, if the United States and the People's Republic of China have agreed in a treaty that each country will have MFN status with respect to international trade, then the United States must treat China at least as well as the country receiving the most favorable treatment from the United States and vice versa.

international trade were first initiated in 1947, with the formation of the General Agreement on Tariffs and Trade (GATT). From then on, countries that had signed the agreement met periodically to negotiate reductions in tariffs (taxes on imports). At the final meeting of GATT members in 1994, the World Trade Organization (WTO) was launched—and replaced GATT.

The establishment of the WTO will ultimately result in tariff reductions of over 40 percent worldwide. The WTO also established an arbitration panel to deal with international disputes over trade issues. Each member nation of the WTO also agreed to grant **most-favored-nation (MFN) status** to every other member nation—meaning that no country can discriminate against any other with respect to trade privileges.

Human Rights and the WTO

In recent years, the WTO has come under attack by human rights activists because WTO member nations must allow favorable trade status to other member nations without regard to their policies on human rights. For example, in the past, the United States often threatened to

CARLSON © 1997 *Milwaukee Journal-Sentinel*. Reprinted by permission of UNIVERSAL PRESS SYNDICATE. All rights reserved.

withdraw China's MFN status unless that country improved its human rights record. In the end, though, the United States always caved in and granted an additional year of such status, thereby benefiting the Chinese export sector. In 2000, the Clinton administration and Congress agreed to grant China *permanent* MFN status so that China could join the WTO.

Supporters of the decision to grant China permanent MFN status argued that increased trade with China may ultimately bring about political and social change in that country. Greater economic freedom for the Chinese may help to loosen the Chinese government's control of its citizens. Human rights groups, in contrast, claimed that the United States, by this action, was essentially giving its stamp of approval to the Chinese government's oppression of its citizens' rights.

AMERICA at odds

Globalization—Good, Bad, or Indifferent?

Globalization, the diffusion of commodities and ideas on a global scale, has been accelerated by the increased use of the Internet to communicate and conduct business. Globalization has fostered a certain degree of cultural homogenization. Whether this is good or bad, most scholars agree that it is the inevitable result of increased global commerce. Globalization is also associated with Americanization—American movies, TV shows, clothing styles, music, and food have invaded every nation to some degree.

Most labor unions oppose globalization, arguing that as restrictions on world trade are lifted, American companies are moving their plants to other nations where they can find cheaper labor. As a result, the demand for American workers—particularly relatively high-paid union workers—is decreasing. Also opposed to globalization are a number of groups that believe that corporate profits have taken priority over human rights and environmental health. Members of several of these groups participated in demonstrations against the WTO at its conference in Seattle in 1999. Although most large businesses support globalization (because they have offices, plants, and workers all over the world), some businesses are against globalization. They have experienced lower profits because of increased competition from abroad.

Because freer international trade has led to lower prices for many consumer goods, consumers in general favor increased globalization. Yet consumers are also employees, some of whom are in unions. Consumers are also shareholders in corporations, some of which are harmed by international competition. Although Republicans have generally favored increased globalization, George W. Bush chose in 2002 to increase tariffs on lower-cost steel imports, thus protecting the American steel industry. Globalization is clearly a complex issue with which Americans will be struggling for many years to come.

Should We Keep Supporting the United Nations?

The United Nations (UN) is now more than fifty years old. It was put together at the end of World War II to promote international cooperation and world peace. Fifty-one nations signed its original charter. Today, it has 191 member states. Its six principal organs are (1) the General Assembly, (2) the Security Council, (3) the Economic and Social Council, (4) the Trusteeship Council, (5) the International Court of Justice (World Court), and (6) the Secretariat. The Secretariat is the administrative body of the organization and has more than 8,500 employees. Not counting the UN's 10,000 consultants and its peacekeeping forces, more than 64,500 people work for the UN.

The diplomatic crisis in 2002 and 2003 over disarming Iraq renewed ongoing debates over the future of the UN. Numerous critics, both in the United States and elsewhere, argue that it is inefficient and ineffective.

Criticisms of the UN

Conservatives on the far right of the political spectrum, such as Pat Buchanan, tend to portray the UN as a central player in an international conspiracy to deprive U.S. citizens of their national rights and liberties. Even conservatives who are not so "conspiracy minded" have argued that UN budgets are shrouded in secrecy and that there is a total lack of accountability. They point out that UN administrators are unwilling to undergo a thorough outside audit. Consequently, many political conservatives believe that the UN needs to be drastically downsized, and not just reformed. Some have suggested that many of the agencies could be privatized.

Critics of the UN also point out that the General Assembly has been dominated by non-Western nations whose political cultures are at odds with the democratic West. These non-

The General Assembly of the United Nations (UN) is composed of representatives of all of the member nations of that body. Each nation is entitled to one vote. On the most important questions, a two-thirds majority vote of those present is required. For other questions, a simple majority vote is sufficient. The name *United Nations* was coined by President Franklin D. Roosevelt in 1941. The term was first used officially on January 1, 1942, when twenty-six nations pledged, in a Declaration by the United Nations, to continue their joint war efforts against Germany, Italy, and Japan and not to make peace separately. The UN Charter was drawn up at a conference held in San Francisco in 1945. (© Wally McNamee/CORBIS)

Secretary of Defense Donald H. Rumsfeld tries to explain the role of UN weapons inspectors to reporters during a Pentagon press briefing on January 15, 2003. Rumsfeld said, "They're not in there to discover things and find things—they're in there to inspect things that the Iraqi government decides to disclose to them." (Department of Defense photo/R. D. Ward)

Western states typically support antimarket economics. Most factions in the General Assembly have often voted against the United States. Additionally, the member nations of the UN have diverse views on such issues as human rights and nuclear proliferation. Because of conflicting political cultures, the UN is often unable to reach consensus on what action should be undertaken in a given situation.

UN Successes

Certainly, many who consider themselves political liberals agree that the UN should undergo reform. A significant group, though, believes that the UN is definitely worth saving. Until the second Gulf War, the United States had been very successful in using the UN as a tool for American diplomacy. The UN has also promoted free trade and helped cultivate democracy in such places as Mozambique.

The payment that the United States is supposed to make to the UN each year is equal to the annualized cost of a single aircraft carrier battle group. That is not very much for the benefits we receive, according to supporters of the UN today. When the United States intervenes along with the UN, we pay less than 30 percent of the cost, and other nations provide most of the troops. Also, U.S. firms provide a significant portion of the goods and services the UN buys, so those purchases generate increases in income in the United States.

UN missions have achieved some great successes, including the World Health Organization's $30 million investment in eradicating smallpox worldwide, which was completed by 1977. Prior to that year, the United States alone spent $350 million a year on immunizations against that disease. Nonetheless, the failure of diplomacy and the UN weapons inspection process in Iraq in 2003 put the UN's future in some doubt.

why does it MATTER?

Foreign Policy and Your Everyday Life

It may seem strange that during a time when the United States is the only superpower left, foreign policy could actually affect your everyday life. But it does, in many ways, some of them subtle and some of them not. The size of our defense budget is a function of foreign policy, and that affects you in many ways.

Spending on Defense

If the nation's policymakers and the president believe that our national security is threatened, more federal dollars will be spent on defense. This is certainly what happened after the terrorist attacks of September 11, 2001. The war on terrorism, including the use of military forces in Afghanistan and Iraq, meant that a larger percentage of the federal budget had to go toward defense. That means that less money is being spent on other government programs, many of which may affect you.

Privacy Is an Issue

The more our foreign policy focuses on controlling terrorism worldwide, the more your day-to-day privacy may be invaded. Currently, the National Security Agency routinely monitors calls to foreign nations, without first obtaining search warrants. Because of the war on terrorism, the federal government has implemented a system to "eavesdrop" on e-mail transmissions. Because e-mail has become pervasive in the majority of Americans' everyday lives, such actual or potential invasions of privacy have become an everyday issue.

Foreign Policy Also Involves Foreign Trade

Part of U.S. foreign policy involves attempts to make world trade freer. The passage of the North American Free Trade Agreement in 1993 and U.S. participation in the World Trade Organization affect your daily life quite directly—you have a wider choice of

foreign goods to purchase, and those goods are sold to you at lower prices.

Taking Action

Many Americans took action to participate in the foreign policy decisions involving the U.S. war in Iraq in 2003. Often, this participation took the form of protests against the war. Indeed, some Americans even went to Baghdad, Iraq, to act as "human shields" in a protest against the U.S.–led war with that nation. The group going to Baghdad included volunteers from France, Britain, Spain, the United States, Italy, Denmark, Belgium, Germany, Switzerland, and Australia. One of these volunteers was Max Salamander of San Francisco. In the photo above, Salamander, shown with his back to the camera, is being hugged by a colleague in Amman, Jordan. (AP Photo/Jamal Nasrallah)

Key Terms

coalition 383

Cold War 379

collective security 379

colonial empire 377

Communist bloc 378

containment 379

Cuban missile crisis 379

détente 380

deterrence 379

foreign policy 373

interventionism 377

iron curtain 378

isolationism 376

Marshall Plan 378

Monroe Doctrine 377

most-favored-nation (MFN) status 390

multilateral 383

mutually assured destruction (MAD) 379

neutrality 377

preemptive war 389

unilateral 383

weapons of mass destruction (WMDs) 384

Western bloc 379

Chapter Summary

1 Foreign policy includes all of the economic, military, commercial, and diplomatic positions and actions that a nation takes in its relationships with other countries. U.S. foreign policy has been guided by both moral idealism and the need to protect our national security.

2 As commander in chief, the president oversees the military and guides defense policy. The president's cabinet, particularly the secretary of state and the secretary of defense, assist the president in foreign policy, as do a number of agencies, including the National Security Council and the Central Intelligence Agency. Congress also plays a significant role in foreign policy.

3 Early U.S. political leaders felt that the best way to protect American interests was through isolationism—avoiding political involvement with other nations. The Spanish-American War of 1898 marked the first true step toward interventionism. By the end of the nineteenth century, the United States had acquired a colonial empire and was acknowledged as a world power.

4 After World War I, the United States again returned to an isolationist foreign policy, which lasted until the Japanese attacked Pearl Harbor in 1941 and the United States entered World War II. The United States emerged from the war as a superpower, along with the Soviet Union. From the late 1940s until the early 1990s, the United States and the Soviet Union engaged in the Cold War—a war of words, threats and warnings, and ideologies. The collapse of the Soviet Union in 1991 brought about the end of the Cold War.

5 Since the end of the Cold War, the greatest threat to the United States has been international terrorism. The terrorist attacks on September 11, 2001, put the United States on the offensive against foreign terrorist networks and rogue nations. The war on terrorism presents the United States with several dilemmas, particularly the extent to which it can act alone or should rely on multilateral cooperation.

6 Reducing the threat presented by nuclear arsenals and the proliferation of other weapons of mass destruction is another challenge to today's political leaders. Although nations, including the United States, have attempted to control arms proliferation through a system of international treaties, the treaties contain few provisions for monitoring compliance. The failure of weapons inspections to contain Iraq's nuclear, chemical, and biological weapons programs led to war and a regime change in that nation in 2003. Preemptive war to halt weapons proliferation is now accepted by many as part of American foreign policy.

7 The establishment of the World Trade Organization (WTO) in 1994 was a significant step in the international effort to reduce tariffs and promote freer trade. The WTO has been controversial because, among other things, member nations are required to grant favorable trading privileges to all other member nations without regard to their human rights records. Some believe that the WTO should impose human rights and environmental requirements on member nations.

8 The United Nations (UN) was created after World War II to promote international cooperation and world peace. One of the issues being debated by Americans today is whether we should keep supporting the UN.

RESOURCES FOR FURTHER STUDY

Selected Readings

Kolko, Gabriel. *Another Century of War?* New York: New Press, 2002. The author, a historian of war, provides a candid and critical look at American foreign policy and presents an assessment of whether this policy offers any hope of attaining greater security for America.

Nye, Joseph S., Jr. *The Paradox of American Power: Why the World's Only Superpower Can't Go It Alone.* New York: Oxford University Press, 2002. The author, dean of Harvard's Kennedy School of Government and former assistant secretary of defense, argues that unless the United States cooperates with the international community, its ability to lead the world will be damaged.

Telhami, Shibley. *The Stakes: America and the Middle East.* Boulder, Colo.: Westview Press, 2002. In this insightful study, the author explains how and why the United States is often viewed as arrogant, self-indulgent, and hypocritical by many in the Arab and Muslim worlds, and why military victories alone will not eliminate the Islamic terrorist threat.

Woodward, Bob. *Bush at War.* New York: Simon & Schuster, 2002. Veteran journalist and investigative reporter Bob Woodward offers a close-up, day-by-day account of decision making by the Bush administration during the three months following the terrorist attacks of September 11, 2001.

InfoTrac Citations

Using your InfoTrac password, access the InfoTrac database at **http://infotrac.thomsonlearning.com**. Once at the site, you can do "key word" searches to locate the following articles, each of which deals with a topic covered in this chapter. The key words to use in your search are indicated in parentheses.

- "Bush Tells United Nations to Show 'Backbone'" (Bush United Nations)

- "Bush Accuses Syria of Harboring Weapons, Iraqi Leaders" (Bush Syria)

- "Ran-goons: Why Isn't Burma on Bush's 'Axis of Evil' List?" (Bush Axis of Evil)

- "'A Work in Progress': Bush's NAFTA Decision to Open U.S. Border Will Mean Profits 'Manana,' but Not Right Now" (Bush Free Trade)

Politics on the Web

You can find news about international events at an interesting Web site sponsored by the Institute for International Economics. You can also get access to the group's working papers at **http://www.iie.com**

- To learn more about national security policy and defense issues, you can go to the U.S. Department of Defense's DefenseLINK site at **http://www.defenselink.mil**

- For information on the U.S. Department of State and its activities, go to **http://www.state.gov**

- If you are interested in U.S. intelligence and terrorism, go to **http://www.spystuff.com/terrorism.html**

- The Global Legal Information Network (GLIN) provides a database of national laws from countries around the world via the Web server of the U.S. Library of Congress. The site consists of more than 54,000 records of legislation enacted from 1976 to the present. To access this site, go to **http://loc.gov/glin/law/guide/nations.html**

- The World Bank's home page offers a wealth of information on international development, research studies containing economic data on various countries, and the like. Go to **http://www.worldbank.org**

- For worldwide news, an excellent site to visit is **http://www.start4all.com**

- The Washburn University Law School and Virtual Law Reference Desk offers, among other things, extensive information on international affairs, including United Nations materials. To access this site, go to **http://washlaw.edu**

Web Resources on Your CD-ROM

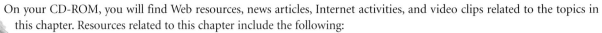

On your CD-ROM, you will find Web resources, news articles, Internet activities, and video clips related to the topics in this chapter. Resources related to this chapter include the following:
- **Values Inventory**—Political Ideology: Should the United States Be the Global Cop?
- **Why Does It Matter?**—Shape Opinion on Foreign Policy with a Letter to an Editor.
- **Updates**—Keep up with the issues in this chapter!
- **Web Resources**—Internet Activities: The U.S., Iraq, and the World Policeman Role; Support for U.S. Unilateralism.
- **Where Do You Stand?**—Dialogue: Should the United States Be the Global Cop?
- **Comparative Politics**—Europe and Foreign Policy.
- **NewsEdge**—Visit this global resource for current events related to this chapter.

chapter 17
state and local politics

CHAPTER OBJECTIVES

After reading this chapter, you should be able to . . .

▶ Summarize some of the differences between state constitutions and the U.S. Constitution.

▶ Describe some of the characteristics of state legislatures and some of the powers that are commonly exercised by state governors.

▶ Define the terms *initiative, referendum,* and *recall* and discuss their use by various states.

▶ Delineate the typical structure of state court systems.

▶ Discuss the primary sources of state and local government revenues.

Are Ballot Initiatives Good for Our Democracy?

Ballot initiatives are viewed as the most obvious form of direct democracy available to Americans today. Voter initiatives have been around since the nineteenth century. In California, the voter initiative was first used in 1911, but it did not become popular until the last few decades.

Today, a number of states use voter initiatives to determine a large variety of issues. Initiatives have been placed on state ballots to legalize physician-assisted suicide, make English the official language of a state, reject bilingual education, deny equal marital rights to same-sex couples, lower property taxes, require drug treatment as opposed to incarceration for nonviolent minor drug offenses, control the sale of guns, liberalize drug laws, and ban cockfighting.

Some believe that we should continue this trend toward allowing voters to participate directly in democracy. Others believe that voter initiatives are undermining our representative government.

Voter Initiatives—The More the Merrier

Those in favor of direct democracy, as opposed to representative democracy, feel that the use of voter initiatives should be supported and indeed expanded across the United States. In their view, initiatives are a way to allow individuals to have a say in their government and participate in important decisions that directly affect their lives. Proponents argue that voter initiatives are a backlash against a political system that rarely, if ever, represents the will of the people. While voter participation in all elections has dropped, the popularity of initiatives has risen. This is no accident. Citizens rightfully mistrust what they see as a very complicated lawmaking system that is too heavily influenced by wealthy special interests.

In the last several years, a number of states have taken steps to make it harder to place initiatives on the ballot. Such efforts are clear proof that politicians are afraid of initiatives.

The more the people can directly participate in government, the better.

Stop the Nonsense—We Chose a Representative Government over Two Hundred Years Ago

Many other Americans argue that the extensive use of ballot initiatives threatens our representative form of government. They contend that the framers chose representative democracy rather than direct democracy for a reason—to avoid the

tyranny of the majority. They point out that initiatives often result in conflicting policies and sometimes in bad law. They also point to the absurdity of overwhelming voters with too many ballot initiatives. In a recent election, Oregonians faced twenty-six initiatives. The state sent each voter a 376-page guide describing these initiatives. Who is going to read all of that? As one Oregonian voter put it, "It's totally confusing to me. I'm not even sure if a 'yes' vote really means 'yes' or 'no.'"

Although ballot initiatives may originally have been a vehicle to express populist outrage, today they are something quite different. They are the favorite short cut for corporations, well-financed activists, and billionaires to get what they want at the expense of others. These rich people have good reason to be so interested in the initiative process—about 40 percent of all ballot initiatives become law. The process is not cheap, though. Gathering the tens or hundreds of thousands of voter signatures needed to get an initiative on the ballot costs money. Professional groups are often paid to do the actual work. Consider one example in Washington State. Microsoft co-founder Paul Allen agreed to buy the Seattle Seahawks football team only if voters would authorize a $425 million publicly financed football stadium and exhibition hall. He spent over $6 million to gather signatures and buy ads.

Finally, voter initiatives bypass the normal research and deliberation that legislators undertake before they enact new laws. In addition, perhaps more important, voter initiatives enable the legislature to avoid facing many tough issues.

Where Do You Stand?

1. If you could ban voter initiatives and allow your elected representatives to make all legislative decisions, would you do so? Why or why not?

2. If you found out that a voter initiative in your state required millions of dollars in financing to get on the ballot, would you be upset?

Interacting with Your CD-ROM Resources

Use your CD-ROM to access resources on the Web, simulations, participation exercises, and video clips. Important resources related to this feature include:

- **Values Inventory**—Political Ideology: Are Ballot Initiatives Good for Our Democracy?
- **Where Do You Stand?**—Dialogue: Are Ballot Initiatives Good for Our Democracy?
- **Web Resources**—Internet Activities: 2002 Ballot Initiatives; The Council of State Governments' Commentary on the 2002 Ballot Initiatives.

INTRODUCTION

The resolution of independence passed on July 2, 1776, states that "These United Colonies are, and of right ought to be, free and independent States." In many ways, the states are independent: each has its own constitution and its own legislative, executive, and judicial branches. In 1787, when our federal system of government was created, the original thirteen colonies were included as "states" in that system. Also included in the American government system were the many local units of government that existed at that time. Since then, other states, cities, and local units of government have been created. The process has not yet ended: more local government units are still being created, while others are being eliminated.

State and local governments play a vital role in the American political system. State constitutions and other laws can tailor government operations and services to meet the needs of a particular state's residents. Numerous policy choices are made at the state and local levels, including choices made by the people themselves to place citizens' initiatives on the ballot— a topic covered in this chapter's opening feature. Many Americans, when they think of government, think of local government units and the services they provide. This is understandable, for local government actions and services are the most pervasive in our daily lives. To understand how state and local governments function in the United States, the best place to start is at the constitutional level.

INTRASTATE COMMERCE Commerce that takes place within state borders. State governments have the power to regulate intrastate commerce.

The U.S. Constitution and the State Constitutions

The U.S. Constitution never explicitly defines the powers of the states; rather, the Tenth Amendment to the Constitution states that the powers not delegated to the national government by the Constitution "are reserved to the States respectively, or to the people." The major reserved powers of the states include the power to regulate **intrastate commerce** (commerce *within* a state) and to exercise police powers. A state's police powers, as discussed in Chapter 3, refer to the state's right to pass and enforce laws in the areas of public safety, health, welfare, and morality.

Opponents of rewriting Alabama's constitution (the nation's longest) gathered on the steps of the state supreme court in 2001 to hear critics of constitutional revision speak. The opponents voiced fears that the foundation of state government was about to be broken, with God thrown out and more taxes and gambling brought in. (AP Photo/Kevin Glackmeyer)

State Constitutions Are Long

The U.S. Constitution is a model of brevity: it consists of only about 7,000 words. State constitutions, however, are typically models of excessive length and detail. Alabama's constitution, which contains 220,000 words, is the longest. Only one state constitution—that of Vermont, which has 6,880 words—is shorter than the U.S. Constitution.

Many Constitutional Changes In contrast to the U.S. Constitution, which has only twenty-seven amendments, many state constitutions have hundreds of amendments. The Texas Constitution, for example, has been amended 409 times. The South Carolina Constitution has 483 amendments. The Alabama Constitution tops the list with 706 amendments. Additionally, whereas the U.S. Constitution has endured for over two hundred years, many states have rewritten their constitutions several times. Louisiana has had eleven constitutions; Georgia has had ten; South Carolina has had seven; Alabama, Florida, and Virginia have had six each; and Texas has had five.

Reasons for Lengthy State Constitutions
The length and mass of detail of many state constitutions reflect the loss of popular confidence in state legislatures between the end of the Civil War and the early 1900s. During that period, forty-two states adopted or revised their constitutions. Constitutions that were adopted before or after that period are shorter and contain fewer restrictions on the powers of state legislatures.

An equally important reason for the length and detail of state constitutions is that the framers of state constitutions have had a difficult time distinguishing between constitutional law and statutory law. (Remember from Chapter 14 that statutory law is law made by legislatures, such as the U.S. Congress or the legislatures of the various states.) Many laws that are clearly statutory in nature have been put into state constitutions.

For example, South Dakota's state constitution has a provision authorizing the establishment of a cordage and twine plant at the state penitentiary. The Texas Constitution includes a pay schedule for state legislators. The Alabama Constitution includes an amendment establishing the "Alabama Heritage Trust Fund." A provision of the California Constitution discusses the tax-exempt status of the Huntington Library and Art Gallery. In New York, the width of ski trails in state parks is a constitutional matter. Obviously, the U.S. Constitution contains no such details. It leaves to Congress the nuts-and-bolts activity of making specific statutory laws.

Amending State Constitutions

Like the U.S. Constitution, most state constitutions can be amended through a process involving amendment proposal and ratification.

Proposing a Constitutional Amendment
Generally, a state constitutional amendment may be proposed in one of three ways: by legislative activity, by a constitutional convention, or by popular demand. Most commonly, amendments are proposed by the legislature. All states authorize their legislatures to propose constitutional amendments. Usually, an **extraordinary majority** of votes—typically two-thirds or three-fifths of the total number of legislators—is required to propose an amendment. In some states, a proposed amendment has to be passed in two successive sessions of the legislature.

A second method of proposing an amendment to a state constitution is by holding a state constitutional convention. On about 250 occasions, states have called constitutional conventions either to write new constitutions or to amend existing ones. This is not surprising, because four-fifths of all state constitutions expressly allow for such conventions. Some states, such as Illinois, New York, Ohio, and Michigan, require that constitutional conventions be called periodically to consider whether changes are needed and, if so, to propose them. Figure 17–1 shows how a constitutional convention must be called in each of the states.

Finally, some states provide that a constitutional amendment may be proposed by the citizens in what is known as an **initiative**—a procedure by which voters propose a new law or constitutional amendment. Eighteen states (Arizona, Arkansas, California, Colorado, Florida, Illinois, Massachusetts, Michigan, Mississippi, Missouri, Montana, Nebraska, Nevada, North Dakota, Ohio, Oklahoma, Oregon, and South Dakota) permit the use of the initiative to propose constitutional amendments. The constitutional initiative allows citizens to place a proposed amendment on the ballot without calling a constitutional convention. The number of signatures required to get a constitutional initiative on the ballot varies from state to state, but it is usually between 5 and 10 percent of the total number of votes cast in the last gubernatorial election. The use of the initiative is an example of direct democracy, as you read earlier in the chapter-opening *America at Odds* feature.

Ratification of a Constitutional Amendment
No matter which method of proposing an amendment is used, all of the states except Delaware require an amendment to be ratified by a majority of the voters in a general election. (To be ratified in Delaware, a constitutional amendment must receive a two-thirds vote by the state legislature in two consecutive sessions.) Generally, amendment proposals coming from the legislature are adopted far more often than those that originate by an initiative.

EXTRAORDINARY MAJORITY More than a mere majority; typically, an extraordinary majority consists of two-thirds or three-fifths of the voting body (such as a legislature).

INITIATIVE A procedure by which voters can propose a change in state and local laws, including state constitutions, by means of gathering signatures on a petition and submitting it to the legislature (and/or the voters) for approval.

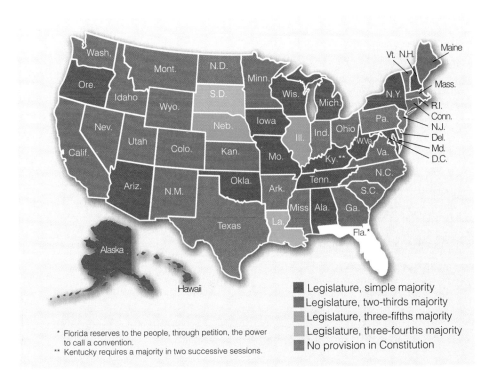

FIGURE 17-1
Provisions for Calling State Constitutional Conventions

Legislature, simple majority
Legislature, two-thirds majority
Legislature, three-fifths majority
Legislature, three-fourths majority
No provision in Constitution

* Florida reserves to the people, through petition, the power to call a convention.
** Kentucky requires a majority in two successive sessions.

Legislatures and Legislators

During the early years of the American republic, the legislative branch of state government clearly was more important than the executive and judicial branches. Most state constitutions mention the legislative branch first. It was initially regarded as the primary method for putting state constitutional law into action. Today, however, state legislatures have lost much of their glow. Many governors—the states' chief executives—have emerged as the leaders of the people in political affairs. Nonetheless, state legislatures remain important forces in state politics and state governmental decision making. The task of these assemblies is to develop and pass laws on such matters as taxes, regulation of business and commerce, and funding for school systems and welfare payments. Allocation of state funds and program priorities are vital issues to residents and communities in every state.

Elements of a Typical State Legislature

All state legislatures, except for that of Nebraska, are bicameral—that is, they consist of two chambers. The size of state legislatures varies dramatically. Alaska has 40 members in its lower house, Delaware has 41, and Nevada has 42; but Pennsylvania has 203, and New Hampshire has 400.[1] There is less diversity in the states' upper houses. These range from 20 seats in Alaska to 67 in Minnesota.[2]

Characteristics of State Legislators

State legislators have been criticized as being less professional and less qualified than the members of the U.S. Congress. The reality is that most state legislators are paid relatively little and given relatively few resources with which to work. A number of states pay their legislators less than $15,000 per year. Table 17–1 on the next page shows how well your state's legislators are paid relative to legislators in other states.

The low salaries for state legislators are partly explained by the fact that whereas members of the U.S. Congress have regular, year-round jobs as congressmen or congresswomen, most state legislators serve actively for erratic periods—full-time for a few months and at odd times

TABLE 17-1
Characteristics of State Legislatures

	Seats in Senate	Length of Term	Seats in House	Length of Term	Years Sessions Are Held	Salary*
Alabama	35	4	105	4	Annual	$10(d)†
Alaska	20	4	40	2	Annual	24,012†
Arizona	30	2	60	2	Annual	24,000
Arkansas	35	4	100	2	Odd	12,796†
California	40	4	80	2	Even	99,000†
Colorado	35	4	65	2	Annual	30,000†
Connecticut	36	2	151	2	Annual	28,000
Delaware	21	4	41	2	Annual	33,400
Florida	40	4	120	2	Annual	27,900†
Georgia	56	2	180	2	Annual	16,200†
Hawaii	25	4	51	2	Annual	32,000†
Idaho	35	2	70	2	Annual	16,646†
Illinois	59	‡	118	2	Annual	55,788†
Indiana	50	4	100	2	Annual	11,600†
Iowa	50	4	100	2	Annual	20,758†
Kansas	40	4	125	2	Annual	76(d)†
Kentucky	38	4	100	2	Even	158(d)†
Louisiana	39	4	105	4	Annual	16,800†
Maine	35	2	151	2	Even	10,815$
Maryland	47	4	141	4	Annual	31,509†
Massachusetts	40	2	160	2	Annual	50,123†
Michigan	38	4	110	2	Annual	77,400†
Minnesota	67	4	134	2	Odd	31,140†
Mississippi	52	4	122	4	Annual	10,000†
Missouri	34	4	163	2	Annual	31,561†
Montana	50	4	100	2	Odd	72(d)†
Nebraska"	49	4	—	—	Annual	12,000†
Nevada	21	4	42	2	Odd	130(d)†
New Hampshire	24	2	400	2	Annual	200(b)
New Jersey	40	4	80	2	Annual	35,000
New Mexico	42	4	70	2	Annual	—†
New York	61	2	150	2	Annual	79,500†
North Carolina	50	2	120	2	Odd	13,951†
North Dakota	49	4	98	4	Odd	111(d)†
Ohio	33	4	99	2	Annual	51,674
Oklahoma	48	4	101	2	Annual	38,400†
Oregon	30	4	60	2	Odd	15,396†
Pennsylvania	50	4	203	2	Annual	61,889†
Rhode Island	50	2	100	2	Annual	11,236
South Carolina	46	4	124	2	Annual	10,400†
South Dakota	35	2	70	2	Annual	12,000#
Tennessee	33	4	99	2	Odd	16,500†
Texas	31	4	150	2	Odd	7,200†
Utah	29	4	75	2	Annual	120(d)†
Vermont	30	2	150	2	Odd	536(w)
Virginia	40	4	100	2	Annual	18,000~
Washington	49	4	98	2	Annual	32,064†
West Virginia	34	4	100	2	Annual	15,000†
Wisconsin	33	4	99	2	Annual	44,333†
Wyoming	30	4	60	2	Annual	125(d)†

*Salaries annual unless otherwise noted as (d)—per day, or (b)—biennium, or (w)—per week.
†Plus *per diem* living expenses.
‡Terms vary from two to four years.
$For odd year; $7,500 for even year.
"Unicameral legislature.
#For two years.
~For members of the Senate (members of the House receive $17,640). Members of both chambers also receive *per diem* living expenses.

SOURCE: Adapted from Council of State Governments, *The Book of the States, 2002–2003* (Lexington, Ky.: Council of State Governments, 2002).

for the remainder of their terms. Consequently, state legislators often have other jobs and look on their legislative duties as a sideline. In some states, including California and New York, the trend is toward making the job of legislator a full-time and adequately paid position and toward providing funds for professional staff and research assistants to help the legislators.

About 40 percent of all state legislators are either lawyers or farmers; many others are business executives. The majority (about three-fourths) of state legislators have a college education. Most state legislators, after serving their terms, either resume their previously held jobs in the private sector or seek other employment in government. In other words, state legislators have a higher rate of turnover than members of the U.S. Congress, who often have lengthy careers.

Terms of State Legislators and Term Limits

As you can see in Table 17–1 on the facing page, legislators serve either two-year or four-year terms. As with the U.S. Congress, state senators are often elected for longer terms than are state representatives. In all but five states—Alabama, Louisiana, Maryland, Mississippi, and North Dakota—representatives are chosen for two-year terms. In any given year, more than 25 percent of the 7,500 state legislators in the country are serving their first term in office.

Many citizens welcome a high turnover rate in their legislatures. Their reasoning is that newer members in a state legislature are more closely attuned to the wishes of their constituents than are legislators who have served for several terms and who tend to view politics as a career. This reasoning underlies the movement toward term limits. At least twenty-four states now limit the terms of their state legislators. Some of these states limit senators to two four-year terms, while representatives in the lower house may serve three two-year terms. Other states impose different limits, such as restricting the terms of all legislators to a total of eight years. The requirements vary from state to state.

Until 1995, many state laws also imposed term limits on members of the U.S. Congress. A Supreme Court decision in 1995, however, held that such limits were unconstitutional because the U.S. Constitution says nothing about limiting the terms of U.S. senators and representatives. The Court stated that the only way term limits can be imposed on national legislators is through an amendment to the U.S. Constitution.[3] Supporters of term limits continue to push for such an amendment.

Direct Democracy

Lawmaking is somewhat different at the state level than it is at the national level. Many states exercise a type of direct democracy through the initiative, the referendum, and the recall—procedures that allow voters to control the government directly. Direct democracy at the state level was first instituted in Oregon before the 1920s. Remember from Chapter 1 that a form of direct democracy emerged in America at an early time in New England town meetings and continues to exist there. (But see this chapter's *Perception versus Reality* feature on the next page for a candid look at how democratic these meetings really were.)

The Initiative

The *initiative* lets citizens themselves propose new laws for the voters' approval. As already mentioned, a number of states now allow the use of the initiative. Eighteen states allow constitutional amendments to be proposed by initiative. Twenty-four states allow the initiative to be used for proposing new statutory laws. This type of initiative is called the *legislative initiative*. As with constitutional initiatives, most states require that a legislative initiative's backers circulate a petition to place the measure on the ballot. A certain percentage of the registered voters in the last gubernatorial election must sign the petition. If enough signatures are obtained, the issue is put on the ballot.

There are two types of initiatives—direct and indirect. A *direct initiative* goes directly on the ballot to be decided by popular vote. An *indirect initiative* goes first to the state legislature.

If the legislature passes the initiative, the measure becomes law and does not go on the ballot. If the legislature does not pass the initiative, the measure is placed on the ballot, and the voters decide the issue.

The Referendum

REFERENDUM A form of direct democracy in which legislative or constitutional measures are proposed by a legislature and then presented to the voters for approval.

The **referendum** is similar to the initiative, except that the issue (or constitutional change) is proposed first by the legislature and then directed to the voters for their approval. Whereas all of the states except Alabama currently provide for the use of the referendum for constitutional changes, only twenty-three states allow changes to statutory law through referenda.

The referendum is often used at the local level to approve local school bond issues and at the state level to amend state constitutions. In a number of states that provide for the referendum, a bill passed by the legislature may be "put on hold" by obtaining petitions with the required number of signatures from voters who oppose it. A statewide referendum election is then held, and if the majority of the voters disapprove of the bill, it is no longer valid.

Initially, the referendum was not intended for regular use. Indeed, it was used infrequently in the past. Its opponents argue that it is an unnecessary check on representative government and that it weakens legislative responsibility. Nonetheless, in recent years, the referendum has become increasingly popular as citizens have attempted to control their state and local governments. Interest groups have been active in sponsoring the petition drives necessary to force a referendum.

perception versus REALITY

Direct Democracy in Early American New England Towns

In the last decade or so, there have been a number of efforts—by historians, political scientists, and other scholars—to penetrate the screen of American mythology to discern "what really happened" in the past. Recently, in his book *The Good Citizen: A History of American Civic Life,*[4] historian Michael Schudson took a close look at New England town meetings and came up with a "reality" that is far different from the usual perception of what happened at those meetings.

THE PERCEPTION

In the early days of this nation, settlers in the New England area organized local governing units called towns. As used here, the word *town* is not just another term for a small community or city. Rather, it is a political unit similar to the county in other regions of America and typically comprises one or more urban communities and their outlying rural areas. Political decisions were made, just as they are today, in *town meetings* attended by the town's residents. Town meetings have often been described as forums for direct democracy, in which all residents could come to the town hall and vote on what taxes would be levied, who should be elected to serve as the town's leaders, what laws should be enacted, and so on.

Although few residents turn out for town meetings today, the town meeting has been used by generations of historians and political scientists as an example of democracy in its purest form. In recent years, the labeling of Internet conferences as "electronic town-hall meetings" marks an attempt to call up the image of the intimate, deliberative democracy practiced in New England town meetings in the past.

THE REALITY

According to Schudson, the reality of the town meeting was far different from the myth that it inspired. For one thing, the meetings were open only to white male residents who owned property and, in some cases, only to church members. And the idea that town meetings were forums for free expression or that they epitomized political freedom, contends Schudson, is "pure bunk." Rather, New England town halls were meant to showcase harmony and consensus. Far from being models of pure democracy, town meetings usually followed the agenda and preferences of the wealthiest residents in the town. The meetings were also not models of political participation, as has often been claimed. In eighteenth-century Massachusetts, for example, attendance at town meetings ranged from 20 to 60 percent of eligible voters. Apparently, then, as now, town meetings suffered from citizen apathy.

What's Your Opinion?

How do you explain the tendency—on the part of Americans as well as others around the globe—to idealize the past? Does such idealization serve any important function in a political culture?

Town moderator John Trzepacz presides over a town meeting in Bakersfield, Vermont. Vermont's Town Meeting Day is an annual exercise in pure democracy in the Green Mountain State's cities and towns. (AP Photo/Rob Swanson)

The Recall

The **recall**—a vote to dismiss an official—is directed at public officials whose conduct is deemed incompetent or grossly unethical. Voters may circulate a petition calling for the removal of such an official, and if the petition obtains a sufficient number of signatures (which may be as high as 25 percent of the number of votes cast in the last gubernatorial election), then a recall election is held.

The recall is authorized in nearly half of the states. Being placed on a recall ballot does not necessarily mean that an elected person is guilty of anything, although charges of criminal activity are often a reason for recalling an official.

RECALL A procedure that allows voters to dismiss an elected official from a state or local office before the official's term has expired.

An executive director of the American Lung Association speaks to supporters of a ballot initiative in Washington state. The 2002 elections offered voters in forty states the chance to decide 202 ballot initiatives and referenda. Of these, the voters approved 67 percent. (AP Photo/Louie Balukoff)

Although the recall is rarely used, it functions as a threat to public officials. Proponents of the recall in the states in which it exists argue that the possibility of recall prevents outrageously inappropriate official behavior. Opponents of the recall argue that it makes officeholders prey to well-financed special interest groups.

The State Executive Branch

The governor is the chief executive officer in each of the fifty states. In addition to her or his role as chief executive, the state governor is also the state's chief legislator and policymaker, chief political-party leader, and chief spokesperson. Some of the most populous states have given their governors great control over the state executive branch. Even a few less populated states, such as Alaska and Hawaii, have made provisions for strong governors.

The formal qualifications for governor in most states are simple. A candidate for governor must be (1) a U.S. citizen, (2) of a certain age (normally, at least twenty-five or thirty years old), (3) a resident of the state for a minimum period of time (normally, five years), and (4) a qualified voter. A few states do not require even these qualifications. For example, Kansas has no formal qualifications for governor. In Ohio, the governor must be a U.S. citizen and a qualified voter, but the state constitution does not specify any residency requirements. In some states, including California, Massachusetts, Ohio, and Wisconsin, one can become governor at the age of eighteen.

Because millions of men and women can meet the formal requirements to become governor, the *informal* requirements are what truly determine who will be elected. No handbook is available to outline these qualifications, but they certainly include name familiarity, political experience, skill in relating to the media, and voter appeal in terms of personal demeanor and personality.

Length of Service

Gone are the one-year terms of office that were so popular in the early days of this nation. Forty-eight states now have the governor serve for a minimum of four years.

Many states limit the number of terms that a governor may serve. Virginia, for example, allows the governor to serve additional terms, but not consecutively. In thirty-seven states, governors may serve no more than two consecutive terms. Four states have an absolute two-term limit.

Governors who choose to run for a second term almost always win. The power of incumbency is great at virtually all levels of government. The all-time record for gubernatorial service is held by Governor George Clinton of New York, who held office from 1777 to 1795 and from 1801 to 1804. He did this by winning seven three-year terms. The modern record goes to Orval Faubus, who was governor of Arkansas from 1955 to 1967—six consecutive two-year terms.

Impeachment and Recall

IMPEACHMENT A formal criminal proceeding against a public official for misconduct or wrongdoing in office.

Removing a state governor by **impeachment** usually requires an indictment by the lower chamber of the legislature, a trial by the upper chamber (in which the senators are the jury members and the state supreme court justices are the judges), and conviction. State constitutions often provide that the chief justice of the state supreme court is to preside at the trial. Only Oregon does not allow the removal of the governor by impeachment.

Impeachment is not impossible, but it is infrequent. Governor Evan Mecham of Arizona was impeached and removed from office in 1988 when he was convicted of mishandling campaign finances and lending $80,000 of the state's money to his car dealership. (He was later acquitted of felony charges.) Since 1900, only four other governors have been removed in such a manner.[5]

About a third of the states provide for removal of the governor by recall. By signing petitions, voters in these states can call for a special election to determine whether the governor (or other state officials) will be removed before the term expires.

Surrounded by New Jersey state legislators, Governor James E. McGreevey signs a bill that targets lenders who take advantage of homeowners. (AP Photo/Brian Branch-Price)

The Powers of the Governor

Whereas the U.S. Constitution defines the president as *the* "executive" of the federal government, most state constitutions describe their governors as "*chief* executive" in state government. The difference between *the* and *chief* may not seem significant, but it is. No one legally shares supreme executive power with the president of the United States. In many states, though, executive power may be shared by several executive officers, such as the lieutenant governor or the treasurer, who are often also popularly elected.

Appointment and Removal Powers
One of the most important executive powers of the governor is the power to appoint and remove state officials. A governor who can appoint her or his own department and agency heads is more likely to be able to coordinate policies and be more powerful than a governor without such powers. A governor who can reward supporters by appointing them to important department and agency positions will have a greater chance of success in carrying out his or her policies. One way to judge a governor's power is to see whether that governor can in fact select and appoint loyal and competent assistants.

A factor that can potentially reduce a governor's ability to appoint loyal followers is the requirement in most states that major appointees be confirmed by the state senate, as part of the system of checks and balances. Some legislatures also set qualifications that appointees must meet in order to assume office. In states that have vigorous two-party competition, legislatures often require that a specified number of members of each commission or board be from each party. As a result, the governor must appoint members of the opposite party during her or his administration.

Power of the Purse
In the early years of this nation, governors had virtually no budgetary powers. In most states today, in contrast, planning and carrying out the budget is a significant responsibility for the governor. Just as the president of the United States prepares an annual budget, so too do many governors prepare annual or biennial budgets. After the governor finishes the budget, it is sent to the legislature for approval.

Once a budget is authorized by the legislature, most governors possess the power to control the pattern of expenditures through executive agencies and departments. Governors often have the power to decide which expenditures will be made in a particular year. A governor

Governors from the various states convene at the National Governors Association (NGA) annual conference. The NGA was founded in 1908 after state governors met with President Theodore Roosevelt to discuss conservation issues. The NGA's mission is to provide a forum for governors to exchange views and experiences among themselves. The group also seeks to implement policies on national issues. (Paul Conklin/PhotoEdit)

may withhold the funding for a particular project if he or she is not satisfied with the way the project is progressing.

Veto Power   Every state has given the governor the power to veto legislation. In some states, however, the governor has only a short time after the legislature passes a bill in which to veto it. The designated period is three days in Iowa, Minnesota, New Mexico, North Dakota, and Wyoming. In a number of other states, it is six or seven days. If the governor does not veto a measure during the designated period, the measure normally becomes law.

In forty-one states, the governor has some provision for a line-item veto. This allows the governor to veto a particular item in a bill with which he or she disagrees, while signing the rest of the bill into law.

A Typical State Court System

Every state has a different court system, but many systems are organized around three or four levels of courts. Any person who is involved in a lawsuit typically has the opportunity to plead the case before a *trial court,* which is on the lowest tier, or level, of state courts. If that person loses the case, he or she usually has the opportunity to appeal the decision to two other levels of courts, called *appellate courts* (review courts, or courts of appeals). About three-fourths of the states have intermediate appellate courts (courts on the level between the trial courts of general jurisdiction and the state's highest court). Every state has a highest court, which is usually called the state supreme court but may be called by some other name.[6]

In most states, a case proceeds first through a trial court with an automatic right to review by an appellate court. If the reviewing court is an intermediate court of appeals, the decision of that court may be appealed to the state's highest review court. Figure 17–2 shows the tiers of a typical state court system.

Each court has certain powers of jurisdiction. Recall from Chapter 14 that jurisdiction refers to a court's power to hear and decide cases. Courts with *limited* jurisdiction can hear only certain types of cases; courts with *general* jurisdiction can hear a broader range of cases.

Limited-Jurisdiction Trial Courts

Most states have local trial courts that have limited jurisdiction, meaning that they can hear and decide only cases involving certain subject areas. These courts are often called special inferior trial courts or minor trial courts. Typical courts of limited jurisdiction are domestic rela-

FIGURE 17-2

A Typical State Court System

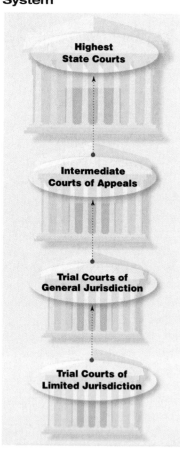

Highest State Courts

Intermediate Courts of Appeals

Trial Courts of General Jurisdiction

Trial Courts of Limited Jurisdiction

tions courts, which handle only divorces and child-custody cases; local municipal courts, which mainly handle traffic cases; probate courts, which handle the administration of wills and estate-settlement problems; and small claims courts. Usually, the minor trial courts do not keep complete written records of trial proceedings.

General-Jurisdiction Trial Courts

State trial courts that have general jurisdiction may be called county courts, district courts, superior courts, or circuit courts. In Ohio, the name is Court of Common Pleas; in New York, it is Supreme Court; and in Massachusetts, Trial Court. (The name sometimes does not correspond with the court's functions. For example, in New York the trial court is called the Supreme Court, whereas in most states the supreme court is the state's highest court.) General-jurisdiction trial courts have the authority to hear and decide cases involving many types of subject matter.

In trial courts, the parties to a controversy may dispute the particular facts, which law should be applied to those facts, and how that law should be applied. If a party is entitled to a trial by jury and requests one, the appropriate issues will be tried before a jury in a trial court. Generally, judges decide *questions of law* (what law applies to the facts of the case and how the law should be applied), and juries decide *questions of fact* (the outcome of the factual dispute before the court). If the trial is held without a jury, the judge decides both questions of law and questions of fact.

Appellate Review

No jury and no witnesses are present during an appellate court's review of a trial court's decision. Rather, when a case is heard on appeal, normally a panel of judges reviews the records of the trial court to determine whether the trial court's judgment was correct. Appellate courts look at questions of law and procedure, but usually not at questions of fact. The decisions of each state's highest court on all questions of state law are final, unless the case can be appealed to the United States Supreme Court.

State Court Judges

In the federal court system, as you read in Chapter 14, all judges are appointed by the president and confirmed by the Senate. It is difficult to make a general statement about how judges are selected in the state court systems, however, because procedures vary widely from state to state. In some states, such as Delaware, all judges are appointed by the governor and confirmed by a majority vote of the upper chamber of the legislature. In other states, such as Alabama, all judges are elected on a partisan ballot. In still other states, such as Kentucky, all judges are elected on a nonpartisan ballot. In a number of states, judges in some of the lower state courts are elected, while judges of the appellate courts are appointed. Additionally, in some of those states in which judges are appointed for their initial terms, if they wish to retain their offices, they must run for reelection.[7]

One of the issues raised by state judicial elections is whether candidates should be free to state their positions on issues when campaigning for judgeships. A stir over this question arose when the Minnesota Supreme Court amended that state's judicial canons, or rules, to prohibit any "candidate for judicial office" from announcing "his or her views on disputed legal or political issues." Critics challenged the Minnesota court's action, contending that the canon violated the First Amendment's guarantee of free speech. When the case ultimately reached the United States Supreme Court, the Court agreed that the canon violated the First Amendment.[8] The Court's decision means that similar canons in other states, such as Pennsylvania, are also invalid.

Judicial campaign posters decorate a tree in the Neshoba County Fair square in Philadelphia, Mississippi. Although federal judges are appointed, many state judges are elected to their posts. (AP Photo/Rogelio Solis)

Another issue raised by state judicial elections has to do with the influence of campaign contributions on judicial decision making, an issue we look at next.

Should All State Court Judges Be Appointed?

In recent state judicial elections, campaign spending amounted to more than $45 million. Unless a judicial candidate is independently wealthy or is running for an uncontested office, he or she cannot wage a campaign without relying on campaign contributions from others. On average, about half of these campaign contributions come from lawyers and law firms—and typically from attorneys who appear before the judge in court. In Wisconsin, 75 percent of all cases that came before the state supreme court over a recent ten-year period involved a lawyer, law firm, company, or other organization that had made campaign contributions to one or more of the supreme court judges.

Many Americans believe that campaign dollars threaten the ability of state judges to be objective and neutral when hearing cases involving the interests of campaign contributors. After all, how can a judge ignore the political implications of certain decisions, especially if they are made near election time?[9] Some have suggested that to maintain judicial neutrality and objectivity, state judges should be appointed—not elected—to their posts. One way of doing this would be to have a commission consisting of lawyers and nonlawyers investigate and evaluate applicants for judgeships. The commission would then submit the most highly qualified candidates to the appointing authority for appointment. This alternative, called merit selection, has already been adopted in thirty-five jurisdictions.[10]

Others do not agree that state judges should be appointed. Business groups, law firms, and others who contribute to judicial campaigns often maintain that they do not support particular judges to curry their favor. Rather, they support the judges because of their legal abilities and fair decision making.

Local Governments

Today, there are about 87,900 local governments in the United States. Local government units include counties, municipalities, school districts, and other units. These governments undertake a variety of services, including public education, police and fire protection, city planning and zoning, public welfare, recreational and cultural activities, and many others. Table 17–2 lists and describes the characteristics of the basic types of local government.

The Legal Status of Local Governments

The U.S. Constitution does not mention local governments, and states are not required by the Constitution to provide local governments at all. Every local government is therefore a creation of its parent state. Just as states can create local governments, so can they disband them. Since World War II, almost twenty thousand school districts have gone out of existence or been consolidated with other school districts—an example of how tenuous the existence of local government is.

Among the many pressing issues for state and local governments today is the need to improve education. These governments have been considering a number of proposed reforms, but exactly how best to improve education remains a divisive issue among Americans. Should the public school system be bolstered, and if so, how? Should states implement voucher systems to give parents and children more educational choice? Should teachers be better trained and held more accountable than they currently are? Indeed, the problems with education were serious enough to prompt the federal government to pass the No Child Left Behind Act in 2002, thus involving the federal government to an even greater extent in an area (education) that traditionally had been governed by state and local governments. As you read in Chapter 3,

TABLE 17-2
Types of Local Government Units

TYPE OF UNIT	CHARACTERISTICS
Municipality	A political entity created by the people of a city or town to govern themselves locally. Almost all municipalities are fairly small cities. About three-fourths of municipal tax revenues come from property taxes. Municipalities rely heavily on financial assistance from both the federal government and the state.
County	The state sets up counties on its own initiative to administer state laws and state business at the local level. A county government's responsibilities may include zoning, building regulations, health, hospitals, parks, recreation, highways, public safety, justice, and record keeping.
New England Town	The New England town is a unique feature of the New England states. In those states, the word *town* refers to a government unit that exercises the combined functions of a municipality and a county. The tradition of the annual town meeting is an example of direct democracy. Those who attend the meeting levy taxes, pass laws, elect town officers, and allocate funds for various activities.
Township	Townships are units that were mapped out by federal land surveys that began in the 1780s. The township operates as a subdivision of a county and performs similar functions. Indiana, New Jersey, New York, and most midwestern states have townships.
Special District	The special district is a one-function local government, such as a school district, that is usually created by the state legislature and governed by a board of directors. Most of the 87,900-plus local governments in the United States are special districts. In addition to school districts, there are special districts for mosquito control, fire protection, cemeteries, and numerous other concerns.

this legislation requires that students take standard assessment tests, that schools be graded in terms of their performance, and that students be permitted to leave poorly performing schools to attend others.

Perhaps one of the most controversial suggestions for educational reform is the use of vouchers. Not only do vouchers raise church-state issues, but they also have implications for the future of the public school system.

AMERICA at odds

Are School Vouchers the Solution?

One way of introducing more choice into the schools is through the use of school vouchers. In a voucher system, parents receive state educational funds to use at any school they wish. If parents prefer to send their children to private schools, they can use the vouchers to help defray tuition costs. The problem is that in those areas that have experimented with voucher systems, many of the private schools at which state vouchers were used were religious schools.

Is this constitutional? Does the use of state funds to pay for education in a religious school violate the establishment clause of the First Amendment? According to the Supreme Court in 2002, not necessarily. In a case challenging the constitutionality of a voucher program in Cleveland, Ohio, the high court held that the program had the "valid secular purpose" of helping children trapped in failing public schools. Furthermore, the government aid reaches religious schools only as a result of the genuine and independent choices of private individuals. Thus, the program did not involve a state-approved religious mission.[11]

Some Americans, especially conservative and religious groups, hailed the Court's ruling as a step toward initiating true competition among schools. According to conservative

Clint Bolick, vice president of the Institute for Justice, a libertarian law firm that represented Cleveland families in the school voucher case, talks to reporters outside the U.S. Supreme Court in June 2002. The Court had just ruled that the Constitution allows public money to underwrite tuition at religious schools as long as parents have a choice among a range of religious and secular schools. (AP Photo/Evan Vucci)

columnist George Will, "socially disadvantaged children had their best day in court" since the *Brown v. Board of Education of Topeka* case was decided by the Court in 1954. Since the Court's decision on school vouchers, suits have been brought in many states to challenge state constitutional provisions that ban public funding for religious schools. Currently, thirty-seven states have such provisions. Others of a liberal stripe argue that if vouchers are made available, so many students will opt for private education that ultimately many public schools will have to close their doors. Perhaps the strongest opponents of school vouchers are the teachers' unions, which insist that vouchers would destroy the public school system.

State and Local Government Revenues

Relatively few limitations are placed on state and local taxing powers. The most obvious one was already discussed in Chapter 3—states cannot tax the operations, land, buildings, or any other aspect of the federal government. In addition, the U.S. Constitution prevents the states from taxing both imports into the United States and exports to other countries. The due process clause of the Fourteenth Amendment also places a restriction on methods of state and local government taxation. Taxes must be imposed and administered fairly and not be so great as to be the equivalent of seizing property. The equal protection clause of the same amendment also forbids unreasonable classifications for the purpose of collecting taxes. For example, a state can collect taxes on smokers by taxing cigarettes, but a state cannot make only blonde-haired citizens pay a state income tax.

Sources of State and Local Revenues

In Figure 17–3, you can see the relative importance of various sources of state and local revenues. The most important tax for most states is the general sales tax. The most important tax at the local level is the property tax. Other sources of state and local government revenues include federal grants, which were examined in Chapter 3; personal and corporate income taxes; and social-insurance contributions.

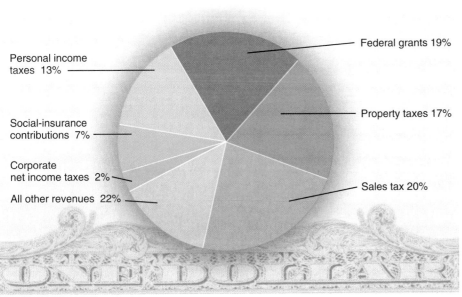

FIGURE 17-3

Sources of State and Local Revenues

Federal grants 19%

Personal income taxes 13%

Property taxes 17%

Social-insurance contributions 7%

Corporate net income taxes 2%

Sales tax 20%

All other revenues 22%

SOURCE: U.S. Bureau of the Census, 2003.

Dwindling State Revenues

During the late 1990s, when the economy was booming, many states embarked on new spending programs to meet new challenges, such as the desire to reduce class sizes in the schools and to help senior citizens pay for prescription drugs. The subsequent economic downturn ended the good times. Indeed, by 2003 the states were undergoing the most severe financial crisis they had experienced in a half-century. All but six of the states faced budget shortfalls. California had the largest shortfall—its revenues covered only about 65 percent of planned expenditures. Even Texas, where George W. Bush's tax cuts helped his political career, now has serious financial troubles.[12]

Unlike the federal government, state constitutions in all states but Vermont require the state government to balance its budget. In other words, the state cannot spend more than it receives in revenues. For many states, this has required severe cuts in spending. States around the country are resorting to desperate measures to balance their budgets. In an attempt to reduce spiraling health-care costs, which climbed overall by 13.4 percent between 2001 and 2002, many states are cutting back on Medicaid benefits and increasing co-payments for health care.[13] Numerous areas now have fewer police officers. Many public schools have seen their budgets cut to the point that they have had to shorten the school year or increase class sizes, or both. In some states, governments have even released felons from prison to save on prison construction and maintenance costs.

Notwithstanding these problems, state and local governments now face an additional burden—providing for homeland defense. The difficulties involved in meeting this challenge are discussed in this chapter's *The Politics of Homeland Security* feature on the next page.

Devolution: Returning Responsibility to the States

A watchword of American politics since the 1990s has been *devolution,* or the transfer of certain national government responsibilities back to state and local governments. The words *back to* are important. They indicate that the responsibilities in question were once the purview of state and local governments.

Over time, as the nation grew, the national government did indeed assume regulatory responsibilities over areas traditionally governed by the states. The problem is, government

The POLITICS of HOMELAND SECURITY

Can the States Afford to Defend the Homeland?

The U.S. Constitution gives Congress the power and authority to provide for the common defense. But much of the burden of homeland defense falls on state and local governments. As mentioned elsewhere in this text, these governments are the "first responders" to crises, including terrorist attacks. Additionally, state and local governments are responsible for detecting, preparing for, preventing, and recovering from terrorist attacks.

THE COST OF HOMELAND DEFENSE

Homeland defense is necessarily a costly undertaking. Firefighting departments need more equipment and training. Emergency communications equipment must be purchased. Funds are needed to secure ports, ensure water safety and airport security, obtain new bomb-detecting equipment, and increase security at nuclear plants and laboratories. Additional law enforcement resources must be obtained. The question is, can the states afford to pay these additional costs?

Clearly, in view of the financial crises that many state governments are facing, this is not the ideal time for those governments to incur additional costs. Yet, as noted in Chapter 3, the Bush administration has increased demands on state and local governments to participate in homeland security. By early 2003, however, the federal government had not been forthcoming with some $3.5 billion in funds that had been promised to the states to help in their efforts.

WASHINGTON TURNS ITS BACK

In February 2003, when the nation's governors traveled to Washington, D.C., for their annual meeting with the president, many governors had hoped that the federal government would come to their assistance. At the least, the states thought that the federal government should reimburse the states for homeland security costs already incurred and provide adequate funding for future efforts at the state and local levels.

President Bush, however, did not offer much help. He explained to the governors that the federal government also had budget problems—the states would simply have to work out their problems on their own.

President Bush makes remarks to governors during the National Governors Association luncheon in the White House on February 24, 2003. (AP Photo/Rick Bowmer)

Are We Safer?

The federal government has provided funds to help the airlines stay in business following the September 11, 2001, terrorist attacks and has passed legislation calling for agricultural subsidies in an amount some deem "historic." Should the federal government also assist the states by giving them grants to help with their expenses? Why or why not?

regulation is costly. By the 1990s, it was apparent that the federal government could no longer meet the costs of its regulatory burden without going further into debt. One result of the federal government's budgetary problems was the increasing use of unfunded federal mandates (requirements in federal legislation, such as an environmental law, with which state and local governments must comply—and for which they must pay). At the same time, there was a growing sentiment that many federal programs, such as welfare, were ineffective at combating the problems facing American society, such as poverty. The solution, according to many, was to give state and local governments more responsibility over areas that have been regulated by the national government since the 1930s.

What does devolution mean for state and local governments? On the plus side, of course, is the ability to tailor programs to meet the needs of citizens in that particular state, including homeland defense needs, which are often different from those of citizens in other areas of the country. On the minus side are the costs of administering programs, such as welfare, that have for decades been the responsibility of the national government. When state governments find it difficult to meet such costs, one option is to pass the costs on to local governments in the form of unfunded state mandates. Just as the federal and state governments have been at odds over unfunded federal mandates (see Chapter 3), now state and local governments are finding themselves at odds over the same issue. Devolution also raises the question as to which government—federal, state, or local—is the appropriate body to handle certain types of problems, such as welfare. Americans continue to be at odds over this issue.

why does it MATTER?

Local Government and Your Everyday Life

There are over 87,900 governmental units in the United States. The majority of them are state and local. The ones that affect you the most are indeed your local governments. As the governments closest to you, they provide services that directly address your needs.

Got a Problem? Don't Call Washington, D.C.

If your garbage is not being collected by your city government when promised, you have to call a local government agency to resolve the issue. If you are not satisfied with its resolution, then you might go to the mayor's office. You certainly won't go to a state or federal government official to solve such a local problem.

Are you dissatisfied with the way your children are being taught in your local school? You have to start by complaining to that school's administration. If you are not satisfied, then you go to the local school board. Calling the president of the United States is not going to help.

Is the road in front of your house covered with potholes? Then you had better call the local agency responsible for road repairs. If nothing happens, you might want to try the county board of commissioners or the township trustees.

Are mosquitoes eating you alive every summer evening? There is probably a local agency in your area responsible for mosquito abatement.

Are your neighbors driving you nuts playing loud music at two o'clock in the morning? You certainly don't call the U.S. Army to report the problem. Rather, you normally will call city or county law enforcement authorities to complain. A local police officer may help you resolve the problem. You may end up in a municipal court suing your neighbors. Or you might use the services of a local mediation agency.

Taking Action

Getting involved in local politics can be as simple as writing a letter to the editor of your local newspaper about an issue concerning your community. Other options include attending a PTA meeting at your local school or going to a city planning commission meeting convened to discuss proposed changes in your neighborhood. There may be opportunities through your local parks department to plant trees or lead nature walks. Many have found it rewarding to work with the Habitat for Humanity program, which builds homes for those in need of housing. The photo above shows a new home being built for a Los Angeles resident by Habitat for Humanity volunteers. (Copyright © David Young-Wolff/Photo Edit)

Key Terms

extraordinary majority 400　　　initiative 400　　　recall 405　　　referendum 405

impeachment 406　　　intrastate commerce 399

Chapter Summary

1 Compared to the U.S. Constitution, state constitutions are lengthy and detailed. State constitutional amendments may be proposed by the state legislature, by a constitutional convention, or by a constitutional initiative proposed by the citizens. All states but Delaware require an amendment to be ratified by a majority of the voters in a general election.

2 All state legislatures, except for that of Nebraska, are bicameral (have two chambers). The size of state legislatures varies significantly from state to state, as do the salaries and terms of state legislators.

3 Many states exercise a type of direct democracy through the initiative, the referendum, and the recall. Twenty-two states allow their citizens to use initiatives to place proposed laws on the ballot for popular vote; in eighteen states, the initiative can be used to propose constitutional amendments. The referendum is similar to the initiative, but the new law or constitutional change is proposed first by the legislature and then directed to the voters for their approval. The recall—a vote to dismiss an official—is aimed at public officials whose conduct is deemed incompetent or grossly unethical. The recall is authorized in nearly half of the states.

4 The governor is the chief executive officer in each state. In most states, the governor serves for a minimum of four years. Many states limit the number of terms that a governor may serve. In all states but Oregon, governors may be removed through impeachment proceedings. About one-third of the states provide for removal of the governor by recall. The powers of the governor include the power to appoint and remove state officials, the power to plan and carry out the budget, and the power to veto legislation.

5 A typical state court system consists of three or four tiers, or levels, and includes trial courts of limited jurisdiction, trial courts of general jurisdiction, intermediate appellate courts (in about three-fourths of the states), and a state supreme court. State judges may be elected or appointed, depending on the jurisdiction. State judicial elections have led to controversy because of the potential influence of campaign contributors on judicial decision making.

6 There are about 87,900 local governments in the United States. Local governments are created by the states and perform a variety of services.

7 States' sources of revenue include general sales taxes and personal income taxes. The most important source of revenue at the local level is the property tax. Federal grants are also important sources of state and local revenues. Declining revenues in 2002 and 2003 have caused many states to experience severe budget crises. The devolution of certain responsibilities from the federal government to state and local governments has also added to state financial burdens.

RESOURCES FOR FURTHER STUDY

Selected Readings

Beyle, Thad L. *State and Local Government, 2003–2004.* Washington, D.C.: CQ Press, 2003. This collection of articles, essays, reports, and news from key publications is topically organized, easy to read, and a good source for learning about current developments in state politics and government.

Finn, Chester E., Jr., *et al. Charter Schools in Action: Renewing Public Education.* Ewing, N.J.: Princeton University Press, 2001. The author looks closely at a development that holds promise for states in dealing with a pressing question—how to improve public education.

Sabato, Larry. *Dangerous Democracy?* Lanham, Md.: Rowman & Littlefield Publishing, 2001. This collection of essays by leading political scientists and other scholars focuses on the increasing use of initiatives by state government and the implications of this development for democratic government.

Tarr, G. Alan. *Understanding State Constitutions.* Ewing, N.J.: Princeton University Press, 2000. As the trend toward states' rights and greater independence from the federal government continues, Americans are searching for a fuller understanding of state governments. This book, which explores state constitutions, offers many insights into the similarities and differences among state governments.

InfoTrac Citations

Using your InfoTrac password, access the InfoTrac database at **http://infotrac.thomsonlearning.com**. Once at the site, you can do "key word" searches to locate the following articles, each of which deals with a topic covered in this chapter. The key words to use in your search are indicated in parentheses.

- "Boom to Bust: For Colleges Now Drowning in Red Ink, the High-Tech Spending Spree of the 1990s Seems Like Ancient History: With State Deficits Soaring and Education Budgets Shrinking, Most Schools Are Just Trying to Hold onto What Computer Assets They Have Left" (State Deficits)

- "The Naked and the Red: Led by a Former Boeing Machinist, Las Vegas Exotic Dancers Are Talking Union" (Nevada Dancers Union)

- "Environmentalists Succeed in Pushing Passage of California Auto Emissions Bill" (California Auto Emissions)

- "National-State Relations: Cooperative Federalism in the Twentieth Century" (New England Town)

Politics on the Web

A good source for information on state news is Stateline.org at **http://www.stateline.org**

- The National Governors Association provides extensive information on developments among the states, state policy positions on various issues, and other state information at **http://www.nga.org**

- Still another source for information on state governments, including some of the challenges that they are currently facing, is the National Conference of State Legislators. Go to **http://www.ncsl.org**

- Another site that gives you information on state and local government can be found at **http://www.statelocalgov.net/statefaq.cfm**

- If you want to find the e-mail address or home page for your state's representative(s) in Congress, go to **http://www.house.gov**

- For e-mail addresses and home pages for your state's senators in the U.S. Senate, go to **http://www.senate.gov**

- To find newspapers that may be online in your state or local area, go to Newspapers Online at **http://www.newspapers.com**

Web Resources on Your CD-ROM

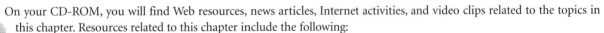

On your CD-ROM, you will find Web resources, news articles, Internet activities, and video clips related to the topics in this chapter. Resources related to this chapter include the following:
- **Values Inventory**—Political Ideology: Are Ballot Initiatives Good for Our Democracy?
- **Why Does It Matter?**—Pick a Local Issue and Discuss It with a Local Government Office.
- **Updates**—Keep up with the issues in this chapter!
- **Web Resources**—Internet Activities: 2002 Ballot Initiatives; The Council of State Governments' Commentary on the 2002 Ballot Initiatives.
- **Where Do You Stand?**—Dialogue: Are Ballot Initiatives Good for Our Democracy?
- **Comparative Politics**—Local Government in France.
- **Video**—Proposition 209.
- **NewsEdge**—Visit this global resource for current events related to this chapter.

Preamble

We the People of the United States, in Order to form a more perfect Union, establish Justice, insure domestic Tranquility, provide for the common defence, promote the general Welfare, and secure the Blessings of Liberty to ourselves and our Posterity, do ordain and establish this Constitution for the United States of America.

Article I

Section 1.   All legislative Powers herein granted shall be vested in a Congress of the United States, which shall consist of a Senate and House of Representatives.

Section 2.   The House of Representatives shall be composed of Members chosen every second Year by the People of the several States, and the Electors in each State shall have the Qualifications requisite for Electors of the most numerous Branch of the State Legislature.

No Person shall be a Representative who shall not have attained to the Age of twenty five Years, and been seven Years a Citizen of the United States, and who shall not, when elected, be an Inhabitant of that State in which he shall be chosen.

Representatives and direct Taxes shall be apportioned among the several States which may be included within this Union, according to their respective Numbers, which shall be determined by adding to the whole Number of free Persons, including those bound to Service for a Term of Years, and excluding Indians not taxed, three fifths of all other Persons. The actual Enumeration shall be made within three Years after the first Meeting of the Congress of the United States, and within every subsequent Term of ten Years, in such Manner as they shall by Law direct. The Number of Representatives shall not exceed one for every thirty Thousand, but each State shall have at Least one Representative; and until such enumeration shall be made, the State of New Hampshire shall be entitled to chuse three, Massachusetts eight, Rhode Island and Providence Plantations one, Connecticut five, New York six, New Jersey four, Pennsylvania eight, Delaware one, Maryland six, Virginia ten, North Carolina five, South Carolina five, and Georgia three.

When vacancies happen in the Representation from any State, the Executive Authority thereof shall issue Writs of Election to fill such Vacancies.

The House of Representatives shall chuse their Speaker and other Officers; and shall have the sole Power of Impeachment.

Section 3.   The Senate of the United States shall be composed of two Senators from each State, chosen by the Legislature thereof, for six Years; and each Senator shall have one Vote.

Immediately after they shall be assembled in Consequence of the first Election, they shall be divided as equally as may be into three Classes. The Seats of the Senators of the first Class shall be vacated at the Expiration of the second Year, of the second Class at the Expiration of the fourth Year, and of the third Class at the Expiration of the sixth Year, so that one third may be chosen every second Year; and if Vaments until the next Meeting of the Legislature, which shall then fill such Vacancies.

No Person shall be a Senator who shall not have attained to the Age of thirty Years, and been nine Years a Citizen of the United States, and who shall not, when elected, be an Inhabitant of that State for which he shall be chosen.

The Vice President of the United States shall be President of the Senate, but shall have no Vote, unless they be equally divided.

The Senate shall chuse their other Officers, and also a President pro tempore, in the Absence of the Vice President, or when he shall exercise the Office of President of the United States.

The Senate shall have the sole Power to try all Impeachments. When sitting for that Purpose, they shall be on Oath or Affirmation. When the President of the United States is tried, the Chief Justice shall preside: And no Person shall be convicted without the Concurrence of two thirds of the Members present.

Judgment in Cases of Impeachment shall not extend further than to removal from Office, and disqualification to hold and enjoy any Office of honor, Trust, or Profit under the United States: but the Party convicted shall nevertheless be liable and subject to Indictment, Trial, Judgment, and Punishment, according to Law.

Section 4. The Times, Places and Manner of holding Elections for Senators and Representatives, shall be prescribed in each State by the Legislature thereof; but the Congress may at any time by Law make or alter such Regulations, except as to the Places of chusing Senators.

The Congress shall assemble at least once in every Year, and such Meeting shall be on the first Monday in December, unless they shall by Law appoint a different Day.

Section 5. Each House shall be the Judge of the Elections, Returns, and Qualifications of its own Members, and a Majority of each shall constitute a Quorum to do Business; but a smaller Number may adjourn from day to day, and may be authorized to compel the Attendance of absent Members, in such Manner, and under such Penalties as each House may provide.

Each House may determine the Rules of its Proceedings, punish its Members for disorderly Behavior, and, with the Concurrence of two thirds, expel a Member.

Each House shall keep a Journal of its Proceedings, and from time to time publish the same, excepting such Parts as may in their Judgment require Secrecy; and the Yeas and Nays of the Members of either House on any question shall, at the Desire of one fifth of those Present, be entered on the Journal.

Neither House, during the Session of Congress, shall, without the Consent of the other, adjourn for more than three days, nor to any other Place than that in which the two Houses shall be sitting.

Section 6. The Senators and Representatives shall receive a Compensation for their Services, to be ascertained by Law, and paid out of the Treasury of the United States. They shall in all Cases, except Treason, Felony and Breach of the Peace, be privileged from Arrest during their Attendance at the Session of their respective Houses, and in going to and returning from the same; and for any Speech or Debate in either House, they shall not be questioned in any other Place.

No Senator or Representative shall, during the Time for which he was elected, be appointed to any civil Office under the Authority of the United States, which shall have been created, or the Emoluments whereof shall have been increased during such time; and no Person holding any Office under the United States, shall be a Member of either House during his Continuance in Office.

Section 7. All Bills for raising Revenue shall originate in the House of Representatives; but the Senate may propose or concur with Amendments as on other Bills.

Every Bill which shall have passed the House of Representatives and the Senate, shall, before it become a Law, be presented to the President of the United States; If he approve he shall sign it, but if not he shall return it, with his Objections to the House in which it shall have originated, who shall enter the Objections at large on their Journal, and proceed to reconsider it. If after such Reconsideration two thirds of that House shall agree to pass the Bill, it shall be sent together with the Objections, to the other House, by which it shall likewise be reconsidered, and if approved by two thirds of that House, it shall become a Law. But in all such Cases the Votes of both Houses shall be determined by Yeas and Nays, and the Names of the Persons voting for and against the Bill shall be entered on the Journal of each House respectively. If any Bill shall not be returned by the President within ten Days (Sundays excepted) after it shall have been presented to him, the Same shall be a Law, in like Manner as if he had signed it, unless the Congress by their Adjournment prevent its Return in which Case it shall not be a Law.

Every Order, Resolution, or Vote, to which the Concurrence of the Senate and House of Representatives may be necessary (except on a question of Adjournment) shall be presented to the President of the United States; and before the Same shall take Effect, shall be approved by him, or being disapproved by him, shall be repassed by two thirds of the Senate and House of Representatives, according to the Rules and Limitations prescribed in the Case of a Bill.

Section 8. The Congress shall have Power To lay and collect Taxes, Duties, Imposts and Excises, to pay the Debts and provide for the common Defence and general Welfare of the United States; but all Duties, Imposts and Excises shall be uniform throughout the United States;

To borrow Money on the credit of the United States;

To regulate Commerce with foreign Nations, and among the several States, and with the Indian Tribes;

To establish an uniform Rule of Naturalization, and uniform Laws on the subject of Bankruptcies throughout the United States;

To coin Money, regulate the Value thereof, and of foreign Coin, and fix the Standard of Weights and Measures;

To provide for the Punishment of counterfeiting the Securities and current Coin of the United States;

To establish Post Offices and post Roads;

To promote the Progress of Science and useful Arts, by securing for limited Times to Authors and Inventors the exclusive Right to their respective Writings and Discoveries;

To constitute Tribunals inferior to the supreme Court;

To define and punish Piracies and Felonies committed on the high Seas, and Offenses against the Law of Nations;

To declare War, grant Letters of Marque and Reprisal, and make Rules concerning Captures on Land and Water;

To raise and support Armies, but no Appropriation of Money to that Use shall be for a longer Term than two Years;

To provide and maintain a Navy;

To make Rules for the Government and Regulation of the land and naval Forces;

To provide for calling forth the Militia to execute the Laws of the Union, suppress Insurrections and repel Invasions;

To provide for organizing, arming, and disciplining, the Militia, and for governing such Part of them as may be employed in the Service of the United States, reserving to the States respectively, the Appointment of the Officers, and the Authority of training the Militia according to the discipline prescribed by Congress;

To exercise exclusive Legislation in all Cases whatsoever, over such District (not exceeding ten Miles square) as may, by Cession of particular States, and the Acceptance of Congress, become the Seat of the Government of the United States, and to exercise like Authority over all Places purchased by the Consent of the Legislature of the State in which the Same shall be, for the Erection of Forts, Magazines, Arsenals, dock-Yards, and other needful Buildings;—And

To make all Laws which shall be necessary and proper for carrying into Execution the foregoing Powers, and all other Powers vested by this Constitution in the Government of the United States, or in any Department or Officer thereof.

Section 9. The Migration or Importation of such Persons as any of the States now existing shall think proper to admit, shall not be prohibited by the Congress prior to the Year one thousand eight hundred and eight, but a Tax or duty may be imposed on such Importation, not exceeding ten dollars for each Person.

The privilege of the Writ of Habeas Corpus shall not be suspended, unless when in Cases of Rebellion or Invasion the public Safety may require it.

No Bill of Attainder or ex post facto Law shall be passed.

No Capitation, or other direct, Tax shall be laid, unless in Proportion to the Census or Enumeration herein before directed to be taken.

No Tax or Duty shall be laid on Articles exported from any State.

No Preference shall be given by any Regulation of Commerce or Revenue to the Ports of one State over those of another: nor shall Vessels bound to, or from, one State be obliged to enter, clear, or pay Duties in another.

No Money shall be drawn from the Treasury, but in Consequence of Appropriations made by Law; and a regular Statement and Account of the Receipts and Expenditures of all public Money shall be published from time to time.

No Title of Nobility shall be granted by the United States: And no Person holding any Office of Profit or Trust under them, shall, without the Consent of the Congress, accept of any present, Emolument, Office, or Title, of any kind whatever, from any King, Prince, or foreign State.

Section 10. No State shall enter into any Treaty, Alliance, or Confederation; grant Letters of Marque and Reprisal; coin Money; emit Bills of Credit; make any Thing but gold and silver Coin a Tender in Payment of Debts; pass any Bill of Attainder, ex post facto Law, or Law impairing the Obligation of Contracts, or grant any Title of Nobility.

No State shall, without the Consent of the Congress, lay any Imposts or Duties on Imports or Exports, except what may be absolutely necessary for executing its inspection Laws: and the net Produce of all Duties and Imposts, laid by any State on Imports or Exports, shall be for the Use of the Treasury of the United States; and all such Laws shall be subject to the Revision and Controul of the Congress.

No State shall, without the Consent of Congress, lay any Duty of Tonnage, keep Troops, or Ships of War in time of Peace, enter into any Agreement or Compact with another State, or with a foreign Power, or engage in War, unless actually invaded, or in such imminent Danger as will not admit of delay.

Article II

Section 1. The executive Power shall be vested in a President of the United States of America. He shall hold his Office during the Term of four Years, and, together with the Vice President, chosen for the same Term, be elected, as follows:

Each State shall appoint, in such Manner as the Legislature thereof may direct, a Number of Electors, equal to the whole Number of Senators and Representatives to which the State may be entitled in the Congress; but no Senator or Representative, or Person holding an Office of Trust or Profit under the United States, shall be appointed an Elector.

The Electors shall meet in their respective States, and vote by Ballot for two Persons, of whom one at least shall not be an Inhabitant of the same State with themselves. And they shall make a List of all the Persons voted for, and of the Number of Votes for each; which List they shall sign and certify, and transmit sealed to the Seat of the Government of the United States, directed to the President of the Senate. The President of the Senate shall, in the Presence of the Senate and House of Representatives, open all the Certificates, and the Votes shall then be counted. The Person having the greatest Number of Votes shall be the President, if such Number be a Majority of the whole Number of Electors appointed; and if there be more than one who have such Majority, and have an equal Number of Votes, then the House of Representatives shall immediately chuse by Ballot one of them for President; and if no Person have a Majority, then from the five highest on the List the said House shall in like Manner chuse the President. But in chusing the President, the Votes shall be taken by States, the Representation from each State having one Vote; A quorum for this Purpose shall consist of a Member or Members from two thirds of the States, and a Majority of all the States shall be necessary to a Choice. In every Case, after the Choice of the President, the Person having the greater Number of Votes of the Electors shall be the Vice President. But if there should remain two or more who have equal Votes, the Senate shall chuse from them by Ballot the Vice President.

The Congress may determine the Time of chusing the Electors, and the Day on which they shall give their Votes; which Day shall be the same throughout the United States.

No person except a natural born Citizen, or a Citizen of the United States, at the time of the Adoption of this Constitution, shall be eligible to the Office of President; neither shall any Person be eligible to that Office who shall not have attained to the Age of thirty five Years, and been fourteen Years a Resident within the United States.

In Case of the Removal of the President from Office, or of his Death, Resignation or Inability to discharge the Powers and Duties of the said Office, the same shall devolve on the Vice President, and the Congress may by Law provide for the Case of Removal, Death, Resignation or Inability, both of the President and Vice President, declaring what Officer shall then act as President, and such Officer shall act accordingly, until the Disability be removed, or a President shall be elected.

The President shall, at stated Times, receive for his Services, a Compensation, which shall neither be increased nor diminished during the Period for which he shall have been elected, and he shall not receive within that Period any other Emolument from the United States, or any of them.

Before he enter on the Execution of his Office, he shall take the following Oath or Affirmation: "I do solemnly swear (or affirm) that I will faithfully execute the Office of President of the United States, and will to the best of my Ability, preserve, protect and defend the Constitution of the United States."

Section 2. The President shall be Commander in Chief of the Army and Navy of the United States, and of the Militia of the several States, when called into the actual Service of the United States; he may require the Opinion, in writing, of the principal Officer in each of the executive Departments, upon any Subject relating to the Duties of their respective Offices, and he shall have Power to grant Reprieves and Pardons for Offenses against the United States, except in Cases of Impeachment.

He shall have Power, by and with the Advice and Consent of the Senate to make Treaties, provided two thirds of the Senators present concur; and he shall nominate, and by and with the

Advice and Consent of the Senate, shall appoint Ambassadors, other public Ministers and Consuls, Judges of the supreme Court, and all other Officers of the United States, whose Appointments are not herein otherwise provided for, and which shall be established by Law; but the Congress may by Law vest the Appointment of such inferior Officers, as they think proper, in the President alone, in the Courts of Law, or in the Heads of Departments.

The President shall have Power to fill up all Vacancies that may happen during the Recess of the Senate, by granting Commissions which shall expire at the End of their next Session.

Section 3. He shall from time to time give to the Congress Information of the State of the Union, and recommend to their Consideration such Measures as he shall judge necessary and expedient; he may, on extraordinary Occasions, convene both Houses, or either of them, and in Case of Disagreement between them, with Respect to the Time of Adjournment, he may adjourn them to such Time as he shall think proper; he shall receive Ambassadors and other public Ministers; he shall take Care that the Laws be faithfully executed, and shall Commission all the Officers of the United States.

Section 4. The President, Vice President and all civil Officers of the United States, shall be removed from Office on Impeachment for, and Conviction of, Treason, Bribery, or other high Crimes and Misdemeanors.

Article III

Section 1. The judicial Power of the United States, shall be vested in one supreme Court, and in such inferior Courts as the Congress may from time to time ordain and establish. The Judges, both of the supreme and inferior Courts, shall hold their Offices during good Behaviour, and shall, at stated Times, receive for their Services a Compensation, which shall not be diminished during their Continuance in Office.

Section 2. The judicial Power shall extend to all Cases, in Law and Equity, arising under this Constitution, the Laws of the United States, and Treaties made, or which shall be made, under their Authority;—to all Cases affecting Ambassadors, other public Ministers and Consuls;—to all Cases of admiralty and maritime Jurisdiction;—to Controversies to which the United States shall be a Party;—to Controversies between two or more States;—between a State and Citizens of another State;—between Citizens of different States;—between Citizens of the same State claiming Lands under Grants of different States, and between a State, or the Citizens thereof, and foreign States, Citizens or Subjects.

In all Cases affecting Ambassadors, other public Ministers and Consuls, and those in which a State shall be a Party, the supreme Court shall have original Jurisdiction. In all the other Cases before mentioned, the supreme Court shall have appellate Jurisdiction, both as to Law and Fact, with such Exceptions, and under such Regulations as the Congress shall make.

The Trial of all Crimes, except in Cases of Impeachment, shall be by Jury; and such Trial shall be held in the State where the said Crimes shall have been committed; but when not committed within any State, the Trial shall be at such Place or Places as the Congress may by Law have directed.

Section 3. Treason against the United States, shall consist only in levying War against them, or, in adhering to their Enemies, giving them Aid and Comfort. No Person shall be convicted of Treason unless on the Testimony of two Witnesses to the same overt Act, or on Confession in open Court.

The Congress shall have Power to declare the Punishment of Treason, but no Attainder of Treason shall work Corruption of Blood, or Forfeiture except during the Life of the Person attainted.

Article IV

Section 1. Full Faith and Credit shall be given in each State to the public Acts, Records, and judicial Proceedings of every other State. And the Congress may by general Laws prescribe the Manner in which such Acts, Records and Proceedings shall be proved, and the Effect thereof.

Section 2. The Citizens of each State shall be entitled to all Privileges and Immunities of Citizens in the several States.

A Person charged in any State with Treason, Felony, or other Crime, who shall flee from Justice, and be found in another State, shall on Demand of the executive Authority of the State from which he fled, be delivered up, to be removed to the State having Jurisdiction of the Crime.

No Person held to Service or Labour in one State, under the Laws thereof, escaping into another, shall, in Consequence of any Law or Regulation therein, be discharged from such Service or Labour, but shall be delivered up on Claim of the Party to whom such Service or Labour may be due.

Section 3. New States may be admitted by the Congress into this Union; but no new State shall be formed or erected within the Jurisdiction of any other State; nor any State be formed by the Junction of two or more States, or Parts of States, without the Consent of the Legislatures of the States concerned as well as of the Congress.

The Congress shall have Power to dispose of and make all needful Rules and Regulations respecting the Territory or other Property belonging to the United States; and nothing in this Constitution shall be so construed as to Prejudice any Claims of the United States, or of any particular State.

Section 4. The United States shall guarantee to every State in this Union a Republican Form of Government, and shall protect each of them against Invasion; and on Application of the Legislature, or of the Executive (when the Legislature cannot be convened) against domestic Violence.

Article V

The Congress, whenever two thirds of both Houses shall deem it necessary, shall propose Amendments to this Constitution, or, on the Application of the Legislatures of two thirds of the several States, shall call a Convention for proposing Amendments, which, in either Case, shall be valid to all Intents and Purposes, as part of this Constitution, when ratified by the Legislatures of three fourths of the several States, or by Conventions in three fourths thereof, as the one or the other Mode of Ratification may be proposed by the Congress; Provided that no Amendment which may be made prior to the Year One thousand eight hundred and eight shall in any Manner affect the first and fourth Clauses in the

Ninth Section of the first Article; and that no State, without its Consent, shall be deprived of its equal Suffrage in the Senate.

Article VI

All Debts contracted and Engagements entered into, before the Adoption of this Constitution shall be as valid against the United States under this Constitution, as under the Confederation.

This Constitution, and the Laws of the United States which shall be made in Pursuance thereof; and all Treaties made, or which shall be made, under the Authority of the United States, shall be the supreme Law of the Land; and the Judges in every State shall be bound thereby, any Thing in the Constitution or Laws of any State to the Contrary notwithstanding.

The Senators and Representatives before mentioned, and the Members of the several State Legislatures, and all executive and judicial Officers, both of the United States and of the several States, shall be bound by Oath or Affirmation, to support this Constitution; but no religious Test shall ever be required as a Qualification to any Office or public Trust under the United States.

Article VII

The Ratification of the Conventions of nine States shall be sufficient for the Establishment of this Constitution between the States so ratifying the Same.

Amendment I [1791]

Congress shall make no law respecting an establishment of religion, or prohibiting the free exercise thereof; or abridging the freedom of speech, or of the press; or the right of the people peaceably to assemble, and to petition the Government for a redress of grievances.

Amendment II [1791]

A well regulated Militia, being necessary to the security of a free State, the right of the people to keep and bear Arms, shall not be infringed.

Amendment III [1791]

No Soldier shall, in time of peace be quartered in any house, without the consent of the Owner, nor in time of war, but in a manner to be prescribed by law.

Amendment IV [1791]

The right of the people to be secure in their persons, houses, papers, and effects, against unreasonable searches and seizures, shall not be violated, and no Warrants shall issue, but upon probable cause, supported by Oath or affirmation, and particularly describing the place to be searched, and the persons or things to be seized.

Amendment V [1791]

No person shall be held to answer for a capital, or otherwise infamous crime, unless on a presentment or indictment of a Grand Jury, except in cases arising in the land or naval forces, or in the Militia, when in actual service in time of War or public danger; nor shall any person be subject for the same offense to be twice put in jeopardy of life or limb; nor shall be compelled in any criminal case to be a witness against himself, nor be deprived of life, liberty, or property, without due process of law; nor shall private property be taken for public use, without just compensation.

Amendment VI [1791]

In all criminal prosecutions, the accused shall enjoy the right to a speedy and public trial, by an impartial jury of the State and district wherein the crime shall have been committed, which district shall have been previously ascertained by law, and to be informed of the nature and cause of the accusation; to be confronted with the witnesses against him; to have compulsory process for obtaining witnesses in his favor, and to have the Assistance of Counsel for his defence.

Amendment VII [1791]

In Suits at common law, where the value in controversy shall exceed twenty dollars, the right of trial by jury shall be preserved, and no fact tried by a jury, shall be otherwise re-examined in any Court of the United States, than according to the rules of the common law.

Amendment VIII [1791]

Excessive bail shall not be required, nor excessive fines imposed, nor cruel and unusual punishments inflicted.

Amendment IX [1791]

The enumeration in the Constitution, of certain rights, shall not be construed to deny or disparage others retained by the people.

Amendment X [1791]

The powers not delegated to the United States by the Constitution, nor prohibited by it to the States, are reserved to the States respectively, or to the people.

Amendment XI [1798]

The Judicial power of the United States shall not be construed to extend to any suit in law or equity, commenced or prosecuted against one of the United States by Citizens of another State, or by Citizens or Subjects of any Foreign State.

Amendment XII [1804]

The Electors shall meet in their respective states, and vote by ballot for President and Vice-President, one of whom, at least, shall not be an inhabitant of the same state with themselves; they shall name in their ballots the person voted for as President, and in distinct ballots the person voted for as Vice-President, and they shall make distinct lists of all persons voted for as President, and of all persons voted for as Vice-President, and of the number of votes for each, which lists they shall sign and certify, and transmit sealed to the seat of the government of the United States, directed to the President of the Senate;—The President of the Senate shall, in the presence of the Senate and House of Representatives, open all the certificates and the votes shall then be counted;—The person having the greatest number of votes for President, shall be the President, if such number be a majority of the whole number of Electors appointed; and if no person have such majority, then from the persons having the highest numbers not exceeding three on the list of those voted for as President, the House of Representatives shall choose immediately, by ballot, the President. But in choosing the President, the votes shall be taken by states, the representation from each state having one vote; a quorum for this purpose shall consist of a member or members from two-thirds of the states, and a majority of all states shall be necessary to a choice. And if the House of Representatives shall not choose a President whenever the right of choice shall devolve upon them, before the fourth day of March next following, then the Vice-President shall act as President, as in the case of the death or other constitutional disability of the President.—The person having the greatest number of votes as Vice-President, shall be the Vice-President, if such number be a majority of the whole number of Electors appointed, and if no person have a majority, then from the two highest numbers on the list, the Senate shall choose the Vice-President; a quorum for the purpose shall consist of two-thirds of the whole number of Senators, and a majority of the whole number shall be necessary to a choice. But no person constitutionally ineligible to the office of President shall be eligible to that of Vice-President of the United States.

Amendment XIII [1865]

Section 1. Neither slavery nor involuntary servitude, except as a punishment for crime whereof the party shall have been duly convicted, shall exist within the United States, or any place subject to their jurisdiction.

Section 2. Congress shall have power to enforce this article by appropriate legislation.

Amendment XIV [1868]

Section 1. All persons born or naturalized in the United States, and subject to the jurisdiction thereof, are citizens of the United States and of the State wherein they reside. No State shall make or enforce any law which shall abridge the privileges or immunities of citizens of the United States; nor shall any State deprive any person of life, liberty, or property, without due process of law; nor deny to any person within its jurisdiction the equal protection of the laws.

Section 2. Representatives shall be apportioned among the several States according to their respective numbers, counting the whole number of persons in each State, excluding Indians not taxed. But when the right to vote at any election for the choice of electors for President and Vice President of the United States, Representatives in Congress, the Executive and Judicial officers of a State, or the members of the Legislature thereof, is denied to any of the male inhabitants of such State, being twenty-one years of age, and citizens of the United States, or in any way abridged, except for participation in rebellion, or other crime, the basis of representation therein shall be reduced in the proportion which the number of such male citizens shall bear to the whole number of male citizens twenty-one years of age in such State.

Section 3. No person shall be a Senator or Representative in Congress, or elector of President and Vice President, or hold any office, civil or military, under the United States, or under any State, who having previously taken an oath, as a member of Congress, or as an officer of the United States, or as a member of any State legislature, or as an executive or judicial officer of any State, to support the Constitution of the United States, shall have engaged in insurrection or rebellion against the same, or given aid or comfort to the enemies thereof. But Congress may by a vote of two-thirds of each House, remove such disability.

Section 4. The validity of the public debt of the United States, authorized by law, including debts incurred for payment of pensions and bounties for services in suppressing insurrection or rebellion, shall not be questioned. But neither the United States nor any State shall assume or pay any debt or obligation incurred in aid of insurrection or rebellion against the United States, or any claim for the loss or emancipation of any slave; but all such debts, obligations and claims shall be held illegal and void.

Section 5. The Congress shall have power to enforce, by appropriate legislation, the provisions of this article.

Amendment XV [1870]

Section 1. The right of citizens of the United States to vote shall not be denied or abridged by the United States or by any State on account of race, color, or previous condition of servitude.

Section 2. The Congress shall have power to enforce this article by appropriate legislation.

Amendment XVI [1913]

The Congress shall have power to lay and collect taxes on incomes, from whatever source derived, without apportionment among the several States, and without regard to any census or enumeration.

Amendment XVII [1913]

Section 1. The Senate of the United States shall be composed of two Senators from each State, elected by the people thereof, for six years; and each Senator shall have one vote. The electors in each State shall have the qualifications requisite for electors of the most numerous branch of the State legislatures.

Section 2. When vacancies happen in the representation of any State in the Senate, the executive authority of such State shall issue writs of election to fill such vacancies: Provided, That the legislature of any State may empower the executive thereof to make temporary appointments until the people fill the vacancies by election as the legislature may direct.

Section 3. This amendment shall not be so construed as to affect the election or term of any Senator chosen before it becomes valid as part of the Constitution.

Amendment XVIII [1919]

Section 1. After one year from the ratification of this article the manufacture, sale, or transportation of intoxicating liquors within, the importation thereof into, or the exportation thereof from the United States and all territory subject to the jurisdiction thereof for beverage purposes is hereby prohibited.

Section 2. The Congress and the several States shall have concurrent power to enforce this article by appropriate legislation.

Section 3. This article shall be inoperative unless it shall have been ratified as an amendment to the Constitution by the legislatures of the several States, as provided in the Constitution, within seven years from the date of the submission hereof to the States by the Congress.

Amendment XIX [1920]

Section 1. The right of citizens of the United States to vote shall not be denied or abridged by the United States or by any State on account of sex.

Section 2. Congress shall have power to enforce this article by appropriate legislation.

Amendment XX [1933]

Section 1. The terms of the President and Vice President shall end at noon on the 20th day of January, and the terms of Senators and Representatives at noon on the 3d day of January, of the years in which such terms would have ended if this article had not been ratified; and the terms of their successors shall then begin.

Section 2. The Congress shall assemble at least once in every year, and such meeting shall begin at noon on the 3d day of January, unless they shall by law appoint a different day.

Section 3. If, at the time fixed for the beginning of the term of the President, the President elect shall have died, the Vice President elect shall become President. If the President shall not have been chosen before the time fixed for the beginning of his term, or if the President elect shall have failed to qualify, then the Vice President elect shall act as President until a President shall have qualified; and the Congress may by law provide for the case wherein neither a President elect nor a Vice President elect shall have qualified, declaring who shall then act as President, or the manner in which one who is to act shall be selected, and such person shall act accordingly until a President or Vice President shall have qualified.

Section 4. The Congress may by law provide for the case of the death of any of the persons from whom the House of Representatives may choose a President whenever the right of choice shall have devolved upon them, and for the case of the death of any of the persons from whom the Senate may choose a Vice President whenever the right of choice shall have devolved upon them.

Section 5. Sections 1 and 2 shall take effect on the 15th day of October following the ratification of this article.

Section 6. This article shall be inoperative unless it shall have been ratified as an amendment to the Constitution by the legis-

latures of three-fourths of the several States within seven years from the date of its submission.

Amendment XXI [1933]

Section 1. The eighteenth article of amendment to the Constitution of the United States is hereby repealed.

Section 2. The transportation or importation into any State, Territory, or possession of the United States for delivery or use therein of intoxicating liquors, in violation of the laws thereof, is hereby prohibited.

Section 3. This article shall be inoperative unless it shall have been ratified as an amendment to the Constitution by conventions in the several States, as provided in the Constitution, within seven years from the date of the submission hereof to the States by the Congress.

Amendment XXII [1951]

Section 1. No person shall be elected to the office of the President more than twice, and no person who has held the office of President, or acted as President, for more than two years of a term to which some other person was elected President shall be elected to the office of President more than once. But this Article shall not apply to any person holding the office of President when this Article was proposed by the Congress, and shall not prevent any person who may be holding the office of President, or acting as President, during the term within which this Article becomes operative from holding the office of President or acting as President during the remainder of such term.

Section 2. This article shall be inoperative unless it shall have been ratified as an amendment to the Constitution by the legislatures of three-fourths of the several States within seven years from the date of its submission to the States by the Congress.

Amendment XXIII [1961]

Section 1. The District constituting the seat of Government of the United States shall appoint in such manner as the Congress may direct:

A number of electors of President and Vice President equal to the whole number of Senators and Representatives in Congress to which the District would be entitled if it were a State, but in no event more than the least populous state; they shall be in addition to those appointed by the states, but they shall be considered, for the purposes of the election of President and Vice President, to be electors appointed by a state; and they shall meet in the District and perform such duties as provided by the twelfth article of amendment.

Section 2. The Congress shall have power to enforce this article by appropriate legislation.

Amendment XXIV [1964]

Section 1. The right of citizens of the United States to vote in any primary or other election for President or Vice President, for electors for President or Vice President, or for Senator or Representative in Congress, shall not be denied or abridged by the

United States, or any State by reason of failure to pay any poll tax or other tax.

Section 2.   The Congress shall have power to enforce this article by appropriate legislation.

Amendment XXV [1967]

Section 1.   In case of the removal of the President from office or of his death or resignation, the Vice President shall become President.

Section 2.   Whenever there is a vacancy in the office of the Vice President, the President shall nominate a Vice President who shall take office upon confirmation by a majority vote of both Houses of Congress.

Section 3.   Whenever the President transmits to the President pro tempore of the Senate and the Speaker of the House of Representatives his written declaration that he is unable to discharge the powers and duties of his office, and until he transmits to them a written declaration to the contrary, such powers and duties shall be discharged by the Vice President as Acting President.

Section 4.   Whenever the Vice President and a majority of either the principal officers of the executive departments or of such other body as Congress may by law provide, transmit to the President pro tempore of the Senate and the Speaker of the House of Representatives their written declaration that the President is unable to discharge the powers and duties of his office, the Vice President shall immediately assume the powers and duties of the office as Acting President.

Thereafter, when the President transmits to the President pro tempore of the Senate and the Speaker of the House of Representatives his written declaration that no inability exists, he shall resume the powers and duties of his office unless the Vice President and a majority of either the principal officers of the executive department or of such other body as Congress may by law provide, transmit within four days to the President pro tempore of the Senate and the Speaker of the House of Representatives their written declaration that the President is unable to discharge the powers and duties of his office. Thereupon Congress shall decide the issue, assembling within forty-eight hours for that purpose if not in session. If the Congress, within twenty-one days after receipt of the latter written declaration, or, if Congress is not in session, within twenty-one days after Congress is required to assemble, determines by two-thirds vote of both Houses that the President is unable to discharge the powers and duties of his office, the Vice President shall continue to discharge the same as Acting President; otherwise, the President shall resume the powers and duties of his office.

Amendment XXVI [1971]

Section 1.   The right of citizens of the United States, who are eighteen years of age or older, to vote shall not be denied or abridged by the United States or by any State on account of age.

Section 2.   The Congress shall have power to enforce this article by appropriate legislation.

Amendment XXVII [1992]

No law, varying the compensation for the services of the Senators and Representatives, shall take effect, until an election of Representatives shall have intervened.

the declaration of independence

In Congress, July 4, 1776

A Declaration by the Representatives of the United States of America, in General Congress assembled. When in the Course of human Events, it becomes necessary for one People to dissolve the Political Bands which have connected them with another, and to assume among the Powers of the Earth, the separate and equal Station to which the Laws of Nature and of Nature's God entitle them, a decent Respect to the Opinions of Mankind requires that they should declare the causes which impel them to the Separation.

We hold these Truths to be self-evident, that all Men are created equal, that they are endowed by their Creator with certain unalienable Rights, that among these are Life, Liberty, and the Pursuit of Happiness—That to secure these Rights, Governments are instituted among Men, deriving their just Powers from the Consent of the Governed, that whenever any Form of Government becomes destructive of these Ends, it is the Right of the People to alter or to abolish it, and to institute new Government, laying its Foundation on such Principles, and organizing its Powers in such Forms, as to them shall seem most likely to effect their Safety and Happiness. Prudence, indeed, will dictate that Governments long established should not be changed for light and transient Causes; and accordingly all Experience hath shewn, that Mankind are more disposed to suffer, while Evils are sufferable, than to right themselves by abolishing the Forms to which they are accustomed. But when a long Train of Abuses and Usurpations, pursuing invariably the same Object, evinces a Design to reduce them under absolute Despotism, it is their Right, it is their Duty, to throw off such Government, and to provide new Guards for their future Security. Such has been the patient Sufferance of these Colonies; and such is now the Necessity which constrains them to alter their former Systems of Government. The History of the present King of Great-Britain is a History of repeated Injuries and Usurpations, all having in direct Object the Establishment of an absolute Tyranny over these States. To prove this, let Facts be submitted to a candid World.

He has refused his Assent to Laws, the most wholesome and necessary for the public Good.

He has forbidden his Governors to pass Laws of immediate and pressing Importance, unless suspended in their Operation till his Assent should be obtained; and when so suspended, he has utterly neglected to attend to them.

He has refused to pass other Laws for the Accommodation of large Districts of People, unless those People would relinquish the Right of Representation in the Legislature, a Right inestimable to them, and formidable to Tyrants only.

He has called together Legislative Bodies at Places unusual, uncomfortable, and distant from the Depository of their Public Records, for the sole Purpose of fatiguing them into Compliance with his Measures.

He has dissolved Representative Houses repeatedly, for opposing with manly Firmness his Invasions on the Rights of the People.

He has refused for a long Time, after such Dissolutions, to cause others to be elected; whereby the Legislative Powers, incapable of Annihilation, have returned to the People at large for their exercise; the State remaining in the mean time exposed to all the Dangers of Invasion from without, and Convulsions within.

He has endeavoured to prevent the Population of these States; for that Purpose obstructing the Laws for Naturalization of Foreigners; refusing to pass others to encourage their Migrations hither, and raising the Conditions of new Appropriations of Lands.

He has obstructed the Administration of Justice, by refusing his Assent to Laws for establishing Judiciary Powers.

He has made Judges dependent on his Will alone, for the Tenure of their offices, and the Amount and payment of their Salaries.

He has erected a Multitude of new Offices, and sent hither Swarms of Officers to harrass our People, and eat out their Substance.

He has kept among us, in Times of Peace, Standing Armies, without the consent of our Legislatures.

He has affected to render the Military independent of, and superior to the Civil Power.

He has combined with others to subject us to a Jurisdiction foreign to our Constitution, and unacknowledged by our Laws; giving his Assent to their Acts of pretended Legislation:

For quartering large Bodies of Armed Troops among us:

For protecting them, by a mock Trial, from Punishment for any Murders which they should commit on the Inhabitants of these States:

For cutting off our Trade with all Parts of the World:

For imposing Taxes on us without our Consent:

For depriving us, in many cases, of the Benefits of Trial by Jury:

For transporting us beyond Seas to be tried for pretended Offences:

For abolishing the free System of English Laws in a neighbouring Province, establishing therein an arbitrary Government, and enlarging its Boundaries, so as to render it at once an Example and fit Instrument for introducing the same absolute Rule into these Colonies:

For taking away our Charters, abolishing our most valuable Laws, and altering fundamentally the Forms of our Governments:

For suspending our own Legislatures, and declaring themselves invested with Power to legislate for us in all Cases whatsoever.

He has abdicated Government here, by declaring us out of his Protection and waging War against us.

He has plundered our Seas, ravaged our Coasts, burnt our towns, and destroyed the Lives of our People.

He is, at this Time, transporting large Armies of foreign Mercenaries to compleat the works of Death, Desolation, and Tyranny, already begun with circumstances of Cruelty and Perfidy, scarcely parallelled in the most barbarous Ages, and totally unworthy the Head of a civilized Nation.

He has constrained our fellow Citizens taken Captive on the high Seas to bear Arms against their Country, to become the Executioners of their Friends and Brethren, or to fall themselves by their Hands.

He has excited domestic Insurrections amongst us, and has endeavoured to bring on the Inhabitants of our Frontiers, the merciless Indian Savages, whose known Rule of Warfare, is an undistinguished Destruction, of all Ages, Sexes and Conditions.

In every state of these Oppressions we have Petitioned for Redress in the most humble Terms: Our repeated Petitions have been answered only by repeated Injury. A Prince, whose Character is thus marked by every act which may define a Tyrant, is unfit to be the Ruler of a free People.

Nor have we been wanting in Attentions to our British Brethren. We have warned them from Time to Time of Attempts by their Legislature to extend an unwarrantable Jurisdiction over us. We have reminded them of the Circumstances of our Emigration and Settlement here. We have appealed to their native Justice and Magnanimity, and we have conjured them by the Ties of our common Kindred to disavow these Usurpations, which, would inevitably interrupt our Connections and Correspondence. They too have been deaf to the Voice of Justice and of Consanguinity. We must, therefore, acquiesce in the Necessity, which denounces our Separation, and hold them, as we hold the rest of Mankind, Enemies in War, in Peace, Friends.

We, therefore, the Representatives of the UNITED STATES OF AMERICA, in General Congress Assembled, appealing to the Supreme Judge of the World for the Rectitude of our Intentions, do, in the Name, and by the Authority of the good People of these Colonies, solemnly Publish and Declare, That these United Colonies are, and of Right ought to be, Free and Independent States; that they are absolved from all Allegiance to the British Crown, and that all political Connection between them and the State of Great-Britain, is and ought to be totally dissolved; and that as Free and Independent States, they have full Power to levy War, conclude Peace, contract Alliances, establish Commerce, and to do all other Acts and Things which Independent States may of right do. And for the support of this declaration, with a firm Reliance on the Protection of divine Providence, we mutually pledge to each other our lives, our Fortunes, and our sacred Honor.

supreme court justices since 1900

Chief Justices

Name	Years of Service	State App'd From	Appointing President	Age App'd	Political Affiliation	Educational Background*
Fuller, Melville Weston	1888–1910	Illinois	Cleveland	55	Democrat	Bowdoin College; studied at Harvard Law School
White, Edward Douglass	1910–1921	Louisiana	Taft	65	Democrat	Mount St. Mary's College; Georgetown College (now University)
Taft, William Howard	1921–1930	Connecticut	Harding	64	Republican	Yale; Cincinnati Law School
Hughes, Charles Evans	1930–1941	New York	Hoover	68	Republican	Colgate University; Brown; Columbia Law School
Stone, Harlan Fiske	1941–1946	New York	Roosevelt, F.	69	Republican	Amherst College; Columbia
Vinson, Frederick Moore	1946–1953	Kentucky	Truman	56	Democrat	Centre College
Warren, Earl	1953–1969	California	Eisenhower	62	Republican	University of California, Berkeley
Burger, Warren Earl	1969–1986	Virginia	Nixon	62	Republican	University of Minnesota; St. Paul College of Law (Mitchell College)
Rehnquist, William Hubbs	1986–	Virginia	Reagan	62	Republican	Stanford; Harvard; Stanford University Law School

*Source: Educational background information derived from Elder Witt, *Guide to the U.S. Supreme Court*, 2d ed. (Washington, D.C.: Congressional Quarterly Press, Inc., 1990). Reprinted with the permission of the publisher.

Associate Justices

Name	Years of Service	State App'd From	Appointing President	Age App'd	Political Affiliation	Educational Background
Harlan, John Marshall	1877–1911	Kentucky	Hayes	61	Republican	Centre College; studied law at Transylvania University
Gray, Horace	1882–1902	Massachusetts	Arthur	54	Republican	Harvard College; Harvard Law School
Brewer, David Josiah	1890–1910	Kansas	Harrison	53	Republican	Wesleyan University; Yale; Albany Law School
Brown, Henry Billings	1891–1906	Michigan	Harrison	55	Republican	Yale; studied at Yale Law School and Harvard Law School
Shiras, George, Jr.	1892–1903	Pennsylvania	Harrison	61	Republican	Ohio University; Yale; studied law at Yale and privately
White, Edward Douglass	1894–1910	Louisiana	Cleveland	49	Democrat	Mount St. Mary's College; Georgetown College (now University)

Associate Justices (continued)

Name	Years of Service	State App'd From	Appointing President	Age App'd	Political Affiliation	Educational Background
Peckham, Rufus Wheeler	1896–1909	New York	Cleveland	58	Democrat	Read law in father's firm
McKenna, Joseph	1898–1925	California	McKinley	55	Republican	Benicia Collegiate Institute, Law Dept.
Holmes, Oliver Wendell, Jr.	1902–1932	Massachusetts	Roosevelt, T.	61	Republican	Harvard College; studied law at Harvard Law School
Day, William Rufus	1903–1922	Ohio	Roosevelt, T.	54	Republican	University of Michigan; University of Michigan Law School
Moody, William Henry	1906–1910	Massachusetts	Roosevelt, T.	53	Republican	Harvard; Harvard Law School
Lurton, Horace Harmon	1910–1914	Tennessee	Taft	66	Democrat	University of Chicago; Cumberland Law School
Hughes, Charles Evans	1910–1916	New York	Taft	48	Republican	Colgate University; Brown University; Columbia Law School
Van Devanter, Willis	1911–1937	Wyoming	Taft	52	Republican	Indiana Asbury University; University of Cincinnati Law School
Lamar, Joseph Rucker	1911–1916	Georgia	Taft	54	Democrat	University of Georgia; Bethany College; Washington and Lee University
Pitney, Mahlon	1912–1922	New Jersey	Taft	54	Republican	College of New Jersey (Princeton); read law under father
McReynolds, James Clark	1914–1941	Tennessee	Wilson	52	Democrat	Vanderbilt University; University of Virginia
Brandeis, Louis Dembitz	1916–1939	Massachusetts	Wilson	60	Democrat	Harvard Law School
Clarke, John Hessin	1916–1922	Ohio	Wilson	59	Democrat	Western Reserve University; read law under father
Sutherland, George	1922–1938	Utah	Harding	60	Republican	Brigham Young Academy; one year at University of Michigan Law School
Butler, Pierce	1923–1939	Minnesota	Harding	57	Democrat	Carleton College
Sanford, Edward Terry	1923–1930	Tennessee	Harding	58	Republican	University of Tennessee; Harvard; Harvard Law School
Stone, Harlan Fiske	1925–1941	New York	Coolidge	53	Republican	Amherst College; Columbia University Law School
Roberts, Owen Josephus	1930–1945	Pennsylvania	Hoover	55	Republican	University of Pennsylvania; University of Pennsylvania Law School
Cardozo, Benjamin Nathan	1932–1938	New York	Hoover	62	Democrat	Columbia University; two years at Columbia Law School
Black, Hugo Lafayette	1937–1971	Alabama	Roosevelt, F.	51	Democrat	Birmingham Medical College; University of Alabama Law School
Reed, Stanley Forman	1938–1957	Kentucky	Roosevelt, F.	54	Democrat	Kentucky Wesleyan University; Foreman Yale; studied law at University of Virginia and Columbia University; University of Paris
Frankfurter, Felix	1939–1962	Massachusetts	Roosevelt, F.	57	Independent	College of the City of New York; Harvard Law School
Douglas, William Orville	1939–1975	Connecticut	Roosevelt, F.	41	Democrat	Whitman College; Columbia University Law School
Murphy, Frank	1940–1949	Michigan	Roosevelt, F.	50	Democrat	University of Michigan; Lincoln's Inn, London; Trinity College
Byrnes, James Francis	1941–1942	South Carolina	Roosevelt, F.	62	Democrat	Read law privately
Jackson, Robert Houghwout	1941–1954	New York	Roosevelt, F.	49	Democrat	Albany Law School

Associate Justices (continued)

Name	Years of Service	State App'd From	Appointing President	Age App'd	Political Affiliation	Educational Background
Rutledge, Wiley Blount	1943–1949	Iowa	Roosevelt, F.	49	Democrat	University of Wisconsin; University of Colorado
Burton, Harold Hitz	1945–1958	Ohio	Truman	57	Republican	Bowdoin College; Harvard University Law School
Clark, Thomas Campbell	1949–1967	Texas	Truman	50	Democrat	University of Texas
Minton, Sherman	1949–1956	Indiana	Truman	59	Democrat	Indiana University College of Law; Yale Law School
Harlan, John Marshall	1955–1971	New York	Eisenhower	56	Republican	Princeton; Oxford University; New York Law School
Brennan, William J., Jr.	1956–1990	New Jersey	Eisenhower	50	Democrat	University of Pennsylvania; Harvard Law School
Whittaker, Charles Evans	1957–1962	Missouri	Eisenhower	56	Republican	University of Kansas City Law School
Stewart, Potter	1958–1981	Ohio	Eisenhower	43	Republican	Yale; Yale Law School
White, Byron Raymond	1962–1993	Colorado	Kennedy	45	Democrat	University of Colorado; Oxford University; YaleLaw School
Goldberg, Arthur Joseph	1962–1965	Illinois	Kennedy	54	Democrat	Northwestern University
Fortas, Abe	1965–1969	Tennessee	Johnson, L.	55	Democrat	Southwestern College; Yale Law School
Marshall, Thurgood	1967–1991	New York	Johnson, L.	59	Democrat	Lincoln University; Howard University Law School
Blackmun, Harry A.	1970–1994	Minnesota	Nixon	62	Republican	Harvard; Harvard Law School
Powell, Lewis F., Jr.	1972–1987	Virginia	Nixon	65	Democrat	Washington and Lee University; Washington and Lee University Law School; Harvard Law School
Rehnquist, William H.	1972–1986	Arizona	Nixon	48	Republican	Stanford; Harvard; Stanford University Law School
Stevens, John Paul	1975–	Illinois	Ford	55	Republican	University of Colorado; Northwestern University Law School
O'Connor, Sandra Day	1981–	Arizona	Reagan	51	Republican	Stanford; Stanford University Law School
Scalia, Antonin	1986–	Virginia	Reagan	50	Republican	Georgetown University; Harvard Law School
Kennedy, Anthony M.	1988–	California	Reagan	52	Republican	Stanford; London School of Economics; Harvard Law School
Souter, David Hackett	1990–	New Hampshire	Bush, G. H. W.	51	Republican	Harvard; Oxford University
Thomas, Clarence	1991–	District of Columbia	Bush, G. H. W.	43	Republican	Holy Cross College; Yale Law School
Ginsburg, Ruth Bader	1993–	District of Columbia	Clinton	60	Democrat	Cornell University; Columbia Law School
Breyer, Stephen G.	1994–	Massachusetts	Clinton	55	Democrat	Stanford; Oxford University; Harvard Law School

party control of congress since 1900

Congress	Years	President	Majority Party in House	Majority Party in Senate
57th	1901–1903	T. Roosevelt	Republican	Republican
58th	1903–1905	T. Roosevelt	Republican	Republican
59th	1905–1907	T. Roosevelt	Republican	Republican
60th	1907–1909	T. Roosevelt	Republican	Republican
61st	1909–1911	Taft	Republican	Republican
62d	1911–1913	Taft	Democratic	Republican
63d	1913–1915	Wilson	Democratic	Democratic
64th	1915–1917	Wilson	Democratic	Democratic
65th	1917–1919	Wilson	Democratic	Democratic
66th	1919–1921	Wilson	Republican	Republican
67th	1921–1923	Harding	Republican	Republican
68th	1923–1925	Coolidge	Republican	Republican
69th	1925–1927	Coolidge	Republican	Republican
70th	1927–1929	Coolidge	Republican	Republican
71st	1929–1931	Hoover	Republican	Republican
72d	1931–1933	Hoover	Democratic	Republican
73d	1933–1935	F. Roosevelt	Democratic	Democratic
74th	1935–1937	F. Roosevelt	Democratic	Democratic
75th	1937–1939	F. Roosevelt	Democratic	Democratic
76th	1939–1941	F. Roosevelt	Democratic	Democratic
77th	1941–1943	F. Roosevelt	Democratic	Democratic
78th	1943–1945	F. Roosevelt	Democratic	Democratic
79th	1945–1947	Truman	Democratic	Democratic
80th	1947–1949	Truman	Republican	Democratic
81st	1949–1951	Truman	Democratic	Democratic
82d	1951–1953	Truman	Democratic	Democratic
83d	1953–1955	Eisenhower	Republican	Republican
84th	1955–1957	Eisenhower	Democratic	Democratic
85th	1957–1959	Eisenhower	Democratic	Democratic
86th	1959–1961	Eisenhower	Democratic	Democratic
87th	1961–1963	Kennedy	Democratic	Democratic
88th	1963–1965	Kennedy/Johnson	Democratic	Democratic
89th	1965–1967	Johnson	Democratic	Democratic
90th	1967–1969	Johnson	Democratic	Democratic
91st	1969–1971	Nixon	Democratic	Democratic
92d	1971–1973	Nixon	Democratic	Democratic
93d	1973–1975	Nixon/Ford	Democratic	Democratic
94th	1975–1977	Ford	Democratic	Democratic
95th	1977–1979	Carter	Democratic	Democratic
96th	1979–1981	Carter	Democratic	Democratic
97th	1981–1983	Reagan	Democratic	Republican
98th	1983–1985	Reagan	Democratic	Republican
99th	1985–1987	Reagan	Democratic	Republican
100th	1987–1989	Reagan	Democratic	Democratic
101st	1989–1991	G. H. W. Bush	Democratic	Democratic
102d	1991–1993	G. H. W. Bush	Democratic	Democratic
103d	1993–1995	Clinton	Democratic	Democratic
104th	1995–1997	Clinton	Republican	Republican
105th	1997–1999	Clinton	Republican	Republican
106th	1999–2001	Clinton	Republican	Republican
107th	2002–2003	G. W. Bush	Republican	Democratic*
108th	2003–2005	G. W. Bush	Republican	Republican

*Effective June 2001.

	TERM OF SERVICE	AGE AT INAUGURATION	PARTY AFFILIATION	COLLEGE OR UNIVERSITY	OCCUPATION OR PROFESSION
1. George Washington	1789–1797	57	None		Planter
2. John Adams	1797–1801	61	Federalist	Harvard	Lawyer
3. Thomas Jefferson	1801–1809	57	Democratic-Republican	William and Mary	Planter, Lawyer
4. James Madison	1809–1817	57	Democratic-Republican	Princeton	Lawyer
5. James Monroe	1817–1825	58	Democratic-Republican	William and Mary	Lawyer
6. John Quincy Adams	1825–1829	57	Democratic-Republican	Harvard	Lawyer
7. Andrew Jackson	1829–1837	61	Democrat		Lawyer
8. Martin Van Buren	1837–1841	54	Democrat		Lawyer
9. William H. Harrison	1841	68	Whig	Hampden-Sydney	Soldier
10. John Tyler	1841–1845	51	Whig	William and Mary	Lawyer
11. James K. Polk	1845–1849	49	Democrat	U. of N. Carolina	Lawyer
12. Zachary Taylor	1849–1850	64	Whig		Soldier
13. Millard Fillmore	1850–1853	50	Whig		Lawyer
14. Franklin Pierce	1853–1857	48	Democrat	Bowdoin	Lawyer
15. James Buchanan	1857–1861	65	Democrat	Dickinson	Lawyer
16. Abraham Lincoln	1861–1865	52	Republican		Lawyer
17. Andrew Johnson	1865–1869	56	National Union†		Tailor
18. Ulysses S. Grant	1869–1877	46	Republican	U.S. Mil. Academy	Soldier
19. Rutherford B. Hayes	1877–1881	54	Republican	Kenyon	Lawyer
20. James A. Garfield	1881	49	Republican	Williams	Lawyer
21. Chester A. Arthur	1881–1885	51	Republican	Union	Lawyer
22. Grover Cleveland	1885–1889	47	Democrat		Lawyer
23. Benjamin Harrison	1889–1893	55	Republican	Miami	Lawyer
24. Grover Cleveland	1893–1897	55	Democrat		Lawyer
25. William McKinley	1897–1901	54	Republican	Allegheny College	Lawyer
26. Theodore Roosevelt	1901–1909	42	Republican	Harvard	Author
27. William H. Taft	1909–1913	51	Republican	Yale	Lawyer
28. Woodrow Wilson	1913–1921	56	Democrat	Princeton	Educator
29. Warren G. Harding	1921–1923	55	Republican		Editor
30. Calvin Coolidge	1923–1929	51	Republican	Amherst	Lawyer
31. Herbert C. Hoover	1929–1933	54	Republican	Stanford	Engineer
32. Franklin D. Roosevelt	1933–1945	51	Democrat	Harvard	Lawyer
33. Harry S Truman	1945–1953	60	Democrat		Businessman
34. Dwight D. Eisenhower	1953–1961	62	Republican	U.S. Mil. Academy	Soldier
35. John F. Kennedy	1961–1963	43	Democrat	Harvard	Author
36. Lyndon B. Johnson	1963–1969	55	Democrat	Southwest Texas State	Teacher
37. Richard M. Nixon	1969–1974	56	Republican	Whittier	Lawyer
38. Gerald R. Ford‡	1974–1977	61	Republican	Michigan	Lawyer
39. James E. Carter, Jr.	1977–1981	52	Democrat	U.S. Naval Academy	Businessman
40. Ronald W. Reagan	1981–1989	69	Republican	Eureka College	Actor
41. George H. W. Bush	1989–1993	64	Republican	Yale	Businessman
42. William J. Clinton	1993–2001	46	Democrat	Georgetown	Lawyer
43. George W. Bush	2001–	54	Republican	Yale	Businessman

*Church preference; never joined any church.

†The National Union Party consisted of Republicans and War Democrats. Johnson was a Democrat.

**Inaugurated Dec. 6, 1973, to replace Agnew, who resigned Oct. 10, 1973.

‡Inaugurated Aug. 9, 1974, to replace Nixon, who resigned that same day.

§Inaugurated Dec. 19, 1974, to replace Ford, who became president Aug. 9, 1974.

	RELIGION	BORN	DIED	AGE AT DEATH	VICE PRESIDENT	
1.	Episcopalian	Feb. 22, 1732	Dec. 14, 1799	67	John Adams	(1789–1797)
2.	Unitarian	Oct. 30, 1735	July 4, 1826	90	Thomas Jefferson	(1797–1801)
3.	Unitarian*	Apr. 13, 1743	July 4, 1826	83	Aaron Burr	(1801–1805)
					George Clinton	(1805–1809)
4.	Episcopalian	Mar. 16, 1751	June 28, 1836	85	George Clinton	(1809–1812)
					Elbridge Gerry	(1813–1814)
5.	Episcopalian	Apr. 28, 1758	July 4, 1831	73	Daniel D. Tompkins	(1817–1825)
6.	Unitarian	July 11, 1767	Feb. 23, 1848	80	John C. Calhoun	(1825–1829)
7.	Presbyterian	Mar. 15, 1767	June 8, 1845	78	John C. Calhoun	(1829–1832)
					Martin Van Buren	(1833–1837)
8.	Dutch Reformed	Dec. 5, 1782	July 24, 1862	79	Richard M. Johnson	(1837–1841)
9.	Episcopalian	Feb. 9, 1773	Apr. 4, 1841	68	John Tyler	(1841)
10.	Episcopalian	Mar. 29, 1790	Jan. 18, 1862	71		
11.	Methodist	Nov. 2, 1795	June 15, 1849	53	George M. Dallas	(1845–1849)
12.	Episcopalian	Nov. 24, 1784	July 9, 1850	65	Millard Fillmore	(1849–1850)
13.	Unitarian	Jan. 7, 1800	Mar. 8, 1874	74		
14.	Episcopalian	Nov. 23, 1804	Oct. 8, 1869	64	William R. King	(1853)
15.	Presbyterian	Apr. 23, 1791	June 1, 1868	77	John C. Breckinridge	(1857–1861)
16.	Presbyterian*	Feb. 12, 1809	Apr. 15, 1865	56	Hannibal Hamlin	(1861–1865)
					Andrew Johnson	(1865)
17.	Methodist*	Dec. 29, 1808	July 31, 1875	66		
18.	Methodist	Apr. 27, 1822	July 23, 1885	63	Schuyler Colfax	(1869–1873)
					Henry Wilson	(1873–1875)
19.	Methodist*	Oct. 4, 1822	Jan. 17, 1893	70	William A. Wheeler	(1877–1881)
20.	Disciples of Christ	Nov. 19, 1831	Sept. 19, 1881	49	Chester A. Arthur	(1881)
21.	Episcopalian	Oct. 5, 1829	Nov. 18, 1886	57		
22.	Presbyterian	Mar. 18, 1837	June 24, 1908	71	Thomas A. Hendricks	(1885)
23.	Presbyterian	Aug. 20, 1833	Mar. 13, 1901	67	Levi P. Morton	(1889–1893)
24.	Presbyterian	Mar. 18, 1837	June 24, 1908	71	Adlai E. Stevenson	(1893–1897)
25.	Methodist	Jan. 29, 1843	Sept. 14, 1901	58	Garret A. Hobart	(1897–1899)
					Theodore Roosevelt	(1901)
26.	Dutch Reformed	Oct. 27, 1858	Jan. 6, 1919	60	Charles W. Fairbanks	(1905–1909)
27.	Unitarian	Sept. 15, 1857	Mar. 8, 1930	72	James S. Sherman	(1909–1912)
28.	Presbyterian	Dec. 29, 1856	Feb. 3, 1924	67	Thomas R. Marshall	(1913–1921)
29.	Baptist	Nov. 2, 1865	Aug. 2, 1923	57	Calvin Coolidge	(1921–1923)
30.	Congregationalist	July 4, 1872	Jan. 5, 1933	60	Charles G. Dawes	(1925–1929)
31.	Friend (Quaker)	Aug. 10, 1874	Oct. 20, 1964	90	Charles Curtis	(1929–1933)
32.	Episcopalian	Jan. 30, 1882	Apr. 12, 1945	63	John N. Garner	(1933–1941)
					Henry A. Wallace	(1941–1945)
					Harry S Truman	(1945)
33.	Baptist	May 8, 1884	Dec. 26, 1972	88	Alben W. Barkley	(1949–1953)
34.	Presbyterian	Oct. 14, 1890	Mar. 28, 1969	78	Richard M. Nixon	(1953–1961)
35.	Roman Catholic	May 29, 1917	Nov. 22, 1963	46	Lyndon B. Johnson	(1961–1963)
36.	Disciples of Christ	Aug. 27, 1908	Jan. 22, 1973	64	Hubert H. Humphrey	(1965–1969)
37.	Friend (Quaker)	Jan. 9, 1913	Apr. 22, 1994	81	Spiro T. Agnew	(1969–1973)
					Gerald R. Ford**	(1973–1974)
38.	Episcopalian	July 14, 1913			Nelson A. Rockefeller§	(1974–1977)
39.	Baptist	Oct. 1, 1924			Walter F. Mondale	(1977–1981)
40.	Disciples of Christ	Feb. 6, 1911			George H. W. Bush	(1981–1989)
41.	Episcopalian	June 12, 1924			J. Danforth Quayle	(1989–1993)
42.	Baptist	Aug. 19, 1946			Albert A. Gore	(1993–2001)
43.	Methodist	July 6, 1946			Dick Cheney	(2001–)

federalist papers no. 10 and no. 51

The founders completed drafting the U.S. Constitution in 1787. It was then submitted to the thirteen states for ratification, and a major debate ensued. As you read in Chapter 2, on the one side of this debate were the Federalists, who urged that the new Constitution be adopted. On the other side of the debate were the anti-Federalists, who argued against ratification.

During the course of this debate, three men well known for their Federalist views—Alexander Hamilton, James Madison, and John Jay—wrote a series of essays in which they argued for immediate ratifcation of the Constitution. The essays appeared in the New York City Independent Journal *in October 1787, just a little over a month after the Constitutional Convention adjourned. Later, Hamilton arranged to have the essays collected and published in book form. The articles filled two volumes, both of which were published by May 1788. The essays are often referred to collectively as the* Federalist Papers.

Scholars disagree as to whether the Federalist Papers *had a significant impact on the decision of the states to ratify the Constitution. Nonetheless, many of the essays are masterpieces of political reasoning and have left a lasting imprint on American politics and government. Above all, the* Federalist Papers *shed an important light on what the founders intended when they drafted various constitutional provisions.*

Here we present just two of these essays, Federalist Paper *No. 10 and* Federalist Paper *No. 51. Each essay was written by James Madison, who referred to himself as "Publius." We have annotated each document to clarify the meaning of particular passages. The annotations are set in italics to distinguish them from the original text of the documents.*

#10

Federalist Paper No. 10 is a classic document that is often referred to by teachers of American government. Authored by James Madison, it sets forth Madison's views on factions in politics. The essay was written, in large part, to counter the arguments put forth by the Anti-Federalists that small factions might take control of the government, thus destroying the representative nature the republican form of gov-ernment established by the Constitution. The essay opens with a discussion of the "dangerous vice" of factions and the importance of devising a form of government in which this vice will be controlled.

Among the numerous advantages promised by a well-constructed Union, none deserves to be more accurately developed than its tendency to break and control the violence of faction. The friend of popular governments never finds himself so much alarmed for their character and fate as when he contemplates their propensity to this dangerous vice. He will not fail, therefore, to set a due value on any plan which, without violating the principles to which he is attached, provides a proper cure for it. The instability, injustice, and confusion introduced into the public councils have, in truth, been the mortal diseases under which popular governments have everywhere perished, as they continue to be the favorite and fruitful topics from which the adversaries to liberty derive their most specious declamations. The valuable improvements made by the American constitutions on the popular models, both ancient and modern, cannot certainly be too much admired; but it would be an unwarrantable partiality to contend that they have as effectually obviated the danger on this side, as was wished and expected. Complaints are everywhere heard from our most considerate and virtuous citizens, equally the friends of public and private faith and of public and personal liberty, that our governments are too unstable, that the public good is disregarded in the conflicts of rival parties, and that measures are too often decided, not according to the rules of justice and the rights of the minor party, but by the superior force of an interested and overbearing majority. However anxiously we may wish that these complaints had no foundation, the evidence of known facts will not permit us to deny that they are in some degree true. It will be found, indeed, on a candid review of our situation, that some of the distresses under which we labor have been erroneously charged on the operation of our governments; but it will be found, at the same time, that other causes will not alone account for many of our heaviest misfortunes; and, particularly, for that prevailing and increasing distrust of public engagements and alarm for private rights which are echoed from one end of the continent to the other. These must be chiefly, if not wholly, effects of the unsteadiness and injustice with which a factious spirit has tainted our public administration.

In the following paragraph, Madison clarifies for his readers his understanding of what the term faction means.

By a faction I understand a number of citizens, whether amounting to a majority or minority of the whole, who are united and actuated by some common impulse of passion, or of interest, adverse to the rights of other citizens, or the permanent and aggregate interests of the community.

In the following passages, Madison looks at the two methods of curing the "mischiefs of factions." One of these methods is removing the causes of faction. The other is to control the effects of factions.

There are two methods of curing the mischiefs of faction: the one, by removing its causes; the other, by controlling its effects.

There are again two methods of removing the causes of faction: the one, by destroying the liberty which is essential to its existence; the other, by giving to every citizen the same opinions, the same passions, and the same interests.

It could never be more truly said than of the first remedy that it was worse than the disease. Liberty is to faction what air is to fire, an aliment without which it instantly expires. But it could not be a less folly to abolish liberty, which is essential to political life, because it nourishes faction than it would be to wish the annihilation of air, which is essential to animal life, because it imparts to fire its destructive agency.

The second expedient is as impracticable as the first would be unwise. As long as the reason of man continues fallible, and his is at liberty to exercise it, different opinions will be formed. As long as the connection subsists between his reason and his self-love, his opinions and his passions will have a reciprocal influence on each other; and the former will be objects to which the latter will attach themselves. The diversity in the faculties of men, from which the rights of property originate, is not less an insuperable obstacle to a uniformity of interests. The protection of these faculties is the first object of government. From the protection of different and unequal faculties of acquiring property, the possession of different degrees and kinds of property immediately results; and from the influence of these on the sentiments and views of the respective proprietors ensues a division of the society into different interests and parties.

The latent causes of faction are thus sown in the nature of man; and we see them everywhere brought into different degrees of activity, according to the different circumstances of civil society. A zeal for different opinions concerning religion, concerning government, and many other points, as well of speculation as of practice; an attachment to different leaders ambitiously contending for pre-eminence and power; or to persons of other descriptions whose fortunes have been interesting to the human passions, have, in turn, divided mankind into parties, inflamed them with mutual animosity, and rendered them much more disposed to vex and oppress each other than to co-operate for their common good. So strong is this propensity of mankind to fall into mutual animosities that where no substantial occasion presents itself the most frivolous and fanciful distinctions have been sufficient to kindle their unfriendly passions and excite their most violent conflicts. But the most common and durable source of factions has been the various and unequal distribution of property. Those who hold and those who are without property have ever formed distinct interests in society. Those who are creditors, and those who are debtors, fall under a like discrimination. A landed interest, a manufacturing interest, a mercantile interest, a moneyed interest, with many lesser interests, grow up of necessity in civilized nations, and divide them into different classes, actuated by different sentiments and views. The regulation of these various and interfering interests forms the principal task of modern legislation and involves the spirit of party and faction in the necessary and ordinary operations of government.

No man is allowed to be a judge in his own cause, because his interest would certainly bias his judgment, and, not improbably, corrupt his integrity. With equal, nay with greater reason, a body of men are unfit to be both judges and parties at the same time; yet what are many of the most important acts of legislation but so many judicial determinations, not indeed concerning the rights of single persons, but concerning the rights of large bodies of citizens? And what are the different classes of legislators but advocates and parties to the causes which they determine? Is a law proposed concerning private debts? It is a question to which the creditors are parties on one side and the debtors on the other. Justice ought to hold the balance between them. Yet the parties are, and must be, themselves the judges; and the most numerous party, or in other words, the most powerful faction must be expected to prevail. Shall domestic manufacturers be encouraged, and in what degree, by restrictions on foreign manufacturers? Are questions which would be differently decided by the landed and the manufacturing classes, and probably by neither with a sole regard to justice and the public good. The apportionment of taxes on the various descriptions of property is an act which seems to require the most exact impartiality; yet there is, perhaps, no legislative act in which greater opportunity and temptation are given to a predominant party to trample on the rules of justice. Every shilling with which they overburden the inferior number is a shilling saved to their own pockets.

It is in vain to say that enlightened statesmen will be able to adjust these clashing interests and render them all subservient to the public good. Enlightened statesmen will not always be at the helm. Nor, in many cases, can such an adjustment be made at all without taking into view indirect and remote considerations, which will rarely prevail over the immediate interest which one party may find in disregarding the rights of another or the good of the whole.

The inference to which we are brought is that the causes of faction cannot be removed and that relief is only to be sought in the means of controlling its effects.

In the preceding passages, Madison has explored the causes of factions and has concluded that they cannot "be removed" without removing liberty itself, which is one of the causes, or altering human nature. He now turns to a discussion of how the effects of factions might be controlled.

If a faction consists of less than a majority, relief is supplied by the republican principle, which enables the majority to defeat its sinister views by regular vote. It may clog the administration, it may convulse the society; but it will be unable to execute and mask its violence under the forms of the Constitution. When a majority is included in a faction, the form of popular government, on the other hand, enables it to sacrifice to its ruling passion or interest both the public good and the rights of other citizens. To secure the public good and private rights against the danger of such a faction, and at the same time to preserve the spirit and the form of popular government, is then the great object to which our inquiries are directed. Let me add that it is the great desideratum by which alone this form of government can be rescued from the opprobrium under which it has so long labored and be recommended to the esteem and adoption of mankind.

According to Madison, one way of controlling the effects of factions is to make sure that the majority is not able to act in "concert," or jointly, to "carry into effect schemes of oppression."

By what means is this object attainable? Evidently by one of two only. Either the existence of the same passion or interest in a majority at the same time must be prevented, or the majority, having such coexistent passion or interest, must be rendered, by their number and local situation, unable to concert and carry into effect schemes of oppression. If the impulse and the opportunity be suffered to coincide, we well know that neither moral nor religious motives can be relied on as an adequate control. They are not found to be such on the injustice and violence of individuals, and lose their efficacy in proportion to the number combined together, that is, in proportion as their efficacy becomes needful.

From this view of the subject it may be concluded that a pure democracy, by which I mean a society consisting of a small number of citizens, who assemble and administer the government in person, can admit of no cure for the mischiefs of faction. A common passion or interest will, in almost every case, be felt by a majority of the whole; a communication and concert results from the form of government itself; and there is nothing to check the inducements to sacrifice the weaker party or an obnoxious individual. Hence it is that such democracies have ever been spectacles of turbulence and contention; have ever been found incompatible with personal security or the rights of property; and have in general been as short in their lives as they have been violent in their deaths. Theoretic politicians, who have patronized this species of government, have erroneously supposed that by reducing mankind to a perfect equality in their political rights, they would at the same time be perfectly equalized and assimilated in their possessions, their opinions, and their passions.

In the following six paragraphs, Madison sets forth some of the reasons why a republican form of government promises a "cure" for the mischiefs of factions. He begins by clarifying the difference between a republic and a democracy. He then describes how in a large republic, the elected representatives of the people will be large enough in number to guard against factions—the "cabals," or concerted actions, of "a few." On the one hand, representatives will not be so removed from their local districts as to be unacquainted with their constituents' needs. On the other hand, they will not be "unduly attached" to local interests and unfit to understand "great

and national objects." Madison concludes that the Constitution "forms a happy combination in this respect."

A republic, by which I mean a government in which the scheme of representation takes place, opens a different prospect and promises the cure for which we are seeking. Let us examine the points in which it varies from pure democracy, and we shall comprehend both the nature of the cure and the efficacy which it must derive from the Union.

The two great points of difference between a democracy and a republic are: first, the delegation of the government, in the latter, to a small number of citizens elected by the rest; secondly, the greater number of citizens and greater sphere of country over which the latter may be extended.

The effect of the first difference is, on the one hand, to refine and enlarge the public views by passing them through the medium of a chosen body of citizens, whose wisdom may best discern the true interest of their country and whose patriotism and love of justice will be least likely to sacrifice it to temporary or partial considerations. Under such a regulation it may well happen that the public voice, pronounced by the representatives of the people, will be more consonant to the public good than if pronounced by the people themselves, convened for the purpose. On the other hand, the effect may be inverted. Men of factious tempers, of local prejudices, or of sinister designs, may, by intrigue, by corruption, or by other means, first obtain the suffrages, and then betray the interests of the people. The question resulting is, whether small or extensive republics are most favorable to the election of proper guardians of the public weal; and it is clearly decided in favor of the latter by two obvious considerations.

In the first place it is to be remarked that however small the republic may be the representatives must be raised to a certain number in order to guard against the cabals of a few; and that however large it may be they must be limited to a certain number in order to guard against the confusion of a multitude. Hence, the number of representatives in the two cases not being in proportion to that of the constituents, and being proportionally greatest in the small republic, it follows that if the proportion of fit characters be not less in the large than in the small republic, the former will present a greater option, and consequently a greater probability of a fit choice.

In the next place, as each representative will be chosen by a greater number of citizens in the large than in the small republic, it will be more difficult for unworthy candidates to practice with success the vicious arts by which elections are too often carried; and the suffrages of the people being more free, will be more likely to center on men who possess the most attractive merit and the most diffusive and established characters.

It must be confessed that in this, as in most other cases, there is a mean, on both sides of which inconveniencies will be found to lie. By enlarging too much the number of electors, you render the representative too little acquainted with all their local circumstances and lesser interests; as by reducing it too much, you render him unduly attached to these, and too little fit to comprehend and pursue great and national objects. The federal Constitution forms a happy combination in this respect; the great and aggregate interests being referred to the national, the local and particular to the State legislatures.

In the remaining passages of this essay, Madison looks at another "point of difference" between a republic and a democracy. Specifically, a republic can encompass a larger territory and a greater number of citizens than a democracy can. This fact, too, argues Madison, will help to control the influence of factions because the interests that draw people together to act in concert are typically at the local level and would be unlikely to affect or dominate the national government. As Madison states, "The influence of factious leaders may kindle a flame within their particular States but will be unable to spread a general conflagration through the other States." Generally, in a large republic, there will be numerous factions, and no particular faction will be able to "pervade the whole body of the Union."

The other point of difference is the greater number of citizens and extent of territory which may be brought within the compass of republican than of democratic government; and it is this circumstance principally which renders factious combinations less to be dreaded in the former than in the latter. The smaller the society, the fewer probably will be the distinct parties and interests composing it; the fewer the distinct parties and interests, the more frequently will a majority be found of the same party; and the smaller the number of individuals composing a majority, and the smaller the compass within which they are placed, the more easily will they concert and execute their plans of oppression. Extend the sphere and you take in a greater variety of parties and interests; you make it less probable that a majority of the whole will have a common motive to invade the rights of other citizens; or if such a common motive exists, it will be more difficult for all who feel it to discover their own strength and to act in unison with each other. Besides other impediments, it may be remarked that, where there is a consciousness of unjust or dishonorable purposes, communication is always checked by distrust in proportion to the number whose concurrence is necessary.

Hence, it clearly appears that the same advantage which a republic has over a democracy in controlling the effects of faction is enjoyed by a large over a small republic—is enjoyed by the Union over the States composing it. Does this advantage consist in the substitution of representatives whose enlightened views and virtuous sentiments render them superior to local prejudices and to schemes of injustice? It will not be denied that the representation of the Union will be most likely to possess these requisite endowments. Does it consist in the greater security afforded by a greater variety of parties, against the event of any one party being able to outnumber and oppress the rest? In an equal degree does the increased variety of parties comprised within the Union increase this security. Does it, in fine, consist in the greater obstacles opposed to the concert and accomplishment of the secret wishes of an unjust and interested majority? Here again the extent of the Union gives it the most palpable advantage.

The influence of factious leaders may kindle a flame within their particular States but will be unable to spread a general conflagration through the other States. A religious sect may degenerate into a political faction in a part of the Confederacy; but the variety of sects dispersed over the entire face of it must secure the national councils against any danger from that source. A rage for paper money, for an abolition of debts, for an equal division of property, or for any other improper or wicked project, will be less apt to pervade the whole body of the Union than a particular member of it, in the same proportion as such a malady is more likely to taint a particular county or district than an entire State.

In the extent and proper structure of the Union, therefore, we behold a republican remedy for the diseases most incident to republican government. And according to the degree of pleasure and pride we feel in being republicans ought to be our zeal in cherishing the spirit and supporting the character of federalists.

Publius
(James Madison)

#51

Federalist Paper No. 51, which was also authored by James Madison, is one of the classics in American political theory. Recall from Chapter 2 that a major concern of the founders was to create a relatively strong national government but one that would not be capable to tyrannizing over the populace. In the following essay, Madison sets forth the theory of "checks and balances." He explains that the new Constitution, by dividing the national government into three branches (executive, legislative, and judicial), offers protection against tyranny.

To what expedient, then, shall we finally resort, for maintaining in practice the necessary partition of power among the several departments as laid down in the Constitution? The only answer that can be given is that as all these exterior provisions are found to be inadequate the defect must be supplied, by so contriving the interior structure of the government as that its several constituent parts may, by their mutual relations, be the means of keeping each other in their proper places. Without presuming to undertake a full development of this important idea I will hazard a few general observations which may perhaps place it in a clearer light, and enable us to form a more correct judgment of the principles and structure of the government planned by the convention.

In the following two paragraphs, Madison explains that to ensure that the powers of government are genuinely separated, it is important that each of the three branches of government (executive, legislative, and judicial) should have a "will of its own." Among other things, this means that persons in one branch should not depend on persons in another branch for the "emoluments annexed to their offices" (pay, perks, and privileges). If they did, then the branches would not be truly independent of one another.

In order to lay a due foundation for that separate and distinct exercise of the different powers of government, which to a certain extent is admitted on all hands to be essential to the preservation of liberty, it is evident that each department should have a will of its own; and consequently should be so constituted that the members of each should have as little agency as possible in the appointment of the members of the others. Were this principle rigorously adhered to, it would require that all the appointments for the supreme executive, legislative, and judiciary magistracies should be drawn from the same fountain of authority, the people, through channels having no communication whatever with one another. Perhaps such a plan of constructing the several departments would be less difficult in practice than it may in contemplation appear. Some difficulties, however, and some additional expense would attend the execution of it. Some deviations, therefore, from the principle must be admitted. In the constitution of the judiciary department in particular, it might be inexpedient to insist rigorously on the principle: first, because peculiar qualifications being essential in the members, the primary consideration ought to be to select that mode of choice which best secures these qualifications; second, because the permanent tenure by which the appointments are held in that department must soon destroy all sense of dependence on the authority conferring them.

It is equally evident that the members of each department should be as little dependent as possible on those of the others for the emoluments annexed to their offices. Were the executive magistrate, or the judges, not independent of the legislature in this particular, their independence in every other would be merely nominal.

One of the striking qualities of the theory of checks and balances as posited by Madison is that it assumes that persons are not angels but driven by personal interests and motives. In the following two paragraphs, which are among the most widely quoted of Madison's writings, he stresses that the division of the government into three branches helps to check personal ambitions. Personal ambitions will naturally arise, but they will be linked to the constitutional powers of each branch. In effect, they will help to keep the three branches separate and thus serve the public interest.

But the great security against a gradual concentration of the several powers in the same department consists in giving to those who administer each department the necessary constitutional means and personal motives to resist encroachments of the others. The provision for defense must in this, as in all other cases, be made commensurate to the danger of attack. Ambition must be made to counteract ambition. The interest of the man must be connected with the constitutional rights of the place. It may be a reflection on human nature that such devices should be necessary to control the abuses of government. But what is government itself but the greatest of all reflections on human nature? If men were angels, no government would be necessary. If angels were to govern men, neither external nor internal controls on government would be necessary. In framing a government which is to be administered by men over men, the great difficulty lies in this: you must first enable the government to control the governed; and in the next place oblige it to control itself. A dependence on the people is, no doubt, the primary control on the government; but experience has taught mankind the necessity of auxiliary precautions.

This policy of supplying, by opposite and rival interests, the defect of better motives, might be traced through the whole system of human affairs, private as well as public. We see it particularly displayed in all the subordinate distributions of power, where the constant aim is to divide and arrange the several offices in such a manner as that each may be a check on the other—that the private interest of every individual may be a sentinel over the public rights. These inventions of prudence cannot be less requisite in the distribution of the supreme powers of the State.

In the next two paragraphs, Madison first points out that the "legislative authority necessarily predominates" in a republican form of government. The "remedy" for this lack of balance with the other branches of government is to divide the legislative branch into two chambers with "different modes of election and different principles of action."

But it is not possible to give to each department an equal power of self-defense. In republican government, the legislative authority necessarily predominates. The remedy for this inconveniency is to divide the legislature into different branches; and to render them, by different modes of election and different principles of action, as little connected with each other as the nature of their common functions and their common dependence on the society will admit. It may even be necessary to guard against dangerous encroachments by still further precautions. As the weight of the legislative authority requires that it should be thus divided, the weakness of the executive may require, on the other hand, that it should be fortified. An absolute negative on the legislature appears, at first view, to be the natural defense with which the executive magistrate should be armed. But perhaps it would be neither altogether safe nor alone sufficient. On ordinary occasions it might not be exerted with the requisite firmness, and on extraordinary occasions it might be perfidiously abused. May not this defect of an absolute negative be supplied by some qualified connection between this weaker department and the weaker branch of the stronger department, by which the latter may be led to support the constitutional rights of the former, without being too much detached from the rights of its own department?

If the principles on which these observations are founded be just, as I persuade myself they are, and they be applied as a criterion to the several State constitutions, and to the federal Constitution, it will be found that if the latter does not perfectly correspond with them, the former are infinitely less able to bear such a test.

In the remaining passages of this essay, Madison discusses the importance of the division of government powers between the states and the national government. This division of powers, by providing additional checks and balances, offers a "double security" against tyranny.

There are, moreover, two considerations particularly applicable to the federal system of America, which place that system in a very interesting point of view.

First. In a single republic, all the power surrendered by the people is submitted to the administration of a single government; and the usurpations are guarded against by a division of the government into distinct and separate departments. In the compound republic of America, the power surrendered by the people is first divided between two distinct governments, and then the portion allotted to each subdivided among distinct and separate departments. Hence a double security arises to the rights of the people. The different governments will control each other, at the same time that each will be controlled by itself.

Second. It is of great importance in a republic not only to guard the society against the oppression of its rulers, but to guard one part of the society against the injustice of the other part. Different interests necessarily exist in different classes of citizens. If a majority be united by a common interest, the rights of the minority will be insecure. There are but two methods of providing against this evil: the one by creating a will in the community independent of the majority—that is, of the society itself; the other, by comprehending in the society so many separate descriptions of citizens as will render an unjust combination of a majority of the whole very improbable, if not impracticable. The first method prevails in all governments possessing an hereditary or self-appointed authority. This, at best, is but a precarious security; because a power independent of the society may as well espouse the unjust views of the major as the rightful interests of the minor party, and may possibly be turned against both parties. The second method will be exemplified in the federal republic of the United States. Whilst all authority in it will be derived from and dependent on the society, the society itself will be broken into so many parts, interests and classes of citizens, that the rights of individuals, or of the minority, will be in little danger from interested combinations of the majority. In a free government the security for civil rights must be the same as that for religious rights. It consists in the one case in the multiplicity of interests, and in the other in the multiplicity of sects. The degree of security in both cases will depend on the number of interests and sects; and this may be presumed to depend on the extent of country and number of people comprehended under the same government. This view of the subject must particularly recommend a proper federal system to all the sincere and considerate friends of republican government, since it shows that in exact proportion as the territory of the Union may be formed into more circumscribed Confederacies, or States, oppressive combinations of a majority will be facilitated; the best security, under the republican forms, for the rights of every class of citizen, will be diminished; and consequently the stability and independence of some member of the government, the only other security, must be proportionally increased. Justice is the end of government. It is the end of civil society. It ever has been and ever will be pursued until it be obtained, or until liberty be lost in the pursuit. In a society under the forms of which the stronger faction can readily unite and oppress the weaker, anarchy may as truly be said to reign as in a state of nature, where the weaker individual is not secured against the violence of the stronger; and as, in the latter state, even the stronger individuals are prompted, by the uncertainty of their condition, to submit to a government which may protect the weak as well as themselves; so, in the former state, will the more powerful factions or parties be gradually induced, by a like motive, to wish for a government which will protect all parties, the weaker as well as the more powerful. It can be little doubted that if the State of Rhode Island was separated from the Confederacy and left to itself, the insecurity of rights under the popular form of government within such narrow limits would be displayed by such reiterated oppressions of factious majorities that some power altogether independent of the people would soon be called for by the voice of the very factions whose misrule had proved the necessity of it. In the extended republic of the United States, and among the great variety of interests, parties, and sects which it embraces, a coalition of a majority of the whole society could seldom take place on any other principles than those of justice and the general good; whilst there being thus less danger to a minor from the will of a major party, there must be less pretext, also, to provide for the security of the former, by introducing into the government a will not dependent on the latter, or, in other words, a will independent of the society itself. It is no less certain than it is important, notwithstanding the contrary opinions which have been entertained, that the larger the society, provided it lie within a practicable sphere, the more duly capable it will be of self-government. And happily for the *republican cause,* the practicable sphere may be carried to a very great extent by a judicious modification and mixture of the *federal principle.*

Publius
(James Madison)

spanish equivalents for important political terms

A

Acid Rain: Lluvia Acida

Acquisitive Model: Modelo Adquisitivo

Actionable: Procesable, Enjuiciable

Action-Reaction Syndrome: Sídrome de Acción y Reacción

Actual Malice: Malicia Expresa

Administrative Agency: Agencia Administrativa

Advice and Consent: Consejo y Consentimiento

Affirm: Afirmar

Affirmative Action: Acción Afirmativa

Agenda Setting: Agenda Establecida

Aid to Families with Dependent Children (AFDC): Ayuda para Familias con Niños Dependientes

Amicus Curiae Brief: Tercer persona o grupo no involucrado en el caso, admitido en un juicio para hacer valer el intéres público o el de un grupo social importante.

Anarchy: Anarquía

Anti-Federalists: Anti-Federalistas

Appellate Court: Corte de Apelación

Appointment Power: Poder de Apuntamiento

Appropriation: Apropiación

Aristocracy: Aristocracia

Attentive Public: Público Atento

Australian Ballot: Voto Australiano

Authority: Autoridad

Authorization: Autorización

B

Bad-Tendency Rule: Regla de Tendencia-mala

"Beauty Contest": Concurso de Belleza

Bicameralism: Bicameralismo

Bicameral Legislature: Legislatura Bicameral

Bill of Rights: Declaración de Derechos

Blanket Primary: Primaria Comprensiva

Block Grants: Concesiones de Bloque

Bureaucracy: Burocracia

Busing: Transporte Público

c

Cabinet: Gabinete, Consejo de Ministros

Cabinet Department: Departamento del Gabinete

Cadre: El núcleo de activistas de partidos políticos encargados de cumplir las funciones importantes de los partidos políticos americanos.

Canvassing Board: Consejo encargado con la encuesta de una violación.

Capture: Captura, Toma

Casework: Trabajo de Caso

Categorical Grants-in-Aid: Concesiones Categóricas de Ayuda

Caucus: Reunión de Dirigentes

Challenge: Reto

Checks and Balances: Chequeos y Equilibrio

Chief Diplomat: Jefe Diplomático

Chief Executive: Jefe Ejecutivo

Chief Legislator: Jefe Legislador

Chief of Staff: Jefe de Personal

Chief of State: Jefe de Estado

Civil Law: Derecho Civil

Civil Liberties: Libertades Civiles

Civil Rights: Derechos Civiles

Civil Service: Servicio Civil

Civil Service Commission: Comisión de Servicio Civil

Class-Action Suit: Demanda en representación de un grupo o clase.

Class Politics: Política de Clase

Clear and Present Danger Test: Prueba de Peligro Claro y Presente

Climate Control: Control de Clima

Closed Primary: Primaria Cerrada

Cloture: Cierre al Voto

Coattail Effect: Effecto de Cola de Chaqueta

Cold War: Guerra Fría

Commander in Chief: Comandante en Jefe

Commerce Clause: Clausula de Comercio

Commercial Speech: Discurso Comercial

Common Law: Ley Común, Derecho Consuetudinario

Comparable Worth: Valor Comparable

Compliance: De Acuerdo

Concurrent Majority: Mayoría Concurrente

Concurring Opinion: Opinión Concurrente

Confederal System: Sistema Confederal

Confederation: Confederación

Conference Committee: Comité de Conferencia

Consensus: Concenso

Consent of the People: Consentimiento de la Gente

Conservatism: Calidad de Conservador

Conservative Coalition: Coalición Conservadora

Consolidation: Consolidación

Constant Dollars: Dólares Constantes

Constitutional Initiative: Iniciativa Constitucional

Constitutional Power: Poder Constitucional

Containment: Contenimiento

Continuing Resolution: Resolució Contínua

Cooley's Rule: Régla de Cooley

Cooperative Federalism: Federalismo Cooperativo

Corrupt Practices Acts: Leyes Contra Acciones Corruptas

Council of Economic Advisers (CEA): Consejo de Asesores Económicos

Council of Government (COG): Consejo de Gobierno

County: Condado

Credentials Committee: Comité de Credenciales

Criminal Law: Ley Criminal

D

De Facto **Segregation:** Segregación de Hecho

De Jure **Segregation:** Segregación Cotidiana

Defamation of Character: Defamación de Carácter

Democracy: Democracia

Democratic Party: Partido Democratico

Détente: No Spanish equivalent.

Dillon's Rule: Régla de Dillon

Diplomacy: Diplomácia

Direct Democracy: Democracia Directa

Direct Primary: Primaria Directa

Direct Technique: Técnica Directa

Discharge Petition: Petición de Descargo

Dissenting Opinion: Opinión Disidente

Divisive Opinion: Opinión Divisiva

Domestic Policy: Principio Político Doméstico

Dual Citizenship: Ciudadanía Dual

Dual Federalism: Federalismo Dual

E

Economic Aid: Ayuda Económica

Economic Regulation: Regulación Económica

Elastic Clause, or Necessary and Proper Clause: Cláusula Flexible o Cláusula Propia Necesaria

Elector: Elector

Electoral College: Colegio Electoral

Electronic Media: Media Electronica

Elite: Elite (el Selecto)

Elite Theory: Teoría Elitista (de lo Selecto)

Emergency Power: Poder de Emergencia

Enumerated Power: Poder Enumerado

Environmental Impact Statement (EIS): Afirmación de Impacto Ambiental

Equal Employment Opportunity Commission (EEOC): Comisión de Igualdad de Oportunidad en el Empleo

Equality: Igualdad

Equalization: Igualación

Era of Good Feeling: Era de Buen Sentimiento

Era of Personal Politics: Era de Política Personal

Establishment Clause: Cláusula de Establecimiento

Euthanasia: Eutanasia

Exclusionary Rule: Régla de Exclusión

Executive Agreement: Acuerdo Ejecutivo

Executive Budget: Presupuesto Ejecutivo

Executive Office of the President (EOP): Oficina Ejecutiva del Presidente

Executive Order: Orden Ejecutivo

Executive Privilege: Privilegio Ejecutivo

Expressed Power: Poder Expresado

Extradite: Entregar por Extradición

F

Faction: Facción

Fairness Doctrine: Doctrina de Justicia

Fall Review: Revision de Otoño

Federal Mandate: Mandato Federal

Federal Open Market Committee (FOMC): Comité Federal de Libre Mercado

Federal Register: Registro Federal

Federal System: Sistema Federal

Federalists: Federalistas

Fighting Words: Palabras de Provocación

Filibuster: Obstrucción de Iniciativas de Ley

Fireside Chat: Charla de Hogar

First Budget Resolution: Resolució Primera Presupuesta

First Continental Congress: Primér Congreso Continental

Fiscal Policy: Político Fiscal

Fiscal Year (FY): Año Fiscal

Fluidity: Fluidez

Food Stamps: Estampillas para Comida

Foreign Policy: Política Extranjera

Foreign Policy Process: Proceso de Política Extranjera

Franking: Franqueando

Fraternity: Fraternidad

Free Exercise Clause: Cláusula de Ejercicio Libre

Full Faith and Credit Clause: Cláusula de Completa Fé y Crédito

Functional Consolidation: Consolidación Funcional

G

Gag Order: Orden de Silencio

Garbage Can Model: Modelo Bote de Basura

Gender Gap: Brecha de Género

General Law City: Régla General Urbana

General Sales Tax: Impuesto General de Ventas

Generational Effect: Efecto Generacional

Gerrymandering: División arbitraria de los distritos electorales con fines políticos.

Government: Gobierno

Government Corporation: Corporación Gubernamental

Government in the Sunshine Act: Gobierno en la Acta: Luz del Sol

Grandfather Clause: Cláusula del Abuelo

Grand Jury: Gran Jurado

Great Compromise: Grán Acuerdo de Negociación

H

Hatch Act (Political Activities Act): Acta Hatch (Acta de Actividades Políticas)

Hecklers' Veto: Veto de Abuchamiento

Home Rule City: Régla Urbana

Horizontal Federalism: Federalismo Horizontal

Hyperpluralism: Hiperpluralismo

I

Ideologue: Ideólogo

Ideology: Ideología

Image Building: Construcción de Imágen

Impeachment: Acción Penal Contra un Funcionario Público

Inalienable Rights: Derechos Inalienables

Income Transfer: Transferencia de Ingresos

Incorporation Theory: Teoría de Incorporación

Independent: Independiente

Independent Candidate: Candidato Independiente

Independent Executive Agency: Agencia Ejecutiva Independiente

Independent Regulatory Agency: Agencia Regulatoria Independiente

Indirect Technique: Técnica Indirecta

Inherent Power: Poder Inherente

Initiative: Iniciativa

Injunction: Injunción, Prohibición Judicial

In-Kind Subsidy: Subsidio de Clase

Institution: Institución

Instructed Delegate: Delegado con Instrucciones

Intelligence Community: Comunidad de Inteligencia

Intensity: Intensidad

Interest Group: Grupo de Interés

Interposition: Interposición

Interstate Compact: Compacto Interestatal

Iron Curtain: Cortina de Acero

Iron Triangle: Triágulo de Acero

Isolationist Foreign Policy: Política Extranjera de Aislamiento

Issue Voting: Voto Temático

Item Veto: Artículo de Veto

J

Jim Crow Laws: No Spanish equivalent.

Joint Committee: Comité Mancomunado

Judicial Activism: Activismo Judicial

Judicial Implementation: Implementación Judicial

Judicial Restraint: Restricción Judicial

Judicial Review: Revisión Judicial

Jurisdiction: Jurisdicción

Justiciable Dispute: Disputa Judiciaria

Justiciable Question: Pregunta Justiciable

K

Keynesian Economics: Economía Keynesiana

Kitchen Cabinet: Gabinete de Cocina

L

Labor Movement: Movimiento Laboral

Latent Public Opinion: Opinión Pública Latente

Lawmaking: Hacedores de Ley

Legislative History: Historia Legislativa

Legislative Initiative: Iniciativa de Legislación

Legislative Veto: Veto Legislativo

Legislature: Legislatura

Legitimacy: Legitimidad

Libel: Libelo, Difamación Escrita

Liberalism: Liberalismo

Liberty: Libertad

Limited Government: Gobierno Limitado

Line Organization: Organización de Linea

Literacy Test: Exámen de Alfabetización

Litigate: Litigar

Lobbying: Cabildeo

Logrolling: Práctica legislativa que consiste en incluir en un mismo proyecto de ley temas de diversa ídole.

Loophole: Hueco Legal, Escapatoria

M

Madisonian Model: Modelo Madisónico

Majority: Mayoría

Majority Floor Leader: Líder Mayoritario de Piso

Majority Leader of the House: Líder Mayoritario de la Casa

Majority Opinion: Opinión Mayoritaria

Majority Rule: Régla de Mayoría

Managed News: Noticias Manipuladas

Mandatory Retirement: Retiro Mandatorio

Matching Funds: Fondos Combinados

Material Incentive: Incentivo Material

Media: Media

Media Access: Acceso de Media

Merit System: Sistema de Mérito

Military-Industrial Complex: Complejo Industriomilitar

Minority Floor Leader: Líder Minoritario de Piso

Minority Leader of the House: Líder Minorial del Cuerpo Legislativo

Monetary Policy: Política Monetaria

Monopolistic Model: Modelo Monopólico

Monroe Doctrine: Doctrina Monroe

Moral Idealism: Idealismo Moral

Municipal Home Rule: Régla Municipal

N

Narrow Casting: Mensaje Dirigído

National Committee: Comité Nacional

National Convention: Convención Nacional

National Politics: Política Nacional

National Security Council (NSC): Concilio de Seguridad Nacional

National Security Policy: Política de Seguridad Nacional

Natural Aristocracy: Aristocracia Natural

Natural Rights: Derechos Naturales

Necessaries: Necesidades

Negative Constituents: Constituyentes Negativos

New England Town: Pueblo de Nueva Inglaterra

New Federalism: Federalismo Nuevo

Nullification: Nulidad, Anulación

O

Office-Block, or Massachusetts, Ballot: Cuadro-Oficina, o Massachusetts, Voto

Office of Management and Budget (OMB): Oficina de Administració y Presupuesto

Oligarchy: Oligarquía

Ombudsman: Funcionario que representa al ciudadano ante el gobierno.

Open Primary: Primaria Abierta

Opinion: Opinión

Opinion Leader: Líder de Opinión

Opinion Poll: Encuesta, Conjunto de Opinión

Oral Arguments: Argumentos Orales

Oversight: Inadvertencia, Omisión

P

Paid-for Political Announcement: Anuncios Políticos Pagados

Pardon: Perdón

Party-Column, or Indiana, Ballot: Partido-Columna, o Indiana, Voto

Party Identification: Identificación de Partido

Party Identifier: Identificador de Partido

Party-in-Electorate: Partido Electoral

Party-in-Government: Partido en Gobierno

Party Organization: Organización de Partido

Party Platform: Plataforma de Partido

Patronage: Patrocinio

Peer Group: Grupo de Contemporáneos

Pendleton Act (Civil Service Reform Act): Acta Pendleton (Acta de Reforma al Servicio Civil)

Personal Attack Rule: Regla de Ataque Personal

Petit Jury: Jurado Ordinario

Pluralism: Pluralismo

Plurality: Pluralidad

Pocket Veto: Veto de Bolsillo

Police Power: Poder Policiaco

Policy Trade-Offs: Intercambio de Políticas

Political Action Committee (PAC): Comité de Acción Política

Political Consultant: Consultante Político

Political Culture: Cultura Política

Political Party: Partido Político

Political Question: Pregunta Política

Political Realism: Realismo Político

Political Socialization: Socialización Política

Political Tolerance: Tolerancia Política

Political Trust: Confianza Política

Politico: Político

Politics: Política

Poll Tax: Impuesto Sobre el Sufragio

Poll Watcher: Observador de Encuesta

Popular Sovereignty: Soberanía Popular

Power: Poder

Precedent: Precedente

Preferred-Position Test: Prueba de Posición Preferida

Presidential Primary: Primaria Presidencial

President Pro Tempore: Presidente Provisoriamente

Press Secretary: Secretaría de Prensa

Prior Restraint: Restricción Anterior

Privileges and Immunities: Privilégios e Imunidades

Privatization, or Contracting Out: Privatización

Property: Propiedad

Property Tax: Impuesto de Propiedad

Public Agenda: Agenda Pública

Public Debt Financing: Financiamiento de Deuda Pública

Public Debt, or National Debt: Deuda Pública o Nacional

Public Interest: Interes Público

Public Opinion: Opinión Pública

Purposive Incentive: Incentivo de Propósito

R

Ratification: Ratificación

Rational Ignorance Effect: Effecto de Ignorancia Racional

Reapportionment: Redistribución

Recall: Suspender

Recognition Power: Poder de Reconocimiento

Recycling: Reciclaje

Redistricting: Redistrictificación

Referendum: Referédum

Registration: Registración

Regressive Tax: Impuestos Regresivos

Relevance: Pertinencia

Remand: Reenviar

Representation: Representación

Representative Assembly: Asamblea Representativa

Representative Democracy: Democracia Representativa

Reprieve: Trequa, Suspensión

Republic: República

Republican Party: Partido Republicano

Resulting Powers: Poderes Resultados

Reverse: Cambiarse a lo Contrario

Reverse Discrimination: Discriminación Reversiva

Rule of Four: Régla de Cuatro

Rules Committee: Comité Regulador

Run-off Primary: Primaria Residual

S

Safe Seat: Asiento Seguro

Sampling Error: Error de Encuesta

Secession: Secesión

Second Budget Resolution: Resolución Segunda Presupuestal

Second Continental Congress: Segundo Congreso Continental

Sectional Politics: Política Seccional

Segregation: Segregación

Select Committee: Comité Selecto

Selectperson: Persona Selecta

Senatorial Courtesy: Cortesia Senatorial

Seniority System: Sistema Señiorial

Separate-but-Equal Doctrine: Separados pero Iguales

Separation of Powers: Separación de Poderes

Service Sector: Sector de Servicio

Sex Discrimination: Discriminación Sexual

Sexual Harassment: Acosamiento Sexual

Slander: Difamación Oral, Calumnia

Sliding-Scale Test: Prueba Escalonada

Social Movement: Movimiento Social

Social Security: Seguridad Social

Socioeconomic Status: Estado Socioeconómico

Solidary Incentive: Incentivo de Solideridad

Solid South: Súr Sólido

Sound Bite: Mordida de Sonido

Soviet Bloc: Bloque Soviético

Speaker of the House: Vocero de la Casa

Spin: Girar/Giro

Spin Doctor: Doctor en Giro

Spin-Off Party: Partido Estático

Spoils System: Sistema de Despojos

Spring Review: Revisión de Primavera

Stability: Estabilidad

Standing Committee: Comité de Sostenimiento

Stare Decisis: El principio característico del ley común por el cual los precedentes jurisprudenciales tienen fuerza obligatoria, no sólo entre las partes, sino tambien para casos sucesivos análogos.

State: Estado

State Central Committee: Comité Central del Estado

State of the Union Message: Mensaje Sobre el Estado de la Unión

Statutory Power: Poder Estatorial

Strategic Arms Limitation Treaty (SALT I): Tratado de Limitación de Armas Estratégicas

Subpoena: Orden de Testificación

Subsidy: Subsidio

Suffrage: Sufrágio

Sunset Legislation: Legislación Sunset

Superdelegate: Líder de partido o oficial elegido quien tiene el derecho de votar.

Supplemental Security Income (SSI): Ingresos de Seguridad Suplementaria

Supremacy Clause: Cláusula de Supremacia

Supremacy Doctrine: Doctrina de Supremacia

Symbolic Speech: Discurso Simbólico

T

Technical Assistance: Asistencia Técnica

Third Party: Tercer Partido

Third-Party Candidate: Candidato de Tercer Partido

Ticket Splitting: División de Boletos

Totalitarian Regime: Régimen Totalitario

Town Manager System: Sistema de Administrador Municipal

Town Meeting: Junta Municipal

Township: Municipio

Tracking Poll: Seguimiento de Encuesta

Trial Court: Tribunal de Primera

Truman Doctrine: Doctrina Truman

Trustee: Depositario

Twelfth Amendment: Doceava Enmienda

Twenty-fifth Amendment: Veinticincoava Enmienda

Two-Party System: Sistema de Dos Partidos

U

Unanimous Opinion: Opinión Unánime

Underground Economy: Economía Subterráea

Unicameral Legislature: Legislatura Unicameral

Unincorporated Area: Area no Incorporada

Unitary System: Sistema Unitario

Unit Rule: Régla de Unidad

Universal Suffrage: Sufragio Universal

U.S. Treasury Bond: Bono de la Tesoreria de E.U.A.

V

Veto Message: Comunicado de Veto

Voter Turnout: Renaimiento de Votantes

W

War Powers Act: Acta de Poderes de Guerra

Washington Community: Comunidad de Washington

Weberian Model: Modelo Weberiano

Whip: Látigo

Whistleblower: Privatización o Contratista

White House Office: Oficina de la Casa Blanca

White House Press Corps: Cuerpo de Prensa de la Casa Blanca

White Primary: Sufragio en Elección Primaria/Blancos Solamente

Writ of *Certiorari*: Prueba de certeza; orden emitida por el tribunal de apelaciones para que el tribunal inferior dé lugar a la apelación.

Writ of *Habeas Corpus*: Prueba de Evidencia Concreta

Writ of *Mandamus*: Un mandato por la corte para que un acto se lleve a cabo.

Y

Yellow Journalism: Amarillismo Periodístico

Notes

Chapter 1

1. A summary of this study is available at the National Opinion Research Center's Web site. Go to **http://www.norc.uchicago.edu/new/pats.htm**.
2. Bryan Chambers, "America Shows Its Colors," *The Herald-Dispatch,* September 11, 2002.
3. Wallace Baine, "The Other Patriotism," March 13, 2002. You can view this and other articles by Wallace Baine at **http://www.wallacebaine.com**.
4. Marci Elliot, "FGCU Library Director Reprimanded for Stance on Patriotic Stickers," *Naples Daily News,* September 20, 2001.
5. Tony Francetic, "No Policies Change after Flag Incident," *Central Michigan Life,* October 24, 2001.
6. The Pew Research Center study, "What the World Thinks in 2002," as well as a number of other recent surveys, can be accessed at the Web site for the Pew Research Center for the People and the Press at **http://people-press.org**.
7. Gallup poll, October 29, 2002.
8. Harold Lasswell, Politics: Who Gets What, When, and How (New York: McGraw-Hill, 1936).
9. Charles Lewis, *The Buying of Congress* (New York: Avon Books, 1998), p. 346.
10. For other examples, see Robert J. Samuelson, "Think Again: Rich Special Interests Don't Rule in America," *International Herald Tribune,* April 19, 2000, p. 8.
11. The extent of special interests' influence in Washington, D.C., has led some scholars to conclude that Congress has indeed been "bought" by campaign contributors. See, for example, Jeffrey H. Birnbaum, *The Money Men: The Real Story of Fund-Raising's Influence on Political Power in America* (New York: Crown Publishers, 2000).
12. Congress passed the Flag Protection Act of 1989 after the Supreme Court had ruled in *Texas v. Johnson, 491 U.S. 397 (1989), that a state law prohibiting* the burning of the American flag was unconstitutional.
13. *United States v. Eichman,* 496 U.S. 310 (1990).
14. In Mississippi, voters agreed to keep the state flag that prominently displays the Confederate emblem. In Georgia, a similar struggle over the Confederate battle emblem that has been part of that state's flag since 1956 resulted in a compromise: the Confederate emblem was reduced to one of five tiny flags from Georgia's history along the bottom of a new state flag.
15. As quoted in Fareed Zakaria, "The Answer? A Domestic CIA," *Newsweek,* May 27, 2002, p. 39.
16. Edward Badolato, interview by Gwen Ifill, The NewsHour with Jim Lehrer, Public Broadcasting System, November 18, 2002.
17. Interview on This Week with George Stephanopoulos, ABC News, November 24, 2002.
18. See, for example, Thomas Sowell, The Quest for Cosmic Justice (Riverside, N.J.: Free Press, 1999).
19. The Public Agenda study, as well as a number of other recent surveys, can be accessed at Public Agenda's Web site at **http://www.publicagenda.org**.

Chapter 2

1. The first *European* settlement in North America was St. Augustine, Florida (a city that still exists), which was founded on September 8, 1565, by the Spaniard Pedro Menéndez de Ávilés.
2. Archaeologists have recently discovered the remains of a colony at Popham Beach, on the southern coast of what is now Maine, that was established at the same time as the colony at Jamestown. The Popham colony disbanded after thirteen months, however, when the leader, after learning that he had inherited property back home, returned—with the other colonists—to England.
3. John Camp, *Out of the Wilderness: The Emergence of an American Identity in Colonial New England* (Middleton, Conn.: Wesleyan University Press, 1990).
4. Jon Butler, *Becoming America: The Revolution before 1776* (Cambridge, Mass.: Harvard University Press, 2000).
5. Paul S. Boyer *et al., The Enduring Vision: A History of the American People* (Lexington, Mass.: D. C. Heath, 1996).
6. Corsets are close-fitting undergarments that were worn at the time by both men and women to give the appearance of having a smaller waist. Whalebone was inserted in the corsets to make them stiff, and lacing was used to tighten them around the body.
7. Much of the colonists' fury over British policies was directed personally at King George III, who had ascended the British throne in 1760 at the age of twenty-two, rather than at Britain or British rule *per se.* If you look at the Declaration of Independence in Appendix B, you will note that much of that document focuses on what "He" (George III) has or has not done. George III's lack of political experience, his personality, and his temperament all combined to lend instability to the British government at this crucial point in history.
8. *The Political Writings of Thomas Paine,* Vol. 1 (Boston: J. P. Mendum Investigator Office, 1870), p. 46.
9. The equivalent in today's publishing world would be a book that sells between eight and ten million copies in its first year of publication.
10. As quoted in Winthrop D. Jordan *et al., The United States,* 6th ed. (Englewood Cliffs, N.J.: Prentice Hall, 1987).
11. Many historians believe that the term *United States* was coined in a series of articles written in the 1770s by Thomas Paine. See, for example, A. J. Ayer, *Thomas Paine* (New York: Atheneum, 1988), p. 42.
12. Some scholars feel that Locke's influence on the colonists, including Thomas Jefferson, has been exaggerated. For example, Jay Fliegelman states that Jefferson's fascination with the ideas of Homer, Ossian, and Patrick Henry "is of greater significance than his indebtedness to Locke." Jay Fliegelman, *Declaring Independence: Jefferson, Natural Language, and the Culture of Performance* (Stanford, Calif.: Stanford University Press, 1993).
13. See, for example, Robert A. Dahl, "Liberal Democracy in the United States," in *A Prospect of Liberal Democracy,* ed. William Livingston (Austin, Tex: University of Texas Press, 1979).

14. Well before the articles were ratified, many of them had, in fact, already been implemented. The Second Continental Congress and the thirteen states conducted American military, economic, and political affairs according to the standards and form specified later in the Articles of Confederation. See Robert W. Hoffert, *A Politics of Tensions: The Articles of Confederation and American Political Ideas* (Niwot, Colo.: University Press of Colorado, 1992).

15. Madison was much more "republican" in his views than Hamilton. See Lance Banning, *The Sacred Fire of Liberty: James Madison and the Founding of the Federal Republic* (Ithaca, N.Y.: Cornell University Press, 1995).

16. The State House was later named Independence Hall. This was the same room in which the Declaration of Independence had been signed eleven years earlier.

17. Charles A. Beard, *An Economic Interpretation of the Constitution of the United States* (New York: Macmillan, 1913; New York: Free Press, 1986).

18. Morris was partly of French descent, which is why his first name may seem strange. Note that naming one's child *Gouverneur* was not common at the time in any language, even French.

19. As cited in Wendy McElroy, "Constitutional Intentions," *Ideas on Liberty,* June 2000, p. 15.

20. See Randall Robinson, *The Debt: What America Owes to Blacks* (New York: Dutton, 2000).

21. "*Courant* Complicity in an Old Wrong," *Hartford Courant,* July 4, 2000.

22. As quoted in Tamar Lewin, "Calls for Slavery Restitution Getting Louder," *The New York Times,* June 4, 2001.

23. *Ibid.*

24. Some scholarship suggests that the Federalist Papers did not play a significant role in bringing about the ratification of the Constitution. Nonetheless, the papers have lasting value as an authoritative explanation of the Constitution.

25. The papers written by the Anti-Federalists are now online (see the *Politics on the Web* section at the end of Chapter 2 for the Web URL). For essays on the positions, arranged in topical order, of both the Federalists and the Anti-Federalists in the ratification debate, see John P. Kaminski and Richard Leffler, *Federalists and Antifederalists: The Debate over the Ratification of the Constitution,* 2d ed. (Madison, Wisc.: Madison House, 1998).

26. Beard, *An Economic Interpretation of the Constitution,* p. 299.

27. Jim Powell, "James Madison—Checks and Balances to Limit Government Power," *Freeman,* March 1996, p. 178.

28. The concept of the separation of powers is generally credited to the French political philosopher Montesquieu (1689–1755), who included it in his monumental two-volume work entitled *The Spirit of Laws,* published in 1748.

29. The Constitution does not explicitly mention the power of judicial review, but the delegates at the Constitutional Convention probably assumed that the courts would have this power. Indeed, Alexander Hamilton, in *Federalist Paper* No. 78, explicitly outlined the concept of judicial review. In any event, whether the founders intended for the courts to exercise this power is a moot point, because in an 1803 decision, *Marbury v. Madison,* the Supreme Court claimed this power for the courts—see Chapter 14.

30. As quoted in David Firestone, "Top Bush Aides Urge No Change in Security Plan," *The New York Times,* July 12, 2002.

31. See the summary of the Homeland Security Bill issued by the House Select Committee on Homeland Security at its Web site, **http://hsc.house.gov/legislation/final.asp.**

32. Eventually, Supreme Court decisions led to legislative reforms relating to apportionment. The amendment concerning compensation of members of Congress became the Twenty-seventh Amendment to the Constitution when it was ratified 203 years later, in 1992.

33. See the *Politics on the Web* section at the end of this chapter for a Web site where you can access the constitutions of other nations online.

34. In 1989, protesters calling for political reforms gathered in Beijing's Tiananmen Square. The government imposed martial law and ordered the army to quell the protest, resulting in a blood bath in which at least two hundred protesters were killed.

Chapter 3

1. *United States v. Oakland Cannabis Buyers' Co-op*, 532 U.S. 483 (2001).

2. *Conant v. Walters*, 309 F.3d 629 (2002).

3. Text of an address by the president to the National Conference of State Legislatures, Atlanta, Georgia (Washington, D.C.: The White House, Office of the Press Secretary, July 30, 1981).

4. An excellent illustration of this principle was President Dwight Eisenhower's disciplining of Arkansas governor Orval Faubus when he refused to allow a Little Rock high school to be desegregated in 1957. Eisenhower federalized the National Guard to enforce the court-ordered desegregation of the school.

5. 5 U.S. 137 (1803).

6. 4 Wheaton 316 (1819).

7. 9 Wheaton 1 (1824).

8. *Hammer v. Dagenhart*, 247 U.S. 251 (1918). This decision was overruled in *United States v. Darby*, 312 U.S. 100 (1941).

9. *Wickard v. Filburn*, 317 U.S. 111 (1942).

10. *McLain v. Real Estate Board of New Orleans, Inc.*, 444 U.S. 232 (1980).

11. See, for example, Edward H. Crane, "GOP Pussycats," *Forbes*, November 13, 2000, p. 36.

12. Richard Wolf, "States See Washington Trying to Grab Power," *USA Today*, July 24, 1998, p. 4A.

13. 514 U.S. 549 (1995).

14. *Printz v. United States*, 521 U.S. 898 (1997).

15. *United States v. Morrison*, 529 U.S. 598 (2000).

16. 527 U.S. 706 (1999).

17. *Kimel v. Florida Board of Regents*, 528 U.S. 62 (2000).

18. *Board of Trustees of the University of Alabama v. Garrett*, 531 U.S. 356 (2001).

19. Curt A. Levey, "States' Rights Are Also Civil Rights," *The National Law Journal*, December 4, 2000, p. A27.

20. National Governors Association statement on "Federalism, Preemption, and Regulatory Reform," December 2, 2002. You can view this and other statements by the National Governors Association at its Web site, **http://www.nga.org**.

21. Albert H. Cantril and Susan Davis Cantril, *Reading Mixed Signals: Ambivalence in American Public Opinion about Government* (Washington, D.C.: Woodrow Wilson Center Press, 1999).

22. Donald F. Kettl, "Dots Unconnected," The Century Foundation, July 9, 2002. You can read this and other articles on federalism challenges to homeland security at the Century Foundation Homeland Security Project's Web site at **http://www.homelandsec.org**.

23. Daniel Henninger, "New Balance: Homeland Security Will Drastically Reshape American Government," *The Wall Street Journal*, November 22, 2002.

24. Although Louisiana prohibited minors from purchasing alcohol, it did not prohibit bars and alcohol retailers from selling alcohol to minors. Not until 1996, when President Bill Clinton threatened to withhold $1.7 million in federal highway funds from Louisiana, did that state fully comply with the drinking-age requirement.

Chapter 4

1. *Planned Parenthood v. American Coalition of Life Activists*, 290 F.3d 1058 (9th Cir. 2002).

2. Title VII of the Civil Rights Act of 1964 outlaws racial and gender discrimination in the workplace. Title IX of the Higher Education Amendments of 1972 makes gender discrimination in the classroom unlawful for institutions that receive federal funds. The courts, the Equal Employment Opportunity Commission, and the Office of Civil Rights of the Department of Education have all found sexual harassment to be a form of unlawful gender discrimination under Title VII and Title IX. Most states also have laws prohibiting sexual harassment in the workplace and at state institutions.

3. Quoted in Patrick Healy, "Harvard Law Plan on Speech Causes Stir," *Boston Globe,* November 19, 2002.

4. "Meeting Minutes of the Wesleyan Student Assembly Meeting, 2002–2003," October 2, 2002, p. 10. You can view this document at the Web site of the Wesleyan Student Assembly, **http://www.wesleyan.edu/wsa**.

5. See the article by Shannon P. Duffy, "Right to a 'Redneck' T-Shirt," *The National Law Journal*, October 14, 2002, p. A4.

6. You can access Georgetown University's student handbook online at **http://www.georgetown.edu/student-affairs/handbook/index.html**.

7. 330 U.S. 1 (1947).

8. 370 U.S. 421 (1962).

9. 449 U.S. 39 (1980).

10. *Wallace v. Jaffree*, 472 U.S. 38 (1985).

11. See, for example, *Brown v. Gwinnett County School District*, 112 F.3d 1464 (1997).

12. *Santa Fe Independent School District v. Doe*, 530 U.S. 290 (2000).

13. 393 U.S. 97 (1968).

14. *Edwards v. Aguillard*, 482 U.S. 578 (1987).

15. *Freiler v. Tangipahoa Parish Board of Education*, 201 F.3d 602 (5th Cir. 2000).

16. 403 U.S. 602 (1971).

17. *Mitchell v. Helms*, 530 U.S. 793 (2000).

18. *Simmons-Harris v. Zelman*, 234 F.3d 945 (6th Cir. 2000).

19. *Zelman v. Simmons-Harris*, 536 U.S. 639 (2002).

20. *Holmes v. Bush* (Fla.Cir.Ct. 2002). For details about this case, see David Royse, "Judge Rules School Voucher Law Violates Florida Constitution," *USA Today*, August 6, 2002, p. 7D.

21. *Newdow v. U.S. Congress*, 292 F.3d 597 (2002).

22. See Marie Failinger, "Indivisible Day and the Pledge of Allegiance: One Nation under God?" *Journal of Lutheran Ethics*, July 10, 2002.

23. See Howard Fineman, "One Nation, under . . . Who?" *Newsweek*, July 8, 2002, p. 20.

24. 98 U.S. 145 (1878).

25. For more information on this case, see Bill Miller, "Firefighters Win Ruling in D.C. Grooming Dispute," *Washington Post*, June 23, 2001, p. B01.

26. *Schenck v. United States*, 249 U.S. 47 (1919).

27. 341 U.S. 494 (1951).

28. *Brandenburg v. Ohio*, 395 U.S. 444 (1969).

29. *Liquormart v. Rhode Island*, 517 U.S. 484 (1996).

30. For more information on this case, see Samuel Maull, "Judges Rule against 2 Accused of Praising Sept. 11 Attacks," *Washington Post*, March 31, 2002, p. A6.

31. 413 U.S. 15 (1973).

32. *Reno v. American Civil Liberties Union*, 521 U.S. 844 (1997).

33. *American Civil Liberties Union v. Reno*, 217 F.3d 160 (2000).

34. *American Library Association v. United States*, 201 F.Supp.2d 401 (2002).

35. *Ashcroft v. Free Speech Coalition*, 535 U.S. 234 (2002).

36. 249 U.S. 47 (1919).

37. 268 U.S. 652 (1925).

38. 484 U.S. 260 (1988).

39. *Smith v. Collin*, 439 U.S. 916 (1978).

40. *City of Chicago v. Morales*, 527 U.S. 41 (1999).

41. *Gallo v. Acuna*, 14 Cal.4th 1090 (1997).

42. Brandeis made this statement in a dissenting opinion in *Olmstead v. United States*, 277 U.S. 438 (1928).

43. The state of South Carolina challenged the constitutionality of this act, claiming that the law violated states' rights under the Tenth Amendment. The Supreme Court, however, held that Congress had the authority, under its commerce power, to pass the act because drivers' personal information had become articles of interstate commerce. *Reno v. Condon*, 528 U.S. 141 (2000).

44. 410 U.S. 113 (1973). Jane Roe was not the real name of the woman in this case. It is a common legal pseudonym used to protect a party's privacy.

45. See, for example, the Supreme Court's decision in *Lambert v. Wicklund*, 520 U.S. 1169 (1997). The Court held that a Montana law requiring a minor to notify one of her parents before getting an abortion was constitutional.

46. *Schenck v. ProChoice Network*, 519 U.S. 357 (1997); and *Hill v. Colorado*, 530 U.S. 703 (2000).

47. *Stenberg v. Carhart*, 530 U.S. 914 (2000).

48. Yochi J. Dreazen, "Abortion Protesters Use Cameras, Raise New Legal Issues, Lawsuits," *The Wall Street Journal*, May 28, 2002.

49. *Washington v. Glucksberg*, 521 U.S. 702 (1997).

50. This report, titled "Surveying the Digital Future" and based on an extensive study of attitudes concerning Internet use, was published in 2000 by the UCLA Center for Communication Policy. It is available on the Internet at **http://www.college.ucla.edu/InternetReport**.

51. Jeffrey Rosen, *The Unwanted Gaze: The Destruction of Privacy in America* (Westminster, Md.: Random House, 2000).

52. Jeffrey Rosen, "A Watchful State," *The New York Times Magazine*, October 7, 2001.

53. *Ibid.*

54. Steven Brill, "The Biggest Hole in the Net," *Newsweek*, December 30, 2002, p. 48. Brill is also the author of *After: How America Confronted the September 12 Era* (New York: Simon & Schuster, 2003).

55. For more on the American Civil Liberties Union's position on national ID cards, visit its Web site at **http://www.aclu.org/Privacy/PrivacyMain.cfm**.

56. Brill, "The Biggest Hole."

57. Amitai Etzioni, *The Limits of Privacy* (New York: Basic Books, 1999).

58. 372 U.S. 335 (1963).

59. *Mapp v. Ohio*, 367 U.S. 643 (1961).

60. 384 U.S. 436 (1966).

61. *Moran v. Burbine*, 475 U.S. 412 (1986).

62. *Arizona v. Fulminante*, 499 U.S. 279 (1991).

63. *Davis v. United States*, 512 U.S. 452 (1994).

64. *Dickerson v. United States*, 530 U.S. 428 (2000).

Chapter 5

1. *Grutter v. Bollinger*, 123 S.Ct. 617, *cert.* granted (2002); and *Gratz v. Bollinger*, 123 S.Ct. 602, *cert.* granted (2002). For more information about these cases, see Linda Greenhouse, "Supreme Court to Revisit Colleges' Diversity Efforts," *The New York Times*, December 3, 2002.

2. Neil L. Rudenstine, "Student Diversity and Higher Learning," in Gary Orfield and Michal Kurlaender, eds., *Diversity Challenged: Evidence of the Impact of Affirmative Action* (Cambridge, Mass.: Harvard Education Publishing Group, 2001).

3. *Michael M. v. Superior Court*, 450 U.S. 464 (1981).

4. See, for example, *Craig v. Boren*, 429 U.S. 190 (1976).

5. *Orr v. Orr*, 440 U.S. 268 (1979).

6. *Mississippi University for Women v. Hogan*, 458 U.S. 718 (1982).

7. 518 U.S. 515 (1996).

8. 163 U.S. 537 (1896).

9. 347 U.S. 483 (1954).

10. 349 U.S. 294 (1955).

11. *Swann v. Charlotte-Mecklenburg Board of Education*, 402 U.S. 1 (1971).

12. *Keyes v. School District No. 1*, 413 U.S. 189 (1973).

13. *Milliken v. Bradley*, 418 U.S. 717 (1974).

14. *Riddick v. School Board of City of Norfolk*, 627 F.Supp. 814 (E.D.Va. 1984).

15. 515 U.S. 70 (1995).

16. Edward Glaeser and Jacob L. Vigdor, "Racial Segregation in the 2000 Census: Promising News," The Brookings Institution Center on Urban and Metropolitan Policy, April 2001. You can access this report at **http://www.brookings.edu/dybdocroot/es/urban/census/glaeserexsum.htm**.

17. Bureau of Labor Statistics, 2002. For more information, visit the Current Population Survey at the Web site of the Bureau of Labor Statistics, at **http://www.bls.gov/cps/home.htm**.

18. Jay P. Greene, "Choosing Integration," *The Wall Street Journal*, July 8, 2002.

19. Erica Frankenburg and Chungmei Lee, "Race in American Public Schools: Rapidly Resegregating School Districts," a publication of the Harvard University Civil Rights Project, August 8, 2002. To view the full report, go to **http://www. civilrightsproject.harvard.edu/research/k12_ed.php**.

20. For the most recent statistics on voter registration, visit the Web site of the Federal Election Commission at **http://www.fec.gov**.

21. Early women's rights conventions were usually referred to as "woman's rights" conventions.

22. See *Meritor Savings Bank, FSB v. Vinson,* 477 U.S. 57 (1986); and *Harris v. Forklift Systems, Inc.,* 510 U.S. 17 (1993).

23. *Oncale v. Sundowner Offshore Services,* 523 U.S. 75 (1998).

24. *Faragher v. City of Boca Raton,* 524 U.S. 775 (1998).

25. The Supreme Court upheld these actions in *Hirabayashi v. United States,* 320 U.S. 81 (1943); and *Korematsu v. United States,* 323 U.S. 214 (1944).

26. John Derbyshire, "At War, At First Glance: Racial Profiling, Burning Hotter," *The National Review,* October 15, 2001, p. 42.

27. On December 16, 2002, citizens and nationals of Iran, Iraq, Libya, Sudan, and Syria were required to register. On January 10, 2003, the program was expanded to include citizens or nationals of Afghanistan, Algeria, Bahrain, Eritrea, Lebanon, Morocco, North Korea, Oman, Qatar, Somalia, Tunisia, Yemen, and the United Arab Emirates. The program was expanded again on January 16, 2003, to include citizens or nationals of Bangladesh, Egypt, Indonesia, Kuwait, and Jordan.

28. 414 U.S. 563 (1974).

29. This siege was the subject of Dee Brown's best-selling book, *Bury My Heart at Wounded Knee* (New York: Holt, Rinehart, & Winston, 1971).

30. *County of Oneida, New York v. Oneida Indian Nation,* 470 U.S. 226 (1985).

31. *Kimel v. Florida Board of Regents,* 528 U.S. 62 (2000).

32. *Board of Trustees of the University of Alabama v. Garrett,* 531 U.S. 356 (2001).

33. 517 U.S. 620 (1996).

34. 438 U.S. 265 (1978).

35. 515 U.S. 200 (1995).

36. 84 F.3d 720 (5th Cir. 1996).

37. See, for example, *Johnson v. Board of Regents of the University of Georgia,* 106 F.Supp.2d 1362 (S.D.Ga. 2000); and *Smith v. University of Washington School of Law,* 233 F.3d 1188 (9th Cir. 2000).

38. *Coalition for Economic Equity v. Wilson,* 110 F.3d 1431 (9th Cir. 1997).

Chapter 6

1. Some constitutional scholars have been reexamining the theory that only state militias have the right to bear arms, concluding that the founders may have intended individuals to have this right. See, for example, William Glaberson, "The Right to Bear Arms: A Second Look," *The New York Times,* May 30, 1999, p. 3.

2. *Printz v. United States,* 521 U.S. 898 (1997).

3. Taken from the NRA Web site: **http://www.nra.org**.

4. For an interesting discussion of the evolution of the right to bear arms in England, see Joyce Lee Malcolm, T*o Keep and Bear Arms: The Origins of an Anglo-American Right* (Cambridge, Mass.: Harvard University Press, 1996).

5. *United States v. Emerson,* 46 F.Supp.2d 598 (N.D.Tex. 1999).

6. Andrew Lyons, "Anxiety Drives Increased Florida Gun Purchases," *The Daytona Beach News-Journal,* January 23, 2003.

7. *Democracy in America,* Vol. 1, ed. by Phillip Bradley (New York: Knopf, 1980), p. 191.

8. Pronounced ah-*mee*-kus *kure*-ee-eye.

9. David Truman, *The Governmental Process* (New York: Knopf, 1951); and Robert Dahl, *Who Governs?* (New Haven, Conn.: Yale University Press, 1961).

10. Fred McChesney, *Money for Nothing: Politicians, Rent Extraction and Political Extortion* (Cambridge, Mass.: Harvard University Press, 1997).

11. The Agricultural Adjustment Act of 1933 (declared unconstitutional) was replaced by the 1937 Agricultural Adjustment Act, which later was changed and amended several times.

12. "A Tale of Two Lobbies," *The Economist,* October 19, 1996, p. 20.

13. "Overboard on Gun Control," *The Wall Street Journal Europe,* October 23, 1996, p. 6.

14. Data on PAC contributions can be accessed at the Web site of the Federal Election Commission at **http://www.fec.gov**.

15. Brennan Center for Justice Policy Committee on Political Advertising, "Five New Ideas to Deal with the Problems Posed by Campaign Appeals Masquerading as Issue Advocacy," May 2000. You can read this report online at **http://www.brennancenter.org/programs/cmag_temp/cmag_recs.html**.

16. Jeff Gerth and Sheryl Gay Stolberg, "Medicine Merchants Cultivating Alliances: With Quiet, Unseen Ties, Drug Makers Sway Debate," *The New York Times,* October 5, 2000.

17. Mark Hosenball, "Flo's Big-Dollar Backers," *Newsweek,* September 25, 2000, p. 26.

18. Sheila Kaplan, "When the Grass Has No Roots," *U.S. News & World Report,* October 9, 2000, p. 23.

19. *United States v. Harriss,* 347 U.S. 612 (1954).

Chapter 7

1. G. Bingham Powell, *Elections as Instruments of Democracy: Majoritarian and Proportional Visions* (New Haven, Conn.: Yale University Press, 2000).

2. Mark Shields, interview by Margaret Warner, *The NewsHour with Jim Lehrer,* Public Broadcasting System, November 15, 2002.

3. Letter to Francis Hopkinson written from Paris while Jefferson was minister to France, as cited in John P. Foley, ed., *The Jeffersonian Cyclopedia* (New York: Russell & Russell, 1967), p. 677.

4. From the names of the twins in Lewis Carroll's *Through the Looking Glass and What Alice Found There,* first published in London in 1862–1863.

5. "A Notable Minority Challenges the System," *Public Perspective,* September/October 2000, p. 27; and Gallup/CNN/*USA Today* poll conducted in July 1999.

6. The term *third party,* although inaccurate (because sometimes there have been fourth parties, fifth parties, and so on), is commonly used to refer to a minor party.

7. Today, twelve states have multimember districts for their state houses, and a handful also have multimember districts for their state senates.

8. H. Ross Perot and John Hagelin of the Natural Law Party challenged the decision in court, without success. *Perot v. Federal Election Commission,* 97 F.3d 553 (D.C.Cir. 1996).

9. *USA Today,* February 23, 1999, p. 6A. See also Albert R. Hunt, "The Me-Too—Or Yes-But—Republicans," *The Wall Street Journal,* February 25, 1999, p. A19.

10. Richard Darman, *Who's in Control? Polar Politics and the Sensible Center* (New York: Simon & Schuster, 1996).

11. CNN/*USA Today*/Gallup poll, January 2002.

12. Shields, interview.

13. Quoted in Edmund L. Andrews, "Washington Talk; George W.'s Worst Fear: A W-Shaped Recession," *The New York Times,* August 22, 2002.

14. In most states, a person must declare a preference for a particular party before voting in that state's primary election (discussed in Chapter 9). This declaration is usually part of the voter-registration process.

15. Larry M. Bartels, "Partisanship and Voting Behavior, 1952–1996," *American Journal of Political Science,* Vol. 44 (January 2000).

16. For an interesting discussion of the pros and cons of patronage from a constitutional perspective, see the majority opinion versus the dissent in the Supreme Court case, *Board of County Commissioners v. Umbehr,* 518 U.S. 668 (1996).

17. Kathleen Hall Jamieson, *Everything You Think You Know about Politics . . . and Why You're Wrong* (New York: Basic Books, 2000).

18. If that candidate loses, however, the chairperson is often changed.

Chapter 8

1. As reported in *Public Perspective,* July/August 2001, p. 11.

2. Robert Weissberg, *Why Politicians Should Ignore Public Opinion Polls,* policy analysis dated May 29, 2001, the Cato Institute, Washington, D.C.

3. See Doris A. Graber, *Mass Media and American Politics,* 6th ed. (Chicago: University of Chicago Press, 2001).

4. *The Gallup Report,* April 28, 1999.

5. *The Gallup Report,* May 21, 1999.

6. John M. Benson, "When Is an Opinion Really an Opinion?" *Public Perspective,* September/October 2001, pp. 40–41.

7. Robert B. Reich, "The Unending War," *The American Prospect,* December 17, 2001.

8. Norman Ornstein, *The Permanent Campaign and Its Future* (Washington, D.C.: AEI Press, 2000).

9. As quoted in Karl G. Feld, "When Push Comes to Shove: A Polling Industry Call to Arms," *Public Perspective,* September/October 2001, p. 38.

10. As quoted in Owen Ullman, "Why Voter Apathy Will Make a Strong Showing," *Business Week,* November 4, 1996.

11. Kathleen Hall Jamieson, *Everything You Think You Know about Politics . . . and Why You Are Wrong* (New York: Basic Books, 2000), pp. 80–81.

12. As quoted in Ullman, "Why Voter Apathy Will Make a Strong Showing."

Chapter 9

1. As cited in Peter Coy, "Electoral College, Hail to Thee," *Business Week,* November 4, 1996, p. 42.

2. This word *caucus* apparently was first used in the name of a men's club, the *Caucus Club* of colonial Boston, sometime between 1755 and 1765. (Many early political and government meetings took place in pubs.) The origin of the word is unknown, but some scholars have concluded it is of Algonquin origin.

3. *California Democratic Party v. Jones,* 530 U.S. 567 (2000).

4. Cited in Yvonne Abraham, "Democratic National Convention Has Price Tags, Details Galore for 2004," *The Boston Globe,* December 17, 2002.

5. Cited in Lydia Saad, "Gore Gains in Race for President as Result of Democratic Convention," *Gallup Poll Analyses,* August 21, 2000.

6. George F. Will, "Conventional Journalism," *Newsweek,* September 2, 1996.

7. Tom Johnson, "Do Conventions Still Rate Big TV Coverage?" *USA Today,* July 31, 2000, p. 17A.

8. See "Capital Wrapup," *Business Week,* November 11, 2002. For more about groups founded by the families of September 11 victims, visit the following Web site: **http://www.familiesofseptember11.org**.

9. Center for Responsive Politics, 2003. Data showing the relationship between spending and winning, as well as other information on campaign expenditures, are available at the center's Web site at **http://www.opensecrets.org**.

10. This act is sometimes referred to as the Federal Election Campaign Act of 1972 because it became effective in that year. The official date of the act, however, is 1971.

11. 424 U.S. 1 (1976).

12. Center for Responsive Politics, 2003.

13. *Colorado Republican Federal Campaign Committee v. Federal Election Commission,* 518 U.S. 604 (1996).

14. Quoted in George Will, "The First Amendment on Trial," *The Washington Post,* December 1, 2002, p. B07.

15. Charles Lewis, *The Buying of the Congress: How Special Interests Have Stolen Your Right to Life, Liberty, and the Pursuit of Happiness* (New York: Avon Books, 1998).

16. Jeffrey H. Birnbaum, *The Money Men: The Real Story of Fund-Raising's Influence on Political Power in America* (New York: Crown Publishers, 2000), pp. 3–4.

17. Fox expresses these views in an article posted online at **http://www.thisnation. com/question/036.html**.

18. Shortly after the U.S. 2000 elections, Fenton Bresler, a British barrister (attorney) and journalist now living in the United States, explored this question. His comparison of the two systems is the basis for this feature. See Fenton Bresler, "Could Brits Do Better?" *The National Law Journal,* November 27, 2000, p. A20.

19. In 1824, no candidate received a majority of electoral votes; John Quincy Adams was elected president by the House of Representatives. Rutherford B. Hayes lost the popular vote in 1876, but, after the resolution of an electoral dispute, ultimately won a majority of electoral votes. In 1888, Benjamin Harrison lost the popular vote, but won a majority of electoral votes.

20. For a more detailed account of the 2000 presidential elections, see *36 Days: The Complete Chronicle of the 2000 Presidential Election Crisis* (New York: Times Books, 2001), by correspondents of the *New York Times.*

Chapter 10

1. "Terrorism Transforms News Interest," *Pew Research Center for the People and the Press Survey Reports,* December 18, 2001. You can view this report and others at the Pew Research Center's Web site at **http://www.people-press.org**.

2. George Kennedy, "Perspectives on War: The British See Things Differently," *Columbia Journalism Review,* March/April 2002.

3. "Return to Normalcy? How the Media Have Covered the War on Terrorism," *Project for Excellence in Journalism Reports and Surveys,* January 28, 2002. You can view this report and others at the Web site of the Project for Excellence in Journalism and the Committee of Concerned Journalists, **http://www. journalism.org**.

4. "Terror Coverage Boosts News Media's Images," *Pew Research Center for the People and the Press Survey Reports,* November 28, 2001.

5. Harold Evans, "Reporting in the Time of Conflict," essay presented as part of the Newseum War Stories Exhibit, May 18–September 30, 2001. Also available online at **http://www.newseum.org/warstories/essay/warcorrespondent.htm**.

6. Bernard Cohen, *The Press and Foreign Policy* (Princeton, N.J.: Princeton University Press, 1963), p. 81.

7. Marc Fisher, "And Let's Not Forget the Band-Aids," *The Washington Post,* February 13, 2003, p. B01.

8. Interestingly, in the 2000 campaigns, a Texas group supporting George W. Bush's candidacy paid for a remake of the "daisy" commercial, but the target in the new ad was Al Gore—see the photo caption on page 230.

9. The commission's action was upheld by a federal court. See *Perot v. Federal Election Commission,* 97 F.3d 553 (D.C.Cir. 1996).

10. Doris Graber, *Mass Media and American Politics,* 5th ed. (Washington, D.C.: Congressional Quarterly Press, 1997), p. 59.

11. Kerry Fehr-Snyder, "TV, Radio Win Big on Proposition Ads," *The Arizona Republic,* October 29, 2002.

12. S. Robert Lichter, Stanley Rothman, and Linda S. Lichter, *The Media Elite* (New York: Adler & Adler, 1986).

13. Kathleen Hall Jamieson, *Everything You Think You Know about Politics . . . and Why You're Wrong* (New York: Basic Books, 2000), pp. 187–195.

14. Survey conducted by the Pew Research Center for the People and the Press, October 2000.

15. Calvin F. Exoo, *The Politics of the Mass Media* (St. Paul: West Publishing Co., 1994), pp. 49–50.

16. Jamieson, *Everything You Think You Know about Politics,* pp. xiii–xiv.

17. According to a survey conducted by the Pew Research Center for the People and the Press from April 24 to May 11, 1998.

18. "Self-Censorship: How Often and Why," *Pew Research Center for the People and the Press Survey Reports,* April 30, 2000.

19. *Ibid.*

20. Frank Newport, "Number of Americans Who Feel News Coverage Is Inaccurate Increases Sharply," *Gallup News Service,* December 8, 2000.

21. Franklin D. Gilliam, Jr., and Shanto Iyengar, "Prime Suspects: The Influence of Local Television News on the Viewing Public," *American Journal of Political Science,* Vol. 44 (July 2000).

22. These studies are discussed in Mikal Muharrar, "Media Blackface: 'Racial Profiling' in News Reporting," *Extra!,* September/October 1998.

23. Martin Gilens, *Why Americans Hate Welfare: Race, Media, and the Politics of Antipoverty Policy* (Chicago: University of Chicago Press, 1999).

24. Muharrar, "Media Blackface."

25. University of California at Los Angeles Internet Report, October 2000. This report is online at **http://www.college.ucla.edu/InternetReport**.

26. *Ibid.*

27. Brigid McMenamin, "Humbled by the Internet," *Forbes,* July 27, 1998.

28. A summary of this report is available online at **http://www.people-press.org/ online00rpt.htm**.

29. N. Rebecca Donatelli, as quoted in *Business Week,* August 30, 1999, p. 54.

30. John Simons, "Inside U.S. Presidential Campaign 2000: The Internet Is the New Battleground," *The Wall Street Journal,* May 25, 1999, p. 10.

31. "South Korea Claims Net 'Super' Status," *BBC News World Edition,* November 6, 2002.

32. As cited in Doug Struck, "Blacklisted on the Web, Fifty-Eight Candidates Lose in South Korean Vote," *International Herald Tribune,* April 15–16, 2000, p. 5.

33. Alex Zoghlin, "These Websites Need Improvement," *Fortune,* March 6, 2000, pp. 86–87.

Chapter 11

1. These states are Alaska, Delaware, Montana, North Dakota, South Dakota, Vermont, and Wyoming.

2. 369 U.S. 186 (1962).

3. 376 U.S. 1 (1964).

4. See, for example, *Davis v. Bandemer,* 178 U.S. 109 (1986).

5. *Amicus curiae* brief filed by the American Civil Liberties Union (ACLU) in support of the appellants in *Easley v. Cromartie,* 532 U.S. 234 (2001).

6. See, for example, *Shaw v. Reno,* 509 U.S. 630 (1993); *Miller v. Johnson,* 515 U.S. 900 (1995); *Shaw v. Hunt,* 517 U.S. 899 (1996); and *Bush v. Vera,* 517 U.S. 952 (1996).

7. *Easley v. Cromartie,* 532 U.S. 234 (2001).

8. For a discussion of the role of political parties in the selection of congressional candidates, see Gary Jacobson, *The Politics of Congressional Elections,* 5th ed. (New York: Longman Publishers, 2001).

9. *Powell v. McCormack,* 395 U.S. 486 (1969).

10. Quoted in John Samples and Patrick Basham, "Election 2002 and the Problems of American Democracy," *Policy Analysis,* September 5, 2002.

11. Some observers maintain that another reason Congress *can* stay in session longer is the invention of air conditioning. Until the advent of air conditioning, no member of Congress wanted to stay in session during the hot and sticky late spring, summer, and early fall months.

12. David Broder, "The New GOP Take on Term Limits," *The Washington Post,* January 5, 2003, p. B07.

13. A term used by Woodrow Wilson in *Congressional Government* (New York: Meridian Books, 1956 [first published in 1885]).

14. See the statement by the Office of Management and Budget (OMB), "Charting a Course for the Federal Budget," which is one of the budget documents for fiscal year 2004. It is available at the OMB's Web site, **http://www.whitehouse.gov/omb/budget/fy2004/charting.html**.

15. Jonathan Karl, "Cooking the Books Is an Old Recipe for Uncle Sam," *The Wall Street Journal,* July 22, 2002, p. A14.

16. Quoted in Karl, "Cooking the Books."

17. *Ibid.*

18. In 2003, President Bush's budget projections extended only five years, as had been the practice before 1996.

19. Jeffrey H. Birnbaum, "The Return of Big Government: Federal Spending Is Skyrocketing, but Shockingly Little of It Is Related to September 11," *Fortune,* September 16, 2002, p. 112.

Chapter 12

1. Several Supreme Court cases have addressed whether the federal government can enter into treaties that contain provisions that violate the restrictions or requirements of the Constitution. See, for example, *Geofroy v. Riggs,* 133 U.S. 258 (1890); *U.S. v. Wong Kim Ark,* 169 U.S. 649 (1898); *Asakura v. City of Seattle,* 265 U.S. 332 (1924); *Reid v. Covert,* 354 U.S. 1 (1957); and *Boos v. Barry,* 485 U.S. 312 (1988).

2. Lyndon B. Johnson, *The Vantage Point: Perspectives of the Presidency, 1963–1969* (New York: Henry Holt & Co., 1971).

3. *Newsweek* poll, October 1996.

4. Franklin D. Roosevelt, as quoted in *The New York Times,* November 13, 1932.

5. Marvin Olasky, "Sex and the Presidency," *The Wall Street Journal—Europe,* January 27, 1998.

6. Forrest McDonald, *The American Presidency: An Intellectual History* (Lawrence, Kans.: University Press of Kansas, 1994), p. 179.

7. Versailles, located about twenty miles from Paris, is the name of the palace built by King Louis XIV of France. It served as the royal palace until 1793 and was then converted into a national historical museum, which it remains today. The preliminary treaty ending the American Revolution was signed by the United States and Great Britain at Versailles in 1783.

8. *Clinton v. City of New York,* 524 U.S. 417 (1998).

9. As cited in Lewis D. Eigen and Jonathan P. Siegel, *The Macmillan Dictionary of Political Quotations* (New York: Macmillan, 1993), p. 565.

10. The Constitution does not grant the president explicit power to remove from office officials who are not performing satisfactorily or who do not agree with the president. In 1926, however, the Supreme Court prevented Congress from interfering with the president's ability to fire those executive branch officials whom he had appointed with Senate approval. See *Myers v. United States,* 272 U.S. 52 (1926).

11. Richard E. Neustadt, *Presidential Power: The Politics of Leadership* (New York: John Wiley, 1980), p. 10.

12. As quoted in Richard M. Pious, *The American Presidency* (New York: Basic Books, 1979), pp. 51–52.

13. A phrase coined by Samuel Kernell in *Going Public: New Strategies of Presidential Leadership,* 2d ed. (Washington, D.C.: Congressional Quarterly Press, 1992).

14. Congress used its power to declare war in the War of 1812, the Mexican War (1846–1848), the Spanish-American War (1898), World War I (U.S. involvement lasted from 1916 until 1918), and World War II (U.S. involvement lasted from 1941 until 1945).

15. William S. Cohen, "Why I Am Leaving," *The Washington Post National Weekly Edition,* January 28–February 4, 1996, p. 29.

16. See, for example, Thomas E. Cronin and Michael A. Genovese, *The Paradoxes of the American Presidency* (New York: Oxford University Press, 1998).

17. *Ibid.,* p. 108.

18. See the writings of Aubrey Immelman, a political psychologist and associate professor of psychology at the College of St. Benedict and St. John's University, at **http://www.csbsju.edu/uspp/Publications&Citations/Publications.html**.

19. James Klurfeld, "The Really Big Story: Bush's Awesome Power," *Newsday,* December 26, 2002.

20. "U.S. Places New Curbs on Weapons Data; Secrecy Watchdogs Warn of Rule's Broader Uses," *The Washington Post,* March 22, 2002, p. A3.

21. As quoted in Thomas E. Cronin, *The State of the Presidency,* 2d ed. (Boston: Little, Brown, 1980), p. 11.

Chapter 13

1. Geoffrey F. Segal, *Cato Handbook for Congress: Policy Recommendations for the 108th Congress* (Washington, D.C.: The Cato Institute, January 22, 2003), p. 327.

2. For further information on the AFSCME's position on privatization, go to **http://www.afscme.org/srkplace/salelc.htm**.

3. This definition follows the classical model of bureaucracy put forth by German sociologist Max Weber. See Max Weber, *Theory of Social and Economic Organization,* Talcott Parsons, ed. (New York: Oxford University Press, 1974).

4. It should be noted that although the president is technically the head of the bureaucracy, the president cannot always control the bureaucracy—as you will read later in this chapter.

5. "The Political Hacks' Ultimate Fantasy Book," *Fortune,* March 3, 1997, p. 46.

6. Christopher C. DeMuth, "After the Ascent: Politics and Government in the Super-Affluent Society," Francis Boyer Lecture, American Enterprise Institute, Washington, D.C., February 15, 2000.

7. George Melloan, "Disturbing Trends for America's Rule of Law," *The Wall Street Journal,* November 2, 2002, p. A11.

8. Trucking associations and other business groups sued the EPA, claiming, among other things, that the EPA had to take economic costs into account when issuing new rules. Ultimately, the case reached the Supreme Court, which held that the EPA did not have to take such costs into consideration when creating new rules. *Whitman v. American Trucking Associations,* 531 U.S. 457 (2000).

9. Anne B. Fisher, "One Welfare Program That Won't Die," *Fortune,* November 27, 1995, p. 40.

10. See the White House Press Release of May 13, 2002, at **http://www.usda.gov/news/ releases/2002/05/farmbill2002.htm**.

11. As quoted in Bob Norton, "Why Federal Programs Won't Die," *Fortune,* August 21, 1995, p. 35.

12. As quoted in Laura Parker et al., "Secure Often Means Secret," *USA Today,* May 16, 2002, p. 2A.

13. As quoted in George Melloan, "Bush's Toughest Struggle Is with His Own Bureaucracy," *The Wall Street Journal,* June 25, 2002, p. A13.

Chapter 14

1. Pronounced *ster*-ay dih-*si*-ses.

2. 347 U.S. 483 (1954).

3. See *Plessy v. Ferguson,* 163 U.S. 537 (1896).

4. Although a state's highest court is often referred to as the state supreme court, there are exceptions. In the New York court system, for example, the supreme court is a trial court, and the highest court is called the New York Court of Appeals.

5. Pronounced jus-*tish*-a-bul.

6. *Raines v. Byrd,* 521 U.S. 811 (1997).

7. *In re Sealed Case,* 310 F.3d 717 (For.Int.Surv.Ct.Rev. 2002).

8. Pronounced sur-shee-uh-*rah*-ree.

9. Between 1790 and 1891, Congress allowed the Supreme Court almost no discretion over which cases to decide. After 1925, in almost 95 percent of appealed cases the Court could choose whether to hear arguments and issue an opinion. Beginning with the term in October 1988, mandatory review was virtually eliminated.

10. 84 F.3d 720 (5th Cir. 1996).

11. 5 U.S. (1 Cranch) 137 (1803). The Supreme Court had considered the constitutionality of an act of Congress in *Hylton v. United States,* 3 U.S. 171 (1796), in which Congress's power to levy certain taxes was challenged. That particular act was ruled constitutional, rather than unconstitutional, however, so this first federal exercise of judicial review was not clearly recognized as such. Also, during the decade before the adoption of the federal Constitution, courts in at least eight states had exercised the power of judicial review.

12. Jeffrey A. Segal and Harold J. Spaeth, *The Supreme Court and the Attitudinal Model* (New York: Cambridge University Press, 1993), p. 65.

13. 536 U.S. 304 (2002).

14. Antonin Scalia, *A Matter of Interpretation* (Ewing, N.J.: Princeton University Press, 1997).

15. *U.S. Airways v. Barnett,* 535 U.S. 391 (2002).

16. As cited in Linda Greenhouse, "The Competing Visions of the Role of the Court," *The New York Times,* July 7, 2002, p. 3.

17. 514 U.S. 549 (1995).

18. *Federal Maritime Commission v. South Carolina State Ports Authority,* 535 U.S. 743 (2002).

19. John T. Noonan, Jr., *Narrowing the Nation's Power: The Supreme Court Sides with the States* (Berkeley: University of California Press, 2002).

20. Simon Lazarus, "The Most Dangerous Branch," *The Atlantic Monthly,* June 2002, p. 24.

Chapter 15

1. *Weems v. United States,* 217 U.S. 349 (1910).

2. *Lockyer v. Andrade,* 123 S.Ct. 1166 (2003); and *Ewing v. California,* 123 S.Ct. 1179 (2003).

3. President's remarks to West Ashley High School, Charleston, South Carolina, July 29, 2002. You can read a transcript of the president's speech at **http://www.whitehouse.gov/news/releases/2002/07/20020729-6.html**.

4. Jocelyn Y. Stewart, "Charity Meals Debated in L.A.," *The Los Angeles Times,* January 13, 2003.

5. For an argument in support of this view, see Ethan Nadelmann, "Rethinking the War on Drugs," *The Oregonian,* January 18, 1998, p. 1B.

6. The National School Safety Center's Report on School Associated Violent Deaths, December 20, 2002. You can access this report online at **http://www.nssc1.org/ savd/savd.pdf**.

7. See the analysis of the Economic Growth and Tax Relief Reconciliation Act of 2001, released by the Urban Institute and the Brookings Institution, 2002. You can access this report at **http://www.taxpolicycenter.org/taxfacts/ overview/egtrra.cfm**.

8. Robert J. Samuelson, "The Rich and Everyone Else," *Newsweek,* January 27, 2003, p. 57.

Chapter 16

1. Mackubin Thomas Owens, "The Price of the Pax Americana," *The Wall Street Journal,* September 12, 2000. You can access other articles and editorials by Professor Owens at **http://www.ashbrook.org/columns/owens**.

2. As quoted in John Mack Faragher *et al., Out of Many: A History of the American People,* 2d ed. (Upper Saddle River, N.J.: Prentice Hall, 1997), p. 412.

3. *Public Papers of the Presidents of the United States: Harry S Truman, 1947* (Washington, D.C.: U.S. Government Printing Office, 1963), pp. 176–180.

4. The containment policy was outlined by George F. Kennan, the chief of the policy-planning staff for the Department of State at that time, in an article that appeared in *Foreign Affairs,* July 1947, p. 575. The author's name was given as "X."

5. This statement was part of the National Security Strategy of the United States, which was submitted to Congress in September 2002. You can access the full text of the strategy at **http://www.whitehouse.gov/nsc/nssall.html**.

6. Victor Davis Hanson, "America Must Go It Alone," *The Wall Street Journal,* August 6, 2002, p. A20.

7. You can access the full text of this report at **http://www.newamericancentury.org/ defensenationalsecurity.htm**.

8. You can access the full transcript of President Bush's speech at **http://www. whitehouse.gov/news/releases/2002/10/20021007-8.html**.

9. See the transcript of Hans Blix's presentation to the United Nations Security Council on March 7, 2003, available online at **http://www.un.org/apps/news/ infocusnewsiraq.asp?NewsID=414&sID=6**.

10. See the remarks made by President Bush on national missile defense on December 13, 2001, at **http://www.whitehouse.gov/news/releases/2001/ 12/20011213-4.html**.

11. You can access the most recent statistics on Russia's declared nuclear warheads at **http://www.nti.org/db/nisprofs/russia/weapons/stockpil.html**.

12. As cited in *The Economist,* January 22, 2000, p. 34.

13. "Ban the Bug Bomb: New Horrors Are Certain If the Convention on Biological Weapons Is Not Strengthened," *The Economist,* November 23, 1996, p. 19.

14. Steven R. Weisman, "Preemption: Idea with a Lineage Whose Time Has Come," *The New York Times,* March 23, 2003.

15. Quoted in Weisman, "Preemption."

16. Letter of Thomas Jefferson to Carmichael and Short, 1793.

17. You can access a transcript of this speech at the following Web site: **http://www.house.gov/paul/congrec/congrec2002/cr090402.htm**.

Chapter 17

1. New Hampshire developed a strong dislike of government beyond its towns' borders when it was ruled directly from England as a royal colony. Its House of Representatives has at least one member for each town regardless of population. It is the third largest legislature in the English-speaking world, topped only by Congress and the British Parliament.

2. *The Book of the States, 2002–2003* (Lexington, Ky.: Council of State Governments, 2002).

3. *U.S. Term Limits v. Thornton,* 514 U.S. 779 (1995).

4. Michael Schudson, *The Good Citizen: A History of American Civic Life* (New York: Free Press, 1998).

5. William Salzer of New York in 1913, James E. Ferguson of Texas in 1917, J. C. Walton of Oklahoma in 1923, and Henry S. Johnston of Oklahoma in 1929.

6. In New York, the state's highest court is called the Court of Appeals. In Texas and Oklahoma, there are two "highest" appellate courts. In Texas, for example, state district court decisions can be appealed to either the Texas Supreme Court or the Texas Court of Criminal Appeals, depending on the type of case.

7. *The Book of the States, 2002–2003.*

8. *Republican Party of Minnesota v. White,* 436 U.S. 765 (2002).

9. For a discussion of other negative consequences and implications of judicial elections, see Derek Bok, "Too Many Beholden Judges," *The National Law Journal,* November 25, 2002, p. A8.

10. Cynthia Gray, "Judging by the Merits," *The National Law Journal,* May 27, 2002, p. A17.

11. *Zelman v. Simmons-Harris,* 436 U.S. 639 (2002).

12. Jackie Calmes, "Bush's Home State Faces Budget Mess," *The Wall Street Journal,* January 22, 2002, p. A4.

13. Robert Pear, "Most States Cutting Back on Medicaid, Survey Finds," *The New York Times,* January 14, 2001, p. A20.

A

ABSOLUTE MONARCHY A form of monarchy in which the monarch has complete and unlimited power as a matter of divine right.

ACTION-REACTION SYNDROME For every government action, there will be a reaction by the public. The government then takes a further action to counter the public's reaction—and the cycle begins again.

ADJUDICATE To render a judicial decision. In regard to administrative law, the process in which an administrative law judge hears and decides issues that arise when an agency charges a person or firm with violating a law or regulation enforced by the agency.

ADMINISTRATIVE AGENCY A federal or state government agency established to perform a specific function. Administrative agencies are authorized by legislative acts to make and enforce rules to administer and enforce the acts.

ADMINISTRATIVE LAW The body of law created by administrative agencies (in the form of rules, regulations, orders, and decisions) in order to carry out their duties and responsibilities.

ADMINISTRATIVE LAW JUDGE One who presides over an administrative agency hearing and who has the power to conduct legal hearings and make legal determinations.

ADMINISTRATIVE PROCESS The functions—including rulemaking, enforcement, and adjudication—undertaken by administrative agencies in administering the law.

AFFIRMATIVE ACTION A policy calling for the establishment of programs that involve giving preference, in jobs and college admissions, to members of groups that have been discriminated against in the past.

AGENDA SETTING The first stage of the policymaking process, which consists of getting an issue on the political agenda to be addressed by Congress.

AGENTS OF POLITICAL SOCIALIZATION People and institutions that influence the political views of others.

AMERICAN CREED The principles set forth in a document written by William Tyler Page in 1917 and based on the Declaration of Independence.

ANTI-FEDERALISTS A political group that opposed the adoption of the Constitution because of the document's centralist tendencies and because it did not include a bill of rights.

ANTITRUST LAW The body of law that attempts to support free competition in the marketplace by curbing monopolistic and unfair trade practices.

APPELLATE COURT A court having appellate jurisdiction that normally does not hear evidence or testimony but reviews the transcript of the trial court's proceedings, other records relating to the case, and the attorneys' respective arguments as to why the trial court's decision should or should not stand.

APPORTIONMENT The distribution of House seats among the states on the basis of their respective populations.

APPROPRIATION A part of the congressional budgeting process that involves determining how many dollars will be spent in a given year on a particular set of government activities.

ARTICLES OF CONFEDERATION The nation's first national constitution, which established a national form of government following the American Revolution. The articles provided for a confederal form of government in which the central government had few powers.

ATTACK AD A negative political advertisement that attacks the character of an opposing candidate.

AUSTRALIAN BALLOT A secret ballot that is prepared, distributed, and counted by government officials at public expense; used by all states in the United States since 1888.

AUTHORITY The ability to exercise power, such as the power to make and enforce laws, legitimately.

AUTHORIZATION A part of the congressional budgeting process that involves the creation of the legal basis for government programs.

AUTOCRACY A form of government in which the power and authority of the government are in the hands of a single person.

B

BIASED SAMPLE A poll sample that does not accurately represent the population.

BICAMERAL LEGISLATURE A legislature made up of two chambers, or parts. The United States has a bicameral legislature, composed of the House of Representatives and the Senate.

BILL OF ATTAINDER A legislative act that inflicts punishment on particular persons or groups without granting them the right to a trial.

BILL OF RIGHTS The first ten amendments to the U.S. Constitution. They list the freedoms—such as the freedoms of speech, press, and religion—that a person enjoys and that cannot be infringed on by the government.

BLANKET PRIMARY A "wide open" primary in which each voter receives a single ballot listing each party's candidates for each nomination.

BLOCK GRANT A federal grant given to a state for a broad area, such as criminal justice or mental health programs.

BUREAUCRACY A large, complex, hierarchically structured administrative organization that carries out specific functions.

BUREAUCRAT An individual who works in a bureaucracy; as generally used, the term refers to a government employee.

BUSING The transportation of public school students by bus to schools physically outside their neighborhoods to eliminate school segregation based on residential patterns.

C

CABINET An advisory group selected by the president to assist with decision making. Traditionally, the cabinet has consisted of the heads of the executive departments and other officers whom the president may choose to appoint.

CAMPAIGN MANAGER The person who coordinates and plans a political candidate's campaign and the strategy that will be used for it.

CAMPAIGN STRATEGY The comprehensive plan for winning an election developed by a candidate and his or her advisers. The strategy includes the candidate's position on issues, slogan, advertising plan, press events, personal appearances, and other aspects of the campaign.

CASE LAW The rules of law announced in court decisions. Case law includes the aggregate of reported cases that interpret judicial precedents, statutes, regulations, and constitutional provisions.

CATEGORICAL GRANT A federal grant targeted for a specific purpose as defined by federal law.

CAUCUS A meeting held by party leaders to choose political candidates. The caucus system of nominating candidates was eventually replaced by nominating conventions and, later, by direct primaries.

CHECKS AND BALANCES A major principle of American government in which each of the three branches is given the means to check (to restrain or balance) the actions of the others.

CHIEF DIPLOMAT The role of the president in recognizing and interacting with foreign governments.

CHIEF EXECUTIVE The head of the executive branch of government. In the United States, the president is the head of the executive branch of the federal government.

CHIEF OF STAFF The person who directs the operations of the White House Office and who advises the president on important matters.

CHIEF OF STATE The person who serves as the ceremonial head of a country's government and represents that country to the rest of the world.

CIVIL DISOBEDIENCE The deliberate and public act of refusing to obey laws thought to be unjust.

CIVIL LAW The branch of law that spells out the duties that individuals in society owe to other persons or to their governments, excluding the duty not to commit crimes.

CIVIL LIBERTIES Individual rights protected by the Constitution against the powers of the government.

CIVIL RIGHTS The rights of all Americans to equal treatment under the law, as provided for by the Fourteenth Amendment to the Constitution.

CIVIL RIGHTS MOVEMENT The movement in the 1950s and 1960s, by minorities and concerned whites, to end racial segregation.

CIVIL SERVICE Employees of the civil government, or civil servants.

CLASSICAL LIBERALISM Liberalism in its traditional form. Like modern liberalism, classical liberalism stressed political democracy, constitutionally guaranteed civil liberties, political equality, free political competition, and separation of church and state. Unlike modern liberalism, classical liberalism opposed government intervention in the economy and stressed free enterprise, individual initiative, and free trade.

CLOSED PRIMARY A primary in which only party members can vote to choose that party's candidates.

CLOTURE A method of ending debate in the Senate and bringing the matter under consideration to a vote by the entire chamber.

COALITION An alliance of individuals or groups with a variety of interests and opinions who join together to support all or part of a political party's platform.

COLD WAR The war of words, warnings, and ideologies between the Soviet Union and the United States that lasted from the late 1940s through the early 1990s.

COLLECTIVE SECURITY A national defense and security policy that involved the formation of mutual defense alliances, such as the North Atlantic Treaty Organization, with other nations.

COLONIAL EMPIRE A group of colonized nations that are under the rule of a single imperial power.

COMMANDER IN CHIEF The supreme commander of the military forces of the United States.

COMMERCE CLAUSE The clause in Article I, Section 8, of the Constitution that gives Congress the power to regulate interstate commerce (commerce involving more than one state).

COMMERCIAL SPEECH Advertising statements that describe products. Commercial speech receives less protection under the First Amendment than ordinary speech.

COMMON LAW The body of law developed from judicial decisions in English and U.S. courts, not attributable to a legislature.

COMMUNIST BLOC The group of Eastern European nations that fell under the control of the Soviet Union following World War II.

COMPETITIVE FEDERALISM A model of federalism devised by Thomas R. Dye in which state and local governments compete for businesses and citizens, who in effect "vote with their feet" by moving to jurisdictions that offer a competitive advantage.

CONCURRENT MAJORITY A principle advanced by John C. Calhoun that states that democratic decisions should be made only with the agreement of all segments of society affected by the decisions. Without their agreement, a decision should not be binding on those whose interests it violates.

CONCURRENT POWERS Powers held by both the federal and state governments in a federal system.

CONCURRING OPINION A statement written by a judge or justice who agrees (concurs) with the court's decision, but for reasons different from those in the majority opinion.

CONFEDERAL SYSTEM A league of independent sovereign states, joined together by a central government that has only limited powers over them.

CONFEDERATION A league of independent states that are united only for the purpose of achieving common goals.

CONFERENCE In regard to the Supreme Court, a private meeting of the justices in which they present their arguments with respect to a case under consideration.

CONFERENCE COMMITTEE A temporary committee that is formed when the two chambers of Congress pass separate versions of the same bill. The conference committee, which consists of members from both the House and the Senate, works out a compromise form of the bill.

CONFERENCE REPORT A report submitted by a congressional conference committee after it has drafted a single version of a bill.

CONGRESSIONAL DISTRICT The geographic area that is served by one representative in Congress.

CONSENSUS A general agreement among the citizenry (often defined as an agreement among 75 percent or more of the people) on matters of public policy.

CONSERVATISM A set of beliefs that includes a limited role for the national government in helping individuals, support for traditional values and lifestyles, and a cautious response to change.

CONSERVATIVE One who subscribes to a set of political beliefs that includes a limited role for government, support for traditional values, and a preference for the status quo.

CONSTITUTIONAL CONVENTION The convention (meeting) of delegates from the states that was held in Philadelphia in 1787 for the purpose of amending the Articles of Confederation. In fact, the delegates wrote a new constitution (the U.S. Constitution) that established a federal form of government to replace the governmental system that had been created by the Articles of Confederation.

CONSTITUTIONAL LAW Law based on the U.S. Constitution and the constitutions of the various states.

CONSTITUTIONAL MONARCHY A form of monarchy in which the monarch shares governmental power with elected lawmakers; the monarch's power is limited, or checked, by other government leaders and perhaps by a constitution or a bill of rights.

CONTAINMENT A U.S. policy designed to contain the spread of communism by offering military and economic aid to threatened nations.

CONTINUING RESOLUTION A resolution, which Congress passes when it is unable to pass a complete budget by October 1, that enables the executive agencies to keep on doing whatever they were doing the previous year with the same amount of funding.

COOPERATIVE FEDERALISM The theory that the states and the federal government should cooperate in solving problems.

COUNCIL OF ECONOMIC ADVISERS (CEA) A three-member council created in 1946 to advise the president on economic matters.

CREDENTIALS COMMITTEE A committee of each national political party that evaluates the claims of national party convention delegates to be the legitimate representatives of their states.

CRIMINAL LAW The branch of law that defines and governs actions that constitute crimes. Generally, criminal law has to do with wrongful actions committed against society for which society demands redress.

CUBAN MISSLE CRISIS A nuclear stand-off that occurred in 1962 when the United States learned that the Soviet Union had placed nuclear warheads in Cuba, an island ninety miles off the U.S. coast. The crisis was defused diplomatically, but it is generally considered the closest the two Cold War superpowers came to a nuclear confrontation.

CYBER DEMONSTRATION A labor protest, or demonstration, organized and executed by the use of e-mail communications among labor union members.

D

DE FACTO **SEGREGATION** Racial segregation that occurs not as a result of deliberate intentions but because of past social and economic conditions and residential patterns.

DE JURE **SEGREGATION** Racial segregation that is legally sanctioned—that is, segregation that occurs because of laws or decisions by government agencies.

DELEGATE A person selected to represent the people of one geographic area at a party convention.

DEMOCRACY A system of government in which the people have ultimate political authority. The word is derived from the Greek *demos* (people) and *kratia* (rule).

DEREGULATION The removal of regulatory restraints on business.

DÉTENTE A French word meaning a relaxation of tensions. Détente characterized the relationship between the United States and the Soviet Union in the 1970s, as the two Cold War rivals attempted to pursue cooperative dealings and arms control.

DETERRENCE A policy of building up military strength for the purpose of discouraging (deterring) military attacks by other nations; the policy of "building weapons for peace" that supported the arms race between the United States and the Soviet Union during the Cold War.

DEVOLUTION In the context of American politics, the transfer to the states of some of the responsibilities assumed by the national government since the 1930s.

DICTATORSHIP A form of government in which absolute power is exercised by a single person who has usually obtained his or her power by the use of force.

DIPLOMAT In regard to international relations, a person who represents one country in dealing with representatives of another country.

DIRECT DEMOCRACY A system of government in which political decisions are made by the people themselves rather than by elected representatives. This form of government was widely practiced in ancient Greece.

DIRECT PRIMARY An election held within each of the two major parties—Democratic and Republican—to choose the party's candidates for the general election.

DISSENTING OPINION A written opinion by a judge or justice who disagrees with the majority opinion.

DIVERSITY OF CITIZENSHIP A basis for federal court jurisdiction over a lawsuit that arises when (1) the parties in the lawsuit live in different states or when one of the parties is a foreign government or a foreign citizen, and (2) the amount in controversy is more than $75,000.

DIVINE RIGHT THEORY A theory that the right to rule by a king or queen was derived directly from God rather than from the consent of the people.

DIVISION OF POWERS A basic principle of federalism established by the U.S. Constitution. In a federal system, powers are divided between units of government (such as the federal and state governments).

DOMESTIC POLICY Public policy concerning issues within a national unit, such as national policy concerning welfare or crime.

DOUBLE JEOPARDY To prosecute a person twice for the same criminal offense; prohibited by the Fifth Amendment in all but a few circumstances.

DUAL FEDERALISM A system of government in which both the federal and state governments maintain diverse but sovereign powers.

DUE PROCESS CLAUSE The constitutional guarantee, set out in the Fifth and Fourteenth Amendments, that the government will not illegally or arbitrarily deprive a person of life, liberty, or property.

DUE PROCESS OF LAW The requirement that the government use fair, reasonable, and standard procedures whenever it takes any legal action against an individual; required by the Fifth and Fourteenth Amendments.

E

EASY-MONEY POLICY A monetary policy that involves stimulating the economy by expanding the rate of growth of the money supply. An easy-money policy supposedly will lead to lower interest rates and induce consumers to spend more and producers to invest more.

ECONOMIC POLICY All actions taken by the national government to smooth out the ups and downs in the nation's overall business activity.

ECONOMIC REGULATION Government regulation of natural monopolies and inherently noncompetitive industries.

ELECTOR A member of the electoral college.

ELECTORAL COLLEGE The group of electors who are selected by the voters in each state to officially elect the president and vice president. The number of electors in each state is equal to the number of that state's representatives in both chambers of Congress.

ELECTORATE All of the citizens eligible to vote in a given election.

ELECTRONIC MEDIA Communication channels that involve electronic transmissions, such as radio, television, and, to an extent, the Internet.

ENABLING LEGISLATION A law enacted by a legislature to establish an administrative agency; enabling legislation normally specifies the name, purpose, composition, and powers of the agency being created.

ENCRYPTION SOFTWARE Computer programs that enable the user to encode ("encrypt") data to prevent access to the data by unauthorized persons.

ENTITLEMENT PROGRAM A government program (such as Social Security) that allows, or entitles, a certain class of people (such as the elderly) to receive special benefits. Entitlement programs operate under open-ended budget authorizations that, in effect, place no limits on how much can be spent.

EQUAL EMPLOYMENT OPPORTUNITY A goal of the 1964 Civil Rights Act to end employment discrimination based on race, color, religion, gender, or national origin and to promote equal job opportunities for all individuals.

EQUAL PROTECTION CLAUSE Section 1 of the Fourteenth Amendment, which states that no state shall "deny to any person within its jurisdiction the equal protection of the laws."

EQUALITY A concept that holds, at a minimum, that all people are entitled to equal protection under the law.

ESPIONAGE The practice of spying, on behalf of a foreign power, to obtain information about government plans and activities.

ESTABLISHMENT CLAUSE The section of the First Amendment that prohibits Congress from passing laws "respecting an establishment of religion." Issues concerning the establishment clause often center on prayer in public schools, the teaching of fundamentalist theories of creation, and government aid to parochial schools.

EVOLUTIONARY THEORY A theory that holds that government evolved gradually over time as families first joined together into clans, then into tribes, and then into a larger, more formal unit.

***EX POST FACTO* LAW** A criminal law that punishes individuals for committing an act that was legal when the act was committed but that has since become a crime.

EXCLUSIONARY RULE A criminal procedural rule requiring that any illegally obtained evidence will not be admissible in court. The rule is based on Supreme Court interpretations of the Fourth and Fourteenth Amendments.

EXECUTIVE AGREEMENT A binding international agreement, or pact, that is made between the president and another head of state and that does not require Senate approval.

EXECUTIVE OFFICE OF THE PRESIDENT (EOP) A group of staff agencies that assist the president in carrying out major duties. Franklin D. Roosevelt established the EOP in 1939 to cope with the increased responsibilities brought on by the Great Depression.

EXECUTIVE ORDER A presidential order to carry out a policy or policies described in a law passed by Congress.

EXECUTIVE PRIVILEGE An inherent executive power claimed by presidents to withhold information from, or to refuse to appear before, Congress or the courts. The president can also accord the privilege to other executive officials.

EXPRESSED POWERS Constitutional or statutory powers that are expressly provided for by the Constitution or by congressional laws.

EXTRAORDINARY MAJORITY More than a mere majority; typically, an extraordinary majority consists of two-thirds or three-fifths of the voting body (such as a legislature).

F

FACTION A group or clique within a larger group.

FEDERAL MANDATE A requirement in federal legislation that forces states and municipalities to comply with certain rules.

FEDERAL OPEN MARKET COMMITTEE (FOMC) The most important body within the Federal Reserve System; the FOMC decides how monetary policy should be carried out by the Federal Reserve.

FEDERAL QUESTION A question that pertains to the U.S. Constitution, acts of Congress, or treaties. A federal question provides a basis for federal court jurisdiction.

FEDERAL SYSTEM A form of government in which a written constitution provides for a division of powers between a central government and several regional governments. In the United States, the division of powers between the national government and the fifty states is established by the Constitution.

FEDERALISM A way of organizing separate states into a single political system in such a way that each can maintain its fundamental political identity. Federalism emphasizes negotiated policymaking among the member states. The United States has a truly federal system because the

Constitution specifically describes how power to make and implement policy should be shared by the national government and the state governments.

FEDERALISTS A political group, led by Alexander Hamilton and John Adams, that supported the adoption of the Constitution and the creation of a federal form of government.

"FIGHTING WORDS" Words that, when uttered by a public speaker, are so inflammatory that they could provoke the average listener to violence.

FILIBUSTERING The Senate tradition of unlimited debate, undertaken for the purpose of preventing action on a bill.

FIRST BUDGET RESOLUTION A budget resolution, which is supposed to be passed in May, that sets overall revenue goals and spending targets for the next fiscal year, which begins on October 1.

FIRST CONTINENTAL CONGRESS The first gathering of delegates from twelve of the thirteen colonies, held in 1774.

FISCAL FEDERALISM The power of the national government to influence state policies through grants.

FISCAL POLICY The use of changes in government expenditures and taxes to alter national economic variables, such as the employment rate and price stability.

FISCAL YEAR A twelve-month period that is established for bookkeeping or accounting purposes. The government's fiscal year runs from October 1 through September 30.

FORCE THEORY A theory that holds that government originated when strong persons or groups conquered territories and forced everyone living in those territories to submit to their will.

FOREIGN POLICY A systematic and general plan that guides a country's attitudes and actions toward the rest of the world. Foreign policy includes all of the economic, military, commercial, and diplomatic positions and actions that a nation takes in its relationships with other countries.

FREE EXERCISE CLAUSE The provision of the First Amendment stating that the government cannot pass laws "prohibiting the free exercise" of religion. Free exercise issues often concern religious practices that conflict with established laws.

FUNDAMENTAL ORDERS OF CONNECTICUT America's first written constitution, developed by some of the Pilgrims who left the Massachusetts Bay Colony and settled in what is now Connecticut. The document provided for an assembly of elected representatives from each town and for the popular election of a governor and judges.

FUNDAMENTAL RIGHT A basic right of all Americans, such as all First Amendment rights. Any law or action that prevents some group of persons from exercising a funda-mental right will be subject to the "strict scrutiny" standard, under which the law or action must be necessary to promote a compelling state interest and must be narrowly tailored to meet that interest.

G

GENERAL ELECTION A regularly scheduled election to elect the U.S. president, vice president, and senators and representatives in Congress; general elections are held in even-numbered years on the first Tuesday after the first Monday in November.

GERRYMANDERING The drawing of a legislative district's boundaries in such a way as to maximize the influence of a certain group or political party.

GLASS CEILING The often subtle obstacles to advancement faced by professional women in the workplace.

GOVERNMENT The individuals and institutions that make society's rules and that also possess the power and authority to enforce those rules.

GOVERNMENT CORPORATION An agency of the government that is run as a business enterprise. Such agencies engage in primarily commercial activities, produce revenues, and require greater flexibility than that permitted in most government agencies.

GREAT COMPROMISE A plan for a bicameral legislature in which one chamber would be based on population and the other chamber would represent each state equally. The plan, also known as the Connecticut Compromise, resolved the small-state/large-state controversy.

I

IDEOLOGUE An individual who holds very strong political opinions.

IDEOLOGY A set of beliefs about human nature, social inequality, and government institutions that forms the basis of a political or economic system.

IMPEACHMENT A formal criminal proceeding against a public official for misconduct or wrongdoing in office.

IMPLIED POWERS The powers of the federal government that are implied by the expressed powers in the Constitution, particularly in Article I, Section 8.

INCOME REDISTRIBUTION The transfer of income from one group to another; income is taken from some people through taxation and given to others.

INDEPENDENT EXECUTIVE AGENCY A federal bureaucratic agency that is not located within a cabinet department.

INDEPENDENT EXPENDITURE An expenditure for activities that are independent from (not coordinated with) those of a political candidate or a political party.

INDEPENDENT REGULATORY AGENCY A federal bureaucratic organization that is responsible for creating and implementing rules that regulate private activity and protect the public interest in a particular sector of the economy.

INHERENT POWERS The powers of the national government that, although not expressly granted by the Constitution, are necessary to ensure the nation's integrity and survival as a political unit. Inherent powers include the power to make treaties and the power to wage war or make peace.

INITIATIVE A procedure by which voters can propose a change in state and local laws, including state constitutions, by means of gathering signatures on a petition and submitting it to the legislature (and/or the voters) for approval.

INSTITUTIONS Organizations and establishments in a society that are devoted to the promotion of a particular cause. Some of the institutions in our government are the legal system, Congress, and the social welfare system.

INSTRUCTED DELEGATE A representative (such as a member of Congress) who is expected to mirror the views of those whom he or she represents (such as a congressional member's constituents).

INTEREST GROUP An organized group of individuals sharing common objectives who actively attempt to influence policymakers in all three branches of the government and at all levels.

INTERGOVERNMENTAL LOBBY A special interest lobby formed by governors, mayors, highway commissioners, and others for the purpose of obtaining federal funds for state and local governments.

INTERSTATE COMMERCE Trade that involves more than one state.

INTERVENTIONISM Direct involvement by one country in another country's affairs.

INTRASTATE COMMERCE Commerce that takes place within state borders. State governments have the power to regulate intrastate commerce.

IRON CURTAIN A phrase coined by Winston Churchill to describe the political boundaries between the democratic countries in Europe and the Soviet-controlled communist countries in Eastern Europe.

IRON TRIANGLE A three-way alliance among legislators, bureaucrats, and interest groups to make or preserve policies that benefit their respective interests.

ISOLATIONISM A political policy of noninvolvement in world affairs.

ISSUE AD A negative political advertisement that focuses on flaws in an opposing candidate's position on a particular issue.

J

JUDICIAL REVIEW The power of the courts to decide on the constitutionality of legislative enactments and of actions taken by the executive branch.

JUDICIARY The courts; one of the three branches of the federal government in the United States.

JURISDICTION The authority of a court to hear and decide a particular case.

JUSTICE COURT A local court with limited jurisdiction; justice courts typically hear minor civil and criminal cases, perform marriages, and legalize documents.

JUSTICE OF THE PEACE A local judicial official who presides over the activities of a justice court; often popularly elected for a short term.

JUSTICIABLE CONTROVERSY A controversy that is not hypothetical or academic but real and substantial; a requirement that must be satisfied before a court will hear a case.

K

KEYNESIAN ECONOMICS An economic theory proposed by British economist John Maynard Keynes that is typically associated with the use of fiscal policy to alter national economic variables. Keynesian economics gained prominence during the Great Depression of the 1930s.

KITCHEN CABINET The name given to a president's unofficial advisers. The term was coined during Andrew Jackson's presidency.

L

LABOR FORCE All of the people over the age of sixteen who are working or actively looking for jobs.

LEGISLATIVE RULE An administrative agency rule that carries the same weight as a statute enacted by a legislature.

LEMON TEST A three-part test enunciated by the Supreme Court in the 1971 case of *Lemon v. Kurtzman* to determine whether government aid to parochial schools is constitutional. To be constitutional, the aid must (1) be for a clearly secular purpose; (2) in its primary effect, neither advance nor inhibit religion; and (3) avoid an "excessive government entanglement with religion." The *Lemon* test has also been used in other types of cases involving the establishment clause.

LIBEL A published report of a falsehood that tends to injure a person's reputation or character.

LIBERAL One who subscribes to a set of political beliefs that includes the advocacy of active government, government intervention to improve the welfare of individuals, support for civil rights, and political change.

LIBERALISM A set of political beliefs that includes the advocacy of active government, government intervention to improve the welfare of individuals, and civil rights.

LIBERTY The freedom of individuals to believe, act, and express themselves freely so long as doing so does not infringe on the rights of other individuals in the society.

LIMITED GOVERNMENT A form of government based on the principle that the powers of government should be clearly limited either through a written document or through wide public understanding; characterized by institutional checks to ensure that government serves public rather than private interests.

LITERACY TEST A test given to voters to ensure that they could read and write and thus evaluate political information; a technique used in many southern states to restrict African American participation in elections.

LOBBYING All of the attempts by organizations or by individuals to influence the passage, defeat, or contents of legislation or to influence the administrative decisions of government.

LOBBYIST An individual who handles a particular interest group's lobbying efforts.

LOOPHOLE A legal way of evading a certain legal requirement.

M

MADISONIAN MODEL The model of government devised by James Madison in which the powers of the government are separated into three branches: executive, legislative, and judicial.

MAGISTRATE A local judicial official who presides over the activities of a magistrate's court; often popularly elected for a short term.

MAGISTRATE COURT A local court with limited jurisdiction, usually in a small town or city.

MAGNA CARTA The great charter that King John of England was forced to sign in 1215 as protection against the absolute powers of the monarchy. It included such fundamental rights as trial by jury and due process of law.

MAJORITY LEADER The party leader elected by the majority party in the House or in the Senate.

MAJORITY PARTY The political party that has more members in the legislature than does the opposing party.

MALAPPORTIONMENT A condition that results when, based on population and representation, the voting power of citizens in one district becomes more influential than the voting power of citizens in another district.

MANAGED NEWS COVERAGE News coverage that is manipulated (managed) by a campaign manager or political consultant to gain media exposure for a political candidate.

MANDATORY PREFERENCE POLL A form of the preference poll in which delegates to the national party convention are selected at a state convention, and the delegates must vote for the candidate chosen by the voters.

MARKUP SESSION A meeting held by a congressional committee or subcommittee to approve, amend, or redraft a bill.

MARSHALL PLAN A plan providing for U.S. economic assistance to European nations following World War II to help those nations recover from the war; the plan was named after George C. Marshall, secretary of state from 1947 to 1949.

MASS MEDIA Communication channels, such as newspapers and radio and television broadcasts, through which people can communicate to mass audiences.

MAYFLOWER COMPACT A document drawn up by Pilgrim leaders in 1620 on the ship *Mayflower*. The document stated that laws were to be made for the general good of the people.

MEDIA Newspapers, magazines, television, radio, the Internet, and any other printed or electronic means of communication.

MEDIATING INSTITUTIONS Institutions that assume a mediating role between Americans and their government. Mediating institutions include political party conventions (which decide who will be candidates for political office) and network news organizations (which determine what political events should be reported to the public).

MINORITY LEADER The party leader elected by the minority party in the House or in the Senate.

MINORITY PARTY The political party that has fewer members in the legislature than does the opposing party.

MINORITY-MAJORITY DISTRICT A congressional district whose boundaries are drawn in such a way as to maximize the voting power of a minority group.

MIRANDA WARNINGS A series of statements informing criminal suspects, on their arrest, of their constitutional rights, such as the right to remain silent and the right to counsel; required by the Supreme Court's 1966 decision in *Miranda v. Arizona*.

MODERATE With regard to the political spectrum, a person whose views fall in the middle of the spectrum.

MODERN LIBERALISM A political ideology that stresses political democracy, constitutionally guaranteed civil liberties, political equality, free political competition, and separation of church and state. Unlike classical liberalism, modern liberalism supports the notion that the national government should take an active role in solving the nation's domestic problems and in protecting the interests of poor and disadvantaged groups in society.

MONARCHY A form of autocracy in which a king, queen, emperor, empress, tsar, or tsarina is the highest authority in the government; monarchs usually obtain their power through inheritance.

MONETARY POLICY Actions taken by the Federal Reserve Board to change the amount of money in circulation so as to affect interest rates, credit markets, the rate of inflation, the rate of economic growth, and unemployment.

MONROE DOCTRINE A U.S. policy, announced in 1823 by President James Monroe, that the United States would not tolerate foreign intervention in the Western Hemisphere, and in return, the United States would stay out of European affairs.

MOST-FAVORED-NATION STATUS A status granted by a clause in an international treaty. Generally, most-favored-nation clauses are designed to establish equality of international treatment. For example, if the United States and the People's Republic of China have agreed in a treaty that each country will have most-favored-nation status with respect to international trade, then the United States must treat China at least as well as the country receiving the most favorable treatment from the United States and vice versa.

MULTICULTURALISM The belief that the many cultures that make up American society should remain distinct and be protected and even encouraged by our laws.

MULTILATERAL Involving more than one side or nation.

MUTUAL-ASSURED DESTRUCTION (MAD) A phrase referring to the assumption, on which the policy of deterrence was based, that if the forces of two nations are equally capable of destroying each other, neither will take a chance on war.

N

NARROWCASTING Catering media programming to the specialized tastes and preferences of targeted audiences.

NATIONAL CONVENTION The meeting held by each major party every four years to select presidential and vice presidential candidates, to write a party platform, and to conduct other party business.

NATIONAL PARTY CHAIRPERSON An individual who serves as a political party's administrative head at the national level and directs the work of the party's national committee.

NATIONAL PARTY COMMITTEE The political party leaders who direct party business during the four years between the national party conventions, organize the next national convention, and plan how to obtain a party victory in the next presidential election.

NATIONAL SECURITY COUNCIL (NSC) A council that advises the president on domestic and foreign matters concerning the safety and defense of the nation; established in 1947.

NATURAL RIGHTS Rights that are not bestowed by governments but are inherent within every single man, woman, and child by virtue of the fact that he or she is a human being.

NECESSARY AND PROPER CLAUSE Article I, Section 8, Clause 18, of the Constitution, which gives Congress the power to make all laws "necessary and proper" for the federal government to carry out its responsibilities; also called the elastic clause.

NEGATIVE EXTERNALITY An effect of private decision making, such as pollution, that imposes social costs on the community. Negative externalities resulting from business decisions are often cited as reasons for government regulation.

NEGATIVE POLITICAL ADVERTISING Political advertising undertaken for the purpose of discrediting an opposing candidate in the eyes of the voters; attack ads and issue ads are forms of negative political advertising.

NEGOTIATED RULEMAKING A type of administrative agency rulemaking in which the industries that will be affected by the new rule participate in the rule's formulation.

NEUTRAL COMPETENCY The application of technical skills to jobs without regard to political issues.

NEUTRALITY A position of not being aligned with either side in a dispute or conflict, such as a war.

NEW DEAL A program ushered in by the Roosevelt administration in 1933 to bring the United States out of the Great Depression. The New Deal included many government spending and public-assistance programs, in addition to thousands of regulations governing economic activity.

NEW FEDERALISM A plan to limit the federal government's role in regulating state governments and to give the states increased power to decide how they should spend government revenues.

NOMINATING CONVENTION An official meeting of a political party to choose its candidates. Nominating conventions at the state and local levels also select delegates to represent the people of their geographic areas at a higher-level party convention.

NORTHWEST ORDINANCE A 1787 congressional act that established a basic pattern for how states should govern new territories north of the Ohio River.

O

OBSCENITY Indecency or offensiveness in speech or expression, behavior, or appearance; what specific expressions or acts constitute obscenity normally are determined by community standards.

OFFICE OF MANAGEMENT AND BUDGET (OMB) An agency in the Executive Office of the President that assists the president in preparing and supervising the administration of the federal budget.

OFFICE-BLOCK BALLOT A ballot that lists together all of the candidates for each office.

"ONE PERSON, ONE VOTE" RULE A rule, or principle, requiring that congressional districts must have equal population so that one person's vote counts as much as another's vote.

OPEN PRIMARY A primary in which voters can vote for a party's candidates regardless of whether they belong to the party.

OPINION A written statement by a court expressing the reasons for its decision in a case.

ORAL ARGUMENT An argument presented to a judge in person by an attorney on behalf of his or her client.

P

PARLIAMENT The name of the national legislative body in countries governed by a parliamentary system, as in England and France.

PARLIAMENTARY DEMOCRACY A form of democracy in which the lawmaking and law-enforcing branches of government overlap. In Great Britain, for example, the prime minister and the cabinet are members of the legislature, meaning that they both enact and enforce the laws.

PARTISAN POLITICS Political actions or decisions that are influenced by a particular political party's ideology.

PARTY ELITE A loose-knit group of party activists who organize and oversee party functions and planning during and between campaigns.

PARTY IDENTIFIER A person who identifies himself or herself as being a member of a particular political party.

PARTY PLATFORM The document drawn up by each party at its national convention that outlines the policies and positions of the party.

PARTY TICKET A list of a political party's candidates for various offices.

PARTY-COLUMN BALLOT A ballot (also called the Indiana ballot) that lists all of a party's candidates under the party label; voters can vote for all of a party's candidates for local, state, and national offices by making a single "X" or pulling a single lever.

PATRONAGE A system of rewarding the party faithful and workers with government jobs or contracts.

PEER GROUP Associates, often those close in age to oneself; may include friends, classmates, co-workers, club members, or church group members. Peer group influence is a significant factor in the political socialization process.

PICKET-FENCE FEDERALISM A model of federalism in which specific policies and programs are administered by all levels of government—national, state, and local.

PLURALIST THEORY A theory that views politics as a contest among various interest groups—at all levels of government—to gain benefits for their members.

PLURALITY A situation in which a candidate wins an election by receiving more votes than the others but does not necessarily win a majority (over 50 percent of the votes). Most federal, state, and local laws allow for elections to be won by a plurality vote.

POCKET VETO A special type of veto power used by the chief executive after the legislature has adjourned. Bills that are not signed by the president die after a specified period of time and must be reintroduced if Congress wishes to reconsider them.

POLICE POWERS The powers of a government body that enable it to create laws for the protection of the health, morals, safety, and welfare of the people. In the United States, most police powers are reserved to the states.

POLICYMAKING PROCESS The procedures involved in getting an issue on the political agenda; formulating, adopting, and implementing a policy with regard to the issue; and then evaluating the results of the policy.

POLITICAL ACTION COMMITTEE (PAC) A committee that is established by a corporation, labor union, or special interest group to raise funds and make contributions on the establishing organization's behalf.

POLITICAL ADVERTISING Advertising undertaken by or on behalf of a political candidate to familiarize voters with the candidate and his or her views on campaign issues.

POLITICAL AGENDA The issues that politicians will address; often determined by the media.

POLITICAL CONSULTANT A person who, for a large fee, devises a political candidate's campaign strategies, monitors the campaign's progress, plans all media appearances, and coaches the candidate for debates.

POLITICAL CULTURE The set of ideas, values, and attitudes about government and the political process held by a community or nation.

POLITICAL PARTY A group of individuals outside the government who organize to win elections, operate the government, and determine policy.

POLITICAL SOCIALIZATION A learning process through which most people acquire their political attitudes, opinions, beliefs, and knowledge.

POLITICS The process of resolving conflicts over how society should use its scarce resources and who should receive various benefits, such as wealth, status, health care, and higher education. According to Harold Lasswell, politics is the process of determining "who gets what, when, and how" in a society. According to David Easton, politics is "the authoritative allocation of values" in a society.

POLL TAX A fee of several dollars that had to be paid in order to vote; a device used in some southern states to prevent African Americans from voting.

POLL WATCHER A representative from one of the two major political parties who is allowed to monitor a polling place to make sure that the election is run fairly and to avoid fraud.

POWER The ability to influence the behavior of others, usually through the use of force, persuasion, or rewards.

PRECEDENT A court decision that furnishes an example or authority for deciding subsequent cases involving identical or similar facts and legal issues.

PRECINCT A political district within a city (such as a block or a neighborhood) or a portion of a rural county; the smallest voting district at the local level.

PREEMPTION A doctrine rooted in the supremacy clause of the Constitution that provides that national laws or regulations governing a certain area take precedence over conflicting state laws or regulations governing that same area.

PREEMPTIVE WAR A strategy of striking against an enemy before the enemy is able to launch an attack. It characterizes the foreign policy of the George W. Bush administration in the war on terrorism.

PREFERENCE POLL A method of voting in a primary election in which the names of the candidates for the nomination and the delegates appear separately, and voters cast separate votes for candidates and for delegates.

PRESIDENTIAL DEMOCRACY A form of democracy in which the lawmaking and law-enforcing branches of government are separate but equal, as in the United States.

PRESS CONFERENCE A scheduled interview with the media.

PRESS SECRETARY A member of the White House staff who holds press conferences for reporters and makes public statements for the president.

PRIMARY A preliminary election held for the purpose of choosing a party's final candidate.

PRIMARY SOURCE OF LAW A source of law that establishes the law. Primary sources of law include constitutions, statutes, administrative agency rules and regulations, and decisions rendered by the courts.

PRINT MEDIA Communication channels that consist of printed materials, such as newspapers and magazines.

PRIVATIZATION The replacement of government agencies that provide products or services to the public by private firms that provide the same products or services.

PROBABLE CAUSE Cause for believing that there is a substantial likelihood that a person has committed or is about to commit a crime.

PUBLIC DEBT The total amount of money that the national government owes as a result of borrowing; also called the national debt.

PUBLIC OPINION The individual attitudes or beliefs about politics, public issues, and public policies that are shared by a significant portion of adults; a complex collection of opinions held by many people on issues in the public arena.

PUBLIC OPINION POLL A numerical survey of the public's opinion on a particular topic at a particular moment.

PUBLIC POLICIES Plans of action to support or achieve government goals that are designed to improve the lives of citizens.

PUBLIC SERVICES Essential services that individuals cannot provide for themselves, such as building and maintaining roads, providing welfare programs, operating public schools, and preserving national parks.

PUBLIC-INTEREST GROUP An interest group formed for the purpose of working for the "public good"; examples of public-interest groups are the American Civil Liberties Union and Common Cause.

PUSH POLL A campaign tactic used to feed false or misleading information to potential voters, under the guise of taking an opinion poll, with the intent to "push" voters away from one candidate and toward another.

PUSH TECHNOLOGY Software that enables Internet users to customize the type of information they receive from Web sources. The information is "pushed" to the user automatically as it is put on the Web.

Q

QUOTA SYSTEM A policy under which a specific number of jobs, promotions, or other types of selections, such as university admissions, must be given to members of selected groups.

R

RACIAL PROFILING A form of discrimination in which law enforcement assumes that people of a certain race are more likely to commit crimes. Racial profiling has been linked to more frequent traffic stops of African Americans by police, and of increased security checks in airports of Arab Americans.

RADICAL LEFT Persons on the extreme left side of the political spectrum who would like to significantly change the political order, usually to promote egalitarianism. The radical left includes socialists, communists, and, often, populists.

RADICAL RIGHT Persons on the extreme right side of the political spectrum. The radical right includes reactionaries (who would like to return to the values and social systems of some previous era), fascists (who pursue strongly nationalistic policies), and libertarians (who believe in no regulation of the economy and individual behavior, except for defense).

RANDOM SAMPLE In the context of opinion polling, a sample in which each person within the entire population being polled has an equal chance of being chosen.

RATING SYSTEM A system by which a particular interest group evaluates (rates) the performance of legislators based on how often the legislators have voted consistently with the group's position on particular issues.

RATIONAL BASIS TEST A test (also known as the "ordinary scrutiny" standard) used by the Supreme Court to decide whether a discriminatory law violates the equal protection clause of the Constitution. Few laws evaluated under this test are found invalid.

REALIGNING ELECTION An election in which the popular support for and relative strength of the parties shift so that either (1) the minority (opposition) party emerges as the majority party or (2) the majority party is reestablished with a different coalition of supporters.

RECALL A procedure that allows voters to dismiss an elected official from a state or local office before the official's term has expired.

REFERENDUM A form of direct democracy in which legislative or constitutional measures are proposed by a legislature and then presented to the voters for approval.

REGULATION The exercise of government powers to influence the social and economic activities of a society.

REPRESENTATIVE DEMOCRACY A form of democracy in which the will of the majority is expressed through smaller groups of individuals elected by the people to act as their representatives.

REPRESENTATIVE GOVERNMENT A form of government in which representatives elected by the people make and enforce laws and policies.

REPUBLIC Essentially, a term referring to a representative democracy—in which the will of the majority is expressed through smaller groups of individuals elected by the people to act as their representatives.

REREGULATION The act of regulating again. In the 1990s, certain groups began to call for the reregulation of industries that were deregulated in the 1970s and 1980s in order to avoid the unintended results of some of the earlier deregulatory policies.

REVERSE DISCRIMINATION The assertion that affirmative action programs that require preferential treatment for minorities discriminate against those who have no minority status.

RULE OF LAW A basic principle of government that requires both those who govern and those who are governed to act in accordance with established law.

RULEMAKING The process undertaken by an administrative agency when formally proposing, evaluating, and adopting a new regulation.

RULES COMMITTEE A standing committee in the House of Representatives that provides special rules governing how particular bills will be considered and debated by the House. The Rules Committee normally proposes time limitations on debate for any bill, which are accepted or modified by the House.

S

SABOTAGE A destructive act intended to hinder a nation's defense efforts.

SAMPLE In the context of opinion polling, a group of people selected to represent the population being studied.

SAMPLING ERROR In the context of opinion polling, the difference between what the sample results show and what the true results would have been had everybody in the relevant population been interviewed.

SEARCH ENGINE A special computer program that allows users to perform "key word" searches of documents on the Internet. Popular search engines include Yahoo, WebCrawler, Excite, Infoseek, HotBot, and Lycos.

SECESSION The act of formally withdrawing from membership in an alliance; the withdrawal of a state from the federal Union.

SECOND BUDGET RESOLUTION A budget resolution, which is supposed to be passed in September, that sets "binding" limits on taxes and spending for the next fiscal year, which begins on October 1.

SECOND CONTINENTAL CONGRESS The congress of the colonies that met in 1775 to assume the powers of a central government and establish an army.

SEDITIOUS SPEECH Speech that urges resistance to lawful authority or that advocates the overthrowing of a government.

SELF-INCRIMINATION Providing damaging information or testimony against oneself in court.

SEPARATE BUT EQUAL DOCTRINE A Supreme Court doctrine holding that the equal protection clause of the Fourteenth Amendment did not forbid racial segregation as long as the facilities for blacks were equal to those provided for whites. The doctrine was overturned in the *Brown v. Board of Education of Topeka* decision of 1954.

SEPARATION OF POWERS The principle of dividing governmental powers among the executive, the legislative, and the judicial branches of government.

SEXUAL HARASSMENT Unwanted physical contact, verbal conduct, or abuse of a sexual nature that interferes with a recipient's job performance, creates a hostile environment, or carries with it an implicit or explicit threat of adverse employment consequences.

SHAYS' REBELLION A rebellion of angry farmers in western Massachusetts in 1786, led by former Revolutionary War captain Daniel Shays. This rebellion and other similar uprisings in the New England states emphasized the need for a true national government.

SINGLE-MEMBER DISTRICT SYSTEM A method of election in which only one candidate can win election to each office.

SIT-IN A tactic of nonviolent civil disobedience. Demonstrators enter a business, college building, or other public place and remain seated until they are forcibly removed or until their demands are met. The tactic was used successfully in the civil rights movement and other protest movements in the United States.

SLANDER The public utterance (speaking) of a statement that holds a person up for contempt, ridicule, or hatred.

SOCIAL CONFLICT Disagreements among people in a society over what the society's priorities should be with respect to the use of scarce resources.

SOCIAL CONTRACT A voluntary agreement among individuals to create a government and to give that government adequate power to secure the mutual protection and welfare of all individuals.

SOCIAL REGULATION Government regulation across all industries that is undertaken for the purpose of protecting the public welfare.

SOCIAL WELFARE POLICY All government actions that are undertaken to give assistance to specific groups, such as the aged, the ill, and the poor.

SOFT MONEY Campaign contributions that are made to political parties, instead of to particular candidates.

SOLIDARITY Mutual agreement with others in a particular group.

SOUND BITE In televised news reporting, a brief comment, lasting for only a few seconds, that captures a thought or a perspective and has an immediate impact on the viewers.

SPEAKER OF THE HOUSE The presiding officer in the House of Representatives. The speaker has traditionally been a long-time member of the majority party and is often the most powerful and influential member of the House.

SPECIAL ELECTION An election that is held at the state or local level when the voters must decide an issue before the next general election or when vacancies occur by reason of death or resignation.

SPIN A reporter's slant on, or interpretation of, a particular event or action.

SPIN DOCTOR A political candidate's press adviser who tries to convince reporters to give a story or event concerning the candidate a particular "spin" (interpretation, or slant).

STAGFLATION A condition that occurs when both inflation and unemployment are rising.

STANDING COMMITTEE A permanent committee in Congress that deals with legislation concerning a particular area, such as agriculture or foreign relations.

STANDING TO SUE The requirement that an individual must have a sufficient stake in a controversy before he or she can bring a lawsuit. The party bringing the suit must demonstrate that he or she has either been harmed or been threatened with a harm.

STARE DECISIS A common law doctrine under which judges normally are obligated to follow the precedents established by prior court decisions.

STATUTORY LAW The body of law enacted by legislatures (as opposed to constitutional law, administrative law, or case law).

STORE AND FORWARD PROCEDURE A process by which information is divided into separate packets, transmitted over the Internet, and then reassembled at the destination. The procedure was devised to ensure that information, once transmitted, could be rerouted and retrieved in the event of a nuclear attack.

STRAW POLL A nonscientific poll; a poll in which there is no way to ensure that the opinions expressed are representative of the larger population.

SUBCOMMITTEE A division of a larger committee that deals with a particular part of the committee's policy area. Each of the standing committees in Congress has several subcommittees.

SUFFRAGE The right to vote; the franchise.

SUPREMACY CLAUSE Article VI, Clause 2, of the Constitution, which makes the Constitution and federal laws superior to all conflicting state and local laws.

SUSPECT CLASSIFICATION A classification based on race, for example, that provides the basis for a discriminatory law. Any law based on a suspect classification is subject to strict scrutiny by the courts—meaning that the law must be justified by a compelling state interest.

SYMBIOTIC RELATIONSHIP The complex relationship that exists between political consultants and the media during political campaigns; derived from the biological term *symbiosis.*

SYMBOLIC SPEECH The expression of beliefs, opinions, or ideas through forms other than speech or print; speech involving actions and other nonverbal expressions.

T

TERRORISM The random use of staged violence at infrequent intervals to achieve political goals.

THIRD PARTY In the United States, any party other than one of the two major parties (Republican and Democratic) is considered a minor party, or third party.

THREE-FIFTHS COMPROMISE A compromise reached during the Constitutional Convention by which it was agreed that three-fifths of all slaves were to be counted both for tax purposes and for representation in the House of Representatives.

TOTALITARIAN A term describing a dictatorship in which a political leader (or group of leaders) seeks to control almost all aspects of social and economic life. Totalitarian dictatorships are rooted in the assumption that the needs of the nation come before the needs of individuals.

TRACKING POLL Polls that are taken almost every day toward the end of a political campaign to find out how well the candidates are competing for votes.

TRADE ORGANIZATION An association formed by members of a particular industry, such as the oil industry or the trucking industry, to develop common standards and goals for the industry. Trade organizations, as interest groups, lobby government for legislation or regulations that specifically benefit their groups.

TREASON As enunciated in Article III, Section 3, of the Constitution, the act of levying war against the United States or adhering (remaining loyal) to its enemies.

TREATY A formal agreement between the governments of two or more countries.

TRIAL COURT A court in which trials are held and testimony taken.

TRUSTEE In regard to a legislator, one who acts according to his or her conscience and the broad interests of the entire society.

TWO-PARTY SYSTEM A political system in which two strong and established parties compete for political offices.

TYRANNY The arbitrary or unrestrained exercise of power by an oppressive individual or government.

U

UNICAMERAL LEGISLATURE A legislature with only one chamber.

UNILATERAL In international relations, an action undertaken by one nation.

UNITARY SYSTEM A centralized governmental system in which local or subdivisional governments exercise only those powers given to them by the central government.

V

VETO A Latin word meaning "I forbid"; the refusal by an official, such as the president of the United States or a state governor, to sign a bill into law.

VETO POWER A constitutional power that enables the chief executive (president or governor) to reject legislation and return it to the legislature with reasons for the rejection. This prevents or delays the bill from becoming law.

VITAL CENTER The center of the political spectrum, or those who hold moderate political views. The center is vital because, without it, it may be difficult, if not impossible, to reach the compromises that are necessary to a political system's continuity.

W

WARD A local unit of a political party's organization, consisting of a division or district within a city.

WATERGATE SCANDAL A scandal involving an illegal break-in of the Democratic National Committee offices in 1972 by members of President Richard M. Nixon's reelection campaign staff. Before Congress could vote to impeach Nixon for his participation in covering up the break-in, Nixon resigned from the presidency.

WEAPONS OF MASS DESTRUCTION (WMDs) Nuclear, chemical, and biological weapons that can inflict massive civilian casualties and pose long-term health dangers to human beings.

WEB BROWSER The name given to software that allows Internet users to navigate through the World Wide Web. Web browsers enable users to browse, or "surf," across many Web sites through a system of hypertext links. Two of the most popular Web browsers today are *Netscape Navigator* and *Internet Explorer*.

WESTERN BLOC The democratic nations that emerged victorious after World War II, led by the United States.

WHIP A member of Congress who assists the majority or minority leader in the House or in the Senate in managing the party's legislative preferences.

WHISTLEBLOWER In the context of government employment, someone who "blows the whistle" on (reports to authorities) gross governmental inefficiency, illegal action, or other wrongdoing.

WHITE HOUSE OFFICE The personal office of the president. White House Office personnel handle the president's political needs and manage the media.

WINNER-TAKE-ALL SYSTEM A term used to describe the electoral college system, in which the candidate who receives the largest popular vote in a state is credited with all that state's electoral votes—one vote per elector.

WRIT OF *CERTIORARI* An order from a higher court asking a lower court for the record of a case.

WRIT OF *HABEAS CORPUS* An order that requires an official to bring a specified prisoner into court and explain to the judge why the person is being held in prison.

WRITE-IN CANDIDATE A candidate whose name is written on the ballot by the voter on election day.

Segregation, 345
de facto, 104–105, 106
de jure, 104, 106
persistent, 106
in today's schools, 106
Self-censorship, 235
Self-incrimination, 94–95
Semiclosed primary, 205
Semiopen primary, 205
Senior citizens. *See* Older Americans
Separate-but-equal doctrine, 103, 325–326
Separation of powers, 38, 247
Seven Years' War, 24
Sexual harassment, 111–112
Shays, Daniel, 30
Shays' Rebellion, 30
Sherman, Roger, 26, 32
Sherman, William Tecumseh, 33
Siegelman, Don, 184
The Sierra Club (SC)
litigation used by, 143
profile of, 135
Sit-ins, 106, 107
Slander, 85
Slaves, slavery
abolition of, 33, 103
Civil War and, 59–60
Confederate flag as symbol of, 10
Great Britain and, 32
as presidential election issue, 164
reparations and, 33–34
three-fifths compromise and, 32
trade and, 32
United States Constitution and, 11, 32–33
Small Business Administration (SBA), 309
"Smart cards," 93
Smith, Tom, 2
Smith, Will, 141
Smith Act (1940), 84–85
SNCC (Student Nonviolent Coordinating
Committee), 106, 108
Sniper shootings, 130
Snow, John, 291
Social conflict, 3
Social contract, 22
Social Democrats (Germany), 166
Social Security, 355–357
benefits from, 118, 266, 356
Europe's problems with, 356
government spending on, 8, 355
old-age, survivors', and disability
insurance (OASDI) and, 355
as political issue, 229, 355, 356, 357
privatization and, 157, 320, 356–357
problems with, 355–356
as "sacred cow," 355
saving, 157
as social insurance program, 355
taxes for. *See* Social Security tax(es)
trust fund and, 265
Social Security Act, 93
Social Security Administration, 314
Supplemental Security Income (SSI)
program of, 316
Social Security tax(es), 355, 365
drop in, 356

Earned Income Tax Credit (EITC)
program and, 360
Socialist Labor Party, 165
Socialist Party, 165
Socialist Workers Party, 165
Socialists, 195
Social-welfare policy, 354–361
Aid to Families with Dependent Children
(AFDC) and, 358
defined, 354
Earned Income Tax Credit (EITC)
program and, 360
food stamps and, 359
Temporary Assistance to Needy Families
and, 358
Socioeconomic status. *See* Economic status
Soft money, 212–213
contributions of, growth of, illustrated,
213
defined, 213
Software
filtering, 87
push technology and, 238
Solid South, 194
Solidarity, 159
Somalia, American intervention in, 372, 380
Sound bite, 228
Souter, David, 324, 335, 336, 341
South Africa, civil law system in, 327
South Korea
cyber politics in, 240, 241
"Koreagate" scandal and, 145
Korean War and, 286
relations with North Korea and, 241
Southern Christian Leadership Conference
(SCLC), 106
Sovereign immunity, 63, 119, 120, 342–343
Sovereignty, popular, 36–37
Soviet Union. *See also* Russia
arms control treaties and, 380
Cold War and, 378–380
Cuban missile crisis and, 379
dissolution of, 273, 372, 380
relations with U.S. and, 379–380, 389
Strategic Arms Limitation Treaty (SALT I)
signed by, 380
totalitarian dictatorship in, 6
World War II and, 378
Spaeth, Harold, 340
Spain
American colonies settled by individuals
from, 22
American conflict with, westward
expansion and, 377
President Bush's Iraq policy supported by,
390
slave trade and, 32
Spanish-American War and, 377
Spanish-American War, 377
Speaker of the House, 157, 254–255, 295
Speaker *pro tempore* of the House, 255
Special election, 216
Special session, 253
Speech
commercial, 85
freedom of, 75, 333

candidate's funding of own campaign
and, 212
challenge to Bipartisan Campaign
Reform Act of 2002 and, 214
civil liberties in everyday life and, 96
hate speech and, 74
issue advertising by interest groups
and, 143
issue advocacy by interest groups and,
213
limitations on, 84–85
physicians' recommending marijuana
use and, 50
talk radio and, 233–234
hate, 74
seditious, 84
symbolic, 84
unprotected, 85–87
Speedy trial, 94
Spin, 232
Spin doctors, 232
Splinter political parties, 163, 165
Split-ticket voting, 216
SSI (Supplemental Security Income)
program, 357
Stagflation, 364
Stalin, Josef, 6
Stamp Act (1765)(Great Britain), 24
Standing committee, 257
Standing to sue, 328–329
Stanton, Elizabeth Cady, 109, 110
Star Chamber, 331
"Star Wars" (strategic defense
initiative)(SDI), 380
Stare decisis, 325, 337, 344
START I (Strategic Arms Reduction Treaty),
388
START II, 388
State(s)
constitutions of, 27–28, 326, 399–400
amending, 399, 400–401
courts of. *See* State court system
government of. *See* State government(s)
moving from one state to another, 45
party organizations in, 169
primary elections in, 205
regulation by, 50, 312, 317
rights of
federalism and, 51, 59–60
Supreme Court and, 63, 119, 120,
342–343
secession and, 59–60
sovereign immunity and, 63, 119, 120,
342–343
supreme court of, 328, 330
transformed from colonies, 27–28
treaty and, 5, 57
State Building and Construction Trades
Council of California, 142
State court system
appellate courts of, 408, 409
judges of, 409–410
supreme (highest) court of, 328, 330
trial courts of, 408–409
general-jurisdiction, 408, 409
limited-jurisdiction, 408–409

Table of Contents
and Chapter Opening Photo Credits

ix © Photo Courtesy of The Capital Region USA, Inc.; x Library of Congress; xi White House Photo by Eric Draper; xii Library of Congress; xiv Photo courtesy of AFL-CIO; xv Photographed by Paul Corbit Brown for the U.S. Census Bureau; xvii Library of Congress; xviii Library of Congress; xix © Photo Courtesy of The Capital Region USA, Inc.; xx © Photo Courtesy of The Capital Region USA, Inc.; xxi © Photo Courtesy of NASA; xxii © Photo Courtesy of The Capital Region USA, Inc.; xxiii U.S. Census Bureau; xxiv U.S. Marine Corps photo by Sgt. Mauricio Campino; xxv Photographed by Marty Leuders for the U.S. Census Bureau; 1 © Grant V. Faint/The Image Bank/Getty; 19 © The Library of Congress; 49 © AP Photo/The Decatur Daily/John Godbey; 73 © AP Photo/Lawrence Jackson; 99 © AP Photo/Marcio Jose Sanchez; 129 © AP Photo/Steve Miller; 151 © AP Photo/Mark Humphrey; 175 © Michael Newman/PhotoEdit; 201 © AP Photo/Oscar Sosa; 223 © AP Photo/LM Otero; 245 © Photo Courtesy of The Capital Region USA, Inc.; 271 © AP Photo/Ken Lambert; 299 © NASA; 323 © James P. Blair/CORBIS; 349 © AP Photo/J. Scott Applewhite; 371 © AP Photo/Jerome Delay; 397 © AP Photo/Rich Pedroncelli.

New Version 2.0! America at Odds CD-ROM
Your essential study partner!
Works interactively
with this book!

The ultimate in interactive learning, this CD-ROM links the issues presented in this book to an interactive module for *each* chapter of the text. As you participate in the CD-ROM's simulated dialogues, activities, and exercises, you'll experience the excitement of truly active citizenship. All the tools to help you do your best in this course are right here!

From each chapter's pull-down menu you can access these features:

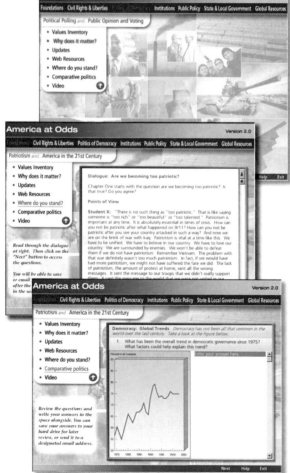

- **Values Inventory** quizzes help you look deeply at your own opinons, giving you new ways to re-evaluate or reinforce your stand on important issues. "Values Inventory" sections in every chapter-opening "America at Odds" section in this book (and again at the end of every chapter) guide you to the CD-ROM.

  By taking the quizzes before and again after reading the text chapter, you can evaluate whether your stance on the chapter-opening "America at Odds" issue has changed based on your new knowledge.

- **Why Does It Matter?** participation activities may very well surprise you with how intimately the government is a part of nearly every aspect of your life. Many of these are linked to the chapter-opening "America at Odds" features in this book.

- **Updates** keep the CD-ROM current with updates to the Web resources and more.

- **Web Resources** expand coverage of the chapter-opening issues by taking you online to related sites and asking incisive follow-up questions.

- **Where Do You Stand?** dialogues among three hypothetical students conclude with questions for analysis that guide you in thinking through these issues. The CD-ROM's "Where Do You Stand?" debates are linked directly to this book's "Where Do You Stand?" sections located in the chapter-opening "America at Odds" boxes.

- **Comparative Politics** exercises enrich your understanding of U.S. politics and government through comparisons with systems around the world. Many of these exercises are linked to this book's "Comparative Politics" boxes and include InfoTrac® College Edition and Internet references.

- **Video** segments with follow-up questions for analysis also help you to solidify your thinking on important issues.